Flight Paths

Dene Ward

DeWard Publishing Company

Flight Paths: A Devotional Guide for Your Journey

P.O. Box 6259, Chillicothe, Ohio 45601
800.300.9778
www.deward.com

Cover design by Jonathan Hardin.

The preponderance of Bible quotations are taken from the American Standard Version. Any emphasis in Bible quotations is added.

Reasonable care has been taken to trace original sources for any excerpts and quotations appearing in this book and to document such information. For material not in the public domain, fair-use standards and practices were followed. Should any attribution be found to be incorrect or incomplete, the publisher welcomes written documentation supporting correction for subsequent printings.

Printed in the United States of America.

ISBN: 978-1-936341-11-5

Preface

In 2005, my mom began to lose her vision. It has always been bad, and she had been transferred to a world-renowned doctor a couple of years earlier, but that was the year the major surgeries started. Doctors told her that the surgeries likely wouldn't be successful; even if they were, they would merely postpone the inevitable. There was no going back. There was no getting better. Short of Divine Intervention, she was headed down the path to blindness. (So far, the surgeries have been successful and the inevitable has, thank God, been postponed.)

Music notes aren't known for their large size, so it wasn't long before this malady forced her to retire from her successful career as a private piano and voice teacher, a studio she operated in our house so she would be home for my brother and me. Moments in life such as this bring with them two basic options: sink into depression or endure. She chose endurance.

Having spent nearly as long teaching Bible classes as music, she focused her energies on that. In 2007, at Dad's urging, she started writing e-mail devotionals for anyone who was interested in receiving them. They were faithfully sent out three times a week—vacations and subsequent surgeries notwithstanding—to a growing number of people. It wasn't long before the readership was measured in the hundreds rather than the dozens. In addition to the growing list, some of her readers would immediately forward her message to the entire congregation with whom they assemble. And then her devotions began to pop up in church bulletins and on blogs.

Mom is always surprised to hear of the success her little e-mail idea has had. But if you ask anyone who has studied under her during the last 30 years, you will find that she is the *only one* who is surprised.

It wasn't too long after she began writing that Daniel DeGarmo and I started DeWard Publishing Company with the publication of my own book. When it became clear that Mom would make it to 365 devotions, it became obvious to both of us that we should publish this as a daily devotional. She, I believe, was already thinking about the same thing, which made her easy to convince. What you hold in your hand is the result of her efforts.

The schedule of devotions is set to the 2011 Calendar. You will, for example, find a Labor Day devotion on September 5. In other years, it will not match up exactly, but none of the thematic devotions will be far off, regardless of what year it is. We've also included a February 29 devotion, for those reading in a Leap Year.

You will find this to be different from some daily devotional books; it is a little thicker than most. This is because you will not simply find short, feel-good fluff in these devotions. Instead, you will encounter thought provoking, character challenging, deep articles that usually cannot be contained to a single page—even with all of the layout tweaking and fudging I did to make each one as short as possible. But take the extra minute or two to read these slightly-longer devotions and you will find it rewarding and yourself enriched for having done so.

Nathan Ward | November 2010 | Tampa, Fla.
Content Manager | DeWard Publishing Company

January 1

Maybe I Should Be Committed!

I seem to have a little more time on my hands these days. This vision problem has forced me to close my in-home music studio after 35 years. My husband Keith suggested that I should spend some time writing devotional pieces. For some reason, he thought I talked enough to fill up 365 pages. After living with me for more than 35 years, I cannot fault him there, but this is something I must think about seriously. If I say I will do something, I believe I must follow through. That's the way I was raised.

Commitment has become a rare commodity in our society. Maybe it is the prevalence of instant gratification through things like credit cards (no more waiting to save up the money for something) and society's acceptance of sexual relationships outside of the marriage bond (no more waiting for the wedding). Perhaps it has something to do with the blame game—it's never my fault if I do not have the self-control to see something through. If the teachers had been more interesting, I would have made better grades. If the boss were more reasonable, I could keep a job. If my wife had not been a nag, if my husband had been more responsible, this marriage might have lasted.

Jesus said we should think about it before we commit to anything. He said when you commit, then run out on your commitment, you become a laughingstock. Funny how our society does not see it that way any more. Jesus did not mean to say that you should think of every possible thing that might happen before you make a commitment. Let me tell you, as many things as I considered before Keith and I married, I never in a million years imagined half of what we have been through. Shooting snakes? Chasing pigs? Milking a cow? Living without running water for a month? Bandaging bullet wounds? Sometimes I think the Lord had me wired for a different century than I wound up in.

Making a commitment means that after you consider all the possibilities, you make up your mind that no matter what happens, you will follow through as long as you are physically able. It means the same thing when we commit our lives to him. We may never face the kind of persecution that the first century Christians did, but how are we doing when people accuse us of being full of hate just because we have standards of morality and stick with them? Are we committed enough to take that?

All this rambling is simply putting off the decision I must make. Here goes: I will commit to writing these for a whole year. Since you are reading this, I assume you are making the commitment to read them all. The question is, can we both become better by doing this? Commitment is nothing if growth and change do not follow.

> *For which of you, intending to build a tower, does not first sit down and count the cost, whether he has enough to complete it? Otherwise when he has laid a foundation and is not able to finish, all who behold begin to mock him, saying, "This man began to build and was not able to finish." Or what king as he goes to encounter another king in war, will not sit down first and take counsel whether he will be able with ten thousand to meet him who comes against him with twenty thousand? And if not, while the other is still a great way off, he sends a delegation and asks for terms of peace. So therefore whosoever of you that renounces not all that he has, he cannot be my disciple.*
>
> Luke 14.28–33

January 2

A Puzzle Every Moment

That is how my doctor describes me: "She's a puzzle every moment." At least that's what he says when I am present. I wonder what he says when I cannot hear and he is once again at a loss for what to do next.

In the past seven years I have learned more about eyes than I ever wanted to know. At least one doctor has told me I can open up my own practice soon.

I was born severely hyperopic and nanophthalmic with anatomical narrow angle. I also have narrow angle glaucoma, as opposed to the more common open angle variety. The zonules in my left eye are weak. The sclera is thick. My corneas are among the steepest ever measured at the University of Florida School of Medicine, and the eyeballs the smallest. My anterior chamber is too shallow and I have a shallow retina detachment in the right eye. Because the angles are too narrow, the vitreous humor is backing up and raising pressure. I have had two iridotomies, four iridoplasties, two lens replacements, and two trabeculectomies, after which I went into aqueous misdirection and needed nearly half a dozen capsulotomies and anterior hyloidotomies. There is talk of a vitrectomy and a CPC (cytophotocoagulation) procedure. I have one piece of hardware in my right eye and three in my left, including a capsular tension ring and a 50 micron shunt, which leaves me with an elevated bleb. My epitheliums are being "crucified," in the doctor's words, by the medications.

See what I mean about learning? Three or four years ago I only knew what a couple of those polysyllabic words meant, and not many more of the shorter ones.

But the more I learn, the more amazed I am by the complexity of the human eye, and the foolishness of so-called learned men who believe it all just "happened." If one part of your eye does not work right, you will probably lose your vision. So how in the world did the eyeball evolve? The eyeball had to exist and work right from the beginning or those blind creatures would not have survived long enough to reproduce and adapt. Here is the real puzzle: How can anyone believe that something as amazing as the human body just happened by accident?

Pardon me if I choose to be a little less foolish and believe in a Creator. The very complexity of all creation and the various relationships that must exist for both sides to survive, scream Eternal Intelligence far louder than I ever could.

Tell your children. Tell your neighbors. Creationists are not ignorant fanatics. In fact, we are the only ones who make any sense at all.

For you did form my inward parts;
You did cover me in my mother's womb.
I will give thanks unto you, for I am fearfully and wonderfully made;
Wonderful are your works;
And that my soul knows right well.

Psalm 139.13–14

January 3

The Scarlet Woman and Her Scarlet Cord

Rahab was a harlot, what we would call a prostitute. I have come across many commentators who have tried their best to turn her into an "innkeeper," but the word just won't allow it.

The Hebrew word in Joshua 2.1 is *zanah.* It is also translated *commit fornication, go awhoring, play the harlot, play the whore, whorish, whore, etc.* It is used in Leviticus 19.29; Hosea 4.13; Exodus 34.16; Isaiah 23.17 and many other places where the meaning is quite clear. In the New Testament, the word is *porne*, in James 2.25 for example, and I do not imagine I need to tell you the English word we get from that Greek one. This same word is translated *whore* in Revelation 17.1, 15–16; 19.2. Rahab was a harlot—no ifs, ands, or buts about it.

So what is the problem with commentators who insist on "innkeeper"? The same one the Pharisees had. If Jesus was the Messiah, how could he possibly associate with publicans and sinners? If Rahab was a harlot, how could she possibly be in the genealogy of Christ? Yet they talk about the grace and mercy of God like they understand it better than we do.

And sometimes we are no better. Whom do we open our arms to when they walk through our doors? Whom do we actively seek and label "good prospects for the gospel?" Yet the people we choose to shun are the people who understand grace because they understand their need for it. We are a bit like the rich, young ruler, who, though he knew something was missing in his life despite all the laws he kept faithfully, still thought his salvation depended upon something he could *do.*

Rahab showed her dependence on God with a scarlet line she hung from her window. Did you know that word is only translated "line" twice in the Old Testament, counting this occurrence in Joshua 2.21? The other translations are *expectation* (seven times such as Psa 62.5), *hope* (23 times, such as Jer 17.13; Psa 71.5), and *the thing that I long for* (once, Job 6.8). I do believe it was a literal rope of some sort, but it seems more than passing coincidence that the word most of the time has those other meanings. I have often wondered what her neighbors thought of that cord hanging there, but every day Rahab was reminded of the salvation she did not deserve, that she hoped for, longed for, and expected to receive when those people marched into the land.

When we get a little too big for our britches, a little too proud of our pedigree in the kingdom, maybe we need to hang a scarlet cord in our windows to remind us what we used to be, and what we have waiting for us *in spite of that.*

> *But when the kindness of God our Savior, and his love toward man, appeared, not by works done in righteousness, which we did ourselves, but according to his mercy he saved us, through the washing of regeneration and renewing of the Holy Spirit, which he poured out upon us richly through Jesus Christ our Savior, that being justified by his grace we might be made heirs according to the hope of eternal life.*
>
> Titus 3.4–7

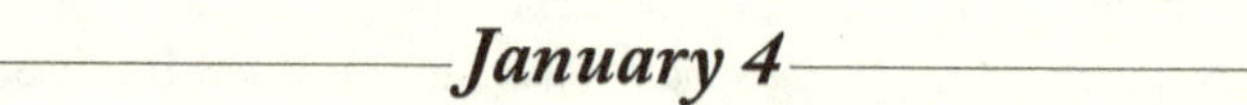

January 4

Accent on Speech

In spite of the fact that my husband claims to be a Southerner (he is really an Arkansas hillbilly and I had to teach him the proper way to eat grits), he regularly makes fun of my accent. This from the guy to whom perfect strangers point and say with amazement, "You sound just like Jimmy Stewart!" He says folks from the Deep South are the only ones who can take a three letter word, put three syllables in it, and take three full seconds to say it. Ham, for instance: hay—ee—yum.

Actually I have noticed how my speech has changed over my lifetime. I was born around Orlando, not the Orlando you know now, but pre-Disney Orlando, which was a small town then, full of people with rural roots, and only a few pretentious folks over in the Winter Park section—the white-gloved folks who knew how to stick their pinkies out when they drank tea. Back then I probably had a true Southern accent.

I spent the last eight years of my growing up life and the first year of married life in Tampa, so my accent began to even out some. Then two years in Illinois farmland put a real spin on it. For the last 30 years I have lived back in Florida—not the cosmopolitan Florida the rest of the world knows about, but rural, north central Florida, where the possums and coons still rummage at night, the bobcats scream, and the hound dogs bay at the moon. I don't think I have pronounced the "g" on an -ing word in at least 20 years.

God's people have had similar problems throughout the ages. Nehemiah was horrified at the effect foreign people were having on his brethren, and used their language problem as a symbol for things much worse: "In those days also I saw the Jews that had married women of Ashdod, Ammon, and Moab; and their children spoke half in the speech of Ashdod and could not speak in the Jews' language, but according to the language of each people" (Neh 13.23–24).

I have always heard this passage used to point out that some use Bible words the wrong way, mixing up pastors with preachers, and fellowship with donuts. But it is more important for me in my daily life to think about this: I should not allow the language around me to affect the way I speak. God's children should be speaking blessing, not cursing; words of understanding, not words of judgment; words of praise, not words of criticism. Can I turn a cashier's day around with a friendly hello rather than a cold empty look? Can I make a waitress's feet hurt a little less with friendly conversation, rather than a gruff complaint? Can I give my wavering brother or sister an encouraging word rather than an unfeeling push over the edge of temptation? The condemnation of the language of Ashdod means a whole lot more than just mixing up a few definitions.

Today, and every day Lord, help my accent to be that of a Christian.

A soft answer turns away wrath. ...The tongue of the wise utters knowledge correctly. ...A gentle tongue is a tree of life. ...A man has joy by the answer of his mouth, and a word spoken in due season, how good it is. ...Pleasant words are like a honeycomb: sweet to the soul and health to the bones.

Selections from Proverbs 15 and 16

January 5

A Big Stink

I was nearly out of lotion and saw a sale—some fancy stuff for the same price as good old Lubriderm. I stood there at the display amid way too many choices. How do you decide between apple pomegranate, vanilla fluff, gingerbread, sugar plum, lemon twist, and blue ocean? Well, I was afraid the last one would make me smell like salt cod so that was a no-brainer.

I picked up the gingerbread tube and thought I would just flip open the top and give it a sniff. Nothing. I do have more trouble these days smelling things because of all the medications. So I decided to give the tube a light squeeze so a puff of scented air from inside the tube would give me a better whiff.

Instead of air, a big glop of orange creamsicle-colored lotion shot straight into the air and arced over to the catchall shelf of sorts that I carry in front of me. Plop! A big orange spot appeared on my bright blue sweater.

Wait! Is anyone looking? Did anyone see? I looked around guiltily and then, because I had nothing else with me, started wiping if off with my finger. The sweater was dark enough and nubby enough that the spot no longer showed, but I had a big dollop of lotion to get rid of and the best I could think was to just rub it into my hands and arms. I am sure the security people were laughing their heads off as they viewed the monitor that picked up this *I Love Lucy* moment.

You know what? I did not like the smell. A friend later asked me if I had spilled machine oil all over myself. No, just gingerbread body lotion, and I carried it about with me for a long eight hour day because I had a doctor's appointment afterward. Yuck!

Let that be a lesson to you. Sometimes we start wondering what we are missing out there in the big, bad world. I have been good all my life—brought up "in the church," taught to obey all authorities—parents, teachers, policemen—memorized all the no-nos for a Christian, and the scriptures to go along with them. If all those things out there are so bad, why do so many spend their lives pursuing them? What do they know that I don't? Just one little whiff is all I want.

But that little whiff can easily become a big glop of smelly stuff that we carry with us far longer than the actual experience lasts. Consequences can raise a big stink in your life. In fact, they can ruin your life, and even the lives of those you love and have no desire to hurt.

It is not a question of what those folks out there know that *you* don't; it's a question of what you know that *they* don't—that sin is deceptively easy to fall into and sometimes impossible to get out of. God will forgive you, but he will not wash away the consequences—like ruined relationships, like destroyed trust, like physical diseases or injuries, like jail time and a record that follows you everywhere.

Though I did not really like it much, that little glop of lotion did not smell quite *that* bad when it landed on my sweater. But as the day grew longer, it began to reek. Sin will do exactly the same thing.

> *There is no soundness in my flesh because of your indignation; there is no health in my bones because of my sin. For my iniquities have gone over my head; like a heavy burden, they are too heavy for me. My wounds stink and fester because of my foolishness, I am utterly bowed down and prostrate; all the day I go about mourning. For my sides are filled with burning, and there is no soundness in my flesh. I confess my iniquity; I am sorry for my sin. Do not forsake me, O Lord! O my God, be not far from me! Make haste to help me, O Lord, my salvation!*
>
> Selections from Psalm 38

January 6

Parsley on Your Plate

Because of health circumstances, my teaching has been limited lately, but I remembered the other day a certain fifth grade Bible class—students who are now in college or out working in the world. (My, how time flies!) We studied a workbook that used that old standby phrase "the Christian graces," describing the passage in 2 Peter 1.5–7.

Although this phrase is nowhere found in the Bible, when one grows up hearing things over and over, one tends to accept them without question. Before teaching that lesson I decided to do a word study. Imagine my surprise to discover that use of the word "grace" meant "an embellishment, adornment, enhancement, or garnish." In other words, graces are something not essential to the entity in question, but which make it more attractive. Like that parsley next to your steak dinner at a restaurant—it just makes the plate pretty. The steak is still a steak without it. Are we still Christians without these characteristics? Is that what we want these children to believe about Christianity?

Even my fifth-graders were able to pick out these phrases in the context of the list: they "make you to be not idle or unfruitful" (v 8); "he who lacks these things is blind" (v 9); "if you do these… you shall never stumble" (v 10); "thus you shall be richly supplied… the entrance into the eternal kingdom" (v 11).

And the traits which do this? Virtue, knowledge, self-control, perseverance, godliness, brotherly kindness, love. Can one be a Christian without loving others? Without controlling himself? Without persevering to the end?

Maybe some of us treat these things like parsley on our plates of Christianity, but my fifth-graders decided that we should call them "the requirements of being a Christian." I think they are right. Truly, *out of the mouths of babes...*

> *Yes and for this very cause adding on your part all diligence, in your faith supply virtue, and in your virtue knowledge, and in your knowledge self-control, and in your self-control perseverance, and in your perseverance godliness, and in your godliness brotherly kindness, and in your brotherly kindness love. For if these things are yours and abound, they make you to be not idle or unfruitful unto the knowledge of our Lord Jesus Christ. For he that lacks these things is blind, seeing only what is near, having forgotten the cleansing from his old sins. Wherefore, brethren, give the more diligence to make your calling and election sure, for if you do these things, you shall never stumble, for these shall be richly supplied unto the entrance into the eternal kingdom of our Lord and Savior Jesus Christ.*
>
> 2 Peter 1.5–11

January 7

God's Country

People always call places like Tennessee and North Carolina "God's Country," but no one says anything remotely like that about rural north central Florida. All we have is Spanish moss dripping off huge, ancient live oaks, whose wingspan is broader then my house, tall pencil-slim pines standing like silent rows of soldiers in the woods, knobby-kneed cypresses wading in the swamps whose heavy silence is punctuated only by the plop of bullfrogs in the water, rolling green pasture land dotted with grazing black Angus, and always something blooming, no matter what time of year it is. Not long ago I heard our resident hawk family again, and in just a few weeks, while everyone else is still in the throes of winter, the cardinals and hummingbirds will be back, azaleas and dogwoods blooming so heavily no one can even catch sight of their greenery. Not too bad for a place no one calls "God's Country."

But neither here nor any of those other places compare to the real "God's country." God promised Abraham a land He later described to Moses as "a good land and a large... a land flowing with milk and honey" (Exod 3.8). Abraham's descendants waited 400 years for that Promised Land. But even Abraham knew that the real Promised Land was still to come. That is why he could endure, stay faithful, and even pass the horrible test of offering his son.

Paul had to scold the Corinthians more than once for having "carnal" minds. Not carnal in the sense of illicit pleasures, but carnal in that they were more concerned with this life and the physical aspects of it than in spiritual things. Only carnally minded people become jealous for showy spiritual gifts, sue one another, brag about who baptized them, and bring enough to feed an army for their family's Lord's Supper, just so they can show off. Too often we, too, get caught up in the here and now and forget that this is merely a short, temporary motel stop on the way to a far better and permanent home.

I have just come from the funeral of a man who understood that. He never lived in a fancy home or had an expensive car. He often worked two jobs to keep his family fed. He landed on the shores of Northern France in June 1944 and marched all the way to Berlin. He endured many illnesses. He buried a ten-year-old daughter. But he would have told you he lived a good life, because he knew the physical doesn't last. His eyes were focused elsewhere, and nothing that happened here could get him down.

We should all learn what he knew: no place on this earth should mean more to us, no person should come between us, and no thing should ever deter us from our journey to God's Country. Praise God! My father-in-law has made it home.

> *By faith Abraham, when he was called, obeyed to go out unto a place which he was to receive for an inheritance, and he went out, not knowing where he went. By faith he became a sojourner in the land of promise as in a land not his own, dwelling in tents, with Isaac and Jacob, the heirs with him of the same promise, for he looked for the city which has the foundations, whose builder and maker is God...they desire a better country, that is a heavenly one, wherefore God is not ashamed of them to be called their God, for he has prepared for them a city.*
>
> Heberws 11.8–10, 16

January 8

Have You Given Up Yet?

It's been a week. How are you doing on those New Year resolutions? Sometimes we make it past the first few days, sometimes a whole month before we are back to our old habits. And next year we make the same resolutions all over again, only to fail again.

Too often the same thing happens with our spiritual lives—we make resolutions at our conversion and find that the next day we are still having the same old problems, and sooner or later fall into the same traps. But Jesus tells us the trick to making resolutions stick.

"If anyone would come after me, let him deny himself, and take up his cross daily, and follow me" (Luke 9.23).

This verse has been misunderstood so long you may have missed the point. The cross you bear is not some problem or disability you may have. I may soon be blind, but that is not my cross to bear. The cross is something you take up voluntarily. I certainly did not choose to have these eye diseases. Other people are blind who are not Christians, and they are *not* taking up a cross for Jesus.

"I have been crucified with Christ and it is no longer I that live, but Christ who lives in me" (Gal 2.20). The cross symbolizes death. Taking up your cross is about choosing to crucify yourself. "For if we have become united with him in the likeness of his death, we shall be also in his resurrection, knowing this, that our old man was crucified with him that the body of sin might be done away, that we should no longer be in bondage to sin, for he that has *died* has been justified from sin" (Rom 6.5–7).

And Jesus says I must do it *daily*. Those twelve step programs are right. You must never think, can I go without a drink for the rest of my life? You would give up right away. The question is, can I do without a drink *today?* And the alcoholic is encouraged. Of course I can. Then tomorrow he wakes up and says, Can I do without a drink *today?* And he does. Then the next day and the next, and before he knows it, like my good friend and brother Joe, he has done without a drink for more than 20 years!

So forget those New Year resolutions. Take up your cross *daily:* make a New *Day* resolution. Can I crucify myself and let Christ live in me just for today? Of course, I can. Then tomorrow, do it again. Then the next day, and the next. Put it right in there with brushing your teeth every morning—something you do without fail—and pretty soon you will have lived a better life for longer than you ever dreamed possible!

> *For I have been crucified with Christ, and it is no longer I who live, but Christ lives in me; and that life which I now live in the flesh I live in faith, which is in the Son of God, who loved me and gave himself for me.*
>
> Galatians 2.20

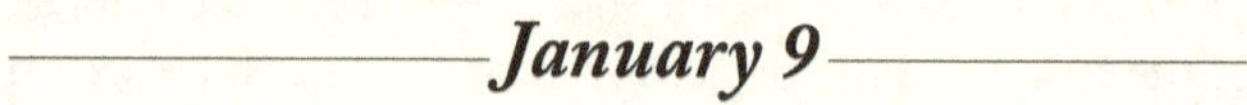

January 9

Bird Watching

In the last couple of years, my life has really slowed down. I am no longer able to teach piano and voice lessons because I cannot read the students' music well enough. This means fewer teachers' meetings, and no more competitions to prepare for, sweat over, and pray about—I had the usual bunch of cardiac kids who waited till the last minute to pull it off.

My jog has also become a walk, at times with a big sturdy walking stick to steady myself when I stumble over something I did not see.

And I am paying more attention to the birds on our property. Though I cannot always see them, I have learned many of their calls, and can now identify quail, doves, owls, whippoorwills, hawks, blue jays, crows, titmice, wrens, woodpeckers, and hummingbirds—and I don't mean the pecking and humming of the last two, but their actual vocal sounds. And now that I recognize all of those, the ones I have not yet identified are more distinct when I hear them. There is one out there that sounds like a bad flutist.

My son thinks it is pretty amazing when I say things like, "There's a wren in the live oak outside your old bedroom window." But would I know where he was if I could not hear him? What is the most amazing thing of all is that my Heavenly Father knows where each and every bird is whether it sings or not. And that means He knows where I am, both physically and spiritually. He knows, not just because He is able to know, but because He *cares* to know. And that is the greatest security a child of God can have. "Yes for me, for me He careth."

Are not five sparrows sold for two pence? And not one of them is forgotten in the sight of God. But the very hairs of your head are numbered. Fear not. You are of more value than many sparrows.

Luke 12.6–7

January 10

Camouflage

The other morning I was outside feeding the dogs when I got a bit of a shock. Wood smoke from the chimney swirled around in the cold north breeze, rustling the one or two brown leaves still hanging on the sycamore. My breath billowed around me even thicker than the smoke and my hands ached from the cold. The frost on the ground crunched beneath my feet, and the cold dampness coming through my shoes turned my toes to ice cubes. Suddenly I heard my neighbor's lawn mower roar into life. My subconscious mind immediately went to work and without even thinking about it I was humming the old *Sesame Street* tune, "One of these things is not like the other, one of these things just isn't the same. . . ."

Yes, I do live in Florida, but up here in north Florida your mower sits gathering dust, leaves, spider webs, and other assorted natural trash from November 1 till March 1, and sometimes beyond. What in the world was he mowing? I wondered.

I never did find out, but it struck me that if I had driven by he would have looked odd sitting on a lawn mower with a heavy jacket, gloves, and a wool hat. I wonder if he worried about what the people who drove by his yard thought about him.

You think not? You're probably right. Something needed to be done that involved a lawn mower and so he did it. It's really no one else's business what it was and why he felt the need to do it. Then why in the world do we get so uncomfortable when we look different to the world?

We always direct thoughts like this to the young, but peer pressure works on every age, not just teenagers. Isn't that why we become uncommonly quiet when certain topics of conversation come up among our friends in the world? We Americans often argue about our right to be individuals, usually quoting from works like *1984,* calling Big Government laws we don't like "Orwellian" because they take away the rights of the individual. Then when the time comes to actually stand up and be an individual, to act differently than the mainstream of society, to talk differently, dress differently, live differently, we are just as bad as a teenager who wants to do what "everyone else is doing." Like a chameleon, we want to camouflage ourselves and blend in.

So, can I really do this? Do I have the strength to stand out in a crowd? Can I be the one that every *Sesame Street* viewing child can point out as "not the same?" God expects me to do just that. In fact, he says, that if I live by the standards his Son taught I will not be able to help being different. Some people will hate me for it; but others will respect me for it. And maybe a few will be influenced to change their own lives. We cannot have that influence if we are busy putting on our camo gear every morning before we go out. Yes, the snipers might get us if we go out in blaze orange, but the ones who are looking for a way out of the woods might see us too.

> *Beloved I beseech you as sojourners and pilgrims to abstain from fleshly lusts which war after the soul; having your behavior seemly among the Gentiles; that wherein they speak against you as evil-doers they may by your good works which they behold, glorify God in the day of visitation.*
>
> 1 Peter 2.11–12

January 11

Blaming God

It seems that more and more I hear people blame God for all their ills, even people who claim to be Christians. I think the first time this really struck home was a day many years go when I was passing out gospel meeting invitations to neighbors. I met a woman about a half mile down the road from where I lived who could hardly get past hello before she was telling me how God had let her down. She had prayed and prayed for her father's health, but "God let him die anyway." Now what do I say? I tried to sound sympathetic and asked how old he had been.

"Eighty-six," she said. I did my best not to look stunned. Eighty-six is certainly not an early death. I wondered what age would have suited her, or did she just expect God to allow him to live forever? The thing is, she made the same mistake everyone does. We do not die because of God. We die because of Satan and sin, and the fact that we all partake in that sin: "Therefore as through one man sin entered into the world, and death through sin, and so death passed unto all men *for that all sinned*" (Rom 5.12).

But babies do not sin, some will say. No, but they live in a world dominated by it, and so the innocent also suffer. But to even ask the question is still to miss the point. As Jeremiah said, even standing in the midst of destruction, "It is because of Jehovah's loivingkindnesses that we are not consumed, because his compassions fail not" (Lam 3.22).

If not for God there would be *nothing* good in this world at all. There would be thorns, but no beautiful roses attached; there would be stingers, but no sweet honey made by the bee. Without God this world would be a horrible, dark, desperate, heartrending, agonizing place—a true Hell on earth.

Everyone dies, but it isn't God's fault. Everyone has illness, pain and suffering of some kind, but God didn't cause it. To blame Him is to place ourselves with Adam, who, instead of confessing, instantly turned and blamed the woman, who then instantly turned and blamed the serpent. God did not cause their expulsion from the garden any more than He caused the disease I have. Satan did.

Are you reasonably well this morning? Can you still get around? Do you have a faithful spouse? Do you have healthy children? Do you have children who are faithful Christians and have raised even more faithful Christians? Do you have faithful brethren? Do you have a roof over your head? Are you worried about eating too much, instead of having anything to eat at all? Do you have a hope of Heaven? Maybe you could not say yes to all those questions, but for *anything* you did say yes to, God is the reason. Blame Him for those things.

Every good and perfect gift is from above, coming down from the Father of lights, with whom can be no variation, neither shadow that is cast by turning.

James 1.17

January 12

A Good Sport

Due to my congenital eye problems, I grew up reading in my room instead of playing outside with the other kids. That may sound odd—reading when one has an eye problem—but, you see, reading was safe. As long as I had my coke bottle glasses I could sink back into my imagination and see the world. Whenever I tried to play with the other children, I always tripped over something I did not see, fell and skinned my knees, or got hit in the face with whatever ball we were playing with at the time because I could not see it coming, sometimes breaking those expensive glasses.

Then I married a man, and had two boys. Here I was with a house full of men and had absolutely no experience either playing sports or watching them—well, I tried to watch football once when I was about 10. It looked to me like two bunches of men who every minute or so ran into each other and fell down. I did enough of that myself, and could not see the attraction at all.

But I wanted a close relationship with my family, so I started sitting with them on Saturday afternoons, watching what they watched—football and basketball. Although I still do not have any idea what a "pick and roll" is, or why in the world they call a guy a tackle and then forbid him to do exactly that, I can now identify a naked bootleg and tell when a charge is not a charge, but a blocking foul. The boys got a big kick out of teaching these things to Mom.

I went to that trouble because I cared about my family relationships. Do I care for my neighbors as well? Or have I bought into the egocentric American notion that the world should operate on my schedule and according to my desires, and no one else has any legitimate problems, or any other rationale for what they do other than to aggravate me and get in my way?

Will I ask the man next door about his golf game, while studiously avoiding the old joke about golf being "a good walk ruined"? When I meet the lady across the street at the mailbox, will I ask to see her latest crocheted creation, even though I don't know the name of a single stitch, and can barely sew a straight line on a machine? If I want to develop the kind of relationships that will become closer and deeper, and perhaps eventually lead them to the Lord, I hope I will. These things may seem insignificant, but they pave the way for things that are anything but.

What lives will you and I try to touch today?

For though I was free from all men, I brought myself under bondage to all, that I might gain the more. And to the Jews I became as a Jew that I might gain Jews; to them that were under the law, as under the law, not being myself under the law, that I might gain them that are under the law; to them that are without law as without law, not being without law to God but under law to Christ. To the weak I became weak, that I might gain the weak. I have become all things to all men that I may by all means save some. And I do all things for the gospel's sake, that I might be a joint partaker thereof.

1 Corinthians 9.19–23

January 13

Parts of Speech

I came across a reference to a Stephen Crane short story in which he stated that a certain character was not even a noun, but only an adverb. I have never read that story, so I found myself pondering what in the world he must have meant by that. My mind wandered all over, eventually to spiritual matters. How could one be an adverb instead of a noun?

Then it struck me. What is it the apostle John says of God? Not that He acts lovingly, but that He *is* love. It is one thing to act in a loving manner on occasion, and quite another to be the very embodiment of love.

If someone said of me that I had acted rudely, I would hope it was a momentary lapse in my usual behavior. However, if someone said I was rudeness personified, it would mean that courtesy was a momentary lapse; that my habit was to behave rudely in practically every situation. One is a stronger accusation than the other by far. You can apologize for one. The other requires a complete change in character.

If someone called you a Scrooge, you would instantly understand that they think you are greedy and miserly. The Bible uses similar language when it uses terms like "sons of disobedience." It is not that difficult a concept to grasp.

So how would people describe me this morning? Am I kindness personified? Am I the embodiment of wisdom? Or am I the epitome of childishness, or pettiness, or malice? What noun are you?

And then there is this further consideration: can I even become a noun? Am I too inconsistent or too weak to become what God requires of me on a regular basis? Can I ever hope to have someone say of me, "She is love," or, "She is joy," or "She is faith?"

A small thought for the morning, but one that could make a huge difference in our lives.

For the love of Christ constrains us; because we thus judge, that one died for all, therefore all died; and he died for all, that they that live should no longer live unto themselves, but unto him who for their sakes died and rose again. ...Wherefore if any man is in Christ, he is a new creature: the old things are passed away; behold, they are become new.

2 Corinthians 5.14–15, 17

Teamwork

I ran a piano and voice studio off and on—between babies and moves—for 37 years, the last 23 in a row in one place with no "offs." I entered my students into several evaluations and competitions a year. About 20 years ago, I discovered a state competition for students who made "superior" ratings at the district level. I asked around and two well-meaning teachers told me that I needn't bother taking my students because no one from Union County could possibly win. Winners usually came from the Miami area, students of retired concert artists, students with a concert career in mind, willing to practice for several hours a day.

Always looking for motivation, at my next student meeting I told them about the competition and passed along the opinions, "Your students can't possibly win." Their reaction began with head-shaking confusion followed by red-faced indignation, and finally, steely-eyed determination. From that point on they had a mission.

Unfortunately, our first trip proved my friends correct. We won absolutely nothing. Besides the disadvantages I mentioned before, the groups we competed in were sometimes as large as 80 with only one winner and three or four honorable mentions chosen from "superior" rated students all across the state. But they did not give up—they learned to do better.

And sure enough, the next year we had a winner. Every year after that we brought home at least one winner, and one year we outdid every other group in the state: nine students with performance wins (one of whom was my son Nathan), three state officers elected, including state vice-president and president (Nathan), and a $200 summer music camp scholarship winner (did I mention that Nathan won that?).

How did they manage this? Things that had never made any difference to them at all suddenly became important. We taped their performances at lessons and they would sit and pick themselves apart—I seldom said a word. All of a sudden they could hear that their tempo was not steady, that their melody got lost in the underlying harmonies, that their dynamic shading was practically nonexistent; that their vocal placement was wrong, that their diphthongs were too wide, that their tone was unsupported.

Most importantly I think, this group became a team. Several times during the year the students listened to one another and gave critiques. The ones performing did not let their pride get in the way because someone was telling them they were not perfect—they were anxious to hear how to do better, and after the taping exercise, realized that we do not all see (or hear) ourselves correctly. And it worked. They began to win. And success breeds success.

They even came up with their own uniforms—black pants or skirt, white shirt, and Looney Tunes tie. This little outfit started with just one duet team and gradually spread. It finally got to the point where new students were asking me when they got their "uniforms." And whenever a child was without something—especially the tie, which some had trouble finding—there would be the "passing of the ties" between rooms and events as they raced to perform, so that no one would be without. It was amazing to me to see this happen among children, with no prompting whatsoever. The last few years as I sat in the audience, I heard other parents and teachers around me saying, "Uh-oh. They're from the group with the ties," as one of my ensembles approached the piano. Even the ones who never won anything viewed the "outfit" as a badge of honor. It meant they belonged to a group who did win, and that meant they won, too.

Do I really need to make an application here? What if the church acted like this group of children? What if we all had the attitude, "Please tell me how to do better?" "Please tell me exactly what I'm doing wrong." What if we all "rejoiced with those who rejoiced" instead of becoming envious? What if we all viewed being a part of the Lord's body as an honor? What if we all looked Satan right in the face and said, "I can too do it!" And then did.

There should be no schism in the body; but the members should have the same care one for another. And if one member suffers, all the members suffer with it; or if one member is honored, all the members rejoice with it. Now **you** *are the body of Christ and each is a member of it.*

1 Corinthians 12.25–27

January 15

Teamwork (2)

While my students did win solo awards in piano solo, art song, and musical theater, our specialty seemed to be piano ensembles. The point of an ensemble is not just to play the right notes at the right time, but to make a piano duet sound like one person with four hands and a trio like one person with six. Not an easy thing to do when one partner plays with a heavy hand and the other with light finger work, one with the ebb and flow of rubato and the other the steadiness of a machine.

My teacher friends laughed at me when they saw all my students make a point to approach the piano together, sit at the same time, put their hands on and off the keys at the same time, then stand together and leave together. I guess they never thought about whose students were bringing back trophies and whose weren't. The point of all that togetherness was to infuse oneness into them. Your performance starts from the moment your names are called; that single four- or six-handed creature acted as one from then till they hit their seats in the audience afterward.

The performance aspects were trickier. Who has the melody? Does the partner have a counter-melody or an oom-pah-pah chordal accompaniment? Does the partner enter with the same melody a few bars later? How can the one with the steady underlying rhythm make it stable enough to help the syncopated partner, without overpowering him? Are the dynamics terraced or interlaced? How each partner plays his part depends upon the answer to all those questions. What a lot to remember and listen for.

I had one duo that excelled at all of this. They played together for ten years and by the time the older graduated from high school, I was positive they were even breathing in sync while they performed. They played pieces where one partner got up, walked around the piano and sat down to play again; then later in the piece got up and went back to his original position, all without stopping, without errors, and without one of them falling off the bench! They played pieces where the one higher on the keyboard picked up his hand and put it between the other's two hands and then continued playing, without a hitch. If you were not watching, you would not know anything had happened. Once they played a piece where one's left hand was on the black keys above the other's right hand on the white keys, and they never once got in each other's way. Now that's teamwork. (Did I mention that Nathan was one of the partners?)

Perfecting the piece was not enough for them. They even created entrances, with both walking down opposite aisles exactly together and approaching the judges' bench with a flourish precisely at the same time in the middle of the front row. At the end of the piece they each crossed the outside hand to bounce off the last note with the inside hand, and held their hands up for exactly the same three count—nonverbally. They simply knew each other that well.

And I remember my baby duet. A little step-brother and -sister act in the Primary 1 category performing "O Susanna." When one had the melody the other played softer; when the other came in with the melody, the first one pulled her tone way down almost instinctively, and then back up again when it was her turn. These were eight-year-olds, mind you, and it was flawless, seamless, and so amazing the judges looked at each other as soon as it happened. I knew then we had it, and sure enough, we did.

That is what teamwork is all about. You know that old coach's saying, "There is no *I* in team?" Unfortunately, many people still manage to spell *me,* and the team is never as unified as it could be. Teamwork means doing what is best for the group. It means constantly putting someone else ahead of me. It means making an objective judgment of what is most important at a given time and not forcing my issues to the forefront if they are less critical than another's. It means not complaining if I don't have the lead and trying to horn my way in anyway. It means not whining when I don't get the praise I think I deserve. If one of my students had said, "I don't care if I don't have the melody. I am just as important as her, so I'm playing my chords just as loudly," they would have never won anything. In fact, they would never have gotten a superior at the district level and not made it to the state competition. What's best for me will very often ruin it for everyone else. And we all need to have that feeling. If we do, no one feels left out or unappreciated.

Why is it that we cannot see these things when we are the ones involved? Are we really so dense? Is it pride? Is it arrogance? Is it our rights-oriented society? Whatever it is, we need to get over it, so the church can once again "make known the manifold wisdom of God" (Eph 3.10), and we, through our unity, can cause the world to believe (John 17.21).

Doing nothing through faction or through vainglory, but in lowliness of mind, each counting other better than himself, not looking each of you to his own things, but each of you also to the things of others.

Philippians 2.3–4

January 16

The Fall

I have been going up the step from the back porch into the laundry room for 25 years. I never look down, and I never fall—until the other morning. And as I fell I just had time to say to myself, "There is nothing you can do about this," and splat! Rug rash on both elbows and one knee. In fact, the right knee hit so hard that a layer of skin embedded itself into my leggings, and when I pulled them off to check for bleeding, the skin stuck to them instead of me. Worst abrasion I ever had in my life, plus achy hip, achy neck, and a headache that started in the afternoon and would not leave no matter what I took. At least I did not break anything, not even the floor. Do I need any more proof that Keith did not marry me for my grace?

And yet, as rough a fall as that was, it is nothing compared to a spiritual fall. And should I think that a saved person cannot fall, hear Paul's warning to the Galatian brethren: "You who would be justified by the law are severed from Christ; you are fallen away from grace" (Gal 5.4). If they can be severed from Christ, they were once in Him; if they can fall from grace, they once stood waist deep in it. As Paul said earlier in the epistle, I should not listen to anyone who tells me otherwise, not even an angel from heaven.

And that fall will not bring skinned knees and aching necks. "For if, after they have escaped the defilements of the world through the knowledge of the Lord and Savior Jesus Christ, they are again entangled in them and overcome, their last state is worse than the first" (2 Pet 2.20). That fall will cost my soul. My bruises and abrasions will eventually heal, but spiritual injuries will not, without repentance.

Isn't it interesting how many physical terms the Holy Spirit uses to get across his point? Perhaps any physical fall we take should make us stop and examine where we stand spiritually as well. We might stop just in time, one step before the edge, and save ourselves a headlong spiritual fall that will cost us more than a little skin.

> *They also that seek after my life lay snares for me, and they that seek my hurt speak mischievous things, and meditate deceits all the day long...In you O Jehovah, do I hope. You will answer, O Lord my God. For I said, lest they rejoice over me. When my feet slip, they magnify themselves against me. For I am ready to fall, and my sorrow is continually before me...Forsake me not, O Jehovah. O my God, be not far from me. Make haste to help me, O Lord, my salvation.*
>
> Psalm 38.12, 15–17, 21–22

January 17

Mrs. Job

I find Job to be one of the most perplexing books in the Bible. After trying many years to understand it, I have come up with this: the book of Job does not answer the question of why bad things happen to good people; it is merely God saying, "You do not need to know why. You just need to trust me no matter what."

We all know the story. In an attempt to make Job renounce God, Satan took away every good thing in his life. What did he lose? Seven sons, three daughters, 7,000 sheep, 3,000 camels, 500 yoke of oxen, 500 female donkeys (remember, wealth was measured mainly by livestock in the patriarchal times), many servants, standing in the community, and even his health. About the only things he didn't lose were his house (42.11), his wife, and his closest friends—if you can call them that. In fact, when you think about it, Satan probably knew those people would be a help in his own cause, and that is why he left them. He certainly would not have left Job with a support system if he could have helped it.

And that brings us to Mrs. Job. Now let's be fair. When Job lost everything, so did she. And as I have grown older I have learned to be very careful about judging people who are going through any sort of traumatic experience.

Keith and I have been through a lot together. I have had to take food off my plate and put it on my children's plates because they were still hungry and there was no more. We have dug ditches next to each other in a driving rainstorm to keep our house from washing away. I have held a convulsing child as he drove 90 mph to the emergency room 30 miles away. We have carried all the water we used in the house back and forth for a month because the well collapsed and we could not afford to repair it. I have bandaged the bullet wounds he sustained as a law enforcement officer. But all that happened over a period of 30 years, not in one day. And *never* have I lost a child, much less all of them. What I would do if I were Mrs. Job, I do not know. What I *should* do is easy to say, but however glibly it rolls off my tongue, that does not mean I would have the strength to do it.

She was suffering just as much as her husband. But somehow, Job hung on, while his wife let her grief consume her. Job actually lost his wife in an even more painful way than death because she failed the test of faith.

So what happened to her afterward? Job did have a wife or he would not have had more children (42.13). Without further evidence to the contrary, the logical assumption is that it was the same wife. Since they had a continuing relationship perhaps he is the one who helped her, and she repented both of her failure to be a "helper suitable" and of her faithlessness.

So what should we learn about sharing grief as a couple? What I hope we would all do when grief and suffering assail our homes is support one another. The thing that Job did not have from anyone is the thing that should make all single people desire a good marriage: support and help. Troubles should pull us together, not tear us apart. What I cannot lift by myself, I can with help. Sometimes he is the reason she makes it over a personal hill and other times she is his light to make it through the dark places, and that is how God intended it.

Now here is the question for each of us. If Satan were going to test my spouse, would he take me, or leave me?

> *Two are better than one, because they have a good reward for their labor. For if they fall, the one will lift up his fellow, but woe to him who is alone when he falls and has not another to lift him up. Again, if two lie together, then they have warmth, but how can one be warm alone?*
>
> Ecclesiastes 4.9–11

January 18

Dancin' in the Fryin' Pan

I thought it was just because I was a classical voice teacher who, since I live in a rural county in the South, spent a lot of time on diction—clean enunciation, and particularly those wide Southern diphthongs. What is the point of singing if no one can understand the words? So I thought it was just because I was sensitive to it that I kept noticing that I could not understand the words in a lot of pop music. Finally, one day when we were listening to a "Best Of..." tape in the car, I asked them, "Is he really saying 'dancin' in the fryin' pan?'"

"No, mom. It's dancin' an' prancin'," accompanied by exaggerated eye rolls and head shakes as only teenagers can.

Recently I discovered a whole website devoted to "Misheard Lyrics." I feel vindicated at last.

But pop music is not the problem. The singers are the problem. Most of us can tell stories of our children just beginning to sing our hymns and the often hilarious mistakes they make.

In the middle of the grocery store one morning, three-year-old Nathan said, "Sing the song about the sandals, mom."

"Sandals? A church song?"

"Yes. All other ground is sinking sandals, other ground is sinking sand."

Lucas at the same age asked his grandfather to sing the song about the peas. "He whispers sweet peas to me." And a few months later I heard him singing, "When the roll is called under the water."

Do you wonder if God has the same problem understanding our singing? Not as long as we sing and make melody with our hearts (Eph 5.19), rather than muttering half-memorized words on automatic pilot. What about our prayers?

Once in a women's class, a dear friend was praying and had trouble with a certain phrase. No matter how she tried, it kept coming out backwards to what she intended. Finally she just said, "Lord, you know what I mean!"

Of course He does. Why was that such a revelation and comfort to me? Because we spend so much time legislating prayer, telling folks which person of the Godhead they can and cannot pray to, what things they can and cannot ask for, and what things they *must* say if they expect their prayer to get past the ceiling when the real problem is, we don't pray enough. No wonder! Everyone's afraid of doing it wrong. Just as the Pharisees made the Law of Moses a burden (Matt 23.4), we are making what should be one of our greatest comforts in this life, a burden instead.

Just pray! We have an intercessor, a mediator who is on our side and pleads our cases. He is not standing their just waiting to stamp my particular prayer, "Disqualified!" and send it back unheard. There are no misheard prayers in Heaven.

> *For there is one God,* ***one mediator*** *between God and man, himself man, Christ Jesus, who gave himself a ransom for all.*
>
> *And he who searches the hearts knows what is the mind of the spirit, because he makes intercession for the saints according to the will of God.*
>
> *These things says the Son of God. ...I am he who searches the reins and the hearts.*
>
> 1 Timothy 2.5–6; Romans 8.27; Revelation 2.18, 23

Thar He Blows!

If you have ever tried to take care of an infant's stuffy nose with one of those rubber ball suction devices, you—and your child—know the importance of the day he actually learns to blow his nose, even if you do have to hold the Kleenex for him.

Lucas must have been about 18 months old when he learned. He was so thrilled he could not get enough of it. I caught him grabbing a hanging bath towel at the hem, which was the only place he could reach, and blowing his nose on it. Then he came running to me, for hugs and kisses I assumed; but no, as soon as I picked him up, he grabbed my shirt and blew his nose on it. When I finally realized what was up, I saw him just as he made a beeline for a clean pile of laundry waiting to be folded, and caught him before he could jump into the basket and blow his nose all over everything. It was suppertime, though, when I realized that teaching him nose-blowing etiquette was of paramount importance. I sat him in the high chair and he promptly reached out and blew his nose on—no, not his napkin—his biscuit!

Now when I have a cold I am glad I can blow my nose, but it's no big deal. Lucas, on the other hand, had learned something new. It made his life so much easier and he was excited to practice it. Now where am I going with this one?

Two people walk into the meetinghouse on Sunday morning. One comes in with a ho-hum expression, sits near the back, tries not to fall asleep, and leaves looking much as he did when he arrived. Another comes in smiling, hugs everyone in sight, sits near the front taking copious notes, asks questions in class, and even stays afterward with more questions. Which is the "mature" Christian and which is the babe in Christ? Isn't it sad that we all know the answer to that one?

Why have we "mature" Christians—or should I just say "old" converts?—lost our enthusiasm? Why is it that we need to learn from the babes the joy of salvation, the diligence of study, and the satisfaction of serving others, when *we* should be giving *them* the example? Why is it that the ones who should least understand the importance of salvation are the ones who appreciate it the most? Have we forgotten what we know, or are we just bored with it? Are we, like the Pharisees, so enamored with our own sense of righteousness that we actually think we have saved ourselves?

Unfortunately for the babes, many will learn from our example and become just like us. Let's rekindle the fire. There is a reason for the term "revival," and it is not an unscriptural word. Let's start behaving like mature Christians ought to behave, like children of God who live lives of joy and are thrilled to be able to call God their Father and Jesus their older brother. Isn't that amazing?

Turn us, O God of our salvation, and cause your indignation toward us to cease. Will you be angry with us forever? Will you draw out your anger to all generations? Will you not revive us again that your people may rejoice in you? Show us your lovingkindness, O Jehovah, and grant us your salvation.

Psalm 85.5–7

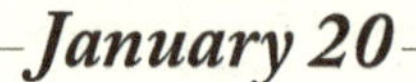

January 20

Jesus' Laws of Motion

Perhaps you remember Newton's second law of motion from high school physics (or is it the third?—Hey! At least I can remember the law): for every action there is an equal and opposite reaction.

Sometimes we live our lives by this law as well. We constantly react to what others do, and excuse it because of what the other person did first. Christianity is a life of action not reaction. *My actions should not depend upon what other people do, but upon what is right and what is wrong.* Any time I let someone else's behavior "cause" me to do something; I am actually letting that person control me. How often have I said, "He made me so mad?" No, he didn't. I *let* myself get angry. When I stand before the throne of God, I will not be judged on other people's deeds but upon mine, no matter what the other guy did first.

Most of us know this, and readily spout the appropriate answers when called upon in Sunday morning Bible study, but when we get out in the world things are always "different." No, they are not. These things apply to my relationship with my next door neighbor, my co-workers, my family, yes, even to that driver up in front of me! Then there is the matter of poor service in a restaurant, or a delay in the doctor's office, or a faulty product that needs returning. All of these offer me a chance to *act* as a Christian, not *reac*t as an unbeliever who has no self-control. Yes, in our society we are allowed to voice our concerns over shoddy service and merchandise, but Christians never have the right to make a scene or be verbally abusive. By letting others control me, I am showing how weak I truly am, not how strong.

Christians control themselves—they do not let others do it. Is this easy? Not with Satan constantly whispering in my ear, "He had it coming." Like Eve, I often listen to him. But this is how important ignoring that whisper is: I must constantly ask myself why I have acted as I have. If the answer starts, "Because he/she/they…" I am condemned already.

Jesus' Laws of Motion

For this is acceptable, if for conscience toward God a man endures griefs, suffering wrongfully. For what glory is it if, when you sin and are buffeted for it, you shall take it patiently? But if, when you do well and suffer for it you shall take it patiently, this is acceptable with God. For hereunto were you called: because Christ also suffered for you, leaving you an example, that you should follow his steps; who did no sin, neither was guile found in his mouth; who, when he was reviled, reviled not again, when he suffered, threatened not, but committed himself to him that judges righteously.

And as you would that men should do to you, do you also to them likewise. And if you love those who love you, what thank have you? For even sinners love those who love them. And if you do good to them that do good to you, what thank have you? For even sinners do the sane. And if you lend to those of whom you hope to receive, what thank have you? Even sinners lend to sinners, to receive again as much. But love your enemies and do them good, and lend, never despairing, and your reward shall be great, and you shall be sons of the Most High, for he is kind toward the unthankful and evil.

1 Peter 2.19–23; Luke 6.31–35

January 21

The Bodyguard

I have had several surgeries in the past two or three years, mainly eye surgeries. Each time I have had to carefully work my way back into my physical regimen. I believe that God expects me to keep this body he gave me as fit as I can so I can serve him as long and well as possible. One of my regular activities is walking. After eye surgeries, the challenge is to see where I am going, and I use an old rake handle as a walking stick to steady myself when I stumble.

My six-year-old red heeler, a color of Australian cattle dog, has figured out that I have some sort of a problem, and she has become my "protector." When our neighbor to the west came down a few weeks ago with his brush-hog to mow the majority of our five acres, I was out walking. She usually walks the first lap of six on my half-mile-plus loop, scares up all the critters—especially the snakes—then sits in the shade, watching, while I finish. That day, she stayed with me for the entire walk, and any time I got within 100 feet of the tractor, she went after that mower with a vengeance. We were afraid she would get hurt, so I altered my walk to stay on one side of the property and the neighbor worked the other half until I finished. Then my canine bodyguard retreated under the porch till the next time I came outside.

One Saturday, I was walking while Keith used the little rider on the acre we keep mown around the house. Every time our paths started to intersect, she would charge across the field from wherever she happened to be, cut between us, and bark and nip at his wheels, even though she is scared to death of the mower, and runs from it otherwise. (I wonder if she thought it had already eaten Keith.)

Today, another neighbor was using his brush-hog on his side of the south fence, and we passed one another three or four times along the fence while I walked. Magdi headed for him every time we got close and barked and jumped at the fence until I was safely by. Then she followed after me, and stayed at my heels until the next lap brought us back to the fence, where she repeated her performance. Once he lifted the front bucket right at her, and she slowly rose on her hind legs, barking even louder, till he put it back down. The way my 40 pound red-headed protector takes such good care of me warms my heart, especially since she is so afraid herself of those vicious green monsters that inhabit our fields and woods! I don't know how she knows that I am not quite up to par, but she is making it her business to watch out for me.

As heartwarming as all that may be, it is nothing compared to the assurance I have that my Heavenly Father looks out for me. The evidence I have in the past year alone is amazing, but all I have to do is open His Word to see the most astonishing care of all—He gave His Son for my soul.

For I am persuaded that neither death, not life, nor angels, nor principalities, nor things present, nor things to come, nor powers, nor height, nor depth, nor any other creature, shall be able to separate us from the love of God, which is in Christ Jesus our Lord.

Romans 8.38–39

January 22

Audience Participation

Have you ever said as you left the meetinghouse on Sunday morning, "I didn't get much out of the worship today?"

Just examine that statement for a moment. We are there for our group worship, the worship we are commanded to do when we are "gathered together." Who is it that we are worshipping? I don't think it's me, and I don't think it's you. When it comes to the worship aspect, I think it matters what *God* thinks of it, not us.

We sit in an auditorium with a raised platform in front of us. Several different men take turns standing before us to lead us in various aspects of our worship to God. Sometimes that gives us the mistaken idea that *we* are the audience. No, *we* are the performers. God is the audience, and if He "doesn't get much out of our worship," it's our fault, not His, nor that of the men who try so hard to lead us, and seldom get anything but complaints for their efforts.

What would you think of a performer who gave a lackadaisical performance, who acted like he couldn't care less that someone was watching him? If I paid good money for a ticket, I would want my money back. I wonder if that's what God thinks as we "worship" by barely mumbling through our songs, daydreaming during prayers, and making faces at the babies in front of us during the sermons. I wonder if He would like to have back what it cost Him for us to be able to come before Him and worship Him. You see, He is watching our performance; *He* is the audience. It doesn't really matter if I don't like the songs chosen, if I think the prayer is too long, if I think the sermon is boring. What matters is, did I worship God with all my heart in spite of those things? That's what this Audience grades us on. I don't want Him to ask for a refund.

So this Sunday as I leave the meetinghouse I should ask myself this, "How well did I worship my God this morning?" Whether or not this is all there is to my worship is another matter entirely, but this question certainly makes a good start on answering that one too, don't you think?

> *Oh Jehovah, truly I am your servant; I am your servant, the son of your handmaid. You have loosed my bonds. I will offer to you the sacrifices of thanksgiving, And will call upon the name of Jehovah. I will pay my vows unto Jehovah, Even in the presence of all his people. In the courts of Jehovah's house, In the midst of you, O Jerusalem, Praise Jehovah.*
>
> Psalm 116.16–19

January 23

Mirror, Mirror

I have discovered a new body part. It is called the "forgetter." A few weekends ago, it ran in overdrive. On Saturday morning I melted the butter, then forgot to put it in the pecan waffle batter. I preheated the waffle iron on high, then forgot to turn it down to medium. Tough black waffles were not what I planned for breakfast.

On Sunday morning I seasoned the roast with salt, pepper, fresh thyme and marjoram, browned it in olive oil, chopped some onions, garlic, and celery and sautéed them in the drippings, deglazed the pan, then put everything back in with potatoes and carrots. Sounds like a great cooking show, right? I set the temperature on the oven, set the timer to start while we were gone, and walked out of the house without turning it on! I knew we were in trouble when I walked in and sniffed and that aroma that instantly makes your stomach stand up and beg was missing.

I always used to think the passage in James about the man who looks into the mirror and then walks away forgetting what he saw, was a little farfetched. But now I regularly look at myself in the mirror every morning, walk away and get sidetracked making a bed or sorting laundry, taking a phone call or paying a bill, and forget to comb my hair until I look again a couple of hours later. Lucky for me I have a head full of curls and the style these days is to look like your hair has not seen a comb for three weeks. Celebrities pay big bucks for such a look. So I can get by, right? Everyone will think I just have the same hairstyle as some glamorous movie star. When I looked out and said good morning to the meter reader the other day, the look he gave me said he was not fooled a bit.

So it is not as difficult now to realize that people can look at the mirror of God's word and walk away, forgetting to change themselves. They are as easily distracted by the "cares and riches and pleasures of this life," as I am by assorted housekeeping duties, and the Word is choked out of them (Luke 8.14). But change is the essence of repentance; it is the point where self is pushed aside, and obedience and service to the Lord becomes my reason for living. If I can see in God's word what I need to be and do, and then walk away without doing it, I have not turned my life over to Him—I have not been converted, or else I have turned my back on that commitment like an unfaithful spouse. That is why the Old Testament prophets call it spiritual adultery.

Sometimes I forget because I *want* to forget. In a culture where self-control is a scarce commodity, it's easier to say, "That's just the way I am." It's even easier to never look in the mirror in the first place because I do not want to see anything wrong with myself. But God won't be fooled any more easily than my meter reader was.

Remember to look in the mirror this morning, and don't forget what you see.

But be doers of the word and not hearers only, deluding yourselves. For if anyone is a hearer of the word and not a doer, he is like a man seeing his natural face in a mirror; for he sees himself and goes away, immediately forgetting what kind of man he saw. But he who looks into the perfect law of liberty, and so continues, being not a hearer that forgets, but a doer who works, this man shall be blessed in his doing.

James 1.22–25

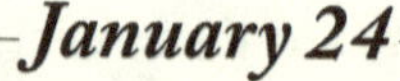

January 24

Learning to Work

If there is one thing Keith taught our sons, it is how to work. Living on five acres with a huge garden, several animals, and a wood-burning stove for heat, but only rakes, shovels, hoes, a wheelbarrow, and a *push* mower to work with—no, it was not self-propelled, and we had no tractors or other power equipment—meant they had chores that had to be done or the family suffered. They certainly did not appreciate the lesson then, but they have thanked him several times since they left home and entered the work force. More than once I have had their bosses thank me for my sons, adding things like, "I wish I had a store full of them."

Lucas, my older son, is now in management with a large grocery chain. He often laments the workers he has to deal with, who have no sense of responsibility, showing up late or not at all, who never anticipate needs, never see what needs doing on their own, or who simply lollygag around with no sense of urgency or efficiency. The saddest ones, he says, are the young ones who really want to do a good job, but whose parents have never taught them how, either by assigning chores, or actually expecting them to be done well and on time. The ones who irritate him the most are the ones who think showing up and clocking in means they *are* working, even if all they do is stand in the halls and talk.

God has called us to work in his vineyard. I am sure he is patient with those who need to learn how to work. But some treat their job in the vineyard as an entitlement that precludes any notion of actual labor. As long as they clock in (submit in baptism, show up on Sunday morning—choose your application), they are "earning" their paycheck. We have forgotten that the only "wages" we can *earn* is death. Eternal life is a precious gift, and how we work in the vineyard is directly proportionate to our gratitude for it. Am I standing in the halls talking, or am I wearing myself out laboring for the Lord?

Let us therefore labor to enter in that rest, that no man fall after the same example of disobedience.

Hebrews 4.11

January 25

Other People's Trash

When we first moved here, the land was a pristine wilderness. We were the only ones back here in the woods, half a mile off the highway. People often asked, "How in the world did you even find this spot?" If it hadn't been for the sign on the highway, we never would have.

Fast forward to the last few years. The deeds on the rest of the parcels of acreage are finally clear and others have bought and moved in. Oh, for the money to have bought it all way back then....

As you come down our drive now, you pass one plot in particular where you wonder if you missed the "Junkyard" sign. Empty fertilizer sacks, empty feed sacks, broken buckets with all their pieces, torn potato chip bags and candy bar wrappers, shattered plastic milk jugs, toys in various states of disrepair, gardening tools, rusty tractor parts and old horse trailers, torn screen segments, pieces of hose draped over fences, broken down appliances, seldom- or no longer-driven vehicles including a burnt-out semi tractor, and piles of pure garbage dot the landscape. I knew we were in trouble the first week these folks moved in, when a used disposable diaper sat in the yard for days, and then they mowed over it, scattering it to the winds.

When you say anything to them, the standard reply is, "This is our land. We can do with it what we want. It's no business of yours."

But it is. Every time the wind blows I must go around with a trash bag and pick up the litter than blows over or through the fence onto our property. Every time a strong rain comes, more is washed down around the gate. And should we ever decide to sell, the mere fact that any prospective buyer must go past that mess to get to us, will lower our property value. Keith explained this last fact to them one day, and they said, "Huh? Why?"

Sometimes I also fail to see how my life is anyone else's business. It's easy to say, "This doesn't hurt anyone, so why can't I do it?" or, "Why does it matter how I let my attitude show? They can just ignore me." In real life, that is impossible. I do affect everyone who comes into contact with me. I can make their days better or worse. I can say something that will help or hinder. I can do something that comforts or hurts. What I cannot do is something that has no affect at all—it is simply impossible.

My trashy neighbors have actually done me a lot of good. I find myself thinking about these things more and more, wondering whom I am affecting every day, and hoping it is for the good. I hope hearing about them will help you today too.

Your boasting is not good. Do you not know that a little leaven leavens the whole lump? Clean out the old leaven that you may be a new lump, as you really are unleavened. For Christ, our Passover Lamb, has been sacrificed. Let us therefore celebrate the festival, not with old leaven, the leaven of malice and evil, but with the unleavened bread of sincerity and truth.

1 Corinthians 5.6–8

January 26

Define These Words

I mentioned once before a certain fifth grade class I taught, and the lesson we had on 2 Peter 1.5–7. In trying to explain these characteristics, the requirements of being a Christian as they preferred to call them, I did a lot of word study. Three of those words, and the way the children chose to make applications of them, have especially stuck with me after all these years.

Look up "virtue" in a Greek dictionary or lexicon and you are likely to find the phrase "moral excellence." But this does not do a thing for a ten-year-old or for many adults either. I finally came up with "doing right because it *is* right, not because someone is watching or you are afraid of the consequences." Or as the children put it, "Virtue is when you *want* to be good." They easily came up with example after example. Probably my favorite was, "It isn't virtue when you slow down to the speed limit because you see a police car." Children can be brutal!

Another word we looked up was "knowledge." We all feel so lacking here. It was such a relief to discover that this use of the word signifies an active searching and desire for the truth—something even the newest Christian can have—and very often has more of than the one who has been sitting on his pew for 40 years. The children understood right away that this word was not a measure of knowledge but of devotion, and came up with examples even more easily than they had for "virtue." Just how often do we sit down for some real study, not just a read-through? Do we spend more time in front of the TV than we do with our Bibles? Are our Bible class lessons done as faithfully as our "homework?"

Then there was godliness. How many times have I heard this defined as "a short form of godlikeness?" Children these days are so worldly wise that even they understood that you cannot make an argument based on the construction of an English word when the word was originally written in Greek! Godliness means my entire life is focused toward God. Everything I say, think, or do must put Him first. If I make any decision in life without first asking how it will affect my service to God, I am not godly.

The children's example? If deciding to buy a new car means I cannot give as I should to the Lord, then I should not buy a new car! Simplistic, you say? Too much "this world"? Well, they were only children after all, but doesn't their example clearly show how godliness should pervade our everyday lives? And isn't that exactly what we adults have the most trouble with—applying spiritual principles to specific circumstances in our everyday lives, even when it hurts?

Virtue, knowledge, and godliness: hard to define? Not to a ten-year-old. Hard to do? That depends on us.

Virtue*: Servants, be obedient unto them that according to the flesh are your masters with fear and trembling, in singleness of your heart, as unto Christ; not in the way of* *eye-service, as men-pleasers, but as servants of Christ, doing the will of God from the heart, with goodwill, doing service as unto the Lord, and not unto men, knowing that whatever good thing each one does, the same shall he receive from the Lord.*

Knowledge: *Putting away therefore all wickedness, and all guile, and hypocrisies, and envies, and all evil speaking, as newborn babes long for mother's milk, you long for the spiritual milk which is without guile, that you may grow thereby unto salvation.*

Godliness: *For they that are after the flesh mind the things of the flesh, but they that are after the spirit, the things of the spirit. For the mind of the flesh is death, but the mind of the spirit is life and peace.*

Ephesians 6.5–8; 1 Peter 2.1–2; Romans 8.5–6

January 27

Where Are the Cookies?

Several years ago, a prominent female politician angered many American women when she answered a reporter about her choice of career over homemaking by saying, "Well I suppose I could have stayed home and *baked cookies*." Most of us read a sneer in her tone and, as I remember it, her office was inundated with homemade cookies baked and sent by outraged homemakers.

One of the things I decided to do as a homemaker was to keep a cookie jar filled with homemade cookies, and for the most part I have. Chewy oatmeal raisin, spicy gingersnaps, crumbly peanut butter, sparkly snickerdoodles, decadent triple chocolate, wonderful almond crunch cookies that always surprise people and steal the show, and all those variations of the All-American chocolate chip: Toll House, Neimann Marcus, peanut butter chocolate chip, double chocolate chip, oatmeal chocolate chip, and death by chocolate chocolate chip. My boys would come home from their friends' houses talking about how deprived they were—all they had were Oreos.

My younger son Nathan was especially fond of cookies. As a toddler, he would pull up a chair to stand in so he could "help" me make cookies—help that usually involved tasting the dough to make sure it was good, and then "cleaning" the beaters. When he was in high school, I bought him a shirt that said, THE BIG QUESTIONS: WHO AM I? WHY AM I HERE? WHAT IS MY FATE? WHERE ARE THE COOKIES?

Eventually that chubby, tow-headed, blue-eyed cherub became a long, lean man who went off to college. The first time he came home he brought a friend with him. He immediately led the buddy to the counter where the cookie jar always sat. "See? I *told* you there would be cookies." Until he married I would bake cookies and save a dozen each week in a freezer bag until I had four or five kinds, then mail them to him and start all over. This was one serious cookie connoisseur. I am not sure what else made an impression on him, but I know he will remember that I loved him enough to make cookies for him.

I am reminded of David after his small army defeated the Amalekites. Not all of his men were as righteous as he. Several "wicked men and base fellows" did not want to share the spoils with the men who had stayed at camp, guarding their belongings. David said, "You shall not do so, my brothers, with that which Jehovah has given us... the share of him who goes down to the battle shall be the same as he who tarried by the baggage; they shall share alike, and it was from that day forward a statute and ordinance in Israel" (1 Sam 30.23–25). David understood the value of those who did the behind-the-scenes work, the jobs others considered less important, and which seldom received glory or recognition.

Think about Dorcas. Stephen, the deacon and great preacher, had been killed not long before. James the apostle, a cousin of Jesus himself, would be next. But who did Peter raise from the dead? Not the powerful speakers who performed miracles, but a widow who made clothes for the poor (Acts 9.36–42). Surely *God* was saying that what we consider small and unimportant tasks are actually some of the greatest of all.

Never underestimate the importance of baking cookies.

For whosoever shall give you a cup of water to drink because you are Christ's, truly I say to you, he shall not lose his reward.

Mark 9.41

January 28

The Tablecloth

My grandmother crocheted a lace tablecloth for me many years ago. She was quite a lady, my grandmother. She was widowed in her 40s, left behind with two of her five children still at home. She met the bills by doing seasonal work in the citrus packing sheds of central Florida, standing on her feet 10–12 hours a day, six days a week in season, and then working in a drugstore, a job she walked to and from for nearly 30 years. She delivered prescriptions, worked the check-out, even made sodas at the fountain.

It was a small town and once, a woman, whom she knew was not married, came in looking for some form of birth control. My grandmother told her, "No! Go home and behave yourself like a decent woman should." No, she did not lose her job over that. She merely said what every other person there wished they had the nerve to say back in those days. She lived long enough to see the shame of our society that no one thinks it needs saying any more.

As to my tablecloth, most people would look at it and think it was imperfect. She crocheted with what was labeled "ivory" thread, but she could never afford to buy enough at once to do the whole piece. So after she cashed her paycheck, she went to the store and bought as much as her budget would allow that week and worked on it. The next week, she went back and did the same, always buying the same brand labeled "ivory." Funny thing about those companies, though—when the lot changes, sometimes the color does too, sometimes only a little, but sometimes "ivory" becomes more of a vanilla or even crème caramel. The intricately crocheted squares in my tablecloth are not all the same color, even though the thread company said they were.

Some people probably look at it and wonder what went wrong. All they see is mismatched colors. What I see is a grandmother's love, a grandmother who had very little, but who wanted to do something special for her oldest grandchild. I revel in those mismatched squares because I know my grandmother thought of me every week for a long time, spent the precious little she had to try to do something nice, and, as far as I am concerned, succeeded far beyond her wildest dreams.

If it were your grandmother, you would think the same I am sure. So why is it we think Almighty God cannot take our imperfections and make us into great men and women of faith? Why is it we beat ourselves to death when we make a mistake, even one we repent of and do our best to correct? Do we not yet understand grace? Are we so arrogant that we think we don't have to forgive ourselves even though God does? Yes we should understand the enormity of our sin, repenting in godly sorrow, over and over, even as David did, but prolonged groveling in the pit of unworthiness can be more about self-pity and lacking faith in God to do what he promised than it is about humility. The longer we indulge in it, the less we are doing for the Lord, and Satan is just as pleased as if we had gone on sinning. Either way helps him out.

The next time you look into a mirror and see only your faults, remember my tablecloth. When you give God all you have, he can make you into something beautiful too.

And God is able to make all grace abound unto you, that you, always having all sufficiency in everything, may abound unto every good work.

2 Corinthians 9.8

The Lost Art of Meditation

What do you do in your spare time? Yes, I hear you laughing, but I have come to the conclusion that as Christians we need to make sure we have some of that precious commodity. Not because "I just have to have some time for me," but because I just have to have some time with God.

So what would we do if we had a few spare minutes alone? Prayer comes to mind, of course, but another important activity is meditating, or musing on God's word. In Genesis 24.63 Isaac went out in the evening to the fields where he could be alone to meditate. David made time too, even in the midst of tending sheep, leading an army, and running a kingdom. When he was in the wilderness he meditated *in the night watches* (Psa 63.6). He anxiously looked forward to those times (Psa 119.148).

Perhaps it is most difficult for mothers to find time to meditate. Our entire day, from the moment we rise to the moment our heads hit the pillow again at night, is filled with "Mom, can you…," "Honey, will you…," and, "Ma'am you need to…" until our minds are run ragged. But even when we are alone we sabotage ourselves. When the family leaves for work and school and the baby is napping, we turn on the TV "for company." When we drive, we turn on the radio. When we exercise, we slip on the headphones. I have decided that one of the nicest things God did for me was to *not* furnish me with a dishwasher. Do you know how much meditation can be accomplished over a sink full of soapy water?

Mary, as young and inexperienced as she was, gives us the perfect example—even as a new mother making the time to meditate, pondering things in her heart (Luke 2.19, 51). The word "ponder" means to put one thing with another. But look at these other places where the same word is used (but translated by another English word), all in the book of Acts: 4.15—they *conferred* among themselves; 17.18—certain philosophers *encountered* him; 18.27—he *helped* them; 20.14—when he *met* us. In all these cases words or people were put together (pondered) with a purpose—to learn, to assist, to come to an understanding. So pondering God's word is an attempt "to put it all together" in our minds. Anyone who thinks they can read it through once and get the whole picture will be sadly disappointed!

Meditation is not for the shallow-minded, but you do not need to be an intellectual either. The greatest benefit of meditation is the sheer depth of understanding one can eventually come to about God, the nature of his kingdom, and the beauty of his plan (Psa 143.5). One can find himself in a place he never dreamed existed years before when he so confidently knew all the Bible stories, the "plan of salvation," and "the five acts of worship" (Psa 49.3; 119.99); and he can still see below him an awe-inspiring depth that makes Bible study once again vital and exciting (Psa 119.15). Meditation can spawn a prayer (Psa 5.1–3) making that part of our lives richer and deeper as well. In the end it can bring us acceptance by our God (Psa 19.14).

So make some spare time today. Get up earlier, stay up later, take off those earphones or turn off the radio. Spend some time meditating. You don't have to twist yourself into a pretzel to gain a deeper understanding of the True God and his Word.

> *Blessed is the man who walks not in the counsel of the wicked, nor stands in the way of sinners nor sits in the seat of scoffers. But his delight is in the law of Jehovah, and in his law does he meditate day and night. And he shall be like a tree planted by the streams of water, that brings forth its fruit in its season, whose leaf also does not wither; and whatsoever he does shall prosper.*
>
> Psalm 1.1–3

January 30

An Unheated Bathhouse

After camping for many years in both Florida and Georgia state parks, I can give you a list of advantages and disadvantages in each. In Florida parks you can actually reserve a specific campsite that meets your own needs and preferences. In Georgia parks you can only reserve "a site"; you learn to arrive right at check-out time so you have more choices. Otherwise you may wind up without enough level ground for your 16' x 10' tent, and an up close and personal view of your neighbors.

But Georgia parks do have this advantage—their bathhouses are heated in the cool seasons. I suppose Florida parks must live up to the State's image as "warm." The ceilings in the bathhouses are about 12 feet high and the top four feet of wall is screen—whatever the temperature is outside, it is inside too, sometimes cooler since the concrete walls tend to hold in the cold. In summer that may be nice, but in winter it's for the birds—penguins, in this case.

Yet in Florida we do have some chilly days, and in North Florida we have several downright cold days. On our last January camping trip to Anastasia State Park on the northeast coast, highs were in the 50s and lows in the 30s, and taking a shower was literally a bone-chilling experience. To make matters worse, every time I arrived at the bathhouse, the door was propped open and the ceiling fan spinning, its chain way out of my reach. If grandma had been right about the cold and wet making you sick, we would have been terminal by the end of our stay. No amount of pretending could make those temperatures any warmer. All the ceiling fans, screens and other accoutrements of tropical warmth could not make the goosebumps and shivers disappear. It was *cold.* And our Canadian campsite neighbors agreed.

Don't we sometimes do the same in our spiritual lives? I once saw a man open his closed fist over the collection plate, *and nothing came out.* We may think our pretending is not quite as obvious as that, but God sees our hearts better than my eyes saw that man's empty hand. We sit on a pew on Sunday morning, but what are we doing on Monday morning? We follow along as the preacher cites passages, but do we open our Bibles at home? We bow our heads during prayer, but does God hear from us the rest of the week? Our hands are not empty when we open them over the basket, but are our arms open to the needy, the discouraged, the hurting every other day?

God will not be fooled by the accoutrements of modern Christian living any more than my goosebumps were fooled by screens, a whirling ceiling fan and a big sign that said FLORIDA. Let us turn on the heat in our lives—the heat of passion in our worship, and the warmth of heartfelt compassion toward others.

Take heed that you do not your righteousness before men, to be seen of men, else you will have no reward with your Father who is in heaven. When you do your alms, sound not a trumpet before you as the hypocrites do...that they may have glory of men...When you pray, you shall not be as the hypocrites, for they love to stand and pray in the synagogues and on the corners of streets that they may be seen of men. Moreover when you fast, be not as the hypocrites, of a sad countenance, for they disfigure their faces that they may be seen of men to fast. But you, when you fast, anoint your head, and wash your face, that you be not seen of men to fast, but of your Father who is in secret, and your Father who sees in secret, shall reward you.

Matthew 6.1–6, 16–18

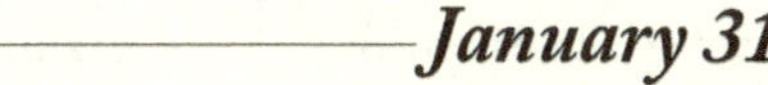

January 31

When Sparks Fly

Many, many years ago we rented an old frame house with rollercoaster wooden floors, leaky, drafty, 15 foot ceilings, and, unfortunately, a bad wiring system. We did not know about the faulty wiring until one by one our appliances started going out. One of the last was the television, an ancient, secondhand model. When its replacement blew the minute we turned it on, and the next, which had worked fine in the store, did the same, things began to fall into place—the electric skillet, the vacuum cleaner, the washing machine, and the electric mixer all had died in the week or two before. A friend came with a voltmeter and we discovered that we were getting 145 volts in the 110 outlets and 290 in the 220s.

A call to the electric company brought an inspection. It wasn't the old wiring after all; it was the transformer, which meant the electric company was at fault and paid for all the appliances, at depreciated value, of course, but at least we had a little help. I'll tell you this, though—never since then have I had a mixer that could whip egg whites in ten seconds flat.

Sometimes I feel like I need a little extra voltage, don't you? Life has its difficult moments, and it seems the older you are and the less strength your body has to deal with it, the more difficulty it must withstand. But spiritually speaking, that should not be the case. Age means experience, which means wisdom, which means things are handled better and more easily, right?

Lucas recently repeated something he had heard from someone somewhere. "Sometimes the discretion of wisdom is just the result of being too tired to act." I identified with the thought immediately. I wonder how many times I have been complimented for my restraint in handling things when the momentary lag of weariness just gave me enough time to think first, or maybe when it just plain overwhelmed me enough to keep me still and out of trouble.

I feel sometimes like I need a spark, that extra voltage that made a stiff meringue faster than I ever had before. We all tend to become complacent, to take for granted the spiritual blessings we have, even salvation. It usually shows in our anemic zeal and ho-hum worship.

And we get tired of the fight. Yet again someone has belittled the Word of God, or taken his name in vain, or simply treated sin as normal and anyone who thinks otherwise as a bigoted fanatic. After fighting for God for so many years, feeling like we are making no headway at all in a world dominated by sin, we just sit back and let it happen. What good will it do anyway?

You never know. More than once I have spoken out alone, only to suddenly find several others standing next to me—people who were too fearful to speak until they heard someone else. I have found out, many days after the fact, that when I stood for the truth, or acted like a Christian is supposed to act in the face of mistreatment, that it helped someone else do the same later on. And many, many more times, I have been the fearful one who was helped simply by seeing a warrior for righteousness take on Satan and his minions single-handedly.

So take some spiritual vitamins today. Pray, read the scripture, meditate in your break time, call a brother or sister and revel in their love—that's why they are there, that's why God gave us each other. Put a jolt of extra voltage in your spiritual life and don't give in to weariness. You do make a difference for the Lord.

You are righteous, O Jehovah, and upright are your judgments. You have commanded your testimonies in righteousness and very faithfulness. My zeal has consumed me because my adversaries have forgotten your word. Your word is very pure, therefore shall your servant love it. I am small and despised, yet I do not forget your precepts. Your righteousness is an everlasting righteousness and your law is truth.

Psalm 119.137–142

February 1

Home of the Soul

We live in a mobile society. The first 11 years of our marriage we lived in five places, and we fully expected that to continue. Neither of us dreamed that our children would go through the same school system for their entire 13 years of schooling, and we would one day look around and say, "We've been here 25 years now!"

It isn't much by worldly standards, just five acres half a mile off a county road with a "manufactured home" on it. But it isn't square footage and high end building materials that make a home. Would you like a tour?

Over to the west sits the doghouse Keith and the boys built together. It has housed five dogs and three cats now—you see, it is an original design, the cats had the second floor of this special pet condo. A bright green swing hangs under the grape arbor. Keith built the arbor and Lucas made the swing in high school shop class. I make muscadine jelly with the grapes—Welch's doesn't even come close. A live oak shades us from the afternoon sun—Nathan fell out of it one Saturday while on the rope swing and broke his arm. Daylilies bloom bright as a yellow sun in a bed I dig up every five or six years, thin out by giving the excess bulbs to friends, and then replant.

Off to the southwest a blueberry patch furnishes us with pies, cobblers, jam, muffins, and pancakes every May. Beyond it a wooded acre includes four huge live oaks growing so close together that two little boys can barely fit between them. But this "fort" gave them plenty of cover from wild Indians and assorted other bad guys.

The open field lies to the south, a place that has seen hundreds of football, basketball, and baseball games. Croquet played on a green tabletop lawn? Forget it. We played "ultimate croquet" with slopes, molehills, armadillo holes, paper plate sized sycamore leaves, pine cones, twigs, and other assorted obstacles. It was a whole lot more interesting.

Off to the southeast sit the old pigpen and the site of the old chicken pen, where the boys learned how to take care of dependent animals, and where the food we eat really comes from. They also learned that there is a good reason to keep the pigpen way out to the southeast!

The garden has moved a few times as we not only rotate crops but entire plots as well. It was another source of learning—about sowing and reaping, about growth, about hard work, about sharing. To the east the creek, which is actually a run, now sits dry as a bone because of the several years of drought, but when the boys were young it always had water in it and they took a dip every so often on a hot summer afternoon.

Isn't it odd how something that is not that valuable to anyone else can mean the world to you? I think we have lost that in a society that no longer even furnishes much of a yard for children to play in. I hope that does not make us lose the impact of some of the descriptions of Heaven, especially those that depict it as a re-creation of the Garden of Eden.

I will one day have to leave this place, and that will be a difficult day. I once had some roses, big beautiful bushes weighed down with pink and white blooms all summer. But between the Storm of the Century in March '93, the several years of drought, and the natural bacteria in the ground in this area, they have gradually faded and died.

You know that old song, "Where the Roses Never Fade?" One day I will have my "roses" again, and they will never die, and neither will we. And we will *never* have to leave.

> *And he showed me a river of water of life, bright as crystal, proceeding out of the throne of God and of the Lamb in the middle of the street; and on this side of the river, and on that was the tree of life bearing twelve kinds of fruit, yielding its fruit every month; and the leaves of the tree were for the healing of the nations. And there shall be no curse any more, and the throne of God and of the Lamb shall be there, and his servants shall serve him and they shall see his face, and his name shall be on their foreheads. And there shall be night no more and they need no light of lamp, neither light of sun for the Lord God shall give them light. And they shall reign forever and ever.*
>
> Revelation 22.1–5

Me and My Shadow

I wonder what Punxatawny Phil saw this morning. According to folklore, when this 120-year-old groundhog leaves his burrow on Gobbler's Knob each February 2, his shadow, or lack thereof, predicts the length of winter. If he sees his shadow, there will be six more weeks of cold. This has never made much sense to me. The only way to see your shadow is on a sunny day. It would make far more sense if the day was cloudy and gray and he did not see his shadow. A cold gray day should mean *more* winter, not less. Besides, how can Phil predict my weather from more than 1,000 miles away? My own local weatherman changes his five day forecast every 12 hours, and still misses it half the time.

The idea of shadows is used a lot in the scriptures. I was raised on the concept of "foreshadowing"—items under the Old Covenant used as types of things in the New (Heb 8.5; 10.1; 1 Cor 5.7–8, *etc.).* I think I had the notion that esoteric concept was the primary use of the word "shadow" in the Bible.

Then I discovered Psalm 102.11, 144.4, and Ecclesiastes 8.13. Our lives are depicted as shadows that decline and pass away. Have you ever stood outside when a breeze was blowing those puffy cotton ball clouds across the sky? One minute you are in the sun and the next in the shade—one minute you have a shadow and the next you don't. Life is just as ethereal in several ways. One moment you are basking in the warmth of happiness and good times; the next your life is dark and gray with trials. One minute you are here, and the next you are gone. Remember not to lay up treasures for this world, but for the lasting one to come.

The word is also used in terms of protection, hiding in the "shadow" of God. David conveys thoughts like these in Psalm 17.8; 36.7; and 57.1. Jeremiah uses the figure in Lamentations 4.20. In a hot land with several desert areas, the protection of shade is important and that figure spoke volumes to these people. Down here in Florida we have a healthy respect for shade which can make a 10 to 15 degree difference in the temperature. We will walk the entire length of two parking lots in order to park a car in the miniscule shade of a thin-limbed sapling. I wonder why so few are interested in the huge cooling shadow of a loving God.

But then maybe I do understand. When you step into the shadow of someone who is bigger than you, your own shadow disappears. Our lives "are hid with Christ" (Col 3.3). Maybe we just cannot stand the notion of giving up self. We want to retain just a touch of independence. "That's just who I am," becomes an excuse for our failure to overcome sin and become new creatures. We fail to realize that we have merely swapped dwelling in the protective shadow of God for dwelling in the outer darkness of the Devil.

Think today about shadows—about the interesting study of Old Testament items foreshadowing those in the New; about the fleeting nature of life, like a shadow dissolving when a cloud sails across the sun; about the great protection found in God's shadow. Think too about hiding yourself in the larger shadow of a Big Brother whose life we must emulate if we ever hope for that Father's protection, and a life that is no longer as ephemeral as a shadow.

He that dwells in the secret place of the Most High shall abide under the shadow of the Almighty. I will say of the LORD, He is my refuge and my fortress: my God; in Him will I trust.

Psalm 91.1–2

Germ Warfare

A few Sundays ago I listened to some wonderful prayers in our group worship. However, something struck me that day and not for the first time. In our Bible study prayer we prayed for "forgiveness of sins." In our "opening prayer" we prayed for "forgiveness of sins." In our "closing prayer" we prayed for "forgiveness of sins." I suddenly looked around me and thought, "What in the world has everyone been doing in the past two hours?"

I think in our efforts to avoid any resemblance to the doctrine I grew up calling "the impossibility of apostasy," we have done ourselves a grave disservice and a very discouraging one as well. As a child I saw good men who often prayed, "Lord forgive us, because we know we sin every day." Or "all the time." Or "so often." I used to look at them and wonder what it was they were doing. I never saw them sin, or heard anyone else say they saw them sin either. I began to feel like sin must be some sort of miasma that follows you around and then, *bang!* when you least expect it, it infects you like some kind of airborne germ.

That is not the Bible definition of sin. "Everyone who does sin, does lawlessness, and sin is lawlessness" (1 John 3.4). No, I am not gong into some heavy theology. I don't think I need to. John plainly teaches that sin is something you do. Now sin may involve wrong thinking, too, but still it is a specific thing. It is not some sort of germ you catch without ever knowing it. By making it into that sort of thing, we make ourselves miserable, living a life of despair instead of hope. God said you can control yourself. He said you can overcome. He said you can live a godly life. Give yourself a break! God does.

Does that mean we won't sin? Of course not. But why in the world do we feel so compelled to always add the negative, especially when we are talking to one another? We should be encouraging one another, not trying to build stumbling-blocks of cynicism and pessimism. Of course, using the correct definition of sin, something we actually do and can quantify verbally, forces us to specifically repent of actual things we have done, instead of being able to say, "Lord, I know I sin a lot, and probably don't even know it when I do, so please forgive me." Maybe that is the real problem—too much pride to admit the wrong we do, and actually try to become better people. If you never know when the germ is going to get you, it's not your fault right? But that's not the way it works, at least not to someone sincerely trying to grow as a Christian.

I know that when I sin and realize it, I feel so heartbroken and ashamed that, like David, I ask for forgiveness again and again, but should someone who has been a Christian for a decade, who is supposed to have grown in strength, need to pray for forgiveness three times for three different sins in two hours' time? I hope not. If we really are "sinning all the time," we need to take a serious look at our lives. Theologians have a name for that doctrine too. It's called "total depravity." When a society became totally depraved, "sinning all the time," God destroyed it. Sodom, Assyria, Babylon, Rome, even the whole world in Genesis, except for one man who walked with God, and found grace in the eyes of the Lord. If Noah could do it, so can we.

> *Let not sin reign in your mortal body that you should obey the lusts thereof; neither present your members unto sin as instruments of unrighteousness, but present yourselves unto God, as alive from the dead, and your members as instruments of righteousness unto God. For sin shall not have dominion over you, for you are not under law, but under grace.*
>
> Romans 6.12–14

February 4

All Right

Whenever someone asks how I am doing these days, I usually find myself saying, "All right." Yes, I understand that "How are you?" is generally a greeting, not a question, but most of the time people are really asking, and I do not want them to be sorry they did. "All right," seems to answer the question in all respects without beginning a litany of troubles. Things are not good and may never be again, but I am not now in the middle of another crisis.

Look at that phrase carefully, though. "All right." Isn't it odd that it has come to mean that things are *not* all right? Not actually bad, but just "all right." Certainly not "great."

Do you remember the poem "Pippa's Song" from Robert Browning's *Pippa Passes?* The last line says, "God's in His Heaven, all's right with the world." The context of that poem is interesting. Pippa is an orphan in a crime-ridden neighborhood in Asolo, Italy, where even the pillars of the community live lives of moral decadence. Yet her viewpoint is that, despite all the evil in the world, we can still know that God is in his Heaven, and thus everything is "all right," in the true meaning of those two words, not their presently understood mediocrity.

Especially if we interpolate a word in there, "God's *back* in his Heaven and all's right with the world," we Christians can know the same thing.

God, who became the Son, left Heaven for us, going so far as to give up his equality with God the Father (Phil 2.6–7), suffering the same trials and temptations we do in life, yet refusing to give in to sin (Heb 4.15). He died a torturous death (Acts 2.23). Then, just as Satan thought he had won the ultimate victory, it was snatched out of his hands when Jesus rose from the dead (1 Cor 15.1–8). Forty days later he ascended back into Heaven (Acts 1.3, 9). And all of that happened so we could be forgiven, so we could live an abundant life here, and so we could have Eternal Life in the hereafter.

So remember today and every day, regardless how your life is going, regardless how you may feel, regardless the horrible tragedies Satan may have unleashed around us, "God's [back] in his Heaven, and all's right with the world."

> *Therefore let us also, seeing we are compassed about with so great a cloud of witnesses, lay aside every weight of sin that so easily besets us, and run with patience the race that is set before us, looking unto Jesus, the author and perfecter of faith, who for the joy that was set before him, endured the cross, despising shame, and has sat down at the right hand of the throne of God.*
>
> Hebrews 12.1–2

February 5

Good Queen Jezebel

Now that I have your attention with that title, you can take the jaw out of your lap. On second thought, save yourself some trouble and leave it there, because I am about to shock you again: we all need to be more like Jezebel.

Jezebel was smart. She knew Ahab wanted Naboth's vineyard, but she knew better than to just have him killed. Someone might have rebelled at the murder of an innocent man. So she took care to have "witnesses," even though they were false witnesses, so everything would look "right." We should not be deceitful in order to get what we want, but we are commanded to be "wise as serpents" when the good of the Lord's work requires it. Jesus did not thumb his nose at all the traditions of his time, just those that were diametrically opposed to the intent of God's Law. And he was the master at answering a question with a question, putting the questioner on the spot. Paul learned well from his Master. Remember those speeches that always seemed to be just right for the person and the cause? Sometimes we "cut off our noses to spite our face," bragging about our zeal in doing so, when the Lord's work suffers for it.

Jezebel was loyal to her husband. She even went as far as murder for him. How loyal are we? Will we go out of our way to do even innocuous things for our spouses? Or is it just too much trouble and he or she ought not to be so picky in the first place? Do we never even allow thoughts of infidelity to enter our minds, or do we consider those harmless as long as we do not act on them? What kinds of things do we say about them in the break room at work or the neighborhood coffee party? What do our children hear us say? Disloyalty can be shown in many ways.

Jezebel was loyal to her god. She converted an entire nation to Baal. How concerned are we about our neighbors' souls? Do we even mention the True God to them? Are we careful to keep our relationships with them in such a state that they will come to us when a spiritual need arises? Jezebel was ready to avenge her god by killing Elijah for his having killed the prophets of Baal (1 Kgs 19.2). Both her and Elijah's loyalty was measured by their willingness to fight for God (or a god). Do we stand up to oppose false teachings and immorality in our society, or are we afraid to stir things up?

She implanted her values into her children—so well that they followed in her footsteps all their lives. The problem, of course, was her values. How much effort do we put into teaching our children God's Law, even when we know it could cost them their souls if we do not? Or are we too busy supplying physical needs, and cultural "enrichment"?

Of course, none of us want to be like Jezebel in her wickedness, but remember Jesus' parable about the unrighteous steward: "The sons of this world are for their own generation wiser than the sons of light" (Luke 16.8). Learn your lessons from whomever you can. Just make sure your application is righteous.

> *My son, if you will receive my words and lay up my commandments with you, so as to incline your ear unto wisdom and apply your heart to understanding, yes if you will cry after discernment, and lift up your voice for understanding, if you seek her as silver, and search for her as for hidden treasure, then you shall understand the fear of Jehovah, and find the knowledge of God. For Jehovah gives wisdom. Out of his mouth comes knowledge and understanding.*
>
> Proverbs 2.1–6

February 6

A Life of Joy

We have a new puppy. Chloe is an Australian cattle dog, a companion for our six-year-old Australian. They are great dogs, playful, loyal, and smart—too smart sometimes for their owners' good!

Magdalene, our older dog, seems to enjoy the little one, even though she did have to growlingly remind her yesterday that her tail was *not* a chew toy. They both walk with me now, Chloe struggling with her short legs and puppy-plump tummy to keep up, and we look like a parade as we make our morning laps. Magdi has developed some arthritis in her hips so they sit out after the first two rounds, but Chloe still had excess energy this morning. She wanted to be with Magdi, but wanted to run too, so she compromised by running circles around the patient older dog, by turns prancing and ripping back and forth, turning on a dime, as that breed is capable of doing, and yipping playfully. I thought, as I rounded my last bend and came upon this scene that no matter what the scientists tell me about dogs not having emotions, if she did not have it, Chloe was managing a very good impression of pure, unadulterated joy.

First century Christians had that feeling in spades. I did a study on joy recently. Do you know what surprised me? Not a single time does the New Testament say their joy was caused by the physical things in this life—not their health, their wealth, their careers, their homes, not even the weather—is listed as a cause for their joy at all. If it's in there, I missed it.

What caused their joy? Hearing the gospel (Acts 13.52); being baptized (Acts 8.39); having a hope (Rom 12.12); being counted worthy to suffer dishonor for Christ (Acts 5.41); being afflicted (2 Cor 7.4); being persecuted and having their possessions confiscated (Heb 10.32–34); being put to grief through trials (1 Pet 1.6–9); becoming partakers of the suffering of Christ (1 Pet 4.12–16)—whoa, now! What's going on here? Are these a bunch of masochists or what?

The problem is that we confuse joy with happiness. *Hap*-piness comes because of things that *hap*-pen, as does un-*hap*-piness. Joy is an overriding foundation for how we live our lives. I may experience *moments* of unhappiness, but as long as I do not let them overcome my *life* of joy, I am able to survive with that joy intact. I may lose my belongings, lose a loved one, contract a serious illness, even face death, and still not lose my joy.

All those things that caused joy in the early Christians are based upon having a Savior who has gone through every type of problem I ever will have (Heb 4.15), and more than that, gave up an incomprehensible position (Phil 2.6–7), and separated himself from the Father for the first time in all Eternity (Matt 27.46), all so I could have salvation. Anything I have to face in this life, no matter how dire, is petty compared to that. That is why I should only experience moments of grief. To make a "career" of sadness is to devalue everything He went through for me. Nothing I have to face is worse than He faced so that I might some day be in a place where joy will reach its full potential.

Maybe, as Thoreau said in *Walden*, "The mass of men lead lives of quiet desperation," but not Christians. We lead lives of joyful anticipation.

Beloved, do not think it strange concerning the fiery trial among you, which comes upon you to prove you, as though a strange thing happened to you; but insomuch as you are partakers of Christ's sufferings, rejoice, that at the revelation of his glory also you may rejoice with exceeding joy.

1 Peter 4.12–13

February 7

Meat Loaf

There are probably as many recipes for meat loaf as there are families who eat it. Up until a few years ago, I thought the only excuse for making meat loaf was the sandwiches you made with the leftovers. In fact, I was happy to forego eating it at all the first night, and use it only for sandwiches the next day.

Then I found a recipe for Southwestern Meat Loaf. It's still meat loaf—ground meat, finely chopped vegetables, filler, binder of eggs and dairy, seasonings, and a tomato product on top.

Instead of white or yellow onions you use scallions. Instead of bell pepper, open a can of chopped green chiles. Instead of bread crumbs or oatmeal, grind up corn tortillas in the food processor. Instead of milk, sour cream fills the dairy bill with the usual eggs. Along with the usual salt and pepper, sprinkle in chili powder, cumin, and chopped fresh cilantro. Instead of ketchup, mix three tablespoons of brown sugar in a cup of salsa. Pour a quarter cup of that over the top; save the rest for heating and passing with the finished loaf. Fifteen minutes before it's done, sprinkle it with Monterey Jack cheese instead of cheddar. Voila! (Or whatever the Mexican word for that is.)

You know what? It still looks like meat loaf, smells like meat loaf, and tastes like meat loaf, just with a different accent, one we happen to prefer. But if someone else came up with a recipe using chunks of beef, broth, potatoes, onions, and carrots we would all think he was nuts to call it meat loaf. It bears no resemblance to the meat loaf pattern—it's beef stew.

For some reason, that made me think about God's plan for the church. We can find verse after verse where the apostles, particularly Paul, tell us that God expects us to follow a pattern in each congregation—1 Corinthians 4.17; 7.17; 16.1 and 2 Timothy 1.13, just to name a few. But sometimes we mistake an expedient for a flaw in the pattern, and try to legislate where God did not.

Take the Lord's Supper for instance: grape juice and unleavened bread on the first day of the week. What kind of grapes must the juice come from? What sort of flour must the bread be made of? Most of the time here in America, we use juice made from Concord grapes. They did not have Concord grapes in first century Jerusalem. The grapes they had in Corinth were probably different, too. Today we use wheat flour, usually bleached, all-purpose, white flour. Most likely the early Christians in Palestine used barley flour, and I bet there was nothing white about it—pure, whole grain was all most of them could afford. (Funny how that is the expensive kind today!) In Rome the Christians might have used semolina flour. But there is one thing for certain—everywhere in the world, grapes of some sort are available, and everywhere in the world people eat bread. All they have to do is press the grapes and remove the leavening from the bread recipe.

Following a pattern does not mean we make rules God did not. Two women can each make a dress from the same pattern. One uses satin and trims it in lace; the other can only afford gingham and trims it with rickrack. Did they both follow the pattern? Are the sleeves the same length in the same place? Is the neckline the same? Do they both have a gathered skirt, or is one A-line? Oops. That one changed the pattern. It's really not that hard to tell, is it?

And that is how we tell if a church is following the pattern. Sometimes we try to force every church into satin and lace, when they are really more suited to gingham and rickrack. But the essentials are there. It is not my job to go around making judgments about details (cultural expedients) as long as the basic pattern is sound.

But that pattern does matter. It has always mattered with God. Read about Nadab and Abihu, Uzzah, or King Uzziah. Then let's make sure we have found a group of people who do their best to follow God's pattern, and who do not add their own rules to God's. After all, meat loaf is meat loaf is meat loaf. But beef stew isn't!

Even as Moses is ***warned of God*** *when he is about to make the tabernacle, See, said he, that you make all things according to the pattern which was shown you in the mount.*

Hebrews 8.5

February 8

Canoe Trip

On our last camping trip we stayed on the Blackwater River in the Florida panhandle, "the last white sand river in the country," according to the brochures. We decided to take advantage of a local outfitter and rented a canoe. For the price they transport you upriver 11 miles so that when you get to your destination, your vehicle is waiting for you, and you can pull the canoe onshore and leave on your own schedule.

It was a crisp winter morning, with a sky so clear and blue you wondered if God had simply done away with clouds forever. We put in on a white sand beach and headed off with our paddles dipping rhythmically at first, but eventually lying across our laps for the bulk of the trip as we drifted along with the current.

We saw turtles by the dozen, sunning on logs near the shore, ducks splashing ahead of us by the river's edge, a heron that seemed to taxi across the top of the water before its take-off, and an owl that took flight from a huge cypress branch as we passed him. We scared up one poor water bird of some sort that would fly on ahead, and then as we came round the next bend, fly again. I felt sorry for the poor fellow.

If he had only flown inland 20 or 30 feet and waited for us to pass, he could have stayed where he was. I wondered how far from home he finally ended up.

We passed small streams emptying noisily into the bigger river, and backwaters that sat still and quiet, forested with cypress knees, and impervious to the river's current. I am happy to report that we saw no alligators at all.

About noon we pulled onto a white sand bar, sat in the shade of a scraggly myrtle, and dug into a backpack for a lunch of biscuits and sausage leftover from breakfast and a canteen of water. We wandered around and found some deer tracks by the water's edge, freshly made we knew, because it had rained the night before.

Then a half hour or so later, as we drifted on down the river, we suddenly found ourselves tangled among the branches of a cypress that had fallen into the river. We had not kept a lookout and floated right into it. Since we were there anyway, and stuck, we had a snack of tangerines, dropping the peels into the water to see if fish enjoyed that sort of thing. Evidently they don't, so we extricated ourselves from among the branches and once again caught the current going downriver.

That stop made a small respite but today it makes a big point. We spent most of the four and a half hours on the water drifting. We seldom put our oars in unless we saw something ahead that we wanted to avoid, usually fallen trees in the water, some just under the surface scraping the bottom of the canoe. Sometimes as we came round a bend, the current would send us toward shore and we had to paddle to keep from bottoming out. Usually it was no problem to stay out of trouble. That one time was a result of becoming so entranced with our surroundings that we did not notice what lay ahead.

That is probably the way we wind up getting in trouble in our spiritual lives too. We get distracted by things, not necessarily sinful things, but things that keep our attention too long from the direction we should be going. When you are looking around, you can't paddle straight, so you wind up drifting where the current takes you, and in this world, that may be a dangerous place. More likely it will be into a bend in the river where the current swirls around in a slow, endless eddy, leading you nowhere.

So be careful of your surroundings today, be careful that the things of this world do not take too much of your time and energy away from things of the next world. You need to be involved in this world—how else can your light shine? But you do not need to wrap yourself up in it to the point that it squeezes out your spirituality and concern for Eternity. When visiting a lonely widow, cooking for a family burdened by illness, studying the Bible, or assembling with the saints becomes simply one more thing on a "to do" list, on the same plane as the PTA meeting, the piano lesson, and the Little League schedule, the priorities of life need a serious overhaul, even if it means giving up something.

Don't drift into the fallen logs and trees that will scrape up your soul. Don't let the bottom of your canoe bump against things that could tip you and drown out your spirituality. Don't bottom out, mired in the mud of life's responsibilities. Don't spend so much time looking at the world as you pass it by, that it winds up meaning more to you than the one you are supposed to be headed for.

> *And that which fell among the thorns, these are they that have heard, and as they go on their way they are choked with cares and riches and pleasures of this life, and bring no fruit to perfection.*
>
> Luke 8.14

Have You Stopped Praying?

Sometimes I think in our efforts to be so careful about doing exactly what God has said to do, we ruin perfectly simple commands with all sorts of convoluted logic. I recently heard one of those old notions again: since we cannot pray 24 hours a day, "Pray without ceasing," *must* mean to be in a prayerful attitude all the time. When I was a child I never did understand that, but I assumed I would when I grew up. I still don't. It says "pray," not be in a prayerful attitude, and exactly what is a prayerful attitude anyway? I know for a fact that you cannot be in a prayerful attitude 24 hours a day any more than you can pray like that.

Have you ever tried to play a 40 page Beethoven sonata from memory? Believe me; trying to remember the fingering and the notes, not to mention getting the nuances just right, takes all the concentration you can muster. How about singing German lieder? As an American who does not speak the language, trying not only to remember words that sound like gibberish to me, but knowing when the "ch" sound is a frontward cat hiss and when it is a backward throat scrape, takes all the brain power I have. I am sure that some of the things you do take equal concentration. And I defy anyone to have a prayerful attitude while they are asleep! One of the works of the Holy Spirit was to take God's words and put them into words we humans could understand (1 Cor 2.6–13). The way to understand 1Thessalonians 5.17 is simply to use words and phrases the way they are ordinarily used.

Suppose you have a checkup with your doctor. He says your cholesterol and blood pressure are both up, and asks, "Have you stopped taking your medicine? Have you stopped exercising?" No, you tell him, but instead of believing you he says, "How can you lie to me like that? I am standing right here in front of you and you are neither exercising nor taking your medicine at this very moment!" I hope you would get a new doctor immediately because you certainly cannot communicate with this one. You have not stopped taking your medicine because you still take every dose on schedule. You have not stopped exercising because you walk every morning. Nothing has caused you to change those habits. Just because you are not doing it at that particular moment does not mean you have "ceased," *and anyone with common sense would know that.*

How about a Biblical example? Daniel prayed three times a day, Daniel 6.10. When his enemies tricked the king into making the law that anyone caught praying to anyone besides him would be cast into a den of lions, *did Daniel cease to pray?* We all know he did not. He still prayed three times a day.

So the passage means "Don't stop praying." If you begin to have one problem after another, don't blame it on God and stop praying. If unbelievers make fun of you, calling you a superstitious fool for believing in a higher power, don't be embarrassed and stop praying. If you have great successes, don't start relying on yourself, forgetting that God can take it away in a flash—remember the great privilege you have, and don't stop praying. *Pray without ceasing.*

> *Bow down your ear, Oh Jehovah, and answer me, for I am poor and needy. Preserve my soul, for I am godly. Oh my God, save your servant, who trusts in you. Be merciful unto me, O God, for I cry unto you all day long.*
>
> Psalm 86.1–3

February 10

That You May Teach Your Children

The one and only time I went to the Florida College Summer Camp was when I was eight. It was held on campus and I had the first floor dorm room in Sutton Hall that looks out toward what I knew later as Upper Division Dorm.

The last night of camp, when all the parents came to pick us up, the counselors staged a "Bible Bee." We all stood in a circle, beginning with the youngest on to the oldest. Someone asked Bible questions around the circle and if you missed the question you sat down. After about 30 minutes there were five of us left—me, all alone on the "kiddy" side of the nearly depleted circle, and, on the other side, four teenagers who looked as big as adults to me.

I only remember one question. I was flabbergasted when a 16 year old could not answer, "Who was thrown into the lion's den?" The question came to me next, and I actually felt embarrassed for the boy when I answered, "Daniel." That was as far as I got. You would think I would remember the question that did me in, but I don't. I do remember that I could hardly comprehend what was being asked, so it must have been a doozy.

Eventually, one of the older teenagers won the bee, and I could not understand why so many people came up to me saying how impressed they were. Except for that last question they were all so easy. You see, it had absolutely nothing to do with me, and everything to do with my parents.

My sister and I were raised knowing the importance of Bible knowledge. My mother was a first-generation Christian and back then did not have the teaching resources I had available when I was raising my children. But judging by that "bee," she and my father, who was only second-generation himself, did a much better job of teaching than most who had more advantages. They answered all the questions we asked, helped us when we needed it, and made sure we did our Bible lessons. They bought us a big beautiful Bible story book. I did not realize then how expensive it was, but now I can look back and appreciate how lavishly they spent on us and why, especially given our un-lavish lifestyle. They even allowed us to stay up 15 minutes late so we could read it every night, and later our own Bibles, before bed. That certainly instilled its importance to me. Because of their diligence, I cannot understand parents who allow their children—no matter how old they are—to get in the car on Sunday morning without checking to see that they have their lesson books and their Bibles, and without making sure the lessons were done the night before.

Something just as important—I always saw my parents doing their own lessons, whether it involved doing a workbook or reading a passage of scripture. Their Bibles and class materials always had a special place on the shelf by the carport door. If it was not there, they were studying, or they were at class. None of this "I forgot" business. And they talked about the scriptures on days other than Sunday and Wednesday. We grew up knowing that you were supposed to think about these things every day.

That is how I did so well at the Summer Camp Bible Bee. Like I said, it really had nothing at all to do with me.

> *...having been reminded of the unfeigned faith that is in you, which dwelt first in your grandmother Lois, and in your mother Eunice, and I am persuaded in you also.*
>
> 2 Timothy 1.5

February 11

That You May Teach Your Children (2)

Someone recently asked me what I thought a kindergarten aged child should know about the Bible. All I can tell you is from my own experience.

I believe they should know about God, Jesus, and the Holy Spirit—and that all of those beings *love* him no matter what. They should know every major Bible story, and be able to name the books of the Bible, the apostles, the sons of Jacob, and the judges. They should have some major memorizing done, individual verses here and there, and larger passages as well, *e.g.*, Psalm 23, the beatitudes, scriptures like Romans 12.1–3 and good old John 3.16. And those things should be explained as well as a five or six year old can understand them, which may be more than you think. They should have a large repertoire of spiritual songs, not just children's songs, but some of the hymns from the songbook as well. They should be praying several times a day.

The person who asked looked at me, dumbfounded. "That's impossible," he said. No. It's not. I could do most of that, and my children could do all of it. I can still hear five-year-old Lucas reciting the twenty-third psalm, and three-year-old Nathan singing all five verses of "Twust and Obey."

What's that? "It isn't about learning facts." Of course, it isn't. But tell me, which do you teach first, critical analysis of the poetry of Keats versus that of Milton, or memorizing the alphabet? They will never understand faith till they see it working in the life of Abraham; or courage, until they know the stories of David and Esther; or unselfish devotion until they hear about Ruth gleaning in the field. Isn't that why God put those facts there in the first place? "things... written aforetime were written for our learning" (Rom 15.4).

And you know what works even better? Learning about the generosity of Barnabas and then seeing a father like mine, who gave so generously that the IRS audited him. And learning about the compassion of Dorcas and then a seeing a mother like mine, who took food off her table to give to a neighbor whose husband was killed in an automobile accident, and then organized a food drive for that same neighbor and her five small children.

And as to the amount I think a child should know so early? The problem is not a child's capacity. *The problem is adults underestimating their capacity.* And maybe the problem is we do not want to spend the time it takes to do this. This is not something you accomplish in 15 minutes a day of "quality time," that great myth that has been foisted on American parents. God never expected that meager amount to be the time we spend teaching our children.

> *Hear, O Israel: Jehovah our God is one Jehovah. And you shall love Jehovah your God with all your heart and with all your soul, and with all your might. And these words which I command you this day shall be upon your heart;* ***and you shall teach them diligently unto your children, and shall talk of them when you sit in your house and when you walk by the way, and when you lie down, and when you rise up. And you shall bind them for a sign upon your hand, and they shall be for frontlets between your eyes, and you shall write them on the doorposts of your house, and upon your gates.***
>
> Deuteronomy 6.4–9

I think that pretty well covers it all, don't you?

The Welcome Mat

About 20 years ago, we spent a long weekend camping in one of our north Florida parks. It was cold that November, the coldest weather we had ever camped in, and I was busily trying to remember to pack enough cold weather clothes to keep us warm, especially for a night outdoors. Unfortunately, I forgot the garment bag that held our Sunday clothes.

Not attending services that Sunday morning in the nearby town was not an option for us. We raised our boys the way I was raised—on Sundays we went to the assembly of the saints, period. No one ever even thought to say, "*Will* we attend today?"

So we walked into the services that morning in jeans and flannel shirts. We did not even have on our "best" jeans, because we learned early that camping could be a dirty, staining experience. It was not quite so bad for the guys—one or two other men did not have on ties—but there I was, the only woman in the place without a dress and heels. And without exception, the women looked at me, turned their heads, and walked away. None of them ever did speak to me, even after Keith spoke knowledgeably in Bible class, and we obviously knew the hymns. I tried not to be judgmental, but I kept wondering if they thought we were some poor, down and out family, who had stopped, "just to try to get some money." You know why? Because I had thought the same thing in the past about others who looked like us.

I wanted to stand up and say, "My husband preached full time for ten years and is a deacon. I teach Bible classes and have some Bible class literature in the bookstores. My children can probably answer more Bible questions than you can!" I wanted to rub their noses in the fact of their discrimination. But I didn't. Instead, I pondered my own guilt, and wondered if I would have done any better.

So take a minute and think about your own behavior on Sunday mornings. Whom do you rush to greet? Whom do you leave standing, feeling awkward and unwelcome? Which ones may need the Lord the most? In fact, which ones might the Lord himself have welcomed the most fervently? Would we have stood with the Pharisees, rebuking him for eating with sinners? And weren't we, in our suits and ties, dresses and heels, once in the same condition? And couldn't we find ourselves there again, if we do not follow his example?

My brethren, hold not the faith of our Lord Jesus Christ, the Lord of glory, with respect of persons. For if there comes into your assembly a man with a gold ring, in fine clothing, and there comes in also a poor man in vile clothing, and you have regard to him who wears the fine clothing, and say, "Sit here in a good place," and you say to the poor man, "Stand there," or "Sit under my footstool," do you not make distinctions among yourselves and become judges with evil thoughts? Listen, my beloved brethren, did not God choose those who are poor as to the world to be rich in faith, and heirs of the king-

dom which he promised to them who loved him? Howbeit, if you fulfill the royal law according to the scripture, "Thou shalt love thy neighbor as thyself," you do well, but if you have respect of persons, you commit sin, being convicted by the law as transgressors. For judgment is without mercy to him who shows no mercy.

James 2.1–5, 8–9, 13

February 13

Lost in the Cracks

You remember that strange commercial where the woman's guests keep disappearing, and we discover they have all fallen into the crack of her sofa and are living down there? Keith put his hands down the crack of the narrowest upholstered chair in the house and, like a magician pulling a rabbit out of his hat or endless scarves out of his sleeves, he kept coming up with the oddest things—a Ghiradelli dark chocolate square wrapper, two unpopped popcorn kernels, three red hots, two broken rubber bands, four shelled but shriveled peas, a nail file, a ballpoint pen, three quarters, three dimes, three nickels and five pennies, a fifteen inch square red bandanna, a twelve by five decorator pillow, and a co-ax cable connector. I am afraid to try the much broader backed sofa—there really might be people living down there.

I know we have all experienced that feeling of being "lost in the cracks." We have all had applications, letters, requests, complaints, and worst of all, payments, lost in the paper shuffle of doctor's offices, large corporations, and government agencies. Depending upon the issue, it could cause anything from the minor annoyance of a simple delay to the more serious problems of cut-off utilities or destroyed credit ratings. It's a helpless feeling, and a lonely one, to know you have done everything right and *still* this has happened—and no one seems to care.

Now just imagine your reaction if you had *not* done everything right. You filled out the wrong form with the wrong information, sent it to the wrong address with the wrong amount of money, and you did it all two years late. Not only that, but everything you did wrong you did that way on purpose. Yet a week later you receive everything you had asked for anyway with promises of more whenever you needed it.

You would shake your head and say, "This can't be possible," and you would be right.

But isn't that exactly what we receive with God? In spite of our best efforts to wreck our lives, to sink into the depths of sin and be lost among the myriads who are content to live there, his searching hand will find us if we just reach out and take it. We will never be lost in the cracks.

And Jehovah said, Go through the midst of the city, through the midst of Jerusalem, and set a mark upon the foreheads of the men that sigh and that cry over all the abominations that are done in the midst thereof. And to the others he said in my hearing, Go through the city after him and smite; let not your eye spare, neither have pity, and slay utterly… but come not near anyone upon whom is the mark.

The firm foundation of God stands having this seal, The Lord knows those who are his.

Ezekiel 9.4–6; 2 Timothy 2.19

February 14

Heart to Heart

Today is a day for lovers, or so the merchandisers of the world say. Do Keith and I do anything special? You better believe it. It's usually nothing huge—a card, a homemade gift, a bouquet of handpicked wildflowers, a special dessert. We don't try to single-handedly support Madison Avenue. Sometimes Keith simply takes the day off and we spend time together talking—what a novel idea, especially for some married folks! Not because we celebrate some Catholic "saint" or because we feel pressured by society, but because we take every opportunity to revel in our love. How do you think we have managed to put up with each other for all these years?

Romance is not an un-Biblical concept. While the description of the body in several passages in the Song of Solomon may not appeal to our Western ears, it is still used in the courtship rituals of some Eastern countries today. The Proverb writer speaks of romance like this: "There are three things which are too wonderful for me, yes, four which I do not understand: the way of an eagle in the air, the way of a serpent upon a rock, the way of a ship in the middle of the sea, and the way of a man with a maid" (30.18–19).

The writer of Ecclesiastes tells us to "live joyfully with the wife whom you love all the days of your life of vanity, which he has given you under the sun… for that is your portion in life" (9.9). "Live joyfully" is an injunction; it is not passive. Do not wait for it; initiate it yourself. These passages were originally spoken to couples whose marriages were arranged. Imagine what God expects of those of us who chose our own spouses after "falling in love."

Two or three times a week as I clean out Keith's lunchbox in the evening, I find red, heart-shaped love notes he has cut out of some office scrap paper and written—I know he has taken time out of a busy day to think of me. And he usually calls during his lunch hour.

Eating a nice dinner out is in our budget only a couple of times a year—and that is up from the early days of our marriage—but I can make a four course meal for two for the price of one entrée in an upscale restaurant, and enjoy doing it. Several times a year, we dress up, get out the china, light the candles, and have a meal I have worked on all day. When the boys were little, I fixed them their own special meal—more along the lines of pizza than boeuf bourguignon—then explained how they could help mommy and daddy have a special time together by going to bed early, and staying there. Besides the reward of their favorite meal, they could stay up late reading and talking to one another. We occasionally heard thumps and giggles long after we would have ordinarily put a stop to it, but never once did they not fulfill their part of the bargain by interrupting us because we stressed to them how important their part was and they were thrilled to do it.

Marriage is a high maintenance relationship. If you neglect it, it goes downhill in a hurry. Do something today, no matter how small it may be—and whether or not the other one reciprocates—to keep that from happening. Make sure it is something that will mean something to your spouse, not just to you! Men and women are different that way (as if you hadn't noticed). Then choose another time to do it again—not just your anniversary or Valentine's Day. Do it sometimes for no good reason at all. Or isn't keeping your marriage alive reason enough?

God *expects* you to romance one another.

Drink waters out of your own cistern, and running waters out of your own well. Should your springs be dispersed abroad, and streams of water in the streets? Let them be for yourself alone, and not for strangers with you. Let your fountain be blessed and rejoice in the wife of your youth. As a loving hind and a pleasant doe, let her breasts satisfy you at all times, and be ravished always with her love.

Proverbs 5.15–19

February 15

Target Practice

Being married to a law enforcement officer who is also a certified firearms instructor means you get free shooting lessons—whether you want them or not. I have learned many things, and used them—just ask the snake community in this area. I am sure they know all about the crazy lady who shoots till they quit wiggling.

I also learned that even handguns, especially big handguns like Keith's .45 magnum (think Matt Dillon) can have a kick. I haven't dared try it because of my experience with his smaller .357 revolver. I am a pianist. Good pianists use their wrists like shock absorbers—they go down as you approach the keyboard and pull up the instant the key has been struck. That is what creates a smooth, warm tone rather than a harsh, jarring one. A loose wrist is a must for pianists, but is not good when you are shooting a big gun. For one thing, the recoil on a loose wrist hurts; for another you nearly give yourself a black eye with the barrel as it swings back at you. I simply cannot seem to keep a stiff arm when shooting!

That may not be something you need to worry about since most of you are not pianists. But a basic rule for everyone is: if you want to hit the target, you have to aim at it first. You would be surprised how many do not aim correctly—it's all about sight alignment. But even that presupposes that one has the sense to aim at the target.

Unfortunately, many of us do not have that kind of sense when we attempt to become better people. An old saying goes, "Aim at nothing and that's what you will hit every time." We go around "trying to get better," or "trying to do better," but we will never *be* better till we can answer the question, "Better at *what?*" Unfortunately, that means we have to ditch the pride and actually list our faults—specifically, not abstractly. And when we mess up, we must be willing to acknowledge it.

I have heard this statement all my life, usually from people who have been Christians a long time: "If I have done anything wrong, then I'm sorry." That's supposed to be a confession? What that is, is someone who knows better than to claim perfection, but who thinks he has it anyway!

Here is my chore today: make a list of my faults and weaknesses—*specific* problems I have. It may be obvious things like lying, gossiping, drinking, or losing my temper. But it might also be things like being oversensitive, assuming the worst about people, holding a grudge and trying to get even—treating people the way they treat me. Whatever I list, pray about them, find some scriptures that deal with them, meditate on those. At the end of the day, make an honest assessment of how I did and [probably] pray for forgiveness. Keep at it every day. Make a note of the particular circumstances that cause me to fail. When I see them beginning, get away if I can. If it is impossible, immediately slow down and think before every word or action. And always remember: "The Lord is at hand [right next to me]" (Phil 4.5).

That is a lot to do, especially every day. But remember—the only way to hit a target is to aim at it. God bless us all as we try to become what He would have us be.

Wherefore also we make it our aim, whether at home or absent, to be well-pleasing unto him. For we must all be made manifest before the judgment-seat of Christ; that each one may receive the things done in the body, according to what he has done, whether it is good or evil.

2 Corinthians 5.9–10

February 16

Just a Cold

It was just a cold. The first day I lost my voice and sneezed a lot. The second day I started coughing, a deep cough that felt like it scraped the bottom of my lungs. The third day I started wheezing and my temperature rose over 100. The fourth day the headache started. The fifth day my shoulders, neck, and back began aching and I could not get comfortable no matter how or where I lay or sat. The sixth day it climbed into my head. I could no longer breathe, smell, or taste. The seventh day I lost my hearing and my ears began to ache. Meanwhile, all the other symptoms continued. The eighth day my temperature fell a degree below normal, but I felt a little better—very little. Eventually it did go away, but the cough lingered for weeks. Why in the world do we always say, "It was *just* a cold?"

Maybe it's habit.

"I was *just* ten minutes late."

"I was *just* ten miles over the speed limit."

"It was *just* a song service."

"It was *just* a little fib."

"I was *just* so tired and frustrated."

"It was *just* this once."

Always excusing ourselves with that little word, making every bad judgment call or "little" sin unimportant—where does it stop? How big do they have to be before we stop using that word?

What could God have said about us? David knew full well when he said in the Psalm 8, "What is man that you are mindful of him, and the son of man that you care for him?" Indeed, God could have said, "They're *just* people. Why bother?" and we would have had no answer for that, especially the way we so often use that word to rationalize less than stellar behavior.

Yet Jehovah, the Word, and the Spirit got together before they made anything else, and came up with a plan so that they could keep fellowship with men, no matter how sinful they had become. That plan involved sacrifice on their parts, but it made men once again presentable to them. For some reason, they thought we were worth it.

Think about that the next time you try to excuse yourself with that word "just."

I give you thanks, O Lord, with my whole heart; before the gods I sing your praise. I bow down toward your holy temple and give thanks to your name for your steadfast love and your faithfulness, for you have exalted above all things your name and your word. On the day I called, you answered me; my strength of soul you increased. All the kings of the earth shall give you thanks, O Lord, for they have heard the words of your mouth, and they shall sing of the ways of the Lord, for great is the glory of the Lord. ***For though the Lord is high, he regards the lowly****, but the haughty he knows from* *afar. Though I walk in the midst of trouble, you preserve my life; you stretch out your hand against the wrath of my enemies, and your right hand delivers me. The* LORD *will fulfill his purpose for me; your steadfast love, O* LORD, *endures forever. Do not forsake the work of your hands.*

Psalm 138

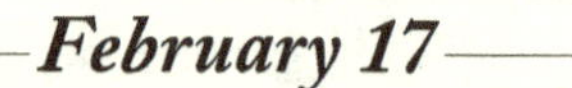

February 17

Johnny Can't Read

It's been more than 50 years since Rudolf Flesch wrote *Why Johnny Can't Read.* Someone had finally been brave enough to say out loud, "Modern education methods are not working."

There was a sudden push in the universities for all teachers in every subject to be able to teach reading as well. Even in music education, I was required to come up with methods to teach word reading while at the same time teaching music reading—a bit like trying to teach English and Math simultaneously. I haven't noticed that is has helped. We have a newspaper columnist who keeps track of the English, spelling, and word choice errors in his own paper. His list never seems to shorten.

The other day, I heard a sportscaster, who was *speculating* about a certain team's future in the season ahead, say, "Of course, I realize we are living in the *speculum* here." And if you know what a speculum is, you know that it is not the sort of thing you want to be living in! That same day another sportscaster said he was "efforting" to give us an unbiased view of things. Then there are the want-ads: we recently noticed a "12 gage shotgun" for sale, along with a "chester drawers."

So in many cases, Johnny still can't read, but I think in the case of many Christians it is more a matter of "Johnny *won't* read."

In nearly every overseas mission I have heard of, the biggest need is for Bibles in that particular language. Those people, to whom Bibles are rare and precious, crave them the most and read them the most. Most of us have several Bibles in our homes, gathering dust, spending more time in the car seat traveling back and forth to the meetinghouse than being read.

How do I know? The same way I know that sportscaster made a low score on the vocabulary portion of his SAT. When I hear that Jacob had to wait 14 years before he could marry Rachel, that David saw Bathsheba bathing on the rooftop, and that the wise men showed up at the stable the night Jesus was born, I know someone is not reading. When I hear people say, "Money is the root of all evil," and "Pride goes before a fall," thinking they are quoting scripture, I know they are not reading those scriptures they claim to live by.

And here is an excellent point—many do know their scriptures backwards and forwards, inside and out, yet they don't allow them to penetrate their hearts. But how can they ever reach our hearts, if we never read them in the first place?

I look at a cookbook four or five times a week to feed my family well. What and how often am I reading so I can feed their souls even better?

And all the people gathered themselves together as one man into the broad place that was before the water gate; and they spoke unto Ezra the scribe, to bring the book of the law of Moses, which Jehovah had commanded to Israel. ...And Ezra opened the book in the sight of all the people, (for he was above all the people); and when he opened it, all the people stood up... and they read in the book, the Law of God, distinctly, and they gave the sense so that they understood the reading.

Till I come, give heed to reading.

Nehemiah 8.1, 5, 8; 1 Timothy 4.13

February 18

To the Rescue!

After a hard day and a bad night, I was late getting up the other morning. Already behind, I decided to start a load of laundry before dressing. As I stood there in the laundry room I thought I heard someone outside calling from a long way off. I almost didn't—I was behind and did not need the interruption—but finally I opened the door. Calling is not the word. Screaming is more like it. "No! No! Oh noooooo!" a voice I finally realized was my neighbor's pierced the morning mist through the woods and across the creek.

As fast as I could, I pulled on a pair of jeans, grabbed a sweater, slipped on shoes, and put the cell phone in my pocket. Despite the early morning gloom of the woods, I made it to the creek without stumbling. Providence, surely, since I trip over everything now. Across the narrow stream the house stood quiet and peaceful. Either everything was okay, or everyone was already dead.

Not being one of those stupid girls in the horror movies who go down into the basement to check out the noise without a second thought, I stood there watching as I called on the cell. No answer. Well, that wasn't good. So I crossed the wooden bridge and opened the gate.

Now I had to be on the lookout as well for the Great Dane, whose ears peak at eyeball level on me. Not to mention the German shepherd and the blood hound. Finally I saw vague figures moving over by the stable in the field fenced off from the main yard. No one seemed frantic. So I slipped around the house expecting them to come around the other side any moment, but no one was there and no one showed up in the few seconds I waited.

As I turned to go back to the carport door I always use, the Dane in the house spotted me through the front window and his basso profundo bark rattled the walls. I knew no one had gotten into *that* house, so my heartbeat slowed a bit. My neighbor saw me herself then, and called from the back door. I had, indeed, gotten there after the excitement was over. Her husband had left before daylight, forgetting to put the two big outside dogs in the horse field before the men hired to do some tree work had arrived. She is 67 and shorter than I by three or four inches, but had tried to do it herself, and was knocked over by the happy, excited dogs and hit her head on the board fence. Another neighbor had gotten to her first, which was just as well. Only a man could have handled all those big, excited animals, and I think the hired men had to help him—that is who I had seen.

I thought, as I made my way back through the woods, as scared as I had been, I had not hesitated at all to go see about my neighbor. Yet how many times have I ignored the cries of distress from my neighbors whose souls are in jeopardy? No, they do not actually cry out. You see that distress in their eyes. You hear their desire for the peace you have in their questions, in their comments about how you handle problems better than they do.

But instead of opening the door to listen, we are too busy with everyday chores to even notice. We have our families to think about. We have our own problems. As one church told Keith a long time ago when he asked for a few dollars to print gospel meeting announcements and pass them out door to door, "They know where we are. They will come if they are interested. No need wasting the Lord's money like that."

Are we really listening to their calls for help? Will they be calling someone else because we didn't pay good enough attention and were slow to react? Are we afraid we will waste "the Lord's" money? Why do we think it is there? He certainly doesn't need it.

Pay attention to those around you today. Be sure you are really listening.

Whosoever shall call upon the name of the Lord shall be saved. How then shall they call on him in whom they have not believed? And how shall they believe in him whom they have not heard? And how shall they hear without a preacher? And how shall they preach, except they be sent? Even as it is written, how beautiful are the feet of them that bring glad tidings of good things!

Romans 10.13–15

Old Time Religion

I don't know how many times in my life I have heard people say the Law of Moses was a matter of form religion only, that the heart did not matter to God one way or the other. How anyone could think this of a religion whose mantra seemed to be "Thou shalt love the Lord your God *with all your heart,* and *with all your soul,* and *with all your might*" (Deut 6.5) is beyond my comprehension. Yet all of us have blind spots where what we have heard all our lives keeps us from seeing things right under our noses.

Here is a list of passages to read at your convenience in the next week. It will amaze you, stun you, and forever more settle the matter. God expected his people to live the Law every day of their lives, not just on the Sabbath. He has always wanted their hearts. See Isaiah 1.11–17; 29.13; 30.8–14; 58.13–14; 66.1–2; Jeremiah 7.8–10; 8.8–9; 22.3–4; Ezekiel 33.13, 30–33; 34.1–31; Hosea 6.4–6; 10.12; 12.6; Amos 5.11–15; 8.4–10; Micah 6.6–8.

Yes, form was important to God. It showed exactly how much faith and devotion his people had to obey him in even the smallest details. As God told Moses, "See that you make things according to the pattern which was shown you in Mount [Sinai]" (Exod 25.40). Jesus even said the Pharisees were right to be careful to follow the Law exactly: "Whatever [the Pharisees] bid you, do and observe… for these things [tithing even their herbs] you ought to have done" (Matt 23.1, 23). But he went on to say that the heart was even more important: "You have left undone the weightier matters of the Law, justice, mercy, and faith." God expected their obedient following of the pattern of worship to match an obedient life of righteousness, coming from a pure heart of faith, love, and mercy. He flatly told them that none of their worship would be accepted otherwise.

Why do you think Jesus was so angry with the scribes and Pharisees? They prided themselves on knowing and keeping the Law, but they seemed totally ignorant of those scriptures listed above. He quoted several of those passages to them (Matt 9.13; 13.14–15; 15.8–9), ending with, "Go learn what this means," the ultimate insult to a scribe, a "teacher" of the Law.

Those Jewish leaders were still under the Law at the time. Do we, who have a better covenant, a better priest, and better forgiveness, think God will expect any less of us? God demands more than simply following His law to the letter. He expects a life of service from us, "Inasmuch as you have done this unto the least of these my brothers, you have done it also unto me" (Matt 25.40). Let's not sit on our pews congratulating ourselves because we are following all the rituals correctly, if we have left so much else undone throughout the week. As Peter reminds us in 1 Peter 4.17, judgment will begin with us. We had better make sure our hearts are ready for it.

I hate, I despise your feasts, and I will take no delight in your solemn assemblies. Yes, though you offer me your burnt offerings and meal offerings, I will not accept them, neither will I regard the peace offerings of your fat beasts. Take away from me the noise of your songs, for I will not hear the melodies of your viols. But let justice roll down like waters, and righteousness as a mighty stream.

Amos 5.21–24

February 20

Of Doves and Serpents

We have shared our lives with a lot of animals over the years. Two who grew up with our boys were Bart and Abby. Bart was a big, friendly, yellow lab, who trotted up to anyone who would pet him, and wagged his tail so hard his whole rear end swayed. Even in his senior years, he got as excited as a puppy every time any of us called him. If you stopped petting him, he would carefully place his head under your dangling hand to remind you he was still there.

I remember one morning when Abby, the black and white "Gateway" cat, walked up to him. They had already established a friendly, if cautious, relationship, even rubbing noses upon occasion, but Bart knew to stand still with his muscles bunched until he discovered what mood Abby was in. Sure enough, Abby nuzzled sweetly, stroking Bart's huge leg with a tiny white paw. As soon as Bart relaxed, Abby walked around behind him, lifted a paw, and whapped his rear end hard enough to send him running.

Abby had been fooling us since we first got him at the age of six weeks. We named him Abigail, and by the time we discovered there was more hiding beneath his fur than we had first thought, he knew his name, and we were stuck trying to find a male version of Abby. Abigail became Abner, at least on the vet's records. He learned early how to get what he wanted. If we were walking outside and he decided he needed to be held, he would throw himself bodily in front of us on the ground. If we stepped around him, he would follow along and do it again until he finally wore us down and we picked him up.

Those two pets always reminded me of Jesus' admonition to be "wise as serpents and harmless as doves." The Lord expects us to have no malice toward anyone, always willing to help those who need it, whether they deserve it or not. On the other hand he also expects us to be on guard. It is hard to strike an even balance. Some lean toward naiveté and others toward cynicism, each one rationalizing himself and criticizing the other, when possibly what they both need is moderation—it isn't that you choose only one side of this coin; it's that you flip it as the occasion requires.

Jesus never let himself be caught in the traps of the scribes and Pharisees, but he was willingly led to the cross "as a lamb to the slaughter."

Sometimes I hear prudence castigated as a lack of faith. Jacob prayed that God deliver him from the hand of Esau, then the next morning, sent gifts to appease his brother, Genesis 32.11ff. Many impugn his faith because of that. But tell me, as my son Nathan likes to point out, if you saw a known murderer in your front yard, wouldn't you go inside and lock the door before you prayed? In fact, might you not call 911 as well? How easily we judge when it is someone else's neck on the chopping block. Was Paul faithless when he escaped his enemies in Damascus over the wall in a basket? Why didn't he stay if he had faith that God would care for him? In fact, he went on to Jerusalem after Agabus told him he would be imprisoned there. What was the difference? It may be difficult to know, but as long as we take the time to consider all of our decisions, putting our service to God at the top of the list instead of such things as financial success, as long as we live our lives by a faith that trusts no matter what, He will be pleased.

> *Jehovah is on my side; I will not fear: What can man do unto me? It is better to take refuge in Jehovah than to put confidence in man.*
>
> Psalm 118.6, 8

February 21

Monday Morning

It's another Monday. Am I ready for the week ahead? If I assembled with my brethren yesterday, and our assembly accomplished the purpose God meant it to when he ordained it, I should be not only ready, bur "revved up and rarin' to go."

On a Monday, you ask incredulously? Maybe you did not get out of Sunday what you were supposed to. So what is the purpose of our assembling together? It may not be what you have always thought.

I think our best verse is good old Hebrews 10.25, only forget the way we always use it, shaking our fingers in the faces of those who miss services. Start with the verse ahead: "Let us consider one another to provoke to love and good works... exhorting one another... ."

Too often we focus all our attention on the assembly as if that is the whole of our service to God. What it should be is refueling, so we can go out and continue to serve during the week. Romans 12.1 is key to understanding this: "Present your bodies a living sacrifice, holy, acceptable to God, which is your spiritual worship."

You probably have a version that says "spiritual service," but that word can also be translated "worship." It is worship when I go about my daily life serving my family, serving my brethren, and serving others as well. Everything I do is worship to God, not just those few hours a week. By compartmentalizing our religion to a certain day, time, and place, we are giving God those lame sacrifices Malachi talks about in Malachi 1.8. God expects our all, all the time—not just on Sundays. And he has given us our brethren to encourage us and keep us on the right track when we meet together, "provoking one another to love and good works." "One another" means we are all doing it, not just the preacher. Did you do your part to help someone else or did you just go to be entertained?

Somehow we think rituals are the only things that qualify as worship. Many passages in the Old Testament mention the people praying, or singing, or sacrificing, and *then* "they worshipped," almost as if those other acts were not worship (*e.g.*, 2 Chron 29.29–30). And maybe there is a point there: we can do all those things, at the "right time," in the "right place" (translation: on a pew inside a building with a certain sign over the door), and still not be worshipping. Worshipping is prostrating the heart before God, not the body, and he expects us to do that all day long, every day.

So am I ready to worship God again this week, all week? If I refueled myself, drained out and changed the old dirty oil and filter, and vacuumed out the grime and dust of life, I should be able to serve God with all my might—whatever level that is in my stage of life at this particular time—and make it through another week in a world that should be foreign to my nature, instead of comfortable. And then I will be anxious for another day of replenishment next Sunday, because the need will be so obvious to me.

Through him then let us offer up a sacrifice of praise to God ***continually*** *but to do good and to communicate forget not; for with such sacrifice God is well pleased.*

Hebrews 13.15–16

One Too Many Trips to the Wishing Well

Down here in north Florida we don't look at the calendar to tell the season. We generally have about five months of summer, nearly three months each of spring and fall, and four–six weeks of winter.

Since I moved to the country I have noticed that each season has its own feel and smell. About the first week of October the morning air becomes crisp and dry, for Florida anyway, and I know fall has arrived. It may leave a week later, but we know that by the first of November it is generally here to stay.

Then shortly before the holiday season I will be greeted by the smell of wood fires and a damp cold that seeps into your bones. I lived in Illinois for two years so I know what below zero weather is like, but even up there you could quickly run the trash out in your shirtsleeves at 45 degrees. Down here that same temperature will set your teeth chattering in just a few short minutes. It's winter!

Sometime around Valentine's Day the warm sunshine on your back spreads like a soothing ointment, and soon the air is heavy with the perfume of azaleas, dogwoods, gardenias, wisteria and the first roses of the year. Rakes scratch the ground and black plastic bags stack up in every yard. The acrid smell of burning leaves fills the air and the spring green of new leaves lights up the sky. Jack Frost may paint your garden one more time in March, but spring has definitely sprung!

By the first of May a wet morning fog drips on until about 10:00, and the flower smells have mellowed into the watermelon smell of new-mown grass. Just standing outside for ten minutes will leave your hair damp with both humidity and perspiration. The long, hot summer has begun.

It has taken awhile but now I relish every change of season. I used to wish away the long, humid summers precisely because they were that way. Then when my children started school, I wished away the rest of the year because the summer was the only time I had them to myself. But I spent the first part of my life wishing it away as well. I couldn't wait to start school. Then I couldn't wait for college. Then I couldn't wait to get married. Then I couldn't wait to have children. And now what? I have an empty nest and my life is more than half over. Is that why we say that middle age brings wisdom? Why did it take so long for me to figure this out?

God wants us to enjoy our lives. Yes, we suffer trials and even some minor persecution. But as much as is possible He expects us to live well and laugh well, to "love life and see good days" (1 Pet 3.10). "This is the day which Jehovah has made; rejoice and be glad in it" (Psa 118.24). "He has made everything beautiful in its time, also he has set eternity in their hearts" (Ecc 3.11). "Behold that which I have seen to be good and comely is for one to eat and to drink and to enjoy good in all his labor wherein he labors under the sun, all the days of his life which God has given him, for this is his portion" (Ecc 5.18). Finally, I have learned to take joy in every day.

If you are still young, don't wish your life away. It may seem that your children will never grow up, that you will never have time for yourself and your spouse again, that everything you really want is somewhere out there in the future. Take a minute and look around. God wants you to enjoy the present. If you cannot learn that now, then when those future things come along, you won't know how to enjoy them either. I have seen so many who are never satisfied with what they have, and who ruin the time they have left looking for something better. Learn to be happy and content because one of these days you may find yourself wishing you had back all those days you wished away in the first place.

> *He that would love life and see good days, let him refrain his tongue from evil, and his lips that they speak no guile; let him turn away from evil and do good; let him seek peace and pursue it. For the eyes of the Lord are upon the righteous, and his ears unto their supplication. But the face of the Lord is upon those who do evil.*
>
> 1 Peter 3.10–12

February 23

Hot Air Balloons

That is exactly what our lungs are—hot air balloons. Most of the time we only use a small amount of their capacity. That is why taking a deep breath can have such a profound effect. We are not used to having that much oxygen in our systems all at once. I have heard that when a person actually begins to use his lungs to their capacity, those who have not smoked in years are suddenly expelling it. It sat at the bottom of their lungs all that time. I don't know if that is true, but I would not be surprised.

When teaching voice lessons, one of the biggest challenges is to teach people how to breathe, and then how to manage all that air. Taking a deep breath will not accomplish a thing if you just whoosh it all out with the first note you sing. If you take too big a breath, you will not be able to control how much you let out at once. Because you have filled to capacity, the minute you apply any pressure at all with your diaphragm, you will lose close to half of it on the first word. It is far better to fill to about 90 percent—you will still have far more than you are used to having. You will also have the ability to mete out what you need and sing all the way through a phrase without gasping for air in front of your audience.

When I thought about that, suddenly I understood a word I had been ignoring in one of those oft-quoted passages: "for out of the *abundance* of the heart the mouth speaks" (Matt 12.34). We usually just say, "You can't speak what you don't feel," which may be true, but it is possible to have things come out in ways you never intended at all.

I remember riding to a gospel meeting with another couple many years ago. I was in the backseat with the other woman, while Keith sat up front with the man. Motion sickness can hit me at the drop of a hat. I tried to be polite and actually look at the woman whenever I spoke to her, but that looking back and forth to the side, all that scenery rushing past behind her head, along with the larger sense of lateral sway in the backseat, was taking a toll on me. Finally I said, "I'm sorry. I just can't look at you any more; it's making me sick."

You see what I mean. Sometimes the bad things that come out of your mouth are perfectly innocent.

But Jesus said, "Out of the *abundance* of the heart, the mouth speaks." Aha! I looked up that word. It's a nice long Greek word, also translated, "remain," as in something that remains over and above what is needed. In Matthew 14, Jesus fed 5,000 people with five loaves and two fish. He not only fed them, but he fed them so *abundantly* that "they all ate and were filled and they took up *that which remained* [that long Greek word] of the broken pieces, twelve baskets full" (v 20). The word is also translated "exceed," "enough and to spare," and "abound," as in "the grace of God... *abounds* to the many" (Rom 5.15). How much grace do you want God to give you? I hope he gives me more than just barely enough, and the use of this word proves it will be plenty.

So what comes out of my heart is what I stuff it with, what I cram in there every day, filling it to the brim and overflowing. And, just like when I take too deep a breath and the pressure from my diaphragm makes too much air gush out all at once, when I am under pressure, what I have crammed into my heart is what will come out. Is it bitterness for what I have had to endure? Anger at God for the trials he allows? Resentment of everything and everyone because of how my life has turned out? Or is it love, humility, kindness, generosity, contentment, and faith?

Whatever it is, there is no denying what I have been storing away when all of a sudden it bursts upon the scene in a gust of hot air.

> *Whoever winks the eye causes trouble, but a babbling fool will come to ruin. The mouth of the righteous is a fountain of life, but the mouth of the wicked conceals violence. When words are many, transgression is not lacking, but whoever restrains his lips is prudent. The tongue of the righteous is choice silver; the heart of the wicked is of little worth. The lips of the righteous feed many, but fools die for the lack of sense*
>
> Proverbs 10.10–11, 19-21

February 24

The Refrigerator Door

Some things are just not supposed to happen. Sooner or later you will have a flat tire. Sooner or later your AC will quit on you. Sooner or later the washer will stop washing and the dryer will stop drying. None of these things are pleasant, but they all happen to everyone. When it happens, you groan and then get on with the business of life. But some things are just not supposed to happen.

I was putting some things in the refrigerator the other day. Usually the door swings shut by itself, but this time, as I twisted to get the next item, it swung all the way open. Then it quietly fell off its hinges and tumbled shelf side down, dumping pickles, olives, ketchup, three kinds of mustard, Worcestershire and soy sauces, homemade jelly, butter, cream cheese, and my super special ordered-from-California eye medicine onto the floor, leaving the rest of the refrigerator wide open and humming. For a moment I just stood there, stunned. We have been through several refrigerators—a couple of cheap ones that came with the apartment or trailer we were renting at the time, and a couple of secondhand ones. But this one was a recommended model we bought new. Never have we had a refrigerator door fall off, not even the inexpensive or used ones. Refrigerator doors *do not* fall off.

Don't you know that is how God feels at times? We can find several passages where he laments our actions, saying, "This is not supposed to happen," at least in substance, if not verbatim. James 3.10 is a prime example: "Out of the same mouth comes forth blessing and cursing. My brothers, these things ought not so to be." James tells us we should not bless God and then curse man because when we curse a man made in the image of God, we might as well be cursing God. Yikes! That puts another spin on it, doesn't it? Understand, we are not talking about using four letter words here, but about maliciously wishing evil upon a person. We are not supposed to do it—not even to other drivers! And James acts like we ought to know this *without being told: we should not be cursing men!*

Unfortunately, we do not know, or willfully ignore, many such things. We should know God is our Creator and worship Him, but for some reason that is hotly debated even among intelligent people. We should know God's law; He has made it available and easy enough to understand. But even in the church we have "seasoned" Christians who cannot find their way from Acts to Habakkuk without getting lost somewhere in Ephesians, and who think John wrote several "Revelations."

I wonder if God does what I did the other morning, stand there in shock, staring at a door-less refrigerator, with my mouth hanging open, thinking, "What? That just doesn't happen." Unfortunately, it does. You wonder if God is really all that surprised any more. Tell you what, let's work on a real surprise for Him—let's make sure *we* don't do any of those things from now on.

> *The ox knows his owner, and the ass his master's crib; but Israel does not know, my people do not consider.*
>
> *Yes, the stork in the heavens knows her appointed times; and the turtledove and the swallow and the crane observe the time of their coming; but my people know not the law of Jehovah.*
>
> Isaiah 1.3; Jeremiah 8.7

The Laundry Room

I just figured it up and the load of clothes bouncing and clicking around in my dryer right now is about number 16,000. That is only a family of four, and only two for the last several years, but it does include three boys out in the country!

Depending upon our lifestyles, we all become adept at removing certain stains. In my case they are crankcase oil, garden dirt, blueberries, grapes, and tomato sauce. Some of the stains are seasonal, such as the cranberry sauce that inevitably stains my lace tablecloth in November. Sometimes it's something you never really expected, like the time Lucas had to move a 50 pound wheel of red, wax-coated cheese and the only way to get a good hold of it was to hug it to his chest. He came home in a white shirt streaked with red dye. Yes, I got it out, but it took three tries.

We all use different remedies: ammonia, dish detergent, alcohol, stain remover, bleach—depending upon the stain and the fabric. But sometimes even the best laundresses shake out the wet laundry expecting clean results, only to find a faint shadow of the stain still on the cloth. I don't know about you, but if I can tell where the stain used to be, I didn't do a good enough job.

God has a stain remover, too. What is so absolutely amazing is that His cleaning fluid ought to cause stains of its own. He uses blood! But that blood washes us clean, leaving no mark whatsoever. His forgiveness is so complete that we can never tell where the sin used to be. Unless, of course, we spill that cranberry sauce yet again. Then when we approach his mercy seat and he once again sprinkles that precious blood, there we are—spotless before our Father, and only because of our Savior's personal cleansing agent.

So how many loads have you done? Every time you put yet another load in, put a load in God's laundry too. If you aren't the launderer in your home, think about it when you shed those dirty clothes. They may not seem all that dirty, especially if you sit behind a desk all day, but take a look at the collar, guys. Then think about what our God does for you as well.

These are they who came out of the great tribulation, and they washed their robes, and made them white in the blood of the Lamb.

Come now and let us reason together, says the Lord. Though your sins be as scarlet, they shall be as white as snow; though they be red like crimson, they shall be as wool.

Revelation 7.14; Isaiah 1.18

Dignity or Passion?

Keith began losing his hearing in his early 20s. He received his first hearing aid when he was 27, and we had only been married six months. At this point, nearly 37 years later, the doctors say he is now "profoundly deaf," which means he has reached the 90 percent mark. He can stand next to the phone and not hear it ring. He can wash his face, reach for the towel, and walk out of the bathroom, not realizing the water is still running full blast. He has a tendency to be loud and sometimes monotone because he can no longer hear himself or his tone of voice. If he were home alone and a fire broke out while he was asleep, he would not hear the smoke alarm even though it hangs right outside our bedroom door.

He used to play the violin more than passably well, but violin requires an ear. He used to lead singing, but now he changes key in the middle of a phrase without realizing it. He can no longer hear prayers, sermons, announcements, or comments in Bible classes without reading lips. Hearing is a constant crossword puzzle where his mind fills in the blanks left by his hearing and lip reading—often creating humorous misunderstandings, but that is another story. All this means that in order to hear he must work hard. You think a conversation with friends is relaxing. For him it is exhausting. If he is not feeling well or is already tired, he cannot hear at all, period, because he is not up to the wearying chore of having to "listen" to all the other things he must besides words.

All of this breaks my heart because I can foresee a time when this man, who loves Jehovah God and his word more than life itself, will no longer be able to actively participate in the group worship of his brethren.

Michal, the wife of David, would be thrilled to be in my shoes. She was Saul's daughter, a princess royal and now a king's wife, enamored with the dignity of her position. How do I know? Look at 2 Samuel 6. She was married to a man who loved God with all his heart, a man who wrote poetry to God by the yard and sang to Him every day. Mothers, here is the role model for your little boys. David was a man's man in every sense of the word—a warrior king who killed wild animals practically bare-handed, and engaged in heart-pounding, daring battles with the enemies of God—but a man who did not believe that religion made him a sissy.

After David captured Jerusalem, he brought the ark of Jehovah in, and was so thrilled that his passionate worship had him dancing in the street. Michal saw him from her window, and later scolded him, "How you distinguished yourself in front of the maidens of Israel today, like any other common man in the streets!"

David answered, "It was the Lord who chose me above your father... I will celebrate before the Lord. I will become even more undignified than this—I will humiliate myself in my own eyes, but by these same slave girls I will be held in honor." David understood two things. First, that it was not *his* dignity Michal was worried about, it was *hers*. And second, God demands that pride be left behind when we worship him. God wants worship with passion. Despite what you may have heard about the Old Law, he always has. If I let my pride hold me back, I may as well not bother. I have always found it interesting that the passage telling us to do things "decently and in order" (1 Cor 14.40) is in the same context as the one that makes it plain that amens from the assembly were the rule not the exception (v 16).

Do you elbow your husband when he says, "Amen?" Do you shush him when he sings loudly because you think he is off-key? Is that any different than Michal? If you have found a man who understands that faith has nothing to do with weakness and everything to do with strength, who loves the Lord enough to humble himself and worship unashamedly, praise God for your good fortune and encourage him in his worship. You never know when he might no longer be able to do so.

As the hart pants after the water brooks, so pants my soul after you, O God. My soul thirsts for God, for the living God; when shall I come and appear before God? My tears have been my food day and night, while they continually say unto me, Where is your God? These things I remember and pour out my soul within me, how I went with the throng and led them to the house of God with the voice of joy and praise, a multitude keeping holyday.

Psalm 42.1–4

February 27

Lemon Juice

Do you know that it is practically impossible to find plain old banana ice cream in the grocery store? You can find banana split ice cream and banana cream pie ice cream, but not plain banana. So when overripe bananas were on sale a few weeks ago, Keith bought some to make ice cream. As we were in the middle of mashing bananas I added a splash of lemon juice and suddenly we were having a conversation about it. He was just sure I had ruined his banana ice cream and made it sour—why the whole thing would curdle now, didn't I know that?

The past few weeks he has started watching me do things and asking questions for the inevitable day when he will need to take over. In the past, he has never known that I add a splash of lemon juice to a lot of things, his favorite apple pie, his favorite blueberry crisp, his favorite peach cobbler, his favorite crab cakes, and I could go on and on. Lemon juice is one of those things that brighten flavors and make things taste better, even though you don't actually taste the lemon—similar to salt in baked goods. Any good cook knows that if you leave the salt out of the cookies or the cake or the pie crust or the biscuits, none of them will be fit to eat. You don't know it is in there, but you sure know it if it isn't.

I have a feeling we treat God's blessings that way sometimes. We never really notice all the good things we have, but I bet if they suddenly disappeared we would. Oh yes, we often thank God for the really big things like salvation and grace, but what if you got up to a black and white world tomorrow morning? Have you ever really thought about the blessing of color? We thank God every day for the food on our tables, but what if suddenly you could no longer taste it? Let me tell you, I have had that problem with these eye medications and it is awful. About the only thing good about it was a ten pound weight loss in two weeks, but there comes a point when even that is not a blessing.

You see, God is responsible for everything good, even the seemingly small, unimportant things. When your life takes a turn for the worse, it is easy to forget that and blame God. But by remembering that there are still good things, like color and taste, like flowers and butterflies, like puppies and kittens, like rain on the roof and a breeze in the trees, like a *real* vine-ripened tomato, you can know that God is still there, He is still giving you blessings. They may be blessings like lemon juice in banana ice cream or salt in cookies: just because you don't notice them, doesn't mean He doesn't care.

> *You visit the earth and water it, you greatly enrich it; the river of God is full of water. You provide their grain for so you have prepared it. You water its furrows abundantly, settling its ridges, softening it with showers and blessing its growth. You crown the year with your bounty, your wagon tracks overflow with abundance. The pastures of the wilderness overflow, the hills gird themselves with joy, the meadows clothe themselves with flocks, the valleys deck themselves with grain; they shout and sing together for joy.*
>
> Psalm 65.9–13

February 28

What I've Always Believed

Accepting new truths can be difficult sometimes. Especially if I learned it from "good old brother So-and-So" or my parents, it becomes nearly impossible to think they might have been wrong about anything. Or, irrationally, I might think that accepting something different from what they believed makes them wrong, but not accepting it somehow keeps them right. When I hear others refusing clear truth for these reasons, I wonder if they do not realize what they are saying about their mentors or their parents. Surely they believe these people had enough intellectual integrity to change their minds if someone showed them clear evidence otherwise, don't they? In that sense, what they are doing is no longer loyalty, but an insult.

Jesus spent an entire sermon undoing people's misconceptions, things "they had always been taught." "You have heard it was said… but I say unto you…" peppered what we call the Sermon on the Mount. These concepts were not foreign to the Law, as we sometimes seem to believe; it has always been wrong to lust after a woman, and it has always been wrong to verbally abuse someone, as well as the other things Jesus listed. He was simply undoing the misinterpretations of the scribes and rabbis. They changed a guideline of the heart that should have led to sincere, overflowing service to God and mankind to nothing more than "the least I have to do mechanically to remain in good standing with God."

The Pharisees did not accept Jesus for exactly this reason: He did not match the picture of the Messiah and his kingdom they had always believed in. No matter that He quoted and explained scriptures to them, they would not listen. What was this? A king who was poor, who did not own property, who led no mighty army? It did not help that Jesus' version of the kingdom stripped them of the power they hoped to have, and the status they currently enjoyed. A kingdom where publicans, harlots, Samaritans, and Gentiles were equal with them? Impossible!

Because of that bias, they refused the scriptures that were laid before them, and became more and more incensed until they were willing to commit murder to remove the teacher and the doctrine that distressed them so. Would we have so adamantly refused the truth just because it was not "what I've always heard" or worse, perhaps, "not what I want to hear?" Do we, too, have misconceptions about the King and His Kingdom?

Every time we talk to a neighbor about the gospel, we expect him to readily give up his lifelong beliefs simply because we show him a scripture. Shouldn't we be willing to do the same? The next time someone comes at a scripture from a different angle than I have always heard, I need to catch myself before I instantly reject his point. I need to listen with an open mind. Growth implies change. When was the last time I changed my mind about something in the scriptures? Do I really think I know it all? If good old brother So-and-So who taught me is half the brother he ought to be, he would be upset with me if I weren't willing to consider a different view than his.

> *And the brethren immediately sent away Paul and Silas by night to Berea, who, when they arrived, went into the synagogue of the Jews. Now these were more noble than those in Thessalonica in that they received the word with all readiness of mind, searching the scriptures daily to see whether these things were so. Many of them, therefore, believed….*
>
> Acts 17.10–12

February 29
(when necessary)

Leap of Faith

My boys were typical boys. They played outside more than in. They had their own variations of football, baseball, and basketball for two players, or three when their dad was home. They swam like fish, climbed trees, and traipsed through the woods exploring. Since they have grown up, my hair has turned grayer and curled tighter listening to some of the things they did that I never knew about.

Their dad encouraged them in their daring feats. He wanted them to grow up to be strong men who would not flinch when a job needed doing, even if it was dirty, difficult, or a little scary.

I remember many times when he would hold out his arms and they would jump into them. As they learned to swim, he stood out in the deeper water and they leapt as far as they could, with him reaching to pull them out at the last minute. Gradually he moved back farther and farther, and they were swimming to him before they realized it.

Once Lucas climbed a tree with a rotten limb. He found out when the limb beneath his feet broke under him, leaving him hanging by the limb above, his feet a good ten or twelve feet off the ground. We were sitting nearby when we heard the crack and the "whump!" of the falling branch.

Keith walked over to see what he could do. Nothing, as it turned out, except stand beneath his son to break the fall. When he was certain he was in the right place, he told Lucas to let go, and he did, nothing doubting—and nothing broken on either of them when the whole thing was over.

My sons never doubted their father. If he told them to jump, they did. If he told them to let go, they did. They knew beyond a shadow of a doubt that he would catch them and keep them from harm. Why in the world can't we have that same faith in God? Keith could have made an error in judgment; he could have miscalculated what needed to be done to save his sons, or just missed when they jumped. God can't, and He won't.

How would you feel if your child told you he did not believe you would help him? How would you feel if he showed absolutely no trust at all in your promises? How do you think God feels when we do that to Him?

It's called a "leap of faith" because that is what it takes—faith. When we won't do it, we don't have it. It is as simple as that. It has nothing to do with wisdom or good stewardship or common sense. It simply means we don't trust God enough to take care of us. Sometimes what He asks of us seems foolish and impractical. Those words mean nothing to Him, except to describe the people who think their own wits are better than His promises. How foolish and impractical can you get?

For you are my lamp, O Jehovah; And Jehovah will lighten my darkness. For by you I run upon a troop; By my God do I leap over a wall. As for God, his way is perfect: The word of Jehovah is tried; He is a shield unto all them that take refuge in him. For who is God, save Jehovah? And who is a rock, save our God?

2 Samuel 22.29–32

March 1

Flight Paths

A few years after we moved to this spot of country, I was startled one morning by a low rumbling that, over the next few minutes, grew louder and louder. It seemed to come from above, but could not be a plane, I reasoned, because it was taking so long to pass by. I stepped outside and there, to my amazement, flew the Budweiser blimp, so low over our field I felt like I could hold a conversation with the pilot.

We must be on a regular flight path because we have seen that blimp several times, along with all sorts of planes from props to airliners, and helicopters galore. The military also uses our area for drills of some sort, sometimes in groups and other times a lone pilot putting his jet through the routine loops, leaving a tangled skein of contrails behind. Except for the military planes, they all follow the same southerly course across our field, almost as if there were lane markings in the sky.

I have spent a lot of time sitting on the shaded carport, itself in the deep shade of live oaks, killing time, day after day, waiting to see if this latest surgery has worked, and knowing that even if it has it will only last a couple of years. This disease has a regular flight path, just like all those flying machines that pass over us. The optic nerve in the left eye is now 60 percent destroyed. Once gone, those nerve endings can never come back. That led me to contemplate the notion of fate or, as theologians call it, predestination.

Despite what the majority say, the Bible does not teach that God has already decided which of us He will save, and is now resting easy in His recliner watching the show He set in motion. But one thing has been predetermined for a couple of thousand years now—the victory has already been won. It is up to me to follow the flight path that my Savior created, that will inevitably lead me to share in His glory. I must not be detoured by this world, either its pleasures or its problems. Either one could lead to a crash landing far short of the goal.

For this we say to you by the word of the Lord, that we who are alive, that are left till the coming of the Lord, shall in no way precede those who have fallen asleep. For the

Lord himself shall descend from Heaven with a shout, with the voice of the archangel, and with the trump of God, and the dead in Christ shall rise first; then we who are alive, that are left, shall together with them be caught up in the clouds to meet the Lord in the air; and so shall we ever be with the Lord.

1 Thessalonians 4.15–17

March 2

The Bird Feeder

Before this last surgery, Keith built a bird feeder outside the window next to my favorite chair—a metal trough about five feet long on a wooden frame. I must admit I have enjoyed this thing a whole lot more than I expected to. We keep it filled with birdseed and Keith hung a cylinder of suet over it as well.

First the cardinal couple came to dine. They spend their time in the trough with the seed. The suet is not their cup of tea, so to speak, but several others seem to prefer it. A hummingbird came and hovered next to it, trying his best to figure out how to get the nectar out of it, but finally gave up and flew back to the hummingbird feeder on the other side of the house.

Then the catbird came calling. He stood under it, with the bottom of it just out of reach. First, he tried the hummingbird's trick, but a catbird cannot hover, he quickly found out as he fell with a splat into the trough. Then he started jumping up and down, trying to peck when he reached the height of his jump, once again falling into the trough, this time nearly doing a backward somersault. Poor bird, I hope he didn't hear me laughing at him, but you never think about a bird being so awkward as to fall on his backside. Maybe he did hear me, because he left and did not come back for a long time.

The next morning I looked out and a wren had landed on top of the hanging suet and calmly leaned down, pecking away. Every so often he looked around as if to say, "See? This isn't so hard." After a few days he had pecked away most of his sure-footing. The top of the suet was no longer flat, so gradually one foot would slide down and hang onto the side. Every morning he pecked away until finally there was no room at all on the top and both feet clung to the side of the suet. Then came the day he got a little too self-confident. I looked out and he was hanging upside down from the bottom of the suet. His little feet curled in tightly and deeply and he seemed to have a good hold, but he had not reckoned with his desire to eat. He pecked so hard that he pushed himself off the suet and he, too, landed on his back in the trough. Was he embarrassed? No way. He just hopped back up on the side and kept pecking. There are things more important than saving face.

Along came a little gray titmouse with his gray crest, big ringed eye, and the slimmest breast I had ever seen on a bird. He too, figured out how to land on the suet, hang on, and peck. Then one morning the suet cylinder fell and lay across the trough. Back comes the catbird ready for an easy meal. The titmouse arrived shortly after and must have known something about catbirds. He sat in the azalea and squealed ferociously until he finally scared the catbird away. As soon as the titmouse had eaten and left, the big coward came back, but not long afterward the cardinal couple flew at him and off he went again.

All of this makes me think about our efforts to feast on the bread of life. Do we mind looking a little foolish sometimes in our eagerness to learn and grow spiritually? Do we give up after one or two tries if things are more difficult than we expected? Are we too frightened to admit we live on the Word of God—afraid we won't be accepted by our peers, afraid we will be ridiculed, afraid no one will like us any more, afraid it may cost us socially, economically, or maybe some day, even physically?

The little birds at my feeder teach me profound lessons every day. Sometimes I need a prod to be more like the feisty little titmouse or the ingenious little wren who couldn't care less how his hunger for suet makes him look. Sometimes I need to be reminded that there are more important things than what everyone thinks about me, and that fear of others can make you look the most ridiculous of all. Indeed, if a tiny little titmouse can scare away a big old catbird all by himself, why can't I make Satan's minions run away, especially with all the Help I have at hand?

As newborn babes long for the spiritual milk which is without guile, that you may grow thereby unto salvation.

1 Peter 2.2

March 3

A Really Good "Bad Example"

Poor old Martha. How many times does she serve as a bad example from the pulpit or in women's Bible studies? She's even had one of those studies named after her—*Martha, Martha*—and it isn't a compliment!

Jesus spent many hours, in fact, many days, in the company and home of those three siblings, Mary, Martha, and Lazarus. You do realize it was probably Martha's house: "And a certain woman named Martha received him into *her* house" (Luke 10.38), which means the sacred duty of hospitality lay squarely on her shoulders. No wonder she was so consumed by it.

But consider this wonderful attitude of Martha's: Jesus, for whom she has labored so hard, comes into her home and delivers a scolding that is recorded for all posterity simply because she works so long to give him her best (or so it appears), and still she serves him. How many of my sisters might have thought, "The ungrateful lout! See if I ever invite him here again." I would have been hard-pressed not to think those words myself. Do you think you wouldn't have thought them? How do you feel and react when your husband indicates that he does not like a meal you have worked on for several hours? Aha! I thought so.

But Martha did not react that way. She changed. I know this because she served him again, shortly before his death (John 12), and though Mary was once again sitting at his feet, Martha never uttered a complaint against her. And Jesus did not correct Martha, which proves that it was not the serving itself that was the problem, it was the attitude.

Perhaps it was simply that she had decided what Mary needed to be doing instead of focusing on herself. Some of us are more suited to being Marys and some to being Marthas. The Lord had a physical body that needed serving. It was not wrong for Martha to feed and house him. It was wrong, though, for *her* to decide what Mary's obligations were and then resent her for not fulfilling them. That was between Mary and the Lord, *not* between the two sisters. When we all take care of our own duties to the best of our abilities, the Lord will be served in every area.

And here is another thing for which to praise Martha. Imagine the Lord spent as much time in your home as he did with these three beloved friends of his. Just how many times would he be scolding you? I would be lucky not to have more than *one a day* recorded in my case, much less one in about three years' time. Yet this poor woman, who served him faithfully, who corrected her attitude when he spoke to her, who had the faith to say, "If you had been here my brother would not have died, and even now I know that whatever you ask of God, God will give you" (John 11.21–22), this woman we hold up for all generations as a bad example.

I hope in my lifetime I can do as well as she did.

> *Jesus said unto [Martha] I am the resurrection and the life; he who believes on me, though he die, yet shall he live; and whoever lives and believes on me shall never die. Do you believe this? She said unto him, Yes, Lord, I have believed that you are the Christ, the Son of God, even he who comes into the world.*
>
> John 11.25–27

Caution: Lexicon Ahead

Bible study is one of my favorite pastimes. We are blessed to live in an era when all sorts of tools are available that make research fairly easy, and much less tedious than ever before. They also make it much more dangerous. It is easy for me to read a commentary, lexicon, or Bible dictionary and suddenly think I have become a great scholar, when the truth is, not only am I not instantly a Hebrew or Greek scholar, I am not even a good English scholar!

Some of us studied Latin in high school and learned why it is called a "dead" language—it is no longer spoken and therefore no longer changes. A living language changes every day. Take the word "silly." We know it means "absurd, foolish or stupid." Did you know that it originally meant "happy and blessed"? How about "lewd"? It now means "sexually unchaste;" originally it meant "a common person as opposed to clergy." "Idiot" now has the specific meaning of "someone whose mental age does not exceed three," and a colloquial meaning of "a foolish or stupid person." Originally it meant "someone in private station as opposed to someone holding public office." So 500 years ago, most of us could have been described as silly, lewd idiots and we would not have taken offense!

The same changes are true of every language, including Greek and Hebrew. When you search for meanings in a lexicon, be sure you find out what meaning the word had when it was written in the scriptures. In fact, that is why I usually limit my studies to the various ways a word was translated into English. *Psallo* once meant "to pull out one's hair," but by the time Ephesians 5.19 and Colossians 3.16 were written it had gone through several changes and simply meant "to sing praises." That is why we sing to God instead of standing before Him pulling out our hair!

Another thing to be careful of is root words. A lot of arguments have been made based on the root of a Greek word. Let me just give you a quick example in English to show you how dangerous this can be. Do you know what the root word for "nice" is? The Latin *nescius. Nescius* means "ignorant"! Think about that the next time someone tells you how nice you look on Sunday morning.

We do all sorts of other things that we think are so smart and really are not. We talk about compound words as if just knowing the two parts to one will instantly enlighten us to the real meaning of a Greek word. Not necessarily. How about "pineapple?" The bush certainly does not look like a pine, and the fruit neither looks, tastes, nor smells like an apple! Truly, a little knowledge can be a dangerous thing.

Then there are those simplistic definitions we often use. "Faithful means full of faith." Really? Ask someone whose spouse has been "unfaithful" what that word means and you are much more likely to get an accurate and useful definition.

And what does all this have to do with anything? God chose to use His written word to communicate His will to us. I need to be very careful how I use it. Translations are fine. Jesus used one—the Septuagint, the Greek translation of the Old Testament, completed about 200 BC. However, I must be careful in my study lest I think that learning a few things makes me an authority. I know it is a cliché, but it is so true—the more I learn, the more I realize I do not know. But God has made sure I know what I *need* to know.

We have in our hands the Words of Life. Be careful with them.

> *...many of his disciples went back and walked no more with him. Jesus said therefore unto the twelve, Would you also go away? Simon Peter answered him, Lord, to whom shall we go? You have the words of eternal life.*
>
> John 6.66–68

March 5

The Right Question

A few weeks ago I told you the story of a camping trip when I forgot our Sunday clothes, and the chilly reception we received in that church on Sunday morning. Occasionally I receive a little feedback, and I was happy that no one sent the question, "What church was that?" In fact, in all these years, whenever I have told the story no one has asked. Good for you.

First, that church probably no longer exists. Oh, I happen to know that a church still meets in that building. But it is not the same group of people. Some have died and gone on. Some have moved out; some have moved in. But I imagine that all the ones who are still there have grown into better people. Twenty years can make a difference in anyone's life.

And the problem of the group that did exist then was not that they made a mistake in their judgment about why we were there. It did not matter why we were there. Someone should have greeted us warmly and welcomed us into the building whether we were poor people down on our luck, so to speak, or Christians who accidentally left their Sunday clothes hanging in the garment bag on a doorknob somewhere in the house. If someone had greeted us, but only because they recognized us from a meeting sometime in the past, that would have been wrong too.

But as to asking, "Where was that?" the right question is the one the apostles asked when Jesus told them one of them would betray him. As much as they failed to comprehend the kingdom, despite his teaching and their knowledge of Old Testament prophecy, as much as they still fought among themselves about who would be the greatest *even that very night*, they did not start glancing around the table and whispering among themselves things like, "I bet it's Levi. I told Jesus you could never trust a tax collector."

No. Matthew tells us, "And they were exceeding sorrowful and began to say to him *every one,* Is it I, Lord?" (26.22). Mark tells us they asked him "one by one" (14.19).

So when I hear a particularly pointed sermon, I shouldn't look around to make sure brother Whozit is there to hear it because he really needs it. I shouldn't look across the aisle at sister What's-her-name with a "So there!" expression on my face.

What is it we say about approved apostolic example? We use it to nail all sorts of false doctrines, but how about nailing ourselves?

"Is it I, Lord?"

> *Judge not that you be not judged. For with what judgment you judge you shall be judged, and with what measured you mete, it shall be measured unto you. And why do you behold the mote that is in your brother's eye, but consider not the beam that is in your own eye? Or how will you say to your brother, "Let me cast the mote out of your eye," while the beam is in your own eye? You hypocrite! First cast the beam out of your own eye and then you may see clearly to cast the mote our of your brother's eye.*
>
> Matthew 7.1–5

March 6

A Hawk of My Own

Last spring we watched a hawk couple build a nest right over our garden. Every day we were out planting and watering, they were carrying twigs trailing Spanish moss up to the lowest fork, 30 feet up the pine tree just east of the plowed plot of dirt we work all summer. By the time our plants were poking up through the dirt, the mother was sitting on the nest. She sat so low and blended in so well, it took a pair of binoculars and a steady hand to see her at all. The father faithfully brought her food every evening, and would often sit on the branch next to the nest as she sat on her eggs, protecting her, I suppose.

About four weeks later, I saw the mother hop off the nest one morning and a day or so after heard tiny cheeps as I stood under the tree. In a few days, a white downy head appeared, and soon another one. The next three weeks we watched as the parents brought them food, kept them warm, and at times sat on the rowdy babies so they would not fall out of the tree! Soon both babies were sitting up in the nest, at times peering over at me while I picked, hoed, watered, and all the other chores involved in gardening. They were getting so big it took both parents to bring enough food, and their white down was turning brown.

And then one morning, one of them was gone. At first it did not go far. It sat in the trees across the fence from the nest-tree. It was bigger, but had more muted coloring, so we assumed it was a female, and big sister would call out to her little brother all through the day, telling him he could fly too, or so I anthropomorphically presumed. Then big sister and parents were gone most of the day, mom and dad teaching the first one how to hunt, and only coming back in the evenings to feed the smaller one in the nest, who always greeted them with the most pitiful little squeaks of happiness.

He seemed so lonely I started talking to him every morning when I was out, and he usually sat up, cocked his head back and forth, and peered over the edge of the nest at me, until I went inside. I assumed he would be flying in a day or so, but no, after a week, he was still there. He often flapped his wings, big, strong wings I knew could carry him easily, but he seemed afraid. In fact, one morning he hopped out of the nest onto the limb and lost his balance. It was funny to see him wave his wings like a human waving his arms in circles, trying to catch his balance—and he did, and hopped back in that nest as quickly as he could.

Then about ten days after his big sister flew, I went out to the garden and the nest was empty. I felt like his mother, not knowing whether to cheer or cry. I was sure he was gone forever. Then suddenly I heard him, and there he sat in the same tree, but fifteen feet higher! He stayed there the whole time I was out in the garden, but in the evening he was gone.

The next morning, I walked my path and heard him again. High in the air he circled over me then settled on a limb only seven or eight feet off the ground, and directly across the fence from where I stood, calling. As soon as I reached that point in my walk and started talking, he hushed and sat there cocking his head again, until I told him it had been nice talking with him, but I really needed to finish my walk and today's garden work. He called awhile longer while I walked, sometimes changing trees to be nearby, but eventually flew off.

Every day that summer he would come back in the mornings and find a tree near me so we could talk awhile. He eventually figured out where I disappeared and once landed on the roof of the porch where we could see him and he could see us through the window while we ate. Then things happened. I had some surgeries, some complications, and for a few weeks was unable to walk. He disappeared and winter came. Now I *knew* he was gone for good.

Late in January I heard him outside one morning. Yes, when you have heard one hawk often enough, you can actually tell him apart from the others. I ran outside and called out to him. He stopped and listened, then flew away. It had been long enough, I suppose, that his natural fear of man had taken over, but it was still a nice moment in the day. But ever since that day, if I am late getting outside to walk, I hear him calling from high in the sky, and he flies overhead for most of the time I am walking. He will not let me get close, but he will land in trees close to the house to call at least, until I come outside.

I think God allows natural things to happen when we need them—things that encourage us, that help us overcome a temptation or get past a bad moment in the day; brethren we see in our day in unusual places, paths that cross when they can most help one another. I am a long way out and not likely to have those sorts of things, but maybe God has sent me this hawk. I know he reminds me of one of my favorite passages in the Bible—even though he is a hawk and not an eagle. But we will never get the benefit of those providential things if we are not paying attention.

So be aware today of the things that happen, the people you see, and the thoughts that cross your mind—maybe even that hymn that goes round and round in your head like a broken record. Maybe it was Heaven sent.

> *They that wait on Jehovah shall renew their strength; they shall mount up with wings as eagles; they shall run and not be weary; they shall walk, and not faint.*
>
> Isaiah 40.31

March 7

Taking Medicine

My dog hates taking her medicine. Whether it is the monthly squirt of heartworm medication or the monthly application of flea and tick preventive, it takes two of us to do it—one to hold her down and the other to do the dirty work. Not even a treat at the end will dampen her withering glare when it's over. We have betrayed her and she makes sure we feel her scorn.

Actually, I think that is pretty normal. Which is why, when someone I know has tried to admonish a brother and someone else says, "Now he [the sinner] is upset," I want to say, "Well, duh." No one likes to be corrected. I certainly don't, no matter how hard the other guy tries to be nice about it.

And no one I know likes to be the corrector. In spite of what we may hear about all those "bad attitudes" people supposedly have when they correct others, everyone I know approaches the ordeal with fear. They know they will more than likely lose a friend, be attacked, or wind up with a damaged reputation. Why is it that when a godly person rebukes a sinner and the results are less than optimal, that we automatically believe the sinner's version of events, rather than the godly person's? That's not even logical.

So when it comes to taking spiritual medicine, I need to remember three things:

First, be brave. God says when I see someone in sin and I do not warn them, he will hold *me* accountable. "When I say to the wicked, O wicked man, you shall surely die, and you do not speak to warn the wicked from his way, that wicked man shall die in his iniquity, *but his blood will I require at your hand*" (Ezek 33.8). Regardless of the grief it is likely to cause me, God expects me to care enough about a soul to try anyway.

Second, be charitable in my judgment of a corrector. Believe that he did his best, and went with the best attitude. That poor fellow took the risk of a no-win situation because he cared; he deserves my support, not my criticism. Besides, if I thought I could do better, why didn't I?

And finally, when it comes my turn to take the medicine, swallow my pride along with the pill, no matter how bitter it is, recognizing that someone cared enough about my eternal destiny to try to help me. After all, medicine will make you feel better in the end, won't it?

> *Brethren, if a man be overtaken in any trespass, you who are spiritual restore such a one in a spirit of gentleness; looking to yourself, lest you also be tempted.*
>
> Galatians 6.1

A Little Shack in the Woods

Out here in the sticks we are surrounded by hundreds of acres of pine woods planted by the paper companies. Do not let anyone tell you that we are depleting our forests by using so much paper. Old growth forests are not used for paper goods; they are used for that pretty furniture you own. The paper companies regularly plant the trees they send to the mills, and more trees grow in the United States now than when Columbus landed.

I always get a start when I pass a wooded section that has been standing for several years, and find that it has been taken down, soon to be replanted with small saplings. And more often than not, when the trees are removed, a rundown wooden shack sits in the open, formerly hidden by the rows and rows of 60 foot tall pines. The porch sags, the roof waffles, the windows are paneless, with dangling shutters or none at all. There are no power lines and no well tanks. These dilapidated houses may have been empty nearly a hundred years.

I find myself wondering who lived there. None of these places could be more than 20' by 20', many appreciably smaller, probably with one or two rooms, three at the most. Kitchens were often on the back porch because of the heat and humidity in this area; families bathed in wash tubs in the kitchen or on the back porch, and outhouses were the plumbing of the day. Did a young couple raise a family there? In those days, they often had as many as nine or ten children. When it rained they all had to play inside!

And when it rained the roof leaked. When the winter wind blew, it seeped in between the board or log walls. And no telling what might crawl in through the cracks in the floor boards—if there was even a floor. Yet I know happy families lived there, and good citizens grew up from such poverty. I know some of those elderly people and they talk of those days with a lot of smiles and chuckles.

Yet here I sit, complaining because sometimes on a clear, still day in the country your electricity goes out for no apparent reason, and if the wind blows at all you can count on it. No electricity means no air conditioning and no well pump. Whenever a new neighbor moves in between me and the highway, the phone company will inevitably cut my line when they put in the new one. And I don't have a thing to wear! Well, if I lost ten pounds I might. I wonder if those folks who lived in that shack had enough food to even worry about getting too heavy.

These little shacks are reminders to me to be grateful for what I have, and not to covet the material blessings of another. I can be happy anywhere. I can raise godly children anywhere. I can make a good marriage anywhere. I can be a child of God no matter where I live or how. But no mansion on earth will make me happy if that is all I care about.

Godliness with contentment is great gain, for we brought nothing into this world for neither can we carry anything out; but having food and covering we shall with that be content.

1 Timothy 6.6–8

March 9

The Dead Possum

Possums, or more properly "opossums," can be a nuisance. They rummage in the garbage, they poke about in the shed, and they ramble into the garden destroying perfectly good melons with a bite or two out of each one. That is one reason we have dogs, and Magdi has done better than any other at solving the problem. For awhile we had to bury one every day; she must have come across some sort of Possumopolis out in the woods.

One morning Keith found yet another as he was leaving for work, but he was so late he had no time to properly dispose of it. It was my turn to do the honors. I have come a long way in 36 years, but I still won't pick up a dead thing, even with big thick gloves. So I got the shovel.

I am glad my neighbors are not close. I stuck the shovel edge down by the possum and pushed, assuming it would just slide under the offensive creature so I could carry it out to the woods and let nature do the disposal work. Instead, the shovel just pushed the possum along. I tried again, and again, and again. Every time I pushed, the possum moved farther and I wound up following it in a circle around the field. This possum might as well have been alive it was making such a merry chase.

Meanwhile Magdi stood to the side. She looked at me like I was nuts, but she also looked at me like she would really like to have her possum back. Occasionally she lunged at the possum as I made the circle yet again passing her on the right. So there I was pushing a dead possum in a circle around the yard with a shovel, while yelling at the dog at regular intervals, like some sort of bizarre ritualistic dance.

I stopped, winded and frustrated, and found myself next to the oak tree across the driveway from the well. The answer struck me, if only I had the energy left. I pushed the shovel again. Again it pushed the possum, this time right against the tree and the tree held it there for me as the shovel slid beneath it. Success!

I lifted the shovel—and the possum rolled right off of it. Somehow I kept from screaming. Okay, I told myself. You have learned something. Possums are heavy and you have to hold the shovel handle tightly so it won't tip. I tried again, pushing the possum up against the tree and lifting the shovel, this time ready for the shifting weight. Now just to get it to the woods. It was a several hundred yard trip, and that possum at the end of the shovel got heavier and heavier.

About halfway there I knew I was not going to make it, so rather than let the thing drop in a clearing where there were no trees to push against, I carefully lowered the shovel to the ground. As much as I hated to, I had to move my hand farther down the handle, closer to the possum so the weight would be easier to manage. I did, and it was easier, so much easier I could even walk faster without being in danger of losing the possum.

I was already dressed for Bible class and did not want to traipse into the woods among the briars and brush, so I carefully pulled back on the shovel and slung with all my might. So I am not Supergirl. The possum slid off the shovel about five feet into the brush, not much further than the length of the shovel handle. By then, I was ready to call that a great success, and left it.

As shocking as it might sound, that is the way we treat God sometimes. Instead of rushing into His safe and loving embrace, we keep Him at arm's length. Like a teenager who is too embarrassed to act like he loves his parents, we are too embarrassed to let our love for God show to those around us. We don't want to look too weird, too strange, too "fanatical."

Early Christians were known for their good works. In fact, that is how they often gave themselves away to their persecutors. They looked and acted so differently from everyone else. No one else was kind and forgiving, even when mistreated.

Would our godly behavior give us away under similar circumstances, or would it lump us in with the crowd because our religion has not "contaminated" our lives?

Even among ourselves we don't want to say things that might make people look at us askance. It's like the old joke where the new convert sits in the pews saying, "Amen," and "Praise God," only to have some older member take him aside and say, "Son, we don't praise God here."

God wants us close to Him. Think about that for a moment. Our awesome all-powerful Creator wants a relationship with us. He made an incomprehensible sacrifice to make it possible. Maybe we need to be shocked with this analogy, so we will wake up. When we keep Him at arm's length like something disgusting, we are treating God like a dead possum.

Wherefore also He is able to save to the uttermost them that draw near unto God through Him, seeing He ever lives to make intercession for them.

Draw near to God and He will draw near to you.

Hebrews 7.25; James 4.8a

March 10

Rest Area Ahead

I remember folding diapers one day when Lucas was two and Nathan just a few weeks old. I had not had a full night's sleep in the three or four weeks since Nathan's birth—an emergency C-section, which while routine, was still major surgery. The garden was at its height, and laundry was a daily chore along with the usual cooking and cleaning.

During Nathan's morning nap I gave Lucas as much attention as possible. We were learning the alphabet, going through magazines to find pictures of things beginning with that week's letter, practicing how to draw it, and finding it among the words of the book I read to him that day. Our daily Bible lesson included a song I had composed if no ready-made one came to mind, and a dramatic re-creation, either by us or handy stuffed animals which assumed new identities at his command.

Lest anyone think Keith was not doing his share, he was preaching part-time as well as holding down two other part-time jobs and finishing up a degree at the university 20 miles down the road. Then he came home and became Goliath or the "big fish" or whatever large character he needed to be as Lucas recounted his Bible lesson to Daddy. He always gave Lucas his evening bath and watched Nathan while I cleaned up supper dishes. After the babies were in bed, he studied.

On that particular day I was making those intricate folds of bleached white cotton robotically. Nathan was cooing and gurgling on a blanket in the floor, and Lucas was lining up his assorted toy cars and trucks on the other end of the sofa from my stack of diapers. A wave of weariness hit with such force that I leaned my head over on the sofa arm for a second's rest.

Ten minutes later I woke up to little grunts from Nathan. This meant I had approximately 15 seconds to start nursing him before a full-blown howl erupted from that deceptively small set of lungs. What amazed me, though, was that Lucas was in the middle of running a fire engine up my arm and parking it next to my head. Was this what woke me? Obviously not, for there were already five other vehicles parked by my nose. It was my baby's impending distress that woke me from such a deep slumber, not the arm traffic.

That was not the only time exhaustion struck so strongly. Young mothers, I believe, live in a perpetual state of weariness, at least the ones who understand their God-given duties and try to fulfill them. There have been nights when falling into bed and relaxing actually *hurt* for a few seconds.

There are other things that make me weary, not in body but in spirit. A relative's foolish words or actions can cause hurt and turmoil throughout the family. Two supposedly mature brothers or sisters in the Lord who behave like three year olds; an argument over scripture that is punctuated not by, "This is what the scriptures say," but rather, "This is what I think, this is what I feel about it, this is what I am comfortable with"; people who take your much prayed about words and actions in the worst possible light, making petty comments that pierce your heart, and spreading their thoughts to others, who then bring them back to you. Then there is the evening news. These things make you throw up your hands in defeat and say along with the apostle John, "Lord, come quickly."

Rest—if there is anything about Heaven I look forward to more than anything else, it is rest—rest to my soul.

God had promised his people rest when he took them out of Egypt. All they had to do was trust him and obey him, but despite the great signs and wonders done before their eyes, they could not manage that. So God said, "As I swore in my wrath, they shall not enter into my rest" (Heb 4.3). They did enter Canaan, but they did not enter The Rest. They had troubles constantly, from within and without, simply because they did not have the faith it took to obey God. "There remains therefore a Sabbath rest for the people of God" (4.9), a rest like God's rest. The Hebrew writer is careful that we understand the difference. God did not rest because he was tired; he rested because he had finished his work (4.4).

And we have that promise. If we can get past the times that cause us to throw up our hands and shake our heads, the people who make our burdens heavier instead of lighter; if we can manage to stay strong and finish the course, we can rest too. Oh, what a wonderful promise!

For if Joshua had given them rest, he would not have spoken afterward of another day. There remains therefore a Sabbath rest for the people of God. For he who has entered into his own rest has himself also rested from his work as God did from his. Let us therefore give diligence to enter into that rest, that no one fall after the same example of disobedience.

Hebrews 4.8–11

March 11

Judge Righteous Judgment

I have spent several spring weekends judging a piano competition at the University of North Florida. Being a piano and voice teacher, my students were often in similar competitions. A young man once questioned me on the wisdom of this. Wasn't I creating undue stress on my students? Didn't I think that this emphasis on competition would take the joy of music away from them?

I could go on and on about that one, but suffice it to say, I would never have done anything that I believed harmed these children. I never forced any of them to participate in any competition, but I can make this observation from more than 30 years of teaching: the ones who never competed never advanced as quickly, and always quit after two or three years—no exception. The others made rapid progress and the majority of them stuck with it long enough to give a senior recital.

That spurred thoughts of the negative and positive aspects of "judging" in the scriptures. Usually all we hear is "Judge not that you be not judged," and usually from someone who is doing something they ought not to be doing. There are many more occasions where we are either specifically told to judge or to do something that requires making a judgment.

> Mark those that are causing the divisions and occasions of stumbling, contrary to the doctrine which you learned, and turn away from them. (Rom 16.17)
>
> If a man be overtaken in a fault, you who are spiritual restore such a one in a spirit of gentleness. (Gal 6.1)
>
> Shun profane babblings for they will proceed further in ungodliness. (2 Tim 2.16)
>
> Believe not every spirit, but prove the spirits whether they are of God, for many false prophets have gone out into the world. (1 John 4.1)

Making judgments is essential to protecting those we love and saving those in error. I could go on and on, filling up page after page with scriptures like these.

Sometimes judging is required. The trick is to do it properly. Jesus said, "Judge not according to appearance, but judge righteous judgment" (John 7.24). If I read the context of most of those passages above, I will see the guidelines the Holy Spirit has carefully laid out in how to judge righteously.

Being quick to judge others' lives when I do not know the facts, when I am judging only by "how it looks," and when I have never been in their shoes, flies in the face of the love I am commanded to have toward others. In that case, "Judge not that you be not judged" fits me to a tee. But using the excuse "I don't want to judge their situation" when someone is lost in sin, is a cop-out that will not please the Father who watches over us.

> *Deliver them that are carried away unto death; and those that are ready to be slain, see that you hold back. If you say, Behold, we did not know this, does not he who weighs the hearts consider it? And he who keeps the soul, does he not know it? And shall he not render to every man according to his work?*
>
> Proverbs 24.11–12

Ordinarily, I stay away from *The Message.* It is a paraphrase that takes far too many liberties with the scriptures; but I must say, I like its interpretation of the above, with my own added phrase—hey, if he can paraphrase, so can I!—"Rescue the perishing; don't hesitate to step in and help. If you say, 'Hey, that's none of my business,' [I don't want to judge], will that get you off the hook? Someone is watching you closely, you know—Someone not impressed with weak excuses."

So there it is—I must judge, but carefully, wisely, *righteously.*

March 12

A Surprising Source of Hilarity

I have been studying giving lately and came across an interesting tidbit. In 2 Corinthians 9.7, when Paul says "God loves a cheerful giver," the Greek word there, translated "cheerful," is *hilaron.* You can see it, can't you? Two English words we get from that are hilarious and hilarity. *God loves a hilarious giver!*

It isn't enough just to not grumble when we give, no matter what we are giving or when, be it money, time, goods, or encouragement, on Sunday mornings or individual opportunities during the week. It isn't enough not to begrudge the things we are giving up when our sharing deprives us of them. One of the reasons God says we should work is so we will "have whereof to give to him who needs" (Eph 4.28), *not* so we can have everything our hearts desire.

Would you say a movie was "hilarious" if you chuckled once or twice? Would you call a joke "hilarious" if it simply made you smile? The word is a joyousness that bubbles over, that cannot be controlled, that you do not *want* to control. *Vine's* describes it as a "joyfulness that is prompt to act." You don't need a cattle prod to make this person give; the joy he feels in giving takes care of it automatically.

I grew up seeing someone stand before our assemblies saying, "Separate and apart from the Lord's Supper," just before passing the basket. But no matter how much I heard that phrase, as a child I always thought there were three elements to the Lord's Supper. And though now, as an adult, I know better, the fact that we pass the plate within minutes of that ritual keeps me quiet and solemn when I put that check in. I wonder if we ought not to at least *smile* when we do it. Look at one another and share the joy of sacrificing a little something to the Lord. In this blessed country we get precious little chance to feel *any* pain on his behalf.

On Sunday morning, when that basket comes by, look at someone near you with gladness in your heart. And if you hear someone laughing, smile. Maybe someone's joy has finally overflowed.

> *But this I say, he who sows sparingly shall also reap sparingly; and he who sows bountifully shall reap also bountifully. Let each man do according as he has purposed in his heart, not grudgingly or of necessity, for God loves a cheerful [joyous, bubbling over, prompt to act,* ***hilarious****] giver.*
>
> 2 Corinthians 9.6–7

March 13

And He Called the Name of that Place…

I have done more traveling than I really care to lately—in less than two years' time 7,000 miles to either family funerals or experimental surgeries, and all in an automobile. I have started noticing place names that are a bit unusual. Now Florida does have its own peculiarities. Have you ever heard of Two Egg, Florida? As we traveled through Mississippi recently, we came across an exit for Dry Creek Water Park. I am not sure I would want to go down their water slide. Then there was Aux Arc, Arkansas. If you have not had French lessons, or, as in my case, taught French art song, where the judges dock your students severely for mispronunciation, you may not get it. "Au" in French is pronounced "oh", and an "x" at the end of a word is not pronounced at all unless it comes before a word beginning with a vowel, in which case it is pronounced as a "z." So Aux Arc is pronounced "Ozark." Sounds like someone got a little cute. Then there was Toad Suck Park. I do not even want to contemplate how that one got its name.

I am reminded of my readings, in Genesis especially, how various places were named. Almost always it had to do with something that happened there, and in the case of God's people, usually included a reference to God in their lives.

After Abraham offered Isaac (Gen 22) in all but actual deed, he called the mountain "Jehovah-jirah," meaning "Jehovah will provide," for indeed God did provide an offering. When Jacob fled Esau, he dreamed of angels ascending and descending a ladder, and the next morning set up a pillar, poured oil upon it and called it "Beth-El," meaning "house of God" (Gen 28). When he returned to the land 20 years later, he called for all the foreign gods to be disposed of, for his family to purify themselves, and built an altar, calling it "El-beth-El," "the God of Bethel" (Gen 35). In Genesis 33.20 he bought a parcel of land and spread his tent there, calling it "El-Elohe-Israel," "God, the God of Israel."

So if we were going to name our homes, whether they be small apartments in the city, homes in the suburbs, or acreage in the country, what would we call them? Is God a big enough part of our lives to figure in their names as he was to the old patriarchs? Would "Beth-El" be suitable because God is regularly spoken to and the Lord is spoken of in our homes? Could we call it Jehovah-jirah because we understand that all we have is provided by God and his providence? Could we call it "El-Elohe-Ward," "God the God of the Wards" (or your own particular last name)? Or would we, as Isaac did when the Philistines feuded with him over the watering holes, have to name our wells "Esek," ("Contention") and "Sitnah," ("Enmity") (Gen 26)? What emotions are our homes filled with?

It is an interesting exercise to think about giving our homes a name. Try it, and see if it doesn't help you make yours a better home for your family, and a wonderful place for anyone to visit

> *But will God in very deed dwell on the earth? Behold, heaven and the heaven of heavens cannot contain you, how much less this house that I have built! Yet have respect unto the prayer of your servant and to his supplication, O Jehovah my God, to listen unto the cry and to the prayer which your servant prays before you this day: that your eyes may be open toward this house night and day …and hear in heaven your dwelling-place, and when you shall hear, forgive.*
>
> 1 Kings 8.27–30

March 14

Chloe and the Butterfly

Chloe is growing quickly. She is now seven months old and about two-thirds the size of our seven year old Australian cattle dog. Sometimes I have to look twice to tell which one I am looking at. Yes, I know that does not mean much considering the state of my vision these days, but I *know* these dogs.

Chloe, however, is still very much a puppy. She will bring her football to you to throw over and over, or her old rag to play tug-o-war again and again after she manages to yank it away from you. You will always wear out before she does. She prances and cavorts, romps and darts, and any other word in a thesaurus describing playfulness.

A few weeks ago she started chasing butterflies. We have all sorts our here in the country, black and orange monarchs, yellow and black swallowtails, sapphire blue and black hairstreaks, and the ubiquitous canary yellow sulphurs that flit all over, changing direction almost faster than your eye can follow. Those are Chloe's favorites to chase, maybe because they are smaller. Some of the swallowtails are nearly as big as her head.

Yesterday morning, after Magdi had already left my side, and Chloe was still prancing along, another yellow butterfly flitted into our path. Just as usual, Chloe chased it. And then, when she least expected it, she caught it. The look on her face was shock, then panic as the butterfly evidently kept on flitting inside her mouth. Without hesitation, she opened her mouth and the butterfly flew out, none the worse for wear, and Chloe happily resumed the chase.

I thought then, once again, of Jesus' admonition to become as little children. Was this yet another way that children are superior to adults, at least in the kingdom? They do not realize that, with their feet firmly planted on the ground, they should not be able to catch something that can fly. They do not know when something is supposed to be impossible. They do not know the meaning of "illogical." They do not know what science has and has not discovered. How often do we let our maturity in the world rob of us our childhood in the kingdom? How often have I uttered that pessimistic comment, "It'll never work"? How often do we look at a new Christian, especially one who has come from a difficult background, and say, "He won't last"? How often do we look at the physical to judge the spiritual—placing our trust in things that look strong and effective on the outside, and never allowing childlike trust to take a chance on God's power—and why, oh why, do we even consider that "taking a chance"? Why do we refuse to pray for the impossible?

Magdi often plays with Chloe, especially in the cool of the evening, but more often she is content to sit and watch. She keeps a good humor about her most of the time, but sometimes Chloe's high spirits annoy her. When Chloe is chasing a butterfly, not paying attention to where her romps take her, and she runs right over

Magdi, she is often rewarded with a growl, or even a nip. When Magdi actually snorts, it seems for all the world like a grumpy old woman saying, "When will she grow up? She will never catch the thing, and she is always getting in the way and causing me trouble."

I suppose Magdi doesn't remember the day she jumped over three feet off the ground and caught a bird on the wing. I mourned the beautiful cardinal, but her form was beautiful, elegant, and to see a dog jump higher off the ground than she is tall and catch a flying bird is amazing. You see, Magdi was a puppy once, too.

Maybe only silly little puppies chase butterflies and birds; but then, only puppies *catch* them.

> *Woe to those that…rely on horses, and trust in chariots because they are many, and in horsemen because they are very strong, but they look not unto the Holy One of Israel, neither seek Jehovah.*
>
> *Jesus, looking upon them said, With men it is impossible, but not with God; for all things are possible with God.*
>
> Isaiah 31.1; Mark 10.27

March 15

Attitude Shmattitude

Long ago and far away I remember someone saying, immediately after a sermon on the subject, "Attitude shmattitude. I am sick and tired of hearing about attitude."

I thought to myself, "And you, sir, certainly have a bad one."

Hanging by one of the magnets on my refrigerator is a quote by Charles Swindoll that ends, "We have a choice every day regarding the attitude we will embrace for that day. We cannot change our past… we cannot change the fact that people will act in a certain way. We cannot change the inevitable. The only thing we can do is play on the one string we have, and that is our attitude. …I am convinced that life is 10 percent what happens to me and 90 percent how I react to it. And so it is with you… we are in charge of our attitudes."

My neighbor recently returned from a trip to Alaska, a trip she and her husband have wanted to make for a long time. They flew to Anchorage, then rented an RV and traveled the state for two and half weeks. As they were returning the RV, ready to fly back home, she fell in the parking lot, face down. It was a nasty fall. The emergency room doctor put 14 stitches in her face. Five of her front teeth were knocked out, and she is still, after two months, receiving the dental repair work for that, already totaling $10,000. She needed a doctor's note before the airline would allow her on the plane to fly home. She was in a wheelchair, of course, and the other passengers were staring out of the corners of their eyes—being too polite to stare straight on. (We've all done it.) Her husband finally told everyone she had had a run-in with a grizzly bear, and she looked so bad someone actually believed it.

You know what she said after she told me about it? "It's okay. It was the last day not the first, so our trip wasn't ruined. I can't eat very well, so I've lost about 20 pounds. I can't chew on my nails, and for the first time in my life I have nice looking nails. And I fell so flat I'm lucky I didn't break my nose as well."

She put me to shame. She had come up with four blessings in her mishap, when I wonder if I would have been doing anything but moaning.

As Christians our attitudes do make the difference. The way we handle adversity should make people ask us, "How can you do that? What is your secret?"

Those early Christians knew the secret. They rejoiced "that they were counted worthy to suffer dishonor" (Acts 5.41); took "pleasure" in all their sufferings "for Christ's sake" (2 Cor 12.10); "received the word in much affliction with joy" (1 Thes 1.6); and "took joyfully the spoiling of their possessions" (Heb 10.34). How? They had their priorities straight, and that kept their attitudes straight. They truly believed a better place awaits us.

That is what faith requires: "For he who comes to God must believe that he is and that he is a rewarder of those who seek after him" (Heb 11.6). Sometimes I think we focus so much on the first part of that, that we miss the second part. If I want this world and its "stuff" so badly, then maybe I don't really believe there is a reward waiting for me. If I do not have the attitude of Paul that "to die is gain," then my faith is an empty shell. Why in the world do I bother?

Attitude, shmattitude. Don't get sick and tired of hearing about it. It can help you make it successfully to the end, which is really only a beginning that will never end.

But call to remembrance the former days in which, after you were enlightened, you endured a great conflict of sufferings, partly being made a gazingstock both by reproaches and afflictions, and partly becoming partakers with them that were so used. For you both had compassion on them that were in bonds and took joyfully the spoiling of your possessions, knowing that you have for yourselves a better possession and an abiding one.

Hebrews 10.32–34

March 16

Spots before My Eyes

When people start doing things to your eyes, taking things out and putting things in, cutting into them, pouring chemicals into them, you start seeing strange things.

A week after one of the operations I had at the Cincinnati Eye Institute I started seeing gold circles as thin as thread right in front of me. At first I thought I was going through some sort of spider web, although I had never seen a golden one to be sure, but I started waving my hand in front of my face trying to brush it away right in the hotel lobby. When I looked up, the girl behind the front desk was watching me over her glasses with her eyebrows trying to crawl into her hairline. She managed to put on her professional face then and check us out.

Even now I sometimes see sparkling lights in dark corners, and furtive movements on the periphery of my vision. I was sitting in the assembly one Sunday when I was positive I saw rats running along the housing for the indirect lighting on the walls near the ceiling. After I had similar experiences seeing things in the blinds by my chair and out the window next to the dining table, I finally realized it was just another visual anomaly resulting from all the surgery and other treatments I have endured lately.

But the more frightening problem is the black spot—a "pressure phenomenon," as one resident calls it. When I see it, I know the pressure is up. Some days it is bigger than others, also a bad sign. The pinprick-sized spot becomes a nail hole, or even a bolt hole. The first time I saw it, I thought it was a gnat, and I went around all day trying to shoo it away. Finally it dawned on me that this gnat was always in the same place. It only appeared to move because I changed what I was looking at, but I bet I looked pretty funny those few hours before I figured it out.

I wish that spot would go away. On days when it does, I feel a lot better both physically and mentally. Weariness and stress seem to be the worst aggravators of the problem. It reminds me of Lady Macbeth, who succumbed to such guilt over prodding her husband to murder the king that she saw a spot of blood on her hands, and no matter how many times she wiped them, it would not come off. "Who would have thought an old man could bleed so much?" she asks during her famous speech about "the spot."

We have a spot too—one that will not go away, no matter how many times we wipe it, no matter how many times we wash our hands before the world as Pilate did, no matter how strong the soap we use.

Nowadays, mental health experts recognize the signs of guilt and the problems it causes. Their solution is to deny the existence of sin and therefore, remove guilt altogether. Now that's handy, isn't it? All I need to do to avoid feeling bad about doing wrong is believe that it is right. So who gets to decide what is right? What if I don't like your version of sins, especially if it makes your sins legal and mine illegal? Only One is qualified to decide what is right and what is wrong.

And, coincidentally, only one thing will make that guilt go away, and only one person can do it for us. In fact, He requires it of anyone who wants to follow Him. No matter how many times we tell ourselves that wrong is actually right, if we don't let Him rid us of the spot of sin, the guilt will eat us alive just as it did that fictional Lady.

Get rid of the spot while you still can. There will come a time when the offer is rescinded.

Husbands love your wives, even as Christ also loved the church and gave himself up for it, that he might sanctify it, having cleansed it by washing of water with the word, that he might present the church to himself glorious, not having spot or wrinkle or any such thing, but that it should be holy and without blemish.

Ephesians 5.25–27

March 17

Timetable

Hide not your face from me in the day of my distress: Incline your ear unto me; In the day when I call answer me speedily. (Psa 102.2)

I don't know how many times I have said that to God, or at least something similar. "Now, God. Please take care of this now!" Yet another sentence in the same prayer was probably something like, "Please be patient with me, I'm really trying." Avenge me of my adversaries immediately, but don't avenge my sins for Yourself until I have had time to repent—a self-serving double standard if there ever was one.

God does not operate on my timetable. He does not operate on yours. Because He inhabits eternity (Isa 57.15) He sees and knows when the time is right. He is not limited by living only in the present.

Can you explain the fact that God did not send Nathan to David for about a year after his sin with Bathsheba? Uriah was dead, David had married Bathsheba, and the child they made together had been born. Perhaps God knew it would take that long for David to be receptive to Nathan. Perhaps He knew that holding his small son in his hands would make David's heart softer. Who knows why, but that is the way God chose to do it, while in a similar circumstance the Corinthian church was commanded to withdraw from an adulterous brother the next time they met together.

As for us, sometimes we cannot know why God allows things to happen when and as they do. I can often see later on that things turned out better than if they had happened on my schedule instead of God's, but nearly as often I cannot. I am left to wonder. The good that has been accomplished may not become evident until I am dead and gone. I simply must trust that God knows best.

Patience in the Bible is not about waiting quietly. The patience of Job was noisy indeed. Patience in the Bible is about endurance, about keeping on till the end, about being steadfast even when you don't understand, and about trusting God's timetable when your own makes a lot more sense to you.

Think of Noah who built that ark waiting for God's promised flood for 120 years. I wonder what his neighbors were saying after just one year, or how much they sneered after ten, much less 120. Think about Abraham, who received a promise that was not fulfilled in his lifetime, or for a thousand years afterward. Think about Sarah and Elizabeth, women who wanted children more than anything else, but did not receive them until old age had made it seem impossible. For a Being who inhabits eternity, "impossible" does not apply, and time is immaterial. Remember them and wait on the Lord. He will save you, in His way, and in His time.

> *I believe that I shall look upon the goodness of the* Lord *in the land of the living! Wait for the* Lord*; be strong, and let your heart take courage; wait for the* Lord*!*
>
> Psalm 27.13–14

March 18

The Strongest Woman in the Bible

I bet you've never heard of Rizpah. Her story actually begins in Joshua 9.

The first cities the Israelites conquered after they entered Canaan were Jericho and Ai (Joshua 6, 8). In spite of what we would consider primitive communications, the word spread, and just as Rahab had heard about the Red Sea, a nation of people called the Gibeonites, who lived just north of present day Jerusalem, had heard about the Israelites and Jehovah's promise to help them drive out all the Canaanites (9.24). Gibeonites were Hivites, a tribe of Canaanites, so they qualified for destruction, and they knew it.

They chose several men to act as ambassadors, packed up moldy bread, old clothes and shoes, and carried old wineskins. When they arrived at the Israelite encampment, they said, "We've come a long way. Look, everything was new when we started, and our food fresh." They wanted to make a pact: "We will be your servants forever, if you will spare us." Instead of going to God, the Israelites believed these people, and were deceived into making the covenant, swearing by Jehovah.

As their punishment, God held Israel to the deal. Years later, Saul killed some of the Gibeonites. They came to David for justice in 2 Samuel 21. Two of Saul's sons by his concubine Rizpah, and five of his grandsons by his older daughter Merab were given to the Gibeonites for execution. I cannot imagine the despair in these mothers' hearts as their sons were taken to their deaths. But even more, I cannot imagine the strength it took for one of them to do what came next.

The Law stated that a body should not be left hanging overnight (Deut 21.22–23). But those men's bodies hung out there day after day. Rizpah took it upon herself to care for the remains, not just of her sons, but of another woman's sons as well, until someone took notice and obeyed God's Law. This woman, who had been a king's wife (a concubine is a *wife* of second rank), living in relative luxury for many years, sat out in the open, 24/7, chasing away vultures by day and packs of snarling, scavenging jackals by night "from the beginning of harvest till the rains fell again"—*possibly as long as six months!* Now add to that physically taxing and dangerous chore the overpowering, nauseating smell and the hideous sight of seven decomposing bodies, in the heat of summer, and above all, the heart wrenching pain of knowing that two of those bodies were her sons. Finally, David noticed, and buried them.

Being a good parent requires strength and sacrifice, and huge quantities of time. It involves a lot of humbling dirty work. But no messy diaper or pool of vomit to clean up can come close to what this woman endured for her children. Surely with Rizpah as an example, we can do whatever is required of us for the good of our children. We can give up our selfish desires when necessary. We can administer tough love, even when it hurts. We can take the time to teach them right from wrong, and teach them God's word day in and day out, rather than expecting the church to do our God-given duty for us.

Rizpah could not save her sons' lives, but even after their deaths, she did more, endured more for them than some parents will do for their children who are alive and well every day in their comfortable homes.

> *Set your heart unto all the words which I testify unto you this day, which you shall command your children to observe to do, all the words of this law, for it is no vain thing for you,* ***because it is your life.***
>
> Deuteronomy 32.46–47

March 19

A Visit to the Vet

We have had a cat more often than not in the past 20 years. All of them were pretty good about doing their work, as most barn cats are—it comes naturally to them to keep the rodents out of the feed sacks. But because they are outdoor cats, they do not have quite the same affinity for human contact as house cats. In fact, it seems that the less they have to do with us, the better they do their job.

So when it comes time to take this sort of cat to the vet for its shots and checkups, the process is a real adventure. I remember once, when we put the cat in a box we had carefully aerated, drove 20 miles to the vet, opened the box and there was no cat. We drove back home and found her sitting on the steps, licking her paws, and looking at us with a look of disdain. "Where have you been?" she seemed to be saying with a smirk. We still don't know how she got out. Her name was Jezebel. Maybe that explains it.

When we got Jasper we invested in a carrier. The first time I used it, I discovered that this was still not going to be easy. I sat on the porch and called him. He inched his way forward and I just held out my hand until he finally relaxed and let me pet him. After a minute or so, I picked him up and tried to put him in the crate. Immediately, all four sets of claws sprang out and grasped the edges of the opening. It looked like a cartoon as I tried pushing him in while he hung on to the doorframe for dear life. No way was this cat going in there willingly.

Then I got smart, I thought, and put some food in the carrier. Jasper smelled it immediately, and stuck his head inside. I waited patiently as more and more of him disappeared into the box, then quickly shut the door; but somehow in that tiny space, he managed to turn around and slip out before I could get the clasp fastened.

By then, he was getting suspicious. He was too leery to even come near me, so I waited a bit. About a half hour later I grabbed a towel and laid it on the porch floor next to me. By then, he was feeling generous again and sauntered up to me for a scratch. After a few minutes, he lay next to me on the towel. With a quick motion, I flipped the towel over his whole body and dumped him unceremoniously into the upended carrier, The little bit of time it took for him to get his claws out of the towel gave me enough time to shut the door without him escaping. Finally we went to the vet.

Wouldn't you know it, when we got to the vet, he wouldn't come out of the carrier? The vet had to dump him out. And when she was finished with him and let him go, he scrambled back in as fast as he could. Little stinker.

In spite of his unwillingness to go to the vet, it kept him healthy. The shots still worked, even though he really didn't want them. It doesn't work that way with righteousness. You can do things that look like righteousness all day long, but if you are doing them from a bad heart, they won't do a thing for your soul.

We seem to have a mistaken idea about the Old Law, that all they had to do were "right things," and that their hearts did not matter. Yet over and over you find instances where the heart most certainly did matter. "Take from among you an offering unto Jehovah; *whosoever is of a willing heart,* let him bring it" (Exod 35.5). That is just one example among many.

Doesn't it mean more to you that Lord offered himself for us willingly? "No one takes [my life] away from me, but I lay it down of myself. I have power to lay it down, and I have power to take it again" (John 10.18). How much would it mean in terms of love if he had done it because he was forced to?

That is how God looks at us too. How much more does it mean to you when your child brings you a wildflower he picked in the field "just because" than when he sends that expensive arrangement on Mother's Day, a day when the world practically forces it on him? A buttercup on a Tuesday is far superior to a dozen roses the second Sunday in May.

God will not force us to obey him, much less to love him. He has never accepted the letter of the law without the heart.

> *And you, Solomon my son, know the God of your father and serve him with a whole heart and with a willing mind, for the LORD searches all hearts and understands every plan and thought. If you seek him, he will be found by you, but if you forsake him, he will cast you off forever.*
>
> 1 Chronicles 28.9

March 20

The NeverEnding Story

When my boys were young they were enchanted with a movie called *The NeverEnding Story.* You see, when the movie ended it started all over again, and then again, and again.

Maybe it's because I am a woman that I never saw the appeal. All I could think of was housework—laundry that needs washing over and over, shirts that need ironing again and again, dust that keeps settling, meals that need cooking three times a day. Oh for something that when I finish with it will stay finished!

I think the Old Testament Jews understood a little. Have you ever read the complex procedure for the Day of Atonement? You should sometime, and then think about the promise of a forgiveness that lasts forever.

Every year the sins that were forgiven the year before were once again remembered against God's people, and every year the pile grew bigger and bigger. At least when I do the laundry, I know a shirt that I washed and ironed will not be back in the hamper until it has once again been worn. Imagine if everything you ever washed got dirty again the next week just because clean would not stay clean!

The first century Jewish Christians surely appreciated the blessing of forgiveness far better than we can. They had been waiting for that promise to be fulfilled for hundreds of years.

> Behold the days come, says Jehovah, that I will make a new covenant with the house of Israel and with the house of Judah, not according to the covenant that I made with their fathers in the day that I took them by the hands to bring them out of the land of Egypt. ...But this is the covenant that I will make... says Jehovah: I will put my law in their inward parts and in their heart will I write it, and I will be their God and they shall be my people, and they shall teach no more every man his neighbor and every man his brother saying, Know Jehovah, for they shall all know me, from the least of them unto the greatest of them, says Jehovah; for I will forgive their iniquity *and their sins will I remember no more.* (Jer 31.31–34)

A high priest was coming who would offer himself, a perfect sacrifice that would cleanse each sin forever. That pile of guilt would no longer build up on each one, becoming heavier and heavier, needing yet another sacrifice every year. Think what that must have meant to a people who through the years had seen oceans of blood pouring down that manmade altar, knowing that next year, the same thing must happen again, not only for new sins, but for exactly the same old ones as well. What a relief.

And what a relief for us to know that God forgives and forgets, and that because of that wonderful blessing we can enjoy another "Never-Ending Story" that will remind *us* of a blessing, instead of a burden.

> *And they indeed have been made priests many in number because by death they are hindered from continuing; but he, because he abides forever, has his priesthood unchangeable. Wherefore also he is able to save to the uttermost those who draw near to God through him, seeing he ever lives to make intercession for them. For such a high priest became us, holy, guileless, undefiled, separated from sinners, and made higher than the heavens, who needs not daily, like those high priests to offer up sacrifices, first for his own sins, and then for the sins of the people, for this he did once for all, when he offered up himself.*
>
> Hebrews 7.23–27

Nicknames

His name was Joseph. He came from an island off the coast, but had family in the city, and had come to worship at the two feast days, probably staying with his close relative Mary. While he was there he saw and heard amazing things: people speaking languages they had never studied, something that looked like fire but wasn't, something that sounded like a tornado but wasn't, and a sermon that both astonished and convicted him. He wound up staying in town, along with several thousand others who had become part of God's new kingdom, the one they had been waiting for so long.

Despite their previous plans, they all chose to stay so they could learn, so they could grow, so they could mature before they went off on their own to spread the word in a world of sin, a world, they were told, that would reject them more often than accept them. It wasn't long till the practical needs of several thousand homeless people with no income could no longer be ignored.

Those who lived in the city helped as much as they could. They took people in and collected funds to buy extra food and clothing. Men were chosen to see to these needs. Joseph helped as well, selling off extra property he owned, and donating the full amount to the group.

But that was not all he did. Here was a man who excelled at encouragement, consolation, exhortation. He was the first to give a pat on the back when it was needed, a hug, a kind word, a stern word, a teaching word, a "rah-rah" from the sidelines, a second chance to those whom others had given up on. In fact, he became so good at it that the apostles gave him the nickname, "son of encouragement/consolation/exhortation," whatever your version says in Acts 4.36. And forever more in the scriptures, that is how we know him—Barnabas. Did you even know that was not his real name?

Whenever I think of that man, I wonder what nickname the apostles would give me? Whiny Winnie? Gossip Gail? My-Way Martha? Grumpy Gert? Cold-hearted Colleen? Hotheaded Harriet? Wondering about that will give your character a real shot in the arm. I'd much rather have something like Generous Joyce or Compassionate Kate.

Your assignment for today? Try to figure out what they would call you. Be honest. You can always change that name, just by changing yourself.

> *A good name is rather to be chosen than great riches, and loving favor rather than silver and gold.*
>
> Proverbs 22.1

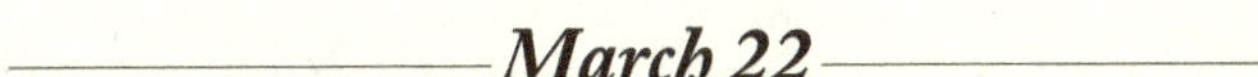

March 22

Chicken and Dumplings

I was reading a cooking magazine a few months ago which claimed to have formulated the best recipe for chicken and dumplings—one of my family's favorite meals, as well as a great way to stretch a dollar of the weekly grocery budget. Halfway through the article I found a big problem.

This magazine is based in Boston; its editor from Vermont. I already had a suspicion what their "best" recipe would contain—big puffy dumplings resembling drowned biscuits. In the South we prefer flat "slicker style" dumplings, akin to noodles or pasta, enriched with egg yolks and butter, even chicken fat if possible.

Sure enough, near the end of the article we readers were informed that the panel of tasters greatly preferred the "Yankee style" dumplings (that was their wording, not mine), "except for two holdouts from Kentucky." Really? Do you suppose if the magazine had been based in Atlanta, with the panel predominantly Southern, that the results might have been overwhelmingly in favor of the Southern style dumplings "except for two holdouts from Connecticut"?

Taste has a lot to do with your background, what you grew up eating, what your parents did and did not like, and what was available in your area. My boys loved fried okra. Some of the friends they brought home from college didn't even know what it was, and were almost afraid to try it. We are blessed to live in a society so wealthy that we can choose what we like and don't like. For most of us, eating has more to do with pleasure than necessity.

Unfortunately, that spoiled attitude has spilled over into our spiritual lives. We think we can take it or leave it as we choose, without ill effect; and if we take it, we think we can choose *how* we take it. Our Creator doesn't get to choose how He wants to be served. We get to choose how, when, where, even if. We get to choose which parts of this law we want to follow, and which we want to ignore. We can even interpret it any way we like, even if our interpretation ignores the context or plainly contradicts another part of it. We get to do all this choosing and He must be satisfied with what *we* want, and what *we* like. No wonder anthropologists talk about Deity as something each culture creates.

Yes, each culture creates gods they want to worship, but that is not Deity. Until we understand that the concept of Deity does not involve our likes and dislikes at all, we will never be approved by that Deity. As long as we think our opinions matter, we are not serving God, we are simply serving ourselves.

God is immutable. Truth is absolute. Obedience is not a request but a demand. We *can* choose to disobey, but the consequences will not be pleasant.

> *Thus says Jehovah, the King of Israel, and his Redeemer, Jehovah of hosts: I am the first, and I am the last; and besides me there is no God. And who, as I, shall call, and shall declare it, and set it in order for me, since I established the ancient people? and the things that are coming, and that shall come to pass, let them declare. Fear not, neither be afraid: have I not declared unto you of old, and showed it? and you are my witnesses. Is there a God besides me? yea, there is no Rock; I know not any.*
>
> Isaiah 44.6–8

March 23

The Devil Cat

I believe I may have mentioned before the black and white cat we had many years ago, Abby. It was not long before he developed the reputation of a scoundrel for the way he treated our gullible lab Bart, and Nathan called him "the devil cat" for he had many devilish ways.

Sometimes I like to take a break from gardening or housework and sit in the swing under the grape arbor. Truly I plan to sit for only a few minutes! But Abby would seize the opportunity, jump into the swing beside me and start purring. Once that purring started I could not help but pet him, and he would creep closer, often placing one paw in my lap. Then he would look up with that sweet furry face, purring even louder. Do you know how relaxing it is to pet a purring cat? Before I knew it, he was in my lap, and a half hour had gone by, along with all my good intentions.

He also liked to pretend he was a lion. Our garden was the Serengeti. Whenever I went out to pick he would creep along, hidden in the pea and bean rows, stalking my feet. When he decided that the gazelles were least aware that he, the king of the beasts, was upon them, he would attack. The first time it happened, my instant reaction was to kick, and he landed about 20 feet away in the cucumbers. Talk about clueless; the look on his face was almost worth the blood he had drawn. After that he learned to be gentler in his play, but I also learned to keep an eye on the moving shadows among the beans.

This leads me to that other lion, who goes about "seeking whom he may devour" (1 Pet 5.8). James tells us to "resist the devil and he will flee from you" (4.7). Try booting him across the garden and see if he doesn't leave you alone for awhile. If you are lucky he will land in the okra patch and itch so much for the next few days that you will be the last thing on his mind!

But watch out, just like my little lion, he will try a new tack and visit you again. There may come a time when you have to flee instead of fighting (1 Cor 6.18; 2 Tim 2.22). Other times he will get you because he is so cute or handsome or personable or comfortable, and before you know it, you are doing something you had no intention of doing. "Even Satan fashions himself as an angel of light. It is no great thing therefore if his ministers also fashion themselves as ministers of righteousness" (2 Cor 11.14–15). (Have you ever seen a really ugly false teacher?)

Our world likes to view Satan as a laughable boogey man made up by irrational fanatics. It is easy to forget he is real. He is out there. Like a hungry lion, he wants you!

Finally, brethren, be strong in the Lord, and in the strength of his might; put on the whole armor of God that you may be able to stand against the wiles of the devil. For our wrestling is not against flesh and blood, but against the principalities, against the powers, against the world rulers of this darkness, against the spiritual hosts of wickedness in the heavenly places. Wherefore take up the whole armor of God that you may be able to withstand in the evil day, and having done all, to stand.

Ephesians 6.10–13

March 24

Exercise or Atrophy?

Several years ago, the heel of my right foot became so swollen and sore I could hardly walk, and if I banged it against anything I nearly lost my lunch. So I needed what the podiatrist called a retrocalcanealexostectomy. In plain English, they detached the Achilles tendon, removed a wad of extraneous tissue that my body had created to try to pillow the pain, sawed off the back of my heel, which had calcified into a walnut-sized knob, then reattached the tendon with what amounted to a "hollow wall anchor." It was nearly a year before I walked normally.

When they took the cast off the right leg, the difference in the calf muscles was amazing. Crutches for two months followed by a cane for another two or three, means no exercise, and no exercise equals atrophy. The right calf was half the size of the left, and totally limp. For the next four years that did not matter too much; I still had a good left leg. Then the left foot did the same thing and here we go again—more surgery.

Now I had two wimpy calf muscles. Guess what you need when you try to reach something on the top shelf and need to stand on your toes? Guess what it feels like when you try to do that automatically, without thinking, with those sore heels and limp calf muscles? Yeow!

So for the last year or so I have been trying to get those muscles back into shape. The first time I tried toe raises, nothing happened! I concentrated hard and told myself to stand on tiptoe, and still nothing happened! So now I am determined. I found some exercises that I can do without trying to stand on my toes, that still make my calf muscles ache and burn. Last week I actually went up about a half inch off the floor. Kind of hard to tell with your eyes a little over five feet higher than your feet, but I am pretty sure, based on what I could and could not reach on the top shelf. Progress! There is no stopping me now. I will be tiptoeing through the tulips by May.

So how about your spiritual muscles? You know what? They atrophy just like those physical muscles. When was the last time you actually did a real Bible study on your own? I mean work, with a pen and paper, not just reading commentaries and doing a copy and paste job on your computer. In education classes they always told us that writing things down was a big key to information retention. Taking notes makes you hear the words again, saying them in your head as your write; then you feel yourself forming each letter of each word, and see them again after they are written. The more senses that are involved, the more likely you are to learn and remember.

Of course, putting knowledge into action is what makes it worthwhile. There is the meditation, the decision making and actual living based upon your newfound knowledge, and the teaching as you share what you learn. The more you learn and do, the stronger you become. Soon you will be tiptoeing through the pages of the Bible with more and more ease, more and more confidence, and *more and more ability to live like God wants you to.* Pick up your Bible and exercise a little.

> *For when by reason of time you ought to be teachers, you have need again that someone teach you the rudiments of the first principles of the oracles of God, and have become such as those who need milk and not solid food. For everyone who partakes of milk is without experience of the word of righteousness, for he is a baby. But solid food is for full-grown men, those who* ***by reason of use have their senses exercised to discern good and evil.***
>
> Hebrews 5.12–14

March 25

Stinkbugs

While I have kept three or four potted herbs on my steps for several years, it has only been a short while that I have grown an herb garden—two kinds of parsley, three kinds of basil, plus thyme, oregano, marjoram, dill, sage, cilantro, rosemary, mint, and chives.

I'm still learning some things the hard way. Dill must be planted in late fall because it cannot tolerate the heat of a Florida summer. Basil will stop growing when the weather cools, whether you protect it from the frost or not. Oregano is a ground runner and needs a lot of room. You must snip your chives from the bottom—not just trim off the tops—if you expect them to replenish. One recipe for pesto will decimate a basil plant for at least two weeks. Always give mint its own separate bed, or better still, pot, because it will take over the joint if you don't.

And, Keith hates cilantro. Although I am not exactly sure how he knows this, he says it tastes "like stinkbugs." We discovered this when I sprinkled chopped fresh cilantro over a turkey tortilla casserole. Now cilantro does have a distinctive flavor. While it bears a close physical resemblance to Italian flat-leaf parsley, the strongest flavored parsley, its flavor is probably ten times stronger than that herb. There *is* such a thing as too much cilantro. On the other hand, a lot of people like it in moderation, including me. I guess there is no accounting for tastes.

And that is why some people reject Jesus. At least they realize that accepting Him means accepting his teachings—making Him Lord—unlike some who seem to think He will accept anything we do. To some people life tastes sweeter when we do things His way. The difficult times become easier to bear, and the good times more than we dared hope for. But other people see in Him a restrictive cage denying them all the pleasures of life. Their focus on the here and now keeps them from seeing the victory of Eternity, but even worse, they are blinded by Satan to the true joys a child of God can have in this life as well. "And exercise yourself unto godliness; for bodily exercise is profitable for a little, but godliness is profitable for all things, *having the promise of the life that now is,* and of that which is to come" (1 Tim 4.7–8). We can have joy, peace, hope, love, and fellowship with both God and the best people on earth, *while* on this earth.

But they just can't see it. I guess to them, godliness tastes like stinkbugs. Like I said, there is just no accounting for tastes.

For we are a sweet smell of Christ unto God, in them that are saved, and in them that perish; to the one a smell from death unto death, and to the other a smell from life unto life.

2 Corinthians 2.15–16

March 26

Peek-a-boo

Sitting next to a window by a bird feeder can give you a feeling of omniscience.

The first time I added stale biscuits to the birdseed, Magdi smelled them and wormed her way through the azaleas. I noticed because of the scuffling against the side of the house. I watched as she stood on her hind legs, trying to reach the biscuits. She never knew I was there until I growled, "Nnnnnnnnno!" with a prolonged and ever increasing N sound. The poor thing tucked her tail and ran so fast the azaleas shook for a full five minutes.

Then there is the squirrel. He has always approached from the east side of the feeder, and unless I am right there can sneak up and eat as much as a foot long line of seed before I catch him. A thump on the wall sends him scampering away. The first time I caught him he tried again a few minutes later, so I hit the window right next to him. I think his leap missed the azaleas entirely as he fled the scene.

One morning he thought he had this Unseen Force fooled. After I thumped the wall, he retreated down the leg of the feeder only a few inches. How did I know? Because his tail stood straight up next to it, a good six inches above the edge. I let him think he had the advantage for a minute or so, and when he had barely crept onto the board again, gave the wall an extra hard thump. No more squirrel for a week after that.

The other morning, he came up with a new tack. I was sitting in my chair when suddenly I saw two little paws appear over the outside edge of the feeder, but on the *west* end. A moment later a furry head came up over the edge in a squirrelly pull-up. This time I had some help. The cardinals in the azaleas all swooped down on him at the exact moment I chose to tap the window in front of him. He fell back into the azaleas with all fours spread, his eyes wide, and what I am sure was an amazing squirrel scream, frantically twisted and turned in mid-air like a cartoon character spinning his wheels, and finally hit the ground running.

Was that the end of this interloper? No, he keeps trying. Like a baby who covers his face with his blanket and thinks he is hidden, the squirrel still has hope that one day he will be able to dine to his heart's content and no one will see.

He is just like us. No matter how many times we talk about the "omniscience" and "omnipresence" of God, we still think we can hide from him. Why else do we keep doing what we do? We are no better than Adam and Eve hiding after their disobedience, though every Bible class I have been in scoffs openly at them when the subject arises.

We quote "the Lord is at hand" (Phil 4.5), and then behave as if we don't really believe it. Do we not realize what that means? The Lord is within arm's length, always—that's what it means. He is standing next to us at the kitchen counter, sitting across the office desk from us, standing in the line at the grocery store with us, or sitting in the front seat of the car beside us. He sees what we do, hears what we say, knows what we feel and think. If we really believed it, wouldn't it make a difference? We are sometimes no better than a dumb animal that thinks it can eventually find a way to hide if it just keeps trying, and just like a small child playing peek-a-boo, whose limited perspective keeps him from realizing what others can see.

Remember today who is at your side. It isn't a threat; it's an asset, a blessing that will help us be who and what we really want to be.

The eyes of Jehovah are in every place, keeping watch upon the evil and the good.

Proverbs 15.3

March 27

Mud Rooms

When I was younger and looked at house plans, I used to see small rooms called "mud rooms" on the blueprints. I never really understood them until I lived two years in Illinois. In Florida the ground never freezes. It is wet with the dew most mornings and dries before noon. Up north the ground must thaw out every spring, and just like that frozen container of homemade tomato sauce on my kitchen counter, it stays wet until it does. Day after day I wiped up mud and scraped off boots. Now I really understood mud rooms and wished for one. At least all the guests were aware of the problem as well and left their shoes at the door without having to be asked.

That reminds me of the symbolism involved in Exodus 3.5: "Take off your shoes from your feet, for the place where you stand is holy ground." While I cherish the confidence to approach God as a loving Father, while I am thrilled to see our young people revel in that closeness, I worry that we have forgotten what awe and reverence really mean, that we do not understand the requirements of holiness. Our lives have gotten so casual we cannot even comprehend the difference between the sacred and the profane—it has nothing to do with four letter words. It means we give our service to God—every day, not just on Sundays—special care, special preparation, and special effort, not just some haphazard, slapdash, last minute, half-hearted stab at it. It means there is a part of me that is afraid *not* to take off my muddy shoes before I enter into God's presence. And that fear is not a watered down variety called simply "respect." Even in a vision, the prophet Isaiah was so awestruck by God's presence that he exclaimed, "Woe is me for I am undone, for I am a man of unclean lips who dwells in the midst of a people of unclean lips and I have seen the King, Jehovah of hosts" (Isa 6.5).

The same book that proclaims that we can come in boldness (Heb 4.16), states that we should approach with reverence and awe because *Our God is a consuming fire* (Heb 12.28–29). Paul also says in 2 Corinthians 5.11 "Knowing therefore the terror of the Lord. . . ." It is this sort of fear that will motivate me to holy living when my will power weakens, and love and gratitude are not quite enough to do the job.

Don't ever forget to take off those muddy shoes before coming before the Creator of the Universe.

> *For great is Jehovah and greatly to be praised: He is to be feared above all gods. For all the gods of the peoples are idols, But Jehovah made the heavens. Honor and majesty are before him: Strength and beauty are in his sanctuary. Ascribe unto Jehovah, you kindred of the peoples, Ascribe unto Jehovah glory and strength. Ascribe unto Jehovah the glory due to his name: Bring an offering and come into his courts. Oh worship Jehovah in holy array: Tremble before him all the earth.*
>
> Psalm 96.4–9

Wading in the Water

We found this plot of land only because Keith drove down the highway one day and saw a sign pointing off to the east: FIVE ACRES FOR SALE BY OWNER. When he stopped he could barely tell that a trail led off the highway, over a shallow rise and on into the woods beyond. Being in the market for a place to put our home, we followed it one day, driving carefully over a bumpy track and eventually onto a grassy downhill slope, hoping we would not bottom out in an unseen gopher hole or mushy spring. Half a mile later, we stood under some big old live oaks draped with Spanish moss, knee deep in grass and weeds, with an open field just over the pushed-up fence row. About a month later, this became home.

When you move onto unimproved land, you discover quickly the value of roads. Roads are built above the general lay of the land, usually ditched on the sides. A new neighbor, who has become a good friend, suggested that we have the septic tank man scrape down the fence row behind the house, which left a path several feet above the rest of the land. We did not use it, instead driving across the top of the property on the grass to the front door. The summer rains began shortly after we moved in, followed by a nearby hurricane, and after having another neighbor pull the car out of the mud with his tractor at least three times, we began using the raised fence row as our driveway. That is why to this day, you pull up to the back of the house instead of the front.

Another problem lay just a couple hundred feet off the highway—a low spot you never noticed until it rained four or five inches. Overnight the land around it drained and made a pond between us and the road. There was no way to go around because of the neighbor's fences, and the low spot was a bowl that could not empty. For a couple of months in August and September, we parked by the highway, waded through the pond, and walked the rest of the half mile to the house.

Sundays were particularly interesting. We all dressed the top half of ourselves, then put on shorts, and carried towels. After walking to the offending body of water, we waded through slowly, careful not to splash mud on the Sunday clothes above our waists, then got into the car, dried off, and finished dressing. When we came home, we reversed the process. Returning from evening services was particularly thrilling, hoping nothing deadly swam by us in the knee deep water and using flashlights to make sure we didn't step on any snakes as we trudged to the house in the dark, with buzzing mosquitoes for company.

Keith worked for years on that spot. An acquaintance did roofing and often had piles of old gravel that needed to be hauled off. Keith would stop by his work site in the evenings, load gravel into his pickup bed with a shovel he always had, bring it home and unload it before coming back to the house. There must be a good three feet of gravel beneath the dirt there now, for 50 feet along that low spot. Eventually he dug a ditch off to the side all the way to the highway—using nothing but a shovel, a 200 foot long ditch, in places hip-deep—so the water would drain. Finally, we could count on getting through, regardless how much it rained. The people who have moved in have no idea how much they owe him.

I remember thinking, especially as I struggled to put on pantyhose in the front seat of the car, or as I fearfully followed the bouncing beam of a flashlight through the north Florida woods at night, that I had better not ever hear anyone else's excuses for not assembling with their brethren.

But I also remember this—not a single time did we even see (or hear) a snake on those scary evenings. Before that, when we could drive through, we saw several, even rattlesnakes and cottonmouths, but nothing on any pedestrian return trip from evening services.

Not a single time did we have to make that half mile walk in the rain. Certainly it had rained beforehand or the pond would not have been there, and often it rained more after we returned home, but we never got wet on our walks. Yes, that was a trying time, but it could have been worse. God knew what we could handle and He expected us to do just that—handle it. In return, He took care of us and never allowed it to be more of a burden than we could overcome.

Too many times we view our troubles from the wrong side and fail to see God's helping hand. Even when we think otherwise, He is there, guiding us and making things bearable. Sometimes we won't realize that till long after the trial is over. Remember that the next time a difficulty arises. I guarantee that as long as you are faithful, God is too, and one of these days you will see that as clearly as through a newly cleaned window.

We have had many difficulties since then, but I find myself looking back on what now seems minor compared to our more recent problems. If we had not waded through the water, if we had not followed a flashlight through the woods, could we have made it through what came after? Probably not, and a wise Father knew that. I find myself thinking, God, can I please have another pond to wade through? But the days of puddles are past. Rivers lie ahead, and we know we can get across them now, in part because of a muddy pond 25 years ago.

Be free from the love of money, content with such things as you have; for He has said, I will in no way fail you, nor in anyway forsake you. So with good courage we say, The Lord is my helper; I will not fear; what shall man do to me?

Hebrews 13.5–6

March 29

Side Effects

Have you ever really listened to one of those commercials about various prescriptions drugs?

"Do not take Wonderdrug if you cannot sit, stand, or lie for longer than an hour, if you are pregnant or might become pregnant, if you have high blood pressure, low blood pressure, heart problems, trouble breathing, or during months beginning with J or ending with R. Wonderdrug has been known to cause dizziness, memory loss, headaches, earaches, toothaches, infectious diseases, cancer of all sorts, liver damage, bleeding ulcers, stroke, seizures, heart attack, acne, warts, and, in rare occasions, death." In some cases the remedy sounds truly worse than the disease. I must say, though, I was stopped in my tracks the other day when one commercial warned that the drug might cause "increase in gambling." Surely they were just trying to get my attention, right?

Lately, I have had so many chemicals poured into me that I have had to wonder about the remedy in my case as well. Atropine, Predforte, Phenylephrin, Zymar, Erithromycin, Alphagan, CoSopt, and Travatan, plus four others by three other doctors, all at the same time, a total of about 60 doses a day at one point. And then there were the accompanying side effects: light sensitivity, erratic heartbeat, dry mouth, dizziness, loss of taste, not to mention the eating away of the top layer of my eyeball (epithiliopathy) not once, but twice since then, after it had healed! Believe it or not, stopping the medication would have been worse, though sometimes I was strongly tempted to do so.

Pouring chemicals into your body is not good. If your body is working correctly, don't.

It is no different with sin. Sin may be attractive. It may look good, but you will sooner or later suffer the side effects: guilt, shame, and spiritual death. As David wrote, "For my iniquities have gone over my head; as a heavy burden they are too heavy for me. My wounds are loathsome and corrupt because of my foolishness" (Psa 38.4–5).

Righteousness, on the other hand, offers no painful side effects to the sin-sick soul. Instead we receive peace, boldness, strength, hope, joy, and life. These are not unnatural to the soul; unlike lives of sin, this is the way God intended us to live from the beginning.

Don't be fooled by the labels the world attaches to sin, labels like "fun," "security," and "love." Jesus did not call Satan a liar without cause. Instead, live joyfully, at peace with God, with all the guilt and shame removed from your shoulders. That is what life in Christ is all about.

Being therefore justified by faith, we have peace with God through our Lord Jesus Christ, through whom we have had our access by faith into this grace wherein we stand, and we rejoice in hope of the glory of God.

Romans 5.1–2

March 30

Inside Out

Oh the pains of learning to dress yourself.

I remember my little boys, determined that they no longer needed Mom's help, carefully laying out their shirts on the bed. As soon as they saw their favorite superhero or cartoon character looking at them, they just knew they had it right. So they leaned over, grabbed the hem, and slipped the tee shirt over their heads, only to look down and see the blank backside of the shirt swathing their tummies. So they ripped it off over their heads and tried again. This time it was on front side to the front, but inside out.

Sometimes they wore it out the door inside out before I could catch them.

We had lessons on seams and labels, and finally they figured it out, more often than not anyway. As we all grow up, though, we must learn that "inside out" is the way a Christian is supposed to operate every day.

Babies have only their own perspectives. If they cannot see you, then you cannot see them. If they cannot feel it, it cannot be felt and is not important. If they want it, no one else should have it. Eventually we learn to think from other perspectives, those outside of our own. We realize that just because I cannot see you with my covered up eyes, that does not mean my whole body is hidden.

Eventually, we learn to think about others' feelings, turning our thoughts "inside out." At least, that is the way it is supposed to work. Too many times though, we operate as if the feelings inside ourselves are the only ones that matter, ready to excuse ourselves without giving the other person the same benefit.

If I cut someone off in traffic, it is because I am late for an important appointment. If the other guy does it to me, it is because he is an inconsiderate jerk.

If I snap at my spouse, it is because I have had a rough day, I'm tired and have a headache. If he does it to me, it is because he is a louse.

If I don't speak to a brother when I walk in the meetinghouse door, it is because I have a lot on my mind and did not see him. If he does not speak to me, it is because he has something against me.

My opinion is carefully thought out and makes sense; yours is ridiculous—how can you possibly be so dumb?

Thinking and feeling inside out is hard to do. It takes work and thought, two things 21st century Americans try to avoid at all costs. Christians are supposed to be different. Oh the pain of learning to think like Christ, who "counted not being on an equality with God a thing to be grasped, but emptied himself, taking the form of a servant." But if he is my Lord, my seams and labels will show; everyone will know I belong to him. If they cannot tell, I have my religion on backwards!

If there is therefore any exhortation in Christ, if any consolation of love, if any fellow-

ship of the Spirit, if any tender mercies and compassions, make full my joy, that you be of the same mind, having the same love, being of one accord, of one mind; doing nothing through faction or through vainglory, but in lowliness of mind each counting other better than himself; not looking each of you to his own things, but each of you also to the things of others.

Philippians 2.1–4

March 31

Prognosis

Twice now I have stood in an emergency room waiting for a doctor to tell me whether or not I would be a relatively young widow, 42 the first time, 48 the second. It is amazing what changes a few unexpected moments can bring about in your attitude. Suddenly you realize what is important. Suddenly the little annoyances of living together every day disappear. You would give anything to pick up after him one more time or put up with an annoying bit of male humor. There is nothing quite like the feeling when the doctor looks into your eyes and says, "He'll live."

When you get that reprieve something else happens as well. The next few days, weeks, even years if you allow it to last that long, are sweeter than ever. You revel in those evenings when you can still walk hand in hand around your garden, throw tennis balls for the dogs to chase, or pick wildflowers to fill an empty vase on the countertop. You understand that an exciting life has nothing to do with going places or having things, but rather in being together for as long as possible. And you find yourself bewildered when those around you don't get it; when they magnify petty grievances or imagined slights into relationship-breaking arguments or silences. What is wrong with these people, you find yourself thinking. Why does it take a tragedy to make us behave like mature adults?

All of us face spiritual emergencies. All of us struggle with temptations, with suffering, and with trials. Sometimes we come through those trials in good shape physically. Other times we may suffer disabilities, the loss of status or worldly goods, the loss of loved ones, even the loss of our own physical lives.

Our souls often lie behind the curtains in a spiritual emergency room. The Great Physician stands over us, comforting us, assuring us that He understands and has, in fact, borne the same woes on His shoulders. He has everything we need to get through this, including the most wonderful prognosis of all.

It will keep us from bitterness because we know that these things are only temporal and fleeting, whether it feels that way right now or not. It will keep us from drowning in sorrow because we know we will see the one we have lost again. It will keep us from throwing our faith away in a moment of despair because, when we believe his words, hope rises to conquer even the forces of Satan.

There is nothing quite like the feeling when He looks into your eyes and says, "You'll live."

> *And the witness is this, that God gave unto us eternal life, and this life is in his Son. He who has the Son has the life; he who has not the Son of God has not the life. These things have I written unto you that you may know that you have eternal life, unto you who believe on the name of the Son of God.*
>
> 1 John 5.11–13

A Little Grace

On a recent camping trip, we had one full day of rain. Twenty-three hours in a tent went faster than we had expected since we had taken books to read, crossword puzzles to do, and a Boggle game. But at supper time we needed more room and a table to cook on, so we took our food and our propane stove down to the pavilion in that State Park and fixed our meal.

A nine-year-old girl pulled her bike into the shelter as the rain picked up. She talked for a few minutes, and then we asked her name.

"Grace," she replied.

“"Hmmm," began Keith, "that means full of mercy and compassion. Is that you?"

She gave a wry grin beyond her years and said, "I don't think so."

We talked awhile longer, and then she politely excused herself. Later I thought, "How incredibly honest." Could I look at myself and give such an assessment without making qualifications and rationalizations? I doubt it. And woe to anyone who tries to do it for me. No *grace* to him!

But here is the irony—as an innocent child, this little girl Grace is a whole lot closer to the ideal of grace than I am. Yet as a child of the God who gives grace abundantly, I must strive the harder to emulate my Heavenly Father, giving grace to all I meet just as He does for us—even though, as the very definition of the word states, we do not deserve it.

Today let us all remember to be as generous as our Father, giving grace where none is due.

By grace are you saved through faith, and that not of yourselves, it is the gift of God.

Above all things be fervent in your love among yourselves, for love covers a multitude of sins...minister among yourselves as good stewards of the grace of God.

Ephesians 2.8; 1 Peter 4.8, 10

April 2

Worship Isn't Free

Neither will I offer burnt offerings unto Jehovah my God which cost me nothing.

Second Samuel 24 relates the numbering of the Israelites as commanded by David. To make a long story short, this sin caused a pestilence sent from God as punishment. God then told David to offer up a sin offering at a threshing floor owned by Araunah.

Aranauh saw the king's entourage headed his way and went out to greet them, wondering what he could do for his king. When David explained and asked to buy the property so he could offer the sacrifice, Araunah said, "Oh no, lord. Everything is yours for the taking, including the oxen for the burnt offering."

Then David uttered those words above, "I will not offer burnt offerings to the Lord which cost me nothing." It isn't worship, David meant, when it isn't mine to give. It isn't worship when it's an extra I keep on the shelf for emergencies. It isn't worship if it isn't something I need for myself. Service to God should cost me something.

I wonder what David would say were he alive today. I bet I know some things he would *not* say.

"We have a gospel meeting this week? I'll go if it's convenient."

"The price of gas has gotten too steep to make that extra Bible study this week."

"That's just too early for me to have to get up in the morning."

"It's a song service tonight? I don't like to sing anyway."

"It's on the way to my activity, so I can stop by the hospital for a quick visit, otherwise. . . ."

"My neighbor mentioned wanting to ask me about some problems he is having, and I wanted to watch that ball game. Maybe tomorrow night."

It doesn't have to be inconvenient to count as service; if it did, the most pious time to assemble would be 2:00 AM. However, if convenient service is all we ever give, you wonder if it truly deserves that description, "service."

Did you ever offer assistance and have someone say, "Well, only if it isn't any trouble?" Have you said it yourself? Don't deny someone the right to "pay" for the offerings they give. It *is* often trouble to help someone out—it's supposed to be! How much trouble they go to for someone else is a measure of their commitment to the Lord (Matt 25.40). The same standard is a measure of your commitment as well.

Since we do operate our assemblies on a system of expedients, it is too easy to think that everything should be convenient. Surely God doesn't really expect our service to Him to cost us time, money, or pleasures and recreation that are good and wholesome. We *may* understand the concept of sacrificial giving on the first day of the week, but how much do we understand the concept of sacrificial giving every day of our lives?

Because of all He has done for me, I should be willing and anxious to say, "I will not offer to the Lord that which costs me nothing."

> *Wherefore, receiving a kingdom that cannot be shaken, let us have grace, whereby we may offer service well-pleasing to God with reverence and awe: for our God is a consuming fire.*
>
> Hebrews 12.28–29

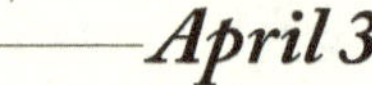

April 3

Wandering Eyes

In February my eyes went to Auckland, New Zealand. Last year they went to Singapore. In the two years before that, they traveled to Honolulu, Lisbon, Amsterdam, London, and Brandenburg, Germany. I suppose it is ironic that although my eyes have been to all those places, I have never seen any of them, and never will. The magic of digital photography, videotape, and DVDs have taken my eyes to far away, exotic places, and because of that, medical magic will help others.

I have heard many speak badly of doctors whose conferences take them to places like these; things like, "I wish I could count my vacation as a business deduction." Have you ever seen one of the programs for these conferences? Yes, there are sightseeing tours arranged for the doctors (which they pay for), but they are sandwiched in between seminars, lectures, demonstrations, and panel discussions that you and I could never make heads nor tails of because we did not sign what amounted to a mortgage in order to attend years of medical school, nor have to pay an annual six figure malpractice insurance premium to protect ourselves from those who think doctors should be perfect.

For any who complain, I hope you never need to rely on two doctors who live a thousand miles apart having met one another by chance several thousands of miles away from their homes in order to save your sight, or worse, your life. Let them sightsee a little. It's worth it, if not to you, then to some poor soul somewhere.

That was extra. Here is my point today: I will never see those places, except in pictures. Abraham did not even have pictures as evidence when he left his home at God's command. He had no deed in his hand when he believed God would give him the land of Canaan, nor did Isaac and Jacob, or their wives. But we are told, "These all died in faith, not having received the promises, but *having seen them and greeted them from afar*" (Heb 11.13). Amazing faith, we think. There was nothing that even *hinted* to them that they would inherit that land. At times they were run off it, even threatened if they stayed, but they still believed God would keep his promise.

That's what we do today, isn't it? Some might think we have it even harder. At least the three patriarchs eventually stood on actual land—dirt and grass and watering holes, with trees growing and animals wandering about. We must believe in something we can't see or touch. Oh, really. Do you think they didn't believe in that place too? "And having confessed that they were strangers and pilgrims on this earth. ...They desire a better country, that is, a heavenly one, wherefore God is not ashamed... to be called their God, but he has prepared for them a city" (Heb 11.13, 16).

Their faith went beyond the physical, just as ours should. It may be a tall order, but look at all those who have gone before us and managed it. Why is it we treat the faith requirement as some sort of burden? "Don't lose faith," we say when someone has a problem, creating yet another problem for them. Faith should be an asset. It causes hope, and how many people have lived longer lives because a doctor gave them a little thing called hope?

The hope we have is for something even better. Unlike all those amazing places my eyes have been but I have never seen, this is one I *will*_see, the most amazing place of all, forever.

> *For in hope were we saved, but hope that is seen is not hope; for who hopes for that which he sees? But if we hope for that which we see not, then do we with patience wait for it.*
>
> Romans 8.24–25

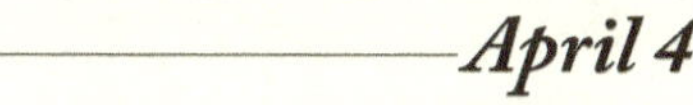

April 4

Unexpected Results

If you read through the histories of the early church, especially during the persecutions, you will see that everyone found the behavior of Christians totally inexplicable. Despite pain and death, they never acted the way people expected them to act. They did not denounce their Savior, and the ones who survived did not try to avenge their mistreatment.

God's people did not suddenly become pliant and merciful in the first century. It began long before. David is a prime example in his careful treatment of Saul, a mad king who was out to destroy him. Maybe that is where the little maiden learned her first lessons about mercy.

We do not know exactly when, how, or where, but a band of Syrian soldiers raided an Israelite town and took many people captive, among them a little girl. Eventually she wound up in the home of Naaman, the captain of the very army who kidnapped her and possibly even killed members of her family, serving his wife. I don't know how old she was, but she was probably far older in mind and actions than children her age nowadays because of what she had been through. She was old enough to remember her homeland and to know about the power of God and his prophet Elisha.

Soon she discovered that her new master had leprosy, a disease so dreaded in her own country that the people who had it were sent away and quarantined. What would you have thought? "Good! Serves him right. Get him, God." I can easily see those thoughts going through my mind, especially if the last view I had of my home was painted with the blood of my family. What was the last thing you wanted to "get even" with someone about? Can it even hold a candle to what this girl must have experienced?

But no, she tells her mistress, "Would that my lord were with the prophet who is in Samaria! He would cure him of his leprosy" (2 Kgs 5.3).

Excuse me? This man is an enemy of God's people, at that time a physical kingdom with physical enemies. God's standing orders often included wiping out those enemies. Yet she wants to save this man, who could easily kill more of God's children? She was obviously too young to know what she was doing.

But Elisha wasn't. And God certainly knew whom he was healing as Naaman dipped himself into the Jordan River. This was no mistake caused by a naïve child. The mercy she showed was exactly what God wanted of her.

And so the unexpected result, mercy from a captive toward her captor, made for yet another unexpected result. Naaman, the heathen army captain, said, "Behold now I know that there is no God in all the earth, but in Israel" (v 15).

Sometimes in our zeal to fight for God, we forget that He knows best. When will we ever learn that with God, we should expect the unexpected?

You have heard that it was said, you shall love your neighbor, and hate your enemy: but I say unto you, love your enemies, and pray for those who persecute you; that you may be sons of your Father who is in heaven: for he makes his sun to rise on the evil and the good, and sends rain on the just and the unjust. For if you love those who love you, what reward have you? Do not even the publicans the same? And if you salute your brethren only, what do you more? Do not even the Gentiles the same? You therefore shall be perfect, as your heavenly Father is perfect.

Matthew 5.43–48

April 5

Heavy Lifting

Keith has become my porter. Depending on my condition at any given moment, high eye pressure, foggy vision, post-op, etc, I am not supposed to lift more than 10–20 pounds. The ten pound limit is a real problem. A grocery sack with a bag of sugar and a bag of flour weighs ten pounds. If the bagger adds anything else, I am over the limit. That makes for a lot of trips back and forth to the car.

So Keith does a lot of carrying. He even insists on carrying my purse sometimes, which I assured him weighs only four pounds—I checked it to make sure.

The Lord has promised to carry our burdens, but we don't want to turn them over to him. The worries are not that big a deal to give up; it's all the emotional baggage from the past that for some reason we cannot seem to part with. You would think it was a treasured heirloom.

Just imagine the troubles the Lord might have had if people had been so reluctant in the first century. Just look at the apostles. How in the world would Simon the Zealot and Matthew the publican have ever gotten along if they had not ridded themselves of their "baggage"? These men came from opposite poles in ideology, and Simon was certainly passionate about it. Yet they learned to trust one another and get along.

Yes, it took a little help from Barnabas for the Jerusalem church to accept their former persecutor, the man who turned them over to their tormentors and executors, but they did. How much more difficult would it have been for the gospel to be preached to all the world if they had rejected Saul of Tarsus? Would *we* have so easily accepted this former enemy into our midst?

How many times do we let our pasts affect how we treat one another? Can I not trust a brother because a long time ago someone hurt my feelings? Do I expect the worst of even my brothers and sisters in Christ because in the past someone disappointed me? Do I judge everyone as "out to get me" because at one time someone was? Too many times the people we claim to love have to pay for what someone they never even knew did to us simply because we cannot let it go.

Jesus expects that when I become his disciple I will put all that extra baggage on him. There may be times when I am tempted to pick it up again, but if I have taken on his burden—"take my yoke upon you and learn of me… for my yoke is easy and my burden is light" (Matt 11.29–30)—I won't have room for anything else.

So the question is, are you truly his disciple? Whose burden are you trying to carry today, his light one or your heavy one? If you are having trouble getting along with someone, especially someone you are supposed to love and trust, I bet I know the answer to that one.

Humble yourselves, therefore, under the mighty hand of God so that at the proper time he may exalt you, casting all your anxieties on him, because he cares for you.

1 Peter 5.6–7

April 6

Climbers

Have you seen the commercial where the father is playing hide and seek and finds his little boy up near the ceiling as his mother says, "We have a climber?" I have one too.

Lucas, my older son, climbs. If there is anything around taller than he is, he is on it without even conscious thought. When he was a teenager, I would hear him call from outside. When I got there, I could not see him anywhere. Finally I would hear laughter coming from above me—way above me. If there is a tree on our property he has not climbed, it was just not big enough to hold him. I should have known.

When he was about eight months old and had just started pulling up on things and walking around them while hanging on (four weeks later he let go!), I had a cake sitting on my countertop, freshly frosted and ready for a potluck. The kitchen I had at the time was a horseshoe shape, with a lower eating bar on the side of the leg of the counter that faced the family room. I just turned around toward the other leg of the counter for two minutes, wiping up crumbs. Someone had left a chair pulled out (we won't say who is guilty of never pushing his chair in). Lucas pulled up on the chair, lifted a little leg, climbed into it, pulled himself up on the bar, then up onto the countertop and was literally two inches from planting his little fist in the cake as he crawled across the countertop when I turned around, gasped, and grabbed him.

If you had seen an eight month old baby, still crawling on the floor, and the height of the countertop, you would have thought the cake was safe too. There was no way he would ever get near it, especially not that fast. But for him, there was no way he could *not* get to it if he wanted it badly enough.

Too many times we give up without trying. We look at the difficulty ahead of us and say, "I can't." We excuse our faults by blaming God, *I'm only human. I can't help it.* You know what that translates to? "God made me this way. It's His fault I can't do any better." What way exactly did God makes us? "And God created man in His own image, in the image of God did he make him" (Gen 1.27). Seems like a pretty good way to be made to me. Every excuse we can come up with is just as baseless as this one.

I can't handle this, God. You're asking too much. Which means God is *not* faithful. He *will* ask more than I can bear. "There has no temptation taken you but such as man can bear; but God is faithful, who will not suffer you to be tempted above that you are able" (1 Cor 10.13).

How can you allow this to happen, God? Which means God *can* be tempted with evil, and he *does* tempt us. "Let no man say when he is tempted, I am tempted of God, for God cannot be tempted with evil, and he himself tempts no man" (Jas 1.13).

Every day I have to fight this battle. It's just too hard for me. Which means you can sin with impunity? "Watch, stand fast in the faith, behave like men! Be strong" (1 Cor 16.13).

I quit. I just can't do it. Oh? "I can do all things through Christ who strengthens me" (Phil 4.13).

There was a little baby once who was just old enough to recognize a cake when he saw it. It did not matter that it was up three or four times higher than his head. It did not matter that he had to work hard to get there. It did not matter that it was dangerous going. He could have fallen and hurt himself badly at any time. Did he care? No, he wanted that cake and was determined to have it.

Isn't Heaven a little more important than a piece of cake?

April 7

A Frightening Prayer

In his third epistle, John prays what has to be the most frightening prayer in the Bible. "Beloved I pray that in all things you may *prosper and be in health, even as your soul prospers*" (v 2).

Have you ever wondered what might happen if God suddenly answered that prayer—that your body and your economic life may be as healthy as your soul? Those of us who prosper financially, might suddenly be living a hand to mouth existence, while others who can barely make ends meet might find their bank accounts overflowing. Are we more concerned with our IRAs, annuities, and money market accounts than with the "unfathomable riches of Christ" (Eph 3.8)? What was it Jesus said to the rich man who was more concerned with his physical wealth than his spiritual wealth? "'You fool! This night is your soul required of you, and all the things you have prepared, whose will they be then?' So is he who lays up treasure for himself but is not rich toward God" (Luke 12.20–21).

But what about the physical health angle of that prayer? Some of us who are fat and sassy might instantly become pale and emaciated. Some of us might even fall over dead! But there might be others, frail and chronically ill, who suddenly become as hale and hearty as the great athletes of the world.

If we want to be able to pray John's prayer, we need to get our souls in shape. Do they get the proper nourishment or do they fast several days a week? Do our souls have to be force-fed? Do we "exercise our senses" every day, "discerning between good and evil," or do we sit like couch potatoes, taking in with a glazed look everything the world has to offer? Are we willing to take our medicine when we need it, or do we deny our faults and blame everyone else as if that will make them go away?

If a righteous man stands up Sunday morning and prays this prayer fervently—that everyone there will suddenly be as prosperous in wealth and healthy in body as they are in soul—will we jump up and beg him to stop because we know the results of the "effectual fervent prayer of a righteous man" (Jas 5.16)?

Think about it; it might change your life.

> *For this cause I bow my knees unto the Father from whom every family in heaven and in earth is named, that he should grant you according to the riches of his glory that you may be strengthened with power through his Spirit in the inner man, that Christ may dwell in your hearts through faith, to the end that you, being rooted and grounded in love, may be strong to apprehend with all the saints what is the breadth and length and height and depth, and to know the love of Christ which passes knowledge that you may be filled unto all the fullness of God.*
>
> Ephesians 3.14–19

Southernisms

The term "Southernism" usually refers to a trait of language or behavior that is characteristic of the South or Southerners. I have a cookbook, *Cooking Across the South* compiled by Lillian Marshall, which extrapolates that definition to include certain Southern recipes as well, particularly older recipes. She includes in that list things like hominy, frocking, poke sallet, and tomato gravy. If you are from north of the Mason-Dixon Line, I am sure you are scratching your head at some of those things, wondering just what in the world they are besides strange.

In the same vein, I wondered if we could stretch that idea to something we might call "Christianisms," things a Christian would do that might seem peculiar to someone who isn't one. Like never using what the world now calls "colorful language"; like remaining calm and civil when someone mistreats you, doing, in fact, something nice for them; like not cheating on your taxes; like giving back the change that a cashier overpays you; like paying attention to the speed limit and other laws of the land even if there is not a trooper behind you; like cooking or cleaning house for an invalid; like making time for the worship on Sunday morning and arriving at the ball game late even if those tickets did cost a small fortune; like being careful of the clothing you choose to wear; like choosing not to see certain movies or watch certain television shows; like thinking that spending time with other Christians is far more enjoyable than things like "clubbing"—these are my idea of Christianisms. I am sure you could add more to the list.

In the cookbook, I must admit, are many things I have never heard of, despite being a born and bred Southerner—frocking, for one. You see I came along at a time when the South was starting to change, especially my part of it. Disney changed everything. Orlando used to be a one-horse town instead of the metropolis it has become. I actually learned how to drive in Tampa on what is now I-275. Can you imagine letting a first timer do that? My part of the South has become less "southern" as the years have passed. So, while I had roots in the traditions of the Deep South, I have lost familiarity with many of them.

Wouldn't it be a shame if we got to that point with "Christianisms?" When you read that list I made, did you stop somewhere along the line and say, "Huh? Why would anyone do that?" Have we allowed the "worldisms" to take the place of concepts and behaviors that ought to be second nature to us? Can we even compose a list of things that make us different or have we become assimilated?

Try making a list of the "Christianisms" in your life today. Make sure you can come up with some, and if not, maybe it's time to make a few changes.

Do all things without grumbling or questioning, that you may be blameless and innocent, children of God without blemish in the midst of a crooked and perverse generation, among whom you shine as lights in the world, holding fast to the word of life.

Philippinas 2.14–16a

April 9

The Pottery Barn

Many years ago on one of our camping trips to the mountains, Keith and I visited a pottery barn, where a potter was busily working at the wheel. We watched him try for several minutes to make a certain type of curve at the lip of the vessel he was making, but every time the lip collapsed. Finally he shook his head and muttered something about the clay having a fault in it. So he changed his plans and made another vessel. It was still a useful pot I am sure, but it did not have that intricate lip that would have made it more beautiful and unique.

Suddenly, I understood a whole lot better all those passages in the Bible about the potter and the clay, and how God can use us without forcing His will on us. God wants us all to be beautiful creations which He can use to accomplish His purpose, but when through our own freewill we rebel, He simply changes His mind and makes us into something else, something not quite as pretty, not quite as special, but usable nonetheless.

We may become so rebellious that we actually think we can keep God from using us, but that is not the case. Some doctrines talk about foreordination in a way that actually limits God. It makes Him need to control everything in order to accomplish His ends. You do realize that notion came from Augustinianism, and Augustine got it from paganism. Remember the doctrine of fatalism from the Greek goddesses called Fates? The scriptures teach instead about a God so powerful that He can use us in spite of the fact that we are able to choose our courses of action. He does not have to control us to bring His plan to fruition. That is truly awesome power.

So make no mistake about it—God *will* use us, but it is up to us *how* He will use us. Personally I would rather be a beautiful vase with an intricate, unique design, or even a plain, practical, but necessary and honorable cooking pot, than some sort of "second option." How would you like to be a spittoon, or maybe a chamber pot? You see, we are all clay in the potter's hand. It's only *what* He makes of us that we have any real choice about.

Now in a great house there are not only vessels of gold and silver, but also of wood and earth, and some unto honor and some unto dishonor. If anyone therefore purge himself... he shall be a vessel of honor, sanctified, meet for the Master's use, prepared unto every good work

2 Timothy 2.20–21

April 10

A Full Service Station

Many years ago, as we drove back from a visit with Keith's parents in Northwest Arkansas, we stopped in a small town for gas. It was an older station, no convenience store attached, just the usual glass-windowed office and two service bays. Before Keith could get out of the car, a young man ran out and asked which octane level we wanted, and proceeded to fill the tank. The boys, who were young teenagers, were amazed.

"Wow!" one of them said. Then he immediately followed it with, "Look Mom! He's cleaning our windshield!"

Before he was finished, the young man had also checked the oil and battery, added some water to the radiator, and taken our credit card to run it through the machine. He returned with it standing up looking at us from the top of a blue plastic clipboard which held the receipt for Keith to sign. Never once did we have to get out of the car. I immediately flashed back to my own childhood, when pumping gas was for attendants at "service" stations, which did not have to advertise themselves as "full service"—everyone understood that was what you got when you stopped there, something neither of my boys had ever seen in their lives.

And that is what a Christian is supposed to be—a "full service" station. Christians focus on the needs of others; they fill the needs they see without being asked; they even go beyond what is expected. As Jesus told his followers, "If you love them that love you, what reward have you? Do not even the publicans the same? And if you salute your brethren only, what do you more than others? Do not even the Gentiles the same?" (Matt 5.46–47). Instead of egocentrism, which sees itself as the center of the universe, Christians understand that even their own lives are not about them, but about others.

They know this because of the greatest example of leadership any group has ever had. A leader who "counted not the being on an equality with God a thing to be grasped, but emptied himself, taking on the form of a servant, being made in the likeness of man, and being found in fashion as a man, he humbled himself, becoming obedient unto death, yes, the death of the cross" (Phil 2.6–8). A leader who was willing to do the dirty work, not just the foot washing duties of the lowliest of servants, but also taking on the filthy load of our sins, a load we all contributed to.

For this reason we serve. For this reason we gladly serve. For this reason we serve fully, wearing ourselves out with serving, even unto death.

> *You call me Teacher, and Lord, and you say well, for so I am. If I then, the Lord and the Teacher, have washed your feet, you also ought to wash one another's feet. For I have given you an example, that you also should do as I have done to you. Amen and amen, I say to you, a servant is not greater than his lord, neither one that is sent greater than he who sent him. If you know these things, blessed are you if you do them.*
>
> John 13.13–17

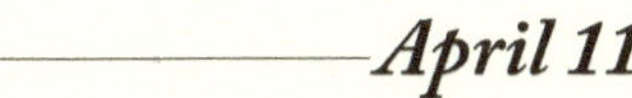

April 11

A Clean Sweep

Now that we have a carport for the first time in 27 years, I find myself wondering if all we did was get something else to keep clean. I know I sweep it every morning I am home and the weather is cooperative. If I miss a day, it's really a mess. A little while ago, after a couple of rainy days, I had an especially large job ahead of me. In places on the edges the dust was caked an inch thick.

I thought I would never finish. I swept several times in each patch and still the dust flew. Finally I looked at Chloe and muttered, "There is enough dust here for God to make a whole person." As my mind is apt to wander into strange places, it was only a second or two before I wondered if I was sweeping some Native American from four or five hundred years ago, or perhaps some Spanish conquistador who never made it home.

Now that's a humbling thought, isn't it? Some day several hundred years from now, someone may be sweeping *me* off *their* carport, or whatever they have by then.

When it comes right down to it that is all these bodies are. As God told Adam, "For dust thou art and unto dust shalt thou return" (Gen 3.19). Too many times we think we are more than that. But answer this: how many billions (or trillions?) have ever lived in all of time, and how many of those do you find in your child's history book? I imagine the percentage would be point zero, zero, zero, zero something—or even less. How can I ever think that I am so important to the world that I would wind up in that tiny group? I will be surprised if anyone remembers me even 20 years after I am gone, much less several hundred.

Thinking too well of myself will do nothing but cause serious trouble. How many relationships are ruined by self-centeredness? How many tyrants came out of an ego that could not be satisfied? How often has the Lord's body suffered schisms because someone thought he was more important than any of his brethren?

If you think about it, it is ironic that the only person who was ever as humble as he should have been is the one who changed history forever. While we claim to follow Him, we evidently don't believe His way is the best. Humility seems to be the most difficult thing we have to learn, and the place we most often fail.

So go sweep your carport today. It might be that you will gain a little perspective.

For if a man thinks himself to be something when he is nothing, he deceives himself.

The dust returns to the earth as it was, and the spirit to God who gave it.

Galatians 6.3; Ecclesiastes 12.7

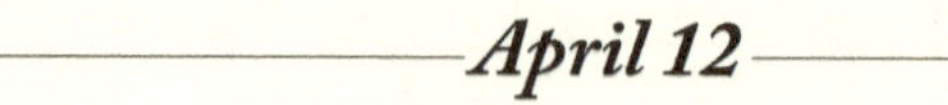

April 12

A New Floor

Among the other things we have dealt with recently is the discovery that I am allergic to dust mites. This is not just a small nuisance. We found out after I ran a low fever for six months, accompanied by horrible headaches. Finally a CAT scan showed that one of my sinuses had been infected for so long that the lining, which should not even show up on a scan, did in fact show up as a gray wall nearly half an inch thick. The doctor operated, ripping out bone and tissue to open up what had become a sealed incubator for anaerobic bacteria.

So we began vacuuming upholstery, washing sheets with a special de-miting solution, and zipping up mattress and box springs in special casings. The doctor also suggested I hire someone to dust for me. That's not going to happen, but I am much more careful when I do the dusting myself.

Keith has also decided that we need to rip out the carpet and put down new flooring. Yes, the doctor says, good idea. Too bad she can't write it out as a prescription we can deduct from the taxes next April.

The money is not the only problem. Do you know what a mess this place is in while we are having this done? Do you know how many things we need to go through and toss, and how many others need to be picked up and moved, or stacked and restacked as progress is made across the house? How about a freezer filled with several hundred pounds of garden produce and meat? How about an antique grand piano? Will I ever again be able to find a certain book in all these bookcases? Just thinking about it stresses me out, and I have an idea that we have not thought about every problem that will arise.

This is exactly the process a person goes through when he makes Christ the new foundation in his life. Those of us who have grown up "going to church" have no real comprehension of what they are facing when we talk to our friends and neighbors. We too often show no sympathy for the upheaval conversion will cause. In fact, the disruption in their lives may be the biggest hurdle they must cross, and the least we can do is be understanding. Too many times we dismiss those poor people, who so desire to have the peace we do, as "not worthy" because they cannot make an instant decision to change themselves, and then do so overnight. "They were not truly converted," we proclaim. Shame on us.

Let's not turn into hecklers instead of helpers. I have seen too many new Christians lose their way because the people who should have been guiding them were moving too fast for them to keep up, and simply grew impatient, leaving them behind. Putting in a new floor is a nuisance. Putting a whole new foundation in one's way of life is a monumental change that deserves help and respect.

And just perhaps, the reason we do not understand is that *our* foundation is not what it should be. Is it habit and comfort, or is it commitment? Maybe I need another kind of new floor as well. Do you?

According to the grace of God which was given unto me, as a wise master builder I laid a foundation, and another builds thereon. But let each man take heed how he builds thereon. For other foundation can no man lay than that which is laid, which is Jesus Christ.

1 Corinthians 3.10–11

April 13

Listen Up!

I sat on the carport today since the spring breeze is still cool, and relatively dry. I was working on Proverbs with my trusty bodyguards lying at my feet, tails occasionally swishing sand across the concrete. When we first moved here, 25 years ago now, it was the quietest place we had ever lived. No neighbors revving up engines of various kinds, no traffic on the highway, certainly no sirens wailing in the air. In the past two or three weeks alone, I have heard sirens three times, which is about as many times as I heard them the whole 25 years before. People are moving here to have what we have, and in the process, destroying it.

But that morning I was suddenly struck by how quiet it was—not exactly like all those years ago, but close. I sat still and really listened; half a dozen different birds sounds, chirps, tweets, squawks, caws, shrieks, and crows; wings flapping in the oaks; a June bug buzzing over our heads in the sycamore, two planes droning overhead, one a jet and the other a single-engine prop; hummingbirds humming and squeaking at the feeder; a semi roaring faintly down the highway to the west beyond the woods, hitting the speed bumps a good half mile away with a rhythmic brrrrump—brrrrump—brump, brump, brump.

Even the dogs seemed to realize how quiet things were, and they sat there with me, watching and listening. Amazing things happen when you sit quietly and just listen. A limb, evidently weakened by age and a recent wind, suddenly cracked and fell just up the driveway, a little flock of sparrows landed barely two feet off the concrete slab, hopping around on the ground as if totally unaware that a human and two dogs were nearby; a pileated woodpecker suddenly swooped down across the drive and landed on the water oak trunk and began pecking for his lunch; a lizard crept out onto the steps and puffed out his red balloon of a throat when he suddenly realized we were there, and a black and yellow swallowtail butterfly landed on an azalea limb close enough for *me* to see its spots.

I have heard that Abraham Lincoln was fond of saying, "Better to be quiet and thought a fool than to open your mouth and remove all doubt." I didn't realize that he was paraphrasing one of the proverbs: "Even a fool when he holds his peace is counted as wise; when he shuts his lips, he is esteemed as prudent" (17.28). I suppose Lincoln's version was a bit more colorful, but you get the point. Amazing things can happen when you keep your mouth shut. People may actually think you are wise!

Someone else has also noted that when your mouth is open, your ears stop working, which is just a cute way of saying that when you are talking you can't listen, and most of us need to do much more listening than talking. I would guess that the majority of times we find ourselves in hot water it is because we talked when we should have been quiet. Is there a problem in the home? At work? With a neighbor? Look back in your mind and 'listen' to what happened. Amazing things can happen when you listen. You will probably see that it all began with a word *not* fitly spoken. As James said: "Let every man be swift to hear, slow to speak and slow to wrath, for the wrath of man does not work the righteousness of God" (1.19–20).

Listening is also a good way to serve others. Don't be so quick to give advice unless it is specifically asked for. Don't be so quick to take over the conversation with how *you* handled something similar. Amazing things can happen when you listen. By having a sympathetic listener, many people can figure their way out of problems on their own, and they will be so grateful for your "help."

Ahem, men—she doesn't want you to fix it, she just wants you to listen. You will become her hero. *Truly* amazing things can happen if you just listen.

And always listen to God. Too many times we are explaining ourselves to him instead. Imagine that. This is God we are talking about and we feel the need to explain something to him? Listen instead. Maybe the problem is we don't want to hear what he has to say to us. So if you do answer back, listen to that too. You might realize your error and repent.

Amazing things can happen when you sit quietly and listen.

> *And Moses said, the Lord God will raise up for you a prophet like me from your brothers. You shall listen to him in whatever he tells you. And it shall be that every soul who does not listen to that prophet shall be destroyed from the people.*
>
> Acts 3.22–23

April 14

Tokens

When was the last time you thought about your baptism? Did you realize that baptism is mentioned in one way or another in well over half the books of the New Testament, and that in the epistles it is a discussion directed toward those who have already been baptized? Why is it then that we relegate it to first principles only, and ignore it the rest of our lives?

Paul told the Colossians that baptism is the "circumcision" of New Testament Israel (2.11–12). Instead of removing a piece of flesh, we remove the "old man of flesh." So what was circumcision to Old Testament Israel?

God told Abraham that circumcision was a token of the covenant between God and his people. "And the uncircumcised male who is not circumcised in the flesh of his foreskin, that soul shall be cut off from his people; he hath broken my covenant" (Gen 17.14).

The Hebrew word for "token," *oth,* is used in a variety of ways in the Old Testament. In Numbers 2.2 it refers to the *banners* that waved over a tribe's encampment to identify them. In Genesis 4.15 it refers to the *mark* God put on Cain as a sign of his protection. In Joshua 2.12 it was the scarlet cord, a *sign* of the bargain between Rahab and the spies. In Exodus 4.8–9 God gave Moses *miracles* to do which showed both the people and Pharaoh that he came from God. In Joshua 4.6 it referred to the pile of stones used to remember the crossing of the Jordan River, a *memorial* that was to be passed down through the generations.

If it was so important, why then did the people discontinue it in the wilderness? "For all the people that came out [of Egypt] were circumcised; but all the people that were born in the wilderness by the way as they came forth out of Egypt, they had not circumcised. For the children of Israel walked forty years in the wilderness, till all the nation, even the men of war that came forth out of Egypt, were consumed, because they hearkened not unto the voice of Jehovah: unto whom Jehovah swore that he would not let them see the land which Jehovah swore unto their fathers that he would give us, a land flowing with milk and honey. And their children, whom he raised up in their stead, these did Joshua circumcise" (Josh 5.5–7).

Maybe I am reading something into this that is not there, but I wonder if God simply did not allow those faithless people to circumcise their children. He certainly took it seriously when Moses did not circumcise his sons (Exod 4.24–26). Only when the faithless generation of Israelites were all dead did Joshua renew this covenant and its token with their children.

So here is our question today: If God were to take similar actions today, would he allow me to have my children baptized? Or would he consider it a travesty of the covenant for someone as faithless as I, someone who no longer lives up to the baptism I took part in, that symbolic resurrection from the death of sin, to try to teach my children about it and what it means? How could I even hope to do so?

The biggest insult a Jew could hurl was "uncircumcised Gentile." That is why they stoned Stephen after he said they were "uncircumcised in heart" (Acts 7.51). They understood that the token of the covenant with God was not supposed to be merely an outward sign, but a symbol of a faithful relationship. What is your baptism to you? Is it merely the last step on the staircase chart of the Plan of Salvation? Or is it a token, a daily reminder to live like a new person, a child of a covenant relationship with God, a relationship that is more precious to you than anything else in the world?

> *In him also you were circumcised with a circumcision made without hands, by putting off the body of the flesh, by the circumcision of Christ, having been buried with him in baptism, in which you were also raised with him through faith in the powerful working of God, who raised him from the dead. And you, who were dead in your trespasses and the uncircumcision of your flesh, God made alive together with him, having forgiven us all our trespasses.*
>
> Colossians 2.11–13

April 15

A Beautifully Made Bed

I well remember my children's first attempt at making their beds. They were so proud of their accomplishment, one I had not even asked them to do, that they came running to get me, and took me to their room by the hand.

There were two twin beds, indeed all made up. The bedspreads hung lopsided, the hem at the head end barely reaching the edge of the bed and the hem at the foot end folding down over itself onto the carpet. Under it, the sheets and blankets sat in piles and rolls, making the bedspread top look like it was laid over Lilliputian foothills. One of the spreads was particularly "off," and I was momentarily at a loss to figure out the problem. At the foot, the bottom sheet showed in a line one to four inches wide. Since the top barely reached the headboard and it was not neatly tucked in under the pillows, that should not have been. Then I realized what was wrong—the whole bedspread was on *sideways.*

"Amazing!" I gushed. "What a fine job you have done." For indeed they had—for a four- and six-year-old who had been given no instruction at all.

The next few mornings I asked if they would like to learn some hints that would make bed making easier. Easier? Of course they would, because it had not taken long for the new to wear off this activity and for it to become simply a chore. So they learned how to make a bed properly, and in time they did reasonably well.

Now imagine if they had shown me that first made bed when they were 14 and 16. Do you think I would have lavished any praise on them? I would have expected a much better eye for detail, and much more care in technique. That does not mean I was lying when I told them at the earlier age that they had done a fine job. They had done a fine job *for their age and experience.*

Now how about us? How old am I as a child of God? But—and here is the crux of the matter—how old do I *act*? How much have I learned and grown, and does it show in the way I behave every day of my life?

We needn't expect the same praise God would give a babe in Christ if we have been Christians for 20 years. If we have been Christians longer than that, we should have made even more progress.

Make no mistake, God does love his children, but he has expectations as well. I must do my best for my Father, trying harder and harder to get better and better. If my "bed making" is still at age four level when I have spent 44 years as his child, he will not be pleased. And if I love him, working to get better is not too much to ask.

...till we all attain unto the unity of the faith, and of the knowledge of the Son of God, unto a full-grown man, unto the measure of the stature of the fullness of Christ: that we may be no longer children, tossed to and fro and carried about with every wind of doctrine, by the sleight of men, in craftiness, after the wiles of error; but speaking truth in love, we may grow up in all things into him, who is the head, Christ.

Ephesians 4.13–15

April 16

Little Miss Piggy

Until we got Chloe, we have always practiced what pet owners know as "self-feeding." You fill up the feed pan and a few days later, when you notice that it is finally empty, you fill it up again. Magdi has always just eaten what she needed to eat and no more, like most animals do. In spite of the fact that she is an athlete who works off an incredible number of calories every day, she has never been tempted to overeat.

Then came Chloe. We kept up with the "self-feeding" once she started eating adult food because we wanted to make sure she got enough. Magdi has a tendency to claim the feed pan as hers and guard it whether she is eating or not. But we should have realized when we stood over Chloe and looked down that she was getting plenty to eat. Instead of a straight line from her shoulders to her hind quarters, there was a significant bulge on each side. When we took her to the vet a couple of weeks ago, the doctor strongly recommended a low calorie diet. Self-feeding does not work with Miss Piggy dining in the doghouse.

In just a couple of weeks of measured daily feeding she has slimmed down. She is much more active, running with Magdi across the fields as they play, and tearing up the ground to greet Keith at the gate when he comes home. She even leapt into the air chasing a bee the other day and managed to get all four feet off the ground a foot or more. We no longer have a piglet with a cold wet black nose and a wagging tail.

God practices a sort of spiritual self-feeding. His word is available to us any time we want it. He has given us elders, wise leaders who see to our more formal spiritual meals, and who take that responsibility seriously. But we can reach into the "pantry" any time we want and snack to our hearts' content. In fact, the shame is that instead of looking pleasantly plump in a spiritual sense, too many of us look like we have been on a fast. When I have labored over a meal for several hours and hardly anyone comes to the dinner table, and those few just pick at their meals, I get a little miffed. Don't you suppose God does, too?

Now, more than any other time in history, and here, more than any other place in the world, we can study the Bible any time we want to. Where is our appreciation of the providence of God? Where is our hunger for the meat of the word? Have we filled ourselves up with the empty calories of pop culture and the simple carbs of modern philosophy to the point that we have no room for real food?

Take a moment today to examine what you are taking into your spirit, what you are filling your soul with, and determine to make a change in your spiritual diet. Jesus called himself the Bread of Life. Aren't we interested in that life at all?

Our fathers ate the manna in the wilderness, as it is written, He gave them bread out of Heaven to eat. Jesus therefore said unto them, Amen and amen, I say unto you, It

> *was not Moses who gave you bread out of Heaven, but my Father gives you the true bread out of Heaven. For the bread of God is that which comes down out of Heaven, and gives life to the world. They said therefore to him, Lord, evermore give us this bread. Jesus said unto them, I am the bread of Life; he who comes to me shall not hunger, and he who believes on me shall never thirst.*
>
> John 6.31–35

April 17

Obstacle Course

A long time ago when I was a young mother, a wise, older woman made me stop and think with a few words that might have sounded harsh, but which she couched with an attitude of love and concern. I had not taken a meal to a sick or grieving family for a long time; I had not taught a children's class for about a year; I had not had anyone in my home for several months; I hadn't even sent a card or made a phone call for awhile. I was a busy young mother. I had laundry to do every day including piles of diapers that never seemed to diminish, meals to fix, a baby to nurse and tend and a toddler to care for and teach, and a home that needed putting in some sort of order if just so we could keep track of where we put things, like the bills that needed paying.

Had this woman had the same problems years before when she was a young mother? I suppose so, but I never even thought about that—all I thought about was my own problems, all the things I needed to do, how tired I was, and how I could not possibly do any of those other things because of the demands of my family and home.

She knew all this, but she still asked this simple question. "What if," she quietly said, "God decided to help you out by taking away all of your excuses?"

After a moment of shock, I suddenly saw my children and my home in another light. Here I was claiming to love them more than anything else, while telling everyone what an obstacle they were in my life, maybe not in words, but certainly in deeds—or lack of them. Yes, serving my family is also serving God, but isn't it hypocritical to then turn around and use that service as a reason *not* to serve others? The last thing in the world I wanted was for God to take them away from me, and I determined that they would no longer be the excuses I offered for not doing what I could.

No, I could not spend hours and hours away from them, nor several hours caring for others directly, but surely I could pick up the phone or write a note when the babies were napping. Surely I could fix an extra casserole when I made one for my family, and send it with someone else to a home where a mother was too sick to do it and the father was out working all day. Surely, I could find *something* I could do.

I think something else happened to my attitude that day, too. I was suddenly aware of all the things that needed doing for others, and looking forward to a time when I could, instead of sitting at home, selfishly dreaming of a time when I could get away from it all and do only for myself. My home was where I wanted to be, but I also knew that I wanted to be doing what I could for others, when I could, for as long as I could, just like that kind sister who taught me a lesson with a simple question.

What kind of excuses have already come out of our mouths today? What if God took them away in the blink of an eye so we could do those things we claim to want to do "if only... ?"

But he said unto him, A certain man made a great supper; and he bade many: and he sent forth his servant at supper time to say to them that were bidden, Come; for things are now ready. And they all with one consent began to make excuse. The first said unto him, I have bought a field, and I must needs go out and see it; I pray have me excused. And another said, I have bought five yoke of oxen, and I go to prove them; I pray have me excused. And another said, I have married a wife, and therefore I cannot come. And the servant came, and told his lord these things. Then the master of the house being angry said to his servant, Go out quickly into the streets and lanes of the city, and bring in the poor and maimed and blind and lame... For I say unto you, that none of those men that were bidden shall taste of my supper.

Luke 14.16–21, 24

April 18

Putting Down Roots

Keith's mother once gave him a tiny orange tree, maybe six inches tall, which she had planted from seed into a coffee can. He brought it home, transplanted it into a black plastic nursery pot and set it next to the shed, continuing to water and feed it until he could find a permanent place for it.

It had grown to a height of three feet when he finally decided where to put it. Bending down, he grabbed the pot with both hands and tugged. Nothing happened. The tree had made its own decision, its roots bursting through the bottom of the pot and digging their way firmly into the ground. It's still there, now over twice as tall as the shed and bearing fruit nearly year round.

Our children are like that little tree. Wherever you leave them is where they will put down roots. The atmosphere you raise them in, the people they spend the most time with, the friends they make and the activities they participate in, whether you are aware of them or not, will all have their effects on your children, and will influence who they eventually become.

Children are growing every minute of every day, not only in body, but also in mind. You cannot set them aside until you have more time, you cannot leave them on their own without guidance, you cannot give them into the charge of another whose belief system does not match yours, and still expect your children to follow in your footsteps. You cannot tell them, not even with all the sincerity you can muster, "Just wait till I finish this degree; just wait till my career is more established; just wait till I can pay off all these bills I ran up, then I will be a good parent to you." If nothing else, you are teaching them exactly what is most important to you—career, status, "things." Meanwhile, they may put down their roots in places you wish they never knew of, with people you wish they had never met, and develop a character that may appall you.

"Where did they learn that?" you might wonder. In the place where you left them while you were too busy to be a parent.

> *Unless the* LORD *builds the house, those who build it labor in vain. Unless the* LORD *watches over the city, the watchman stays awake in vain. It is in vain that you rise up early and go late to rest, eating the bread of anxious toil; for he gives to his beloved sleep. Behold, children are a heritage from the* LORD, *the fruit of the womb a reward. Like arrows in the hand of a warrior are the children of one's youth. Blessed is the man who fills his quiver with them! He shall not be put to shame when he speaks with his enemies in the gate.*
>
> Psalm 127

April 19

Pot-bound

In our quest to diligently teach our children, I think we often overlook something. We care for our children, nurturing both body and soul. Our task, though, is to work our way out of the job. If my 30-year-old child still cannot dress himself, or needs to be reminded to brush his teeth, I have failed miserably. In the same way, our children cannot make it to Heaven on our spiritual coattails.

It is often difficult for a parent to realize that his child's faith should be his own, not an exact replica of the parent's. A child who does nothing but ape his father's opinions has, like the Jews of Isaiah's day, a faith which is "a commandment of men learned by rote" (Isa 29.13), rather than learned by personal study, meditation, and conviction.

Both of my sons have slightly differing views from mine about some passages of scripture. I'm glad. It means they have taken root on their own and, though there is never any guarantee, I feel much more optimistic about their remaining faithful when I am gone. Here is another application to the story of the orange tree my mother-in-law gave us, which rooted itself while we were trying to find a place to put it: children need to have a little freedom in their quest for spirituality, freedom to spread their own roots. Parents who demand exact conformity, treating any difference as a sign of disrespect, are spoon-feeding their children's spirituality while at the same time stunting their growth. They might as well be carrying them off the ground in a black plastic nursery pot so their roots won't branch out. Sooner or later they will become pot-bound and die.

While you expect to shape their values and instill basic concepts of spirituality and faith, God expected that they would ask, "Why?" and that you would give them real and sensible answers. "Because I said so," does have an appropriate time and place in teaching them authority, but not in teaching the word of God. If you cannot tell them why, then when you are gone why should they continue?

Encourage them to study and develop on their own. Treat their discoveries as equally interesting as yours. You may think Paul wrote Hebrews and they may not. You may believe the three-person interpretation of the Song of Solomon and they may prefer the two-person. You may look at Romans 7 as any man without Christ, while they believe Paul is talking about himself before his conversion. Isn't it great? You will most likely have an eternity to discuss these things together and with the authors themselves, while the parents who demanded absolute conformity and automaton feedback, may find themselves looking around, wondering where their children are.

> *And the people came up out of the Jordan on the tenth day of the first month, and encamped in Gilgal, on the east border of Jericho. And those twelve stones, which they took out of the Jordan, did Joshua set up in Gilgal. And he spoke unto the children of Israel, saying, When your children shall ask their fathers in time to come, saying, What mean these stones? Then you shall let your children know, saying, Israel came over this Jordan on dry land. For Jehovah your God dried up the waters of the Jordan from before you, until you were passed over, as Jehovah your God did to the Red Sea, which he dried up from before us, until we were passed over; that all the peoples of the earth may know the hand of Jehovah, that it is mighty; that you may fear Jehovah your God for ever.*
>
> Joshua 4.19–24

April 20

Cutworms

Cutworms are ugly, fat, brown worms that can wreak havoc overnight in a garden. They rise to the surface, wrap themselves around the tender stems of new plants, and cut them off at ground level. In the morning you find plant after plant, cut off and lying on the ground, shriveling in the new dawn.

Gardeners espouse various cures for cutworms. Some place plastic or foil collars around the stems from just above ground level to several inches below. Others insert nails, Popsicle sticks or toothpicks in the ground, one on either side of each stem. We generally just pick up a pile of twigs from the yard and poke them down next to the stems. All these cures work because they keep the worms from being able to surround the stem and cut it down. At least with our way, you don't have to walk the garden removing things that either won't degrade or might be dangerous. Just ask Nathan about toothpicks and bare feet.

These cures work for souls as well. People who face the trials and cares of life alone, without any support or encouragement, might as well have Satan wrap them up in his arms. They are that vulnerable. As vigilant soldiers of Christ we should be on the lookout during times when we find ourselves alone. Are you the only one at school who even claims to be a Christian? The only one at work? The only one in your neighborhood? Make sure you are not too proud to recognize moments of weakness and ask someone for help. Be willing to seek companionship when you need it. In fact, be willing to *run* for it!

And to those who are never alone, who are blessed enough to have a Christian mate or to work in a Christian atmosphere, pay attention to those around you who are not. Find the singles, the widows, the ones who have been left by unfaithful spouses, and be the someone who stands next to her so the devil cannot wrap her up and cut her down. We are too often so involved in our own families that we do not look for or make time for the lonely souls who need us. They are always the "fifth wheel," not a couple, and so they are ignored because they don't fit in. *It is our job to fit them in.*

Look around you today and find a loner. Don't let anyone lose his soul because you didn't even think to wrap him up in your encouraging arms and let him know that he is not alone.

> *Two are better than one, because they have a good reward for their toil. For if they fall, one will lift up his fellow. But woe to him who is alone when he falls and has not another to lift him up! Again, if two lie together, they keep warm, but how can one keep warm alone? And though a man might prevail against one who is alone, two will withstand him—a threefold cord is not quickly broken.*
>
> Ecclesiastes 4.9–12

April 21

Blind Hindsight

Hindsight, rather than being 20/20 and helping us understand better, can often blind us when studying the Bible, particularly the life of Jesus. Every time we see something Jesus did, we see it complete with the Son of God "halo" over his head and miss the effect it would have had on the people then. What they saw was Josh, the son of Joe Carpenter (John 6.42, *Joshua,* of course, being the Hebrew version of *Jesus).*

Let's try this: Imagine five or six of the most stable, godly, faithful Christian women you know. Go ahead, name them out loud—real people you know, with faces you can see in your mind. Now imagine they suddenly started following around some itinerant preacher who vilified the leading men of your congregation (Matt 23), taught things that seemed opposite of what you had heard all your life (Matt 5–6), and actually threw things *and people* out of the meetinghouse (John 2, Mark 11). Not only that, but every time he needed something, these women whipped out their checkbooks and took care of it for him. And he wasn't even handsome (Isa 53.2). What would you think? Have they gone nuts?!

"And it came to pass that he went about through cities and villages teaching... along with certain women who ministered to them of their substance" (Luke 8.1–3).

Susanna, Joanna, Mary Magdalene and others, probably Mary and Martha, and Aunt Salome, too, were those stable, godly, faithful women. "They were following Jesus," we think, "so it was perfectly normal," and miss the sacrifices they made and the courage they had. They were probably the topic of conversation in every home in their communities. Can't you just hear the women gossiping, and the men mocking their husbands? "You mean he actually let's her get away with that? Just who wears the biggest robes in his family, anyway?" They also risked being kicked out of the synagogue, which would have put an end to their social lives and maybe their economic lives as well.

Would I have been as brave? Would you? Are we that brave now, or do we find ourselves saying things like, "We need to be careful what the community thinks about us. We don't want to be controversial. Why, they may think we're fanatics!" *There are times when you just can't worry about what other people think.*

The next time you study, remember, you are looking from only one perspective and sometimes that blinds you to things that should be obvious. Clear your mind and appreciate what these people went through, and try to be as strong as they were.

And who is he that will harm you if you are zealous of that which is good? But even if you should suffer for righteousness's sake, blessed are you and fear not their fear, neither be troubled, but sanctify in your hearts Christ as Lord, being ready always to give answer to every man who asks you a reason concerning the hope that is in you, yet with meekness and fear, having a good conscience that, wherein you are spoken against they may be put to shame who revile your good manner of life in Christ.

1 Peter 3.13–16

A God Made to Order

I had a piano student once who tested my patience often. One day she hopped off the bench, ran to the window, and looked out. "Mom's back," she announced. "I *told* her to come back late so I would have time after lessons to play on the swing!"

I looked at her and said, "It's not the child's job to tell the mom what to do, it's the mom's job to tell the child what to do." She looked at me like I was from another planet. I am happy to report that the story ends well. She learned some discipline and respect for authority, and we developed a good relationship.

But this little girl was right in tune with the times. How often have you heard someone say, "I just can't believe in a God who would...?" Seems they forget who is the Creator and who is the created. People have been making a god to suit themselves for nearly as long as there have been people.

That is one reason Jesus was rejected. He didn't suit their idea of a Messiah. They wanted worldly might, worldly wealth, and worldly status. He was a poor man with no army, who constantly talked about humility. They came to Jesus and said, "Show us a sign and we will believe." What had he been doing but showing sign after sign?

One of my favorite people in the Bible is the blind man of John 9 whom Jesus healed. He is also one of the bravest in the Bible. The rulers questioned him again and again. "How are you able to see? Where did this man come from?" They even brought in his parents and accused them of *pretending* their son was born blind. These men were so desperate to find a way to discredit Jesus that they were coming up with absurdities. Finally the man looked at them and said, "Here is the amazing thing—you don't know where he came from, yet he opened my eyes!" And this man, whose life was really just beginning, was thrown out of the synagogue, ending any sort of normalcy he might have ever had. I think I know who one of the 3,000 on Pentecost was.

Are we any better than those hardheaded rulers of Jesus' day? Do we try to make the church into something other than God intended? What we usually want is a social club with rules of our own making, including what to wear, what to say, and how loud we can say it. What God wants is a dynamic group of believers, whose minds are on the spiritual world not the physical; who understand the severity of God's judgment and believe it is not only their mission to make sure they are saved, but to try to take others with them; people who understand that their worship must include a life of service to others, and who put the unity and good of the body before their own likes and dislikes.

Being a child of God means we don't tell God how to do things; He tells us.

Woe to him who strives with his Maker! A potsherd among potsherds of the earth! Shall the clay say to Him who fashions it, "What are you making?" Does your work say, "He has no hands?" Woe to him who says to his father, "What have you begotten?" or to his mother, "What have you brought to birth?"

But now, O Jehovah, you are our Father; we are the clay, and you the potter, and we are all the work of your hand.

Isaiah 45.9–10; 64.8

April 23

The Car Seat

We traded cars at the end of last year. This one has a few new gadgets on it. You can raise and lower the driver's seat, as well as pull it forward or push it back. You can position the steering column up or down, in or out. Unfortunately I had not yet learned how to do that the first time I climbed in to drive when Keith was at work.

Instead of sliding onto the seat, I fell into a hole. If the seat was not actually sitting on the floorboards of the car, it was close. As I tried to slide my legs under the steering wheel, I realized that it was practically resting on the seat. I sat for a minute fumbling around, and never found the right button, knob, or lever to fix anything. Needless to say, my driving experience that day was far from relaxing. Every time I got in, I fell in, squeezed under the steering wheel, and then spent the entire drive doing pull-ups on it so I could see where I was going.

All of that is because Keith is nearly six inches taller than I, and apparently his favored driving position is sitting on the floor with his knees up around his ears. That is why they make those seats movable—no two people are the same size and shape, and we all have our own definitions of comfort.

We tend to forget that with one another in the church. Depending upon when we first came into contact with the gospel, and the background we brought to the baptistery, we are all in different places in our faith and understanding. While the New Testament strongly hints that God has put a timetable on our learning ("when *by reason of time* you ought to be teachers"), it may not be my place to judge your progress. True, if one has been a Christian 40 years and still craves the milk of the word rather than the meat, there just might be a problem, but most of my impatience with my brothers and sisters has little to do with circumstances so obvious.

The job of the priest under the old law was to "bear gently with the ignorant and erring for he himself also is compassed with infirmity" (Heb 5.2). Aren't we all called priests of God under the new law (1 Pet 2.5)? And Paul says "to the weak I became as weak so that I might gain the weak" (1 Cor 9.22). He did not look down his nose at one who did not yet have his knowledge and comprehension of the plan of God through the ages.

When the church is growing spiritually and has reached a point that change in its traditions becomes expedient for the progress of the gospel, some people have problems with it. They are stuck in a place where traditions in their minds have become laws. It becomes more difficult for them to change those things. Are we patient in our teaching? Do we make ourselves "weak" by understanding how difficult this is for them, and so guide them along with compassion?

Mind you, we are not talking about changing the rules of the road or even how a car operates. You must still drive on the "right" side of the road. You still have to press the accelerator to go and the brake to stop, but some of us shift gears smoothly and automatically, while others need to do it manually, slowly and methodically, one gear at a time.

I usually see all those cars that impatiently pass me a little further down the road. Sometimes they sit on the shoulder with another car behind them, flashing its blue lights. Other times I quietly pull along side of them at the next stoplight as we both obey the law, idling in our separate lanes. So he got there ten seconds ahead of me—big deal. We both followed the rules and ended up in the same place.

We must patiently show one another how to move the car seat so we can all more easily see down the road, so none of us is left sitting in a hole, awkwardly doing pull-ups on the steering wheel, trying to see where he is going.

> *We who are strong have an obligation to bear with the failings of the weak, and not to please ourselves. Let each of us please his neighbor for his good, to build him up. For Christ did not please himself, but as it is written, the reproaches of those who reproached you have fallen on me.*
>
> Romans 15.1–3

April 24

A Piece of Advice

I published my first book of Bible class literature when I was 25 years old. It has weathered well, but I still rewrote the teachers' manual just a few years ago, giving this as one of the reasons: "I have found things I hope no one thinks I still believe. I really have learned better, I promise!"

That is embarrassing, but I suppose it would be even more embarrassing if I had not learned better. That is one problem with writing things down when you are young. They follow you your whole life. I worry about the folks who still have that old manual. What I worry most is that they will have discovered better all by themselves and any influence I may have now will be destroyed because they think I still believe those wrong notions.

When I was young, I was happy to give advice, too. I thought I knew every answer because to me everything was cut and dried, black and white, and I was happy to share my vast knowledge. Unfortunately, my vast inexperience got in the way. I am no longer eager to give advice. When someone approaches me asking for some, I instantly send up a prayer, "Lord, please let it be an easy one this time." I am willing to help whenever someone needs me, but now I take greater care with my choice of words. If you are still eager to offer advice, even when it is not asked for, you need to take a step backwards and think awhile. Realize that God will hold you accountable for the results.

Nowadays we have something else to worry about—the blogosphere. I know many who accomplish good things with their weblogs, but like anything else we do, we need to be careful. You never know who will read it, how young they might be, how inexperienced, how ungrounded, how fragile their souls. Unless you have a foolproof way of limiting access to it, your blog needs to be exactly the way God expects your life to be—a good example that will help and serve, not a poor example that may lead someone astray.

Your blog does not come with a built in "tone of voice." It does not come with a commentary that spells out exactly what you might mean when something clearly has more than one meaning. And realize this: what you perceive as the only possible interpretation of what you have said *isn't!* Your background, culture, and personal baggage make you unable to see in your words alternate interpretations which may be perfectly obvious to others.

I have learned all this the hard way. I do not have a blog, but the many words I have written in this venue and in class literature, and the many I have spoken in classes and speaking engagements have sometimes come back to haunt me, though I regularly pray over them, and have others read them first for any problems they might see. So take this advice, something for once I am happy to share if it will save you from some of the problems I have had—be careful out there. The world is a smaller place than ever before, and you never know who is listening.

Be not many of you teachers, my brethren, knowing that we shall receive heavier judgment.

James 3.1

April 25

Fish Story

Doesn't it seem to you that we are hearing less of those alien abduction stories these days? I enjoy science fiction—especially Orson Scott Card, *The X-Files,* and *Star Trek* in all its various forms—but the fact that these kidnapping tales no longer seem to be *en vogue*, goes a long way to proving that they are more fiction than science. I always wondered about those alien abductors anyway. They seem to practice some sort of "catch and release" program. Is it because they are concerned with the ecology of *Homo sapiens* on the planet *Terra*, or are they just having trouble finding a specimen worth keeping? Maybe we no longer hear these stories because they have just given up on us.

What about you? What about me? Would we be a good catch for some E.T.'s fishing expedition? What sort of bait would it take? Seems to me that the cheaper and more primitive the bait, the dumber the fish. This space traveler would want a fish so smart he would really have to work at it to catch him, wouldn't he? He would want a healthy specimen with no diseases or rare abnormalities. Maybe that's why they stay away from me.

We could go all sorts of directions with this analogy. For example, what sort of bait does it take for Satan to snare you—a cheap, obviously rubber worm, or an expensive, artfully made lure for a really smart fish?

But there is another application I find a lot scarier and more motivating. Does God have a "catch and release" program? I think so, though not like that of the U.S. Fish and Wildlife Service. Size doesn't matter to God, nor does health, wealth, status, or any other physical or economic characteristic. But if we start flip-flopping in God's hands, desperately trying to get back into the waters of sin, He *will* let us go. Yes, we have the promise, "No one is able to snatch them out of the Father's hand" (John 10.29), but that does not preclude God opening His hand so we can walk right out of it if we so choose. Too many scriptures talk about falling away for me to think I have no choice in the matter.

So my prayer every day is that God will be patient with me as a child who sometimes rebels against his parents' rules simply because he does not have the experience and wisdom to see the big picture; that He will chasten my flip-flopping until I finally submit to Him who knows what is best; and that He will never throw me back. Even Jesus used as an analogy for conversion "fishing for men." I don't want to be "the one that got away."

Love not the world, neither the things that are in the world. If any one loves the world, the love of the Father is not in him. For all that is in the world, the lust of the flesh and the lust of the eyes and the vainglory of life, is not of the Father but of the world. And the world passes away and the lusts thereof, but he who does the will of God abides forever.

1 John 2.15–17

Born and Bred

We had never heard of Australian Cattle Dogs until a neighbor gave us a puppy nearly eight years ago. We were so happy with Magdi, we got another one, Chloe, who has just had her first birthday. This breed is one of the newest in existence. As you might guess, they originated in Australia and have wild dingo, Welsh heeler, Australian kelpie, Dalmatian, smooth collie, and bull terrier in their bloodlines. The breed standard was finally set and approved in 1903. That means they will breed true both physically and temperamentally, which is what makes a breed a breed.

What exactly are they bred to do? Herd cattle, of course. They do this by nipping at the cattle's heels, and thus their other name, heelers. As the breed was being developed this caused a few problems. Some mixes made dogs that did not just nip, but bit down and wouldn't let go. Others nipped, but then just stood there and had their heads kicked in by the cattle's hooves. Finally they got the combination that produced a dog smart enough to nip and duck!

Our dogs do their best to herd, in spite of the fact that we have no cows. Magdi started trying to herd the two of us when she was just a few months old. As we walked around the property, she would cut across in front of us trying to turn us in the direction she wanted us to go. We had to be careful not to trip over her. Then whenever we stood still she would lie across our feet so we couldn't go anywhere. Chloe tries to herd Magdi. She nips at her heels all the time until Magdi gets her fill of it and snaps at her. The two of them chase any vehicle that comes down the drive, nipping at its "heels," the back tires. And together they try to herd squirrels. Whenever a squirrel runs up a tree, they are truly mystified—this is *not* the way it is supposed to work.

You know what we are "born and bred" to do? Worship God. He has set eternity in our hearts (Ecc 3.11); he has made his existence obvious through his creation (Psa 19.1–6; Rom 1.19–20). As the writer of Ecclesiastes concluded, "Fear God and keep his commandments for this is the whole of man" (12.13). The fact that people ignore all this and refuse to worship just shows that they are blind, rebellious fools (Jer 5.21–29).

Australian cattle dogs are not house dogs. They are not even yard dogs in today's version of a backyard that takes about 15 minutes to mow. These animals *need* to run. They need property and owners who exercise them more than a walk in the park every day. They are bred for daily prolonged activity. They are also bred to be fiercely loyal to and protective of their masters *for life*—they cannot be adopted by a new family once they have reached adulthood. Their loyalty will always be to their first family. If you take away their place to run and the masters they love, they will be miserable.

Have you noticed how miserable people seem today? Have you seen the perpetual anger that shows itself in road rage, domestic violence, and even the verbal abuse of waitresses and clerks in restaurants and stores? Have you seen how crime is not only growing but blamed on anyone and everyone who had anything to do with the criminal? People simply are not doing what they were "born and bred" to do—serve God and each other. Haven't we seen enough insanely wealthy people satisfying their every desire who are still miserable? When will we ever catch on?

They say that an Australian cattle dog is one of the most intelligent breeds there is, "capable of making decisions regarding himself, his owner and family, his job, and his home territory," according to the American Kennel Club. Sounds to me like they might be smarter than most humans.

> *But ask now the beasts and they shall teach you; and the birds of the heavens, and they shall tell you; or speak to the earth, and it shall teach you; and the fishes of the sea shall declare unto you. Who among all these does not know that the hand of the Lord has done this? In his hand is the life of every living thing and the breath of all mankind.*
>
> Job 12.7–10

Lost in the Woods

About ten years ago, we were camping in a Georgia State Park, one of our favorites actually, private sites, modern bathhouses, beautiful scenery, and great hiking trails. Ah yes, the hiking trails....

We decided one day to do the big trail—up a mountain and back down, seven miles total. So we cooked a hearty breakfast of pancakes, sausage, and coffee, and took off after cleaning up and securing everything against the elements and the wild animals, about 10:00 AM. We carried water and some snacks, and the park map. I am the navigator in the family, and usually the only one with a decent sense of direction. We expected to be back in time for an early supper, about 4:00 PM. With time to build a cook fire, we would be eating by 5:00, and ready for it.

We made the top of the mountain about 1:00, took a few minutes to enjoy the view, eat an apple and a handful of peanuts, then started down the other side. The grade was steep, and we were soon following a trail of switchbacks, but sure we were still on the right path because of the red blazes the park had so thoughtfully sprayed on the trees every so often, and because every turn matched the map. Keith, the one who is always looking for an easier way, looked down the hill to our left and saw yet another switchback. "So let's just take the shortcut down," he said.

Having grown up on the side of a mountain in the Ozarks, he is much surer footed than this flatlander, but he assured me that I could hold on to his shoulders and he would lead the way down safely, and possibly save us a couple hundred yards. So I agreed and willingly followed. We must have cut down through half a dozen switchbacks before the path finally leveled out.

We walked on, and came to a fork in the road that was not on the map. Hmmm. This time he trusted me and my sense of direction, and off we went toward what I knew was south, and thus had to be the right way. A little further on there was another unmapped fork so we took the same direction. And then another, and another. Somehow this did not seem right, and about then I realized that I had not seen a red blaze in a long time. About 4:30 we came to the end of the road—literally. Beyond it lay a fifty foot drop to a creek running full and loud.

Obviously, we had missed something somewhere, but I knew we had not gone the wrong overall direction—we had just wound up on the wrong path. We tried retracing our trail, but going at it backwards through the many forks we had taken, confused even me. We were about resigned to spending the night in the woods. I was exhausted, it was late, and getting colder by the minute. The sweater I had taken off and tied around my waist due to the heat of exercise would not do me much good when the nighttime temperatures hit the 40s. I was determined not to panic, though. I figured the last thing Keith needed was a hysterical woman on his hands. Tomorrow we would get out—somehow.

Finally, he told me to sit and wait while he checked another fork in the road. I didn't tell him that it scared me to death—with his lousy sense of direction it might easily be the last time I ever saw him. But not ten minutes later he came running back. "I found power lines," he said. "They have to lead somewhere."

So we followed them, and about 30 minutes later came out on a gravel road. We followed the lines further and came to a house. Keith knocked on the door and explained our situation. The man was on his way to work the night shift at a local factory and would take us back to camp, "about fifteen miles from here," he added. "You're the second couple in the last month to come out of those woods lost."

We got back to camp at nearly 7:00, exhausted and relieved, and ready to eat, shower, and hit the sleeping bags. The next morning we *drove* to the top of the mountain, then checked out the trail going down, careful to stay on it, watch for blazes, and look at the map. We were sure the park was at fault. But no, at the end of the third or fourth switchback the trail and blazes led straight ahead and down the other side of the mountain. When we had left the trail and cut through those switchbacks to what *looked* like the same trail, we had missed that and had wound up on a mountain bike trail, as yet unfinished, unmapped, and "un-blazed" by the color-coded spray paint. The map was correct; we just did not follow it. At that point we were not ready for another seven mile hike, but the next year we went back to that park and followed the trail carefully the whole way. We got back about 4:30 and never once got lost *because we stayed on the trail and followed the map!*

This one is easy, isn't it? God has given us a map. It does not matter what things may *look* like—*stay on the trail; follow the map!* You may see a trail to the side that seems like the same one. Don't take a shortcut that leads you from what you know is right. If it is the same trail, you will get there eventually. If it is not, you may never find your way back. Always look for the blazes that the faithful who went ahead of you painted for you to follow. You may think you have a great sense of direction—but if you get off track, that won't keep you from getting lost. Or *being* lost, which is what we are all trying to avoid.

Not only has God given you a map, He is out there Himself looking for you. Don't be proud; take advantage of the offer and follow His lead. You will always make it home, no matter how far off the trail you have gotten. The Trailblazer knows the way.

I will seek that which was lost, and will bring back that which was driven away, and will bind that which was broken, and will strengthen that which was sick. …For the Son of Man came to seek and to save that which was lost.

Ezekiel 34.16; Luke 19.10

April 28

This Won't Hurt A Bit

Uh-huh. Sure. I have heard that way too many times in the last few weeks. As much as I like and trust my doctor, he might as well ditch that line. I automatically cringe when I hear it. What follows almost invariably does hurt, at least "a bit," and often more.

What would you expect when they insert six inch sticks halfway into the top of your eye socket and mash all along the top of your eyeball trying to reposition things *inside* your eye? Or when they insert a syringe into the front of your eye and pump in a gel that makes eye pressure increase by 50 percent in just a second or two? Or when they put a needle deep into your eye to ream out a blocked shunt? Or when they laser an eye the size of a marble over 300 times, leaving black burn marks that last for months? And all of this happens while you are awake, with only a couple of numbing drops to deaden the surface of your eye, which also has a fresh surgery incision, and a raw cornea the resident describes as "road rash of the eye."

Sometimes I would like to watch my doctors undergo all of these things, then tell me it doesn't hurt, not even "a bit." I think every patient going through any sort of procedure has those daydreams, especially when they hear, "This won't hurt a bit."

And isn't that why our Savior and High Priest is so precious to us? He does know that life can hurt, that Satan is a frighteningly strong power, that it is not easy to endure this world's sorrows. "Since then the children are sharers in flesh and blood, he also himself in like manner partook of the same, that through death he might bring to naught him that had the power of death, that is, the devil; and might deliver all them who through fear of death were all their lifetime subject to bondage. For truly not to angels does he give help, but he gives help to the seed of Abraham. Wherefore it behooved him in all things to be made like unto his brethren that he might become a merciful and faithful high priest in things pertaining to God, to make propitiation for the sins of the people. For in that he himself has suffered being tempted, *he is able to succor those that are tempted*" (Heb 2.14–18).

So when He says it won't hurt, we know it won't. When He says we can overcome, we know we can. When He says the struggle is worth it, we know it is. Not only has He been through it Himself, but He will go through it again with us.

Hallelujah! What a Savior!

For we have not a high priest who cannot be touched with the feeling of our infirmities, but one who has been in all points tempted like we are, yet without sin. Let us therefore draw near with boldness to the throne of grace, that we may receive mercy, and may find grace to help us in time of need.

Hebrews 4.15–16

Hard Work

Lucas has been transferred and he says the attitude of his workers in this new store is remarkably different from those in his old one. They actually understand the concept of earning a paycheck. In the old store the workers seemed to think that merely showing up not more than a couple minutes late was sufficient to earn their living. They could stand in the halls and talk all they wanted as long as they were there doing it between the start and end of their shifts. Actually working was above and beyond and should earn them a hefty raise every six months.

I am afraid some people who call themselves Christians have the same misunderstanding. They think their "shift" is Sunday morning from 9:00 to noon, and all they have to do is sit in a comfortable seat in an air conditioned building and that should be enough to get them to Heaven, in fact, that should "earn" them Heaven. I mean, what more could God possibly expect than for them to give up a good-sized chunk of their weekends?

They are so mistaken. God expects hard work. Jesus set the example of hard work. He rose early in the morning (Mark 1.35); he often worked through meals (John 4.31–34); he was always looking to the next village, the next person to save (Mark 1.38–39). Finally he was able to say, "I glorified You on the earth, having accomplished the work which You have given me to do" (John 17.4). Do we really think God will expect any less of us?

Paul tells us we should "work heartily [for our masters on earth] as unto the Lord" (Col 3.23), which presupposes that we are actually working hard for the Lord, and need to be told to work that hard for our "masters" as well. Our shift for the Lord begins the day we commit ourselves to Him. It doesn't end until we end.

Paul reminds us to "Give diligence to present yourself approved unto God," (2 Tim 2.15). Diligence means you keep working even if the work is long, difficult, tedious or unpleasant. You cannot take a break; you cannot call in sick; you cannot stop for any reason short of death, and still you have not earned your paycheck. And be glad of that, "For the wages of sin is death, but the free gift of God is eternal life in Christ Jesus our Lord" (Rom 6.23). You really don't want the paycheck you have earned.

And exercise thyself unto godliness: for bodily exercise is profitable for a little; but godliness is profitable for all things, having promise of the life which now is, and of that which is to come. Faithful is the saying, and worthy of all acceptation. For to this end we labor and strive, because we have our hope set on the living God, who is the Savior of all men, especially of them that believe.

1 Timothy 4.7–10

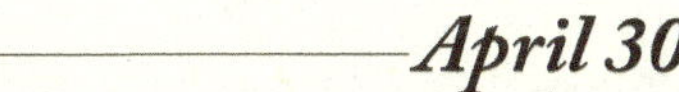

The Proper Process of Incubation

I have started a new study habit, something Keith came up with when he first started preaching full time. He had seen too many of his young preaching brothers be led off the deep end by spending more time in commentaries than in the Word. Every day he read one hour in the Old Testament and one hour in the New. On Sunday mornings he rose early enough to read through the epistles to Timothy and Titus—Paul's instructions to young evangelists—before stepping into the pulpit to "speak as the oracle of God." All this in addition to his regular studies for classes, sermons, and in-home Bible studies with members and non-members alike. All in all he spent nearly 40 hours a week with the Word of God—then he got on with what congregations *think* is a preacher's job.

He had another habit as well, and this is the one I am trying to develop. The book of Proverbs has 31 chapters, a very handy number when you think about it. Seven months of the year have 31 days, and all but one of the others have 30. Whatever day of the month it is, that is the chapter in Proverbs I read. I will get through the entire book seven times in a year, and most of it 12 times. In shorter months I could double up on those ending chapters, but honestly, after a couple dozen proverbs my brain is like an old wet sponge—it gets saturated much too easily. The second chapter's worth just seeps out into a stagnant pool around me. Besides I have studied chapter 31 in depth so many times, reading it every other month or so is enough to renew my interest.

Speaking of proverbs, you probably grew up hearing the old saws like I did, and despite the fact that you rolled your eyes at them like most young people did, you have found yourself repeating them—they *are* true after all. When I was a child someone came up with the fun notion to rephrase them using ten dollar words, leaving everyone to guess the original adage. The only one I can remember is "Never calculate the juvenile poultry before the proper process of incubation has fully materialized." It's easy enough now, but it took a few minutes for a ten year old to come up with the solution. I don't know why someone did this, but for a few minutes, people were once again pondering those wise sayings, and I know that I learned more of them than I would have otherwise.

I have always been amazed by people who can come up with quotes to suit any situation—Shakespeare, poetry, the works of the great philosophers. It would be so much more beneficial to quote the words of God.

Tomorrow is the first day of a thirty-one day month, so why not start this habit with me? I read through the chapter slowly twice, once in my good old 1901 ASV, then in the NIV. I make note of one or two proverbs that really strike me at the time. You see, reading is not enough. You have to go through "the proper process of incubation" for the effects of your study to "fully materialize." You may find some of these materializations in future articles.

Come on. This will be easy. Even if you backslide you can pick it up and start again at any time, even in the middle of the book since there is no plot to worry about. And as long as you have a calendar you won't even need a bookmark.

The proverbs of Solomon, the son of David, the king of Israel: to know wisdom and instruction; to discern the words of understanding; to receive instruction in wise dealing, in righteousness, in justice, and in equity; to give prudence to the simple, to the young man knowledge and discretion; that the wise man may hear, and increase in learning; and that the man of understanding may attain unto sound counsels; to understand a proverb and a figure, the words of the wise and their dark sayings.

Proverbs 1.1–6

May 1

Tick-Tock

I became a mother for the first time on this day in 1977. It seems only yesterday that two hours after the high forceps delivery of a sunny side up (nurse talk for a posterior birth) nine pound three-and-a-half ounce, twenty-two inch boy that the nurse came in, slapped my thigh and said, "Time for a shower!"

"Are you nuts?" I remember asking, not too politely.

Even as big a bundle as he was, he was still too small for those newborn clothes. They swallowed him whole, but he grew into them quickly. Now he is bigger than I am and could carry me around.

Jesus said we need to become "as little children," and many suggestions have been made about what He was referring to, from humility, to total dependence, to being easy to forgive. But when I thought of my son's birthday, it struck me that there is one thing that children do far better than anyone else. In fact, they are made for it—*they grow, and they grow quickly!*

Not too long ago in a women's Bible study, one sister suggested that the reason we don't learn too well, the reason we resist deep study and even complain if a class gets past the things we already know is that we think we have arrived. We are already mature in Christ and there is nothing new to learn. Never mind that we just heard something new and didn't know it—it must not be true if we never heard it before! And it's asking too much for us to actually act like a student and work at learning—reading scriptures, doing research, filling out workbooks.

I have been blessed beyond measure with the classes I have taught. The women in them never complain about the difficult lessons, the number of hours they take and the old chestnuts I debunk—*there is no gate called the Needle's Eye!* They eat up everything I give them, write as fast as their fingers can fly, and have even learned to ask me, "How do you know that?" Good for them!

Do you remember when Paul and Barnabas passed back through the churches of their first journey a second time, appointing elders in every church (Acts 14.21–23)? Those men had only been Christians for about a year. Yet Paul told Timothy the elder should not be a novice (1 Tim 3.6). Would we ever appoint a man to be an elder after only a year? So what's the difference today? Granted they had miraculous gifts back then, but having them and being wise enough to use them properly are two different things—as the Corinthians show us so well; and Paul tells us that having the completed word of God is far superior to spiritual gifts anyway (1 Cor 12.31; 13.8–12). The difference is *they grew,* evidently as fast as children do, while we sit back and complain about the extra effort involved.

If I were told that I had to pass a certain course to keep my job, do you think I would study hard? Of course I would. If I let my driver's license expire and had to retake the test, would I study hard, even though I probably know most of what is in that manual? Yes. I would not want to even take a chance on failing the test. So where are my priorities?

I don't know how much time we have to learn and grow, but God says there is a time for each of us: "For when *by reason of time* you ought to be teachers you have reason again that one should teach you." This is a pass/fail test. What if my time allotment is already past? I'm not taking the chance. How about you?

Of whom we have many things to say, hard of interpretation, seeing you have become dull of hearing. For when by reason of the time you ought to be teachers, you have need again that someone teach you the rudiments of the first principles of the oracles of God, and have become such as need milk, and not of solid food. For everyone who partakes of milk is without experience of the word of righteousness, for he is a baby. But solid food is for full grown men, those who by reason of use have their senses exercised to discern good and evil.

Hebrews 5.11–14

May 2

Growing Basil

I have had a terrible time with my basil this year. It will not grow. It just sits there exactly the same height and with the same number of leaves, day after day. Usually, even though I use it a lot, it becomes a shrub, and I must cut four cups at a time making pesto every couple of weeks to keep up with it. This year I had to ration it in things like my orzo salad with grape tomatoes, green onions, pine nuts, feta, and basil, and the cherry tomato salad with basil, fresh mozzarella, garlic, and balsamic vinegar. Pesto was not even in the forecast, and my late summer marinara may be blander than it has ever been before.

Basil is one of the easiest herbs to grow. Being Mediterranean, it can take the Florida heat and humidity. It may wilt on a hot summer afternoon, but recovers quickly in the evening and looks like new the next morning. It can handle the worst of circumstances. It doesn't even have its own particular pest like parsley has parsley worms. So what is the problem this year? We watered it during the dry weather and fertilized it as usual. I have no idea what happened. Maybe I took it for granted that it was a strong plant needing no special care.

Strong Christians can be like that. People get so used to them being strong that no one checks on them, no one asks how things are going, no one gives them an encouraging word—that's what *they* are supposed to do.

When was the last time you patted an elder on the back and thanked him for his work, maybe even apologized for any trouble or worry you might have caused him? When was the last time you sent him a note or a card of appreciation? How about his wife? She must not only deal with some of the same problems he does, but watch the effect of it all on him—distress etching lines in his face, frustration turning his hair gray a bit too early, his smile all but disappearing over the sorrow for lost souls.

How about the preacher? Even people who don't mean anything by it can say hurtful things, can judge harshly, and can expect the impossible—perfection. Preachers and their wives must watch their children grow up too early as they see their father mistreated over and over, everywhere they go. It's a·wonder any of them stay faithful.

The worst thing you can do to a strong Christian is tell him or her that you know he or she is strong and can take anything. Sometimes they can't. Sometimes it just gets to be too much, and instead of having brethren who will pull them out of the abyss, they must climb out all by themselves because no one thinks they need any help.

Find a strong Christian today and do them a favor—forget they are strong. Treat them as if they needed a boost and then give them one. They will appreciate it more than you can imagine.

> *[And Jehovah said] Charge Joshua and* ***encourage him and strengthen him****, for he shall go over before this people and he shall cause them to inherit this land which you shall see.*
>
> *Wherefore brethren, exhort one another and build each other up, even as you also do. But we beseech you brethren, know* ***those who labor among you****, and are over you in the Lord, and who admonish you.* ***to esteem them highly in love for their work's sake****.*
>
> *[Paul said,] Finally brethren,* ***pray for us****.*
>
> Deuteronomy 3.28; 1 Thessalonians 5.11–13; 2 Thessalonians 3.1

May 3

Shedding

As winter turned to spring this year, we noticed all the usual signs. The azaleas spilled white, red, and all shades of pink and purple blooms under every live oak in sight. The dogwoods made white spotlights in the forests when a sunbeam broke through the gloom. The robins made brief rest stops on their return migration north, and hummingbirds buzzed our feeder, empty since last October, letting us know they were back and ready to be fed. Oak pollen sifted down in a yellow powder all over the car. The temperature and humidity rose as did the gnats, flies, and mosquitoes out of the swamps and bogs. And Chloe started shedding.

Magdi has always shed individual hairs as she rolls in the grass, as she scratches, as we pet or brush her. But Chloe shed in clumps. Whenever she rose, she left behind wads of red fur on the grass or carport, reminding me of the floor of a beauty salon after a haircut. Every time we scratched her head, the clumps stuck to our hands and clothes, or floated off with the breeze as if we had blown red dandelion puffs. Before long she looked like an old sofa with large threadbare patches. Eventually all her winter coat fell off—everything except a two inch fringe running down her hind legs. Now she looks like a canine cowgirl wearing chaps.

But you know what? She is still Chloe, our one-year-old Australian cattle dog. She still loves to eat. She still nips at Magdi's heels. She still chases butterflies and grasshoppers, and plays tug-o-war with ropes and rags. She still has a sweet little face that melts my heart.

When we become Christians, Paul tells us we should lay aside the old self (Eph 4.22), crucify ourselves (Gal 2.20), and become new creatures (2 Cor 5.17). Too many times we do what Chloe did, shed the outer self only. The inside stays the same. We still consider ourselves before others, we still give in to every temptation, we still excuse our poor behavior instead of grabbing hold of the power of Christ to really change who we are. We are still exactly the same person; we just have a new haircut.

Changing is hard—it does not happen overnight. But how many of us can examine ourselves honestly today and see a change from that day we claimed to make a commitment? How long has it been? Even one year should show a significant change for the better, and how many of us have 20, 30, 40 years or more under our belts and still make the same mistakes on a regular basis?

Don't just sweep some hair off the floor today. If you haven't already, start making a real change in yourself.

I beseech you therefore brethren, by the mercies of God, to present your bodies a living sacrifice, holy, acceptable to God, which is your spiritual worship. And be not fashioned according to this world, but be transformed by the renewing of your mind, that you may prove what is the good and acceptable and perfect will of God.

Romans 12.1–2

May 4

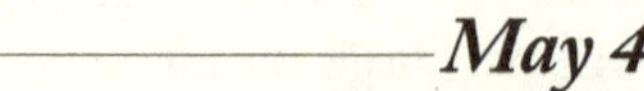

Best Laid Plans

We had another hawk nest this past spring, this one in the pine tree on the northeast corner. We nearly missed it since we seldom go to that side of the property, but suddenly one day, we saw activity in a big ball of leaves, twigs, and moss, and, picking up the binoculars, realized that two baby hawks sat in the nest with wide open mouths, waiting for Mama and Daddy to bring dinner.

We watched them awhile every day, and I spoke to them often enough that they began to recognize my voice and cried when I left. Within a few weeks their white down was gone and they were almost, but not quite ready to fly.

One afternoon I was sitting by the window when lightning struck so close I nearly came up out of the chair. A storm soon followed, and I weathered it with a crossword puzzle and a magnifying glass.

After supper Keith and I went on our regular evening stroll around the place, stopping first by the pine to check on the babies, more like teenagers by then. "Oh no," he said, and after a few more steps I saw it too—a streak of white all the way down the pine. It was the nest tree that had been struck. He put the binoculars to his eyes and said he saw no movement in the nest at all. Then, as he was making his way around the tree to try to catch it from all angles, he came upon them. Both babies had been thrown from the nest to the ground. One was dead, a mangled, broken mass of feathers. The smaller of the two was standing about eight feet away, soaking wet and pitiful looking. Mama perched on a branch across the fence watching. There was no way she could carry a baby this big in her talons back to the nest to feed and tend.

What to do? First, we had to get it up off the ground before Magdi and Chloe saw it. Keith picked up the scared baby, a double handful of feathers with a head as big as my fist. It didn't struggle at all, shell-shocked, I suppose, so we talked to it soothingly as we carried it to the back of the truck and put him inside the camper top. Then, after batting around a few ideas, Keith found an old milk crate, filled it with leaves and moss, and climbed the oak tree nearest the pine that had low enough branches for him to get up into after the ladder steps ran out. He nailed it as high as he could reach.

Meanwhile I went looking for bird food, raw meat in this case, and the only thing I had that was not frozen solid was cubed steak I had bought on sale that morning—still, it was expensive bird food. I put it in the microwave just long enough to get the chill off, but not to cook it. When I dropped a small chunk in the truck by the bird, all he did was look at it for a few seconds. Then his eyes turned to me and never left me, so I kept on talking to him to try to keep him calm.

Keith managed to get up the ladder with him somehow, as I stood on the bottom rung to keep it steady for his one-handed grip. He set the big baby in the box and then tried hand-feeding it. That did it! The hawk knew it was food after that (and nearly had human finger as dessert), so we put more in the homemade nest. We heard Mama again, as she flew back around the old pine, calling for her baby, so we left as quickly as possible.

Now it was time to wait. Would she find him and accept him and feed him again, or had we sealed his fate by handling him? There was no way to know. We had done our best to save him and the rest was up to him and his mother.

The next morning, we stepped outside early and looked toward the tree. Mama must have heard us, for she flew then, but we were overjoyed to see that she had flown from the make-shift nest in the oak tree where she had indeed found her baby. Three days later he flew on his own.

We wonder sometimes how much that bird understood what had happened to it. Why did it have to be his tree that was struck and his brother or sister who was killed? Why did he wind up in a plastic box instead of his cozy, parent-built nest? This is not the way it is supposed to be with hawks!

And we wonder the same things when our life plans are suddenly altered through circumstances we had never even considered—accident, illness, career changes, death of a spouse at a young age. This is not the way we had planned it, this is not what we had wanted for our lives.

I had a dear friend who lived here for several years. This is not where she expected to be, but her husband was killed in a work-related accident, and her only child died suddenly and unexpectedly at a young age. None of this was what she had planned, yet through it all she maintained a level of faith I have yet to reach, and an attitude I want to imitate for the rest of my life.

"I don't understand why God put me here," she once said.

"Charlotte," I told her, "He put you here for me." I can name half a dozen others who feel the same way. Every day, remembering her example helps me cope with the changes that have come my way in the past five years.

Don't ever think that because your plans went awry that you have been forsaken by God. It could very well be that He put you where He did for a reason you may never truly understand, just like that hawk was undoubtedly mystified by what happened to him. But you have the ability to accept your circumstances and make the most of them. God puts you where He wants you for a reason, and giving up hope and ceasing to serve is *not* the solution.

Trust God. Keep serving your neighbors in any way you can, even if it is just to smile and set an example of endurance and peace. Refuse to make excuses for yourself, as Satan would have you do. So your plans were changed? They should not have been that important to you anyway—Christians have far better plans for the future than anything anyone can think up in this life, in this place. Believe it.

Out of my distress I called upon Jehovah: Jehovah answered me and set me in a large place. Jehovah is on my side; I will not fear: What can man do unto me?

Psalm 118.5–6

May 5

Right of Way

Paul wrote a scathing letter to the Corinthian brothers and sisters. This was a church with so many problems many might have refused to call them "sound" nowadays. The root of every problem they had could probably be summed up as "immaturity." Paul, in fact, calls them babes. You know what he would have said in our language? "I could not speak to you as spiritual adults because you are a bunch of big babies!" (1 Cor 3.1).

In chapter six these immature people were taking each other to court. Paul tells them that this only hurts the church's reputation in the world. "What?" he says. "Don't you have any one wise enough to help you settle your disputes? You are doing harm to the church and ought to be willing to suffer wrong instead of making God's kingdom look bad" (my paraphrase).

I don't think that only applies to legal matters. This was recorded for us, and if we are as smart as we think we are, we ought to be able to apply it in all sorts of situations. The problem is, we are Americans, and proud of it. We have rights! And we often insist on those rights, regardless of how it might make others view the body of which we claim to be a part.

And then there are the situations that really have nothing to do with "rights," just convenience or "feelings." I love the insurance commercial that says, "The drivers on the road are *people*. So treat them like they are in your home, not in your way." I wonder if the ad man who came up with that is a Christian. He sounds more like one than some I know who are.

So the next time the person ahead of you in the check-out line takes a long time writing a check, or when the person in the car ahead of you is not as brave as you are about making that left turn across traffic, "take wrong" and "be defrauded" of a few minutes in your day instead of letting him know how much he exasperates you.

What if either of those people walk into services Sunday morning, looking for the truth of God's Word and recognizes you? Exactly how has your "looking out for your rights" affected their hearts? Do you think they are likely to be more or less receptive to the gospel?

What if, at a family gathering or a church potluck someone says something that you find insulting? "Take wrong" or "be defrauded" of your feelings for the sake of the others there, including children whose fun might be ruined when you cause a scene and walk off in a huff, or a visitor someone has brought to the potluck who might now have a bad opinion of the church. In all these cases, just like little children, we often see and care only how things affect us, and not how they will affect others.

If we cannot yield the right of way when it only affects our convenience, what makes us think we can when it is a matter of legal rights? If we cannot sacrifice a few precious feelings, we have already failed the test of whether we would sacrifice our lives. "He who is faithful in little is faithful in much; he who is unfaithful in little, is unfaithful in much" (Luke 16.10).

It takes maturity to yield, especially when you are in the right, especially when the other person is not looking out for your good, especially when you have to suffer wrong, or even just inconvenience, to do so. It also takes maturity to remember this in the heat of the moment. Would Paul call us a bunch of big babies, too?

> *I say this to your shame. Can it be that there is no one among you wise enough to settle a dispute between the brothers, but brother goes to law against brother, and that before unbelievers? To have lawsuits at all with one another is already a defeat for you. Why not rather suffer wrong? Why not rather be defrauded? But you yourselves [by this behavior] wrong and defraud—even your own brothers.*
>
> 1 Corinthians 6.5–8

May 6

Dollars to Doughnuts

My floor is finished. I am thrilled to have my house back to myself after three weeks of sharing it with the installer. He was a nice guy. My dogs loved him. He brought them stale doughnuts every morning.

The morning after he finished I stepped outside to an empty carport and the sound of silence where there should have been the click of claws and pad of paws on concrete, rushing to greet me. I started up the drive and there they were—sitting next to the gate, gazing down the road, obviously pining for the man and his doughnuts.

I called them back. Chloe came more or less eagerly, but Magdi stopped every ten feet or so and looked over her shoulder toward the gate. I had to call and clap my hands every so often to keep her coming my way.

This has happened for several mornings now. I may pet her, and do it often, but I don't give her doughnuts. She has sold her soul to a new master just for a doughnut!

What do we sell ours for? We may even think we have not. Magdi still lives on our property. She still comes when we call. She still allows us to medicate and feed her the healthy stuff, but all the time she is looking over her shoulder toward the gate, yearning for a doughnut.

Are we still showing up at the right places, saying the right things, even acting the right way most of the time, but secretly looking over our shoulders, longing for something else? We needn't even bother trying. "No man having put his hand to the plow and looking back is fit for the kingdom of God; remember Lot's wife" (Luke 9.62; 17.32).

I cannot explain to the dogs that if they lived on a steady diet of doughnuts they would actually die of malnutrition, not to mention the woes that come with obesity. They just know that a nice man gave them something that tasted good.

We should be smarter than a couple of dogs. We should have the sense to know that the things we sell our souls for are not worth the end result—not wealth, not power, not social acceptance, not a physical high that only lasts a moment, not the satisfaction that comes with vengeance or simply putting someone in his place.

Whatever it is we are selling ourselves for, however smart it may appear to the world, however good it may feel, it might as well be doughnuts.

> *Then Jesus said to his disciples, If any will come after me, let him deny himself and take up his cross and follow me. For whoever will save his life shall lose it, and whoever will lose his life for my sake shall find it. For what is a man profited if he shall gain the whole world and lose his own soul? Or what shall a man give in exchange for his soul?*
>
> Matthew 16.24–26

May 7

Cleaning House

Surely I am not the only one who has done this.

You find out that you have company coming in about an hour and the house is a wreck. You were tired, so you left the coffee and dessert dishes in the sink instead of whipping up another sink full of suds at 10:00 the night before, and have only added to them with the breakfast dishes. You did the laundry yesterday, but there were so many errands to run, they are sitting in the basket or hanging from hangers on every doorknob available so the wrinkles will fall out. The garden is coming in so you have left the weekly tub scrubbing, vacuuming, and dusting until some day soon when you are no longer standing in a hot, steamy kitchen for ten hours a day, and the canning supplies litter the kitchen counters, floors, and even the family room sofa. And did anyone make his bed this morning? If they are all male, probably not!

So what do you do? I usually grab another laundry basket and rush through the house throwing everything that is out of place in it, then put it on the guest room bed and shut the door. Spray some bleach solution (that I always have mixed and ready to use) into the showers, as much for the clean smell as anything else, and pull the shower curtains shut. Run a cloth over everything big and obvious (like the grand piano in the living room), and hope no one over six feet tall stands by the top shelves and the refrigerator. Light every good smelling candle in the house and hope that's enough to cover any other "not quite clean" house smell. Run a sink full of soapy water and at least pile everything into it. With canning jars sitting around cooling, it will look like you've been hard at work (and you really have), and are in the midst of cleaning it up. At least you will get points for that!

I have probably fooled a lot of people that way, or else they were just polite. But when it comes to spiritual house cleaning, just getting the outside isn't enough. Oh, we might fool some people who don't really know us very well, but Jesus says "By their fruits you shall know them" (Matt 7.16), so eventually we will give ourselves away if our righteousness is only cosmetic. Just imagine how much God knows—*everything!* "The eyes of Jehovah are in every place, keeping watch upon the evil and the good" (Prov 15.3).

Cleaning the outside is not good enough for Jehovah. It only counts when we clean up our hearts. Then, funny thing, the outside takes care of itself.

> *Woe to you, scribes and Pharisees, hypocrites! For you clean the outside of the cup and of the platter, but within are full of extortion and excess. You blind Pharisees, first clean the inside of the cup and of the platter, that the outside may become clean also. Woe unto you, scribes and Pharisees, hypocrites! For you are like whitewashed sepulchers, which outwardly appear beautiful, but inwardly are full of dead men's bones and all uncleanness. Even so you also outwardly appear righteous unto men, but inwardly are full of hypocrisy and iniquity.*
>
> Matthew 23.25–28

May 8

Battle Scars

Has life left you a few mementos? For me it's silicone lenses, a capsular tension ring, a 50 micron ophthalmic shunt, a metal anchor in each heel, plus the usual stretch marks, wrinkles, gray hairs, numerous surgical scars, and quite a few missing parts. For Keith it's a plastic eye socket, five bullet wound scars, a few wrinkles (very few, dear), and a loss of hair. Our battle scars make our lives sound far more interesting than they actually are.

We live in a culture that wants to erase those marks of life at any cost. I still don't understand why anyone would want to get rid of laugh lines. Does she want people to think she has lived a miserable life? I remember a couple of little boys who were thrilled to death whenever they had a "booboo" to display. I suppose it all depends on how we got those "booboos." I am never quick to show off a bruise I got for being downright stupid.

Paul was proud to mention the scars he earned for the Lord, "Henceforth, let no man trouble me; for I bear branded on my body the marks of Jesus" (Gal 6.17).

What about spiritual battle scars? If we are fighting "the good fight," we ought to have quite a few. I wonder, though, if we have fallen into the trap of our culture. No scar is a good one because no fight is a good fight. Love everyone and accept everything they do. We might as well take the scissors to our Bibles.

If I don't have any spiritual scars, why not? Is it because I run from the fight, too ignorant of the Sword to do battle? Am I too concerned with the opinion of my neighbors to stand up for something unpopular? Is it because I give into temptation too easily? Satan only tempts those he has not caught. Maybe I am just a prisoner of war too cowardly to try to escape.

On the last day, we had better have a few battle scars to show the Lord. We enlisted in an army that fights all day every day. Deserters will not receive the reward.

But we have this treasure in jars of clay, to show that the surpassing power belongs to God and not to us. We are afflicted in every way, but not crushed; perplexed, but not driven to despair; persecuted, but not forsaken; struck down, but not destroyed; always carrying in the body the death of Jesus, so that the life of Jesus may also be manifested in our bodies. For we who live are always being given over to death for Jesus' sake, so that the life of Jesus also may be manifested in our mortal flesh.

2 Corinthians 4.7–11

May 9

Jasmine in the Breeze

Two years ago we planted a jasmine vine. I had always wanted one twining up a trellis by the side of my porch, but being married to a man with allergies made that impossible. That summer, though, he wanted to do anything and everything for me, at least the small things we could afford, so he bought me a jasmine vine. It is not by the porch—I wouldn't let him suffer just for my sake—so it is next to the drive about 75 feet away from the house.

He built one lollapalooza of a trellis out of a cow panel and an antenna mast. It stands about 15 feet in the air. In just two years that dark green vine has grown up and over the top and this time of year is covered with tiny, white blossoms. And the fragrance! When the wind is right, you can smell it 30 feet away. I would know it was there whether I could see it or not—which one day may be important.

I think I would like to be like a jasmine—vines trailing out everywhere, winding in and out of the squares of its "trellis," covered in beautiful blooms, and sending out a sweet smell that tells everyone it is there, even when they cannot otherwise tell. But when I look in "the mirror" I am a long way from that ideal, much pruning and fertilizing still to be done.

If I am going to effect others I need to involve myself with them, whether it is convenient or not. If I am to present a beautiful picture to them, I need to follow in the footsteps of my Savior, who served others to the ultimate degree. If I am to influence those who do not know me, I must influence those who do by an example of love, longsuffering, and faith that continues on even in the face of trials.

The only way to accomplish all of that is to constantly fill myself with His word, to talk with Him often, to make others the center of my life rather than myself, *to watch that tongue of mine!* I must give with no thought of reciprocity from others; give of myself, of my time, of my labor, of my care and consideration, regardless of what others may do.

Oh my, the more I look at this, the more I think I will never make it. But God has made a jasmine vine, a gift from a man who can hardly tolerate them due to the physical discomfort they cause him, yet who gave it nevertheless. That is my inspiration. Every time I walk past it, its sweet fragrance reminds me to pray for help and, in praying, have faith that I will receive.

> *I will heal their backsliding; I will love them freely, for my anger is turned away from them. I will be as the dew unto Israel; he shall blossom as the lily and cast forth his roots as Lebanon. His branches shall spread and his beauty shall be as the olive-tree, and his smell as Lebanon. They that dwell under his shadow shall return; they shall revive as the grain and blossom as the vine; the scent of it shall be as the wine of Lebanon...Who is wise that he may understand these things? Prudent that he may know them? For the ways of Jehovah are right, and the just shall walk in them; but transgressors shall fall therein.*
>
> Hosea 14.4–7, 9

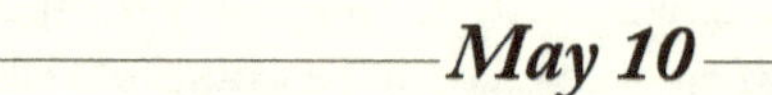

May 10

Bird Songs: Push-Button Music

Lucas bought me a bird book for Mother's Day last year. This was not your average Audubon Society coffee table slab. On the side of the book is a speaker, a push button and a tiny screen. Each page in the book pictures a North American songbird with the usual blurb about its range, habits, and call. Under the bird is a number. When you put the correct number on the screen then push the button, you will hear that particular bird, actual recordings taken by the ornithology lab at Cornell University.

I've heard the ugly squawk of blue jays all my life. It seems fitting for this thug of a bird which bullies smaller birds and steals nests. I'd been hearing a bird with a clear wooden whistle call for years. I was positive it was a cuckoo, based solely on the cuckoo clocks I have heard, but as soon as I checked the cuckoo's sound in my book, I knew I was mistaken. On a whim one day, I punched in the blue jay's number, wondering why in the world it was considered a songbird. Suddenly a wooden whistle came floating out of the speakers. This was a blue jay? This was the sound I had become so enamored with? It had never dawned on me that a bird could make more than one sound.

So blue jays were not the kindest birds in the forest. I loved hearing that loud, clear call of theirs, and the fact that a blue jay could make such a lovely sound was strangely uplifting. I knew I would miss it if suddenly it disappeared.

How many times do we let our judgment of people, especially people we disagree with or have dealt with in less than ideal circumstances, keep us from seeing anything good about them? How many times do we filter our views, not through the rose-colored glasses of kindness, but through a specialty lens we grind ourselves, one of malice that blocks out the good and magnifies the bad? Ounce for ounce, hummingbirds are among the most vicious creatures on earth, actually attempting to impale one another on those long, sword-like beaks as they fight over the feeders we humans put out, yet we ooh and aah over them. I really don't think that the people with whom I have personality conflicts are actually out to murder me, so why can't I see any of the pluses in their characters?

Isn't there a human blue jay in your life? Find that person today and take off the blinders. Do something kind; say something kind. Instead of pushing the button that releases a squawk, push the button that elicits beautiful music. Give him a chance to show his good side. Isn't that what you wish he would do for you?

The wicked one craves evil; his neighbor gets no mercy from him.

Love suffers long and is kind...does not behave itself unseemly, seeks not its own, is not provoked, does not keep track of evil...bears all things, believes all things, and hopes all things...love never fails.

Proverbs 21.10; 1 Corinthians 13.4–8a

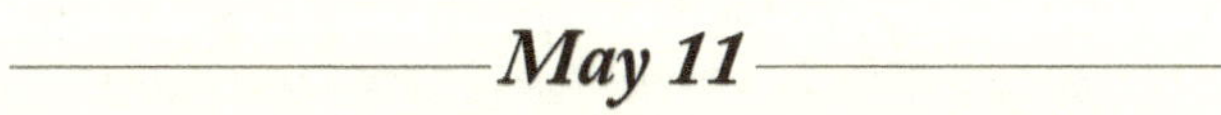

May 11

Bird Songs: The Invisible Owl

When Lucas first gave me the birdsong book, I knew there was one bird I wanted to look up immediately. For two years I had been hearing an owl every morning as I walked the trail around the property. I think I noticed because I was so surprised to discover that they hooted in the daytime too. But unlike the other large birds of prey I had seen, an eagle, an osprey, and the hawk, which still on occasion sits on a tree limb across the fence to talk with me, I had never seen this owl. I had him pictured though—a nearly two foot mottled brown bird with two ear tufts and large yellow eyes that see in the dark.

I found him in the book, a great horned owl, and quickly punched in his number. Imagine my surprise when his call was not quite right. So I checked all the other owls, a screech owl, snowy owl, barn owl, and finally one I had never heard of—a barred owl, slightly smaller, a bit more white streaked in his brown feathers with definite bars across his throat, and a large round head sporting no ear tufts at all. But his sound was unmistakable. This is what I had been listening to for two years, out in the woods beyond the creek. I've still never seen him, but I know he's there, and now I can picture him correctly.

I think as children we develop a mental picture of God from things we have been taught. Sometimes our pictures are mistaken, or at best, simplistic—God is, after all, not easy to explain to a child. As we grow up and learn to study on our own, as we deal with the circumstances of life and meditate on the two together, our picture of God should become clearer, developing into a rich depth of comprehension.

When we rely only on what we have been told and the shallowness of our youthful perceptions fails to mature, our faith may falter in times of trial. Suddenly we can no longer see a God who cares, a God who is powerful and whose plan goes far beyond this short, and to us, too important life. Regardless of the evidence, we fail to see Him there in times of trouble, and what should be visible to us more than others becomes invisible. If we are not careful we will become blind, totally unable to see Him ever again. "I can't believe in a God who would..." is a sign of stunted spiritual growth, *not* increased intellect.

Open your eyes. Examine your life through an overview of faith, not a miniscule sliver of circumstance. Look at the big picture—the evidence is there. I cannot see my owl, but I hear him hooting in the woods and believe. As sure as he is out there, God is too, working in your life through providence, speaking to you in His word, perhaps at a depth you have never been to before. Take the plunge and open your eyes.

Now the king of Syria was warring against Israel, and he took counsel with his servants saying in such and such a place shall you camp. And the man of God sent and told the king of Israel... and the king of Israel was saved not once but twice. And the heart of the king of Syria was troubled... and one of his servants said, Oh king, Elisha the prophet is telling the king of Israel the words that you speak, even in your bedchamber. And he said, Go and see where he is... and it was told him that he was in Dothan. Therefore he sent horses and chariots and a great host, and they came by night and surrounded the city. ...And Elisha's servant said, Alas my lord, what shall we do? And he answered, Fear not, for those who are with us are more than those who are with them. And Elisha prayed and said, Jehovah, I pray you, open his eyes that he may see. And Jehovah opened the eyes of the young man, and he saw, and behold the mountain was full of horses and chariots of fire round about Elisha.

2 Kings 6.8–17

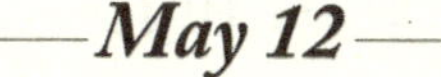

May 12

Bird Songs: The Mourning Dove

The past few mornings I have heard a dove off in the trees just north of the house. His call is a distinctive one, and obviously the reason for his name. He sounds so sad, like he is in mourning for someone he lost. I don't believe I have ever heard any other type of call from this particular bird or any other birdcall so sad.

Then this morning he landed on my feeder. I have seen doves from a distance. They like to stay close to the ground, and when they fly they have a distinctive sound in their "take-off." I know they are doves even though I cannot see them well.

When this one came to eat at our free breakfast bar, I was amused. He has the fattest breast of any bird I have seen yet, which I suppose explains why there is a dove season, and not a cardinal or blue jay or, certainly not, a titmouse season. But his head is tiny and round. He waddled down the feeder, taking his time to eat, then look around, then eat some more. Rather than mournful, this bird looks pretty happy, I thought, almost like a little feathered clown.

Isn't that the dichotomy of a Christian? We mourn for the state of the world, for the state of the people we care about in this world who have not found their way yet, or worse perhaps, those who had found it but lost it again. We mourn that our Savior had to suffer because of that, and we mourn yet more because of the part we played in that suffering. Yet for the same reason, we rejoice. Because of that suffering, we are free, we are saved, we have hope for what would otherwise be unattainable.

And because of that, when the griefs of life come our way, we still have joy, even while the tears run down our faces. Tomorrow our smiles will return. They are permanently etched there while the tears are only temporary; not just joy amid sorrows, but joy overcoming sorrows. Enough so that when others look our way, they will be surprised at how unaffected we are by the sadness around us, just like I was surprised by the jaunty little mourning dove.

Being therefore justified by faith, we have peace with God through our Lord Jesus Christ through whom also we have had our access by faith unto this grace wherein we stand, and we rejoice in hope of the glory of God. And not only so, but we also rejoice in our tribulations, knowing that tribulation works steadfastness, and steadfastness approvedness, and approvedness hope; and hope puts not to shame because the love of God has been shed abroad in our hearts through the Holy Spirit which was given unto us.

Romans 5.1–5

May 13

Lynchpins

"Lynchpin: 1) the pin inserted through an axletree to hold a wheel on; 2) something that serves to hold together the complex."

If the lynchpin is removed, the wheel falls off and the vehicle can longer move; it is useless. Paul tells us that resurrection is the lynchpin to Christianity.

"But if there is no resurrection of the dead, then not even Christ has been raised. And if Christ has not been raised, then our preaching is in vain and your faith is in vain. We are even found to be misrepresenting God, because we testified about God that he raised Christ, whom he did not raise if it is true that the dead are not raised. For if the dead are not raised, not even Christ has been raised. And if Christ has not been raised, your faith is futile and you are still in your sins. Then those also who have fallen asleep in Christ have perished. If in this life only we have hoped in Christ, we are of all people most to be pitied" (1 Cor 15.13–19).

I think we understand that. If Christ has not been raised from the dead, why should we care anything about how he tells us to live? His resurrection is the reason we believe in his Divinity, in his right to tell us how to live, and ultimately in the hope of our own resurrection. Our whole belief system stands or falls on the resurrection.

Paul said a few other things about Christ's death and resurrection in Romans 6: "Or are you ignorant that all we who were baptized into Christ Jesus were baptized into his death? We were buried therefore with him through baptism unto death: that like as Christ was raised from the dead through the glory of the Father, so we also might walk in newness of life. For if we have become united with him in the likeness of his death, we shall be also in the likeness of his resurrection; knowing this, that our old man was crucified with him, that the body of sin might be done away, that so we should no longer be in bondage to sin; for he who has died is justified from sin. But if we died with Christ, we believe that we shall also live with him" (Rom 6.3–8).

Did you catch that? If we were united with him in the likeness of his death, we should also be united with him in the likeness of his resurrection. That new life to which we are resurrected is not the one in the future, but the one we live now, no longer enslaved to sin. Keep on reading in Romans 6. Christ died once and will not have to die again because death no longer has dominion over him. The life he lives now is a life lived "unto God." What does that mean for me? "Even so reckon you also yourselves to be dead unto sin, but alive unto God in Christ Jesus. Let not sin therefore reign in your mortal body, that you should obey the lusts thereof: neither present your members unto sin as instruments of unrighteousness; but present yourselves unto God, *as alive from the dead,* and your members as instruments of righteousness unto God. For sin shall not have dominion over you: for you are not under law, but under grace."

Now that I have been raised in the likeness of his resurrection through my baptism, sin should no longer control me; I should control myself because through Christ I can. If I insist on making excuses for myself, "That's just the way I am," I am denying the power of my resurrection with Christ. If I take Romans 7.15 out of its context, using it as Satan misused scriptures in Matthew 4, saying, "See I want to be good, I just can't help it," when Paul clearly states at the end of this passage that a solution has been found, "Who shall deliver me from this body of death? I thank God through Jesus Christ. There is therefore now no condemnation to those who are in Christ Jesus," I have denied that very deliverance.

When I continue to sin and do nothing to improve myself, I have denied the effects of the resurrection as surely as if I no longer believed in it. It is the same lynchpin, the pin that keeps the wheels from falling off the cart, the pin that keeps my hope in salvation upright and rolling, even on rocky ground or muddy tracks.

Remember the first time you were raised from the dead, that the life you live now you live unto God because sin no longer controls you; you, with the aid of Christ, control it. If you deny the power of the resurrection with ungodly living, then "your faith is futile and you are still in your sins." Live instead like a resurrected creature, and you will make it to the ultimate resurrection.

May 14

Swagger

Have you seen them? Nearly every dramatic television series these days has one—a shot of the team—police, spies, crime scene techs, Robin Hood types, doctors, even lawyers!—walking in a line three, four, five or more abreast, slow motion, grim determination etched on their faces, a breeze off the set blowing just enough to ruffle a curl onto a handsome, stony forehead or whip the jacket aside to show off an outline of chiseled physique. Wow! Who could ever beat these guys?

No matter what you might say otherwise, this obligatory shot must impress us. Otherwise it would not be "obligatory." Why does it succeed? Because it projects a team filled with confidence, strength, and solidarity.

I seldom watch the Power Point on Sunday mornings now because I cannot read most of the passages and the announcements. But I glanced up once a week or so ago, and the shot of our three elders flashed up. We do that so any visitors from the community can recognize them easily. I suddenly remembered all those slow-mo swaggers and wondered what the effect might be if we did one of those. Knowing my humble shepherds as well as I do, I know they would be embarrassed, but I could not help but smile and think, "Our guys could pull it off."

Then I thought to myself, you know what? It might not be such a wild thought. Shouldn't we as Christians have that swagger too? Not because *we* are so good, but because of who would be standing in the middle of our line, perhaps a step or two ahead of the rest of us walking thousands abreast through the world. How could it not have an effect?

There was a time when that Leader did walk the roads with his 12 special followers beside and behind him. But they did not have the swagger necessary for the full effect. They were not as confident as they should have been. Didn't they all fear as the storm raged around their boat, even though they had their Lord with them, who lay calm enough to sleep despite the tossing waves?

They were not as strong as they should have been. Didn't they sleep while he suffered in the garden, and then scatter when he was arrested?

They were certainly not as unified as they should have been. More than once he caught them arguing about who was the greatest.

We are not any better sometimes. At least by the Day of Pentecost, 50 days after they fled in terror from the Roman soldiers, those men finally shaped up. They went on to perform miracles, preach astounding sermons, and face persecution, even to the death.

What about us? When will we mature enough to understand that with the Leader we have, we can *turn the world upside down?* But only if we walk the walk.

Confidence: "I can do all things through him who strengthens me" (Phil 4.13).

Strength: "So that with good courage we say, The Lord is my helper, I will not fear; what shall man do to me? (Heb 13.6).

Solidarity: "That they may all be one, even as you Father are in me and I in you, that they may also be in us, that the world may believe that you sent me" (John 17.21).

If the world is not impressed with us, it is not because of our leader or his message. It is because we have failed him. Any confidence, strength, and solidarity we may have come only from our faith in him. When we are lingering behind, cringing at what lies ahead, or tugging and fussing with one another instead of firmly, confidently striding out to the fight, all the Enemy will do is laugh.

For everyone who has been born of God overcomes the world—and this is the victory that has overcome the world—faith.

1 John 5.4

Another Lion-hearted Man

All my life I have heard David and Peter used as the supreme examples of how great men of God can still fall and repent, and truly they are fine examples. In fact, I often look at Peter as an example of how the church should receive the penitent as well. I bet there is not a church in America today that would choose him as an elder. Someone would always be remembering his past against him. God didn't (1 Pet 5.1), and we need to remember God's disdain for those who will not forgive as he does.

But here is a person I bet you never thought of—Judah. We become so focused on Joseph in the latter chapters of Genesis that we miss a great lesson in this man—how far one can fall, but how much good he can still accomplish if he will only return to God.

If ever there was a man who could blame his parents and his upbringing for his mistakes, here is the one. Judah was an unfavored son of an unfavored wife. His father never even tried to hide his partiality; he virtually rubbed his older ten sons' noses in it. (And I suppose it never crossed their father's mind that if he had given the same love and attention to the others, maybe they would have turned out as well as the two he favored.) Finally, the brothers got rid of their nemesis, the favored brother Joseph, and Judah was right in the mix (Gen 37.25–28).

Then he left the family. Maybe he was sick and tired of the whole lot. Maybe he was trying to outrun his guilt. Maybe it was a little of both. He made some sort of alliance with "a certain Adullamite whose name was Hirah," and married a Canaanite woman (38.1–8). I doubt there was anything else he could have done that would have defied his father more, for in this family, whom you married had been important for generations.

You can read the next few verses in Genesis 38 for yourself if you are not familiar enough with them, how Judah had wicked sons whom God destroyed, and how he eventually cheated his daughter-in-law out of the husband and child the local law said she should have had, a law God killed Judah's son Onan for breaking and eventually incorporated into the law of Moses (Deut 25). So Tamar, the daughter-in-law, disguised herself as a harlot and seduced her father-in-law so she could have the child the law demanded.

When Judah went to Tamar, she was disguised not as an ordinary harlot, but as a temple harlot, another sign of how far Judah had fallen. As a surety for payment he used a signet, a seal worn on a cord around the neck which acted as a personal signature, and his staff, the rod that figured in business transactions and symbolized family or tribal headship. When Tamar disappeared, Judah did not try to find the "harlot" to pay her, but let her keep these two items, giving up the symbols of his family, in effect cutting off his relationship with them for good.

Not only was he no longer in their presence, but he no longer even claimed a connection with the family God had chosen.

When Tamar's pregnancy was discovered, so was Judah's sin because she carried his ID in her hands. "She is more righteous than I." he admitted. The enormity of how far he had fallen finally hit him, as well as the realization that he was the one responsible for his actions, not his biased father; and that if his older brothers were unsuitable to lead the family due to their own sins (Gen 34 and 35.22), then he must.

Judah not only returned to his family, he became pre-eminent among them. He is the one who offered himself as a surety to Jacob when they took Benjamin to Egypt (Gen 43.2–10). He is the one who pled their case before the Egyptian ruler they did not recognize as Joseph (44.14–17). He is the one who offered to stay in prison if Joseph would just let Benjamin go home, showing great concern for his father's welfare (44.18–34), a father, you remember, who had treated him badly.

He became "a lion's whelp" in the inspired words of Jacob (49.9), and this lion-hearted man became the tribal father of the Messiah, his tribe the royal tribe from whom the only good kings God's people ever had came, and his tribe the only one left physically and politically intact when the Messiah finally arrived—Judea.

And so here is another example for us of how forgiving and loving a God we have. It should give us hope that God is patient while we slip and fall, and that he can still make use of even those we consider the greatest of sinners, including ourselves.

> *Judah, you shall your brothers praise, your hand shall be on the neck of your enemies; your father's sons will bow down before you. Judah is a lion's whelp; from the prey, my son, you have gone up; he stoops down, he couches as a lion and as a lioness. Who shall rouse him up? The scepter shall not depart from Judah, nor the ruler's staff from between his feet till Shiloh come; and unto him shall the obedience of the peoples be.*
>
> *...Reuben the firstborn of Jacob, for he was the firstborn, but inasmuch as he defiled his father's couch, his birthright was given to the sons of Joseph, the son of Israel. And the genealogy is not to be reckoned after the birthright, for Judah prevailed above his brothers, and of him came the prince.*
>
> *Jesus... being the son (as was supposed) of Joseph, the son of Heli.... the son of Nathan, the son of David, the son of Jesse...* ***the son of Judah****, the son of Jacob, the son of Isaac, the son of Abraham... the son of Enos, the son of Seth, the son of Adam, the son of God.*

Genesis 49.8–10; 1 Chronicles 5.1–2; Luke 3.23, 31–34, 38

May 16

Lying in the Pews

Once when we were traveling we walked into a meetinghouse and tried to find a place to sit. We were among the first to arrive but pew after pew was already filled with folded shawls, afghans, blankets, Bibles and notebooks. The problem for us is that Keith must sit close enough to be able to read lips or the entire service is lost on him. We are not bashful, so we finally moved aside a blanket and sat down. The owner of the blanket either never arrived that morning or sat somewhere else.

Now I do understand the problem. By the time we load up two Bibles, a notebook, Keith's hearing paraphernalia, my medications, two pairs of glasses, a magnifying glass, a purse, and two jackets I feel like we are moving every Sunday. It would be nice to have two sets of everything and leave one right where we usually sit. If I were alone and older, it would be nice not to have to carry so much. However, suppose we had been visitors from the community that Sunday and felt like we were not welcome to sit wherever we chose because practically every seat was "taken?" A few is not a problem, but maybe we should take a look at the buildings we all meet in and make certain that only a few places appear to be "saved" for someone besides an interested and, we hope, welcome visitor.

Sometimes we leave something much more important in our pews than a Bible or a blanket—our faith, our good behavior, and our desire to operate under the authority of an Almighty God.

Only on Sundays do we think of anyone else, and only the ones announced. The rest of the week we are too busy. Only on Sundays do we stand up for the truth. The rest of the week we don't want to cause a fuss. Only when it involves those "five acts of worship" do we look for the authority of God to act. The rest of the week it never crosses out minds that the same authority will tell us how to live and make important decisions. Only on Sunday are we careful how we approach God, forgetting entirely that we are in his presence every minute of every day.

So what did you leave lying in the pew last Sunday? Be sure to take it home with you this week.

> *Hear this, you who trample on the needy and bring the poor of the land to an end, saying, "When will the new moon be over, that we may sell grain? And the Sabbath, that we may offer wheat for sale, that we may make the ephah small and the shekel great and deal deceitfully with false balances, that we may buy the poor for silver and the needy for a pair of sandals and sell the chaff of the wheat?" Therefore because you trample on the poor and you exact taxes of grain from him, you have built houses of hewn stone, but you shall not dwell in them; you have planted pleasant vineyards, but you shall not drink their wine. For I know how many are your transgressions and how great are your sins—you who afflict the righteous, who take a bribe, and turn aside the needy in the gate. Seek good, and not evil, that you may live; and so the* Lord, *the God of hosts, will be with you, as you have said.*

Amos 8.4–6; 5.11–12, 14

May 17

Birds in the Blueberries

Our blueberries have not been particularly bountiful the past few years. I remember years when over the three or four weeks we were picking, I had enough for four or five pies, two or three dozen giant muffins, blueberry pancakes at least twice, and a dozen jars of jam, and still put 15 full quarts of berries in the freezer for later use. This year after one small batch of blueberry pancakes, half a dozen muffins, one pie and one crisp, I only put up four quarts, with none at all left for jam. Then there was the year not long ago when a late frost on the already blooming bushes did not leave enough for even one muffin. At least this year was better than that one, but if blueberries are antioxidants, we may start rusting soon.

When the blueberries are thin I really hate sharing them with the birds. It would not be so bad if the birds would pick one limb or even one bush out of the twelve we have. But they flit around pecking a blueberry here and a blueberry there. Once a bird has pecked a berry just once, it is useless to us. Yet there is still enough in the one berry for several more pecks if the bird would only take them, and then he would not need to peck so many others!

Satan does the same thing to us. How many faults do you have? How many weaknesses do you fight on a daily basis? If you are a faithful Christian, maybe only a few by now, certainly less than when you started out. But you know what? Satan doesn't need to totally ruin you. He doesn't need to turn you into evil personified. All he needs to do is make you satisfied with just one little fault, only one little thing that you need to work on, because the fewer pecks he makes into your soul, the more likely you are to be satisfied with your progress. You will look at yourself and say, "I'm doing pretty well. This one little thing won't hurt my soul." And so you give in, you make excuses, you say to yourself, "That's just the way I am, and after all, it's not that bad. I haven't killed anyone lately." This is not to minimize the need for grace, just the attitude that says, "I'm satisfied where I am."

So we become a bush full of pecked blueberries, too ruined for those around us to nourish their souls, but not ruined enough for us to think we really need to do something about it. Is that why the church isn't growing? Is that why we no longer have any influence on our neighbors? Is that why our children are falling away and the future looks so grim?

Pecked blueberries are useless. When Satan sends a bird to peck at you, beat him off with a stick if you have to. One peck *can* cost you your soul.

But when the righteous turns away from his righteousness and commits iniquity, and does according to the abominations that the wicked man does, shall he live? None of his righteous deeds that he has done shall be remembered; in his trespass that he has trespassed, and in his sin which he has sinned he shall die. ...I have no pleasure in the death of him who dies, says the Lord. Therefore turn and live.

Ezekiel 18.24, 32

May 18

Glowing in the Dark

I found a verse the other day that intrigued me—"for the kingdom of God is not eating and drinking, but righteousness, and peace, and joy in the Holy Spirit" (Rom 14.17). While the meaning is obvious—in the context of eating meats sacrificed to idols, Paul is telling them that being in the kingdom is a matter of the inner man not the outer man—I still wondered why those three things were chosen among the many traits describing Christians.

Before much longer I found Romans 5.1–3. Those three things are not three separate items, as if they can be chosen one without the other, they are a chain reaction. I am justified (made *righteous*), and as a result have *peace* with God, and that creates *joy* in my life.

Keep reading down to verse 5, then add Romans 12.12 and 15.13 to the mix and you see that joy is inextricably bound with hope. The Greeks did not use "hope" the way we use it, a wish for something that could go either way, but as a confident assurance or, as Keith likes to say, "a vision of a *certain future.*" Along with the apostle John, I should be able to say, "I *know* I am saved; I *know* I have been forgiven; I *know* I have a relationship with God; I *know* I am going to Heaven" (1 John 5.13). Is there anything that should inspire any greater joy?

Being joyful does not mean we may not face sad times; it does not mean we must not ever grieve in a trial. What it does mean is that we will bounce back from those times because joy is the foundation for our lives. If, instead, I come through a trial with an attitude only toward myself, what I have endured, and what I believe others should be doing for me because of it, my joy has turned into bitterness. In fact, *I have not successfully endured that trial at all.*

Whenever I allow something to smother my joy, in at least that much I have allowed that thing to be more important to me than my relationship with God.

This is easier said than done. I used to wonder how to have this joy that everyone kept telling me I was supposed to have. God does not leave us without direction. Colossians 1.9–14 gives us several techniques for having joy. Be filled with the knowledge of Him; walk worthily of the Lord; bear fruit in every good work; give thanks for our salvation. Do you know what that boils down to? Focus on the good things and stay busy serving others.

Joy is like a glow-in-the-dark toy. The more I focus on what God has done for me and what he expects me to do for others, the longer I sit in the light and the stronger my glow will be. But if I sit too long in the shadow of sadness and grief, focusing too long on myself, my joy will begin to fade until eventually it is gone altogether.

If you find yourself alone in the dark today, it's time to come back into the light before your joy disappears, along with the hope that reinforces it. This is a choice *you* make, one that has nothing to do with what happens today or what anyone does to you, but with the path you choose to take regardless.

> *That the proof of your faith, more precious than gold that perishes though it is proved by fire, may be found unto praise and glory and honor at the revelation of Jesus Christ: whom not having seen you love; on whom, though now you see him not, yet believing, you rejoice greatly with joy unspeakable and full of glory: receiving the end of your faith, the salvation of your souls.*
>
> 1 Peter 1.7–9

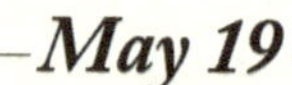

Lightning Bolts

We had a storm a few days ago. That in itself is not unusual. Summer afternoons in Florida often include thunderstorms that go as quickly as they come. This one, though, was not the ordinary storm.

You could hear it coming for about an hour, thunder in the distance, black clouds boiling in an increasing breeze that brought the smell of rain and ozone. Finally the bottom fell out. You could hardly see the bushes right outside the windows it was raining so hard. Afterward, checks on the clock and the rain gauge would show that it rained 1.9 inches in 20 minutes. Before long, we saw the fruit of Keith's hours and hours of backbreaking labor, hauling dirt with a shovel and a wheelbarrow, creating a berm around the house. It looked like we were on an island in the middle of a river, its strong current at least four inches deep as the water rushed down the slope, around the house, and toward the run to the east of us. It would keep running nearly two hours after the rain stopped, and we drained just fine, but meanwhile I found myself humming, "The rains came down and the floods came up."

Suddenly lightning struck in the trees just across the fence to the north. The clap was so loud I screamed, and even Keith, out in the shed without his hearing aids, heard it, and saw a ball of fire at the top of a pine at the same time. He said Magdi shot out from her favorite place under the porch, eyes wide as saucers, circling here and there in the pouring rain looking for someplace safe. He called her into the shed, normally a forbidden place, and petted her dripping and quivering sides until she calmed down. We never saw Chloe until after the storm, but when we did, her tail was plastered down hard between her legs, the end of it curled up under her belly. It didn't come back up for two days.

That reminded me of the Israelites' reaction to God at Mt. Sinai. They were so terrified of the darkness, thunder, and lightning that they begged Moses that

God would no longer speak to them. I find Moses' reply interesting: "Do not fear, for God has come to test you, that the fear of him may be before you that you may not sin" (Exod 20.20).

I think that might just be our problem. We aren't afraid enough any more.

I can remember when a certain phrase was not only forbidden in polite society, it was certainly never said on television or radio. It was considered "taking the Lord's name in vain." Now I hear it all the time, even from children. When ten-year-olds have an abbreviation for it in their text messages, "omg," something has been lost in our reverence for God.

The Word of God is called a book of myths, even by people who claim to live by it, even by some who claim to be its ministers. Religious people are pictured in fiction and drama as bigots, fanatics, hypocrites or maniacs. God, Jesus, Satan, and the struggle against sin are used as comic foils by entertainers. When I start thinking about how far we have gone down this road, it's a wonder to me that lightning isn't popping around us constantly.

We, the people of God, have even taken the concept of "the fear of God" and watered it down to the point that it means nothing more than the respect we might show our own fathers. Isaiah, when he had seen merely a vision of God said, "Woe is me, for I am a man of unclean lips, and I dwell in the midst of a people of unclean lips, for my eyes have seen the King, the Lord of hosts" (6.5). Isaiah was feeling a whole lot more than simple respect. If there was ever a time when he could overcome sin more easily, it was probably in the weeks and months after that vision.

I have a feeling that if we ever stood in the presence of God we would finally understand what the fear of God is all about. Some day we will. I just hope it is not too late.

> *Any one who has set aside the Law of Moses dies without mercy on the evidence of two or three witnesses. How much* ***worse punishment****, do you think, will be deserved by the one who has spurned the Son of God and has profaned the blood of the covenant by which he was sanctified, and has outraged the Spirit of grace? For we know him who said, "Vengeance is mine. I will repay," and again, "The Lord will judge his people." It is a fearful thing to fall into the hands of the living God.*
>
> Hebrews 10.28–31

May 20

Pitting Cherries

I just pitted two pounds of fresh cherries. I *knew* there was a reason I liked blueberries better.

Even with a handy-dandy little cherry pitter, it is still quite a chore. You have to do them one at a time, well over a hundred, and sometimes the pit does not come out the first try. You have to fiddle with the cherry until you get it in there just right—so the little plunger will go right through the center. Then there is the clean-up as some of those wayward pits bounce across the counter and floor, staining everything cherry red.

Not worth it you say? You have obviously never had a cherry pie made with anything but canned cherry pie filling! Some things are worth the trouble. Like children. Like marriage. Like living according to God's rules.

Satan will do everything in his power to make it seem otherwise. He will tell you his reward here and now is greater, like a ready-made store-bought pie. He will tell you that God's reward is mediocre, like a pie you can have in the oven in ten minutes with canned filling and refrigerated pie crust. He will tell you God's reward does not even exist, that there is no such thing as a pie with a homemade crust and fresh cherries—it's all an illusion. Everyone knows pies come in a box in the freezer case!

But God's reward is real; it is better than anything this life and that Enemy have to offer. It takes some effort. Sometimes we fail and have to try again. Sometimes people make fun of us. Sometimes we work till our backs ache and our fingers cramp up, but when you put God's reward on the window sill to cool, everyone knows it was worth it. Even the ones who won't get to taste it.

Blessed are you when men shall hate you, and when they shall separate you from their company, and reproach you, and cast out your name as evil, for the Son of man's sake. Rejoice in that day, and leap for joy, for behold, great is your reward in Heaven.

So that men shall say, "Truly there is a reward for the righteous; truly there is a God who judges the earth."

Luke 6.22–23; Psalm 58.11

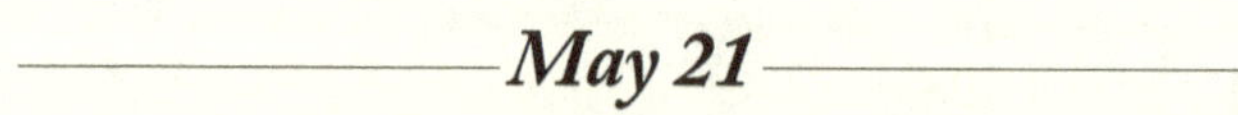

May 21

One Last Grammar Class

Now pay attention! "Irregardless" is not a word; the word is "regardless." "Preventative" and "attentative" are not words; the words are "preventive" and "attentive" without the extra "ta" syllable. You go to an "orientation" session to become "oriented," not "orientated."

You are *not* "laying" in bed. If you were, there would be a pile of eggs there. Today you "lie" there, yesterday you "lay" there, and in the past you "have lain" there.

However, if you are talking about something you put in the bed, then today you "lay" it there, yesterday you "laid" it there, and in the past you also "have laid" it there.

The words are not pronounced "comPARable" and "irrePARable," they are pronounced "COMparable" and "irREParable." And, at least until recently when the lexicographers finally gave up and put it in as an allowed pronunciation, the word was correctly pronounced "off-en" without the T, rather than "off-ten" with the T. At least know that the pronunciation of the word "often" has been corrupted, please.

"Hopefully the weather will clear up" is an impossibility. The weather cannot do anything hopefully, and that is the word being modified in that sentence. What you mean to say is, "I hope the weather will clear up." "Hopefully" used at the beginning of a sentence is almost always wrong.

You cannot "bring" something to a place you are not at; you *take* it there. When you feel ill, you feel "nauseated." When you are "nauseous," *you* are causing nausea in others, although my dictionary tells me that it has been used wrong for so long that they have created a second definition for it.

You know what is so aggravating about all of this? I am *not* a grammarian. I did not have a grammar class after ninth grade. The English classes after that were all literature and writing. Any real grammar scholar could find fault with me. I was, in fact, re-reading an old devotional the other day and found a split infinitive in it. I am just an ordinarily educated person when it comes to grammar. So if I know all these things, what in the world happened? I see and hear them in what purports to be professional speech and writing all the time. It's one thing for us common folks to be less than careful about how we speak, but shouldn't the pros have standards?

Before you start on me for being too picky and fussy, let me remind you that I am in good company. Paul and Jesus both made arguments based on word choice and grammar.

In Galatians 3.16 Paul uses the number of the noun "seed" to prove that Jesus was the fulfillment to the promise to Abraham. "Now to Abraham were the promises spoken, and to his seed. He said not, and to *seeds,* as of many, but as of one, and to thy *seed,* which is Christ." In the first major controversy in the new kingdom, when Jewish Christians were attempting to force Judaism on Gentile Christians as necessary to salvation, that was important. Pretty picky of Paul, wasn't it?

Jesus proved to the Sadducees the resurrection of the dead when he quoted God as He spoke to Moses on Mt. Sinai from the burning bush, "I am the God of Abraham, Isaac, and Jacob." At that point, those men had been long dead, yet God spoke of them in the present tense. Jesus said, "But as regarding the resurrection of the dead, haven't you read that which was spoken to you by God, I am the God of Abraham and the God of Isaac, and the God of Jacob? God is not the God of the dead, but of the living" (Matt 22.31–32), an argument based solely on the tense of a verb. Good thing it had nothing to do with "laying!"

We have a tendency to think of those people in "Bible times" as primitive, ignorant folks. Jesus made a claim of Divinity to them using two words, which of necessity were in the present tense. "Before Abraham was, *I AM,*" (John 8.58). Did they catch something so fussy and nitpicky? I think so. "They took up stones therefore to cast at him." I wonder if today's generation would have just shrugged their shoulders and walked on.

It is permissible to be picky with the Scriptures. We are in good company when we are. Be careful however, that your pickiness is not about pettiness. "Picky" and "petty" are not the same. Jesus and the apostles were one, but not the other. Study the difference, study your scriptures. God did choose words to communicate with us, not subjective feelings. Aren't we glad? There can be no mistake if you have it down in black and white.

> *Truly I say to you, till heaven and earth pass away, one jot or one tittle shall in no way pass from the law till all things are accomplished. Whoever therefore shall break one of these least commandments and shall teach men so, shall be called least in the kingdom of heaven. But whoever shall do and teach them, he shall be called great in the kingdom of heaven.*
>
> Matthew 5.18–19

May 22

Testimonials

We finally gave up and bought one. With my personal situation it seemed inordinately stubborn not to use what could be a real help when I was stuck somewhere unable to get home, or at the doctor's office when out of the blue I needed a procedure. It has happened more than once already. So we bought a cell phone.

We did not buy one of those expensive phones with "plans"; just a cheap little prepaid phone with an hour of talk time good for three months. After nearly a year I can still count the number of times I have used it—without even taking off my shoes!—and I have amassed enough minutes to carry on a peace conference between two double-talking diplomats.

Yet I do keep it handy, and I forgot it was in my sweater pocket the day I happened to think that the load of laundry I was running was perfect for that sweater, and the sweater was dingy around the cuffs from petting dogs and sitting around smoky campfires. So I threw it in the washer as I went by, and found the cell phone in the bottom a half hour later, sparkling clean but dead as a doornail.

Not because we thought it would work, but because we have had to be so frugal for our entire married life, we let the phone dry out completely, then tried charging it. It has worked fine ever since. It even remembered the phone numbers Lucas programmed into it for me. I bet you would like to know the brand, wouldn't you?

I have something else that is a whole lot more valuable than a cell phone, and many times more amazing. Why can't I bring myself to talk about it just as easily? Actually, it has been easier lately. I think we worry too much about how to do it, instead of just letting it happen. Evangelism happens as you live your life.

If I had simply told you that I had this cell phone, it would not have made an impression on you. But when I told you how it has helped me in difficult situations and then how dependable it was in spite of how I abused it, it suddenly became much more interesting, didn't it?

That makes my daily life a much more important part of my Christianity. How can I expect to have any influence when I do not live like I have anything more than anyone else has? If they do not see me overcome, if they do not see me return good for evil, if they do not see joy and contentment regardless of my financial situation, if they do not see peace in my life when others with the same problems are falling apart, my life is not evangelism. In fact, it is quite the opposite. What we perceive as a lack of interest in the gospel may simply be a lack of interest in what we have because of how we are behaving.

Live your life like a testimonial. You will have more opportunity than ever to spread your faith, even without some sort of special "program." People will only want what you have when they see it in action.

> *You are the light of the world. A city set on a hill cannot be hid. Neither do men light a lamp, and put it under the bushel, but on the stand; and it shines unto all that are in the house. Even so let your light shine before men; that they may see your good works, and glorify your Father who is in heaven.*
>
> Matthew 5.14–16

May 23

Clipping Coupons

I have been clipping and redeeming coupons since we got married. I have a file box and a system. I search ads faithfully and use them to plan both my shopping trip and my meals. And I don't fall into the coupon traps—if I don't need it or won't use it, or did not want to try it anyway, I don't buy it. We got by for 50 percent less than most families with teenage boys.

I seldom have one of those shopping trips you hear about, where the woman buys $100 worth of groceries for $2.98, primarily because I do not buy a lot of processed, prepared foods. I have a garden; I bake from scratch. My grocery bill rarely includes anything but staples, meat, paper goods, and the few produce items we do not grow, like onions, potatoes, and garlic. You don't find many coupons for those things, but occasionally I make a "coupon coup." There was the jar of mustard, regularly $1.29, on sale for 99 cents. A 50 cent coupon brought it down to 49 cents. There was the week Publix actually put their bakery's key lime pie on sale for $4.50. I had a $2.50 coupon *plus* they gave away a free loaf of French bread with every pie. So for $2.00 I got a key lime pie (regular $7.49) and a loaf of French bread (regular $1.99). I couldn't have made a key lime pie alone for any less than $4.00, and theirs is nearly as good.

Then I raided the drug store, the popular hang-out for those who are aging. Keith needed glucosamine chondroitin. Thirty dollars a bottle. It was buy one get one, plus I had a $3.00 coupon. We needed vitamins, regular $6.00 a bottle. They were buy one get one, plus I had a $2.00 coupon. They also had my favorite shampoo on sale, one I hardly ever get to buy because it is usually $4.29 a bottle. They had it for $3.00, plus I had a coupon for $2.00 off 2, plus, for buying two, they automatically gave me another $1.00 off anything in the store at the check-out, effectively making the price $1.50 a bottle. Finally we needed some low dose aspirins—$4.69 a bottle. I had a $4.00 coupon, making that 69 cents. Are you keeping track? I bought $86.29 worth of items for $38.19. Don't tell me the time I spend clipping and sorting isn't worth it.

Redeeming coupons brings to mind another sort of redemption. I am always thrilled when I get a high quality item for a low price. I would never pay full price for a crushed box of crackers or a dented can of tomato paste; nor would I for wilted produce—maybe half price for overripe bananas because they still have some use. But top dollar? Forget it.

I am so glad God was not as stingy as I am! He redeemed me, paying full price not for dented cans, crushed boxes, or even overripe bananas. He got the culls, the totally useless, rotten, spoiled produce; he paid top dollar for something no one else would have even considered buying.

I think, when you have "been good" all your life, perhaps "raised in the church," as we are prone to say, it is hard to realize our worthlessness, and really appreciate what has been done for us. An old song goes, "Alas and did my Savior bleed and did my Sovereign die; would he devote that sacred head for such a worm as I?" I noticed that in one of the newer hymnals that last line has been changed to "such a one as I." Unh-unh. We need to get the "worm" back in there, because that is how low we were—totally worthless and disgusting—when Jesus redeemed us, "not with corruptible things, with silver or gold… but with precious blood, as a lamb without blemish and without spot, even the blood of Christ" (1 Pet 1.18–19). Truly the Lord is gracious. In fact, we got the real bargain—precious grace for irregular, damaged merchandise!

> *For while we were weak, in due season Christ died for the ungodly. For scarcely for a righteous man will one die, maybe for a good man someone would dare to die. But God commends his own love toward us, in that, while we were yet sinners, Christ died for us.*
>
> Romans 5.6–8

May 24

Snakes Alive!

In rural north central Florida, snakes are a fact of life. Poisonous snakes are a *big* fact of life. You learn to take precautions, but even then, if you have not seen one in awhile, you become careless. Last summer we were reminded of where we live.

One morning I was walking the mown path around our property, as I do every day, six laps for three-and-a-half miles. Suddenly the weeds to the left of me buzzed. If you have ever heard a rattlesnake in person, you know it does not sound like the ones on TV. It sounds like an angry June bug, a really big, really angry June bug. I leapt sideways about ten feet—in fact, if sideways leaping were an Olympic event, I would have won the gold medal that day.

We never found that one, but not ten days later, the dog alerted us to one in the yard, which Keith shot. Four days later, she found a cottonmouth which escaped her by flattening itself enough to get under the house. Keith had to crawl under there with a flashlight and a pistol for that one. A week later another rattler in the yard met him as he returned from the neighbor's. Four days later a black racer crossed my running path about 30 feet ahead. Two days after that a coachwhip met me at the fence behind the old pigpen when I walked. This was beginning to get eerie. We had never had this many snakes in this short a time, not even the first summer we set up house in this old watermelon field in the piney woods, half a mile off the highway.

Five days later I was folding clothes in the family room and happened to look out the window right next to me. Not five feet from my face, a racer was winding itself up around the TV tower. No, racers are not poisonous. Yes, it was outside and I was inside with not one, but two, glass panes between me and it. But something about that one sent chills up my spine. It was almost more than I could do to go outside that day at all. Somehow I expected to see dozens of snakes slithering up the porch steps and clinging to the screen just waiting to strike when I opened the back door.

But when it was time to walk, I took a deep breath, got the .22 rifle loaded with number 12 shot, leaned it against the tree and set off, with my trusty canine bodyguards bounding up ahead of me to sniff out the critters and, more important, scare away the snakes. Still, I was a lot more alert than usual.

This was a good spiritual reminder as well. We live in a stable society. No natives on the warpath. No marauders on the borders. No wars fought on our home ground. Have we forgotten to be careful? There is still an enemy out there who is *real,* and he will kill our souls if we are not alert. Are we to be so afraid that we shut ourselves away from the world? No, for how could our lights shine and our faith be told? But being cautious never hurt anyone.

When you go out there today, pay attention, stay safe, and when you see the lion, who at least once has masqueraded as a serpent, either shoot him down right there or run!

Be sober, be watchful, your adversary the devil, as a roaring lion, walks about seeking whom he may devour; withstand him, steadfast in your faith, knowing that the same sufferings are accomplished in your brothers who are in the world. And the God of all grace, who called you unto His eternal glory in Christ, after you have suffered a little while, shall Himself perfect, establish and strengthen you.

1 Peter 5.8–10

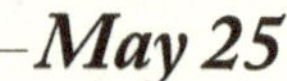

Quicksand

While I was teaching music I was a member of several professional organizations. My favorite was the local group which met seven times a year in members' homes for business, some high-spirited performances, and a potluck lunch. Once we met in a house just off the highway, down a lime rock road. In the middle of the meeting, a rain came up—not just any rain, but one we around here call a "toad strangler." Several inches in less than an hour.

The rain had stopped when it was time to leave and we took off down the dirt road shortcut in a caravan of cars headed to our various studios to meet the students for the day. Suddenly, the cars ahead of me came to a halt, and ladies started climbing out, gathering together and peering up ahead. I turned off the engine and joined the milling crowd at the head of the line.

Water had run across the road. It had not cut a deep rut, and in fact, was a nice shallow-looking, easily fordable stream, but we had all lived in the country long enough to know you don't just drive through water running across an unpaved road. "Someone needs to walk out there and check the road," was the consensus.

Have I mentioned that at 35 I was the youngest in the group by about 30 years? Instantly, all heads turned toward me. Having been silently elected, I slipped off my shoes and started across the newly created waterway. I took five firm steps only to have to grab my skirt and hike it up over my knees as I sank exactly that deep on the sixth. Instantly I had visions of those jungle movies I used to watch on Saturday afternoons as a kid, where the first one in the safari line sinks in the quicksand because, in spite of everyone telling him to be still, he wiggles and squirms and sinks before anyone can even think to cut a vine and use it to pull him out—or if some bright fellow does think of it, 20 people on the other end cannot out-pull the suction of a big mud puddle.

A good minute later it dawned on me that my name was being called, and I still had not sunk any farther. My feet had found a solid layer of hardpan about two feet below the surface so Tarzan swinging to the rescue was totally unnecessary. I made my way back to the group with the most unladylike thwock, thwock, thwock noises as the suction was released with each step. We all carefully backed our cars down the one lane road, turned around in the driveway from where we had started and went the long way home, down the paved state highway.

Hopelessness in the scriptures is often pictured as "sinking." Jeremiah prophesies that Babylon will "sink and shall not rise again because of the evil I will bring upon her" (51.64). Amos warns Israel that they are in for the same punishment: they shall "sink again like the River of Egypt" (8.8; 9.5). And all because of sin. Even Peter, when he tried to walk on water, began to sink because of "little faith" and "doubt" (Matt 14.30–31). And truly, just like sinking in the quicksand (at least in the old grade B movies), there is nothing we can do but hope a savior happens along. Praise God, he has!

The Psalmist pleads "Commit yourself to Jehovah, let him deliver you; let him rescue you, seeing he delights in you" (22.8). In spite of the fact that, like an ignorant city slicker, we walked out into that mud on purpose, in spite of the fact that we ignored warning after warning, and kept right on wiggling and squirming, and even when we have been pulled out before, but keep stepping right back into the same pool of quicksand, Jesus is ready to hold out a hand and save us.

> *Deliver me out of the mire and let me not sink.... Let not the waterflood overwhelm me and swallow me up....Answer me, oh Jehovah, for your lovingkindness is good. According to the multitude of your tender mercies, turn to me; and hide not your face from your servant, for I am in distress; answer me quickly.*
>
> Psalm 69.14–17

May 26

Parsley Worms

I had just checked the day before. How could this be? The herbed rice pilaf was simmering on the stove, and I had run out to the herb garden to cut some parsley to add just before serving. Five healthy Italian flat leaf parsley plants were stripped bare. I leaned to look closer and there they were—four black and green striped parsley worms. They may well have been there the day before, hidden by the bushy leaves, and their green color, the same shade as the parsley stems, but to me it was as if they had eaten them all overnight.

Luckily, the butter, onions, garlic, chicken broth, thyme and toasted almonds gave the pilaf a little flavor at least, and the rest of the meal turned out fine. Enough sauce covered the cider-braised pork chops so that anyone desiring to could spoon it over the rice as well. But it was still missing those pretty flecks of green and the freshness that a good-sized handful of fresh parsley added at the last minute brings. If only I had looked a little closer the day before, even I might have seen those little stinkers.

It can happen to us as easily as to parsley plants. False teachers are charming, logical, and usually attractive people. They will appeal to your sense of justice, common sense, compassion, ego, even your pocketbook, whatever it takes to get your attention and draw you in. Many of them sincerely believe what they teach, having been previously deceived by yet another false teacher. Those are especially difficult to ignore—what seems like an honest and sincere person cannot be the evil wolf Jesus warns us about, can he? "And no marvel; for even Satan fashions himself into an angel of light. It is no great thing therefore if his ministers also fashion themselves as ministers of righteousness" (2 Cor 11.14–15).

So whose fault is it if we are taken in by these people? God makes it clear in both the Old and New Testaments that we are responsible for our own souls.

> A wonderful and a horrible thing has come to pass in the land. The prophets prophesy falsely and the priests bear rule by their means, *and my people love to have it so.* (Jer 5.30–31)
>
> For it is a rebellious people, lying children, *children that will not hear the law of the Jehovah,* that say to the Seers, see not, and to the Prophets, prophesy not right things, but *speak to us smooth things.* (Isa 30.9–10)
>
> For the time will come when they will not endure sound doctrine, but, *having itching ears, will heap to themselves teachers after their own lusts, and will turn away their ears from the truth and turn aside unto fables.* (2 Tim 4.3–4)

Scary, isn't it? Don't think it cannot happen to you and, like my parsley plants, happen quickly. Before the apostles were dead, the first "-ism" was already upon the church. They were fighting the Judaizing brethren, the Gnostics, the Nicolaitans, and others we probably will never know about.

"I am astonished that you are so quickly deserting him who called you in the grace of Christ and are turning to a different gospel, not that there is another one, but there are some who trouble you and want to distort the gospel of Christ" Paul told the Galatians (1.6–7), not 20 years after founding the churches in that area. How about us 2,000 years removed? If there was ever a time for vigilance, for going back to the basics, for attempting to restore the New Testament church as God intended it to be, it is now. So many have strayed so far.

When your elders and preachers seem harsh and intolerant toward a teacher or group, or even toward you, give them a break. Your souls are in their hands. They are seeing things that you, caught up in your emotions and prejudices, might not. Like parents protecting a child from the predators out there in the world, they can see the danger. Instead of adolescently complaining, "You're mean. You don't understand," pay attention. Ultimately, if you choose not to listen to them, the parsley worms will eat up your souls, leaving nothing but useless stems, and God will hold *you* accountable.

> *Beware of false prophets who come to you in sheep's clothing, but inwardly are ravenous wolves. You will recognize them by their fruits. ...Beloved, do not believe every spirit, but test the spirits to see whether they are from God, for many false prophets have gone out into the world.*
>
> Matthew 7.15–16; 1 John 4.1

May 27

Supermom

> *And he came to Lystra and Derbe and behold, a certain disciple was there named Timothy, the son of a Jewess that believed, but his father was a Greek.* (Acts 16.1)
>
> *Having been reminded of the unfeigned faith that is in you, which dwelt first in your grandmother Lois, and your mother Eunice, and I am persuaded, in you also.* (2 Tim 1.5)

Did you see it? Don't feel bad. I missed it too, for years.

Wasn't it great that Eunice taught her son so well? But how many of us are thinking in the back of our minds, "Tsk, tsk, it would have been easier if she had married a child of God to begin to with." I have been guilty of such snap judgments myself over the years, placing these people in my own culture and social customs. Lydia aside, it was not common for a woman to make her own living in those days, in those places. Because of that, to be left alone a widow was to be sentenced to a life of poverty and dependence upon the kindness of others. Look how many passages in the Law made provisions for the widow and orphan. They did not live in a day of insurance policies, pensions, Social Security, and Aid for Dependent Children. If God's people did not follow the Law as he designed it, the widow and orphan would starve.

Parents often arranged marriages, and expecting their daughter to live alone and support herself simply because they could not find a God-fearing husband for her was not an expedient choice for Eunice's parents. Out in the Gentile world with few practicing Jews in the area, the best they could do was find a Greek whom they thought would take good care of their daughter.

And here is what we miss: how do we know there were no Jews to choose from? It was Paul's custom to go to the synagogue first when he came to a town, (Acts 13.5, 14; 14.1; 17.1, *etc*). From the account in Acts, it seems evident that there were no synagogues in Lystra or Derbe. That also means there were fewer than ten Jewish male heads of household in the town, the number necessary to form a synagogue, and not even enough Jewish women to meet down by the river as in Philippi (16.13). Which means there was no Jewish school to send her son to, one of the primary functions of a local synagogue. Besides these obstacles, how many little boys want to "be like Daddy?"

So now you have a woman married to a Greek, who was taught the scripture (Old Testament) so well that she "also believed," meaning she accepted Jesus as the fulfillment of Messianic prophecy, something even the "well-educated" scribes and "pious" Pharisees could not seem to do. And *she* raised a son to do the same, without a righteous man to influence him, without a formal religious education, and without a community of believers from which to draw help and encouragement.

I daresay that none of us has the problems Eunice faced as a mother. In this day when so many want to blame everyone else for their failures, when so many blame the church for the way their children turned out, she is a shining example of what *can* be done, of one who took the responsibility and, despite awesome odds, succeeded.

The world bestows the term "Supermom" for all the wrong reasons. Here is the real thing, one we should be emulating every day of our lives.

And these words which I command you this day shall be upon your heart, and you shall teach them diligently to your children, and shall talk of them when you sit in your house, and when you walk by the way, and when you lie down and when you rise up. And you shall bind them for a sign upon your hand, and they shall be frontlets between your eyes. And you shall write them upon the doorposts of your house and upon your gates.

Deuteronomy 6.6–9

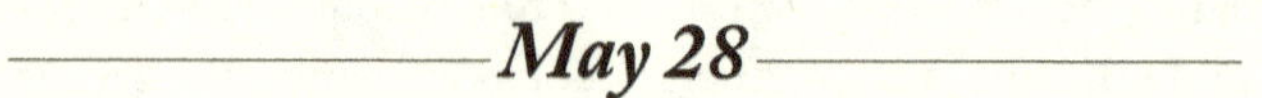

May 28

The Detritus of Life

The torn plastic label from a two-liter bottle, several scraps of both black and white plastic trash bags, the label from a jug of pesticide, the plastic top to a convenience store 44-oz cup, the corner of a corrugated cardboard box, a cracked, black plastic nursery pot, a Wal-Mart bag, a ramen noodle wrapper, a Hershey bar wrapper, a Tootsie Roll wrapper, a Starburst wrapper, a Rice Krispies cereal bar wrapper, a sunflower seed wrapper, six hunks of white batting from some sort of cushion, a Fritos bag, a Subway sandwich bag, a paper Wendy's hamburger wrap, a Krispy Kreme carton, three Little Debbie oatmeal pie wrappers, an empty gallon bleach jug, a used napkin, the Styrofoam from a raw meat package, and piece of a used disposable diaper.

All that is what I picked up on the west side of our property one morning last week, blown over the fence from the neighbors' since my last pick-up two weeks before. You would think their place would look a little better after losing all that, but it didn't even make a dent. I have mentioned them before. These folks must believe that life comes with a built-in maid service. If it does, theirs needs to be fired. Whatever it is they believe, they don't believe they have the responsibility to clean up their own messes.

As much as we like to think we are so much better than that, we often are not. We may not litter the landscape with fast food wrappers and everyday rubbish, but we often leave spiritual and emotional messes in our wake. Broken trust, tattered relationships, bitter disappointments and battered feelings can mark our paths when sin affects our lives. A few unguarded words can hurt instead of heal. A self-centered attitude can trample a heavy heart. Self-righteousness, because of its exaggerated sense of absolutes and conviction in its own virtue, can mercilessly beat a weak soul into giving up the fight.

My neighbors never seem to notice the mess they leave, the cumulative effect of dropping whatever is in hand simply because that is the convenient way to take care of it. I am even worse when, in my headlong rush to please myself or pass judgment, I fail to take the time to stop and look behind. The pieces of souls marking my path should wake me up. They are far more damning than a whole dumpster full of Twinkie wrappers.

What unto me is the multitude of your sacrifices? says Jehovah: I have had enough of the burnt-offerings of rams, and the fat of fed beasts; and I delight not in the blood of bullocks, or of lambs, or of he-goats. When you come to appear before me, who has required this at your hand, to trample my courts? Wash yourself, make yourself clean; put away the evil of your doings from before my eyes; cease to do evil; learn to do well; seek justice, relieve the oppressed, judge the fatherless, plead for the widow. ...Turn to your God: keep kindness and justice, and wait for your God continually. ...If you had known what this means, I desire mercy, and not sacrifice, you would not have condemned the guiltless.

Isaiah 1.11–12, 16–17; Hosea 12.6; Matthew 12.7

May 29

Dragonflies

Keith called me outside one Saturday. I was in the middle of something important and was a little irritated. It is hard enough to do things these days when I have to lean so close, squint so hard, and put up with the resulting headaches trying to see what I am doing. Then he wants to interrupt me, and I will just have to start all over again. But I sighed, a louder one than was called for, and dutifully went outside.

The afternoon sun was waning, for which I was grateful. No matter how dim the day I have to reach for sunglasses nearly all the time now. He took me to a shaded spot on the west side of the field and pointed. Then I saw it, or them as it turned out, probably a hundred dragonflies darting here and there all over the place.

He felt bad for me because I could not see them all the time. In fact, I would not have known what they were had he not told me, but I think my vision of them was the best. He saw them in the shade as well, when they once again became ugly black bugs, but I only saw them as they came out of the shadows, the sun striking their wings and lighting them up like tiny golden light bulbs. Then they would disappear, but more would appear in their place, over and over, darting here and there in movements no one could possibly predict. I think my view was much more magical than his, and therefore far more delightful. We stood there watching them for several minutes. I probably could have stood their longer since I had the better view, a view he would never have because he could see so well.

No matter what we may be going through in this life, God always prepares good things for us, but we will never see them if we always stay inside ourselves, commiserating with ourselves, rewinding over and over the tape of all our troubles till we can recite them from memory to anyone who asks, and even some who don't. There is a silver lining somewhere if we just search, and in the searching who knows what treasures we might find? Besides, it will keep us too busy to complain so much.

Go out there today and look for those silver linings—or the golden dragonflies, or whatever God has specially prepared to help you through this day. You will find them, but only if you have a mind to.

> *You prepare a table before me in the presence of my enemies; you anoint my head with oil; my cup overflows. Surely goodness and mercy shall follow* ***me all the days of my life,*** *and I shall dwell in the house of the* L*ORD* *forever.*
>
> Psalm 23.5–6

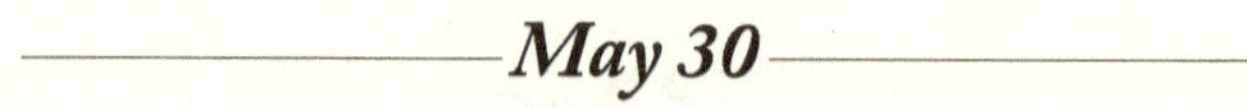

May 30

Recycling

Seems like it happens every 20 years or so—someone thinks they have discovered an amazing new concept that would fix all the problems of the world if everyone would just listen to them. In my college days it was wrapped up in this catchphrase:

teach the Man, not the plan—as if separating Christ from his mission were as easy as slipping skins off scalded tomatoes.

It always boils down to the same old thing: let's talk like Jesus, act like Jesus, and love like Jesus—but never confront like Jesus, rebuke like Jesus, and condemn like Jesus. Let's never be angry with anyone or expect anyone to change his lifestyle because "Jesus loved everyone no matter how bad they were."

Talk like Jesus? How about this? "Get behind me Satan! You are a stumbling-block to me" (Matt 16.23, addressed to one of his apostles). "You are following me not because you saw signs, but because you ate your fill" (John 6.26 to the crowds who followed him). "You are of your father the Devil, and your will is to do your father's desires" (John 8.44, to the believers in Jerusalem). "You serpents, you brood of vipers, how are you to escape the sentence of hell?" (Matt 23.33, to the religious leaders of the day.) Sounds like plain talk to me.

Act like Jesus? "And he looked round about on them *with anger*" (Mark 3.5). "And he made a scourge of cords, and cast all out of the temple, both the sheep and the oxen; and he poured out the changers' money, and overthrew their tables" (John 2.15); "and Jesus entered into the temple of God, and cast out all them that sold and bought in the temple, and overthrew the tables of the money-changers, and the seats of them that sold the doves" (Matt 21.12), the last two, separate instances, years apart. In our culture he would have been arrested.

Love like Jesus? "Neither do I condemn you; go your way and from here on *sin no more*" (John 8.11). "And Jesus, looking upon him, *loved* him, and said, '*One thing you lack*'" (Mark 10.21). Jesus never accepted unchanged lives.

Then there are the ones who try to separate Jesus from his body, "Christ… the head of the church, the savior of the body" (Eph 5.23); and those who try to separate him from his teaching, "Whoever goes onward and abides not in the teaching of Christ, has not God" (2 John 9). And let's not forget that he is the one who will come "in flaming fire, rendering vengeance on those who know not God and obey not the gospel" (2 Thes 1.7–8).

It is the same old thing every time—some folks will only accept Christ on their terms. It is not a matter of "making him the Lord of their lives." Instead, it is a matter of making themselves Lord, and telling Him which parts of him they will and won't accept. The people in John 6 had that problem. When Jesus finally laid it on the line, he did not mollycoddle them or dilute his gospel. Instead, he said, "Does this offend you? …And after this many of disciples turned back and no longer walked with him" (John 6.61, 66).

Did he chase them down? No, he simply turned to the twelve and said, "Will you go also?" (6.67). He was not about to accept anyone who did not accept *all* of Him.

Sooner or later all this nonsense will die down again, but I expect it to reappear in another 15 or 20 years, with someone else thinking he has discovered something new. Our focus then and now should be the focus those 12 had as they stood watching the crowds diminish and realizing, perhaps for the first time, that this calling was not a popular one. That even those they thought were on their side would leave at the first obstacle.

> *Lord, to whom shall we go? You have the words of eternal life.*
>
> John 6.68

May 31

I Forget

They say that anesthesia can cause you some memory problems. I have had so much of it in the past few years that I have started loading up on the green tea because they, the same they I guess, say it will not only help your memory, but will actually revive dying brain cells. If mine are being revived I would hate to think how many were in my brain's ICU just a few weeks ago. I grasp for words I am sure I know at least once or twice a day, walk into a room and then wonder why I'm there, and look at people I have known for years and can tell you everything about—everything except their names. I know there is another supplement that is supposed to help memory too, but I forget what it is.

Speaking of forgetting, I ran a quick search on e-Sword to find all the passages containing the admonition "Forget not," and was surprised how few there were. That tells me that the things I did find must be important.

The proverb writer says to "forget not my law" (3.1), but most of the "forget not" list is in the latter half of the New Testament.

"Forget not to show hospitality" the Hebrew writer tells us (13.2), and I was surprised to find that the actual Greek word for hospitality, *philoxenia*, means *love of strangers.* So when Peter tells us to use hospitality one to another (1 Pet 4.9), he is actually telling us to love each other like strangers. Mull that one over for awhile. I think there must surely be something lacking in how we treat strangers these days.

Later in the same chapter, the Hebrew writer adds "forget not to do good and share what you have, for with such sacrifices God is well-pleased" (13.16). I honestly believe that doing good is easy for all of us, but how about sharing what we have? In fact, Paul told the Ephesians that the reason they were to work was to have to give to others (Eph 4.28). I am not sure how well that sits with the average American, even as wealthy as we are compared to the rest of the world. We can always find an excuse *not* to share that somehow we make sound, not only plausible, but actually righteous.

Then Peter tells us to "forget not" that "a day is as a thousand years with the

Lord and a thousand years as a day" (2 Pet 3.8). Why is that important to remember? Because the world has gone on now for 2,000 years since the promise that the Lord would return, and it is easy to think it always will. Scoffers will always ridicule us for our faith, but even we become complacent, and let our righteousness backslide just a bit here and there, because there is always time to repent. Even if the Lord does not come back during our lifetimes, we should not forget that even young people die, and for all practical purposes, the Lord has come for them.

Some important things to remember, I think, especially if inspired men said so. Whether you drink your green tea or not, make sure you don't forget.

> *Bless the* LORD, *O my soul and all that is within me, bless his holy name. Bless the* LORD, *O my soul, and* ***forget not*** *all his benefits, who forgives all your iniquity and heals all your diseases, who redeems your life from the pit, who crowns you with steadfast love and mercy, who satisfies you with good so that your youth is renewed like the eagle's. …The steadfast love of the* LORD *is from everlasting to everlasting to those who fear him, and his righteousness to children's children, to those who keep his covenant* ***and remember*** *to do his commandments.*
>
> Psalm 103.1–5, 17–18

June 1

Sage Advice

I get these questions so often; let's kill two birds with one stone today.

Q: How do you use all those herbs you grow?

A: Dill is good in any mayonnaise based salad—potato salad, tuna salad, macaroni salad, *etc.* I also use it in my own homemade tartar sauce and deviled eggs.

Basil is good in anything with tomatoes. Throw the leaves of red basil whole in a salad for color and a tasty surprise. When using basil in long cooking items like marinara, be sure to add another sprinkle fresh at the end, just before serving. And anyone with a basil plant needs to learn how to make pesto, the ultimate basil sauce.

Rosemary goes with poultry, pork, and lamb. Sage goes with poultry, pork and beef. Thyme is good with chicken and beef. Tarragon is good with veal and chicken, particularly chicken salad. Use chives when you want a mild onion flavor but not the sharpness of a raw onion. Parsley goes just about anywhere, and not just for garnish.

At Thanksgiving, think of Simon and Garfunkel when you season your bird: "parsley, sage, rosemary, and thyme," but I usually leave rosemary out of the dressing. And the best potatoes you will ever eat are small red potatoes, steamed about

20 minutes with butter, salt, and pepper only, and finished with a heaping handful of mixed chives, parsley, and dill. That will get you started using herbs, and you can experiment to discover more.

Q: How do you take care of herbs?

A: Generally speaking, herbs do not like wet feet, so use well-drained soil. During our recent drought years, I have never gone wrong by watering them every day, and fertilizing at least once a week with a liquid fertilizer for house plants or vegetables.

When you harvest, cut the thickest stems near the bottom. In fact, cut chives at ground level to insure continued growth. Most of the time you only use the leaves. With rosemary and thyme, pull backwards down the stems to remove the leaves easily. If the stem is so tender that it breaks, then just chop it along with the leaves. For other plants, the leaves will easily pull off.

As a general rule, don't let your herbs bloom. Pinch the buds off as they appear, as well as any leaves or stems that get past their prime and turn yellow. Blossoms will take away from the leaves and will turn some herbs bitter.

Now what is all that advice worth? Well, if you don't live in Florida, it is not worth as much as if you do. If you live in South Florida, it might not be worth much either. For you to be sure my advice will work for you, we have to live in the same place. I am in Zone 9 on all those gardening maps, a zone unto itself. We have frosts and freezes fairly often in December and January, and even as late as April or as early as November. On the other hand, once the nighttime temperatures stay above 72, which can happen in early June, the tomatoes stop setting their blooms, and by late June tomatoes and melons may boil in the afternoon sun.

We all understand that you should think about where you get your advice. I use the Union County (Florida) Extension Office. If you live anywhere else, you shouldn't. As many questions as I get, it seems to me that many people are anxious to receive advice on this subject. Why aren't we that smart with spiritual things? I think the answer is a five letter word—pride. How much sense does that make? Wouldn't it be a shame if that kept us from finding help with things much more important that growing and cooking with herbs?

Consider for a moment, the young teenager who was told that she would give birth to the Son of God. Think about the difficulties she was about to face—perhaps the most difficult ones of telling her parents and her betrothed husband that she was pregnant by the Holy Spirit; even if they believed her, the rest of the community could still count to nine and Gabriel was not likely to visit them all. Where did she immediately turn for support and advice? She went to her older, wiser relative Elizabeth, herself a mother-to-be under miraculous and difficult circumstances. She had already dealt with whispers for six months and became an example of reward after long endurance. They shared faith in a common destiny, evidenced by continuing miracles, including the silence of a miraculously stricken Zacharias. Even at her young age, Mary was wise in choosing to whom she would turn for advice.

On the hand we have Rehoboam, Solomon's son, who, instead of listening to the older wiser counselors who had been there with his father, listened to his young hot-headed friends and wound up losing the majority of his kingdom for it (1 Kgs 12.6–11).

God knew we would need help as we lived our lives. That is one reason he set things up as he did—families with older generations to help the younger, and churches with the wisdom of elders and older brethren. Look for people who have more knowledge of the scriptures than you do. Look for people who have had success, who have come safely through the same trials you are facing, who, in other words, live where you do. God has given us ample help if we will only take advantage of it, so much, in fact, that ignorance will be no excuse. It will simply be a mask for pride.

> *Aged women likewise be reverent in demeanor, not slanderers nor enslaved to much wine, teachers of that which is good; that they may train the young women to love their husbands, to love their children, to be sober-minded, chaste, workers at home, kind, being in subjection to their own husbands, that the word of God be not blasphemed: the younger men likewise exhort to be sober-minded. ...Likewise, ye younger, be subject unto the elder. Yea, all of you gird yourselves with humility, to serve one another: for God resists the proud, but gives grace to the humble.*
>
> Titus 2.3–6; 1 Peter 5.5

June 2

The Donkey and the Cow

My neighbor takes as little care of his animals as he does his property. The horses, donkeys and cows all have ribs that show through their skin and sores on their hides, unfortunately, just below the level that the animal control people consider criminal neglect so they will not intervene. I often think to myself that I would like to see those people have to endure the same things as these animals and then decide if it is abuse or not, particularly after those poor creatures have broken through the fence yet again and we must dodge them as they wander the road looking for something to eat. We have even thrown some of our garden refuse over the fence at times to try to help them out.

As I walked up to unlock the gate one morning for an expected visitor, a donkey and a cow stood just across the west fence. The donkey evidently saw a meal on the hoof, walked up to the cow and started chewing its left ear. The cow was not pleased with the situation and turned around. So the donkey started chewing its right ear. The cow yanked its head away and trotted off, with the donkey trailing behind. As soon as the cow stopped, the donkey headed straight for her head and grabbed an ear again. Once again the cow turned around only to have the other ear chomped on. She took off again. I watched this for nearly five minutes before the cow finally headed for the fencerow and quite purposefully stuck her head in a bush.

The donkey tried to get to an ear and found himself struck in the face by the limbs and branches of the wild myrtle and unable to get to the cow's ears. I am afraid I could not help myself—I laughed out loud and cheered for the cow. After a few minutes, the donkey gave up and left, trotting across the field straight for another cow, braying loudly as he went. I had to go about my own business then, but I assume that cow had success as well since, while I still see the outlines of ribs and spines, I have yet to see any of those animals earless.

Sometimes some braying donkey of a human comes along and tries to chew on our ears. I am afraid that too often we let him when we should be turning aside and, if he is persistent, finding a bush to stick our heads into. As long as there is a market for gossip and slander, there will be people to fill the need, and when we listen we are no better than they because we find pleasure in their sin.

Gossip can accomplish a lot, and none of it good. It can ruin friendships, break up families, divide churches, and permanently stain reputations. It has been going on since Satan, the "slanderer," told Eve that God was just a selfish tyrant who did not want to share. Look where that got all of us.

Today, when someone comes to you with the latest "dirt," find a bush and stick your head into it. Don't let that person chew on your ears. Sooner or later he will get the message and move on.

He who goes about as a tale-bearer reveals secrets; therefore company not with him who opens wide his lips.

Proverbs 20.19

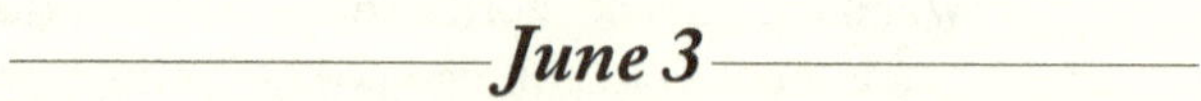

June 3

Up Close and Personal

I had an up close and personal encounter with a wildflower a couple of weeks ago. When we plant a new bed out in the field, we baby it the first year. The point is for them to grow up scattered in the grasses and among other wildflowers in a natural way, but if you don't get them off to a good start, they won't stand a chance with all the competition out there for ground space and rainwater.

So I was weeding the latest patch, which we had let go far beyond the normal time span. I had difficulty even finding some of the small plants amid all the waist high grass and weeds. I had nearly finished, was soaking wet and black up to my elbows, when I noticed one more low-growing weed and bent over to pull it. I did not see the bare stalk of the wildflower right between my feet, leafless and flowerless, standing three feet high. I did not know it was there until, as I bent over, it slid right into my eye like a hot wire. Which eye? The one which most lately has been operated on, the one with the shunt, the capsular tension ring, and the silicone lens, the one that already hurts the most.

The doctor and I spent nearly two weeks fixing me up after this little mishap, checking to see if there was any permanent damage, checking to see if the shunt had been knocked out of place, checking for infection, and worse, for plant fungus. As it turns out, all I had was a hematoma and a laceration, but it was an exciting couple of weeks.

That was too close and personal an encounter with a flower, but we can never be too close and personal with God. I have had to learn that. The prevailing sentiment many years ago seemed to be that we did not want to do or say anything that might make someone apply a religious pejorative to us indicating belief in something other than correct Bible teaching about God, Christ, and the Holy Spirit. Instead of saying, "I'm blessed," instead of saying, "God took care of me," indeed, instead of attributing anything to the providence of God, we said, "I'm lucky." We wouldn't want someone to get the wrong idea, would we?

Where did we come up with that? Read some of David's psalms. He gave God the credit for everything. Read Hannah's song, or Moses and Miriam's after crossing the Red Sea. Since when don't the people of God tell everyone what God has done for them?

Read some of Paul's sermons. He does not seem a bit concerned that someone might use what he says to give credence to false teaching. "You know that idol you have out there?" he asks the Athenians, "the one to the Unknown God? Let me tell you about him." He tells Felix, "But this I confess to you that after the Way which they call a sect, so serve I the God of our fathers" (Acts 24.14). It didn't matter a bit what people called it, as long as he could talk about it. In fact, he used their misconceptions as opportunities to preach the Gospel.

Maybe that is my problem—I don't want to talk about it. It makes me uncomfortable. It has nothing to do with whether someone gets the wrong idea about the Truth, but everything to do with me feeling ill at ease, or downright embarrassed. I don't want to be called a religious fanatic and certainly not a "Holy Roller!" Yes, I want a close, personal relationship with God, as long as no one else knows about it.

But here is the deal: If I am too embarrassed by my relationship with God to even acknowledge it, then He won't acknowledge me either, and *I* am the one with everything to lose.

Go out there today and say or do something that will make someone else curious enough to ask you a question. Then open your mouth and unashamedly tell them how wonderful an up close and personal relationship with your Creator and Savior really is.

> *Everyone therefore who shall confess me before men, him will I also confess before my Father who is in Heaven. But whoever shall deny me before men, him will I also deny before my Father who is in Heaven.*
>
> Matthew 10.32–33

Abracadabra

We tend to think that legalism and emotionalism are the only dangers we need to be wary of in our worship to God. We must be careful that the ritual aspect of our group worship be neither heartless in thought nor perverted by passion. But in 1 Samuel 4–6, God's people found yet another way to distort their spiritual worship.

As was so often the case, the Philistines once again troubled them. They went to battle and promptly lost 4,000 soldiers. What should they do? Talk to God about it? No, they said. Instead, "Let us bring the ark of the covenant of the Lord here from Shiloh that it may save us" (4.3). Not that God may save us, but that *it* may save us, treating it like some sort of magic charm.

When the ark was brought into the camp, the people roared with such a shout that it scared the Philistines. "A god has come into the camp," they said (4.7). Note that there was little difference in the way these pagans thought about the ark and the way the Israelites did. During the next battle 30,000 Israelites lost their lives and the Ark of the Covenant was captured.

The story of how the ark was returned to Israel is an interesting one that would take too much time for this little essay. Suffice it to say that when it found its way home, the Israelites who greeted it said, "Who is able to stand before the Lord, this Holy God?" (6.20). At least a few people had learned a lesson.

Surrounded by paganism on all sides, they had become tainted by its beliefs, many of which were bound up in sorcery and witchcraft. They equated Jehovah with the idols, and the rituals of His worship with the rituals of the heathens.

Do you think that cannot happen to us today? I have lost track of the number of times I have heard a fallen Christian end his litany of faults with the disclaimer, "But I've been baptized!" Somehow that is supposed to keep him safe from the wrath of God, no matter how much he has deliberately provoked that wrath and willingly continues to do so with no intention to change. Baptism, instead of a union of the believer with the sacrifice of his Lord and the resurrection to a new life, has become to such people a ritual performed to break a curse. "Pour the ashes of a rat's tail on a bird's wing, and hop on one foot three times with your eyes closed," would have had as much meaning.

Then there is the matter of the Lord's Supper. Rather than a memorial feast we celebrate with the Lord and our spiritual family, it is treated as a magic potion. "At least I got there in time for the Lord's Supper," is uttered with a "Whew!" and a sigh of relief. Visitors come in late and demand to be served even if the assembly worship is finished. Some members show up only for those "magical" few minutes as if nothing else were worth their trouble.

The same sorts of things happen with prayer, as if it were some magic formula that can only be repeated in certain ways, rather than a pouring out of the heart to a loving Father. And we think we don't have the same problems as those Old Testament Israelites?

Treating God as if He were on the same level as a pagan deity and could be appeased the same way earned those people some of the most scathing indictments in the Old Testament. The danger is that one will think Jehovah can be swapped out in a fair trade. God took care of that notion in the book of Hosea. Israel actually thought that those pagan gods were her source of blessings (2.5), and so God said, "For she did not know that I gave her the grain, and the new wine, and the oil, and multiplied unto her silver and gold, which they used for Baal. Therefore will I take back my grain in the time thereof, and my new wine in the season thereof, and will pluck away my wool and my flax which should have covered her nakedness" (2.8–9). Suddenly, she figured out where it really came from.

Attitudes that treat God and His worship in such a pagan manner are no better. Rather than reverencing God they demean Him. Rather than showing awe for an all-powerful Creator, they minimize that feeling into nothing more than pacifying a petty, capricious tyrant.

Serving our God is a duty certainly, but not one we can fulfill in a slapdash, haphazard fashion just so we get it done in time to avoid the consequences. It is a service He wants us to willingly offer in a careful, obedient, heartfelt manner—an obligation certainly, but also a privilege.

For thus says the LORD, who created the heavens (he is God!), who formed the earth and made it (he established it; he did not create it empty, he formed it to be inhabited!): "I am the LORD, and there is no other. I did not speak in secret, in a land of darkness; I did not say to the offspring of Jacob, 'Seek me in vain. I the LORD speak the truth; I declare what is right.' Assemble yourselves and come; draw near together, you survivors of the nations! They have no knowledge who carry about their wooden idols, and keep on praying to a god that cannot save. Declare and present your case; let them take counsel together! Who told this long ago? Who declared it of old? Was it not I, the LORD? And there is no other god besides me, a righteous God and a Savior; there is none besides me. Turn to me and be saved, all the ends of the earth! For I am God, and there is no other. By myself I have sworn; From my mouth has gone out in righteousness a word that shall not return: 'To me every knee shall bow, every tongue shall swear allegiance.' Only in the Lord, *it shall be said of me, are righteousness and strength; to him shall come and be ashamed all who were incensed against him. In the* Lord *all the offspring of Israel shall be justified and shall glory."*

Isaiah 45.18–25

June 5

Bread Crumbs

Have you discovered *panko* yet? *Panko* is Japanese bread crumbs, an extra light variety that cooks up super-crunchy on things like crab cakes and shrimp. They also cost more than regular bread crumbs, but in certain applications they are worth it. On the other hand a chicken or veal Milanese needs a sturdier crumb to stand up to the lemony butter sauce, an oven fried pork chop needs melba toast crumbs that will cook to a crunch without burning in a high heat oven, and my favorite broccoli casserole needs the faint sweetness of a butter cracker crumb to really set it off.

Although none of these dishes are the food of poverty, using the crumbs and crusts of food rather than tossing them out certainly grew out of the necessity of using whatever was at hand to feed hungry bellies for thousands of years, and now we all do it, even when there is plenty in the pantry. Pies and cheesecakes with graham cracker crumb crusts, anyone? Dressing to stuff your poultry? Bread pudding on a cold winter night? Streusel on that warm coffee cake in the morning? Bread-infused peasant food has even shown up on gourmet cooking shows in the form of panzanella (salad) and ribolita (soup), both of which use chunks of stale bread to bolster their ability to satisfy appetites.

That reminds me of a woman 2,000 years ago who understood the value of leftovers. Her little daughter was demon-possessed, so ill she could not travel, but her mother had heard of someone who might be able to help, who even then was in hiding from the crowds on the border of her country. It took a lot for her to seek him out, first leaving her sick child in someone else's care, then approaching this Jewish rabbi, a type who had either reviled or ignored her all her life; but a desperate mother will make any sacrifice to save her child.

Sure enough, even though she addressed him by the Messianic title, "Son of David," he "answered her not a word" (Matt 15.22–23). Still she persisted, and this time she was insulted—he called her a dog. Oh, he was nicer about it than most, using the Greek word for "little pet dog," *kunarion,* rather than the epithet she usually heard from his kind—*kuno,* ownerless scavenging dogs that run wild in the streets, but still he made her inequality in his eyes obvious.

This woman, though, was ready to accept his judgment of her, "Even the dogs get the crumbs, sir." Moreover, she understood that was all she needed. This man, whose abilities she had heard of from afar, was more than just a man, and even the tiniest morsel of his power was enough to heal her child, even from a distance.

Do we understand that? Do we realize that one drop of God's power can fix any problem we have, and more, do we have the humility to accept our place in His plan, even if it is not what we have planned? Yes, every day I ask for more—more grace, more faith, more of His power to change me and use me, but do I really comprehend His strength? I would say it was impossible to do so, except for the example of this desperate Gentile mother who, like a widow of her nation hundreds of years before her, had more faith, trust, and humility than the religious men of God's chosen people (1 Kgs 17; Luke 4.25–26).

And for this, perhaps, God chose her to foreshadow in the Son's life the crumbling of the barrier between Jew and Gentile, and the inclusive nature of the gospel which had been foretold from the beginning: "in thy seed shall *all* nations of the earth be blessed" (Gen 22.17).

Do I have the faith and humility to accept God's plan for me? One thing is certain—this Gentile mother knew she had nowhere else to turn, and neither do we.

Even God's crumbs are enough to satisfy our every need.

For this cause I bow my knees to the Father… that you… may be strong to apprehend with all the saints what is the breadth and length and height and depth, and to know the love of Christ which passes knowledge, that you may be filled with all the fullness of God… him who is able to do exceeding abundantly above all that we ask or think.

Ephesians 3.14, 17–20

June 6

Weeding the Lilies

My daylilies have been on a roller coaster ride lately. They bloomed so prodigiously, and multiplied so quickly that ten years ago I had to dig them up from their bed by the grape arbor and replant them thinner, planting another bed behind the shed with some of the extras, and still giving away three five-gallon buckets full of bulbs. They bloomed like crazy again, multiplying year by year, until once again they needed thinning.

Four years ago, Keith had to do it for me—after a summer of eye surgeries I was relegated to supervising from a lawn chair. But since then, few have come up and fewer have bloomed. Perhaps we mulched them too well, Keith thought, so he raked off half the mulch this past year to see what would happen. More blooms is what happened, and things seem better. Next year should be another banner year of bright yellow and orange blooms.

I have noticed another thing about these lilies. Even with mulch, the weeds still manage to creep in. The first year I pulled grass till my hands were sore and swollen. Blackberry thorns left them torn and bleeding, even through gloves. The next year I did it again. The third year, things were better—most of the weeds were along the edge. By the fourth year two weedings, one at the beginning of the year, and another near the end, took care of it.

Some day, I would like to think that the weeding won't be necessary at all, but I live in a land of rain and sunshine, warmth even in winter, and humidity that keeps the plants green and moist. Still, it is encouraging to see some progress. I may never have a weed-free flower bed, but at least there are more flowers than weeds these days.

How about me? Am I still pulling out the weeds in my heart? Unfortunately, yes. I do not believe the job will ever be finished. I do believe that there are fewer now than many years ago, and I think I am meant to notice that, that it is not a sign of arrogance to see the improvement in my life. Isn't encouragement a necessary element of growth?

That old saying, "Humility is the thing that as soon as you think you have it, you've lost it," is ridiculous. How else am I to have the impetus to keep going, especially when the job is unending and obviously so? Why is it wrong to recognize my progress? I might as well listen to Satan as to listen to someone say that.

Several times Paul told the people he wrote to that they were doing well, that they had grown, that he was proud of them. James talks about looking in the mirror of God's word to see myself. Am I only supposed to see the faults and none of the good things? That is exactly what leads people to become so despondent they quit trying.

"Might as well be hanged for a sheep as a goat," applies to people who never receive any positive feedback, who are always criticized and told they have done wrong. They think if they are going to receive that kind of response when doing their best, they might as well stop trying so hard. Satan counts on that feeling, and too often we give him the opportunity to make use of it in ourselves and others.

So look at yourself carefully today. Notice the things you still need to work on and do exactly that. But also notice where you have improved and gain some encouragement from it. Maybe the job today won't be quite so tough. If you have had a difficult time lately, that little bit of encouragement may be the thing that gets you through another day.

> *For you know how, like a father with his children, we exhorted each one of you and encouraged you and charged you to walk in a manner worthy of God, who calls you into his own kingdom and glory. And we also thank God constantly for this, that when you received the word of God, which you heard from us, you accepted it not as the word of men but as what it really is, the word of God, which is at work in you believers.*

1 Thessalonians 2.11–13

June 7

The Acid Test

It is a culinary fact that fat tempers acid. That is why some of the world's favorite dishes combine a good helping of both. Melted mozzarella offsets a tomato-y pizza sauce. A cheese-stuffed calzone is almost unbearably rich without a small bowl of marinara to dip it in. A homemade pimento cheese sandwich *screams* for a homemade dill pickle on the side. The South's favorite summer treat, a drippy tomato sandwich on high quality white bread, simply *must* be slathered with a glop of mayo. Fat and acid—the perfect combination; it's why we dip French fries in ketchup and chips in salsa; it's why the favorite toppings for a hot dog are ketchup, mustard, relish, and chili. It's why we put whipped cream on strawberries and why a key lime pie is just about the perfect dessert.

Trials, tribulations, sufferings and afflictions are the acid tests for Christians. No one wants to go through them, yet we all understand that is what makes us stronger, builds up our faith, keeps us able to endure till the end. All of us would be spiritual wimps without them.

What we fail to realize is that God gives us plenty of fat to offset them. How many blessings can you count in your life today, not even considering the most wonderful one of all, your salvation? How many good things happened to you *just this morning*? Did your car start? Did you make it to work safely? Are your children safely ensconced in a safe place? Do you still have a roof over your head? Is there food in your refrigerator? Is the electricity on, the water running and the AC humming away? Are there flowers blooming in your yard and birds singing in the trees? Do you have pleasant memories to calm you in the midst of sorrows? Is there a Bible in your home and are you free to read it whenever you want to? Did you pray to a Father who loves you more than anything else? How many more "fat" items can we come up with? Probably enough to fill even the gigabytes of memory in our computers if we just took the time to think of them. If you have trouble, just ask a three-year-old—they are pros at this.

I don't mean to make light of people's problems with this little analogy—but then again, maybe I do. Paul calls them "light afflictions" in 2 Corinthians 4, and he was including persecution to the death in that context. Compared to the end result, compared to the reward, compared to our Savior's sufferings so we could have that reward, our trials and tribulations are light indeed.

So today, if you are in the middle of a struggle, if the acid is burning your soul, look for the fat God gave you to temper it. Look for everything good in your day, in your life, no matter how small it may seem. If that doesn't work, and sometimes it doesn't, remember the good that will result from your testing, and don't let it be for nothing. Don't let Satan win. The bigger the tomato, the more mayo God smears on, *if you only know where to look.*

> *Wherefore we faint not, for though our outer man is decaying, our inward man is renewed day by day. For this momentary light affliction works for us more and more exceedingly an eternal weight of glory;* ***while we look not at things which are seen, but at the things which are not seen; for the things which are seen are temporal, but the things which are not seen are eternal.***
>
> 2 Corinthians 4.16–18

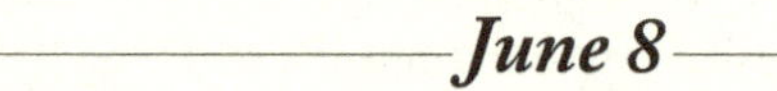

June 8

Advil or Aleve?

I knew he was wrong. I had bought more Aleve just the week before, yet Keith was fussing because we had run out and I needed it after surgery. I pulled myself up out of the chair, went into the bathroom, sat in the floor and began systematically emptying the cabinet under the lavatory, determined to prove him wrong. No Aleve. Four bottles of Advil, but no Aleve.

So later in the evening Keith handed me the pharmacy flyer. On the sixth page I said, "Aha!" and showed him the ad.

He gave me a funny look. "Don't you dare buy any more Advil," he said.

I yanked the paper back and looked again. Sure enough, there was an Advil ad where seconds before I was certain I had seen an Aleve ad.

"Well," he muttered, "now we know how we wound up with so much Advil."

Please don't tell me you haven't done the same thing; it will ruin my illusions.

Yet too many times we do this with the scriptures, and the practice is not new.

If anyone thought they knew God's Word, it was the scribes, Pharisees, and priests. Yet Jesus told them, "You have not his word abiding in you: for whom he sent, him you believe not. You search the scriptures, because you think that in them you have eternal life; and these are they which bear witness of me" (John 5.38–39) Notice: Searching the scriptures is not the same thing as abiding in them. They searched the scriptures, just as we claim to do, and still didn't see what was right in front of their noses. Here is the problem: You must *want* to see the Truth before you *can* see it.

I wanted to see a sale for Aleve. The fact that both products started with a capital A, had five letters, including L and V in each, and each came in a blue or blue-ish carton did not make them the same thing. My pharmacy was not going to give me one for the price of the other, or allow a coupon for one to be used on the other.

Do you think it is easy to give up long held beliefs? I once taught a class where I gave evidence that something they had heard all their lives *might* not be right. The tenacity with which they held on to that old belief, trying to find excuses to still believe it, was amusing because it was something that did not really matter. Yet these were honest women who had time and time again shown a willingness to accept a newly discovered truth. If that can happen so easily to the honest and sincere, just imagine what might happen if you went into your Bible study having already decided what you wanted to find.

You may wind up with a bottle of Advil instead of Aleve, and it just might make a big difference.

> *But they refused to hearken, and pulled away the shoulder, and stopped their ears that they might not hear. Yea, they made their hearts as an adamant stone, lest they should hear the law, and the words which Jehovah of hosts had sent by his Spirit by the former prophets: therefore there came great wrath from Jehovah of hosts.*
>
> Zechariah 7.11–12

June 9

Chili Powder

At the end of the garden season, I dry out my hot chili peppers and make chili powder. I have found a good formula, one part chili pepper, two parts ground cumin, one part dried oregano, and two parts garlic powder. The first few times I made it, I used a blend of Anaheim and cayenne peppers. This year Keith shopped for the chili pepper plants and came home with habaneros. If you know anything about the Scoville heat scale, you know that cayennes, while not at the mild end of the scale, are a couple hundred thousand units removed from habaneros which sit at the hottest end.

To make chili powder, you must first dry the chili peppers, then remove the stems and grind them up. A lot of the heat is in the seeds, so I, being a wimp when it comes to hot peppers, shook out the loose seeds as well—habaneros are hot enough as is. I had enough sense to wear latex gloves while handling these babies, but that is where good sense stopped. When I took the lid off the grinder to see if any pieces remained intact, the cloud of chili powder, totally invisible to the naked eye, rose up into my face. How did I know? My nose started running, my lips started burning, and I sneezed nearly a dozen times. I had pepper-maced myself. I am so very glad I had reading glasses on. I do not know what might have happened to these poor eyes! I know people who don't even use gloves to work with hot peppers, but next time I will reach for a gas mask!

Sin and conscience work the same way. Especially nowadays when sophistication is judged by how little one allows sinful behavior to shock him, we have a tendency to think we can sin indiscriminately and feel just fine about ourselves afterwards. What was it Paul said about the idolatrous pagans? "For when Gentiles who do not have the law, by nature do what the law requires, they are a law to themselves even though they do not have the law. They show that the law of God is written on their hearts, while their conscience also bears witness, and their conflicting thoughts either accuse or even excuse themselves" (Rom 2.14–15). You can't get away from your conscience no matter how sophisticated you think you are.

The scriptures are littered with people who suffered pangs of conscience. Adam and Eve hid themselves after they had sinned. The brothers of Joseph twice confessed their sin against their brother, attributing all the bad things that happened in Egypt with the hostile "Egyptian" ruler as their just recompense. Pharaoh, of all people, said to Moses and Aaron, "This time I have sinned. The Lord is in the right, and I and my people are in the wrong" (Exod 9.27). David sinned more than the once we often focus on. His "heart smote him" after he numbered the people in 2 Samuel 24 and his psalms of repentance after the sin against Bathsheba and Uriah abound with overwhelming guilt.

Herod was so wrought with guilt after killing John that he thought Jesus was John coming back from the dead. Peter's denial caused him to "weep bitterly," while Judas's betrayal led to suicide. Even Paul, a man who surely knew he was forgiven, called himself "the chiefest of sinners" to the end of his life.

And we think we can get away with sin and have it not affect us? Guilt is like that burning chili pepper cloud. You can't see it, but your conscience will still feel its effects, and if you don't deal with it, you will lead a miserable life—at least until you burn that conscience out as if you had "branded it with a hot iron" (1 Tim 4.2).

Do you know how to get rid of the pain of burning chili peppers? Dairy products. If you forget your gloves and those oils get under your nails or in a nick or cut, soak your hands in milk. That is also why there is usually a dollop of sour cream on most Mexican dishes.

Do you know how to get rid of the pain of a burning conscience? Soak it in the blood of Christ. It works wonders.

> *For if the blood of goats and bulls and the ashes of a heifer sprinkling them that have been defiled sanctify unto the cleanness of the flesh, how much more shall the blood of Christ who through the eternal Spirit offered himself without blemish unto God, cleanse your conscience from dead works to serve the living God?*
>
> Hebrews 9.13–14

Rule Books

It happened again the last time I went in. I got another new resident assigned to do the preliminary work-up. Since it was a cornea appointment instead of a glaucoma appointment he had not even planned to check the pressures. I mentioned that my vision was foggy and my eye felt a little different. Could that be caused by higher pressures?

"Oh no," he confidently asserted. "Your pressure would have to be over 50 for that to happen, and you would be throwing up by now."

I looked at him and said, "I've been at 70 before without symptoms." I am not sure he believed me until he went to the next hall over and pulled my other file, the four inch thick one with more notes than he had probably seen on any six patients put together. He read for several minutes and discovered that the obvious course of action for most patients is the worst course for me, and quietly took my pressures. They were indeed high. If nothing else, that day he learned that not all patients follow the rules.

We can be a little like that inexperienced young doctor when it comes to following God's law. We so badly want it all spelled out in black and white for every situation life hands us—it's so much easier than having to think and examine our hearts. That's why we who have led sheltered lives, perhaps growing up in the church as second, third, or even fourth generation Christians who have never had a drink, never let a bad word slip, and never even considered breaking one of the "big" commandments, can be so judgmental about others who still struggle every day. A young Christian who came from a rough background recently said to me, "People in the church look down on me when I talk about battling sin. They say if my faith is genuine, it shouldn't be that way." We carry our rule books, measuring everyone around us, instead of using the sense God gave us, and the love and encouragement he expects of us.

Rule Book people have another problem as well. Despite their protestations of having a true faith because it does so many works, many never truly believe in the grace of God. Some of these poor misguided people worry themselves silly wondering whether they are truly saved. They second-guess every decision they make; they are never confident that they are doing well. Someone has forgotten to read John's first epistle to them, which he wrote "so you may know you have eternal life" (1 John 5.13).

Finally, those folks work so hard to get every little detail right that they often miss the point of the commandment they are trying to follow. The Pharisees are the ultimate example. Even though they began with the simple and righteous desire to follow God's law exactly, they eventually reached the point that they totally missed the focus of the Law. It became a study of minutiae instead of concept. I once read a bit of one their documents discussing the passage, "I meditate on thee in the night watches" (Psa 63.6). The point of the passage is to be thinking on spiritual things all through the day and night, but the next four pages were devoted to various rabbis' arguments about how many night watches there were so they could be sure to meditate exactly that many times! That is what happens when you focus only on the rules and never the heart. Surely none of us wants to be in a group Jesus called "a brood of vipers."

Do not misunderstand me. I believe God has a set of laws He expects us to follow to the letter, but life is not always simple. Sometimes a situation arises that is not cut and dried. We have to actually think about what the right course of action is and make the best possible decision. Sometimes what I feel is right for me may not be what you feel is right for you. It is not situation ethics. It is simply a place where God has not spelled things out, but has left us as His children to pray and meditate, and make a decision from a heart of love and good intentions, and then to trust His grace if we have made a mistake. To do otherwise, or to simply do nothing, would be the sin, and to judge otherwise, would be the self-righteousness Jesus despised.

> *And he spoke also this parable unto certain who trusted in themselves that they were righteous, and set all others at naught: Two men went up into the temple to pray; the one a Pharisee, and the other a publican. The Pharisee stood and prayed thus with himself, God, I thank you, that I am not as the rest of men, extortioners, unjust, adulterers, or even as this publican. I fast twice in the week; I give tithes of all that I get. But the publican, standing afar off, would not lift up so much as his eyes unto heaven, but smote his breast, saying, God, be merciful to me a sinner. I say unto you, This man went down to his house justified rather than the other: for every one who exalts himself shall be humbled; but he who humbles himself shall be exalted.*
>
> Luke 18.9–14

Gone Fishing

We have a neighbor who loves to fish. In fact, he fishes so much that he cannot possibly use all the fish he brings home. Lucky for us! I now have an unending supply, usually of sea trout and shrimp, some of the best stuff out there. When he brings it home, he even cleans it before he calls. Amazing! But someone has to do some messy work in order for anyone to enjoy the fruits of fishing. Unless you go to a fish market, or the seafood section of your local grocer, or, even easier, the freezer case.

Maybe that's our problem—we've been to too many fish markets.

Seems like when we go fishing for men, we don't want anything messy. The only ones we look for are the WASPs with nuclear families, unfettered by problems of any sort. That's where we build our meetinghouses, pass out our meeting announcements, and do our mass mailings. We don't want people with built-in problems, people overcoming addictions, people with messy family lives, people with "big bad sins" in their history. No one wants a "high maintenance" convert who needs our support, our encouragement, our patience, and certainly not our time! In fact, once a long time ago, Keith was chastised for "bringing the wrong class of people to church."

To whom did Jesus go? "Now all the publicans and sinners were drawing near to him to hear him" (Luke 15.1), and I seem to remember a woman who had been married five times and was living with another man (John 4.18). Would we have even given them the time of day?

Jesus only appeals to those who need him, and unfortunately, people who have no "big" problems, no obvious needs, seldom think they need anyone. It usually takes a crisis to wake them up. So why are we so insistent upon turning our efforts to teach the gospel to the very ones who are least likely to listen?

Maybe we no longer want to be fishers of men. The "cleaning" is too messy, too difficult, too heart-wrenching, and too time-consuming. Instead of being fishers of men, as the old saying goes, we just want to be keepers of the aquarium, with a built-in filter (preacher) and someone else to feed the fish (elders and class teachers) so we can swim around in a pretty glass box with plastic mermaids and divers, and live our lives unbothered by things like helping one another grow to spirituality, and scraping the algae off our souls.

Maybe we have forgotten, or never even knew, the mindset of the first century church—a dynamic group of people, spreading God's word to everyone they met, trying to take as many "fish" as they could to Heaven with them, regardless of how messy their lives were.

Maybe someone needs to come fishing for us again.

> *And the scribes of the Pharisees, when they saw that he was eating with the sinners and the publicans, said unto his disciples, "How is it that he eats and drinks with publicans and sinners?" And when Jesus heard it, he said to them, "They that are whole have no need of a physician, but they that are sick. I came not to call the righteous, but sinners."*
>
> Mark 2.16–17

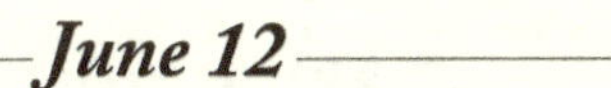

June 12

Picking Up Where We Left Off

We recently had a visit from some old friends we had not seen in 25 years. It was as if it were just yesterday. We spent the time saying, "Remember this one? Remember that one? But whatever happened to so and so? Remember when we went here or there, did this or that?" We started talking and went on for seven hours. We looked at pictures too, usually recognizing old friends in an instant—the eyes never change.

Seven hours, while a good visit, is not enough time to catch up on the entire 25 years since we had seen this couple, or the 31 years since we had seen our mutual friends. Maybe that is why one of the greatest appeals of Heaven is seeing loved ones and friends once again. How many hymns do we sing about it?

> "Dreaming of the comrades that so long have gone..."
> "Saved ones gone to be with Jesus... now are waiting for my coming..."
> "Oh, think of the saints over there, who before us the journey have trod..."
> "If we never meet again this side of Heaven, I will meet you on that beautiful shore."

How many funeral sermons leave us with the hope that once again we will all be together?

It's real, you know. Jesus promised a believing centurion, "Many shall come from the east and the west and shall sit down with Abraham and Isaac and Jacob in the kingdom of Heaven" (Matt 8.11). If their loved ones will see them again, why won't I see mine? After Lazarus's death, Martha said to Jesus, "I know that he will rise again in the resurrection in the last day" (John 11.24). Jesus never said anything to indicate her perception was wrong. It's a real hope, a real promise, one that should get us through the worst temptations and the worst trials successfully.

Isn't it worth any sacrifice or any trial to see a long gone grandparent or parent again, a beloved mate who made the trip ahead of you, or old friends who meant so much to you? That's how it will be, picking up where we left off when they had to say good-bye, if we only want it badly enough.

Beyond the sunset, oh glad reunion,
With our dear loved ones who've gone before.
In that fair homeland we'll know no parting,
Beyond the sunset, forever more.

June 13

Staking Your Tent

We just returned from a long camping weekend. We started camping only after I discovered tents that were completely self-enclosed. Even the floor was sewn into the walls and ceiling. Nothing could get in there but us! For a city girl this was very important. Our first tent was a hexagonal dome. It was put out by a company called Camel, and the brown tent did look a little something like a camel's hump.

Most of the time, we would pack up to come home from a camping trip with the tent still wet from the morning's dew. That meant we had to set it up out in the sunny field once we got home to let it dry out. We never bothered to stake it since it usually dried in under a half hour. As it dried, one of us crawled inside with the portable vacuum to get all the dirt out as well. My younger son Nathan was enjoying that chore once while I hung out sleeping bags and tarps to dry and air out. A little breeze came up and suddenly I was hearing this little voice saying, "What's going on? Hey! *Help!*" I looked up in time to see that self-contained, flat bottomed dome, rolling on its sides across the field in the wind, with my little boy evidently tumbling around inside—and from the sounds of it, not nearly as gracefully as a hamster on its wheel.

At that time he was about 11, still less than 100 pounds, and only about four-and-a-half feet tall. Add to that the fact that the tent was not grounded with stakes, and you had someone ready to be easily tossed around in the wind.

I cannot think of any better reminder to ground myself in the doctrine of Christ. Too many people out there are willing to expound in beautiful moving words that sound good but which could easily upset my faith. Too many times I rely on what I have always known, or on some brother I respect to tell me what to believe. I sit in Bible classes sometimes and shake my head. Whenever a certain topic comes up, I can almost always tell you who will say what, because few have bothered to look at things from a new perspective, to dig a little deeper, to ask questions, to even think it is all right to ask a question without being looked at skeptically. Too many times I have visited women's classes in other places and looked at the cotton candy lesson being studied, wondering if these empty calories are doing anyone's soul any good at all. We call them classes because we are supposed to study deeply and learn new things, not splash around in the shallow end of the pool with the children, trying not to get our hair wet.

The only way to avoid confusion is to ask questions; the only way to grow—and we should all be growing, no matter how long we have been Christians—is to search the scriptures diligently; the only way to build a solid foundation is to learn how to study on my own; the only way to remain steadfast is to gain enough spiritual weight to stake down my tabernacle with stakes I have discovered myself, and hammered deeply into the ground.

Till we all attain unto the unity of the faith and of the knowledge of the Son of God, unto a full-grown man, unto the measure of the stature of the fullness of Christ; that we may be no longer children, tossed to and fro and carried about with every wind of doctrine, by the slight of men, in craftiness, after the wiles of error, but speaking truth in love, may grow up in all things into him, who is the head, even Christ.

Ephesians 4.13–15

June 14, 1974

Today is our anniversary. We like to call it "our" birthday, because 37 years ago we became one new person. It is, in fact, Keith's own birthday as well. He tells me I am the best birthday present he ever received, even now when I am causing him more trouble than ever before.

Do you know what I consider the best present he ever gave me? Security. I am not talking about money. He never promised me a lavish lifestyle. He never promised me a big home, a bottomless bank account, vacations all over the world, or even all over this country. What he did promise was "for richer or poorer, for better or worse, in sickness and in health," and he has kept those promises.

We have had our share of "poorer"; we've certainly had times of "worse"; we have dealt with the "sickness" aspect longer that most realize if you count our increasing disabilities. But he is still here. I can still see well enough in the mirror. Despite bulges, surgery scars, wrinkles, once tight skin that now flaps in the breeze, long black curly hair that is cut short for ease and has turned gun metal gray, and eyes that are now constantly swollen and squinty, and sometimes black, purple, or red, he still tells me I am beautiful. And you know what? Somehow, he makes me believe it.

In spite of his own handicap, which few view with any understanding or compassion at all and which grows worse every day, he pampers me, takes care of me, serves me, guards me, and puts me on a pedestal I don't deserve. I *know* he will never leave me, and that is a gift of comfort beyond all measure.

Yet we do not take each other for granted. We both work hard to make this marriage commitment not just a responsibility but a pleasure as well. Thirty-seven years ago we made promises not just to each other, but to God. We both believe those promises must be kept, and in keeping them, we laugh and love more and more every day.

Being several years older, he frets about who will care for me when he is gone. But we have two sons who have seen his example their entire lives. I don't worry one bit.

Do you young husbands want an example for your marriages? Do you older husbands want to give your wives a wonderful gift? Here it is: security in your love. It will make all the difference in the world.

Husbands love your wives, even as Christ also loved the church and gave himself up for it. Even so ought husbands to love their wives as their own bodies.

Enjoy life with the wife whom you love all the days of your vain life that he has given you under the sun, because that is your portion in life and in your toil which you toil under the sun.

Ephesians 5.25, 28; Ecclesiastes 9.9

June 15

Tony the Waiter

Nearly 40 years ago, shortly after Keith and I became engaged, he took me to the premier restaurant in Tampa, Bern's. Bern's is the kind of restaurant where your waiter is often dressed better than you are, and you hope your actions do not give you away as someone who is totally out of his element. We splurged away a good chunk of Keith's weekly salary on a chateaubriand for two—$40, counting beverages, dessert, tax, and tip. In that day, gas had just risen to 65 cents a gallon, and $35 worth of groceries fed a family of four for a week.

Our waiter, Tony, was an older gentleman with an accent, gray hair, and Old World manners as charming as the fairy tale Prince. At Bern's, diners are seated in various rooms, some larger than others. Ours was small, mostly tables for two, and the three other couples there that night were well-spaced for privacy. Tony was assigned to us and only one other couple.

After taking our order, he always brought each course precisely on time as we finished the one before it. When it came time for the steak, he asked if Keith would like to carve it. We had been holding hands across the table and let go at that question. Immediately, Tony protested. "No, no, no," he said, putting our hands back together. "Tony will carve."

After dinner we had coffee and once, when I put down the half empty china cup at my right elbow and looked up to talk with Keith, I turned back a moment later to a full one. I had never heard Tony even approach the table, much less refill the cup. When I expressed amazement, Keith told me, "He's been standing in that back corner keeping an eye on his two tables the whole time." Needless to say, Tony got an excellent tip, and we still remember him fondly to this day.

I was studying Acts 2.42 the other day and made a discovery that reminded me of Tony: "And they continued steadfastly in the apostles' teaching, and fellowship, breaking of bread and in prayers." Since prayer was the actual subject of my study, I concentrated on that particular item. What did it mean, I wondered, to "*continue* in prayer?"

"Continue" is the same Greek word translated "wait on" in Mark 3.9: "And he spoke to his disciples that a little boat should *wait on* him because of the crowd, lest they should throng him." The multitude was pressing in on Jesus, and he wanted a boat *handy* should he need it, as he did at another time, teaching from the water while the crowd stood on the shore.

What really brought Tony to mind, though, was the use of this word in Acts 10.7: "And when the angel... had departed, [Cornelius] called two of his household servants and a devout soldier of those who *waited on* him continuously." Like Tony, those men stood to the side just in case they were needed. And they must have been needed fairly often, or they would not have been so alert and close by. That is how prayer is supposed to be.

Is that how we treat this gift? Is it something we keep handy and use at the drop of a hat, should some problem come our way? God meant prayer to be there for us continuously. Not that we pray continuously, but that at any moment we may use that gift; that we talk to him through the day, recognize our dependence upon him in all things and the incredible benefits of speaking to him. Like Tony he will be there waiting for anything we need, sometimes even before we express that need.

For our 30th anniversary in 2004, our children gave us a gift certificate to Bern's, the first time we had ever been back. It was another memorable experience, but of course, Tony is no longer there. But unlike Tony, God is still there and always will be.

Keep prayer handy, and use it often. Don't wait for some bedtime ritual if the need should arise in the middle of the day. God wants to help us, and he will, if we but ask.

Out of my distress I called upon Jehovah; Jehovah answered me and set me in a large place. Jehovah is on my side; I will not fear; What can man do unto me?

Psalm 118.5–6

June 16

Green Blackberries

"Mommy, those green blackberries burnt my mouth."

We were picking peas in a field behind a member's farmhouse late one afternoon. We had barely moved to the area and had not had time to plant our own garden, so we were happy to do all the free U-picks our brethren offered. Nathan, who was only 13 months old, was playing up at the house under the watchful care of the grandmotherly farmwife. Three-year-old Lucas wanted to come "help," so he trailed along behind us, picking a pea pod every so often, but usually exploring.

It took a minute for what he had said to register. Then, with a knot of fear growing in my stomach, I calmly asked, "What blackberries? Show me."

He led us back about 20 feet, to a place in the fencerow. Instead of blackberry vines, we saw a four foot high green plant, with spade-shaped leaves and round green berries—nightshade. We dropped our buckets, pulled the plant, scooped him up, and headed for the nearest emergency room, 30 miles east. As soon as we arrived, Keith dropped me at the door. I ran in and practically threw both Lucas and the plant on the registration desk.

"My baby ate this," I managed between gasps.

I had found the trick to immediate action in an emergency room. They ran both him and the plant back behind the swinging doors. I, of course, was taken to Paperwork Central—they never forget the documentation so they will be paid. It probably did not help that I had come straight from the field, sweat, dirt, and all, and so did not look particularly solvent.

Two hours later we left with a completely sobered three-year-old, promising us he would never eat green blackberries again. As far as I know, he hasn't!

So why are we so much less careful about the poison that sickens our souls? Spiritual nightshade surrounds us every day of our lives. Somehow we think we are immune to its effects. We go places we should not, associate with people we should not, dally with things that are as dangerous as a poisonous snake, and pooh-pooh anyone who dares tell us to be careful.

I am not just talking about things like alcohol and sexual immorality. Do you realize that wealth in the scriptures is *never* pictured as anything but dangerous to our souls? But what do we wish for when the subject of wishes comes up? And what do we always say? "I could handle it. I would never use it the wrong way. It would never get the best of me." What do we tell our young people when they say the same things about drugs and alcohol?

Arrogance will always get the best of us in all these cases. Might as well handle a cobra. Might as well drink some cyanide.

Might as well eat a pie made of green blackberries.

For [the] rock [of the wicked] is not as our Rock. ...For their vine is of the vine of Sodom, and of the fields of Gomorrah; their grapes are grapes of gall, their clusters are bitter. Their wine is the poison of serpents and the cruel venom of asps.

Deuteronomy 32.31–33

June 17

A Case of Mistaken Identity

We too often impose our standards, our culture, our way of life on those people who lived thousands of years ago in a place far removed in both custom and time. I have often heard that if Bathsheba had only been a modest woman, David would never have fallen, making her the primary offender, an evil seductress who brought down a man of God. When I did some study, then placed myself in the correct time frame and civilization, I learned a thing or two, and today I am going to be brave enough to share it with you.

First, there was no running water in those days. Now that may seem so obvious as to be ridiculous to mention, but it changes the customs. I discovered in books about social customs in Bible times that it was not at all uncommon for people to bathe outdoors in good weather. Homes had center courtyards and screens were set up to shield the bathers from the eyes of those in the house and on the street. The sexes bathed separately, the women at the same time, then the men. I know that I can still find today people who bathed on the back porch of their homes before they had running water and an indoor bathroom. They took appropriate precautions for modesty too, and were never censured for their actions. Likewise, Bathsheba's actions were socially acceptable and appropriate. There were probably other homes where the same thing was happening. David was the only one at fault here. No one could shield the bathers from someone on a rooftop. Society expected men to be "on their honor." If their actions put them in a place they did not belong, it was up to them to leave, just as it would be today if a man accidentally wandered into a ladies' room by mistake.

Here is another thing we always miss. In those days young women were married off at puberty. The Law made it extremely difficult for a woman who was at all fertile *not* to conceive soon and often (Lev 15.19–28). Uriah and Bathsheba still had no children and we know in hindsight that Bathsheba was able to conceive. I believe that makes a good case for Bathsheba being very young, probably still a teenager. So the king calls for you—not just any king, but the country's hero, a warrior king, and a man over 40 by the way. Even if she were 18 or 19—*even if she were 25*—the intimidation factor had to be huge. Unless you are a woman over 50 who was sexually harassed by a boss back in the days when turning a man in was not common, when it was, in fact, not quite acceptable, don't even talk to me about how Bathsheba should have had the courage to say no. You cannot possibly understand how she must have felt. Yes, I have been there.

When you really study the situation and think about it in its proper time frame and cultural setting, the higher probability is that Bathsheba was not a temptress. More likely, she was a scared young woman who probably felt she had no choice. As it turns out, David was capable of murder, and she was the one looking into his eyes, not us.

Or perhaps there was some ego involved. David was the king and he was handsome. Maybe that excited her, but even if that is true, that intimidation factor just will not go away—David was the final authority in the land. And this was a man who was so cold-blooded about it that he checked to make sure she was "clean" by the Law's standards before he even touched her.

My problems with Bathsheba have more to do with her naiveté. This was a woman who, though she lived in a political milieu, was totally ignorant of how things worked. Her affair with David was just the first time we see this trait, and though we might understand it then if she were indeed a very young teenager, it never seemed to get any better, no matter how long she lived in the palace.

Read the first few chapters of 1 Kings. David is dying and Adonijah is conniving to take the throne, even though it has been promised to her son Solomon. It takes Nathan the prophet to wake her up to what is going on right under her nose. Then a few verses later, after David is dead and Solomon is king, Adonijah asks her for Abishag. Abishag was probably the last of David's concubines. *Everyone* in the kingdom knew that claiming a king's wife was a claim to the throne. That is what Absalom did in the sight of all after he ran David out of the country. But Bathsheba takes the request to Solomon as if it were a simple matter of a request from brother to brother. Solomon understands immediately that his kingdom, God's kingdom, is in danger and has Adonijah killed. Bathsheba should have known too.

So we are back once again to Jesus' command that we are to "be wise as serpents and harmless as doves." This is not just a matter of learning to study better and being careful not to place our own values on a time and place far removed from us, making judgments that may not be valid. There *is* something to be learned from Bathsheba's behavior, though perhaps not the behavior we always condemn. God is not pleased when we act like simpletons, when we fail to see the obvious. He will not save us when we fall into traps that should have been avoided.

Bathsheba did become a faithful wife to David. She did see to his wishes when he became old and physically unable to, even if it did take a nudge from Nathan. Maybe after Adonijah was executed she finally gained a little wisdom in the affairs of her world. It certainly took her long enough.

Brothers, be not children in your thinking. Be infants in evil, but in your thinking be mature.

1 Corinthians 14.20

June 18

Mechanic on Duty

Those piano competitions I spoke of a few weeks ago are fun and uplifting. It is wonderful to hear the future stars of the concert stage make two full days of beautiful music. Which does not mean it was an easy weekend. Ninety percent of the performances we heard were mechanically and technically perfect. Memory lapses were rare and finger slips even rarer. So how do you choose a winner?

Actually, at the end of each session when our panel of three compared notes, we had all picked out the same three or four that distinguished themselves above the others: pianists who played with feeling; who made the melody sound like someone singing; who understood how to shape phrases, not just separate them; who had the musical ear and technical ability to voice their chords; students who played the non-melody hand so far in the background it was as if it were in another room; who knew the difference between a Mozart forte and a Beethoven forte; who understood that rubato meant a proportionate time stretching like the lettering on an inflated balloon, not just a rush followed by a drag. In short, the winners were those who played not only with perfect mechanics, but with artistry as well—they put their hearts into it.

God's people seem to have had a problem with that for a long time. The prophets were constantly reminding them that while God expected absolute obedience, form worship was not acceptable. If perfect mechanics were all that mattered, he could have created a world full of robots to fill the bill. "I hate, I despise your feasts and I will take no delight in your solemn assemblies," God told Israel. "Even though you offer me your burnt offerings and your meal offerings, I will not accept them; neither will I regard the peace offerings of your fat beasts" (Amos 5.21–22). Why? Because it was a mechanical following of ritual. All during their "worship" they were saying, "When will the new moon be gone that we may sell grain, and the Sabbath that we may set forth wheat, making the ephah small and the shekel great, dealing falsely with the balances of deceit; that we may buy the poor for silver and the needy for a pair of shoes, and sell the refuse of the wheat" (8.5–6). Their religion did not affect their hearts and certainly not their everyday lives.

Jesus dealt with their descendants, not only by blood, but in attitude. Were the Pharisees right to require exact obedience to the Law? Jesus said they were: "The scribes and Pharisees sit on Moses' seat. All things whatsoever they bid you, these things do" (Matt 23.2–3). He even praised what we might consider petty exactitude: "You tithe mint, anise, and cumin… these things you ought to have done" (Matt 23.23). But like their ancestors, their heart was not in it. Hear Jesus' whole indictment: "Woe to you scribes, Pharisees, hypocrites, for you tithe mint, anise, and cumin, and have left undone the weightier matters of the law, justice, mercy, and faith; but these things you ought to have done, and not left the other undone."

Correct mechanics are important. A lot of folks in the Bible learned that the hard way. But our hearts are more important, according to Jesus. It is easier to just go down a list and do what we are told than it is to monitor our hearts and keep them in line—but God has never had much truck with laziness either. I didn't give out any prizes for mechanical playing this past weekend. What makes us think God will give them out for mechanical worship?

> *"With what shall I come before the Lord and bow down before the exalted God? Shall I come with burnt offerings, with calves a year old? Will the Lord be pleased with thousands of rams, and ten thousand rivers of oil? Shall I offer my firstborn for my transgressions, the fruit of my body for the sin of my soul? He has showed you, O man, what is good. And what does the Lord require of you, but to do justly, and to love kindness, and to walk humbly with your God?"*
>
> Micah 6.6–8

June 19

Ants

What you don't know won't hurt you.

I didn't know that Keith had taken Chloe's food pan and set it in my chair on the carport when he blew the dust off a few Saturdays ago. He didn't notice that she had left a few kibbles. Neither one of us knew that a few fire ants had gotten in there and they had migrated out to my chair when he disturbed them. I didn't know they had started crawling into my clothes when I sat down there until a few minutes after we walked back into the house. Suddenly I was ripping off my clothes and slapping myself. I wound up with bites on my chest, back, arms, and legs, and a ring of them around my neck. I felt lousy for a day or two, not to mention the aggravating itch.

What I didn't know did in fact hurt me quite a bit.

That seems obvious, but sometimes we act like ignorance is a viable excuse for most anything. And indeed, sometimes it is. A new Christian has a lot to learn. As long as he is studying and praying and trying as hard as he can to learn what he needs to be and do, his prayer for the grace of God will keep him safe. I believe that with all my heart.

But when I have been a Christian for years and years and have done nothing to learn and grow, or have simply stopped, *that* is inexcusable.

Learning new facts can be difficult, especially as I grow older. Trying to see past the superficial to the amazing depth of God's word can mean I must try to comprehend things I have never even thought of before. Yet how many times have I heard "I never heard of such a thing" as the instant dismissal of a new thought in a Bible class? How many times have I heard people complain because a class was "too deep"? What a shameful thing for a Christian to say.

Then we get to the crux of the matter, for applying principles to my life can be as painful as a shirt full of fire ants. Who in the world actually wants to know what they are doing wrong? Why, I've been a Christian 40 years; I'm not about to admit I still have weaknesses I need to confront in anything but a general way.

That is, however, exactly what God expects of us. The shame is that usually the babes in the Word are hungrier to learn and grow than we old-timers. But we had better shape up, sooner rather than later, or ant bites will be the least of our problems.

Hear the word of Jehovah you children of Israel, for Jehovah has a controversy with the inhabitants of the land, because there is no truth or goodness or knowledge of God in the land. My people are destroyed for lack of knowledge. Because you have rejected knowledge, I will reject you.

Hosea 4.1, 6

June 20

Dr. Doolittle

During the weeks after this past surgery I was actually examined one day by two veterinarians. Remember, I am one of the prime teaching tools at the University of Florida Medical School. These young Dr Doolittles were doing research in pain. Their patients cannot tell them how they feel, so they were visiting human post-op cases to ask how they felt after various types of surgery. It was the only way to know how the animals were feeling.

My doctor took them to three different patients, an easy case, a moderate case, and then me—the extreme. I answered their questions with accompanying explanations by my physician, shook their hands, and on they went. Maybe some child's pet bunny rabbit will have an easier time of it because of a ten minute delay in my own case—and putting up with a few jokes afterward.

Isn't that what Jesus did for us? Well, no, not exactly. Instead of asking a few questions, he went through the surgery himself. How else was Deity to understand temptation, fear, pain, anguish, sorrow, desperation, or even relatively petty things like hunger, thirst, and weariness? He did it when he "counted not being on an equality with God a thing to be grasped, but emptied himself" (Phil 2.6–7). He did it by being "tempted in all points like we are" (Heb 4.15). It was really the only way.

And now He knows. Now He can tell His Father in words Deity can understand what it is like to be human. Then He can turn around and tell us how to overcome, how to persevere, how to be "faithful even to the point of death" (Rev 2.10).

Don't make His sacrifice be for nothing.

In the beginning was the Word and the Word was with God, and the Word was God. This same was in the beginning with God. All things were made through him, and without him was not anything made that was made. ...And the Word became flesh and dwelt among us, and we beheld his glory, glory as of the only begotten from the Father, full of grace and truth.

John 1.1–3, 14

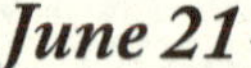

June 21

The Cardinal Family

A male cardinal showed up one spring morning and tried out the bird feeder. He had not eaten long before he left and came back with his mate. He started eating while she sat on the side simply watching, but then he picked up another seed and hopped over to her, gently placing it in her mouth. She ate and afterward continued to eat, the two of them side by side, enjoying a free and easy meal that she now knew was safe.

A few weeks later I noticed that her figure was spreading. Her round breast was more than round. Too much bird seed, I wondered? But no, all of a sudden one morning she was thinner again, and she and her mate came separately instead of together. In fact, she came much less often, and he did a whole lot of back and forth commuting.

Then they showed up with four other cardinals, young ones nearly full-grown, but thinner and with a scruffy plumage, even more muted than Mom's. One female would only sit on the edge of the feeder and quiver her wings so fast they seemed but a blur, leaning forward with her mouth open. Daddy often fed her, one seed at a time, until she was full and flew away. After a week of that, Mom had had enough. How was this one ever going to learn to feed herself? So she often flew at the young one, nearly knocking her off the feeder. Daddy got the message and stopped the "spoon feeding." Sometimes Daddy's little girl tries it again, but Daddy makes her get her own now. What will she do when he is gone if she never has taken care of herself before?

In the evenings the whole family comes to the feeder together. The young ones fly at one another playfully before settling down to eat. Mom and Dad used to eat last, but more often now they jump right in with the "little ones," some of whom are bigger than their parents. The plumage on the males is starting to redden, and, what is more important, they come to eat even when their parents don't. They have learned to shell the seeds, and the flying debris often pings against the windows and out into the azaleas. They have also learned to fend for themselves against the other birds, and when the big bad squirrel comes, they will either gang up on him, or if one is alone, that bird knows it is much better to simply run.

The cardinals have done well. Did you know that those birds are monogamous for life? And they have taught their children well. They know how to take care of themselves. They know when to fight and when to run. They know where to come when they need nourishment, because mama and daddy brought them from the time they were able to fly there behind them. If something ever happens to those parents, I know the young ones will still be visiting me every day. And soon, they will bring their own.

By the way, this lesson is *not* for the birds.

Give ear, O my people, to my law: incline your ears to the words of my mouth. I will open my mouth in a parable; I will utter dark sayings of old, which we have heard and known, and our fathers have told us. We will not hide them from their children, telling to the generation to come the praises of Jehovah, and his strength, and his wondrous works that he has done. For he established a testimony in Jacob, and appointed a law in Israel, which he commanded our fathers, that they should make them known to their children; that the generation to come might know them, even the children that should be born; who should arise and tell them to their children.

Psalm 78.1–6

Naturally Curly Hair

I inherited my hair from my Grandma Ayers. As a teenager I hated it. The style then was long, sleek and straight. Some girls even ironed their hair to remove any hint of natural wave. I never went that far, but twice a week I spent two hours washing it, wrapping it around huge rollers, and sitting under a bonnet dryer trying to get the kink out of it.

The biggest problem with naturally curly hair is that it does what *it* wants to do. I have never been able to take a picture to a stylist and say, "I want my hair to look like that." If it doesn't already do that, it never will.

The biggest blessing with naturally curly hair is that it does what *it* wants to do. I can shower, wash my hair, blow it dry, dress and go in about 35 minutes. There is no sense wasting time on hair that will only do one thing on any given day, depending upon the humidity.

Humidity is the bane of naturally curly hair. I can walk outside on a foggy day and hear it going, "Scrinch! Scrinch! Scrinch!" as each wave turns into a fuzzy ringlet. As a friend once said, I wear a barometer on my head. If I have to go to town on a high humidity day (most days in Florida), I stay away from mirrors. If I were to see what had become of my hair since I left the house I would probably still be in hiding and never make it back home.

During last summer's nomadic tropical storm, an unwelcome guest we thought would never leave, I stepped outside one morning onto the carport to check on the dogs. About a half hour later I looked in the bathroom mirror. My head was covered with corkscrews the size of earthworms dropping onto my forehead, crawling into my ears, and dangling down my neck. The bad part, though, the thing that *no one* ever understands no matter how many times I try to explain it, was the frizz. A halo of gray fuzz stuck out all around the curls a full two inches, like that annoying fuzz around a mohair sweater. This was by far the most extreme "do" my naturally curly hair had ever given me. My head looked bigger than a basketball, and nothing I did could change it.

Most of the time now, I count my hair a blessing, but after all these years of dealing with hair that predetermines how I will look on any given day, I have a special appreciation for the free will God has given us. What I do is my choice not something forced upon me. It doesn't matter who my ancestors were, how I was raised or where, I can still choose to serve God. God reminded his people "Long ago your fathers lived beyond the Euphrates, Terah, the father of Abraham and of Nahor, *and they served other gods*" (Josh 24.2). Abraham's ancestors were idolaters, and he grew up in an idolatrous society, but God still expected his service and devotion. His upbringing and culture were not valid excuses for a lack of faith.

Free will also places a huge responsibility on me in my every day life. It doesn't matter how anyone else treats me, I must treat them in the right manner. It doesn't matter if someone aggravates me, I must not be provoked. It doesn't matter if everything goes wrong today, I must still keep a good attitude and behave like a follower of Christ—a Christian. I now have no excuse for the sin in my life because God gave me the ability to choose otherwise. I cannot blame anything or anyone else.

The thing to do then is decide what I want. A loving Father went to a lot of trouble to make salvation available. A loving Son went through a lot of pain to make it possible to overcome sin. A comforting Spirit went to a lot of work to reveal it all. Now it is up to us—it is our choice one way or the other.

> *For we must all appear before the judgment seat of Christ so that each may receive what is due for what he has done in the body, whether good or evil.*
>
> 2 Corinthians 5.10

June 23

Laryngitis

Keith got a reprieve yesterday—I woke up with laryngitis. A deaf man and a woman barely able to utter a whisper do not make a compatible couple. We struggled through the evening after he came home from work. He would ask a question then walk away until I finally threw something at him to get his attention so he could read my lips as I answered. We would sit at the table together and I would talk without first making eye contact—I had to throw something at him then too. You get the picture. Most of the time a pillow or napkin was within reach, otherwise we might have had a real mess to clean up.

Our biggest problems in life are usually caused by speaking when we should have been quiet. On the other hand, there are times we should speak that we do not, times we get a case of spiritual laryngitis. The more I think about it, the more I realize that my only motivation for having kept quiet at those times was fear.

We preach to our young people about peer pressure, encouraging them to speak up about friends doing wrong, about believing unpopular beliefs, or to simply stand up for those everyone else is picking on as if these were easy things to do. Do we do any better when certain subjects arise among our own peers? Is it so easy to risk losing a friend, losing a sale, losing status in the community, losing the good opinion of people we want to impress? No, we don't do any better most of the time. We are just as afraid to speak out as our children are.

The thing we need to convince our young people of—and ourselves—is that we are afraid of the wrong thing. With knowledge comes responsibility.

If I see you about to do something I know will hurt you and do not say anything, I am guilty of hurting you as much as if I did that hurtful thing to you myself. "If I say to the wicked, 'You shall surely die,' and you give him no warning, nor speak to warn the wicked from his wicked way, in order to save his life, that wicked person shall die for his iniquity, but his blood I will require at your hand" (Ezek 3.18).

If I fail to tell others that I am a Christian, because, like Peter during Jesus' trial, I am afraid of the consequences that might bring me, I have denied my Lord, "Every one therefore who shall confess me before men, him will I also confess before my Father who is in heaven. But whosoever shall deny me before men, him will I also deny before my Father who is in heaven" (Matt 10.32–33).

If I see a wrong and fail to speak out, I am nothing more than a coward. I have become a friend of the unjust man rather than a champion of his victim, and will be included in his curse (Prov 29.24).

Truly, fear gives you spiritual laryngitis. It totally disables you. You become useless to the Lord. *That* is the thing you should fear more than anything else.

> *What I tell you in the darkness, speak it in the light; and what you hear in the ear, proclaim upon the house-tops. And be not afraid of those who kill the body, but are not able to kill the soul: but rather fear him who is able to destroy both soul and body in hell.*
>
> Matthew 10.27–28

June 24

From Bad to Worse

> *This I say therefore, and testify in the Lord, that you no longer walk as the Gentiles also walk, in the vanity of their mind, being darkened in their understanding, alienated from the life of God, because of the ignorance that is in them, because of the hardening of their heart; who being past feeling gave themselves up to lasciviousness, to work all uncleanness with greediness.* (Eph 4.17–19)

In our study of the first century church on Tuesday mornings, the ladies and I have noticed how important purity was to those people. I am not sure we place the same importance on it, and worse, we excuse impurity of all sorts. One of my dear sisters said she had even heard another Christian say it was expecting too much to demand purity from people today, not in a society saturated with hedonism and materialism. Let me tell you, if a Christian could stay pure in a pagan world where fornication was even part of the religious ritual, anyone can stay pure concerning any sin there is. "I can do all things through him who strengthens me" (Phil 4.13).

We were reading together the list in the above passage, a list I had studied several times, when it suddenly struck me that this was not a list at all, it was *a progression.*

The people Paul refers to had "vanity of mind." Most of us who have been in the church for years understand the concept of "vanity"—emptiness. These people had no purpose in life. They moseyed through the day letting life simply "happen." That will not last long. If you have no purpose, you will eventually find one of your own making. It's the only way you can rationalize your existence.

They became "darkened in their understanding." They did not even realize their need. Because they had come up with their own "meaning of life," they were satisfied.

At that point they became "alienated from the life of God." Just across the page from this passage, we are told that God made us alive when we were dead in our sins (Eph 2.5). Our life now is a life of service to Him and others. Our righteous lives look strange to people of the world. Doing things for others? Putting the needs of others ahead of your own? Haven't you heard someone say, "What about yourself?" or, "How can you have any *fun?*" They can no longer comprehend real fulfillment.

And so "because of the hardening of their heart" they refuse to see when others try to tell them what is wrong. They wear a shield so their consciences will not be pricked into realizing what they are doing to themselves.

Eventually they become "past feeling"—they no longer even need the shield over their consciences. They just plain don't care. When you start to talk, they shrug their shoulders. "You have your way, I have mine—now leave me alone."

And so they come to the end—"they give themselves up." At this point, as Peter says, "They cannot cease from sin" (2 Pet 2.14). It will take something akin to a miracle to reach them, if they can be reached at all—probably something terrible.

Truly this is a motivation for keeping oneself pure. How far can I go before I reach the point of no return? Will the next sin be the one that makes it nearly impossible to repent? Do I really want to go through the necessary horror that may be my only chance to wake up?

Don't kid yourself—you are as vulnerable as anyone else. Check this little progression and see where you fall in line. Then get out of line as fast as you can. Nothing says you have to be there at all.

But you did not so learn Christ; if so be that you heard him, and were taught in him, even as truth is in Jesus: that you put away, as concerning your former manner of life, the old man, that waxes corrupt after the lusts of deceit; and that you be renewed in the spirit of your mind, and put on the new man, that after God hath been created in righteousness and holiness of truth.

Ephesians 4.20–24

June 25

Just One Sparrow

After a couple of years, we finally have sparrows at our bird feeder. For some reason, it took them the longest to find us. But which variety? I never realized there were so many until I tried to look these little guys up in my bird book. One afternoon, a sparrow perched on the window ledge right beside me and I looked down on his tiny red-brown cap. Aha! He was a chipping sparrow.

You know what else I noticed? He always has friends with him. What started out as two or three, by the third or fourth day had become a dozen, and the next Saturday afternoon I counted 21 on my five foot long feeder.

On our last camping trip, we threw some biscuit crumbs onto the grass outside the edge of our graveled state park campsite simply because I had heard a dove out there one morning and Keith was hoping to lure him out into the open. I grabbed the binoculars—even though I sat only 15 feet from that grassy spot—and saw a sparrow. No, wait! Not one but two, no—three, no—half a dozen. Keith said, "Look at all those sparrows!" and I answered what I had come to know over the months, "You never see just one sparrow."

This, of course, made me think.

Cardinals? Yes there were always more than one, usually a pair, and when they raise a family nearby they bring them to eat too. They are a bit territorial, though, and will sometimes fly at other birds to knock them away from the food. No one else is supposed to enjoy this privilege.

Titmice? Yes, they come in pairs too. But when other birds arrive, they often sit off in the azalea bushes scolding them with a tiny, high-pitched screech. Even when I go out to add more seed, though the others fly away, the titmice will sit and fuss at me. I keep telling them, "I am giving you a free and easy meal. Be patient!" But scolding seems to be their nature. Nothing anyone else does suits them.

And the catbird? He *always* comes alone. He pecks the suet and flies away as fast as he can. He is the biggest bird to visit my feeder, but he acts like he is afraid of them all. He never interacts with anyone. He is there and gone, almost before your eyes can focus on him. I wonder how he gets any nourishment at all.

But the sparrows? They are not afraid to sit close together and stay long. None of the bigger birds can scare them off. In fact, the doves, which run up and down the feeder, literally "running" birds off more than feeding themselves, cannot run off those sparrows. I saw a dove try to run at a sparrow one day, and the sparrow just sat there, minding his own "eating" business, until the dove at the last minutes had to hop over him to avoid the collision. Meanwhile, there are more and more sparrows coming, and my birdseed bill is growing faster than my grocery budget.

Can we learn anything from all these birds? You can probably see these lessons as easily as I can. Christians are grateful for what they have and enjoy feasting on the word of God. They enjoy each other too. They don't have time to criticize because they are too busy with the business at hand. And most of all, they want to share.

There should never be just one Christian.

So the woman left her waterpot, and went away into the city, and said to the people, Come, see a man, who told me all things that ever I did: can this be the Christ? They went out of the city, and were coming to him. And from that city many of the Samaritans believed on him because of the word of the woman who testified.

John 4.28–30, 39

June 26

Shuffling Along

These days I don't do a lot of reading for pleasure. By the time I do my Bible study and the necessities of life, like balancing the checkbook, paying bills, and making menus and grocery lists, all with the help of a magnifier or two—or three—my eyes are tired, and a headache is not far away. So Keith has started bringing home books on CD from the library.

For awhile I was carting my big boom box from room to room, which got old in a hurry, especially after the doctor said I had to be careful not to carry anything too heavy. So Lucas picked up a portable CD player for me, with earphones and a belt to carry it. Now I can go anywhere and listen to my books, while washing dishes, making beds, folding clothes, sorting coupons, sweeping the carport, or fixing dinner.

There are disadvantages. If you walk into the laundry room while the washer is running, you miss a sentence amid the roar. If the phone rings, you must quickly unzip your holder to get to the pause button before the answering machine picks up on the ringing phone. If the earphone cord is hanging too freely, it will invariably snag on something and be yanked out, leaving you in total silence while the CD plays on. Then there is what happened the other day.

I was washing dishes and had to reach high up to hang a wet Ziploc bag from a shelf to drip dry into the sink so I could use it again another day. I heard a beep, but thought nothing of it. In another minute, the story mentioned something totally out of the blue. A minute or so later a character I had never heard of spoke. I took out the CD player and looked at the window. I had been on track 3 only five minutes before and now I was on 12. That could not possibly be right. I hit the "next track" button and instead of going to 13 it went backwards to 8. Again and it went ahead to 16, then backwards to 5, and then ahead to 10.

Suddenly my slow brain caught on. When I had bumped the countertop with my midsection, I had bumped the "shuffle" button through the belt material, and the player was playing the tracks randomly instead of in order. What a mess! No wonder the story made no sense.

Sometimes we do that with the Bible. It's not just that it must be read in some sort of order. It must be *comprehended* in order. How many times have you tried to set up a Bible study with someone and the first thing he wants to study is the book of Revelation? *You cannot understand the book of Revelation without a working knowledge of prophetic language and an understanding of Old Testament prophecy.* When I hear some of the strange interpretations of that marvelous book going around, I immediately know someone is totally ignorant of those things. The book itself is sandwiched by the promise that the things contained in it "must shortly come to pass" (1.1; 22.6). John expected those early Christians to understand it and be comforted by it in the tribulation which he "shared in" (1.9). Obviously, they knew how to interpret it correctly because they knew their scriptures—with less access to it than we have, I might add.

Then there is the matter of context. I have heard prooftexts taken out of their immediate context so often that when I actually looked them up and read the entire passage for each one, I had "epiphany" after "epiphany." There really is more to them than telling others they are wrong; in fact, many times they speak directly to *us*. Take Matthew 15.9 for example: "In vain do they worship me teaching for doctrine the commandments of men." I have heard that applied to man-made creeds all my life, but start at the top of the chapter and see who Jesus is addressing—not pagans, not Samaritans, or even people who simply worshipped God incorrectly, but scribes and Pharisees, those of God's people who tried their best to obey the Law exactly. In doing so, however, they managed to create traditions—*commandments of men*—that they treated as more important than the Law.

There is also "book context." Don't treat the book of Proverbs like a book of Laws. Proverbs are sayings that are generally true, not always true. "Sacrilege!" I hear someone scream. Look at Proverbs 26.4: "Answer not a fool according to his folly lest you be like him." So? Now look at the very next verse. "Answer a fool according to his folly lest he be wise in his own conceit." Now do you see what I mean? You will definitely treat that book differently than you treat a doctrinal book.

And that leads us to "Bible context." Many people find passages they think excuse them of whatever it is they are doing wrong, and spout them like water out of the blowhole of a whale, ignoring the entire teaching of the Bible. Never interpret a verse in a way that makes it opposite of a plain teaching in another passage. The Bible does not contradict itself. If it does, then why should you care what it says?

Be careful of that "shuffle" button when you study today. It will confuse you as badly as reading a mystery story out of order.

Give diligence to present yourself approved unto God, a workman who does not need to be ashamed, handling correctly the Word of truth.

2 Timothy 2.15

June 27

Automatic Atomizers

In the country you deal with insects on a regular basis, especially the flying kind. Living in the middle of cow pastures, chicken and pig farms, with road kill scattered every couple hundred feet down the rural highway, you don't even want to think about what that fly might have last sat on as it heads straight for the cookies cooling on your countertop.

We found a remedy for this problem many years ago when Keith preached a gospel meeting in a small Arkansas town. It sat right in the middle of rice country where they could have sold mosquitoes by the ton if there had been a market for them. As we ate our breakfasts in the restaurant of the motel the church had put us up in, we saw three or four small wooden ledges in various places around the room, a foot below the ceiling. A small white box on each of them puffed every 15 minutes. Finally we asked one of the waitresses and she told us they were automatic insecticide sprayers, and yes, they did work.

So when we got home we bought one. It is rigged to spray once every 30 minutes for the 12 hours of daylight, and it works like a charm. No more gnats hovering in clouds around the lamps or buzzing our eyes, and no more flies wandering the kitchen looking for tasty landing strips.

Though it is not silent, we never even hear this thing spraying any longer. We are so used to it that it is just a part of the surroundings. When we suddenly start seeing gnats or flies again, we know it has either run out of spray or the battery is dead. Right now I do not remember the last time I heard it spray, but I know it must be working because I do not have any problem with bugs swarming this monitor.

I am afraid we get the same way with God's blessings. Which ones do you notice? Just the big ones, the ones that you especially prayed about yesterday or last week? Does that mean you have not received any today at all? Of course not; it just means that you are so used to all the daily blessings you receive that you no longer even recognize them.

When someone tells me to quit complaining and count my blessings, it usually makes me angry. Maybe that is because I must shamefully admit that I have reached the point of the Pharisees, who seemed to think that they earned their blessings. If anything bad happens, God has let me down. I have been so good and faithful, why did this problem happen to me? When the truth of the matter is, I have sinned too, so why *not* me? In fact, why do I receive any blessings at all because I don't deserve a single one? I have forgotten just how bad sin is, and so I minimize it and maximize my goodness, which Isaiah tells me is no more than "filthy rags," when compared to the holiness of God (64.6).

Because it is so plentiful and so "automatic," I never even notice the good that God sends my way on a daily basis, and gripe and complain because He does not send more or does not send the specific good I want the most as quickly as I want it. If someone looked at a gift I gave him and complained because it was not the brand he wanted or he didn't like the color, I would probably never give him anything else ever again. Think about that for a moment.

It may be trite, but make a list today of all the blessings you take for granted. God sprays them around profligately and we never even notice.

> *Then Job arose, and rent his mantle, and shaved his head, and fell down upon the ground, and worshipped, And said, Naked came I out of my mother's womb, and naked shall I return: the* Lord *gave, and the* Lord *has taken away; blessed be the name of the* Lord*. In all this Job sinned not, nor charged God foolishly.*
>
> Job 1.20–22

June 28

Shelf Life

I never thought about sodas having a shelf life until a couple of years ago. We bought several boxes at a great sale and stacked them out of the way until needed. We put one on the floor of the pantry back behind the potatoes, onions, and other odds and ends that won't fit on a shelf. It takes us two or three months to go through one 12 pack, so by the time we had finished the first few, we had totally forgotten about that one. I only found it because I dropped something that rolled into the back of the pantry and had to pull everything out to find it.

We decided to celebrate our discovery with a soda. It wasn't just flat. It was the worst thing I ever put in my mouth. On a whim, we searched the box, and sure enough, there was a sell-by date that was about a year past.

We all have shelf lives too, as much as we hate to think about it. But instead of viewing this from the perspective of immortality, we seem to view it from the perspective of the shelf life of a bottle of milk. We think we have all the time in the world when our physical lifespans are not even a speck in the vastness of Eternity. Maybe that is why we view death as a tragedy instead of a victory. We keep looking through the wrong end of the binoculars. One of the most difficult things we have to do as Christians is constantly changing our perspectives, re-focusing our hearts from things in plain sight to things which the world cannot, and will not, see.

Second Chronicles 34–35 tell us the story of Josiah, the last good king of Judah. He tried to clean up a Temple that was in disrepair and a worship that was in disarray. As his *reward* God said he would not live to see destruction brought upon Judah.

What?! Dying was a reward? Yes, because this godly man had his perspective correct. He viewed going on to the next life as far preferable to seeing God's people destroyed.

Josiah died in battle at the age of 39. Dying young was his *reward* for faithfulness. What one of us would not look at that fact superficially and say, 'What a tragedy for such a good man to die so young?' Maybe I need to rethink my attitude about death. I may grieve, but faith means my life will not be ruined by the death of a loved one. I may have a little concern about how it will be to die, but faith means I should not be terrified.

I hope I am not coming across as morbid this morning. Maybe having nearly become a relatively young widow twice in the last 11 years has me more aware of the possibilities these days. I simply mean to remind us that we have hopes and comforts the rest of the world doesn't.

I have a shelf life and so do you. It is shorter than we think, and it will mean nothing to us in that first glimpse of Eternity. I imagine we will be glad to be there, and wonder why we worried even a little.

> *For me to live is Christ and to die is gain...I am in a strait between the two, having the desire to depart and be with Christ, for it is far better.*
>
> Philippians 1.21, 23

June 29

How Does Your Garden Grow?

In drought times, not very well. The ground is powder dry. Even my dog raises a dust cloud chasing a tennis ball. In the past three months we have had only six tenths of an inch of rain and that was several weeks ago. We have not even had any dew on the ground in the last month.

Ordinarily, we plant our garden in mid-March, and it is well up and growing by the end of the month. This year we followed the usual pattern, and by April 1 we were replanting—nothing came up in many rows and the rest were sparse. If you are a gardener, you know that squash is the easiest thing in the world to grow. You can practically throw it at the ground and within a month you can supply a city the size of New York. After two weeks we didn't even have one half-inch seedling in the whole row!

So water it, you say? We did. Faithfully. Every evening. Still nothing.

When we decided to replant, we went down the same rows, planting the same things. When we dug new rows, there lay the old seed, looking just like it did when it came out of the package, no germination at all. You know what we discovered? The watering job we did was not deep enough to reach the seeds, in spite of the fact that we spent two hours at it every night.

So we replanted, this time watering the row *before* we covered it, and watering much longer every night since then. The seeds came shoving their way up through the dirt before a week was out, and now some of the old ones are growing too. Some of these rows are experiencing a veritable population explosion. (Beware! Many of you nearby may be constantly visited with bags of produce—including lots of squash!)

Even after 32 years of gardening we learned something. Growth happens with deep watering, not shallow. And it takes an effort to get it as deeply as you should. It's not something you can do with a half-hearted, rushed effort. We're so used to "labor-saving devices" that I wonder if we even recognize real work, because that's what it takes.

God's people in the Old Testament had a watering problem as well. They thought that serving God was simply a matter of following prescribed rituals. Despite daily reciting a passage from the Torah that began "Thou shalt love the Lord thy God with all thy heart," they never got within an inch of their hearts. They "celebrated" the Sabbath, all the time watching the clock, hoping it would be over soon. They offered sacrifices, the lame and blind, and anything else that didn't cost them too much. They fasted, a ritual they called "afflicting the soul," which never once touched their souls.

Now, how is *my* spiritual garden growing? Maybe I need to do some deep watering.

> *Is this the fast I have chosen? The day for a man to afflict his soul? Is it to bow down his head in a rush and to spread sackcloth and ashes under him? Will you call this a fast and an acceptable day to Jehovah? Is not this the fast that I have chosen: to loose the bonds of wickedness, to undo the bands of the yoke, and to let the oppressed go free, and that you break every yoke? Is it not to deal your bread to the hungry, and that you bring the poor that are cast out to your house? When you see the naked that you cover him, and that you hide not yourself from your own flesh and blood? ...If you take away from the midst of you the yoke, the pointing finger, and the malicious talk, and if you draw out your soul to the hungry and satisfy the afflicted soul, then shall light rise in darkness, and your obscurity be as noonday. And Jehovah will guide you continually, and satisfy your soul in the dry places, and make strong your bones and you shall be like a watered garden, and like a spring of water, whose waters fail not.*
>
> Isaiah 58.5–11

June 30

Picking Blackberries

For the past few years wild blackberries have been rare. The vines are there, full of their painful and aggravatingly sticky thorns, but the fruit dries up before it can fully ripen. First the drought of the late '90s, and then the following dry years of this regular weather cycle of wet and dry have meant that when the time is right, usually early to mid-June, there is nothing to pick. The few that might have survived are devoured quickly by the birds.

This year Lucas found some on a nearby service road, and Keith picked enough for one cobbler for the first time in years. Probably because it has been awhile, I think that was the best blackberry cobbler we ever had. Maybe next year I can make jelly too.

Blackberries are a lot of trouble. The thorns seem like they reach out and grab you. I have often come home with bloody hands and torn clothing—you *never* wear anything you might wear elsewhere when you pick blackberries. But that is not the half of it.

You must also spray yourself and your long-sleeved shirt prodigiously with an insect repellent, and tuck the cuffs of your long pants into your socks. No matter how hot the weather, you must be covered. Without these measures chiggers will find their way in and you will be revisiting your time in the woods far longer and in more unpleasant ways than you wish. Ticks are also a problem. Make sure you pick with someone you don't mind checking you over after you get back home, especially your hair. More than once I have had a tick crawl out of my mop of curls several hours later. Mattress "ticking" has nothing to do with those insects and you want to keep it that way.

Finally, you must always carry a big stick or a pistol. I prefer pistols because you don't have to get quite as close to the snake to kill it. Birds love blackberries, and snakes like birds, so they often sit coiled under the canes waiting for their meals to fly in. Keith has killed more than one rattlesnake while picking wild blackberries.

Because of all this, since I have Keith, I seldom pick blackberries any more—I let him do it for both of us. Especially since I stand for hours in a hot kitchen afterward, it seems a fair division of labor. When I am making jelly, straining that hot juice through cheesecloth to catch the plenteous seeds, and ladling that hot syrupy liquid into hot jars isn't much easier than picking them. But wild blackberries are worth all the trouble. Their scent is sweet and heady and their taste, especially in homemade jellies, almost exotic. The purple hands, teeth, and tongue blackberry lovers wind up with are worth it too. If all you have ever had is commercially grown blackberries and store bought blackberry jelly, you really don't know what they taste like.

Why is it that I can make myself go to all this trouble for something good to eat, and then throw away something far more valuable because "it's not worth it"?

Why does teasing my taste buds matter more to me than saving my soul? How many spiritual delicacies have I missed out on because it wasn't worth the trouble?

Serious Bible study can be tedious, but isn't having the Word of God coming instantly to mind when I really need it worth it? When I have taken the time to explore deeply instead of the superficial knowledge most have, isn't it great in the middle of a sermon or Bible class, to suddenly have another passage spring to life right before my mental eyes? "So that's what that means!" is a eureka moment that is nearly incomparable. And while increased knowledge does not necessarily mean increased faith, faith without knowledge is a sham. "Faith comes by hearing and hearing by the word of God" (Rom 10.17). The more scripture you know, the stronger your faith because the more you know about what God has done for us, the more you appreciate it and want to show that appreciation by the service you willingly give.

So many other things we miss out on because we don't want to go to the trouble—cultivating an active prayer life, socializing with brothers and sisters in the faith, helping a new Christian grow, serving the community we live in simply because we care—while at the same time we go to all sorts of trouble for earthly pleasures—sitting in the hot sun on a hard bench amid crude, rowdy people to watch a ball game; searching for a parking space for hours then walking ten blocks in high heels for a favorite meal at a downtown restaurant; standing in long lines at an amusement park, while someone else's ice cream melts on your shirt, and at the same time juggling your own handfuls of fast food, cameras, and tickets, and trying to keep up with rambunctious children. All these things are "worth it." Did you ever ask yourself, "Worth what?" And how long did that pleasure, or whatever your answer is, last?

I would never go to the same amount of trouble for rhubarb that I do for blackberries. That doesn't mean I don't like rhubarb—I make a pretty good strawberry rhubarb cobbler. But rhubarb cannot match blackberries. Spiritually, we too often settle for rhubarb instead of blackberries. You can always tell the ones who don't "settle"—the "purple" fingers from handling the Word of God, and the "purple" teeth and tongues from taking it in on a daily basis and living a life as His servant, give them away.

> *As for the rich in this present age, charge them not to be haughty, nor to set their hopes on the uncertainty of riches, but on God,* ***who richly provides us with everything to enjoy****. They are to do good, to be rich in good works, to be generous and ready to share, thus storing up treasure for themselves as a good foundation for the future,* ***so that they may take hold of that which is truly life.***
>
> 1 Timothy 6.17–19

July 1

Fluff

I suppose it has not escaped your notice that I do not write what I call, "Feel Good Fluff." I do my best writing when I am scolding myself, and unfortunately, that means you get scolded too.

I am more concerned with becoming a better person than with feeling good. Maybe that is because I seldom feel good physically any more, so I am not wedded to the idea that I must always be pumped up spiritually in order to become a more spiritual person.

I have written a few things that I hope have encouraged you. I have written a few things that have made some of you cry, good tears, not bad ones. However, a friend told me once, "I want something that challenges me," and I found myself agreeing with her, and that is what I have tried to do more than anything else. If I keep saying that you are just fine the way you are, will you even bother to try to improve yourself?

As a result, I have lost two or three readers. It makes me think of Ahab who described the prophet Micaiah this way, "I hate him because he does not prophesy good concerning me, but evil" (1 Kgs 22.8), and who once greeted Elijah, "Is it you, you troubler of Israel?" (18.17). Too many folks ignore the fact that *they* are causing their own problems. Like Israel of old they want preachers who say, "Peace, peace, when there is no peace" (Jer 6.14). Like the Galatians' behavior toward Paul, they make those who simply want to help them wonder, "Have I therefore become your enemy because I tell you the truth?" (Gal 4.16).

Pats on the back are good. They serve a purpose. A sermon that makes you shed a tear for the sacrifice that saved you is a helpful thing. It might just sustain you through a temptation that comes your way soon after. I think that is one reason we remember that sacrifice every week.

But emotion fades. That pumped-up feeling can deflate quickly when the realities of life puncture your balloon. You must often sustain yourself with the knowledge that comes from the hard, and often tedious, work of Bible study. You must have the word of God saturating your mind so much that it bubbles up and out of you just when you need it most. You must have prayed often enough that a quick one automatically comes to your lips in difficult circumstances. You must believe because you know logically and with sound evidence that these things are true, not because someone sent you a piece of feel good fluff that won't stand up to an argument by a knowledgeable minister of Satan.

Most of all, you must be willing to listen to those who love you and care about your eternal destiny, whether you want to hear what they say or not—and, in fact, whether they have your good will at heart or not. God has often used the wicked to send his message.

Don't be afraid to be challenged. Don't be afraid to examine yourself for your faults. It will work wonders for your soul.

> *Brethren, if a man be overtaken in a fault, you who are spiritual, restore such a one in the spirit of meekness; considering yourself, lest you also be tempted. Bear one another's burdens, and so fulfill the law of Christ.*
>
> Galatians 6.1–2

July 2

A Niche in Time

Chloe has found her niche. We have never questioned her smarts—her breed is known for them, but we never really figured out what it was she was good at till now.

Magdi, her fellow Australian cattle dog, plays "shortstop" with Keith as he hits tennis balls her way, starting from a crouch and taking off just in time to stop the ball. She plays "outfielder," catching fly balls with her mouth that I would have a problem with if I had a giant mitt. She chases a giant exercise ball around the field, pushing it up on her shoulders and balancing it a few seconds as she runs along. If you tell her to bring you a ball, she will. She is ready for play any time you choose, and even when you don't.

But Chloe? She has no interest in balls. She had much rather sit around chewing on a stick or rolling in the grass. All this exercise stuff is for the birds—or perhaps for less smart dogs?

Then she discovered grasshoppers—the big brown flying kind, as big as small birds. When she happens upon one, she chases it, even as it flies, and leaps into the air to catch it. Then she plops down on the ground immediately and begins crunching. No, she cannot chase balls, and certainly cannot catch high flies, but she can catch big brown grasshoppers just fine. We have noticed that there are fewer of them this year than any other recently.

We all have a gift, a natural ability that God has placed somewhere in all those genes. The trick is to find it. Too many are dissatisfied with the gift they have been given and try to exercise one they do not have. Why? Because, as much as we might talk about humility, we want the flashy gifts that put us in the forefront. A gift for visiting shut-ins and knowing just the right words to say does not garner much attention. Neither does a gift for cleaning—either the meetinghouse or the homes of the sick. But both of those things may make far more difference in someone's life than whether or not a man can lead the singing well or teach a good class.

Yet song leading and teaching seem to be the most desirable gifts in our estimation. We have forgotten their purpose.

Leading a congregation in a song service is not about choosing songs one likes or that he feels show off his ability. It is about enabling a group to more effectively praise God and edify themselves. A good song leader makes thoughtful selections for the occasion, pitches them so that every part can easily sing, and actually *leads* so that the group does not bog down in either tempo or pitch.

Teaching a class is not about standing in front of a group and allowing everyone to have their say, like some sort of verbal traffic cop. A teacher should have prepared long enough and hard enough that anything anyone pops out with off the cuff is far less valuable than what he has prepared. It is more edifying to listen to an enlightening and challenging lecture than to hear yet again what everyone says every time a certain subject comes up, things we could write down before they were even said because we have heard them so many times.

So what is your talent, and more to the point, are you willing to use the one you have, instead of the one you wish you had? If I am griping because everyone gets a turn to teach but me, maybe it's because I am the only one who doesn't realize that I am not any good at it. *What I **am** good at may be far more helpful to my spiritual family.*

Chloe has found her niche, and she is happy to fill it. She doesn't look at Magdi with resentment because we only bat tennis balls for her. She doesn't run around picking up balls lying on the ground, thinking that is the same thing as catching a thirty foot high fly, nor does she stand there barking at the giant exercise ball as if that makes her its master.

God gives us gifts—all of us. It would be singularly ungrateful not to discover them and use them. He gives them so we can help one another get to Heaven. What if you decide you don't like yours and someone misses the trip because of you?

> *For even as we have many members in one body, and all the members have not the same office: so we, who are many, are one body in Christ, and severally members one of another. And having gifts differing according to the grace that was given to us, whether prophecy, let us prophesy according to the proportion of our faith; or serving, let us give ourselves to service; or he that teaches, to his teaching; or he that exhorts, to his exhorting: he that gives, with liberality; he that rules, with diligence; he that shows mercy, with cheerfulness.*
>
> Romans 12.4–8

July 3

Under the Umbrella

Despite its nickname, "The Sunshine State," we have a lot of rain in Florida. One moment it is bright and sunny, and the next it is dark and breezy with angry black clouds boiling in the sky. Within minutes they open up as if Atlas himself were emptying a huge bucket over you. It will rain so hard that visitors often stand at the window watching in fear. Many have never seen anything like a tropical downpour. With us, it is just a matter of course. Less than half an hour later, the sun is out, the pavement steaming, and the puddles already soaking through the sandy soil.

Down here our umbrellas get a work-out. You carry one in each vehicle in case you get caught, and you keep one in the house as well. I have even known a few folks who keep one in the front closet at the meetinghouse. You just never know.

Yet as handy an invention as it is, umbrellas can be awkward. Trying to hold one on your shoulder with your chin while you lean over to unlock the chain on the gate *without getting wet,* is a neat trick I have yet to manage successfully. Something always gets wet—my head, my hand ands arms, my legs, or that part of me that sticks out when I bend over. At best it is clumsy. At worst it is hardly worth the trouble at all, so if it's a light sprinkle, I just leave the umbrella in the car and get wet, but probably not any more wet than I would have gotten anyway. Imagine if you had to carry one all the time. What a nuisance!

Maybe that is why we so often do without our spiritual umbrellas. However, when I turn my life over to God, it is supposed to be just that—my life. Not just Sunday morning, not just moments of crisis, not just times when society and culture say I ought to act in a more spiritual way than usual. Christianity is an umbrella I carry everywhere. It covers every aspect of my life.

I am under its umbrella when I marry, when I raise my children, when I interact with my neighbors. That umbrella should be over me when I drive, when I shop, and when I talk with the repairman or the mechanic. I should be under its influence when the wait at the doctor's office is long, when the order at the restaurant comes out not quite right, and when the bargaining starts at the car lot.

Having that umbrella over my head can be awkward at times. It might mean that I am occasionally taken advantage of. It might mean that my patience is sorely tested. It might mean that I must yield rights that my culture says I have the privilege to. In fact, I might even be ridiculed for carrying an umbrella in a place where no one else does—including a few card-carrying Umbrellians.

Living your life under that umbrella of Christianity has a lot of advantages though. An umbrella offers protection, but only if you keep it open. You can't fold it up and leave it at home when it suits you, then expect it to automatically appear when you need it.

Do have your umbrella with you today? Is it open?

Only let your manner of life be worthy of the gospel of Christ. …For you died, and your life is hid with Christ in God. When Christ, who is our life, shall be manifested, then shall you also with him be manifested in glory.

Philippians 1.27a; Colossians 3.3–4

July 4

Dependence Day

"Do it myself!" What parent has not heard these words from his toddler with mixed feelings? Yes, he is learning to do things for himself, all by himself, without my help. Good for him! Yes, he is learning to do without me. Some day he won't need my help at all. Some day he will experience his own Independence Day, and we will face it with pride in his accomplishment and tears for our own loss at the same time.

And don't we prize that independent feeling ourselves? I have a good friend who is 93. She and I have often bemoaned the fact that people no longer seem to understand the word "need." What they think they "need" is usually just something they "want." It worries us that we are becoming more and more dependent on wealth and the technology it buys. We have said to one another, if someday there is a great catastrophe, most of the country won't know how to survive at all. She has a colorful way of putting it: "They won't even know how to go to the bathroom!"

We have lived in the country for a long time, and I have learned a lot about doing things myself. I don't know when was the last time I bought a jar of jelly at the store. Or pickles. Or canned tomatoes. Or salsa. Or any sort of frozen vegetable at all. I do it myself.

For awhile we had chickens. Until we finally figured out that we were barely breaking even between the cost of feed and the "free" eggs, we gathered jumbos every day, half a dozen or more. Keith milked a cow, and I often had a sour cream pound cake sitting on the countertop, made with our eggs, our homemade butter, and our homemade sour cream. I mashed potatoes we grew with our fresh cream and homemade butter. The ice cream we churned was so rich we often saw flecks of butter in it. I think maybe we gave up the cow the day we actually started feeling our arteries clog as we looked across the table at one another.

A lot of people can and freeze vegetables, jams, and pickles, but it always gave me a little extra pride when I made things that most people never even thought about making, like ketchup from the tag ends of the tomato crop, and chili powder from the cayenne peppers I grew and dried. Lots of folks make applesauce, but not many can their own apple pie filling to use later in the year. Another friend I have makes her own laundry starch. If anything dire does happen in the next few years, my two special friends and I promise to share. I am sure the 93 year old will be happy to tell you how to dig an outhouse.

But that sort of pride and independence can get in the way of our salvation, can't it? There really is nothing we can do to save ourselves. And we must learn to depend upon God—he demands it. He is to be the one we trust, the one we rely on, the one we go to for every need we have, even if our definition of need is really "want."

As long as I think I can manufacture my own salvation and experience a spiritual Independence Day, I will never find myself in God's good graces, or in His grace. This is one case where self-reliance is disastrous. This is one case where we celebrate Dependence Day instead. Have you celebrated yours yet?

> *By grace have you been saved through faith, and that not of yourselves, it is the gift of God.*
>
> Ephesians 2.8

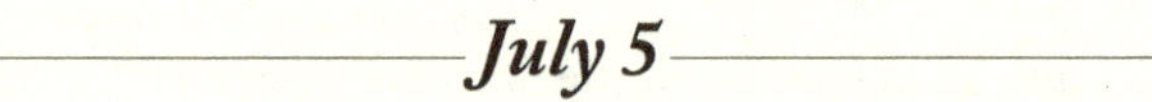

Tending the Garden

This new herb bed with its fancy dirt is taking up a lot of my time. I have gone to a real nursery to find plants, larger and more established (and more expensive) than the discount store 99 cent pots. I have dug trenches for some scalloped stone borders to help keep the encroaching lily bed out of it, and to dissuade any critters that might hide beneath the shed behind the bed from using it as a back door.

I water it every day, and fertilize it every other week. I pull out anything that somehow blows in and seeds itself in my precious black soil.

I have seedlings planted to finish the bed, varieties of herbs that are difficult to find as plants, which I had to carry in and out of the house time and time again due to the fluctuating spring temperatures. Then they were transplanted into ever-increasing sized cups as they outgrew their tiny seed sponges, before finally reaching their permanent home in the herb garden bed.

I have invested so much time, energy, and money into this herb garden that I am not about to let it die.

Why is it that we will work ourselves silly because of a monetary investment, while at the same time neglecting other things much more important to our lives?

How about your marriage? I say to every young couple I know, "Marriage is a high maintenance relationship." Right now, they think they will always be this close, always share every joy and every care. They think there will never come a time when she wonders if he still loves her, or he wonders if she cares at all about the problems he must deal with at work.

Life gets in the way. If you want to stay as close as you are during that honeymoon phase, you have to tend your little garden. Fix his favorite meal. Send her flowers. Put a love note in his lunchbox. Take out the garbage without being asked. Find a babysitter and go out on a date. Just sit down after the kids are in bed and talk to each other. *And listen!* Pray together. Study together. Worship together. Laugh together. Cry together.

What about your relationship with God? Do you think you can maintain a close relationship with someone you don't know? He gave you a whole book telling you who He is (1 Cor 2.11–13). How much time do you spend with it? How often do you talk to Him? How can He help you when you never ask? How can you enjoy being in the presence of someone with whom you have nothing in common? Disciples want nothing more than to become like their teachers (1 Pet 2.21–22; 2 Pet 3.18).

None of that comes without effort. You must spend some time and energy, maybe even make a few sacrifices to cultivate your relationship with God. When you have invested nothing, it means nothing to you, and it shows.

Spend some time today improving your marriage, tending to your family relationships, cultivating your love and care for your brethren, and most of all, caring for your soul—pulling out the weeds, feeding it, nursing it along—so it will grow in a deeper, stronger, more fruitful relationship with your God.

> *Sow to yourselves in righteousness, reap according to kindness; break up your fallow ground; for it is time to seek Jehovah, till he come and rain righteousness upon you.*
>
> Hosea 10.12

July 6

Pots and Kettles

A few weeks ago I got out a pretty dress, put on my heels, found a pretty pair of sparkly, dangling earrings, and dabbed on some lipstick. Keith and I went out to celebrate our anniversary. He trimmed his beard, wore a coat and tie, and polished up his dress shoes. Do you think either one of us for a moment thought that because we chose to dress up for each other on that evening that we didn't love each other the other 364 days of the year? If we had, we would not have been celebrating number 37.

Our assemblies have gotten more casual in dress as the years have gone by. I understand that dress has nothing to do with the heart. Sometimes people clean up the outside when it's the inside that matters. I would never judge a person as being less than devoted to the Lord because he wore jeans to the assembly, or because he waited on the Lord's table without a tie on. I think most of us have gotten past such superficiality.

Recently, though, someone said in my hearing that we needed to realize that we serve God all the time, not just on Sundays and that dressing up on Sundays was a sign of being a "Sunday morning Christian." I certainly agree with the first part of that statement, but I think the second half goes too far.

I still wear a dress to our Sunday morning assemblies because that is what I have done all my life. I see nothing wrong with dressing up—it's one of the few chances I get. It does not mean I don't love the Lord the rest of the week, any more than dressing up for an anniversary dinner means I don't love my husband the rest of the year.

Why is it wrong to judge a person who does not dress up, but perfectly fine to judge a person who does?

That is just a small example of a big problem we *all* have—one way or the other we often do exactly the same things we criticize others for doing. We may be just as judgmental, just as tactless, just as inconsiderate as others. We have just wrapped ourselves in such an aura of self-righteousness that we cannot see it in ourselves. Our vision has been clouded by what we want to see, not what is really there.

I have developed another eye problem—a growth that is fogging up the vision I still have, and which will gradually worsen unless it is removed. Unfortunately, because of all the other conditions, the surgery to remove the growth is as dangerous to my vision as allowing the growth to continue on.

But there is no argument here: it is far more dangerous to our souls to allow that spiritual haze to grow unabated than to remove it. Self-righteousness breeds true, and becomes more and more difficult to see in ourselves as the years go on.

> *Judge not, that you be not judged. For with the judgment you pronounce you will be judged, and with the measure you use it will be measured to you. Why do you see the speck that is in your brother's eye, but do not notice the log that is in your own eye? Or how can you say to your brother, 'Let me take the speck out of your eye,' when there is the log in your own eye? You hypocrite, first take the log out of your own eye, and then you will see clearly to take the speck out of your brother's eye.*
>
> Matthew 7.1–5

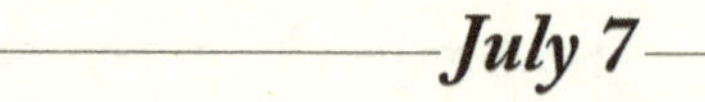

July 7

Party Crasher

When I was 14 a new young doctor came to town, one who was not afraid to "think outside the box." My older doctor turned me over to him and he decided to try contact lenses on me. I had been wearing coke bottle glasses since I was four and my vision declined steadily year after year with the bottoms of the coke bottles getting thicker and thicker.

In those days, hard, nonporous contact lenses were all they had. Usually they were the size of fish scales. Mine were not any broader in circumference but they were still as thick as miniature coke bottle bottoms and nearly as heavy on my eyes. Most people who wore normal lenses could only tolerate them for six to eight hours.

Now add a cornea shaped like the end of a football, a corrugated football at that, and these things were not meant to be comfortable on my eyes, certainly not for the 16–18 hours a day I had to wear them.

So why did I do it? My prescription was +17.25. The doctor told me there was no number on the chart for my vision. ("Chart? What chart? I don't see any chart.") He said if there were, it would be something like 20/10,000, a hyperbole I am sure, but it certainly made the point. Hard contacts were my only hope. If they could stabilize my eyesight, I would last a bit longer. When I was 20, another doctor told me I would certainly have been totally blind by then if not for those contact lenses.

Then soft contact lenses were invented and their popularity grew. But they were not for me. They would not have stabilized my vision. I lost count of the number of times people who wore soft lenses said to me, "I tried those hard ones, but I just could not tolerate them. You are so lucky you can wear them."

Luck had nothing to do with it. My young doctor was smart. He sat me down and said, "The only way you will be able to do this with these eyes is to really want to. You must make up your mind that you will do it no matter what." That was quite a burden to place on a 14 year old, but his tactics worked. Despite the discomfort, I managed, and managed so well that most people never knew how uncomfortable I was. Finally, when what seemed like the one thousandth person told me they just could not tolerate hard lenses, I said, "You didn't need them badly enough." Most of us can do much more than we ever thought possible when we really have to.

Need is a strong motivation. A couple of thousand years ago, it motivated a woman to go where she was not expected, normally not even allowed, and certainly not wanted.

Simon the Pharisee decided to have Jesus for dinner. I read that it was the custom of the day for the leading Pharisee in the town to have the distinguished rabbi over for a meal when he sojourned there. While the man would invite his friends to eat the meal, an open door policy made it possible for any interested party to come in and stand along the wall to listen—any interested *man*, that is. Of course, it was assumed that only righteous men would be interested.

In walked a "sinful" woman (Luke 7). Luke uses a word that does not in itself imply any specific sin, but it was commonly used by that society to refer to what they considered the lowest of sinners, publicans and harlots. The mere fact that she was a woman also caused someone in the crowd to exclaim, "Look! A woman!" in what we assume was horrified shock.

The men were all lying around a low table with their bodies resting on a couch and their feet turned away from the table in the direction of the wall, while their left elbows rested on the table. The woman came into the room, walked around the wall, and began crying over Jesus' feet. Immediately, she knelt to wipe his feet with her hair. I am told that this too was unacceptable. "To unbind and loosen the hair in public before strangers was considered disgraceful and indecent for a woman," commentator Lenski says. We later discover that these were dirty, dusty feet from walking unpaved roads in sandals. How do we know? Because Simon did not even offer Jesus the customary hospitable foot washing.

Then she took an alabaster cruse of ointment, a costly gift, and anointed his feet—not just a token drop or two, but the entire contents—once the cruse was broken open, it was useless as a storage container.

What did Simon do? Nothing outward, but Jesus knew what he thought, and told him a story.

One man owed a lender 500 shillings, and another owed him 50. Both were forgiven their debts when they could not pay. Who, Jesus asked him, do you think was the most grateful? The one who owed the most, of course, Simon easily answered.

And so by using his own prejudices against him, Jesus proved that Simon himself was less grateful to God than this sinful woman. His own actions, or lack thereof toward Jesus was the proof. This man, like so many others of his party, was completely satisfied with himself and where he stood before God. And that satisfaction blinded him to his own need, for truly no one can stand before God in his own righteousness. His gratitude suffered because he did not feel his need. Would he have gone into a hostile environment and lowered himself to do the most menial work a servant could do, and that in front of others? Hardly.

So how much do I think I need the grace of God? The answer is the same one to how far I will go to get it, how much I will sacrifice to receive it, and how much pain I will put up with for even the smallest amount to touch my life. Am I a self-satisfied Simon the Pharisee, more concerned with respectability than with his own need for forgiveness, or a sinful woman, who probably took the deepest breath of her life and walked into a room full of hostile men because she knew it was her only chance at Life?

> *And turning to the woman, he said unto Simon, See this woman? I entered into your house; you gave me no water for my feet: but she has wet my feet with her tears, and wiped them with her hair. You gave me no kiss: but she, since the time I came in, has not ceased to kiss my feet. My head with oil you did not anoint: but she has anointed my feet with ointment. So I say unto you, Her sins, which are many, are forgiven; for she loved much: but to whom little is forgiven, loves little. And he said unto her, Your sins are forgiven. . . .Your faith has saved you; go in peace.*
>
> Luke 7.44–48, 50

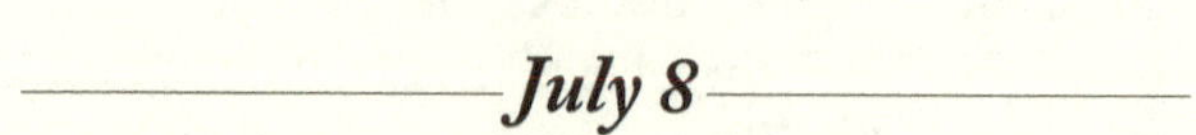

July 8

What Do You Want to Be When You Grow Up?

Sometime back a young lady came up to a friend of mine and said, "I want to be a sweet little old lady when I get older. How do I do that?"

I can imagine myself asking the same question when I was young. I guess I thought there was a magic age, a time when suddenly I would understand everything and feel wise. It hasn't happened yet, and youth left me a long time ago.

My wise friend looked at this young woman and said, "The way to become a sweet little old lady is to be a sweet *young* lady."

She is so right. I can guarantee you that every grumpy old man you know was once a grumpy young one, and every bitter old lady you know was a bitter young one. You will not suddenly become wise just because you have aged, and you will not suddenly become good-natured either. It reminds me of something I heard on an audio book recently: there are no happy endings, only happy people.

And isn't that what we Christians are supposed to be, happy? Yet it seems I meet more and more unhappy Christians. Maybe we do not dwell enough on the hope we have—or maybe we simply don't believe it. If I do believe in that hope, it will show in the things that do and do not upset me, in the things that do and do not discourage me. It will show in how I treat people, even those who are not kind or who actively mistreat me. It will show in the way I put others ahead of myself and my own desires, serving as well as I can in whatever situation I am in. Isn't that what a sweet little old lady does, or a kind and pleasant old man? I have known many in my lifetime. Christians should always become sweet little old ladies and kind and pleasant old men because they believe that here and now is not the end of the matter. They understand that very soon they will see a happy beginning that never ends—*and they believe it.*

If you want to be a sweet little old lady when you grow up, start working on it today, whatever your age, or you will never make it in time.

> *Blessed is the one who finds wisdom, and the one who gets understanding, for the gain from her is better than gain from silver and her profit better than gold. She is more precious than jewels, and nothing you desire can compare with her. Long life is in her right hand; in her left hand are riches and honor. Her ways are ways of pleasantness, and all her paths are peace. She is a tree of life to those who lay hold of her; those who hold her fast are called blessed.*
>
> Proverbs 3.13–18

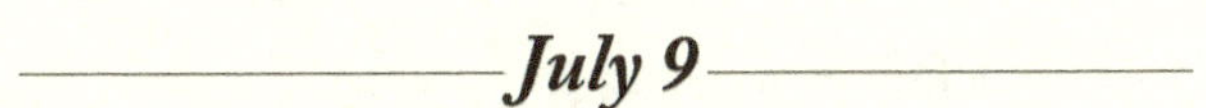

July 9

Root Canals

These things never happen at a good time, but it seems to me that my two root canals outdid themselves for inconvenience.

I had an abscess. My own dentist did not answer, and his message box was full. So I spent the morning searching for a dentist who took our dental insurance. By afternoon I did not care if they did or not—I just needed some relief. So a new dentist saw me and scheduled me for a root canal the next morning. That evening Keith had a stroke and I was at the hospital till 1:30 AM

The next morning, when I considered canceling the procedure, his doctor said, "Go. Take care of yourself so you can take care of him."

That one was not too bad. It was not the reason tears streamed down my face during the whole procedure. I know the dentist must have thought I had lost my mind, though, because at the same time I was struggling not to laugh as that old song ran through my head, "I've got tears in my ears while I lie on my back in my bed when I cry over you." It had been a rough 24 hours and hysteria was close at hand.

The second time, the abscess started the day before I was to leave with my students for state competition. When the dentist heard, he scheduled the procedure for the next week, and sent me on my way with pain killers and antibiotics, as well as his personal phone number. He knew dentists in the city I was headed for and would get me an emergency root canal if I couldn't hack it.

Somehow I managed to accompany eight art songs, eight musical theater numbers and four piano concerti—about 80 pages of music—even though my students had to take turns holding me up in between. Or maybe they were holding me down. The pain killers were doing a number on me and I felt like I was floating.

That root canal, a week later, did not go so well. When the dentist said, "Oho!" I was almost afraid to ask.

"I thought I was nearly finished," he began, "but this tooth has *five* roots instead of four, so here we go again."

Then came the next surprise. That fifth root was covered by calcification. We did not know that meant that the anesthesia had not reached it until the drill burst through covering and hit that live root.

I try to make it a rule not to scream in doctor's offices, but that time I broke the rule.

The only two ways to fix an abscess permanently are to pull the tooth or do a root canal, emptying the tooth of all live material, then crowning it, so it looks and functions like a normal tooth. If you don't get all the way to the bottom, you will still hurt, and another infection will soon follow. They say in the old days that people actually died from those things.

Doing that little job is not pleasant, but if you have been hurting as I had been for days and days, it is definitely worth it.

And pulling it out by the roots is the only way to rid yourself of sin too. David said in the Psalm 36, "Transgression speaks to the wicked deep in his heart; there is no fear of God before his eyes." You can't just put a crown over the tooth and expect it to get well; and so you cannot just put on a cloak of righteousness while your heart still leads you in the same evil direction every day. You cannot take a pain pill and think that will make your tooth well; and so you cannot just sit in a pew on Sunday, not even *every* Sunday, and think that is enough of a change in your life to satisfy God.

You pull the sin out by the roots. You change your habits; you change your associations; you change your schedule; you change your life in whatever way necessary if you have really changed your heart. Then you put down new roots, planted deep in your heart as well, but this time roots of righteousness. When they finally become established it will be as difficult to pull them out as it was to pull out the bad roots, but this time, you won't have to.

The stupid man cannot know; the fool cannot understand this: that though the wicked sprout like grass and all evildoers flourish, they are doomed to destruction forever. ...The righteous flourish like the palm tree and grow like a cedar in Lebanon. They are planted in the house of the L*ORD; they flourish in the courts of our God. They still bear fruit in old age; they are ever full of sap and green, to declare that the* L*ORD is upright; he is my rock, and there is no unrighteousness in him.*

Psalm 92.6–7, 12–15

July 10

Wordplay

I have discovered a little trick to help me get more out of my Bible study. Too often, I read through passages that deal directly with things in my life without even realizing that they do. It just goes right past me. So, after a little meditation, I find something comparable in my own culture and time that I can "plant" into the passage. I am not trying to change the Word of God or make my own "private interpretation." I just want to be able to apply it to me and my problems so I can grow. Here are a couple that have really helped me. The bracketed words are the ones I planted. You might want to read the cited passage before reading these altered ones.

Romans 2.24–25: "For the name of God is blasphemed among [people of the world] because of you, even as it is written. For [baptism] indeed profits if you are a doer of the law, but if you are a transgressor of the law, your [baptism] has become [un-baptism]."

Since circumcision, the token of the Old Covenant, is compared to baptism in Colossians 2.11–12, this was a no-brainer. However, if you press it too far, you could wind up with a theological problem or two, so be careful. The point is to make a passage sing out loud to you! Reading the passage this way I can see that I cannot rely on having once been baptized to save me if my life does not live up to the New Covenant it represents.

1 Corinthians 13.1–3: "[If I go to church three times a week in a certain building with a certain sign over the door] but have not love, I am become a sounding brass or a clanging cymbal. [If I take the Lord's Supper every first day of the week, give more than a tenth, sing loudly, and say amen to every prayer] but have not love, I am nothing. [If I don't cheat on my spouse, lie, drink, or cuss] but have not love it profits me nothing."

As you can imagine, that one really strikes home. How many times do I define faithfulness as "going to church and not doing the big bad sins?" Faithfulness to the Lord involves striving to become like Him, and that means learning a selfless love, not following a learned routine.

I believe the Word of God is alive and relevant to everyone's life; God meant it to be that way. Keeping it limited to another time and culture may make me feel better, but it won't do a thing for my soul. So give yourself some help today with a little wordplay.

> *For the word of God is living and active, and sharper than any two-edged sword, piercing even to the dividing of soul and spirit, of both joints and marrow, and quick to discern the thoughts and intents of the heart.*
>
> Hebrews 4.12

July 11

Deadheads

We live on five acres, but do not have the equipment to handle it sometimes. Most everything we have accomplished has been with a shovel, a wheelbarrow, and Keith's strong back. We certainly don't have a tractor to keep it manicured properly.

We decided a few years ago that we had rather see some splashes of color here and there instead of waist high green grass and assorted head high weeds, so we planted several cans of mixed wildflower seeds around the perimeter of the mown section. The first year they did not do much, but the second year we had a nice showing of coreopsis, gaillardia, and gloriosa daisies. They come up again every spring and have even spread out into the field in a few places.

Four summers ago I started cutting the deadheads and scattering them around. I thought it might be nice to have some up by the gate to greet our guests and scattered a few up there. The next year I had two orange firewheels, the more colloquial name for gaillardia. The year after that we had about six. Last year I quit counting at 20. They were so thick it was hard to tell exactly how many there were—we're talking plants, not blooms, which were many times more than 20. I can hardly wait to see what happens this year.

You've seen deadheads. They are gray or brown, shriveled and dried up. You would never think they had once been beautiful blooms or were any longer valuable at all. But "deadhead" is a most inaccurate name for them. Inside those ugly old blooms lay the potential for thousands more beautiful blooms.

Have you looked in the mirror lately? Some of you are a lot younger than I, but no matter how young you are, you are not as young as you used to be. Someday you will be my age, and most of you will get even older than that. It's easy these days, especially facing a major disability, to think that I am no longer useful in the kingdom. It's easy to say that since I might not be able to get out much any more, that I cannot serve. When you grow older, you will face the same feelings. If you are older, you may be facing them already.

But that is not the case. Just like those dried up flowers, you have the potential to reach thousands through your example. Maybe the only example you are able to give any more is faithfulness—but it is a powerful one, and always needed. You are there when the doors of the meetinghouse are opened if you can drag yourself out at all. Sometimes you are there when you ought not to be. You have been married for 40, 50, 60 years to the same husband or wife, and the devotion between you is still obvious. You sit quietly and never cause any trouble. In Bible classes you make comments that show you have lived by the scriptures. You have children who are faithful to God, to their mates, to the body of Christ, and who are good citizens of this earthly country as well. Do you think none of that counts?

If you are young, you need to start making good use of these resources. Too many times the young are stuck in the self-centered ways of youth, forgetting that older Christians have lived a life every bit as interesting as theirs. Get them to talking sometime about their past. You just might be amazed at what they have been through and survived; things you will probably never face in these prosperous times. And you will find one of the helps God always intended you to have—the wisdom of the aged. I have learned more valuable lessons from quiet people with halos of silver hair than from any pulpit preacher I have ever listened to—and I have heard some pretty good ones.

Setting an example is not something we have a choice about. As long as we are alive we do just that. And it may be the most powerful thing any of us do. You are never shriveled, dried up and useless as far as God is concerned. You are always sowing seeds. Be sure you sow the right ones.

The hoary head is a crown of glory; it shall be found in the way of righteousness.

Proverbs 16.31

July 12

Lessons from the Food Channel

I watch more Food Network shows than any others. I have one favorite I try to never miss, and a couple of others that I will watch if I have the time. Even reruns are good on the Food Channel.

Funny thing, though, I have only tried about three recipes from any of the shows I have watched. That's not three per show; that's three total. The thing I get most from these shows is technique—learning that it takes more salt in your pasta water than you might think to really season it; that you should season every layer of a dish not just the final product so that the dish tastes seasoned not just salty; that meat continues to cook after you take it out of the oven so you must take it out before it's totally done or you end up with tough, dry meat; that in 90 percent of cases fresh herbs are far better than dried; and that real parmagiana reggiano is worth the money—not only does it taste that much better, but you actually use less for the same effect. I didn't realize I was picking these things up until last Thanksgiving when I was told by three separate family members that it was the best turkey and dressing I had ever made.

I started thinking about that, and realized that is the way Satan gets to most of us, too. We don't go out and do all the big, bad sins in the world, following his personal recipes for evil. But if we are not careful, the worldly techniques find their way into our lives. Our perspectives change from the spiritual to the physical. We become more concerned about physical security than spiritual security, more prone to rely on our own acumen than God's promises, more willing to accept sin in others in order to get along.

I can remember preachers making jokes about the King James wording of 1 Peter 2.9: "Ye are… a peculiar people." We think peer pressure is only a problem for teenagers, but none of us wants to be called "peculiar." Four hundred years ago, when the KJV was translated, that word meant "private property." You see, we are supposed to be God's private property, not Satan's. We should be learning God's techniques, not the Devil's. And I guess in the way the word is used today, that *would* make us appear a little peculiar.

In just two or three hours a week, the Food Channel has changed my cooking. Just think what might be happening to us in the many hours a week we are surrounded by those who couldn't care less about spiritual things. Being aware will help us to keep the influence of their techniques minimal. Better still, we should surround ourselves every chance we get with those who would help us learn better spiritual techniques. Let's all help one another get to Heaven.

> *But you are an elect race, a royal priesthood, a holy nation, a people for God's own possession [peculiar], that you may show forth the excellencies of him who called you out of darkness into his marvelous light; who in time past were no people, but now are the people of God; who had not obtained mercy, but now have obtained mercy.*

1 Peter 2.9–10

July 13

Railroad Crossings

Many years ago we lived in an old frame house in front of a train track, on a corner lot right next to the crossing. The boys were four and two, and they loved to run outside as soon as they heard the horn so they could wave to the engineer and watch the cars pass—boxcars, flatcars, tankers, and finally the caboose, usually with another trainman standing on its "back porch," who also received an excited wave. Before a week had passed, those men were craning their necks, looking for the two towheaded little boys so they could be sure to wave back. We learned the train schedule quickly: one every morning about 8:30, one every afternoon about 4:00, and one every Saturday about midnight.

That first Saturday night train took about ten years off my life. I came up out of a deep sleep when the horn sounded. We had only been in the house two days and in the fog of sleep, I did not know where I was or what was happening. Then I heard that train getting closer and closer, louder and louder. I realized what it was then, but my perspective was so out of whack that it sounded like the train was headed straight for the middle of the house. I sat straight up, frozen in terror until it had passed.

Within two weeks I was sleeping through the din. Not even the sudden wail of the horn woke me. During the day it took the tug of a little hand on my shirttail for me to hear the train coming so we could go out and wave. Your mind tunes out what it doesn't want to hear, and does a grand job of it.

How many times do we tune out people? When we learn another's pet peeves, the things he goes on about at the least provocation, we no longer listen. If we have the misfortune to deal with someone who nags, we tune that out. Maybe we should learn the lesson to choose our battles. If we want what we say to matter to people, don't go on and on about the trivial or they will have tuned us out long ago and never hear the things they really need to hear. Parents need to learn that.

Then there is the matter of tuning out God. Oh, we all want to hear how Jesus loved the sinners, but let's not hear His command to, "Go thy way and sin no more." Let's remind ourselves that the apostle Paul was not above preaching to some of the vilest sinners in the known world, "fornicators, idolaters, adulterers, effeminate, abusers of themselves with men, thieves, covetous, drunkards, revilers, extortioners." But let's ignore the fact that he says they *changed:* "such *were* some of you"; let's ignore the fact that he said that in their prior state they were "unrighteous" and could "not inherit the kingdom of God" (1 Cor 6.9–11). That's just one of the many things people don't hear.

Today, maybe we should ask ourselves what it is we don't want to hear. I imagine that it is the very thing we need to hear the most.

Why do you not understand my speech? Because you cannot hear my word. ...He that is of God hears the words of God: for this cause you hear not, because you are not of God.

John 8.43, 47

The Enlightened Ones

We have a tendency to think of ourselves as far more enlightened than those who lived under the Old Law, far more knowledgeable, certainly, of things like the grace of God. Nonsense. Just listen to what Daniel had to say: "For we do not present our supplications before you for *our* righteousness, but for your great mercies' sake" (9.18). Can you think of a better definition of grace?

Those folks also understood that here and now is not what matters, it is only a temporary stop on a journey to the Eternal.

Abraham and Sarah certainly understood that despite their relative wealth in their day and time, it was nothing to compare with what God had in store for them, even far beyond the Promised Land they wandered in. They "died in faith, not having received the promises but having greeted them from afar, and having confessed that they were strangers and pilgrims on this earth" (Heb 11.13).

And Moses, who could had the wealth of Egypt at his disposal, [chose] "rather to share ill-treatment with the people of God than to enjoy the pleasures of sin for a season, accounting the reproaches of Christ greater riches than the treasures of Egypt" (Heb 11.25–26). The "reproaches of Christ"? But he was an Old Testament character! Of course he was, but he still "got it" better than many of us on this side of Malachi.

Even Hannah, a humble woman of Ephraim, was able to recognize in her song of thanksgiving in 1 Samuel 2, "Jehovah makes poor and he makes rich, he brings low and he lifts up, he raises up the poor out of the dust, he lifts up the needy from the dunghill and makes them sit with princes and *inherit the throne of glory.* For the pillars of the earth are Jehovah's and he has set the world upon them. ...Not by his [own] might shall a man prevail." Hannah knew that the circumstances of this life were not what counted—her God was in control and He would reward her.

We could go on and on. Ruth, who left home, family, familiar customs and language—her comfort zone, we might say today—to go to a place where she had nothing to expect but a life of poverty and loneliness, not only as a widow, but also as an alien among God's people. Forget for a moment what actually happened to her. She expected nothing but a hard life. Yet she thought that being able to worship and serve this Jehovah she had learned of with the people He had chosen, was worth giving up any chance at an easier life in her native land. She knew that it was not that physical land that mattered.

So what about us "enlightened" folks? Are we willing to give up anything and everything in this world, willing to endure anything and everything, willing to be different, to think differently, to act differently from everyone else no matter how uncomfortable that may make us, because we understand the importance of the Eternal, or do the tangible things of life tether us to this side of Eternity? To which side of life are you tied today?

In this we groan, longing to put on our heavenly dwelling. For while we are still in this tent, we groan, being burdened—not that we would be unclothed, but that we would be further clothed, so that what is mortal may be swallowed up in life. He who has prepared us for this very thing is God. ...So we are always of good courage. We know that while we are at home in the body, we are away from the Lord, for we walk by faith, not by sight. Yes, we are of good courage, and we would rather be away from the body and at home with the Lord. So whether we are at home or away, we make it our aim to please him, for we must all appear before the judgment seat of Christ, so that each one may receive what is due for what he has done while in the body, whether good or evil.

2 Corinthians 5.2, 4–10

Refreshment

We worked our boys hard when they were growing up, weeding and picking the garden in the heat of a Florida summer, standing in a hot kitchen working the assembly line of produce canning and freezing, mowing an acre's worth of our five with a push mower—not a walk-behind, but a *push* mower—splitting and stacking wood for the wood stove, hauling brush, raking leaves, and dumping them for mulch. After hours of hard labor and buckets of sweat, nothing thrilled them more on a hot summer afternoon than a refreshing dip in a nearby spring.

Springs, even in Florida, are cold. It is almost painful to step into one—they will literally take your breath away. I was one who gradually eased my way in to avoid the shock, but the boys wanted to "get it over with," and usually jumped off the pier, the floating dock, or the rope swing, whatever that particular spring had as a point of entry, and if I was standing too close I "got it over with" too.

One of their favorites was Ichetucknee, probably because that one took up a whole day as we rented tubes and floated down the river from the spring head, leaving the water three hours later when we reached the picnic pavilions. Even by that point in the float, the river was still close enough to the spring that we could chill a homegrown watermelon in its cool shallows while we ate tomato sandwiches and leftover fried chicken; and we never had to worry about snakes or alligators.

We were always the only ones around clothed from our necks to our knees so we got a lot of strange looks. The clothes did not help a bit with the cold. They were for modesty only. Nothing about a freezing wet shirt sticking to your body will keep you warm, even in a patch of sunlight. Yet when I finally got wet enough that a mere splash did not make me squeal, the water was a refreshing respite from the sauna we call summer down here.

Peter told the people of Jerusalem that if they repented they would receive "seasons of refreshing" (Acts 3.19). I am told that the word actually means "breathing," as in catching one's breath after hard labor or exercise. That indicates to me that God is not promising us a life of ease. Yes, we have blessings that others do not have, and that only those who are spiritually minded can even recognize and enjoy, but we will still experience heartache, persecution, illness, and other trials of life. We are expected to wear ourselves out with service to any in need, as long as there is life in us. God has no truck with laziness.

But we have this promise—as surely as ice cold spring water lapping against an overheated body can refresh and renew, we will have refreshment from above that soothes our aches and heals our hurts, that rests our souls with the peace of fellowship with God, and that bestows grace on our tortured spirits.

> *Repent therefore, and turn again, that your sins may be blotted out, that so there may come seasons of refreshing from the presence of the Lord; and that he may send the Christ who has been appointed for you, Jesus.*
>
> Acts 3.19–20

July 16

Where Are You?

We were hiking a mountain trail, sometimes straight up, sometimes straight down. A babbling brook ran to our left at the bottom of a 50 foot ravine, making miniature waterfalls over rocks and roots long before we reached the larger and taller falls, weeping into a pool and running on down the hill. As we made our way over another rise and around a bend, the leaf-strewn trail suddenly dipped and we found ourselves in a cypress swamp. What?!

Oh yes, I remembered, we were not in the mountains after all; we were in Florida. Yet it would have been easy to have fooled a person who had slept through the trip over rivers with names like Suwannee and Ochlockonee, traveling deep into the piney woods of the Big Bend, down to the swamplands. If they had wakened in the campground on the ridge overlooking the river valley below, and walked the first mile of the path, they would have thought they were on the Appalachian Trail somewhere.

But the sight of those huge cypresses, the bottoms of their trunks billowing like the folds of a skirt in the water, their knees standing two and three feet high around them, would have given pause. Suddenly they would realize the shrubbery beneath the trees in the woods wasn't rhododendron and mountain aster, but palmetto and needle palms. The ground wasn't hardwood leaf mold over rock, but pine straw matting over red or yellow clay and sand. This is Florida—perhaps different from most other places in the state, but Florida nevertheless.

Where are you spiritually? Are you where you think you are? Or did you sleep through the first half of your life, and when your spirituality awakened, look around and at first glance think, "Yes, this is the right place," when it was only a close facsimile? Did you find yourself among people who seemed to be doing the right thing and so fail to take a really close look at your surroundings?

Why are you where you are? Is it just because this is where Mom and Dad put you, or because you checked the map and stayed awake for the trip, knowing why you made which turns, and not only how to tell others to get here, but why they should be here with you?

If you are in the mountains of Appalachia, you will need to look out for a few rattlesnakes and copperheads, but those are shy reptiles that will usually run if given the opportunity. In a Florida swamp you will also need to watch out for cottonmouths and alligators. Cottonmouths are notoriously aggressive—they will charge from cover, and then chase you. And alligators move faster than anything that ungainly has a right to. If you are wary of the wrong dangers, you are much more likely to be taken unawares.

God expects you to know where you are spiritually and why you are there. He doesn't want people who are where they are simply out of convenience and family tradition. Where is the service in that?

He expects you to look out for the dangers that might surround you. How can you be alert if the dangers you expect are not the ones in that area?

And how will you ever find God if you are not where you thought you were?

From there you will seek the Lord your God and you will find Him if you search after Him with all your heart and with all your soul.

Deuteronomy 4.29

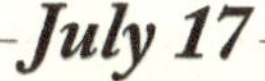

A Poor Excuse

I was in the middle of making an excuse the other morning when suddenly I heard myself. Yes, I was tired, I had a headache, and serious things were whirling around in my mind. So surely my snappy tone of voice was understandable, wasn't it?

Let's check this theory out. Jesus is supposed to be my example. Simply making the claim to be his disciple means I try my best to do what he would do. So if I look at what had to be the worst time of his life on earth, the last 24 hours, then I can measure myself against the true standard.

Over the Passover meal, when his disciples were once again arguing about who would be the most important in the kingdom, he finally lost his cool. "Shut up! I have more important things on my mind than dealing with your petty concerns right now."

He was so concerned about the upcoming trials he would need to endure, he never once thought about what they might be going through, and left them to their fears and confusion. "Grow up!" he told them. "It's high time you figured this out for yourselves."

When one of his best friends betrayed him, the other apostles were still murmuring among themselves about who it must be. "Be quiet," he said. "This isn't about you."

He was obviously in tremendous pain as he hung on the cross, so how could he even begin to worry about his mother and her care? "Can't you quit that sniveling? You're only making things worse."

Well, that's how it might read if it were me going through those trials. Instead, Jesus left an example that shows me there is *no* excuse for poor behavior. Despite what he was going through, the like of which I have never had to endure, he kept his thoughts on others. He kept his voice tempered. He kept his actions loving. Not even his enemies suffered a tongue-lashing of the type I find so easy to dish out when I am upset or do not feel well.

For you see, *God does not allow trials in our lives so we will have excuses for sin.* He allows them so we will grow and get stronger. When I excuse my behavior because of what I am going through, I fail the test. Unless I recognize where I failed and determine not to do it again, I will not get stronger; I will only get weaker. In the process I will make it more likely that the next time I will fail again. And again. And again. Till there is no more need for trials at all because Satan has me exactly where he wants me, and I am too weak to even think about fighting back. Even those I claim to love will know to stay away from me when things are not going well, and so my last avenue of help is also gone.

The sad truth of the matter is the one who is best at making excuses is one poor excuse for a Christian.

For hereunto were you called: because Christ also suffered for you, leaving you an example, that you should follow his steps: who did no sin, neither was guile found in his mouth: who, when he was reviled, reviled not again; when he suffered threatened not; but committed himself to him that judges righteously: who his own self bare our sins in his body upon the tree, that we, having died unto sins, might live unto righteousness; by whose stripes ye were healed. For you were going astray like sheep; but are now returned unto the Shepherd and Bishop of your souls.

1 Peter 2.21–25

July 18

A Bright Spot in the Day

Shortly after this latest surgery, when I had grown weary of sitting in a dark house alone day after day, I donned a couple of pairs of sunglasses and a hat with a broad visor, picked up my walking sticks, and stepped outside. It was still morning so as long as I faced west, the light was tolerable.

The dogs heard me coming and met me at the door, bumping each other out of the way vying for the first pat, tails wagging so hard and fast they might have been declared lethal weapons. When they saw my intent to head out into the open, they took off in that direction, Magdi stiffly romping, an old dog briefly reminded of her youth, and Chloe ripping circles around her, leaving skid marks in the grass.

Right after an eye surgery, the operated-on eye sees nothing but a blur of color for a few weeks. Although the two eyes are separate entities, each with its own plumbing and wiring systems, the other eye experiences some "sympathy pains" and its vision is not as clear as usual either. While I could miss the furniture, so to speak, details were difficult. As far as I could tell there were no individual blooms on the crape myrtles—each was simply one big blotch of color. There were no leaves on the trees—they were just big puffs of green, exactly the way a child would draw them. There were no individual blades of grass—the ground was just painted green, except way out in the field where someone had spilled a bucket of yellow paint.

I headed for that spot, my two bodyguard/playmates scampering around ahead and behind, sniffing up grasshoppers the size of mascara tubes. Our ten paws were soon soaked with dew and breaded with sand. When I got close enough to see my beautiful spot of bright yellow and knelt down, it was a thick oval patch of dandelion blooms about ten feet by six feet, between the mown field and the back fence. Dandelions! I laughed out loud. My spot of beauty was what most people consider bothersome weeds. There ought to be a lesson here, I thought, and maybe this is it.

Not many of us are long stemmed red roses in God's garden, let alone rare and delicate orchids. I have met some fresh-faced petunias whose sincerity is obvious, some formal and well-dressed gladioli who can stand before a crowd and speak without fear, some pleasant and reliable carnations who seem able to function in practically any situation, and some sturdy daisies with a lot of staying power. But some of us are just dandelions, not very popular, not very talented, all too soon developing a cap of fuzzy gray hair. So do we use that as our excuse?

Do we sit back and wait for those other blooms to catch everyone's attention and take care of the business at hand? Do we still do nothing, even those times in our lives when we are the only blossom in a field full of tares and thistles? Even a dandelion looks pretty good there.

That little patch of dandelions gave me the first real laugh I'd had in weeks. It got me out of a dark, lonely house into a world of sunlight (safely at my back), and a cool breeze filled with birdsong. My soul recovered more in five minutes than my body had in the whole week before. What might my day have been like without those humble little plants?

God has a place for all of us and he won't accept excuses for doing nothing. It doesn't matter if someone else is better known, better liked, or even a whole lot more able, especially if those someones are not present when a need arises. Stop looking at yourself and look around you—self-absorption never accomplished anything.

God is the owner of this garden and He doesn't mind a dandelion or two. In fact, it seems like He made more of them than any other flower.

> *Whatever your hand finds to do, do it with your might, for there is no work nor thought nor knowledge nor wisdom in Sheol to which you are going.*
>
> Ecclesiastes 9.10

Shall We?

The difference between the words "shall" and "will" is primarily a legal distinction in America today. We seldom use "shall" in our everyday speech. However, I have heard that in Middle English it was used to distinguish between intent and promise. If one simply said, "I will" do something, it only meant he intended to do so and would do his best. If he said, "I shall," it meant that he would do it one way or the other. "Shall" meant, "I definitely will," "I certainly will," "I most assuredly will," with the "will" underlined, all caps, and bolded. Think about that as you read the following passages from the King James Version, that Middle English so many decry, and think what that means about these things.

> *I will call upon the* L*ORD* *who is worthy to be praised, so* ***shall*** *I be saved from my enemies.* (Psa 18.3)

> *Be of good courage, and he* ***shall*** *strengthen your heart all ye that hope in the* L*ORD*. (Psa 31.24)

> *But God will redeem my soul from the power of the grave, he* ***shall*** *receive me.* (Psa 49.15)

> *For sin* ***shall not*** *have dominion over you, for you are not under law but under grace.* (Rom 6.14)

*Above all taking up the shield of faith wherewith you **shall** be able to quench all the fiery darts of the wicked.* (Eph 6.16)

*But my God **shall** supply all your need according to his riches in glory by Christ Jesus.* (Phil 4.19)

*For the Lord himself **shall** descend from heaven with a shout, with the voice of the archangel and with the trump of God, and the dead in Christ **shall** rise first. (1 Thes 4.16)*

*And God **shall** wipe away all tears from their eyes, and there **shall** be no more death, neither sorrow nor crying, **neither shall** there be any more pain, for the former things are passed away.* (Rev 21.4)

*And there **shall** be no night there, and they need no candle neither light of the sun, for the Lord God gives them light, and they **shall** reign forever and ever; and he said unto me, these sayings are faithful and true.* (Rev 22.5–6)

So the question again is, "Shall we?"
Yes, we most definitely, certainly, assuredly shall!

July 20

That's Different

My neighbor, who has aggravated me with his inconsiderate behavior since he moved in, once again seems to go out of his way to provoke me. So what do I do? I find some way to return the gesture.

This past Sunday morning in Bible class we had discussed Romans 12, including verses 18–19: "As much as in you lies, be at peace with all men. Avenge not yourselves for… vengeance is mine, says the Lord."

I nodded in agreement as the teacher explained the behavior a Christian should exhibit, and eventually became bored and impatient. We all know this. Why is he spending so much time on it?

Now it is Monday—or Wednesday, or some other weekday—and I have left my religious cubbyhole behind. This is real life, we are dealing with, not some ideal that always works out fine. So, despite the fact that I know the "right" answers, I behave the "wrong" way. This is different, I rationalize.

Oh, really? The only difference is that it is *me,* and I give myself a free pass whenever possible. Besides, the vengeance thing is about serious matters, not some minor annoyance, so this does not count. I am not a vigilante, after all.

So if it is so minor, why do I allow myself to be upset by it? Well, because they did it to *me.*

Reading the Word of God is not difficult. Understanding it is sometimes more difficult. But applying it to my life is the most difficult thing of all. I make excuses for myself, ("It's been a rough day"); I flatter myself with good intentions, ("I just want him to learn how it feels"); I try to make my actions seem normal and forgivable, ("It was just an accident, I meant no harm"), all while denying the other person any benefit of a doubt at all.

What I have really done is lower myself to his level. What was that my brain just screamed out at him? Jerk, idiot, lowlife?

I think I hear it echoing back to me.

Be not a witness against your neighbor without cause; and deceive not with your lips. Say not, I will do so to him as he has done to me. ...Say not I will recompense evil; wait for Jehovah and he will save you. ...All the ways of a man are clean in his own eyes, but Jehovah weighs the spirit.

Proverbs 24.28–29; 20.22; 16.2

July 21

A *Worthy* Woman

Proverbs 31 is one of the best known chapters in the Bible—the worthy woman, or as the King James reads, the virtuous woman. I decided to do a study on that word "worthy" and boy, was I surprised. It has a depth of meaning I never suspected.

The Hebrew word *chayil* is used 150 times in the Old Testament. Look at these other words it is often translated by: army, band of men, band of soldiers, company, forces, great forces, host, might, power, strength, substance, valor, war, able, strong, and valiant. When you have a minute today, look up these passages where the word is translated by one of those: Judges 21.10; 1 Chronicles 5.18; 2 Kings 2.16; 2 Chronicles 33.14; 1 Samuel 9.1; 14.48. Of the 150 available, I think that is a good representation. Can you find the word in those verses? If you see one that has anything to do with brave, strong men, that's it: "worthy."

We tend to think of strength and courage as specifically masculine traits, and yes, men may have the monopoly on brute strength, but look through Proverbs 31. Not only does this woman have the strength to survive long, busy days, one after the other with no end in sight, but she has the inner strength to survive life! "Hothouse flowers" who "have the vapors" are not who God had in mind when he created woman.

A woman should have the strength to stand by a man through thick and thin, "in sickness and in health," and all the other things she promised all those years ago, to manage her household (1 Tim 5.14), to teach her children, to help the needy, to serve the saints, and "to stand against the wiles of the Devil, and to quench all the fiery darts of the Evil One" (Eph 6.11, 16).

By using this word in Proverbs 31, both at the beginning of the passage, verse 10 and at the end, verse 29, God is surely telling us that he expects his women to be strong, inside and out.

Ladies, God says there is strength and courage in femininity—don't let anyone tell you otherwise.

> *A* ***worthy [strong, valiant]*** *woman, who can find? Her price is far above rubies. ... She girds her loins with strength, and makes her arms strong. ...Strength and dignity are her clothing and she laughs at the time to come. ...Many daughters have done* ***valiantly*** *but you excel them all. ...Give her of the fruit of her hands, and let her works praise her in the gates.*
>
> Proverbs 31.10, 17, 25, 29, 31

July 22

The Real McCoy

I was watching the sprinkler zzzt-zzzt-zzzt its way across the garden the other day. Usually the end of April and most of May are dry. The afternoon thundershowers don't start until the humidity and temperature both reach the 90s, so to keep the garden alive, we have to irrigate. Keith has various methods he uses, a drip hose, a sprinkler, and simple hand-watering, depending upon the crop and its weaknesses. Some plants are more prone to fungus, so you keep their leaves as dry as possible by hand-watering, directing the water to the bottom of the plant. Sometimes Keith spends as long as two hours in an evening watering.

But as soon as the summer rains start, the garden takes off. It becomes obvious that, despite all the time spent, all we did was help the garden survive until the real thing came along. The plants almost explode they grow so much faster and produce so much better. Chemically the water may be the same, but out here in the country everyone knows that irrigation is a distant second to God's watering.

Should that surprise us? Adam and Eve made themselves aprons of fig leaves. God came along and made them garments of skins. I know which one I had rather wear on a cool evening. Men made gods of stone and wood and metal. Jehovah is a spirit with no beginning or end. I know which one I had rather rely on to take care of me. Under the old covenant, the blood of bulls and goats could only put away the sins for a year at a time. The blood of a perfect, unblemished sacrifice puts them away forever. I know which one I had rather count on for my salvation.

When it comes to God, there is no substitute for the real thing.

> *God understands the way to it, and he knows its place. For he looks to the ends of the earth and sees everything under the heavens. When he gave to the wind its weight, and apportioned the waters by measure, when he made a decree for the rain and a way for the lightning of the thunder, then he saw it and declared it, he established it and searched it out. And he said to man, Behold, the fear of the Lord, that is wisdom, and to turn away from evil is understanding.*
>
> Job 28.23–28

July 23

Beach Towels

As odd as it may seem for a native Floridian, I am not a beach person. Maybe that is why I made the mistake I did.

I was away to a camp retreat for women, when it suddenly dawned on me en route that I had forgotten to pack a bath towel. Rather than delay our progress shopping, we swung by a pharmacy at an exit where we had already stopped for gas, and I picked up the only type of towel they had available—a beach towel.

The next night as I took my turn with the shower shared by 30 other women in our cabin, I discovered that beach towels do not work like ordinary towels. I blotted my wet skin and lifted it to discover all the water droplets sitting on my arm exactly as they had before I used the towel. I tried again, same result. Finally I tried *pushing* off the water. Some, but very little, rolled onto the floor. Slightly encouraged I kept wiping. Eventually I was—well, dry is not the word—but damp instead of soaked. I am positive, though, that most of the drying was a matter of evaporation because I worked at it for nearly 15 minutes.

The strangest things can bring me a moment of inspiration. So when I got home, I did a quick study on the word "wipe." It is an interesting word, in both Testaments.

In the Old Testament the Hebrew word is *machah.* "Jehovah said to Moses, whoever has sinned against me, him will I blot out of my book" (Exod 32.33). "Blot out" is the same word often translated "wiped." Yet in Psalm 51, David uses it when he asks God to "blot out" his transgressions, and in Isaiah 25, God says in a Messianic prophecy that He will "wipe away" His people's tears.

In the New Testament, the word is *exaleipho.* Peter says in Acts 3.19 that we must repent if we expect our sins to be "blotted out." Jesus tells John in Revelation

3.5 that he will not "blot out" the names of those who repent. Then we are told that when we reach our reward "God will wipe away all tears from [our] eyes" (Rev 21.4), all the same Greek word in exactly the same three uses as the Hebrew.

God's mercy is not like a beach towel. He will blot out my sins completely. On the other hand, if I do not live as I should, He will blot me out completely. You cannot use "completely" in one phrase without using it in the other. I cannot say, "Don't blot me out completely. Don't wipe my name out of your book," while expecting God to wipe away my sins as completely as an expensive, absorbent towel wipes the water from my body because His Holy Spirit chose the same word for both actions in two separate languages.

Justice demands that something be blotted out. God's grace makes it possible that it not be the sinner, but merely his sins. Amazing grace indeed.

> *And in this mountain will Jehovah of hosts make unto all peoples a feast of fat things, a feast of wines on the lees, of fat things full of marrow, of wines on the lees well refined. And he will destroy in this mountain the face of the covering that covers all peoples, and the veil that is spread over all nations. He has swallowed up death for ever; and the Lord Jehovah will wipe away tears from off all faces; and the reproach of his people will he take away from off all the earth: for Jehovah has spoken it. And it shall be said in that day, Lo, this is our God; we have waited for him, and he will save us: this is Jehovah; we have waited for him, we will be glad and rejoice in his salvation.*
>
> Isaiah 25.6–9

July 24

Large Letters

I was looking through Galatians 6 the other day and came across that verse that perplexes so many scholars: "See with what large letters I write unto you with my own hand" (v 11). If scholars do not know what it means, I certainly don't, but this is the way my mind wandered that day.

Is Paul talking about writing something with large letters? Did he have a hand injury? I had surgery on my right hand when I was in college. For two months I took notes in classes with my left hand. As a right-hander, I had to write larger than usual in order to maintain any control and be able to read the product. Still, it looked like a kindergartner's printing, but at least I could study for my finals.

But what if, as is more in keeping with my predicament these days, he had to use large letters so he could see what he had written? Maybe that was the case and maybe not, but it made me think of the day I discovered how to change the font size on my PC. What a wonderful day! By upping the font to 18 or 24 point I could actually write emails and articles I could proofread myself. Hurray!

And then I thought, what if poor vision was his problem? In spite of that, without a computer, without a mouse to click on a larger font, without even a typewriter for all that, he managed to write (or dictate) epistles that still leave us studying more and more deeply. That might not have anything to do with Galatians 6.11, but you can see how my mind kept traveling, because that led me to wonder about all those first century brothers and sisters of ours. Without copy machines, they managed to copy those epistles and send them on to the next church. Without airplanes or automobiles, they managed to travel miles and miles on foot, or risk life and limb in a boat no one could possibly mistake for a cruise ship, and carry those messages and minister to those evangelists. Without television, telephone, or radio, without film strips or DVDs, tracts or lesson books, they managed to teach their neighbors and families.

And what happened? Within 30 years they spread the gospel to the entire world (Col 1.5–6, 23). Those people, who had every excuse we don't have, "turned the world upside down" (Acts 17.6).

And here we sit whining because of what we'd like to do if only we could. How many churches, after 30 years, have the same number or fewer members because they have not managed to spread the gospel to just the town they are a part of, much less the whole world? Those people toiled for hours a day just to survive, and still managed to spend time on the *word*. When we finish "just getting by," we spend our time on the *world*. Only one letter difference in those two words, but it certainly is a "large letter," isn't it?

What will you spend your spare time on today?

And you became imitators of us and of the Lord, having received the word in much affliction with joy of the Holy Spirit, so that you became an ensample to all those who believe in Macedonia and Achaia. For from you has sounded forth the Word of the Lord, not only in Macedonia and Achaia, but in every place your faith toward God has gone forth, so that we need not to speak anything.

1 Thessalonians 1.6–8

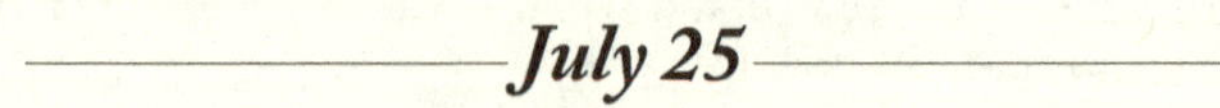

July 25

Automatic Pilot

Did you brush your teeth this morning? Are you sure? Do you really remember it, or are you remembering yesterday morning, or a morning last week? How many other things do we do automatically, without thinking? How about those scary times when you have been driving 10 or 15 minutes and suddenly realize you don't remember that stop sign half a mile from the house or anything else between there and here?

How about your spiritual life? How many things do we do automatically? We have a tendency to condemn that sort of thing, acting without thinking, as if it is hypocrisy, but is that always the case?

I have always been in the same place every Sunday morning of my life, barring illness or injury. No, the physical location may not be the same, but anyone who knows me, knows that on Sunday mornings I am assembling with my brothers and sisters in the Lord at wherever I happen to be. There is never any question what I will do on Sunday morning if I am at all able.

I used to worry about falling asleep in the middle of my final prayer of the day. Surely, "pillow talk" is a close, intimate form of communication. In fact, it is one thing we miss in our marriage—you cannot whisper to a deaf man. So why should I be remorseful about falling asleep while having a comfortable, private moment with my Father? Yes, there are times for more formal, reverential prayers, but who else would I rather be speaking to in my last conscious moments of the day, and why should He be upset with me if I feel so comfortable and easy with Him? It's not like it's the only time we speak. It is, in fact, second nature for me to do so.

"Second nature" is defined as an acquired behavior or trait that is so long practiced as to *seem* natural or inborn. It comes from an old proverb, "Custom (or usage) is a second nature," which was first recorded in 1390.

"First" nature, then, would be things we do instinctively, that *are* inborn. When we are born again into the kingdom of God, it becomes our responsibility to change our behavior, practicing it so frequently, that it eventually becomes our "second" nature, something we do automatically, with hardly any thought at all, but which we had to learn.

In the beginning of my life as a Christian I must consciously make decisions about how to react to others and how to order my new life. Eventually, though, *if I am practicing these things on a regular basis,* that should become easier and easier. How long have I been a Christian yet I still fly off the handle, still say things I should not say, still lower myself to the level of the world by seeking revenge over the silliest things in the most childish ways? I must not be working hard enough to change those habits, for that is what they are, and they can be changed with enough effort, and with the help of Christ. "I can do all things through him who strengthens me" (Phil 4.13).

This does not mean there will no longer be moments of weakness, times when I am more susceptible to my old behaviors. But if those old behaviors are still constant in my life, where is the transformation Paul talks about in Romans 12? Why have I not become more closely "conformed to the image of his son (Rom 8.29)? *Something* about me is supposed to have undergone a permanent change!

Certainly, I must have my mind on my prayers and the words I sing. I must listen consciously and carefully to those who seek to edify me. My worship must not be rote. But there is something to be said for operating on automatic pilot in my spiritual life. At some point it must reach past what I do, and become a matter of *who I am.* If this never happens, then something is missing, and I need to find it—and fix it—soon.

> *Wherefore if any man is in Christ, he is a new creature: the old things are passed away; behold, they are become new.*
>
> 2 Corinthians 5.17

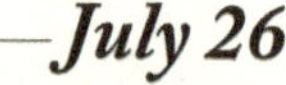

The Coffee Stain

I don't know why, but whenever I drink coffee I have a tendency to drip it on me. I know that, so I am careful. On dark clothes it is not such a big problem, but if I wear white, I usually stay away from the coffeepot.

I was pondering the list of sins in Galatians 5, the works of the flesh, when I thought about that. If you are my age, I am certain you have heard at least one person excuse their behavior by saying that it is not specifically spoken against in the Bible. That is true about a lot of sins. But notice how God carefully ends such lists with words like those in Galatians 5: "And things like these…" (v 21).

We are expected to exercise enough common sense, and to have a heart that is sensitive enough to impurity, that we can know what does and does not belong on the same list of sins and stay away from those things as well, whether God specified them or not. Or are we just a bunch of lawyers looking for loopholes? Give them some credit—even lawyers recognize "the intent of the Law." Yet we often hear things like, "God didn't specify internet pornography so it's not a sin!"

God may not have specified every possible sin, but he gave us plenty of direction about what it is and what it isn't. It is not that difficult to tell, and if someone were to accuse us of being so dim-witted in other areas, we would be insulted. Thus we are back to the question of whether we have a heart that wants more than anything to please God or ourselves.

So let me admonish you today in this way: Even if it's hazelnut, even if it's praline, even if it's Sumatran or Colombian, *or any other flavor like these*, I can still tell it's coffee. More to the point, the flavor won't keep it from staining when it drips. If you plan to wear white robes, stay away from the coffeepot!

> *He who overcomes shall be arrayed in white garments and I shall in no way blot his name out of the book of Life, and I shall confess his name before my father and his angels.*
>
> Revelation 3.5

July 27

Identity Theft

A few weeks ago, Satan finished what he started three years ago and stole my identity. I have packed up the last of my teaching supplies: sheet music, collections, method books, assignment notebooks, theory books, technique books, concerti, history notebooks, listening labs, computer disk theory games, stickers, rhythm instruments, home made music bingo games, magic slates with grand staffs permanently imprinted on them, even my old textbook *How to Teach Piano Successfully.* I have sent them on to a young piano teacher in Ohio, who is just starting out.

I had a weepy moment or two. This part of my life—35 years worth plus all those years learning—is definitely over now. There is no going back; I simply cannot see the music any longer. But I am happy to know that these things will be put to good use—that other little children will learn with them, and that a young preaching couple will have a bit more coming in to help out with a skimpy income. But for a moment the large empty space under my piano made me feel invisible.

I am no longer the piano and voice teacher in Union County.

I no longer open my doors every afternoon to excited little faces, making sure that grubby little hands are washed before touching the keys, but still picking up every ailment my students brought my way—including parvo once, for goodness sake! It must have been all the hugs.

I am no longer playing at weddings half a dozen times a year. I am no longer meeting with my fellow teachers once or twice a month, serving as association officer or chairman of this committee or that.

I no longer take a dozen students to various competitions, crying with them for their losses and cheering for their wins. I no longer spend hours on themed spring programs, gathering up suitable music, matching it to each student's personality, then working out the details, including skits and grand finales.

I no longer present high school seniors in debut recitals with formals and tuxes, long-stemmed red roses, and a glittery reception afterward.

Satan has stolen all of that from me with this disease.

It could have been a real problem for me. I could have sunk into a depression difficult to come out of. Then I remembered my real identity.

> *Behold what manner of love the Father has bestowed on us that we should be called the children of God; and we are.* (1 John 3.1)

> *Listen my beloved brethren did not God choose those who are poor in the world to be rich in faith and heirs of the kingdom which he promised to those who love him?* (Jas 2.5)

> *But you are an elect race, a royal priesthood, a holy nation, a people for God's own possession, that you may show forth the excellencies of him who called you out of darkness into his marvelous light.* (1 Pet 2.9)

> *He has granted unto us precious and exceeding great promises, that through these you may become partakers of the divine nature.* (2 Pet 1.4)

> *The Spirit bears witness with our spirit that we are children of God, and if children, then heirs, heirs of God and joint-heirs with Christ, if so be that we suffer with him, that we may also be glorified with him.* (Rom 8.16–17)

I still have my identity, and so do you. It's the one that counts, the one that Satan cannot steal, the one that will last forever.

Cruciverbalism

I am a cruciverbalist, or at least I try to be. A cruciverbalist is simply an expert at solving crossword puzzles—"cruci" = cross, "verbal" = having to do with words.

I do a dozen crossword puzzles a week, sometimes more. Lucas got me started on the Simon and Schuster books, which besides giving me 225 to work on, are also larger print than the newspapers. After going through seven books in the past four years (yes, that's 1,575 of them) plus any others I can pick up anywhere else, I have become, in Nathan's words, "A treasure trove of useless information."

"Medieval helmet," five letters: armet. What does it look like? I have no idea.

"Betel palm," five letters: areca. Where do they grow? Beats me.

"Anoa's home," seven letters: Celebes. Can I find the Celebes Islands on a map? No, but I know they have an ox there called an anoa!

Sometimes, though, instead of being a "crossword specialist," I become a "cross *word* specialist." That, unfortunately, is a whole lot easier. Just let someone throw me a curveball, upsetting my carefully planned schedule, and I become a real grump. No matter how many times they try to appease me, *I won't let them*. I am upset and that is all I care about at the moment.

I also become cross when I hear secondhand something less than complimentary about myself. My mind starts running in circles as I mentally tell off the one who dared say such a thing, over and over, sometimes even ruining my sleep at night, which serves me right for caring so much about something that really does not matter.

Do you have your cross word specialties? Is it griping about everything? Some people really enjoy complaining. They cannot be happy if they can't be miserable.

Is it passing on gossip? For some people that is the most exciting thing in life. They actually get a rush from it.

Is it sarcasm, open contemptuous mocking of other people's suggestions, ideas, or even their hobbies and interests? Such scorn is disrespect, not teasing.

Is it just plain meanness toward others? I have heard things come out of Christians' mouths that have stopped me in my tracks. I am usually so shocked I just stand there open-mouthed.

I do not like *The Message*. Whenever someone calls it a "translation," I bristle, but for some things it is helpful. We read the Proverbs and they go right over our heads because of the stilted language. I don't do those things! But listen to the following.

"Mean people spread mean gossip. ...Troublemakers start fights, and gossips break up friendships. ...Fools openly spread slander. ...You love malicious gossip, you foul-mouth."

Those are *The Message*'s interpretations of Proverbs 16.27–28; 10.18; and Psalm 52.4. I think he has hit the nail on the head. You see, if I spread mean gossip, I am a mean person. Spreading any gossip makes me a "foul-mouth," a description most of us save for those who use four letter words. It also makes me a fool. And I may not mean to do anything bad, but my words can ruin people's lives.

No one wants to associate with those who constantly scoff, complain, slander, lie, or otherwise cause trouble. Not only do those things not make for peace between brethren, but they will eat at the soul of the listener. It's like purposefully infecting yourself with a lethal virus. You will soon become that person you hate being around for very long at a time, a "cross word specialist."

Pleasant words are a honeycomb, sweet to the soul and health to the bones.

Proverbs 16.24

July 29

Magnifying Glasses

All of a sudden I have a lot of magnifying glasses in my house. A large "Sherlock Holmes" type, another that has a light and fastens to the side of the table, a whole magnifying page that can be laid over a book, and a small one I keep in my purse for fine print in places where I do not want to wrestle with my reading glasses. Sometimes we are tempted to use spiritual magnifying glasses too, and not always in good ways.

Often verses of the Bible are misinterpreted because of the use of the Middle English in the King James Version. Even when newer, just-as-reputable versions come along and put the correct spin on a passage, the old interpretation sticks in the minds of those who learned it as children. 1 Thessalonians 5.22 is one of those verses. "Abstain from all appearance of evil" has come to mean that I must not do or say anything that might possibly be construed as wrong to an observer or listener. "They might think you are ____________." Fill in the blank with practically anything as long as it is a sin.

Even if I did not have better translations to look at, here is my problem with that interpretation: it directly contradicts the admonition of love in 1 Corinthians 13.7—love "bears all things, believes all things, hopes all things." When I love someone I must look at what they have said or done and put the best possible construction on it, not the worst, or my love is a hypocritical love in word only, not in deed. If there is a good way to take what they said, I should take it that way. If there is a plausible excuse for a slight, I should automatically supply it. I am not to take out my magnifying glass and search and search until aha! I have found something I can misconstrue.

Some of the things Jesus did looked awfully wrong to some of the people who saw them! Remember all those times he healed on the Sabbath? Even if he could prove the Old Law said nothing about that, the Pharisees could have correctly said, "But what does it look like?" In fact, one of the rulers told the people, "You can come to be healed six other days in the week. Why come on the Sabbath?" (Luke 13.14). He had a point, didn't he? Why not choose a time when no one would be able to question Jesus' honoring of the Sabbath? I can hear some of my brethren making that point exactly, totally ignoring the plight of this "daughter of Abraham" (13.16). Don't you think Jesus described her that way on purpose? To that ruler she was less important than his traditions, but Jesus made sure he saw her importance in the eyes of God.

In Luke 11 Jesus was invited to a Pharisee's home for dinner and ignored the ritual hand washing before the meal. Since it was a ritual offered by every [Pharisee] host, there was no way he could have done it quietly—he openly refused to do it. In Matthew 12 he allowed his disciples to pluck grain on the Sabbath. In Luke 7 he allowed a sinful woman to touch him. In Luke 15 the Pharisees and scribes murmured, "This man receives sinners and eats with them." And think about this: God even allowed him to be born only six months after his parents married. Imagine what *that* looked like. Imagine what people could have said—in fact what they did say—"*We* were not born of fornication" (John 8.41).

What 1 Thessalonians 5.22 really means, according to the American Standard Version, is "abstain from every *form* of evil" [every shape it takes]. Wherever, whenever, and however evil raises its ugly head, I am to stay away from it.

I need to be very careful. If I am using my magnifying glass just to find faults in you because of the way I think something might look, I need to throw it away.

> *Speak not one against another, brethren. He that speaks against a brother or judges his brother speaks against the law; but if you judge the law, you are not a doer of the law, but a judge. One is the lawgiver and judge, he who is able to save and destroy, but who are you who judges your brother?*
>
> James 4.11

July 30

The Power of the Word

As glad as I am that we no longer seem afraid to talk about the Holy Spirit in our lives these days, I am hearing other things that disturb me, disparaging comments about the Word: "I know it can't be *just* the word of God doing this" paraphrases some of the statements I am hearing. Praise God that his Holy Spirit works in our lives, but do not treat any less respectfully one of His biggest feats: translating the mind of God into words so that we mortals can comprehend what He has done for us and what He wants from us (1 Cor 2.6–12).

Paul calls the gospel "the power of God unto salvation" (Rom 1.16), and an angel told Cornelius to send for Peter who would tell him "words whereby you shall be saved" (Acts 11.14). Peter tells us himself that God's word contains "all things pertaining to life and godliness" (2 Pet 1.3), and the Hebrew writer tells us, "The word of God is living and active, and sharper than any two-edged sword, and piercing even to the dividing of soul and spirit, of both joints and marrow, and quick to discern the thoughts and intents of the heart" (4.12). What can God *not* accomplish with a Word like this?

God told Jeremiah, "Is not my word like fire...and like a hammer that breaks the rock in pieces" (23.29). Have you ever seen the devastation that fire can cause? Can you imagine anything more effective at changing the face of a wall than continually pounding it with a hammer?

In Isaiah we learn how God's word acts on both the good and evil. For those who seek knowledge and understanding, "It is precept upon precept, line upon line, line upon line, here a little, there a little" (28.9–10). And to those "of strange lips, the word of Jehovah be unto them precept upon precept, line upon line, line upon line, here a little, there a little, that they may go and fall backward and be broken and snared and taken" (vv 11–13). In other words, it acts the same way on all of us, but the results depend upon the heart who hears it.

And so it is. After Peter preached on the day of Pentecost, "They were pricked in their hearts" (Acts 2.37), and those who "*received the word* were baptized" (v 41). After Stephen preached the crowd was "cut to the heart" (Acts 7.54), and they stoned him to death (v 58). The same knowledge of God's word that saves some brings death to others (2 Cor 2.14–17). But either way, it is the *Word* that causes the result.

God said the world would call it foolishness to try to save through preaching (1 Cor 1.21). Aren't we guilty of the same thing when we devalue the power of God's word? Jesus was constantly quoting scripture, and in doing so He strengthened himself, defeated Satan, and saved the lost. We should be following in His footsteps, treating God's word with all the deference and respect it deserves, because it is truly the power of God.

For my thoughts are not your thoughts, neither are your ways my ways, says Jehovah. For as the heavens are higher than the earth, so are my ways higher than your ways, and my thoughts than your thoughts. For as the rain comes down and the snow from heaven, and returns not but waters the earth, and makes it bring forth and bud, and gives seed to the sower and bread to the eater, so shall my word be that goes forth out of my mouth: it shall accomplish that which I please, and it shall prosper in the thing for which I sent it.

Isaiah 55.8–11

Doing What Needs to Be Done

I have noticed something about Judges 13 that most people seem to miss. Usually we get into a discussion about Samson's origins, and how his parents were so careful to do what God told them to do even before he was born, a good discussion to be sure. But I like to point out something else that is just as helpful to me as I try to live my life as a disciple of Christ.

I find the difference between Samson's parents amusing. God knew exactly what He was doing when He approached Manoah's wife instead of Manoah himself with the news that they would finally have a son. His wife did run to tell him, as any woman would, but we immediately get the picture of a man so excited he cannot quite think straight. He wants to see this messenger too, so when "the man of God" returns, his wife dutifully brings him. After hearing the same message, Manoah insists on fixing a meal which "the man" says must be an offering to God instead, an offering which is immediately ignited, taking "the man" with it. Wow! This must be an angel! Now Manoah is really excited! "We're going to die!" he screams to his wife.

This calm, practical woman probably sighed before telling him, "Nonsense. If we were going to die, why would he tell us that this was going to happen to us and how to act until then?" The inference is that with this bit of common sense she managed to soothe her frantic husband and then did exactly as she was told, altering her diet so that Samson was indeed a Nazirite "from the womb" as God had promised. Her lack of frenzy did not make her less faithful. She was instead a woman who managed to temper her enthusiasm enough to actually get the job done.

It is a big mistake to judge someone's faith by how loud it is. Too many times we get caught up in the excitement, roused up by the passion, ignited with the zeal, only to have it burn out, leaving us in a pile of ashes, never having accomplished more than a tiny of piece of our mission, if any at all. Towering flames may make a beautiful spectacle, but softly glowing coals cook the meal and heat the home far better, and like them, true faith is usually a quiet one that accomplishes the task, even if it is tedious and disagreeable, and simply never goes out.

Faith is a man who gets up every morning and goes out to provide for his family, whether he likes his job or not. Faith is the woman who cares for her family and her home, as well as the sick and poor in her community, as well as she can, even if the chore gets nasty and no one else notices what she has done. Faith is the teenager who has the maturity and integrity to rise above his fellows—and in spite of his fellows—in choosing the values he will live by. Faith is the retired couple who spend much of their free time visiting and having people in their home, usually people who can never return the favor. Faith is the widow who goes to the meetinghouse on Monday and Thursday to keep the classrooms in order, file the bulletin boards, and run off the newsletter, and has it all taken for granted—or even complained about. Faith is the widower who still comes in every Sunday morning and quietly takes his seat, now empty of the love of his life, but who manages to worship with all his heart anyway, knowing full well that he will see her again.

Real faith is practical. It may not be exciting; it may not make the headlines of the local paper; sometimes it may not even be pleasant; but real people who do what needs to be done with a quiet consistency are the ones we should set up as role models for our children. It takes a far bigger man to do something he may not really like to do simply because it needs doing, than a man who only does the things he enjoys doing. True faith needs neither the acclamation nor the adrenaline rush to endure.

Keep at it. Keep plugging along. Someone is noticing, actually a lot of someones, and your faith will be the example that sustains them as well.

And you, being in time past alienated and enemies in your mind in your evil works, yet now has he reconciled in the body of his flesh through death, to present you holy and without blemish and unreproveable before him: if so be that you continue in the faith, grounded and steadfast, and not moved away from the hope of the gospel which you heard.

Colossians 1.21–23

August 1

Mason Jars

Do people even know what Mason jars are any more? My favorite store has stopped carrying them, and when I finally found them at the local discount store, I could have bought out their entire stock without overdrawing my bank account.

I have a large supply of those clear sturdy jars. Every year I stuff them with pickles, jams, tomatoes, and salsa, place them in a canner and subject them to more heat and pressure than a football coach in the midst of a losing season. Every year they seal and protect as they sit on my shelves for the next few months, then are emptied, washed, and placed back in the shed until I need them again.

This year three or four of them broke. I lifted the lid off the canner, and as I peered into the steam, there they sat, emptied of liquid but looking intact until I tried to lift them out and the bottom stayed in the water, while the sides and lid hung from the canning ring. The contents, now limp and useless, toppled into the canning water. I could hardly complain. These jars have served me well for years. Now that we are only two and I don't need as much, I have plenty of others to take their places on the shelves.

Those broken jars have made canning especially exciting this past year. I never know what I will find when I lift the lids off my two canners. They have also made me think about the way God uses the image of jars in the Bible. As with many other things, He presents them in two ways, one I want and the other I don't.

He tells Isaiah, "Wherefore thus says the Holy One of Israel, Because you despise this word, and trust in oppression and perverseness, and rely thereon; therefore this iniquity shall be to you as a breach ready to fall, swelling out in a high wall, whose breaking comes suddenly in an instant. And he shall break it as a potter's vessel is broken, breaking it in pieces without sparing; so that there shall not be found among the pieces thereof a shard wherewith to take fire from the hearth, or to dip up water out of the cistern" (30.12–14). God's promise of destruction for his rebellious people is frightening, and we must be careful for it does not need to be a national destruction. He can do the same thing to rebellious individuals.

But God also holds out a reward for faithful service that is almost too amazing to believe. "And he who overcomes, and he who keeps my works unto the end, to him will I give authority over the nations: and he shall rule them with a rod of iron, as the vessels of the potter are broken to shivers; as I also have received of my Father: and I will give him the morning star. He who has ears, let him hear what the Spirit says to the churches" (Rev 2.26–29).

I do believe in that reward, and so should you. God has shown us that He will fulfill His promises. That promise in Isaiah is historically verifiable down to the last detail. This one would be too, if history were to continue after it occurs. It won't, but we will.

Now in a great house there are not only vessels of gold and of silver, but also of wood and of earth; and some unto honor, and some unto dishonor. If a man therefore purge himself from these, he shall be a vessel unto honor, sanctified, meet for the master's use, prepared unto every good work.

2 Timothy 2.20–21

August 2

An Outstretched Hand

Keith went out in the dark the other night to check for armadillos. We have found our garden, yard, and flowerbeds torn up nearly every morning for the past two or three weeks, and he was out to rid the world of a few of those pesky critters, a fruitless venture it turned out.

As he stood in the black, heavy, humid air amid the croaking frogs, his eyes not yet used to the dark, he put his left hand down, knowing full well that Chloe's head would find it whether he could see her or not. It did, and he scratched her between the ears and told her what a good dog she was to help with the hunt.

The Bible mentions God's hand being held out as well. Jeremiah speaks of God creating the earth "with great power and an outstretched arm" (27.5). Moses tells the Israelites that same "mighty hand and outstretched arm" brought them out of Egyptian bondage, and thus they should obey His commandments (Deut 5.15ff). Later in their history Ezekiel warns them that, since they disobeyed, His hand would be held out "with wrath poured out" (20.33–34).

That is not the way God wants to hold out His hand. We have all seen animals or children cringe when a hand was held up. It speaks volumes about the kind of treatment they are used to receiving. But God has held His hand out in fellowship from the beginning. We are the ones who ignore it or push it away.

In chapter 11, Hosea tells of God teaching Israel, his son, to walk, and I cannot help but picture a father standing just a step away with his arms outstretched, urging his small child to take that first trusting step into his arms. That is the hand God wants to hold out to us.

The question is do we naturally gravitate to the one who loves us, or do we simply ignore the pleading hand and go about our foolish ways? Chloe is always looking for her master's hand, even in the dark. How about you?

Fear thou not, for I am with you; be not dismayed, for I am your God; I will strengthen you; yea, I will help you; yea, I will uphold you with the right hand of my righteousness.

With a strong hand, and with an outstretched arm; For his lovingkindness endures for ever.

Isaiah 41.10; Psalm 136.12

August 3

What's for Dinner?

We saw a new bird darting in and out of the azalea limbs on the side of the house away from the feeder, a small black bird with a white belly and yellow patches on its wings and tail—an American Redstart, I discovered later, a bug-eater, which explained why he avoided the bird feeder. I don't know why it had never crossed my mind before—no wonder I only saw a few birds there, the same varieties over and over. Birdseed simply does not appeal to all birds. Now if I could figure out a way to keep live bugs there too *and* allow the birds to come and go as they please, I would see a big increase in numbers.

What people see of the gospel in our lives determines who and even *if* we attract others to it. I can remember times past when we were so afraid of unscriptural denominational doctrines that we swung the pendulum too hard in the other direction and wound up being miserable. Since the scriptures plainly teach that it is possible to fall from grace and that humility is necessary for salvation, we never allowed ourselves to say, "I know I am going to Heaven." Why, how arrogant could one be? Don't you know that you can sin so as to lose your salvation? So hope, a confident expectation of salvation, disappeared from our lives.

We treated sin as a constant, a mysterious miasma that afflicted us every day of our lives whether we knew it or not. "Forgive us, Lord, for we know we sin all the time." We thought we could not avoid it no matter how hard we tried, not even with help from the Lord. So we went around looking over our shoulders, wondering when it would attack us and hoping that when we died we would have seen death coming and had time to shoot off a quick prayer for forgiveness.

What did we present to the world? Fear, frustration, hopelessness, anxiety, bitterness, dread, desperation—and then we looked to our neighbors and said, "Hey! Don't you want what I have?" Why were we so surprised when none did?

I think we would attract far more to our "feeder" if we showed them the joy, hope, peace, and love that the first century Christians did. We can because the scriptures plainly teach that we can overcome sin if we will and that God's grace will help us when we fail; they teach that we can be assured of our salvation. God is not sitting up there watching and waiting for us to slip so He can say, "Aha! Gotcha!"

What's on your bird feeder today? The seed of the Word of God, or just a bunch of bugs?

> *My little children, these things write I unto you that you may not sin. And if any man sin, we have an Advocate with the Father, Jesus Christ the righteous: and he is the propitiation for our sins; and not for ours only, but also for the whole world. ...These things have I written unto you, that you may know that ye have eternal life, even unto you that believe on the name of the Son of God.*

1 John 2.1–2; 5.13

August 4

Salad Days

I bought groceries the other day, and as I wandered down the produce aisle, I went past a cart in which the worker had stacked a pile of lettuce heads that were obviously past their prime, browning and wilted. Meanwhile, the line in front of the bagged salads stretched halfway across the produce section. I was headed that way myself—only because they are on sale and I have a coupon, I salved my frugal conscience, certainly not because they are easier.

As I waited my turn, I eased my way past containers of pre-chopped peppers, onions, celery, and garlic. I had seen tubs of already mashed potatoes earlier, and when I scoured the freezer section for shrimp to cook in my bouillabaisse, I had to dig to find some that were not peeled, deveined, and pre-cooked. Everyone wants the easy way these days. Even the last few years I taught piano, it was not unusual for a parent to ask. "How long will it take for my child to learn how to do this?" After 45 years I was still learning! No wonder you hear so much about easy-lose diets, an easy way to a toned body, and easy-read Bibles.

When I was a child, older folks often said, "It's only worth the effort it cost you." God never says being His child will be easy. Even when Jesus says, "My yoke is easy and my burden is light," He is talking in relative terms—it is still a yoke and a burden. But, unlike sin's, His yoke and burden do not come with the built-in weight of guilt, an overriding, insurmountable millstone that will crush your spirit long before it destroys your soul for an eternity. Paul says we will be a servant to something, either to "sin unto death or obedience unto righteousness. …But now being made free from sin and become servants to God, you have your fruit unto sanctification, and the end eternal life" (Rom 6.16, 22). Unlike the fatal weight of sin, this yoke and burden we can "live" with!

The next time I want a salad, I will try to think about that, and buy the whole head, then relax and enjoy the chopping.

Wash me thoroughly from my iniquity and cleanse me thoroughly from my sin. …Purge me with hyssop and I shall be clean; wash me and I shall be whiter than snow. Make me to hear joy and gladness. …Restore unto me the joy of your salvation, and uphold me with your free spirit. …Deliver me from bloodguiltiness, Oh Jehovah, the God of my salvation, and my tongue shall sing aloud of your righteousness.

Psalm 51.2, 7–8, 12, 14

August 5

A Bag of Earrings

A few months ago I went on a trip and, as I was packing, I pulled out my favorite earrings and put them in a plastic bag to take with me. What I did with them after that I have still yet to recall. When I arrived at my destination, they were nowhere in my suitcase or my purse. After returning home, I checked my drawers, my closets, my suitcases—even bags I did not take with me—plus my jewelry box, and the trash can. I thought to myself, I must have had my mind somewhere else and put them in a strange place—like the times I put the milk in the pantry and the peanut butter in the refrigerator—but they will turn up sooner or later. Those earrings have yet to reappear.

Funny how we have such a hard time remembering things we really want to remember but cannot forget those things we ought to forget. Forgiveness is a tricky thing. While I suppose a hurt is impossible to actually forget, forgiveness means we don't continue to dwell on the past, keeping account of wrongs done us by various ones like a bookkeeper with OCD. Yet that is exactly what the Lord expects of us.

When he told Peter his disciples should forgive unto "seventy-times seven" it was a hyperbole, an exaggeration for emphasis. No matter how many times a brother hurts me, I am to forgive. That large a number also emphasizes that I am to do my best to forget. How else could you forgive someone 490 times unless you have forgotten the previous 489? The Lord knew what He was asking of us—continual forgiveness for a brother, even for the same sin, as many times as it takes. He certainly understands the difficulty in that little proposition because He does it for us far more times than that. If we choose a number to stop at, He will too. He has already passed it with us.

Wouldn't it be great if we could forget as easily as we can forget where we put the car keys, or our glasses, or the reason we went into the bedroom to begin with? We forget those things because we so often have our minds on something else and get sidetracked. Do you suppose that might work for forgiving others too?

Put on therefore, as God's elect, holy and beloved, a heart of compassion, kindness, lowliness, meekness, longsuffering; forbearing one another, and forgiving each other, if any man has a complaint against any; even as the Lord forgave you, so also do ye: and above all these things put on love, which is the bond of perfectness.

Good sense makes one slow to anger, and it is his glory to overlook an offense.

Colossians 3.12–14; Proverbs 19.11

August 6

Giving Yourself a Haircut

Anyone who knows what last summer was like, knows that my usual routine was seriously disrupted. In three months' time, I had 28 doctor appointments, a full-blown surgery, and a dozen more procedures. Getting a haircut was the last thing on my mind. In fact, most of the time I could not have cared less how my hair looked. But then it started falling into my face and getting in my eyes, a serious problem for someone with "two very sick eyeballs," as one doctor put it.

So about the middle of July, I cut it myself.

The problem with giving yourself a haircut is you cannot see the back of your head. No matter how much you twist your neck around, the back of your head just keeps getting away from you. And holding another mirror only works if you have three hands—one to hold the second mirror, one to hold your hair, and one to hold the scissors.

So I found myself doing a lot of guesswork. Having curly hair hid most of the mistakes, but is it any wonder that by the first of September my locks were looking a bit ragged? I could hardly wait for someone who could see me from their perspective to even things out a little bit—well, *a lot*, actually.

Isn't it funny that the last thing we want spiritually is for someone to help us even out our lives? For some reason we do not mind going around with ragged lives, and worse, we want to believe they are not ragged at all. We want to believe that what *we* see about ourselves is the way things really are. Please pat down my unruly curl, please tell me to get the green out of my teeth, please unfold my hem, please stuff that facing back into my neckline—you are not a true friend if you let me go out in public this way—but do not under any circumstances tell me my faults, my spiritual imperfections, my sins. You are not my friend if you *do* tell me about those.

Could we be any more illogical? Why is how my hair looks more important than how my soul looks? The eternity caused by a spiritual imperfection is a whole lot longer than the embarrassment of half a day in town shopping with a physical imperfection. We are falling into the sin of the Galatian brethren of whom Paul said, "So then, have I become your enemy by telling you the truth?" (Gal 4.16).

James tells us that we should "confess our faults one to another" (5.16). If we were to call an assembly of the church for the express purpose of allowing everyone to confess their faults in turn, I wonder how many would show up. I wonder how long the service would last. I wonder how many people would suddenly become good students of the scriptures, researching all the words in that verse so they could find a way out of it.

Unfortunately, most of us do not have "the gift to see ourselves as others see us," (apologies to Robert Burns). We do not have three hands to hold the mirror and the hair, and make the correct cuts. That is one reason God gave us each other. Don't you think it's about time we started accepting that gift from one another?

Faithful are the wounds of a friend, but the kisses of an enemy are deceitful.

Proverbs 27.6

August 7

Legacy

I bet if I were to ask you which king set the standard for evil in Israel, without hesitation you would answer, "Ahab," along with his Sidonian wife, Jezebel. Certainly the two of them accomplished a heap of wickedness in their rule of the northern kingdom, everything from idolatry and murder to all sorts of immorality; but you might be surprised at the one who is mentioned most often as a comparison of evil in the scriptures.

Jeroboam was the first king of the northern half of the divided nation. He feared that he would lose the support of the people and they would turn back to the Davidic dynasty in the south, regardless of the fact that God promised him, "If you will hearken to all that I command you, and walk in my ways, and do that which is right in my eyes, to keep my statutes and my commandments, as David my servant did, that I will be with you, and will build you a sure house, as I built for David, and will give Israel to you" (1 Kgs 11.38). Because he did not have faith in that promise, he changed the pattern of worship as set forth in the Law (1 Kgs 12.25–33).

He made a new feast day (vv 32–33), so the people would not be traveling to Jerusalem with all the southerners to worship together (v 27). He began making priests of other tribes than Levi (v 31). He made two new places of worship, Dan and Bethel, conveniently located at both ends of the country, so the people would not feel compelled to travel to Jerusalem—anything to keep them at home and happy. It is important to note, too, that the calves he built were not idols to be worshipped, but graven images by which the people were to worship Jehovah—something Amos and Hosea make more apparent than 1 Kings. This was not rampant idolatry; it was just a change in the pattern of worshipping Jehovah.

So what is the problem? They still worship Jehovah. They still keep feasts to Jehovah, and make sacrifices under the leadership of a priesthood. Yet these were things "devised of his own heart" (v 33), not things that God had ordained. This is the difference: God said through the prophet Ahijah, "Jehovah will raise up a king who will cut off the house of Jeroboam. …For Jehovah will smite Israel, as a reed is shaken in the water, and he will root up Israel out of this good land which he gave to their fathers, and will scatter them beyond the River…and he will give Israel up *because of the sins of Jeroboam, which he has sinned, and in which he made Israel to sin*" (14.14–16). From the point of the northern kingdom's first king, God had decided their fate—they would not stand for the Law, so he would not stand for them.

Now take a few minutes and read these passages: 1 Kings 15.3, 29–30; 16.25–26, 31; 22.51–52; 2 Kings 3.1–3; 10.29–31; 13.1–3, 10–11; 14.23–24; 15.8–9, 17–18, 23–24; 17.20–23. What do they have in common? A phrase similar to this: "And he walked in the ways of Jeroboam the son of Nebat in which he made Israel to sin." Five times a king is said to have done evil "like Ahab," but 16 times the honor goes to Jeroboam. Jeroboam single-handedly caused the destruction of the northern kingdom, and set the standard for evil among all her kings. How? By disrespecting the Law of God. *That* is the legacy of Jeroboam.

Whether we like it or not, we are all leaving a legacy. It may not affect a kingdom, but it will affect our children, and theirs, and theirs, till before you know it, we have affected hundreds. The greatest legacy we can leave is to follow God's pattern for marriage, raising children, worship, and social conduct. If your children are small, now is the time to become conscious of the legacy you are leaving, before it's too late. The frightening thing about legacies is, *they cannot be undone!*

> *But when that generation was gathered to their fathers, there arose a generation that knew not God.* (Jdg 2.10)

Don't let it be your children's generation.

August 8

Knock, Knock

I have been spending a lot of time in doctors' offices and hospitals lately. My ophthalmologist has now transferred me permanently to the University of Florida/ Shands Teaching Hospital where I receive excellent care, and regularly excite the interns. These handsome young men run up and down the halls, grabbing their buddies and saying, "You gotta come! You'll never get another chance to see someone like this!" For a middle-aged, gray-haired, slightly overweight woman, that is quite an ego builder.

Then there are the Fellows. Notice, that is a capital F. I have not quite figured out the whole hierarchy, but these seem to be young doctors who have finished medical school, and are now attached, almost literally, to an older, experienced doctor for a year or so before they go out on their own. I met the latest Fellow a few weeks ago. I go in fairly often—often enough that even the cleaning lady recognizes and greets me. Since it was our first time together, he got to do the initial work-up himself. He tried reading the chart, but my doctor has notoriously bad handwriting, even worse than most doctors—he obviously aced the bad handwriting class that med schools seem to require all doctors to take. The pharmacy regularly has to call the office to find out what he prescribed, and that's his *good* handwriting.

Since this Fellow was having such a tough time of it, I just started talking. He shut the file and listened, and then asked quite a few questions. I have learned more about eyes than I ever hoped to know, including anterior chambers, corneal depths, iris prolapses, capsular tension rings, and zonules. The look he gave me was half surprise and half amusement. Before we were through he said, "In your next life you will be an ophthalmologist."

Opportunity knocked and I was totally oblivious. Let me describe this young doctor and see if you miss it, too. He was medium height, about 5'9", slim build, probably 160. His hair was dark, with heavy eyebrows, his face square and his skin dark as well. His name was Indian, as in Gandhi, not Geronimo. The University of Florida is nothing if not a melting pot. Now think back to what he said. "In your next life. . . ." Even if he no longer believes in his native country's faith, his culture was showing: reincarnation. About six hours later, I realized what I should have said: "In my next life, I won't *need* an ophthalmologist." Here he was, so imbued in his own culture's faith that such a statement would pop out of him, and I, supposedly imbued in mine, missed a golden opportunity to reaffirm what I know to be true.

What do I do? I blame it on my slow mind. I'm getting older, you see, and don't think as quickly as I used to. Nonsense! I had that problem 20 years ago, too. "Old" has nothing to do with it. What has everything to do with it, is a focus on the here and now, rather than on the eternal. I was too concerned about what the doctor would tell me about *this* life to see what I might be able to do about the next one. I was too concerned with *my physical fate* and not concerned at all with the spiritual fate of another.

A few months ago, I did a little study on spiritual immaturity. Do you know what the apostle Paul equates that with? Carnality. "Walking after the manner of men" (1 Cor 3.3). Thinking more about the physical than the spiritual, more about this life than the eternal life to come. As I get more and more mature in Christ, this life should be less and less on my mind. It should be *easier* to think of the "right" thing to say, not harder. Have I not gotten any better at all?

Well, yes, I am some better. I do not rail at God about this illness. I do not ask him, why me? I don't whine—well, not very often anyway. And just when I think I have accomplished something, the Lord sends me a wake-up call. What I *don't* do is not even half of it. My faith should be a positive thing, not a negative thing. Here I had a chance to sow a seed, however small, and I stumbled in what might have been freshly plowed ground and fell flat on my face.

I can hear some saying, "Don't be so hard on yourself. You have serious issues to deal with in your life right now." Didn't Paul have serious issues when he was beaten and thrown into prison? But didn't he sing God's praises and preach to whoever would listen while he was there? Isn't his focus on the spiritual the reason he was able to say "I have learned in whatever state I am to be content" (Phil 4.11)? How else do you handle beatings that flay you open to the bone, stoning, shipwrecks, and betrayal by so-called brethren, to the point of rejoicing that those traitors were preaching the gospel (1.15–18)?

And what shall I more say? for the time will fail me if I tell of Gideon, Barak, Samson, Jephthah; of David and Samuel and the prophets: who through faith subdued king-

doms, wrought righteousness, obtained promises, stopped the mouths of lions, quenched the power of fire, escaped the edge of the sword, from weakness were made strong, waxed mighty in war, turned to flight armies of aliens. Women received their dead by a resurrection: and others were tortured, not accepting their deliverance; ***that they might obtain a better resurrection****: and others had trial of mockings and scourgings, yea, moreover of bonds and imprisonment: they were stoned, they were sawn asunder, they were tempted, they were slain with the sword: they went about in sheepskins, in goatskins; being destitute, afflicted, ill-treated (of whom the world was not worthy), wandering in deserts and mountains and caves, and the holes of the earth. And these all,* ***having had witness borne to them through their faith****, received not the promise, God having provided some better thing concerning us, that apart from us they should not be made perfect.* (Heb 11.32–40)

All of these folks, some of whose names are not even recorded for us, like their father Abraham, desired a better country (v 16), [greeting it] from afar (v 13). And because of that focus on a spiritual life, they were able to meet the challenges of the physical.

Yes, I will see this young man again, probably many times. But I may never again get that golden an opportunity to make a comment that might make him think. But at least next time, I will be listening for the knock.

Are you listening?

August 9

Just A Closer Walk With Thee

Now that it has gotten to be more dangerous, I don't walk with the dogs any longer. I trip over too many invisible roots, step in too many hidden holes, roll along on too many sneaky little pine cones, and therefore either fall or come close too many times a week. Then there are the snakes with their natural camouflage. I wouldn't see one before it struck.

So Keith has bought me an elliptical machine. Actually this gadget is pretty neat. It tells me how many miles I have gone and how many calories I have burned, which is a little disappointing. Oh, for a workout that burns 500 calories in 20 minutes without making you feel like you might die any second!

But it's not the same as walking outside. I miss the fresh air, the waves of wildflower colors in the field, the butterflies flitting across my path, the scent of jasmine wafting along in the breeze. I miss my little furry companions romping on ahead of this tortoise of a human. I will say this for the machine, though—it is a lot closer to the five mile jog I did some 25 years ago than the three mile stroll I have taken with the dogs in the past few years. Whew!

The apostle John called life a walk with God: "If we walk in the light as he is in the light, we have fellowship one with another" (1 John 1.7). Enoch and Noah both "walked with God" in a faithful life (Gen 5.22; 6.9). Paul tells us, "The Lord is at hand" (Phil 4.5). It does help us get through our trials to know he is with us constantly as we go.

Sometimes though we act like this walk is what matters the most. It isn't. This life is the elliptical machine, not the real walk.

Similarly, we often make our lives the destination instead of the walk. We forget that life is just a motel room as we make the trek. Maybe some of us have circumstances in life that make our temporary inn an upscale model, but it is still just that—temporary. You don't put down roots in a Motel 6. You don't even put down roots in a Hilton. You certainly don't file a change of address with the post office. And so our roots are not on this earth.

God wants this life to be good, but we need to remember that no matter how well life here may be going, it is still not the one that matters. There is another walk coming, a walk that is not a journey at all, but a permanent home in a paradise where God will once again visit his people just like He used to every evening in that original home he made. We make this walk every day, so we can take that one forever.

Yet you still have a few names in Sardis, people who have not soiled their garments, and they will walk with me in white for they are worthy. The one who conquers will be clothed thus in white garments, and I will never blot his name out of the Book of Life. I will confess his name before my Father and before his angels.

Revelation 3.4–5

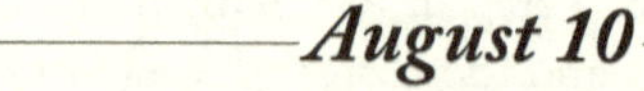

August 10

God's Grapes

August in Florida—the grapes are coming in. Every evening after dinner, Keith and I sit in the shade of the grape arbor in the green swing Lucas made in high school shop class, munching grapes. In Florida grapes are large, thick skinned muscadines and scuppernongs, bronze or a purple so dark it almost looks black. We spit out the more bitter skins, and Chloe and Magdi wander around under our feet scarfing them up like little furry scavengers. When we are too slow to suit them, Chloe wanders back to the vine and picks her own.

Sometimes I think grapes must be God's favorite fruit. The symbolism in the scriptures begins in Genesis where both Judah and Joseph are described as grapevines, and travels on throughout the scriptures. The promise of the Messiah is pictured as a time when "shall sit every man under his vine… and none shall make them afraid" (Mic 4.4). Both Old Testament Israel and New Testament spiritual Israel, the church, are called vineyards (Isa 5.1–7; Matt 20.1–16). Jesus says, "I am the vine" in John 15, and in the memorial feast we partake of every first day of the week, we drink "the fruit of the vine," grape juice, which symbolizes his shedding of blood—not that he simply cut himself and bled one day, but that he died for our sins.

But the symbolism is not always pleasant. In a prophecy about Judah's coming destruction the prophet Zephaniah says, "And their wealth shall become a spoil, and their houses a desolation; yes, they shall build houses, but shall not inhabit them; and they shall plant vineyards, but shall not drink the wine thereof" (1.13).

One of the most terrifying prophecies in the Old Testament also contains the symbolism of grapes and grape juice:

> Who is this that comes from Edom, with dyed garments from Bozrah? He who is glorious in his apparel, marching in the greatness of his strength?
>
> I who speak in righteousness, mighty to save.
>
> Why are you red in your apparel, and your garments like him that treads in the wine vat?
>
> I have trodden the winepress alone; and of the peoples there was no man with me: yes, I trod them in my anger, and trampled them in my wrath; and their lifeblood is sprinkled upon my garments, and I have stained all my raiment For the day of vengeance was in my heart. …And I trod down the people in my anger, and made them drunk in my wrath, and I poured out their lifeblood on the earth. (Isa 63.1–4, 6)

Every evening I once again have the opportunity to reflect on how I want the symbolism of the grapes to manifest itself in my life. Do I want it to be my blood sprinkling the robe of an angry God, who tramples the wicked like grapes in a winepress, or will I accept the blood of the spotless Lamb of God, who died for me, so I can sit under my vine and not be afraid?

Don't ever forget that the choice is ours to make.

> *I am the vine; you are the branches. He who abides in me, and I in him, the same bears much fruit, for apart from me you can do nothing. If a man does not abide in me, he is cast forth as a branch, and is withered, and they gather them and cast them into the fire, and they are burned. If you abide in me and my words abide in you, ask whatever you will, and it will be done unto you. Herein is the Father glorified: that you bear much fruit; and so shall you be my disciples.*
>
> John 15.5–8

August 11

Making Preparations

Funny how you can think you are so prepared and then find out otherwise.

We were going to pack our bag that week, three weeks early, "just in case." But at 7:30 PM, August 10, 2009, Nathan called to tell us we needed to have it packed "Now!" Our grandson had decided to make his arrival nearly four weeks early. So we threw things into a bag and ran out the door, dishes sitting unwashed in the sink, bills left unpaid, the baby gift still "in transit," though I had ordered it in plenty of time for a delivery I expected to be four weeks away. I even had to grab dirty clothes out of the hamper to wash when I got there so I would have enough to wear the week I stayed. So much for thinking we were prepared. Silas Andrew Ward, who made his debut early on August 11, showed us we were not.

We all prepare for things every day. That's why we plan meals and make grocery lists, shop the back-to-school sales, and have retirement plans. So why do we so often fail to prepare the most important things, our souls?

I find myself wondering if, despite our protestations otherwise, we don't truly believe. When we are young, we don't really believe we will die, at least not any time soon. There is plenty of time to prepare. The death of a young friend may shake us for awhile, but how long does that last? Let me tell you, when you finally get to that age you never imagined yourself being, you will understand exactly how short your life is and how blessed you are to still have a chance to prepare. "And just as it is appointed for man to die once, and after that comes judgment" (Heb 9.27).

Maybe we don't really believe in the reward. I think that may be a bigger problem than not believing in the punishment. We think the biggest pleasures we will ever have are here and now, and that is solely because we only have the here and now to judge by—and Satan banks on that, reinforcing the notion every chance he gets with our culture, the media, and the people around us. If we really believed that the reward is far better than anything we could possibly enjoy here, we would try even harder to prepare ourselves for it. "And without faith it is impossible to be well-pleasing to Him; for he who comes to God must believe that He is, *and that He is a rewarder of those who seek after Him*" (Heb 11.6).

The thing about preparation is you never know when you will need it. You wear the seat belt just in case. If you knew you were going to be in an accident, wouldn't you go another way, or simply stay put? Likewise, we never know when God will call us home. You cannot make a reservation for a specific date, then confirm it with a call 24 hours ahead. You simply prepare for something you know will happen some time in the future, *and never underestimate how soon that may be.* Isn't it foolish not to be ready?

Take heed, watch and pray: for you know not when the time is. It is as when a man, sojourning in another country, having left his house, and given authority to his ser-

vants, to each one his work, commanded also the porter to watch. Watch therefore: for you know not when the lord of the house comes, whether at even, or at midnight, or at cockcrowing, or in the morning; lest coming suddenly he find you sleeping. And what I say unto you, I say unto all, Watch.

Mark 13.33–37

August 12

The Assignment Book

All of my piano students had assignment books. For one thing, I could not remember 20 assignments a week, especially not after 30 years of making them. For another, this was their practice record and what they had or had not accomplished showed me how to help them.

I believe in goal-oriented practice. At the beginning, for very young students, the goal was simply to repeat an exercise or practice a piece a certain number of times. The pieces were so short that playing them through that number of times accomplished its purpose—becoming familiar with the keyboard and training the fingers to automatically hit a certain key when the eye saw the note.

The student then progressed to an assignment book charting the number of minutes they practiced. If I asked for 150 minutes in the week, they could divide it however they wished as long as it added up to at least 150 minutes. By this time the exercises were more difficult, the scales more complicated, and the pieces longer, so I usually included detailed instructions on *how* to use those minutes best to accomplish the goal. That is also how I came up with a minute total. If they showed me they could accomplish the same goals in less time, I either upped the goals or lowered the minutes depending upon their age, ability, and interest.

The final level of assignment book was reached by only a few. The pieces were usually several pages long and took months to learn. They were classics requiring far more than simple note-reading and counting. At this level I was teaching talented students to become artists and performers—pianists, not just piano players. It was up to them to pull the pieces apart, working on things like phrase shaping, dynamic nuance, and variations in touch. They chose one such item to work on in a manageable section of the music—say, the exposition section of a sonata instead of the whole ten pages—and when they had accomplished that goal, they were finished with that piece for the day. On its own, practice time had increased from the 15 minutes or so a day for a beginner to something closer to two hours a day.

One day a young lady came in so full of herself I knew something was up. Instead of making me dig through her satchel for the assignment book, she fished it out herself, flipping through to find the correct page and handing it to me with a smug little smile.

I had assigned her 200 minutes of practice for the week, with these additional directions: learn all the black key major scales, hands together, two octaves; memorize the last page of the competition solo she had been working on for two months; and start the rondo movement of her new concerto by playing through the A section everywhere it appeared, in every variation, slowly enough to keep the beat steady and the notes correct.

I looked at the minute total at the bottom of the page—200 minutes, but I had my suspicions. She had practiced, according to her record, 40 minutes exactly on five different days. This was the girl whose previous pages seldom showed more than three days of practice, all with odd numbers like 12, 17 or 21, and whose total had never come close to the assigned number. Each 40 minute entry was written in the same bright blue ink, with the same size numbers, and the same slant, as if she had filled them in at the same time one after the other. The page was clean: no smears, creases, smudges or erasures, as if this was the first time that page had seen the light of day since I wrote out the original assignment.

I kept my suspicions to myself for the moment, smiled, and said, "Let's play." That was where her plan fell apart. Black key majors are the easiest scales to play. She couldn't get past the third note. She could not play the concerto slowly enough *not* to make a mistake and she had exactly two measures of the solo memorized. How she thought she could fool me into thinking she had practiced nearly three-and-a-half hours that week was anyone's guess. After being with me for six years, I couldn't believe she thought I was that dumb.

And yet we think we can fool God into thinking we practice. "For every one that partakes of milk is *without experience* of the word of righteousness; for he is a babe. But solid food is for full-grown men, those who by *reason of use* have their senses *exercised* to discern good and evil" (Heb 5.13–14). If that isn't "practice," I don't know what it is.

If I never improve—if I keep tripping over the same stumblingblock rather than learning to step around it; if I make the same foolish mistakes instead of wising up; if my knowledge remains shallow instead of deepening with understanding through the years; if my faith remains a superficial veneer instead of reaching my heart, how can I even pretend I have been practicing?

Goal oriented practice is self-rewarding when it is followed faithfully. The student himself sees the results and is encouraged to practice more, to gain experience in whatever discipline he is applying himself. Our practice should be goal-oriented too, and we have abundant motivation, both here and beyond. But pretending to work at it will not achieve those goals any more than a silly 13 year old could learn to play a piano concerto by lying about her practice time.

Some of us still think that counting how many times a week we assemble is all the practice we need. But God expects us to get beyond the rote practice of following rules and live the life every minute of every day. He will know when we practice and when we don't. It will be obvious to Him, and maybe to everyone else too.

> *And the Lord said, Forasmuch as this people draw nigh with their mouth and with their lips to honor me, but have removed their heart far from me, and their fear of me is a commandment of men learned by rote; therefore, behold, I will proceed to do a marvelous work among this people, even a marvelous work and a wonder; and the wisdom of their wise men shall perish, and the understanding of their prudent men shall be hid.*
>
> Isaiah 29.13–14

August 13

A Weary Soul

Today is something of a milestone for me. This is the longest I have been without a surgery in the past four-and-a-half years, and it is still less than a year since the last one. In fact, in those four-and-a-half years I have had six major surgeries and 12 minor procedures, many of them even more painful than the big ones. When I realized what this poor body has been through, plus the fact that I have also gotten exactly that many years older, I felt better about myself. No wonder it doesn't take much to wear me out. No wonder my resistance is low and my endurance minimal. You might think otherwise, but it was an uplifting moment.

A couple of summers ago things were really bad. The major surgery had not gone well. Complications had set in within 24 hours. I saw the doctor 14 times in one month and had six more minor surgeries, each one taking more and more out of me. I was about ready to give up. We all know where this is heading, and these surgeries do nothing more than push that time a little further down the road—maybe. When the doctor once again patted my shoulder and said, "We need to do some more," I nearly said, "No. No more. It's not worth all this pain. It won't fix the problem anyway, so why bother?"

George Orwell once said, "The quickest way to end a war is to lose it," (*Polemic*, May 1946, "Second Thoughts on James Burnham").

Do you ever feel that way about life? With all the things happening to him, even Job said, "My soul is weary of my life" (10.1). We all experience those feelings. Illness, financial misfortune, family problems—all these things can sometimes seem insurmountable. Then, when you are completely exhausted, both physically and emotionally, the temptation is to end the war by simply surrendering.

Don't do it. This war has already been won. All we have to do is finish it—do the mop up work, so to speak.

The problem too often is that we try to go it alone, refusing to turn our problems over to the Lord. If we insist on that, we have already lost. We are not alone in this fight. We have a Savior who understands everything we are going through and who will share our loads. Look how far you have already come with His help. Yes, you may be tired, and you may well have good reason to be, but be encouraged by your accomplishments through the abundant help you have been given. "My grace is sufficient for you" (2 Cor 12.9).

Let Jesus carry those burdens for you. He has already borne the biggest one, the sin that would have damned you for eternity. Surely He can handle the others, things which may seem huge to you now, but which eternal perspective will prove small. Some days you may feel like you are just plugging along, but that is all right too, so long as you don't give up.

> *Come unto me, all you that labor and are heavy laden, and I will give you rest. Take my yoke upon you, and learn of me; for I am meek and lowly in heart: and you shall find rest unto your souls. For my yoke is easy, and my burden is light.*
>
> Matthew 11.28–30

August 14

The Lifeline

What shall we say then? Shall we continue in sin, that grace may abound?

Even as early as the writing of Romans 6, Paul was concerned about those who would abuse the incredible gift of the grace of God. Since more sin required more grace to cover it, he feared they would use that as an excuse to sin yet more so they could have more grace (5.20–21).

We still abuse that grace today in much the same way. We misunderstand the purpose of grace, using it to make our lives easier than we have any right to expect. If grace is there to cover our imperfections, we really don't have to try so hard, do we?

Grace is not a safety net; it is, instead, a lifeline. Picture your life as climbing a mountain, a not un-Biblical metaphor, I think. When things get tough, when I tire and want to quit, too many times I just let go, expecting God—*requiring Him*—to catch me when I fall. That is not the way it works.

The Lord came down to make the climb with us. He climbs at the head of the line as the leader, the one who has successfully made the climb before us; hooked to each of us with a lifeline. When my hand slips, when my foothold crumbles beneath me, that line of grace will help me once again gain control as I swing against the face of the mountain, sometimes bouncing hard before I get a new handhold or toehold and can begin the climb again, bruised and sore from my experience. If I become so tired I don't think I can make another step, he will hold out a hand and give me a tug, or even have his Comforting Cohort give me a much-needed kick in the rear. What he will *not* do is tell me to just give up, unhook myself, and fall.

You see, the safety net we often see below is not God's grace; it is not a respite Christ has offered to help us out. Satan is the one holding that inviting net. He is the one who tells us that we can't do it, that we are only human and will never make it to the top. When you give up and say in your misery, "This is just the way I am, I can't help it," he is the one who says, "Of course you can't help it. Quit trying so hard. Unhook yourself and fall into this comfortable net. I won't let you be hurt, banging against the rocks of life like *He* does."

Don't be fooled. That net *is,* in fact, a net. It will trap you with its comfort, its assurance that you are not to blame, and if you are not careful, you will never even start the climb again, much less make it to the top.

God never promised us lives of ease. What He promised was help, enough help to make it through the rough spots. He will hold out His hand and pull, but if you unhook yourself from the lifeline of grace, you have lost the only hope you have.

> *What shall we say then? Shall we continue in sin, that grace may abound? God forbid. We who died to sin, how shall we any longer live therein? ...Let not sin therefore reign in your mortal body, that you should obey the lusts thereof: neither present your members unto sin as instruments of unrighteousness; but present yourselves unto God, as alive from the dead, and your members as instruments of righteousness unto God. For sin shall not have dominion over you: for you are not under law, but under grace.*
>
> Romans 6.1–2, 12–14

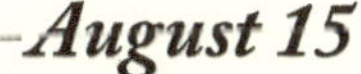

August 15

Pestering God

Every time I go outside Chloe comes running, tail wagging, waiting for me to scratch her head. If my hands are full, she butts the back of my leg with her nose until I manage to free my arms, bend over and scratch her head. If I am taking a load somewhere, she follows along, and I feel that little round nudge constantly all the way until *finally*—I am sure she is thinking—she gets that longed for scratch on the head.

This morning I suddenly wondered if I do that with God. Am I so anxious for

His attention that every morning I can hardly wait to talk with Him? Or do I just leave Him in the back of my mind until I can find a spare minute, and if He is lucky, I might actually have a whole minute?

Yes, Chloe is making a little pest of herself to get my attention, but do you know what? It doesn't bother me a bit. In fact, I find myself hurrying to put down my armload so I can pat her even sooner. It's endearing to have a little creature want you so much. Some days I go outside just to see her run up to me with that swishing tail, and actually sit down and spend a few minutes with her for no other reason than to be with her. I guess that's what happens when your children grow up and the dogs are all you have around to dote on.

What was it Jesus said? "If you then being evil know how to give good gifts to your children, how much more shall your Father who is in heaven, give good things to those who ask him?" (Matt 7.11). I don't for a minute pretend to understand how God feels about things, but Jesus gives us a hint here. If I, an imperfect person who sometimes still allows sin into my life, can love my children enough to give them good gifts, if I can still care enough about a small animal to want to satisfy its desire for attention, what will God not do for me? If that small child's pestering endears him to me because it makes me know he wants to be with me, certainly if it can happen with an animal's little nose bumping my leg, won't my pestering do the same for God?

And to the other side of the question, if I act like God's attention means little to me, why should He give me any of it when I decide I could use it? My mother always says, "If I say to God, 'I'm too busy for you right now,' what's to keep Him from saying that to me?" I think she has a point there.

And he spoke a parable unto them to the end that they ought always to pray, and not to faint; saying, There was in a city a judge, who feared not God, and regarded not man: and there was a widow in that city; and she came often to him, saying, Avenge me of my adversary. And he would not for awhile: but afterward he said within himself, Though I fear not God, nor regard man; yet because this widow troubles me, I will avenge her, lest she wear me out by her continual coming. And the Lord said, Hear what the unrighteous judge says. And shall not God avenge his elect that cry to him day and night and yet he is longsuffering over them? I say unto you, that he will avenge them speedily.

Luke 18.1–8

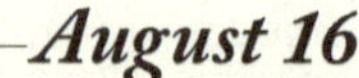

August 16

Sensitivity Training

If there was ever a new church that struggled with its spirituality, it was the church at Corinth. Paul scolded them: "And I, brethren, could not speak to you as to spiritual, but as to carnal, as to babes in Christ. [Read that: "you are acting like a bunch of big babies," and you will get the picture.] I fed you with milk, not with meat, for you were not yet able to bear it, no, *not even now* are you able, for you are still carnal" (1 Cor 3.1–3). We have a tendency to think of things sexual when we see that word "carnal," but Paul tells us in the next phrase or two what it really means: "walking after the manner of men," in other words, being physically minded instead of spiritually minded. He then spent most of that first letter telling them how to become more spiritually minded.

Their struggle over spiritual gifts surely has to be the most obvious example. They actually rated them as to importance, using, of course, carnal measurements—the flashier and showier the better. So Paul spends most of chapter 12 telling them that no one is more important than anyone else. Everyone is useful in the body of Christ, and if any one of them was not there, something would be obviously missing. In chapter 14, when their sense of importance is leading to a confused and disorderly assembly because none will yield his "gift" time to another, he actually gives them specific instructions about how to order things, *all of which are pure common sense if you have the correct object in mind, the edification of the church rather than the glorification of the individual.* He even spells it out several times: if there is no edification, "let them keep silence."

And of course, there is the pitiful business with suing one another, letting things of this physical life effect how they dealt with spiritual brothers and sisters.

Those poor Corinthians at whom we so often shake our heads are not the only ones with these problems. We are beset by the same weaknesses, and the same feelings. In fact, as I was reading and thinking about these things it suddenly struck me that almost any time I take an idle remark as a personal attack, it falls right into the same category.

I believe there is such a thing as being *sinfully* sensitive. Think about it. How many times could Jesus have "gotten his feelings hurt" or "felt insulted"? You could make a list as long as an entire book in the Bible, but he did not allow his feelings to keep him from completing a mission that was more important than anything else in the world.

When I commit myself to being his disciple, don't I promise to follow his example? The problem with being too sensitive is that it causes me to stop what I am doing and spend time on nothing but myself, usually moping or pouting, or even beginning a campaign against the other person. Nothing anyone says to me or about me, or that I might even possibly *construe* to be about me, is an excuse for setting myself up as more important than my mission as Jesus' disciple. As a mature Christian, those things should roll right off me, because my concern is God's glorification, not my own. That is what spirituality is all about. And if we cannot even begin to get a handle on it here, why should we be allowed to live in that exalted state for an Eternity?

Something to think about as we interact with one another today.

Do nothing from rivalry or conceit, but in humility count others more significant than yourselves.

The vexation of a fool is known at once, but the prudent ignores an insult.

Philippians 2.3; Proverbs 12.16

August 17

Prayers Not Prayed

A couple of weeks ago Keith had an appointment with the audiologist at the VA hospital. This meant he was late arriving to work, heading up highway 231 about 9:30 that Friday morning. It takes awhile to park, go through the search checkpoints and all the gates. He arrived at his office in time to hear the news that had just filtered back.

A man in the town had stabbed his girlfriend and fled down that very highway at speeds far exceeding the speed limit and, with apparent intent, hit a van head on. Both drivers were killed instantly. It had happened at 9:40. A ten minute delay anywhere along the road and one of those dead drivers might have been him.

Many times we go through life thinking God has not answered our prayers. Because we are self-oriented and earthly minded, we see only what happens to us or to others right in front of us.

But occasionally we are reminded that God is out there answering prayers we didn't even know to pray.

So many have asked me how I can stay positive in the circumstances in which I find myself. They do not know what I have been told. Five years ago was not the beginning of all this. It is the ending. Many times, many different medical personnel, including three or four doctors famous in their fields, have told me that as severe as my problem is, they do not know how my eyes have lasted this long, how I did not have a crisis long before. God has been answering those unsaid prayers since I was born. He has not let me down; He has given me far more than anyone else in my position had any right to expect.

So today, while you are wondering why God has not answered a prayer you have prayed, when you think He has forsaken you in a time when you need Him most, take a moment to consider all the prayers He has answered that you are unaware of. He knows far better than we what we most need. He is, in fact, answering your other prayers too, but He is not required to keep to your timetable or your methods. Just trust Him. He is there, working while you sleep, while you work, while you play, and while you plan all those big plans that so often exclude Him.

You may never realize what He has truly done for you today, but then just think how horrible it might have been if He hadn't.

Now unto him that is able to do exceeding abundantly above all that we ask or think, according to the power that works in us, unto him be the glory in the church and in Christ Jesus unto all generations for ever and ever. Amen.

Ephesians 3.20–21

August 18

Riding on the Spare

As I was "walking" on my elliptical machine this morning, I suddenly heard several metallic pings on the floor. I got down on my knees and finally found a nut, bolt, and washer. Looking for their proper place on the black machine was hopeless. I knew these eyes would never find it, so my dogs got a surprise. I walked with them for the first time in months. Not for long, though, because I tripped three times in five minutes, once over a root and twice over vines. After that I gave up—this was too dangerous.

So all my careful plans had come to nothing. We bought this machine because I could not walk outside safely any longer and expected that to take care of everything from now on. I can even "walk" on it when I am totally blind, right? The problem is I was counting on something manmade, and sure enough, it let me down. Yes, Keith can put it back together, but how long till this happens again? And how long till it breaks completely? I simply cannot rely on it to work right forever.

Yet we do this all the time with things far more important than taking a walk. We make solid investments, have good life insurance policies, and work for companies with good pension plans. What happens when the economy goes south, when prices double in a few days' time and suddenly that monthly income we had worked so hard to have coming in after retirement will barely cover two weeks?

We take good care of ourselves, having annual check-ups, eating right, taking our vitamins, and exercising regularly. What happens when the tests come back positive?

We can depend upon ourselves for absolutely nothing in this life, but we don't seem to get that. We treat God like the spare tires in our trunks, dinky little donuts we only use when necessary, and only until we can get our own tires fixed up and rolling again. What we fail to realize is when we rely on ourselves we are traveling everywhere on four dinky donuts that could go flat any time, while God has some big steel-belted radials handy if we would only stop and put them on!

God is the only thing you can count on. There is nothing wrong with being good stewards of the blessings God has given us, but there is everything wrong with trusting our own stewardship instead of the Giver of those blessings Himself.

My soul, wait in silence for God only; For my expectation is from him. He alone is my rock and my salvation: He is my high tower; I shall not be moved. With God is my salvation and my glory: The rock of my strength, and my refuge, is in God. Trust in him at all times, you people; Pour out your hearts before him: God is a refuge for us.

Psalm 62.5–8

August 19

One Size Fits All

Could there be a more obvious lie in all of retail sales? "One size fits all." Of course it does, if you call fitting one person like a circus tent around a beanpole and another like a sausage in a casing a couple of perfect fits. There is a reason that a custom tailored suit costs about 200 times more than a one size fits all tee shirt, and it's not just the material.

Yet there is one instance where the phrase is as apt as can be. Sin is a "one size fits all" commodity. "For we before laid charge both of Jews and Greeks, that they are all under sin. …For all have sinned and fall short of the glory of God" (Rom 3.9, 23). And we do not get that sin from some mystical contagion. "Therefore as through one man sin entered into the world, and death through sin, and so death passed unto all men *for that all sinned*" (Rom 5.12). We are under the charge of sin, because we sin, every one of us, no matter how good we think we are.

And sin is sin is sin: "For whoever shall keep the whole law, and yet stumble in one point, he is become guilty of all. For He who said, You shall not commit adultery, also said, You shall not kill. Now if you do not commit adultery, but kill, you have become a transgressor of the law" (Jas 2.10–11). And in that context, James was talking to people who discriminate against others. Bigotry, he meant them to understand, is as bad as adultery and murder.

Even righteous men in the Old Testament understood that the Law could not save them. As sinners, they counted on the grace of God. David wrote a Psalm about it: "Jehovah looked down from heaven upon the children of men to see if there were any who did understand. They were all gone aside; they are together become filthy; there is none that does good, no, not one" (14.2–3). We are all in the same boat—none of us deserve salvation.

But Christ came to offer us a salvation that would fit all of us, too, no matter how many times we have sinned, no matter the heinousness of our sins, as men would categorize them. Christ does indeed fit all, and not only that, His one size is available to all as well, no matter who we are or what our stations in life. All we have to do is put it on. The grace of God will always be a perfect fit.

For the love of Christ constrains us because we thus judge that one died for all, therefore all died; and he died for all that they that live should no longer live unto themselves, but unto him who for their sakes died and rose again.

2 Corinthians 5.14–15

A Biscuit Recipe

A young woman is making biscuits for her new husband. When she tries to roll them out she has a problem—they keep falling apart. It is all she can do to make them stick together long enough to get them on the baking sheet. And when she tries to take them off, they fall to pieces. Her husband tells her, "That's all right. It's the taste that matters," as he gallantly takes a bite, and a little bite is all he can get. They crumble so easily he cannot even butter them. Before long, his plate is filled with crumbs and he has not managed to eat even half a biscuit's worth.

The next morning she calls her mother. "Too much shortening," her mother says. So that evening the new bride tries again. If shortening is the culprit, she reasons, maybe no shortening at all would be even better.

That night, as she slides the biscuits off into the basket, each lands with an ominous thud. Her husband gamely takes a bite, or at least tries to. They might as well be hockey pucks.

I imagine that even non-cooks can see the point here. Each ingredient in the recipe makes a difference; each one is important and must not be left out—the shortening makes the biscuits tender, the flour gives them enough structure to hold together. Why are we smart enough to see that here, but forget it when it comes to spiritual matters?

One group says faith is the only thing we need. Another says strict obedience is the only thing we need. One of them bakes crumbs, the other hockey pucks.

Every generation reacts to the past generation's errors by overcorrecting. Each group is so afraid of making the same mistake that they make another one, and worse, usually sneer at their fathers for missing it so badly, thinking in their youthful arrogance that they have discovered something brand new. What they have usually discovered is the same error another generation made long ago, the error their fathers tried to correct and overdid as well.

Why is it so hard to stop that swinging pendulum in the middle? Why do we arrogantly suppose that the last group did *everything* wrong and we are doing *everything* right.

Does God want faith? Yes, "the righteous shall live by his faith" (Hab 2.4).

Does God want obedience? Yes, "to obey is better than sacrifice" (1 Sam 15.22).

Does God want our hearts? He always has, and why can't we put it all together? "Thanks be to God... that you became *obedient from the heart*" (Rom 6.17).

The Hebrew write equates disobedience with a lack of faith. "And to whom did he swear that they should not enter into his rest but to them who were disobedient? And we see that they were not able to enter in due to unbelief" (Heb 3.18–19).

Can God make it any plainer? He doesn't want crumbs; He doesn't want hockey pucks; He wants a nice tender biscuit of a heart that is firm enough to hold the shape of the pattern used to cut it. Follow the recipe God gave you. When you go about your day today, make sure you have all the ingredients.

> *Woe to you scribes, Pharisees, hypocrites! For you tithe mint, anise, and cumin, and have left undone the weightier matters of the law. But these* [matters of the heart] *you ought to have done, and not left the other* [matters of strict obedience] *undone.*
>
> Matthew 23.23

August 21

The Hero of the Story

I have a problem. I believe that life is a book and I am the hero of the story. Everything anyone does is done with me in mind because I am the central character. Any time I rub shoulders with another person in my daily life, that person did it solely because he wanted to hurt me, or inconvenience me, or insult me, or otherwise bother my life.

What is really happening is that person thinks *his* life is a book and *he* is the hero, and I am the one causing *him* trouble. The things I often get so upset about are nothing more than an accidental crossing of paths or an idiosyncrasy that, in my own self-centeredness, I have decided to take as a personal offense when the other person was not directing it toward me at all.

And in the same vein, I think everything is supposed to turn out wonderfully, a happily ever after for all my goodness and faithfulness, because I am the hero after all. Admit it: you have the same problem. And it can cost us our souls if we are not careful.

I think of John the Baptist, a man whose birth was announced by the same angel who announced Jesus' birth. He gave up any semblance of a normal life to fulfill the mission God gave him. If not for John's preaching, what would have become of Christianity? If it took several years for the men who actually walked with Jesus to figure things out, what of the masses if John had not worked so hard to prepare them for the coming of the kingdom? The thought of 3,000 being baptized on the Day of Pentecost would have been nothing more than a pipe dream.

John also gave up what others might have expected in the way of glory. He watched Jesus begin his ministry and gradually take away many of his own disciples. For all his sacrifice this is the thanks he gets? John did not look for thanks. Indeed, as his ministry waned and an unjust death at about the age of 31 loomed, his remaining disciples came to him complaining about Jesus' growing popularity as if it were an affront to John. "John answered and said, 'A man can receive nothing, except it have been given him from heaven. You yourselves bear me witness that I said, I am not the Christ, but, that I am sent before him. He that has the bride is the bridegroom: but the friend of the bridegroom, who stands and hears him, rejoices greatly because of the bridegroom's voice: this my joy therefore is made full. He must increase, but I must decrease'" (John 3.27–30).

It may have been written many years after his death, but John understood the true meaning of "to them that love God all things work together for good" (Rom 8.28). He understood because he recognized the part that we ignore: "*according to his purpose.* For whom he foreknew, he also foreordained to be conformed to the image of his Son that he might be the firstborn among many brethren: and whom he foreordained, them he also called: and whom he called, them he also justified: and whom he justified, them he also glorified" (vv 29–30). John knew he was not the hero of the story. He knew that he need not expect this life to be a bed of roses with a happy ending.

He also knew that the purpose of God for which he worked was to give everyone the opportunity to be saved, and *that* was the good for which all things worked together. If it took his not being able to have a family, if it took living a meager existence in the wilderness, if it took his murder, he was willing to bear it.

If John could have that attitude, a man who lived a short, strange, sacrificial life and died a martyr by the hand of a ruthless woman and her weak husband, why can't we who live relatively normal, happy, safe lives?

There will be trials. There will be moments of grief. The life we live here may not have the happy ending we always dreamed of, but the purpose of God will make it seem like a mere trifle if we just stop thinking everything is about us, and remember who the real Hero is.

> *Therefore let us also, seeing we are compassed about with so great a cloud of witnesses, lay aside every weight, and the sin which so easily besets us, and let us run with patience the race that is set before us, looking unto Jesus the author and perfecter of faith, who for the joy that was set before him endured the cross, despising shame, and hath sat down at the right hand of the throne of God.*
>
> Hebrews 12.1–2

August 22

The Catbird Seat

It came up in conversation the other day when we were discussing the catbird at my feeder. Where did the expression, "sitting in the catbird seat," come from? So I looked it up.

It is a distinctly American expression, probably because the gray catbird is a North

American bird. Catbirds like to sit in the highest branches of the trees to sing and display. The expression has come to mean being in a superior or advantageous position. One of the first uses found is in a story by James Thurber in which he talks about a batter in a baseball game being "in the catbird seat" with three balls and no strikes.

You know the problem with being "in the catbird seat?" You can get a little too sure of yourself. Obadiah prophesied against the nation of Edom, a country full of mountains, whose inhabitants lived high above any who would try to attack their nearly impregnable rocky dwellings. "The pride of your heart has deceived you, O you who dwell in the clefts of the rock, whose habitation is high; who says in his heart, Who shall bring me down to the ground? Though you mount on high as the eagle, and though your nest be set among the stars, I will bring you down from there, says Jehovah" (Oba 3–4).

The Edomites, though they were brothers of the Israelites through their father Esau, had forgotten that Jehovah made those very mountains they counted on. That meant that He could destroy them with a word if He were of a mind to, and He was. The Edomites were subject to Israel off and on throughout history, and were finally run out of their land completely by the Nabataeans.

It is easy for us to perch ourselves high above others and "display." Like the Jews in John 8, we want to boast of our spiritual heritage and our quest to follow the truth, the whole truth, and nothing but the truth. "We are Abraham's seed, and have never yet been in bondage to any man: how do you say, You shall be made free?" (John 8.33).

They bring it up again in verse 39 and Jesus answers, "If you were Abraham's children, you would do the works of Abraham." Abraham would have denounced them all. What would he say to us, who are supposed to be "Abraham's seed, heirs according to promise?" (Gal 3.29), when pride causes us to place ourselves above the rest of the religious world as if we were more *deserving* of salvation. Jesus warns, "For everyone that exalts himself shall be humbled; and he that humbles himself shall be exalted" (Luke 14.11). Just like those Edomites of old, God can bring us down off that catbird seat.

He can do that because that is where He dwells. "Jehovah is exalted; for he dwells on high: he has filled Zion with justice and righteousness" (Isa 33.5). We count on Him, not on ourselves. "Jehovah also will be a high tower for the oppressed, A high tower in times of trouble" (Psa 9.9). Just as the imagery in Obadiah, He is a high steep place where we are removed from danger.

And in a Messianic passage he tells us that He will take us to new heights. "And Jehovah their God will save them in that day as the flock of his people; for they shall be as the stones of a crown, lifted on high over his land" (Zech 9.16). As children of the Most High God we have an exalted position nothing on this earth can possibly match.

Sitting in the catbird seat is a good thing. Just remember who put you there.

Yea, they shall sing of the ways of Jehovah; For great is the glory of Jehovah. For though Jehovah is high, yet he has respect unto the lowly; But the haughty he knows from afar.

Psalm 138.5–6

August 23

A Blushing Bride

I am an increasingly rare breed—a native Floridian. I never saw snow until we lived two years in Illinois. Talk about culture shock—I won't soon forget the feeling in the pit of my stomach when one of my worried sisters in the Lord asked if I had a heavy winter coat. I showed it to her; it looked new because I seldom wore it down here. She called it a nice "spring coat," and advised me to go shopping.

I soon learned to appreciate the luxuries I had grown up with in winter: warmth—up there we often had lows below zero; sun—I had never before lived in a place that went as long as two weeks with sunless skies and dusk arriving about 4:30... and *green!* Sure the grass may frost off for a couple of weeks down here, and some of the trees lose their leaves, but we still have plenty of green for a lot of the winter. I even learned to appreciate humidity after my entire body chapped through my clothes and I started blowing blood out of my nose.

Of course, I realize that a lot of this depends on what you are used to. We met a man from Massachusetts last February in one of our state parks who told us, "It was almost uncomfortable today." The thermometer might have topped out at 72. I am sure if I had stayed in Illinois longer than two years, I would have become acclimated to the weather and the things I needed to do to make myself comfortable in a different climate.

Becoming accustomed to things can affect our spiritual lives as well. Paul reminds us in 1 Corinthians 5.9–10 that we cannot remove ourselves from the world. In fact we are encouraged to spread the Truth of the Gospel among those very souls, but we are supposed to keep the influence going one way only. When I am no longer shocked at the world's behavior, in fact, when I consider it "normal," the influence has taken a two-way street.

One of the most scathing indictments in the Bible is Jeremiah's accusation, "They were not at all ashamed, neither could they blush" (8.12). Nothing the prophets said could touch these people. They continued in their own stubborn way and never thought anything about it. Many years before, had they seen the direction they were headed, they probably would have been horrified; but they changed so gradually—got used to it—that they did not even realize their sin. Despite that sin, they still stood at God's Temple and worshipped, sure of their good standing with Jehovah (Jer 7.10).

How about us? Have we gotten so used to sin around us that it no longer disturbs us? For the danger, you see, is that because we no longer consider it so reprehensible, we might be tempted to fall into it ourselves. We would never do anything bad, and this is no longer all that bad, so why not?

Historians say that the downfall of any society begins with that society's acceptance of rampant immorality as "the norm." The prophets preached the same about Israel and Judah, and Paul warns the church, Christ's bride, "A little leaven leavens the whole lump" (1 Cor 5.6).

Do not forget how to blush!

> *Forasmuch then as Christ suffered in the flesh, arm yourselves also with the same mind, for he that has suffered in the flesh has ceased from sin, that you no longer should live the rest of your time in the flesh to the lusts of men, but to the will of God. For the time past may suffice to have wrought your desire of the Gentiles, and to have walked in lasciviousness, lusts, winebibbings, revelings, carousings, and abominable idolatries, wherein they think it strange that you do not run with them into the same excess of riot, speaking evil of you, who shall give an account to him that is ready to judge the living and the dead.*
>
> 1 Peter 4.1–5

August 24

An Off Day

Despite all of your kind comments, I have an off day here and there. In fact, I have an off week sometimes. I sit here staring into space, and can think of absolutely nothing to write about. So I come up with something a little mundane, a little trite, something so absolutely so-so I want to trash it, but since I need it, I save it. Sometimes I come back to it in a few months and can finally make something out of it, but other times you get the unvarnished mediocrity as is. Sometimes "mediocrity" is putting it kindly.

Sometimes as Christians we have off days too, or off weeks, or in rare cases off years. We fall short in one way or the other and become depressed over our inability to be what we know we ought to be. That depression can last far too long. Now listen closely: Sometimes we need to give ourselves permission to be human. Not permission to sin, excusing ourselves as if it makes no difference, but permission to forgive ourselves for making a mistake, and then picking up and going on with our lives rather than wallowing in misery. *The amount of time we spend beating ourselves up does not necessarily equal the quality of our repentance.* What it *can* equal is the amount of time we are *not* accomplishing any good for the kingdom because we are so consumed with our despondence.

Depression can paralyze you—just ask those poor souls who are afflicted with clinical depression. Godly sorrow should embody our repentance, but it should not keep us from serving God. If God will forgive me, then isn't it arrogant of me not to forgive myself, and doesn't it serve the needs of Satan far better than getting on with my service to God?

So yes, be upset with yourself when you fail. Do, as the apostle Paul did, buffet your body and make it behave when you are having trouble. Do, as Peter did, go out and weep bitterly at your failures. Do, as David did, repent in heartfelt prayer. But then pick yourself up, dust yourself off, and refuse to indulge in self-pity. Get up and get back to work. When the switch says "off" then the machine isn't working, and when you are having an off day, you aren't either.

> *Have mercy upon me, O God, according to your lovingkindness: According to the multitude of your tender mercies blot out my transgressions. Wash me thoroughly from my iniquity, And cleanse me from my sin. For I know my transgressions; And my sin is ever before me. Against you, you only, have I sinned, And done that which is evil in your sight. ...Hide your face from my sins, And blot out all my iniquities. Create in me a clean heart, O God;* ***And renew a right spirit within me.*** *Cast me not away from your presence; And take not your holy Spirit from me.* ***Restore unto me the joy of your salvation; And uphold me with a willing spirit. Then will I teach transgressors your ways; And sinners shall be converted unto you.***
>
> Psalm 51.1–4, 9–13

August 25

Basil Revisited

As I mentioned before, I have had an awful time growing basil this year. After trying seven or eight different plants, I have ended the summer with two basil plants left alive, each barely six inches tall. I am still rationing out their leaves. Basil is an annual and even if you protect it from the frost, it will eventually give out. We never did have fresh pesto this summer.

Keith happened to say one evening, as he could barely taste the basil in the baked ziti, "What if this had been the first year you had tried to grow it?" Indeed, what if it had? I would probably never have tried again.

This led to a discussion about people. What about that friend you invited to church but who "had a prior commitment"? What about the neighbor you asked to study the Bible with you, but who was "just too busy right now"? How many times did you ask? How many times did you invite? How many times did you even mention the spiritual things in your life to see if they might spark an interest? Do you suppose that maybe those good folks were just having a bad year like my basil plants?

Sometimes I wonder if we don't blurt these invitations out in nervousness or embarrassment, and then feel almost relieved when they are rejected. "Whew! Got that over with. Now I don't have to worry about it any more."

How long did it take for you? How many approaches did you fend off before you finally realized your need? How many times did you "kick against the pricks"? Aren't you glad God didn't give up on you? Aren't you happy he realized that it might just be a bad year for good old Basil, and tried again?

Next year I will still plant Basil in my herb garden. As many abundant years as He has given me, I know that this one was just an anomaly. Don't you think the people you know deserve the same consideration?

> *The Lord is not slack concerning his promise, as some count slackness, but is longsuffering to you, not wishing that any should perish, but that all should come to repentance.*
>
> 2 Peter 3.9

August 26

Old, But Never Useless

A long time ago, Keith was teaching the high school class on Sunday morning, something in Judges or Kings as I remember. He had a young visitor, a visiting preacher's daughter. All of a sudden she asked in a less than respectful tone, "What are you doing teaching from the Old Testament on the Lord's Day? You should always teach from the New Testament on Sundays!" Of course, her father, in a meeting later that week, taught that Psalm 58.6—"Break out the great teeth of the young lions, O Jehovah"—meant that as soon as a child started losing his baby teeth he had reached the age of accountability, so what can you expect?

I can remember a time when the Old Testament was never taught, when in fact, a lot of folks never even carried it. They kept only a thin New Testament in their coat pockets, because "the Old has been nailed to the cross—we don't need it any longer." Don't ever think that knowledge of the Old Testament is now totally unnecessary. How did the apostles teach about Jesus? They taught from the Old Testament. They quoted prophecies extensively and showed how the man Jesus fulfilled them all, and thus was not some ordinary man. Read practically any sermon in Acts and that will become clear. If they do not quote the Old Testament, they allude to it clearly.

When Paul spoke to Timothy about his upbringing—"From a babe you have known the sacred writings which are able to make you wise unto salvation through faith which is Christ Jesus" (2 Tim 3.15)—he was talking about the Old Testament. No one had even started writing the New when Timothy was a small child.

Though teaching facts is essential and the first kind of teaching any child can understand, in the long run teaching facts is not the job of the educator. When all a child knows is facts, his knowledge will always be limited. When you teach a child principles, he will be able to teach himself facts for the rest of his life. When I told my children what to do or not to do, I expected them to eventually use the principles I had taught them to figure out circumstances I had not been able to specifically prepare them for. When they did not, I was disappointed, and usually said something like, "How many times do I have to tell you? You are smarter than this." God spent thousands of years preparing us with principles we can use now. Does He have to tell us everything again? Aren't we smarter than that?

Most any element of the New Testament can be better understood and become more meaningful if you understand its parallel in the Old. I once tried to make a point about the Lord's Supper by pointing out something about the Passover feast. After all, Jesus instituted this feast during a Passover meal using elements from that meal, and Paul says plainly in 1 Corinthians 5.7, "For our Passover has been sacrificed, even Christ." The person I was speaking with totally dismissed my point because the New Testament did not say it word for word. Here was a person who truly had not comprehended the relationship between the testaments and how God had prepared not only the Israelites, but all of us who will take the time necessary to study, for the full glory of the gospel.

The more you know, even things that seem like meaningless details, the more you will comprehend, the more it will touch your heart, the harder you will try to live up to the wonderful blessings we have in Christ Jesus, the fulfillment of the Old Testament.

> *So the law has become our schoolmaster to bring us to Christ, that we might be justified by faith. For the things written aforetime were written for our learning that through patience and comfort of the scriptures we might have hope.*
>
> Galatians 3.24; Romans 15.4

August 27

Out of the Mouths of Babes

Recently someone asked me how I keep from being depressed in my situation. I was so shocked I stumbled a bit in my answer, finally saying, "Well it certainly wouldn't help things, so why would I want to do that?" I got a strange look. I suppose most people think of "depressed" as something you are, not something you do, but that never has made sense to me. All those books, TV shows, and movies revolving around people who fall apart after some sort of shocking revelation, never have made sense to me. So a bad thing has happened. You know what? The laundry still needs washing, the bills still need paying, and the dog still has an appointment at the vet for her rabies shot. I guess I am just a little too practical.

But I remember once, many years ago, when I was unable to keep a tear from leaking out in front of my little boy. We were preparing to move, and after several days of packing and cleaning, and saying good-bye to yet another good friend, it just got away from me. He asked what was wrong.

I never tried to hide things from my children. I told them what I thought they could understand at the time they asked. He would not have understood about the other problems of a move, but he had little friends himself that I knew he would miss, so I said, "It's just sad to leave your friends."

He put his arms around my neck and patted my back. "It's all right, mama. You will always have Jesus."

That nearly undid me for good, but I managed to smile and say, "You are right. And so will you." Then we went on with the task of packing, and managed a laugh or two before long.

As I think back on that now, I believe he had the answer I should have given this friend. Somehow a four year old understood that no matter what happens, we are never alone. What he did not say, but which struck me right between the eyes when I thought about it, was that when we allow ourselves to be depressed over this life, we are being singularly ungrateful to Christ for what He did for us. If this life were all there was, then we ought to be depressed. "If we have only hoped in Christ in this life, we are of all men most pitiable" (1 Cor 15.19). But He gave up a lot so we could have hope for the next life. *I will not slap Him in the face by acting like anything in this life is important enough to take away the joy I have in a relationship with Him.*

That does not mean that some days are not difficult, especially when the pain is worse or the vision is obviously less. But I do not wallow like a pig in the muddy misery. I *choose* not to, in part because a four year old reminded me not to.

From now on, when someone asks, I think I will just use my little boy's answer—which I hope he has not forgotten either. How can I be depressed when I have a Savior who loves me?

For it became him, for whom are all things, and through whom are all things, in bringing many sons unto glory, to make the author of their salvation perfect through sufferings. For both he that sanctifies and they that are sanctified are all of one: for which cause he is not ashamed to call them brethren.

Hebrews 2.10–11

August 28

Guilt by Association

My husband deals with convicted felons every day. It is amazing how many stories he hears that begin, "I didn't do anything. I just went with my friends and then all of a sudden. . . ." It may seem unfair for someone to be punished for simply being in the wrong place at the wrong time, if indeed that is truly what happened, but what about common sense? Why go for a stroll in a snake pit? Wisdom says the consequences will not be worth the adrenalin rush.

We often dally in sin and think nothing of it. We are as bad as young daredevils who think they will never die. "I'm strong; nothing will happen to me. Besides, God knows my heart, and He knows I am not a bad person."

Have you ever looked at the lists of sins scattered throughout the New Testament? It always amazes me the failings I find listed side by side, things I would never have put in the same category.

Look at 2 Timothy 3.2–4: "For people shall be lovers of self, lovers of money, proud, arrogant, abusive, disobedient to parents, ungrateful, unholy, heartless, unappeasable, slanderous, without self-control, brutal, not loving good, treacherous, reckless, conceited, lovers of pleasure rather than lovers of God." Which of us is not sometimes proud, does not sometimes forget to be grateful, or lacks a little self-control in some areas of our lives? Yet the Holy Spirit includes those among the brutal, the ruthless, and the treacherous.

Then there is Romans 1.29–31: "They were filled with all manner of unrighteousness: evil, covetousness, malice, full of envy, murder, strife, deceit, maliciousness; they are gossips, slanderers, haters of God, insolent, haughty, boastful, inventors of evil, disobedient to parents, foolish, faithless, heartless, ruthless." Whoa! Disobedience to parents and gossip included with murder? Boasting and insolence included with hating God? That's a wake-up call we all need.

Another such association literally took my breath away when I discovered it. Look up the Greek word for the Devil—*diabolus*, "Slanderer." That means when I talk about another person, I am becoming exactly what Satan is. Gossip is never inconsequential. Even if it never hurts the one being slandered, a near impossibility, it is certainly affecting the one doing it. You cannot do the works of Satan and come out unscathed.

So be careful when those "little" sins start popping up. Look at the other sins God associates them with. Look who practices them. Being in the wrong place at the wrong time, is just that—wrong.

My little children let no man lead you astray. He who practices righteousness is righteous. He who practices sin is of the devil, for the devil sinned from the beginning. . . .In this the children of God are manifest, and the children of the devil: whoever does not practice righteousness is not of God, neither he who does not love his brother.

1 John 3.7–8, 10

August 29

Sabotage

When I was little and listened to the sick list at church, no matter where we went, there was always someone who was "chronically ill." All that meant to me was they were never at church. I couldn't fathom an illness that never got any better, that gave you good days and bad days, that made you careful not to "overdo" because of the adverse effects that might have on you. Now I understand, and wish I didn't.

I no longer have any social life—my doctor *is* my social life. I see more of him than any of my brothers and sisters in the Lord. I talk on the phone more to his office help than to church folks. I spend more hours sitting in his examining chair than I do in a pew. In fact, they ought to rent me a room there.

And I know this will take a toll on my spirituality. It becomes more and more difficult to keep a good attitude. While I certainly have more time to study, not having a class to prepare to teach makes it less a priority and easy to put off, especially when reading is so difficult. Helping others is nearly impossible, especially when you don't even know what's going on with the brethren any more. So yes, my spirituality is suffering. I struggle to keep it every day. But the circumstances cannot be helped.

What I do not understand is people who do this to themselves on purpose: those who darken the meetinghouse door only enough to keep the elders and deacons off their backs, and leave while the last amen is still echoing down the hall; who never take advantage of the extra Bible studies held in homes, a safe place to ask questions without embarrassment and learn from those who have wisdom and experience in life; who avoid all the social gatherings of the church scheduled between the services, while regularly finding time to be with friends in the world, not to teach, but simply to socialize; who never have a Bible lesson prepared—that's only for the children—who never attend a wedding or funeral so they can "weep with those who weep and rejoice with those who rejoice," those who are healthy enough to jog, to play tennis, to hunt or fish, to go to ball games and sit in the hot sun for hours cheering, but simply do not want more than they consider the bare minimum to get by as a Christian.

Here is the problem with that: there is no such thing as the bare minimum. If Satan can get you to believe that lie, he has sabotaged any chance you have to make it to Heaven. God expects us to give our all, no matter how much that may be; more for some, less for others, depending upon the circumstances of life. It is difficult enough when the minimum *is* your maximum, but doing that to yourself on purpose will only make you miserable in both lives, this one and the one to come.

The early Christians understood that they were spiritual lifelines for each other; they would not let go for anyone or anything. They spent time together, strengthening one another from the beginning, and because of that they were able to withstand horrors we can only imagine. If you wait till the horror is upon you to reach out for that lifeline, it is probably too late.

> *And all that believed were together and had all things common.…And day by day continuing steadfastly with one accord in the Temple, and breaking bread from house to house, they took their food with gladness and singleness of heart, praising God and having favor with all the people. And the Lord added to them day by day those that were saved.*
>
> Acts 2.44, 46–47

August 30

Gratitude, Not Entitlement

I wonder how many of us are so enamored by what we consider a "beautiful" love story, that we miss an even better one. It really should tell us something when we read that Jacob loved Rachel because of her looks. Since when do we teach our children that outer beauty is all that matters?

After the marriages, Leah had children almost immediately. Rachel, of course, wanted children too. Her first resort was to demand them of Jacob, "Give me children or else I die!" (Gen 30.1), as if a man who had already fathered at least four was at fault. Am I being overly critical or doesn't she sound as childish as a little girl threatening to hold her breath if she doesn't get her way?

Then she gave her handmaid to her husband (v 3) for in that culture, the children of one's handmaid were legally your own, and the family already had precedent for such a thing in Hagar. Of course that was less than satisfying, especially since her sister could do the same.

Then she resorted to mandrakes, the local aphrodisiac (v 14), not too surprising from a woman who would steal her father's household gods, I suppose. As you go through chapter 30, pay special attention to the names of the children, what they mean, and what each mother said when they were born. That speaks volumes in itself.

Finally Rachel went to Jehovah. We really have no record of her doing that, but let us give her the benefit of the doubt since the scriptures do say "and God hearkened to [Rachel] and opened her womb" (v 22). Still, her attitude is shown when she greets that child with "Jehovah, give me another one!" and names her son that very sentiment, Joseph, "may God add" (v 24). Compare that to Leah who, when she named Judah, and called to her son every day afterward, was "Praising" Jehovah.

Is that how we treat prayer as well, a last resort? Does God only hear from us when we get desperate or scared or so distressed that we finally realize we have no other hope for a happy ending? Do we demand help from God, then angrily complain when that prayer, which may be the first we have prayed in a week or a month or even longer, does not accomplish what we want? And when we finally do get the desired answer, do we act entitled and fail to express any gratitude at all? After all, we serve God and therefore He is *supposed* to take care of us, right? If we don't get what we want, why should we bother?

Ultimately, Jacob seems to have learned who the better wife was. When Rachel died, she was buried where she fell, even though it was only a day or two's walk from the family burial plot at Machpelah. Jacob himself expected his sons to carry his body back all the way from Egypt. And hear what he says about that: "There they buried Abraham and Sarah his wife, and there they buried Isaac and Rebekah his wife, *and there I buried Leah*" (Gen 49.31). Jacob wanted to be buried next to Leah, the woman he had chosen to place in the family tomb. Finally, he could see a beauty that mattered. I imagine his change of heart had a lot to do with their shared faith in God, and their recognition that He was responsible for every good thing they had. (Study those names!) And didn't God choose Leah as well? "For it is evident that our Lord has sprung out of Judah" (Heb 7.14), who was Leah's son.

God will notice our faith, our desire to talk with Him, our recognition of His providence and care. Prayer is not about entitlement, but gratitude.

Oh give thanks unto Jehovah, for his lovingkindness endures forever.
Oh give thanks unto the God of gods, for his lovingkindness endures forever.
Oh give thanks unto the Lord of lords, for his lovingkindness endures forever.

Psalm 136.1–3

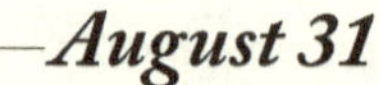

August 31

Faded Jeans

It must be a sign of my "un-hipness." I never have, and I suppose I never will understand the desire to buy pants that look worn out right off the rack, faded, holey and torn. Surely we have reached some sort of social neurosis when a symptom of poverty becomes the popular thing to do for even the wealthiest.

The Holy Spirit did not go in for this obsession either. In 1 Peter 1.4 one of the wonderful things about our inheritance, He says, is that it will not "fade away."

When Disneyworld opened in Florida I was 19 years old. It was the first time

I had been to anything "Disney" at all, and I was entranced. As we rode in on the monorail, I swiveled my head back and forth so much that I was literally "dizzy with delight." I laughed at all the corny jokes in the Haunted House elevator. So much for trying so hard to make everyone think I was now "an adult." I could not get enough of all the fanciful details. I didn't even mind waiting in line! Why they had air conditioning vents blowing out on you as you waited! Isn't that amazing?

The first time I took my children they enjoyed it as much as I had. We had saved money for a year and experienced that park the way it should be experienced, and it was nearly magical, even for us world-weary grown-ups, because we were seeing it again through the eyes of our inexperienced children.

But as my boys grew up and became involved in more and more school activities, they wound up going to Disneyworld for state competitions every year, sometimes twice a year. By their senior years, it was old hat. They spent more time in their hotel rooms than in the park itself. It had become so familiar that it had lost its luster. They even had unused Disney tickets sitting on their desks at home. Can you imagine?

Peter says that will never happen with our inheritance. It will never lose its luster. It will always be a wonder as if new, never trite or stale or boring. Imagine every moment of Eternity being like the first time a small child sees the wonder of a grand amusement park—only so much better, a thousand, a million, a billion times over because it was created by God and not man.

That is the inheritance we have waiting for us. Somehow I don't think we will want it to be used, torn, and full of holes. Looking fresh and new and un-faded every single moment will be just fine.

Blessed be the God and Father of our Lord Jesus Christ, who according to his great mercy begat us again unto a living hope by the resurrection of Jesus Christ from the dead, unto an inheritance incorruptible, and undefiled, and that fades not away, reserved in heaven for you, who by the power of God are guarded through faith unto a salvation ready to be revealed in the last time.

1 Peter 1.3–5

September 1

The Age of Reason

For various reasons I have found myself remembering my junior high years lately. That time of life can be trying. You are not an adult, but you are not a little child either. In fact, you are not sure who you are.

Your body is behaving strangely and you have outgrown the cute stage. You are too fat or too skinny, taller than everyone else or shorter, too loud for the adults in your life, but too quiet to suit your peers. Your hair is too curly or too straight for the current style, and you never know what sort of face will greet you in the mirror each morning.

You begin to feel a need to embrace ideals but you are not sure which ones or why. The ones your peers embrace, even as they strive to rebel from the norm, seem just a little too empty and too "popular." Where is the individuality they say they crave? The ones many teachers press on you seem to come with agendas attached. Do they teach these because they believe them and think they will help you, or because they want disciples?

But the thing we need to think about today is, what about us as parents? Of all people, we should be teaching ideals that will make our children's lives better and their souls secure, but sometimes the things we do make that difficult for a child to see, especially one already confused by his mind and body, and the mixed signals he receives from everyone around him.

Help him out. Live by the ideals you teach. We tell him nothing is more important than his soul, but does he see that in us, or does he see far more time and money given to recreation and status-building than to the Lord, to worthy causes, to needy souls and spiritual pursuits? We tell him his eternal destiny is more important than physical wealth and security, but does he see us sacrifice spiritual matters for those very things time and time again? Does he ever see us engaged in personal Bible study or is the TV on 24 hours a day? Does he hear us preach honesty then hear us brag about cheating the tax man? Does he hear us talk about setting priorities, about being at the meetinghouse every time the door is open, while remembering that you have not spent any time with him, one on one, talking about spiritual things in the past six months or even longer? As young as he is, he understands that there is more to Christianity than sitting on a pew.

Adolescent rebellion is not unusual. It is part of discovering who you are—considering ideas, then rejecting them or accepting them. Don't give your children an easy—and far more obvious reason than you would like to believe—to reject yours.

But as for you, continue in what you have learned and have firmly believed, knowing from whom you learned it and how from childhood you have known the sacred writings, which are able to make you wise unto salvation through faith in Christ Jesus.

2 Timothy 3.14–15

September 2

Popcorn

Popcorn is our snack of choice when watching ball games. We make it the old fashioned way—bacon grease in a large saucepan, bulk popcorn from a large plastic bag, and salt. Heat it over high heat, shaking the pan until it stops popping. The stuff out of the microwave cannot begin to compare.

We still wind up with what the industry calls "old maids," kernels that have not popped. Usually it's the kernel's fault, not the popper's.

They tell me that popcorn kernels are the only grain with a hard moisture-proof hull. That means that not only can moisture not get into the kernel, but the moisture inside the kernel cannot get out either. As you heat them, the steam inside increases until the pressure reaches 135 psi and the heat 180 degrees Celsius (356 for us non-scientists). At that point, the starch inside the kernel gelatinizes, becoming soft and pliable. When the hull explodes the steam expands the starch and proteins into the airy foam we know as popcorn.

I found two theories about old maids. One is that there is not enough moisture in the kernel to begin with; the other is that the hull develops a leak, acting as a release valve so that pressure cannot build enough for the "explosion." Either way, the kernels just sit there and scorch, becoming harder and drier as they cook.

Isn't that what happens when we undergo trials? Some of us use the experience to flower into a stronger, wiser, more pleasant personality. Others of us sit there and scorch in the heat until we dry up completely, no use for God or His people, let alone ourselves. The resulting bitterness is reflected in the cynical way we view the world, the way we continue to wallow in the misery of our losses, and the impenetrable barrier we raise whenever anyone tries to help us. As Israel said when they had forsaken God for idols and knew they would be punished, "Our bones have dried up, our hope is lost, we are clean cut off" (Ezek 37.11). When we refuse to seek God in our day of trouble, when we forget the blessings He has given us even though we deserved none, that is the result.

But God can help even the hopeless. He can bring us back from despair. He can make our hearts blossom in the heat of trial if we remember the lesson about priorities, about what really counts in the end. "If we have only hoped in Christ in this life, we are of all men most pitiable" (1 Cor 15.19), and that is exactly where we find ourselves if we allow anything in this life to steal our faith in God.

Trials are not pleasant; they are not meant to be. They are meant to create something new in us, something stronger and more spiritual. When, instead, we become hard and bitter, we are like the old maids in a bag of popcorn, and when the popcorn fizzles, it's the popcorn's fault.

For our light affliction, which is for the moment, works for us more and more exceedingly an eternal weight of glory; while we look not at the things which are seen, but at the things which are not seen: for the things which are seen are temporal; but the things which are not seen are eternal.

2 Corinthians 4.17–18

September 3

Starting Lineups

It's that time of year—college football season, overlapped and immediately followed by college basketball season. My family will be excitedly quoting stats from September through the first weekend in April—from the first kickoff of the year till the last tip-off.

Of course, I begin hearing about it during spring practice. Who is outplaying whom for which position? Who will the starters be? I bet if one of the players went to the coach and asked, "Do I have to be at every practice to be a starter? Do I have to do extra work in the weight room? Do I have to show up early and stay late shooting baskets?" that he needn't bother checking the list to see if he even *made* the team, much less if he made the starting line-up. And I bet those players do not have to be told so.

My parents recently celebrated their 60th wedding anniversary. I wonder how many they would have made if they had each said, "Now give me a list of what I have to do to be a satisfactory spouse. How many times do I need to remember your birthday? How many times do I need to remember our anniversary? How many times do I need to say I love you? How many times do I even need to be polite?" They never would have married in the first place.

What would my boss think if I showed up tomorrow and asked for a list of the minimum I need to do *not* to lose my job? Hmmm. I think I just lost it, especially since this is something I get *paid* to do.

Service is, by definition, voluntary. Otherwise it is forced labor. It does not expect repayment. It does not seek to know the minimum to get by. Asking that very question does not even cross its mind because it desires to do the most it possibly can, and by doing that often succeeds in doing even more. But it understands from the depth of its soul that even that is not enough.

Here is the problem for those who want to just get by: on God's team, everyone is a starter. Sitting on the bench is not an option. There will be no third-stringers, who never set foot on the field during a game, but still receive a championship ring. Only God's starters get the trophy, and with God you either make the starting lineup or you don't make the team at all.

Now, what was that question you had?

Now beloved, we are persuaded better things of you, and things that accompany salvation, though we thus speak; for God is not unrighteous to forget your work and the love which you showed toward his name, in that you ministered unto the saints and still do minister. And we desire that each one of you may show the same diligence unto the fullness of hope even to the end. That you be not sluggish, but imitators of those who, through faith and endurance, inherit the promises.

Hebrews 6.9–12

September 4

The Trap

If there is one thing the world has wrong about Jesus it's this: the idea that Jesus not only accepts us as sinners but allows us to keep on sinning because He is so kind and loving. And one of their favorite examples is the adulterous woman in John 8. Nonsense!

In the first place, Jesus' attitude toward sin is really just a side issue in this narrative. This is about the Pharisees trying to trap Jesus yet again, and His being able to avoid the snare yet again.

They brought Him a woman who had committed adultery "caught in the very act," they said. "The law of Moses says we should stone her. What do you think?"

Jesus first did what we ought to do 90 percent of the time. He kept His mouth shut. When your mouth is shut, you can think better. And this was an obvious trap, if you just thought about it. His silence also did this: they kept pressing Him until it must surely have become obvious to many who were listening exactly what their motive was as Jesus calmly stooped and wrote in the dirt.

And what was so obvious about the trap? He was approached while he was teaching, a time when there would be many to see and hear His downfall (they hoped), and whatever He had been teaching at the time would have been made ineffective. He was not asked what the Law said, but what He thought. Asking rabbis what they thought about scriptures was not unusual, but if anyone disagreed with Him, perhaps they would no longer listen to Him. They said she was caught in the very act, so where was the man? According to the Law they seemed so concerned about (*i.e.,* Deut 22.22), both should have been brought for judgment, so it was obvious that doing right was the last thing on their minds.

This was the trap: if He says that she deserves to die, He has pronounced the death sentence without the permission of the Roman authorities, which the Jews were not allowed to do, so He is in trouble with the powers that be. If He says otherwise, He is in trouble with the Jewish people who held Him to be a prophet and a righteous man, because He has disobeyed God's law.

But with one sentence, He turns the whole thing around on them. "He who is without sin, let him cast the first stone." I find it hard to believe that these men who would soon murder Him and within a short time afterward imprison, abuse, and murder His followers were at all stung by a guilty conscience. His few words remind them that *the Law* says *they* are to carry out the sentence because they were the witnesses, the ones who caught her "in the very act" (Deut 17.2–7). *The Law* says Jesus could not lift a hand against her until they cast the first stones. So now who is in the trap? Are they willing to follow the Law in spite of the Roman dictum against capital punishment?

And so Jesus once again stooped down to scribble in the dirt, and when He looked up, everyone was gone. And now, He could not accuse her, not because He condoned sin but because there were no witnesses; and He could not stone her, for the same reason. He would not have participated in a travesty of justice anyway, but now He simply could not, according to God's Law.

But what does He say to her? "Go thy way *and sin no more.*"

Jesus never has and never will accept sin. He will accept sinners, but only if they change their lives and begin to live righteously. Even then, when they slip and fall, He expects remorse, repentance, and growth that make those sins farther and farther apart. For each of us, when we lay our sin at His feet, the answer is the same: *Go thy way and sin no more.*

I bet that woman of so long ago did her best not to let Him down again. Can we do any less?

> *My little children, let no man lead you astray. He who does righteousness is righteous, even as he is righteous. He who does sin is of the devil, for the devil sinned from the beginning. To this end was the Son of God made manifest, that he might destroy the works of the devil.*
>
> 1 John 3.7–8

September 5

Labor Day

I've often thought that Keith is a frustrated farmer. If things had worked out differently, perhaps in another era even, that is exactly what he would have been. Working the ground suits him well because he cannot sit still and he doesn't think he has really worked unless he gets filthy in the process.

That garden of his has also done well by us. I do not know how we would have survived without it. Others with teenage boys spent nearly twice as much as we did on groceries and we ate as well or better than they, especially in the middle of summer. For weeks the table was loaded with platters of fresh corn and tomatoes, and bowls of whatever beans or peas were producing at the time, with other extras added in as they ripened—fried okra, cucumber salads, cherry tomato salads, and homemade pickles, fried, or scalloped or "parmagiana-ed" eggplant, peppers stuffed with ground beef, rice, onions, and herbs and baked in a homemade tomato sauce, squash stir-fried or layered in casseroles with cheese sauce and cracker crumbs, homemade biscuits slathered with blueberry jam, muscadine, scuppernong, and blackberry jellies, and anything else I could come up with to use up all the bounty and fill up all the men.

They say there are holidays between May and September. Really? I suppose there are days when Keith does not go to work, but those just mean more work in the garden. We spend Memorial Day snapping green beans and shelling peas, and putting the first of those in the freezer along with the last of the blueberries, and canning blueberry jam. The Fourth of July means corn shucking time—usually the second patch is in by then—and an assembly line in the kitchen putting up a couple dozen quarts. The rest of the summer "break" we spend with yet more "putting up" of pickles, limas, black-eyes, and zipper peas, tomatoes, tomato sauce, salsa, chili powder, herb vinegars, and finally, the muscadine jelly in August. Labor Day means catching up on all the things we had to let go when the fruits and vegetables came in, plus tilling the now spent and bedraggled garden under to help prepare the ground for next year.

We often missed outings, barbecues, and other summer events because of the garden work. Why? Because without that garden we would not have made it. What may be a hobby for some was a necessity for us. Times have been rough and it was the only way to feed our family well for the money we had. I did not buy a jar of tomatoes, tomato sauce, jelly, jam, salsa, or pickles for 20 years. You want to hear some stories? I can tell you how to make one chicken feed your family for four days.

Some of us want to treat our service to God like a hobby, like a garden we don't really need, we just go out and putter around in it when the notion suits us. We fail to realize that it is necessary to our survival. We have mistaken the fact that we have enough in this life to mean that we have enough for the next too, without all that commitment, service, and labor nonsense. So we go out once or twice a week and pull a weed, thinking that is all that is necessary, that God will supply the water and fertilizer for us and give us a bumper crop, which He will reap and can for us to enjoy some time in the future. Why, isn't that what grace is?

As long as Christianity is nothing more than a pleasant little pastime, and the church a nice little social club, we are more than happy to take up some time with it. But we will never reap any rewards until we treat it as a career necessary to keep us and our families alive.

Many of us are willing to throw money at practically any cause. It makes us feel good. What God demands is our time and our labor, things we Americans are often loath to give to anyone but ourselves. There are no holidays for Christians, not until you understand that the blessings a Christian receives make every day a holiday from the curse of sin and the chains of Satan.

> *Therefore, my beloved brothers, be steadfast, immovable, always abounding in the work of the Lord, knowing that in the Lord your labor is not in vain.*
>
> 1 Corinthians 15.58

September 6

Full-Grown

> *But solid food is for full-grown men, even those who by reason of use have their senses exercised to discern good and evil.* (Heb 5.14)

I was amazed to find out that "full-grown" is more often translated "perfect," at least in the ASV. That is ironic to me, because while I will quickly say, "I am not perfect," I would find myself a little miffed if I were called "spiritually immature." At my age? Surely I am a mature Christian by now.

So I looked up that Greek word and the places it is translated "perfect." It quickly became apparent that the word does not mean "sinless." While we understand that the meaning of a word varies according to its context in English, we seem to forget that when it comes to reading the Bible and talking about those Hebrew and Greek words. Yet, in any language, the meaning of a word is limited by its use. And so I read "mature" in every passage I found that word translated "perfect," and found out how to recognize a mature Christian. [When you read all these passages, be sure to read "spiritually mature" every time you see "perfect."]

The maturity level of a Christian is shown by how he treats his enemies (Matt 5.43–48), by how he controls his tongue (Jas 3.2), by how attached he is to his earthly possessions (Matt 19.21). A mature Christian is not easily deceived, not changeable from day to day, and speaks from a motivation of love, even when correcting someone, not from a desire for revenge, or from a feeling of arrogance, and certainly not to cause controversy for the sake of controversy (Eph 4.13–15). A mature Christian will endure, (James 1.4), and in fact, stand fully assured of his salvation (Col 4.12). When I look at those characteristics I can see that I have a way to go before I finally grow up, but at least I have some detailed areas to work on now instead of blindly aiming for some sort of vague idea of maturity or perfection.

One of the residents at the medical school recently told me that I did not look as old as my chart said I was. That was a nice moment in the day, one totally unexpected. Wouldn't if be awful, though, if he had said that I didn't *act* as old as I was? That is where the test comes—not in how long I have been a Christian, but in how much I have grown as one.

> *So we have come to know and to believe the love that God has for us. God is love, and whoever abides in love abides in God, and God abides in him. By this is love [made mature] with us, that we may have confidence in the day of judgment, because as he is so also are we in this world.*
>
> 1 John 4.16–17

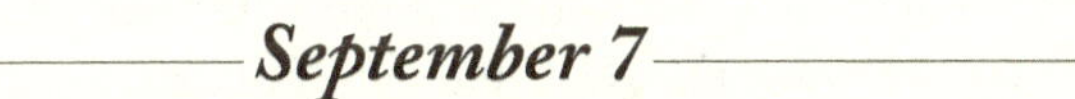

September 7

Product Shrinkage

I reached for a can of tuna the other day and absently read the label: Net Wt, 5 oz. I can remember, and actually have recipes calling for a seven-and-a half ounce can of tuna. I also remember one pound bags of coffee and seven ounce bars of soap.

What happened? The manufacturers attempted to camouflage rising prices by putting less product in similar size containers for the same price. That morning I must have strained a full ounce of water from that five ounce can of tuna. I needed nearly two cans to make the same amount as 30 years ago. Eventually of course, the prices did rise. I can remember tuna for 29 cents a can. Either way, we get less for more.

That makes it even more amazing that the most expensive commodity on earth, the one that cost the death of the Son of God, is free. "To the praise of the glory of his grace, which he freely bestowed on us in the Beloved" (Eph 1.6).

I can recall hearing only one sermon on grace when I was a child. I guess that is why I remember it. I can even remember the building I was sitting in. We have too long ignored the fact that we are saved by grace because we are so afraid someone will think we believe in something unscriptural. Grace is one of the most scriptural topics there is!

But now that I hear more about the grace of God, I am noticing a different problem—we limit the grace of God to forgiveness.

Grace is there to help us live our lives as well. Paul says that when he prayed to Christ to rid him of his "thorn in the flesh," Christ's answer was, "My grace is sufficient" (2 Cor 12.9). In other words, I will help you bear this burden.

Christ went on to say, "For my power is made perfect in weakness." As long as I try to handle things alone I will never make it. But when I make myself weak, allowing Christ to take care of me, I can handle anything. "Therefore," Paul adds, "I will boast all the more gladly of my weaknesses, so that the power of Christ may rest upon me."

And there lies our problem: we so often will not let Him help us. We refuse, in the popular parlance, "to turn it over to God." We keep trying to help ourselves to the point that we do not even see the help He has offered. If it does not match our wants, if it does not look like the help we have envisioned, if it still involves bearing any burden at all, it can't be grace, and so we miss out, and have only ourselves to blame.

God says He will help. What else is it but grace that promises, "God is faithful, who will not suffer you to be tempted above that you are able; but will with the temptation make also the way of escape, that you may be able to endure it" (1 Cor 10.13)? If I do not endure, if I do not overcome, it is because I do not have faith in the grace of God. And that will have a huge impact because if I cannot trust it to help me through this life, how can I trust it to forgive me?

If we are willing to accept it, God will not hold back this gift. He will not decrease the amount of grace He gives. He will, in fact, increase it as we have need. *My grace is sufficient.*

Or maybe it's just that God's grace in any amount is far more powerful than any need we can ever imagine.

> *If the* Lord *had not been my help, my soul would soon have lived in the land of silence. When I thought, "My foot slips," your steadfast love, O* Lord, *held me up. When the cares of my heart are many, your consolations cheer my soul.*
>
> Psalm 94.17–19

September 8

The Milk Cow

In a couple of places where we have lived, a local farmer has allowed Keith to milk his cow. The farmer furnished the cow and the feed, while Keith furnished the labor, and we split the milk. Our cut was usually a gallon a day, which was good with two boys who drank it by the quart. I also used the cream to make our own butter. There is nothing quite like a Southern pound cake made with homemade butter, homemade sour cream, and eggs fresh out of the chicken that morning. Our mashed potatoes were so creamy you might as well have troweled them onto your hips, and the homemade ice cream was so rich it had flecks of butter in it.

When a dairy cow needs milking, it needs milking, period. Keith was away overnight once, not due back till late afternoon the next day. All I could think about was that poor cow. Having nursed babies, I understood her pain. Surely I could take care of this, I thought, and help both of them.

This cow was known to be a kicker. She had only recently gotten used to Keith, finally allowing him to milk her while she ate feed from the trough. I knew the drill, so I got a bucket of feed and headed for the corral. I also knew her penchant for kicking, so I put on Keith's jacket and hat before I left the house. I thought I would look and smell like him and she would never know the difference.

As I headed for the stall she saw me coming, and began a slow walk in my direction. I made my first mistake. Keith always called her with the same phrase every day, so I did too, lowering my voice as much as possible. The cow stopped and looked at me across the fence railing. For a few minutes I thought she had me, but I held up the bucket so the scent of the feed reached her on the breeze, and she started walking again.

After that I kept my mouth shut. I simply poured the feed into the trough and waited for her to put her head down. Then I reached out and started milking. Instantly her head was up again, and she looked over her shoulder at me. I stepped back, keeping a careful eye on her hind legs, ready to jump if she looked like she was even thinking about kicking.

For a long moment we stood there eying one another. Finally, she gave a snort and shake of the head. The jig was up, as they say. For all the world it looked like she was saying, "I really need this right now, so go ahead. But don't think I'm not on to you." She put her head back in the trough, and I began milking again. It was a compromise. She gave me just enough to get the pressure off her aching udder, but not enough so I would think she had not seen through my disguise. A quart later, she stepped back from the trough, and I took both the hint and the milk into the house. When Keith got home, she gladly let him finish the job.

Isaiah had a lot to say about this same point. If a cow—a dumb unreasoning animal—can know its master, why can't we so-called intelligent human beings recognize ours? If a donkey knows where to get its sustenance, why can't we figure out who we must depend upon?

Have you ever seen a cow path? Cows learn when it is time to head for the barn, and they take the shortest route every evening at the same time, following one another down the path, until it is beaten from their hooves and so obvious anyone could follow it. I look around our world every day and marvel at how many smart people don't seem to have a clue where the path is, and what's more, brag about it. Then I look at God's people and cry for all the ones who claim to be His children, but act the same way.

Hear, O heavens, and give ear, O earth; for Jehovah has spoken: I have nourished and brought up children, and they have rebelled against me. The ox knows his owner, and the ass his master's crib; but Israel does not know, my people do not consider.

Isaiah 1.2–3

The Theory of Relativity

Do you want to know what the word "relative" means? Just follow me around for awhile and listen to the doctors.

Many years ago we moved a thousand miles and I went to a new ophthalmologist for the first time. Unfortunately, my file did not make it before the appointment. The doctor looked at my eyes and the contacts I was wearing at the time and shook his head. "Who fit these? He obviously doesn't know what he's doing."

A week later I returned to his office. He had received the file and read it through, noting the nanophthalmic eyes and the incredibly steep corneas. "Your doctor is a genius," he pronounced. "I don't know how he did this. You shouldn't even be able to wear contact lenses, but had he not been able to do it, you would be blind by now." Nothing about my eyes changed, but the doctor's opinion certainly did.

Then there was the difference between the lens implant surgeon in Cincinnati and my glaucoma surgeon. The first considered the lens implant almost a failure because my nanophthalmus had skewed the formulas and I still could not see well. The second considered it a success because I could still see at all.

Only a few weeks ago, I had a visit with the retina guru after a "retina event" as they called it in the glaucoma hall. The tech there declared it impossible for the doctor to be able to see into "these tiny little pupils. You will most certainly need to be dilated." (This, in spite of the fact that my chart is stamped in large, red, capital letters DO NOT DILATE.) The retina doctor knew better than to dilate someone with my symptoms and overruled her. Later, when the glaucoma doctor looked into my eyes, he said, "What are they complaining about? These are nice big pupils." Of course, he has been dealing with them for years.

You see, good for me is bad for you, at least at the ophthalmologist's office.

Many things are like that. If you're from the north, you think Florida winters are warm and springs are hot. If you are from Florida, you think the northeast is arid. You would probably turn to dust the minute you walked into Arizona. And because we understand the concept of relativity, we have a tendency not to see the awfulness of sin, particularly our own. I'm not bad, we think. I haven't murdered anyone, I haven't stolen from anyone. I don't lie—well, at least not big black lies. And there we go excusing ourselves because we can always find someone worse than we are. Paul, in another context, mentions those who "measure themselves by one another and compare themselves with one another," concluding that they are "without understanding" (2 Cor 10.12). We are too, if we think we can get to Heaven by comparing our lives to anything other than God's standard

Nothing is relative when it comes to sin. When we think we can decide which sins need to be repented of and which don't, when we think we can choose a standard of our own, whether a person or a personal credo, when we think we are the ones who get to draw the line, God will not tolerate even what we consider the tiniest of sins. To paraphrase Gertrude Stein, a sin by any other name will still rise as a stench in the nostrils of God.

There is nothing relative about sin. It is a theory that will always prove false.

For whoever shall keep the whole law yet stumble in one point, he has become guilty of it all. For he who said, Do not commit adultery, also said, Do not kill. Now if you do not commit adultery but you do kill, you have become a transgressor of the law. So speak and so do as men who are to be judged by a perfect law of liberty.

James 2.10–12

September 10

Pmr Lru Pgg

No, that is not a typo. Well, it is actually—a typo on purpose. That is what happens when you try to type "One Key Off" with your hands exactly one key off from the correct starting position. Even when you make the right moves with the correct hands you get something that makes no sense, that isn't even pronounceable.

How many times do we do that with the Bible? We start studying in the middle of things, with the most difficult things, with things that do not even apply to our lives. What do we get? A big mess.

If one fundamental fact is wrong, you create a long line of false doctrine—and many through the years have done just that.

If one step in logic is left out, you find yourself believing something so ridiculous, you may eventually lose your faith altogether when you come to your senses, or worse, actually come to believe it so emphatically that you take others down the drain with you. How else do some of these strange cults get their start?

If you get bogged down in things far removed from what you really need to get through life, how will you ever grow?

Isn't it odd that simply being *one key away* can make such a huge difference? Be careful where you put your time studying the scriptures. Match one passage with another. Anytime your interpretation of something does not jive with another scripture, my guess is that you are at least one key off, maybe more.

Start with the simple, start with what you need to believe to be in Christ. Then move to what you need to live your life every day. Worry about Revelation and Zechariah a little further down the road. Find someone you can trust to help you. Elders come to mind, and good Bible class teachers. But whatever you do, be careful where you put your faith. One step away from the truth is not a good place to be.

Hold the pattern of sound words which you heard from me, in faith and love which is in Jesus Christ.

2 Timothy 1.13

September 11

Waiting Rooms

I wish I had a dollar for every hour I have sat in waiting rooms in the past five years, especially at the eye clinic. I had a 3:30 appointment once, and finally saw the doctor at 7:00. Then there was the time we discovered that I needed an emergency procedure. My appointment had been at 11:00. I was finally pronounced fit to leave at 5:30.

The shortest amount of time I have ever spent at the clinic is two hours. Sometimes the doctor is overbooked because he has critical patients who simply must be seen that day; I have been one of those patients. Sometimes he runs late because an emergency arrives that must be worked in; I have been one of those emergencies. I can hardly complain when someone does it to me.

Yet, even the night I had to wait until 7:00, I never doubted that I would be seen. I have never worried that someone would forget I was there and the doctor would leave.

It makes no sense to doubt God either. Sometimes we must wait a long time for the answer to a prayer, but it will come. Sometimes we must endure a trial far longer than we ever expected, but He has not forsaken us. How long did those faithful Jews wait for their Messiah? I have never waited that long for God, have you?

The world thinks that because the promised second coming has not happened in 2,000 years it won't happen at all. They think that proves God doesn't even exist, completely ignoring the evidence of His existence all around them. That makes about as much sense as me deciding my doctor doesn't exist because I have been sitting here waiting for three hours now, and my fellow patient in the next seat has waited four.

My doctor is worth the wait.

If ever anyone was worth a longer wait, it's God.

Knowing this first, that in the last days mockers shall come with mockery, walking after their own lusts, and saying, Where is the promise of his coming? For, from the day that the fathers fell asleep, all things continue as they were from the beginning of the creation. For this they willfully forget, that there were heavens from of old, and an earth compacted out of water and amidst water, by the word of God; by which means the world that then was, being overflowed with water, perished: but the heavens that now are, and the earth, by the same word have been stored up for fire, being reserved against the day of judgment and destruction of ungodly men. But forget not this one thing, beloved, that one day is with the Lord as a thousand years, and a thousand years as one day. The Lord is not slack concerning his promise, as some count slackness; but is longsuffering to you-ward, not wishing that any should perish, but that all should come to repentance.

2 Peter 3.3–9

September 12

Castles in the Sky

Have you ever daydreamed about a perfect life? I suppose most of us have. Enough that mountains of money have been saved so that at retirement couples could live the life they have always dreamed of. Are they really happy? I have this theory: if you cannot be happy living a normal everyday life no matter what your circumstances, you will never be happy living your idea of a perfect life either.

Take a minute now and jot down your idea of a perfect life. Be as specific as possible. Since you are just wishing anyway, you might as well make it good.

Now think about this. As our Creator, God knows what would make us happy. Too often we treat living by His standards as living a miserable existence with no fun allowed at all. But when you think about it, He should know best, shouldn't He? In fact, when He made man, He created a perfect place, a perfect life, a perfect home. Take a look at the Garden of Eden. What did He give His newly created children?

He gave them a beautiful garden that furnished their food and delighted their eyes. I doubt they had truffles, either vegetable or chocolate. I know they did not have *pate de fois gras* or chateaubriand. But they had plenty—and it was certainly organic! (Gen 1.29).

He gave them each other. Not one man with a different woman every night, or one woman with several men. He did not make two men or two women, but one man for one woman for one lifetime (2.24).

He gave them work to do. What?! A perfect place meant having to work? Exactly. Not an all consuming career, but productive work tending the garden that fed them. Not difficult work, as was promised after the fall, but something that fulfilled man's need to pass the time and stay physically fit (2.15).

I assume He gave them some sort of house, but do you realize it is never mentioned in Genesis? Evidently God's notion of paradise for man did not include having a dream house that cost more in taxes and upkeep in a year than most third world families make in a lifetime.

And best of all, He gave them His fellowship. It seems to have been His habit to walk and talk with His children in the cool of the day (3.8).

Now look at your list. Does it match God's list at all? Maybe we need to adjust our thinking—seems to me I have to do a lot of that. I have another theory: if my list is not a whole lot like God's, maybe I won't enjoy Heaven either. Maybe I won't even be allowed to find out.

For he who would love life and see good days, let him refrain his tongue from evil and his lips that they speak no guile; and let him turn away from evil and do good. Let him seek peace and pursue it. For the eyes of the Lord are upon the righteous, and his ears unto their supplication. But the face of the Lord is upon them that do evil.

> *He who has an ear, let him hear what the Spirit says to the churches. To him who overcomes, to him will I give to eat of the tree of life, which is in the Paradise of God.*
>
> 1 Peter 3.10–12; Revelation 2.7

September 13

A Rude Awakening

I was sound asleep when it started. I knew I was asleep but somehow I carried on a regular conversation with myself.

"You are too asleep to do anything about this. Even if you woke Keith up, he could not hear you. Maybe you could point." So I whacked him across the chest with my left arm. He sat straight up in bed shouting, "Hunh? What's happening?" He turned on the light.

By then it had started. I was still asleep, but I was bouncing rhythmically and grunting, "Uh—uh—uh" with every bounce. He thought I was having convulsions and about to die.

"What's wrong? What's wrong? *What's wrong?!*"

I was *still* asleep and could not answer him. Even if I had been awake, I probably could not have said anything. It hurt that badly. Finally I managed to point (still sleeping), and somehow—being married for 37 years maybe?—he figured it out. I had a charley horse. But which leg? He just grabbed the one nearest and started pushing against my heel and rubbing my calf muscle. He got the right leg—actually the left leg—but it *was* the right one.

Finally I woke up. I lifted my toes and pushed against his hand. Five minutes later it was over with, but I still had a knot in my calf muscle the next morning and it took 15 minutes before I could walk flat-footed.

Charley horses must be the worst pain possible for something that is so harmless. They will not kill you—you just wish they would for a minute or two. Then you realize that it will soon be over and everything will be fine.

That is the way the early Christians dealt with trials and persecution. Peter says, "Now for a little while, if necessary, you have been put to grief in many trials." He recognized that they were grievous, they did hurt, but they were only "for a little while." After telling his readers that they would suffer, the Hebrew writer says, "For you have need of patience, that, having done the will of God, you may receive the promise. For *yet a very little while,* He who comes shall come, and shall not tarry" (Heb 10.36–37).

Sometimes that grief is tremendous. It certainly was for those Christians. We all recognize that we must die. We know that one spouse will, in most cases, go before the other. That is normal. We all know that we will bury our parents. That is the natural order. It still hurts, but we understand it. When the unnatural happens, it hurts even more. I have known women who dealt with widowhood in their 30s and 40s. My own in-laws buried a ten-year-old daughter whom cancer had stolen from them. I cannot imagine the pain. I know one good sister who had to endure both of those things—a widow at 40 and an only child, a daughter, who died unexpectedly a long time before she did.

How did they make it? They realized that these trials are transitory. They do not last. That trite old saying is trite because it is true, "This too will pass." Only one thing lasts—the joy we will have as we exist forever with our Father and Savior. Hang on to that hope.

> *Blessed be the God and Father of our Lord Jesus Christ, who according to his great mercy begat us again unto a living hope by the resurrection of Jesus Christ from the dead, unto an inheritance incorruptible, and undefiled, that fades not away, reserved in heaven for you, who by the power of God are guarded through faith unto a salvation ready to be revealed in the last time. Wherein ye greatly rejoice, though now for a little while, if necessary, you have been put to grief in manifold trials, that the proof of your faith, being more precious than gold that perishes though it is proved by fire, may be found unto praise and glory and honor at the revelation of Jesus Christ: whom not having seen you love; on whom, though now you see him not, yet believing, you rejoice greatly with joy unspeakable and full of glory: receiving the end of your faith, the salvation of your souls.*
>
> 1 Peter 1.3–9

September 14

Stupid Is As Stupid Does

I have been thinking about that old saying the past week. I think it means that if I don't want people to think I'm stupid, I should stop acting that way. I thought about it when that snake came back the fourth time.

I looked out one afternoon across the birdfeeder built right up against the house to the azalea bushes just beyond it. One limb looked a little odd. I must have stared at it for ten minutes before Keith noticed, and looked too. "There's a garter snake in the bushes," he said. I had thought so, but could not see it clearly enough to be sure. Finally after three years, a snake had figured out that someone had put an all-you-can-eat bird buffet out for him, and he was sitting there just waiting for his meal to light.

We did not want to hurt the snake. A near relative of his had lived under the house for a few years and kept our rodent population down to something we could handle. We hoped he would do the same, but that did not mean he could go after my birds.

So Keith put on some gloves and knocked him out of the bush. Magdi was on him before we could stop her, but Keith yelled and took the snake away from her, flinging it over the north fence. We were not certain it would have survived her vicious shake—she treats them like a bull whip and usually breaks their backs with only a couple of cracks. Not to worry. Two days later I looked out and there was the snake again.

This time Keith went out with an old rake handle and knocked him off the limb. Magdi knew what was up this time, but despite her increased vigilance, the snake slithered away under the steps and we could not get it to come out.

Until two days after that. I was getting ready to leave that morning and looked out to check the feeder and there he was again. Not being as fearless as Keith, I stood way back and whacked that bush so hard I broke the branches, but once again the snake got away from Magdi.

The fourth time he did not wait two days. He was back in one, and I was home alone again. I grabbed the pole and set off for the bird feeder. I stood there for several minutes thinking he had left because I could not find him through the limbs. Suddenly I thought to step back and look up, and there he was about a foot higher in the bush than he had ever been before. But that meant that when I knocked him out he had farther to fall and must have been a little more addled because Magdi got him before he could crawl away. This time she shook until that snake was a lifeless rubber hose. I could almost hear his spine cracking as she slung it about.

I am sorry about that. I will be sorrier this winter if I have a mouse or two in the house. But really—how long does it take some snakes to learn?

Are we any smarter? How long does it take for us to learn? I have seen Christians put themselves in spiritual danger over and over and over all my life. "I can handle it," they say, despite the Biblical warnings to flee, to abstain, to be watchful; despite the things God lists in black and white as the biggest dangers to our soul—wealth, power, sexual sins, anger, pride, and the tongue. We all think we are different; that we won't be tripped up and fall.

I have seen it happen too many times to ever think it could be different for me. If we choose to defy the odds, sooner or later we will be knocked "out of our tree," and Satan will jump on us and shake us until our spiritual back is broken and we can no longer stand against him.

Stupid is as stupid does.

Now these things happened to them as an example, but they were written down for our instruction, on whom the end of the ages has come. Therefore let anyone who thinks that he stands take heed lest he fall.

1 Corinthians 10.11–12

September 15

Genes

We are now in the middle of jumping through all the insurance hoops to make sure that Silas has not inherited more than his grandmother's neonatal milk allergy. I look into those big blue eyes that sparkle so when he smiles, trying to convince myself that they look more like his grandfather's than mine. Even if they looked exactly like mine, odds are he did not inherit the condition. He may be 100 times more likely to have it than any other baby, but that still makes it a one in a million chance. It happened that way with his uncle. The minute they put him in my arms and I saw his eyes my heart froze, but seven months later we knew he had only inherited the look, not the problem. Still, I would feel horrible if I passed this on to poor little Silas.

There are worse things to pass on to one's children and grandchildren:

> And [Jehoram] walked in the way of the kings of Israel, as did the house of Ahab; *for he had the daughter of Ahab* to wife: and he did that which was evil in the sight of Jehovah. …[Ahaziah] also walked in the ways of the house of Ahab; *for his mother was his counselor to do wickedly*. …And Joram said, Make ready. And they made ready his chariot. And Joram king of Israel… went out to meet Jehu. …And… he said, Is it peace, Jehu? And he answered, What peace, so long as *the whoredoms of your mother Jezebel*… are so many? (2 Chron 21.6; 22.3; 2 Kgs 9.21–22).

Are you familiar with this narrative in the Bible? Start in 1 Kings 16 and read through 2 Kings 11 some night when you want a really good story. It is a little of everything: a family saga; an action-adventure story; a political thriller. It has a villainess of unspeakable cruelty, an underground movement, a mole in the hierarchy, and a hero who saves the day. All of this was brought about by the evil influence Ahab and Jezebel had on their children and grandchildren.

Perhaps the worst of the bunch was Athaliah, their daughter, who reached the point that she could order the murder of "all the seed royal," among them her own grandchildren. I have always thought this woman's crimes especially heinous but now, having held a grandchild in my arms, I know she must have reached a level of moral depravity nearly unheard of, at least among God's people. That is what her parents passed on to her, for the next generation always sees our inconsistencies, the line we will not cross because of the inhibiting baggage we have brought to the table. They see that inconsistency and erase the line, taking what we have taught them to its logical end.

I cannot control whether Silas will inherit my physical condition; but I can control my influence on his spiritual condition. I can set an example of faith that will reinforce his in moments of trial. I can set an example of endurance to bolster his ability to overcome. I can show him how a mature Christian behaves, even when people are less than accommodating. Those things I can do, if I will.

Having children is great motivation to be and do better. Because the end may be in sight and priorities have become clearer, having grandchildren should be the best motivation yet.

I thank God, whom I serve from my forefathers in a pure conscience, how unceasing is my remembrance of you in my supplications, night and day longing to see you, remembering your tears, that I may be filled with joy; having been reminded of the unfeigned faith that is in you; which dwelt first in your grandmother Lois, and your mother Eunice; and, I am persuaded, in you also.

2 Timothy 1.3–5

September 16

A Fine Whine

Americans used to admire "the strong, silent type"—not someone who was uncommunicative, but someone who endured the hardships of life without complaint, a man who always kept a sane head on his shoulders when things got rough. I don't know what has happened, but nowadays strength seems to be measured by how loudly a man can rant and rave about his lot in life and anyone he can blame for it.

Our culture has made whining a world class skill. No, we do not call it whining, but that's what it is. We whine about our jobs, about our neighbors, about our families, about our health, about the government—they give all our hard-earned money to other people, but let them cut one of our entitlement programs and we whine even louder about that. We whine about rising costs, about having to wait in line, about our lifestyles, about the driver in the car in front of us. We whine about the church, about the singing, about the length of sermons, about the preacher, about the elders, and about how hot or cold the building always is. Sometimes I feel like getting out Nathan's violin and accompanying the dirge. At least it would be easier on the ears—and I don't even know how to play!

Look at Numbers 11, the classic example of complaining in the Old Testament. Every place it says weep, weeping, or wept, substitute whine, whining, or whined. That is probably a perfect word for what was going on. Look at Moses' reaction in verse 15. Please allow me to paraphrase: "If this is the way it's going to be, then do me a favor, Lord, and kill me. I can't take it any more." Why anyone would think that whining is a measure of strength is beyond me.

Whining impugns God's goodness. Think of all the things God does for us and gives to us, and still we whine. "Blessed is the man whom you choose and cause to approach unto you, that he may dwell in your courts." How can we complain when we have that blessing? "We shall be satisfied with the goodness of your house, your holy Temple" (Psa 65.4). "Because your lovingkindness is better than life, I will praise you. So I will bless you while I live; I will lift up my hands in your name. My soul shall be satisfied as with marrow and fatness, and my mouth shall praise you with joyful lips" (Psa 63.3–5). A far cry from whining, isn't it?

I may think that I am above the effects of my culture, that I am not influenced by the rampant materialism that often motivates this whining. All I need to do is make a list of things I consider "necessities" to find out otherwise. All I need to do is keep track of all the times I complain during the day to become thoroughly ashamed. God destroyed those who whined against Moses. Why will he accept my murmuring? The poorest among us is wealthier than 90 percent of the rest of the world. Imagine that. And far beyond that, life is good, if for no other reason than I have a Savior. In fact, do I need any other reason?

But even if you should suffer for righteousness' sake, blessed are you; and fear not their fear, neither be troubled, but sanctify in your hearts Christ as Lord.

Neither murmur as some of them murmured and perished by the Destroyer.

1 Peter 3.14–15; 1 Corinthians 10.10

September 17

No Dictionary Needed

I came across a passage a few weeks ago that suddenly spoke to me. I must have read it hundreds of times, but for the first time I really saw it.

Lydia heard the gospel and was baptized. Paul and Silas were traveling and obviously had no place to stay so she said, "If you have judged me to be faithful to the Lord, come into my house, and abide there. And she constrained us" (Acts 16.15).

Lydia was a new Christian. She lived away from her hometown Thyatira. On her own she had discovered a place of prayer by the riverside where she met with other women to worship God. Now Paul and Silas have come along and taught her about the new way, which she accepted with an open heart.

There is a lot there to be admired and spoken about, but consider something with me this morning. She had many things in her way, including this: What Paul and Silas were teaching was obviously not popular among the majority of the people who formed her customer base—they wound up in the Philippian prison as a matter of fact.

But despite her needs as a new Christian, one in less than optimum circumstances, she begged them to let *her* be the one to serve. It was not, "Come show me how wonderful this new way really is by doing as much for me as possible." Instead it was, "What can I do now that I am a Christian? If you don't allow me to serve your needs, you must not think I am really faithful," and with that reasoning she practically forced Paul and Silas to accept her service.

Imagine if we all had that attitude. Imagine if, instead of complaining because "the preacher didn't come see me in the hospital," our attitudes were, "I am so glad to be well again so *I* can help those folks who need me." Imagine if, instead of whining that "the sermon is too long and the singing is boring, and the prayers make me fall asleep," we said, "I wonder if there is any way I can help those men who serve so well and so faithfully." Imagine if, instead of griping about the dead church we had the bad luck to be a part of, we spent our time actively searching for those who need help, and wore ourselves out serving them. Imagine if the church were full of Lydias, instead of people like me (and you?).

Even a new Christian with very little knowledge can do what she did. Faithfulness is not a matter of how much you know; it is a matter of trusting God in whatever circumstances you find yourself and joyfully and willingly serving others. *If you have judged me faithful, allow me to serve you.* When will we get it through our heads that the modern doctrine of Easy Believism did not exist when James wrote,

> *If a brother or sister be naked and in lack of daily food, and one of you say unto them, Go in peace, be warmed and filled; and yet you give them not the things needful to the body; what does it profit? Even so faith, if it has not works, is dead in itself. Yes, a man will say, You have faith, and I have works: show me your faith apart from your works, and I by my works will show you my faith.* (Jas 2.15–18)

No, he was not writing to those who wear the name of Jesus while rejecting His lordship, *James was writing to Christians!*

It doesn't take a great scholar to figure out the true definition of faithfulness, just a Christian who has truly been converted to the greatest Servant ever known.

September 18

Comfort Food

Do a little research and you will find that the term "comfort food" was added to Webster's Dictionary in 1972. It refers to foods that are typically inexpensive, uncomplicated, and require little or no preparation at all; foods which usually bring pleasant associations with childhood, just as an old song can remind one of a long ago romance, or a smell can instantly bring back situations both good and bad.

Comfort foods vary from culture to culture, but in our country usually include things like macaroni and cheese, mashed potatoes, fried chicken, ice cream, peanut butter, and brownies. Folks tend to use comfort foods to provide familiarity and emotional security, or to reward themselves. It's not surprising that many of these are loaded with carbohydrates which can produce a soporific effect as well—comfort food followed closely by the comfort of sleep.

Since it became fashionable I have tried to figure out my own list of comfort foods. Here is my problem: my mother was such a good cook and so adventurous, trying many recipes day after day, that I never had one dish often enough to form an attachment to it. One cooking magazine actually runs the column, "My Mother's Best Meal." I could not possibly pick one. I would need a whole page to list them. So for me it isn't comfort food, it's comfort cooking. When my mind is in turmoil, I cook all day long, trying, I suppose, to recreate the warm, homey, safe atmosphere of my mother's kitchen.

Comfort food works for the soul too. The best part is, you don't have to be a good cook. You just open the word of God and feast. You turn on the water of life and drink to your heart's content. You produce the fruit of the lips in praise to God whenever and wherever you desire. You gather with your brothers and sisters and wallow in a fellowship that has absolutely nothing to do with coffee and donuts.

You can get fatter and fatter with all that spiritual nourishment and still be healthy. In fact, in this context at least, the skinnier you are, the sicker, the sadder, and the weaker you are.

So grab a spoon today, and everyday, and dig in.

Work not for the food which perishes, but for the food which abides unto eternal life, which the Son of man shall give unto you: for him the Father, even God, has sealed.

John 6.27

September 19

Joint-Heirs

Being also ***joint-heirs*** *of the grace of life.* (1 Pet 3.7)

If husbands and wives are supposed to be partners on this journey to Heaven, we sometimes have a funny way of showing it.

One of the most amazing examples Sarah set is not one we often talk about, and when we do, we miss what to me is the most important part. Peter tells us that she called her husband "lord" (1 Pet 3.6). Today that might translate better "sir," but notice the only example Peter had of this: Genesis 18.12, where she is in a tent, away from the three "men" and talking "within herself." When she realizes these men heard her when they normally should not have been able to, she realizes who they are and becomes afraid. Do you get it? When she called him "lord," she was not speaking to Abraham, but about him to herself, behind his back, so to speak, where he could not have heard her if he had wanted to.

Now here is the point ladies, how do we speak about our husbands when they are not around? Can my neighbors list his faults by now as well as I can? Can my children? Can my co-workers relate every mistake he's ever made because I make sure I talk about them? Does anyone who has anything to do with me wonder why I married such a jerk in the first place because that is the impression I have given them about this man I claim to love? I have seen women, as the Proverb writer warns, tear down their houses with their own hands, or in this case, their own mouths.

Do we even stop to consider the pictures others must have of our marriages by the things they see and hear? No one should ever have to endure the embarrassment of standing in my kitchen while I berate my husband in front of them. Do I ridicule and complain about his efforts to support me as well as the gifts he gives me? Do I constantly correct every little detail—even those that do not make a whit's worth of difference—when he tries to tell a story? Do my friends know that I secretly do things he disapproves of? We are not the daughters of Sarah when we act this way.

But Peter does not let the husbands off the hook either. In the same chapter, he tells them, "Dwell with your wives according to knowledge, giving honor to the woman" (v 7). There is nothing honorable about the label, "my old lady." And here is a clue for you: women do not generally appreciate male humor. It is one thing to be able to laugh at yourself, but another thing entirely to have someone constantly make a laughingstock of you. If she asks you not to tell a certain story yet again, or call her by a certain nickname in front of people, then don't—not if you honor her.

I have seen too many a man use up the prime of a woman's life, then somehow think he has "outgrown" her. More likely, his head has outgrown him. But one of the most common complaints I hear is, "She let herself go." That always translates to gaining some weight. You know how she gained that weight? Fixing you the meat and potatoes meals you insist on and carrying your children. Excuse me if the brag that you can still wear the same size jeans as you did in high school does not impress me—the only reason you can do that is you are fastening them six inches lower! No wonder Malachi called such treatment "treachery" (Mal 2.15).

What in the world do we think we are telling people about our marriages and about ourselves when we engage in such insults? After all, we do not live in a culture of arranged marriages—we *chose* our partners. In actuality, we are insulting ourselves.

Peter tells husbands that their treatment of their wives will affect whether their prayers are heard. I have no difficulty believing the same is true for a wife's treatment of her husband. I don't know about you, but I need God to hear my prayers. I ask for forgiveness regularly and it's the only way I know I can get it. How about you?

> *For this cause shall a man leave his father and mother and shall cleave to his wife, and the two shall become one flesh. This mystery is great. …Nevertheless do each one of you love his own wife even as himself, and let the wife see that she reverence her husband.*
>
> Ephesians 5.31–33

September 20

In Case of Emergency

Keith is a firearms instructor for the State Department of Corrections. Whenever he has a class on the range and they run out of ammunition, he makes them pop open their revolvers, allowing the casings to scatter wherever they fall, snap in a speed loader, and start shooting again. Any who empty the casings into their hands get a stern lecture. Why? Because in a state of emergency, you will do what you practice. After gunfights, they have found dead policemen with bullet casings in their hands; men who, on the practice range, took the time to pour the empties into their hands so they wouldn't have to crawl around picking them up later, so that is what they did under pressure, and those few precious seconds when the bullets were flying cost them their lives. There is always time after practice to pick up the brass.

Whenever an emergency arises, whenever you find yourself under extreme pressure, you will always do what you have trained yourself to do.

You will not say, "Oh, I shouldn't take the time to pick up these casings right now. There are bad guys out there trying to kill me so I need to reload as quickly as possible." You will simply do what you have always done. It's why schools and workplaces run fire drills, why the flight attendants tell you how to operate those dangling masks every time you get on a plane, and why the various branches of the armed forces run drills over and over and over.

Why is it important to memorize scriptures, to sing hymns during the day, to talk to God as if He were right there with you all day long? Why is it important to train yourself not to use foul language even when no one else is around, not to lose your temper over even the smallest matters, not to develop dependencies other than God when you are feeling down, not to return evil for evil, even when you are just driving down the road? Because when life's pressures rise, you will do what you practice.

If you curse in private, you will curse for all to hear; but if you pray at the drop of a hat whenever something does not go well, that is what you will do instead. If you have trained yourself to turn the other cheek at the least little grievance, you will more easily do so with the larger ones. If you have filled yourself with the scriptures, those precious words will spring to mind and bail you out of temptation.

In case of emergency, you will do what you have trained yourself to do. Is it time for a spiritual fire drill?

> *With my whole heart have I sought you: Oh let me not wander from your commandments. Your word have I laid up in my heart, that I might not sin against you. Blessed art thou, O Jehovah: Teach me your statutes. With my lips have I declared all the ordinances of your mouth. I have rejoiced in the way of your testimonies, As much as in all riches. I will meditate on your precepts, and have respect unto your ways. I will delight myself in your statutes: I will not forget your word.*
>
> Psalm 119.10–16

September 21

Discerning Taste

If you were to ask the boys what their dog's name was, they would name Bart, the big yellow lab. Bart was born in our dog pen when they were 10 and 12, and all three of them grew up together. Eleven years later, when we finally had to put him down, it was a sad day for all of us, but Lucas put it most succinctly when I asked how he was. "Today my dog died." It did not matter that we already had another one. It did not matter that we had one when he was three, who lived five years, nor did it matter that we had Bart's mother nearly as long as we had him. Bart was the one they played with, the one they rolled around on the ground with, the one they hiked through the woods with, the one they lay their heads on in the field when they were gazing up into the sky at the clouds, talking, dreaming, and planning their lives.

Bart was a good dog, sweet and lovable, and I knew my boys were safe with him. But he was hands down the dumbest dog we ever had. Even his mother (his dog-mother, not me!) got a kick out of tricking him.

Once we laid out a pan of rib bones for them both. If Bart saw anything come out of the house in our hands, he immediately thought it was good food, and usually wolfed it down before he could possibly have tasted it. His mother was well aware of that. As soon as we laid down that pan, she stood up with her ears pricked, and started running down the drive barking. Bart, of course, fell in step beside her and, being bigger with longer legs, soon outran her, heading for the gate. His mother stopped and watched to make sure he was still going all out to get the nonexistent boogey man, then calmly walked back to the pan of ribs. By the time Bart figured it out and came back, Mom had had her fill and she left the remainder for her "little boy" to finish up, which he did in about 30 seconds. He never really seemed to understand what she had done to him, even though we all stood there laughing until our sides nearly split open.

That was Bart for you. Once I threw out some sweet potato skins just to see what would happen. He gulped down three of the four before he realized he didn't like them and quit. Lucas, who could go through a quart jar of my dill pickles in two sittings, once poured the leftover brine into a bowl and took it outside. I am sure this was not just his idea. His little brother seems to be the prankster in the family, and I do recall that Nathan was out there watching too, laughing the most as Bart slurped up about a cupful of the salty, vinegary concoction. He finally stopped and looked at what he was drinking. The worst part was that he also looked at the boys like he was thinking, "You gave this to me, so it must be good. Why don't I like it?" Instant guilt trip!

And then there was the time I threw some trash into the burn barrel and lit it. Bart was so sure it must be good food that he licked the side of that red hot barrel, as I was frantically screaming, "No!" He ran around in circles trying to make his tongue stop burning. I gave him some cold water to drink, but I doubt he really quit hurting for a day or two.

And that is exactly how we do with sin. Our friends are involved in it; society accepts it; it must be okay, and we wolf it down without a second thought. So why is my life falling apart? Why do I feel so bad about what I am doing? It cannot possibly be that this stuff does not taste as good as everyone says it does. Are we being as gullible as that big dumb yellow lab of ours? The answer is probably yes. Unfortunately, we sometimes don't even have the sense he did to finally realize sin does not taste that good and quit. And also unfortunately, one can develop a taste for things that really don't taste very good at all. And sooner or later our tongues will be burned on the garbage we have tried to ingest into our souls.

God does have your good at heart. He will not play any tricks on you. Listen to what He says about how to live your life, and you will find that everything will taste a whole lot better.

Oh taste and see that Jehovah is good; blessed is the man who takes refuge in him. Oh fear Jehovah, you his saints, for there is no want in those who fear him. The young lions lack and suffer hunger, but those who seek Jehovah shall not want for any good thing.

Psalm 34.8–10

September 22

Baby Talk

This morning I sat outside by the remains of last night's fire, drinking my last cup of coffee and petting the dogs. Suddenly I heard the hawk in a tree just across the drive. This was the closest he had come in awhile. I do not know if it was the first hawk that grew up on our property, or his son or grandson, but it was one of those I had talked to as he sat in his nest as a baby. He would never have gotten that close to me otherwise.

No other bird would have talked to me that way either. He didn't call out with the loud, echoing cry of a mature hawk, but with the baby sounds he used to make way up in his nest as I talked to him, the same sounds he always greeted his parents with when they brought him food during the day. This was intimate hawk talk, not formal hawk talk. He still recognized me from his baby days, and knew I was a friend. He knew he could let down his guard and be that little baby hawk one more time.

Sometimes I get tired of being grown up. I get tired of being the mature one who is always supposed to know what to say and how to say it. Sometimes I want to be the little kid who can run to a great big grown-up, spill my heart, and have him tell me everything is going to be all right.

That is exactly what we can do with God. Job said, "My soul is weary of my life; I will give free course to my complaint; I will speak in the bitterness of my soul" (10.1). Job said he could tell God everything, no holding back—"free course." David said, "I pour out my complaint before Him, I show Him my trouble" (Psa 142.2). Both of these strong men of God had moments when they let it all out, just like little children who are afraid and don't understand. Why do I think I need to be any better than they?

My children used to come to me with their troubles, usually small, inconsequential things. But to them, those things were *huge.* I never acted like they were silly to worry over them, but did my best to comfort them, and even fix the things I could fix for them. Most of the things we find ourselves going to God with are inconsequential in His grand scheme of things, but He still treats them as important because they are important to His children. He will listen to even the smallest concern, the pettiest, even the selfish ones, as so many turn out to be.

We never need to hold back with God, especially now, because we have a Mediator who understands how those small things can seem so large. We can run to God any time we need to, and talk as a child to a Father who listens and who cares. It's okay to have a little baby talk with God.

> *For we have not a high priest that cannot be touched with the feeling of our infirmities; but one who has been in all points tempted like as we are yet without sin. Let us therefore draw near with boldness unto the throne of grace, that we may receive mercy, and may find grace to help in time of need.*
>
> Hebrews 4.15–16

September 23

Singing to the Wrens

A wren perched on a branch in a nearby oak sapling as I sat by the fire pit one morning reading. I did not know he was there until he started singing as only wrens can—clear and lovely and loud, especially for such a small bird. I knew I would never see him, but I "sang" back anyway. You don't have to be able to whistle to sing to a bird, evidently. I just copied his pitch and timbre the best I could and sort of "trilled." Immediately he answered back.

We sang back and forth to each other for at least five minutes, then I had to get up to poke the fire, and he flew. Not ten minutes later he was back in the same tree, singing. I answered, and here we went once again, singing back and forth for several minutes.

I have done that with other birds as well. Just imitate their songs, and they will sing right back. Even if you deviate a little, perhaps eight short phrases instead of nine or ending on a high note instead of a low, they will recognize it and return your call.

I am more than happy to sing to a bird. It still puzzles me why it is so hard for me to talk with my fellow human beings, especially about spiritual things—at least I know what they are saying to me. Particularly when *they* start the conversation, why shouldn't it be easy to simply answer?

Birds are not judgmental, you say. Trust me, birds are extremely judgmental. If you don't say what they want to hear, or if you say it too loudly or from too close a position, they will simply up and fly away.

And really, isn't it easy to find something that most humans will talk about?

If you are standing in line and the service is slow, what do you usually talk about with the person behind you? "They really are busy today."

If you are waiting for a bus and it's about to rain, what do you usually say? "Hope that bus gets here before the rain does."

I was checking out at a grocery store the morning of our last anniversary, having laid crabmeat, baby greens, rib eye steaks, shallots, lemons, yellow fingerling potatoes, cremini mushrooms, Granny Smith apples, pecans, and vanilla Haagen-Dazs on the counter. A man I had never seen in my life walked up behind me in line, took one look at the bounty lying there and said, "Man, I want to go home with you tonight!" Before I finished checking out I found out that his wife had died two years before and that the next week would have been their 40th anniversary.

And we can't talk to people.

We *won't* talk to people, even when they start the conversation. Try singing back in his tune instead of ramming another one down his throat. Before long you can begin to deviate a little, and gradually get your points in. Isn't that what Jesus often did?

"Can I have a drink of water?" He asked a woman at a well. Soon they were talking about spiritual water, and soon more people were coming to hear Him.

Don't ignore the wrens in your life. Sing back and make a new friend, and perhaps a new brother.

All your works shall give thanks to you, O Jehovah; and your saints shall bless you. They shall speak of the glory of your kingdom, and talk of your power; to make known to the sons of men his mighty acts, and the glory of the majesty of his kingdom.

Psalm 145.10–12

September 24

Sacrificial Giving

Much of my study lately has been devoted to the early church. I spent a good deal of time in Acts 4 and all of a sudden had an idea. Barnabas and several others were selling property and giving it to the apostles to distribute to the Christians in need. I decided to put that in terms I could understand, with the help of a professional realtor in my area.

Some of those early Christians had houses and sold them. Let's be logical about this: they did not sell the houses they were living in because that would have just exacerbated the problem—more homeless folks to worry about. But let's say they had another house in Jerusalem that they used as a rental property. Today, where I live, any house that is livable will not go for much less than $150,000, and if it is any size at all, $190,000 or more.

Others, particularly Barnabas, sold property. Let's say I have a piece of property that I bought as an investment several years ago. Five acres will cost you about $75,000 in a rural county, but closer to $175,000 in an urban county. In town, zoned commercial, it will get you well over a million and a half. Even a rural property will bring in $350,000 if it also has a livable house and is improved—well, septic, *etc.* We are not talking about these first century Christians making paltry donations; we are not even talking about what we would consider a generous donation. Their giving went far beyond anything I had ever considered before.

Lest some good soul feels convicted and goes out to sell his extra property by Sunday morning, let us hasten to say that this was a time of crisis. Several thousand Christians were homeless and unemployed. They had come for the Jewish feast days, fully expecting to go back home to their trades and dwellings. But in becoming part of the first church, God's promised kingdom, they had much to learn. It would have been inappropriate for someone to say, "Why should I sacrifice my future for them? Let them go back home to their own jobs and houses." God did not want them leaving until they had achieved a solid foundation, something that happened several years later in Acts 8 when "they were scattered abroad… preaching the word."

But I wonder about us, about me, if some crisis should happen to my brethren. What if a hurricane, a tornado, an earthquake, or whatever tragedy is prone to your area, suddenly takes the homes of half the Christians in your city? How much of a sacrifice would you be willing to make? How much would I?

Another crisis fell on the Judean Christians several years later—a famine. Do we really understand this? They had no Publix or Kroger sitting on the street corner that continued to bring in food despite the failure of their own little gardens. People were starving. The Macedonian churches had just been through some affliction that left them poverty-stricken themselves (2 Cor 8.1–3). Yet they did not say, as some might, "Why should we give? Someone needs to take up a collection for us!" They gave anyway. In fact, they *begged* Paul to allow them to give, because those faraway people, whom they had probably never met in their lives, were family to them, brothers and sisters in the Lord. Their secret? They gave themselves to God first. After that, nothing was too much to ask.

What would those early Christians think of us and our giving? Or our excuses for not giving? Yes, we are to be good stewards of our money, but that certainly gets us out of a lot of situations, doesn't it? I praise God that I do know a few twenty-first century Christians who are financially blessed, but who live modestly just so they can find situations they can help with monetarily. It encourages me to do more as well.

Consider these things as you go about your lives today, and especially in the next few weeks. What are you spending your money on? When poverty-stricken Christians can give out of their own need, what can I do out of the gracious plenty I have?

> *Moreover brethren, we make known to you the grace of God which has been given in the churches of Macedonia, how that in much proof of affliction, the abundance of their joy and their deep poverty abounded unto the riches of their liberality. For according to their power… yea and beyond their power, they gave of their own accord, begging us with much entreaty in regard of this grace and the fellowship in the ministering to the saints…but first they gave their own selves to the Lord.*
>
> 2 Corinthians 8.1–5

September 25

Solitary Confinement

I have been alone many times in my life. My vision problem meant I spent a lot of time alone indoors instead of outside playing with other children. We moved a few times, and being naturally reticent, I was slow to make new friends. Being a preacher's wife, and then a law enforcement officer's wife meant I often found myself on the outside looking in—people were often uncomfortable around me. Finally, living out in the country for the past 30 years, where "next door neighbors" can be as far as half a mile away, has also kept me isolated from others. However, I learned a long time ago how to be comfortable with myself. To me, being alone seldom means being lonely.

Far too many people who live in cities, bumping elbows with hundreds of others every day, while never really being alone, are still lonely. Loneliness in the middle of a crowd must be the most debilitating kind there is. When you think no one understands and no one cares, you might as well be on a one man raft in the middle of the ocean.

No Christian should ever feel the burden of loneliness. Apart from the always pleasant surprise of bumping into a brother or sister in the middle of the week "out there in the world," or being warmly welcomed into an assembly far from home, there is that "great cloud of witnesses" who are cheering us on, an Older Brother who has experienced every pain we have, and a Father who will listen any time of day. He is never too busy or too tired for any one of his children.

So if you find yourself feeling lonely, ask yourself why. There is an obligation to reach out for help that the person in the middle of his self-pity wants to deny. "No one loves me" excuses any sort of behavior, we think. But you will never experience the type of loneliness that the Son experienced on your behalf when, solely because of all the sins ever committed—including yours—he was separated from the Father, for God cannot countenance sin; and that Older Brother of ours took them all on his shoulders as he hung on a cross—completely alone *for the first time in all eternity.*

So think again about loneliness and remember that no loneliness you ever experience can match that, and any loneliness you do experience is your own fault—you have placed yourself in solitary confinement. That Brother and that Father are always there, even if the brethren down here sometimes let you down. Reach out and take hold of the comfort and fellowship that is there for the taking.

> *"Behold, Jehovah's hand is not shortened, that it cannot save; neither his ear heavy, that it cannot hear: but your iniquities have separated between you and your God, and your sins have hid his face from you, so that he will not hear. …Him who knew no sin he made sin on our behalf; that we might become the righteousness of God in him. …And about the ninth hour Jesus cried with a loud voice, saying, Eli, Eli, lama sabachthani? that is, My God, my God, why have you forsaken me?"* (Isa 59.1–2; 2 Cor 5.21; Matt 27.46)

God forsook him, and left him hanging there alone because of your sin and because of mine, and so we will never have to be lonely again.

September 26

A Six Inch Pot of Mums

Several years ago I received a pot of rust colored chrysanthemums as a gift. I enjoyed them for many days before they began to fade.

"Well that's that," I thought as I placed them on the outside workbench so Keith could salvage the dark green plastic pot for other uses. By the time he got to them, they were brown and withered, as dead looking as any plant I had ever seen.

Keith cannot stand to throw things away. "It might come in handy," he always says as he pulls things out of the trash. That is why he stuck those dried out flowers in the ground beneath the dining room window. Yet even he was amazed when a few days later green leaves sprouted on those black stems. It was fall, a mum's favorite season, and before long I had twice as many as I had started with.

Fast forward to Thanksgiving, a year later. I now had a bed full of rust colored mums about two feet square. The next year the bed was four feet wide and my amaryllises were swamped. Keith built a raised bed about eight feet square, half of it for the mums and the rest for a plumbago, a miniature rose, and a blue sage. That has lasted exactly one year. The plumbago, rose, and sage have been evicted by the mums and need a new home.

What started as one six inch pot of mums, withered and brown, has become 64 square feet of blooms so thick they sprawl over the timbers of the raised bed into the field surrounding it. Whenever I cut an armful for a vase inside, you cannot even tell where I cut them.

We often fall prey to the defeatist attitude, "What can one person do?" Much to the delight of our Adversary we sit alone in the nursery pot, wither, and die. Yet the influence we have as Christians can spread through our families, our workplaces, our neighborhoods, and our communities. The good deeds we do, the moral character we show, the words we do—and don't—say make an impression on others. Those are the seeds we plant, never giving in to the notion that one person cannot accomplish anything. The attitudes we show when mistreated and the peace with which we face life's trials will make others ask, "Why? Can I have this too? How?"

Plant a seed every chance you get. If a six inch pot of dried up mums can spread so quickly, just think what the living Word of God shown through your life can accomplish.

And he said, How shall we liken the kingdom of God? Or in what parable shall we set it forth? It is like a grain of mustard seed, which, when it is sown upon the earth, though it be less than all the seeds that are upon the earth, yet when it is sown, grows up, and becomes greater than all the herbs, and puts out great branches, so that the birds of the heaven can lodge under the shadow thereof.

Mark 4.30–32

September 27

Thorns in the Flesh

The Lord has made everything for his own purpose, yes, even the wicked for the day of trouble. (Prov 16.4)

Think about that for awhile. If I do not allow the Lord to use me for good, he will use me for evil instead. I cannot refuse to be used; it's one or the other.

A long time ago I studied as many women in the Bible as I could find and tried to discover how they fit into the scheme of redemption. I managed to find a use for every one of them. Then I came to Jezebel and found myself stymied. The only thing I could think was God used her to test his prophet Elijah, and to eventually send him back to his work in Israel with a renewed spirit.

I would hate to think that the only use God could find for me was as a thorn in the flesh of his righteous people, testing their faith. So how do I avoid that?

As in the case of Elijah, discouragement can hamper the work of God. After what seemed like an amazing victory on Mt. Carmel, Elijah awoke the next morning to find that Jezebel was still in charge and his life was still in danger. "Now Ahab told Jezebel all that Elijah had done, and how he had slain all the prophets with the sword. Then Jezebel sent a messenger to Elijah saying, So let the gods do to me, and more also if I make not your life as the life of one of them by tomorrow about this time. And when Elijah saw this, he fled" (1 Kings 19.1–3). What a let-down that must have been. If that great victory had not changed things, what could?

So Elijah ran away to the wilderness where he rested, where an angel fed him, and where God proved to him that Jezebel was *not* the one in charge, and there were still righteous people to stand with him.

Am I just another Jezebel, discouraging God's people in their mission? Do I have a chip on my shoulder that makes me easily offended? Do I sit like a spectator on the bleachers, watching and waiting for the least little thing, quick to complain, unashamed to make a scene, ready to pass judgment on every word and action, and worse, spread that slander to others? Do I march up to the elders, the preacher, the class teachers as if they had to answer to me for anything I find disagreeable, which can be anything and everything, depending upon my mood at the moment?

What purpose do I think that serves other than to try the patience, faith, and endurance of those who must put up with my spitefulness? Why do I think that kind of behavior will help anyone? Would I accept it from anyone toward me?

Every church I have ever been a part of has one of these thorns hidden among them. Don't let it be you. Remember today that God is using you. Make sure that everything you do and say will in some way help His plan to save the world. Your brothers and sisters need your encouragement. Your neighbors need your example of love and service. *That* is what God expects of you—to choose to be a rose instead of a thorn.

A fool shows his annoyance at once, but a prudent man overlooks an insult. There is one whose rash words are like sword thrusts, but the tongue of the wise brings healing.

Proverbs 12.16, 18

September 28

Just Becuase

Do you see it? Sometimes I get to typing too fast. I want to get it down while it's still fresh, or more often, before I forget it, and so the typos pop up all over—mistyped words, missing words, and recently, a homophone I never caught even after several edits.

Other times, though, I have simply taught myself to type something wrong by doing it that way over and over. "Becuase" is a prime example. I type it wrong nearly every time. Even when I slow down, I type it wrong more often than not. The only thing that will ever help is to make myself type it correctly again and again and again. Guess what? I may type it wrong less often, but it will be a problem forever, something I must actively think about every time the word comes up if I hope to do it correctly—all "becuase" I have typed it wrong from the beginning.

Sin works that way too. If you train yourself to do things wrong, or if you train yourself *not* to do things right, you will have that problem for the rest of your life. It isn't just alcoholics and drug addicts who must fight their problems every day, it's plain old sinners too.

Have you always used vulgar language? Don't expect it to clean itself up just because you became a Christian. The words are too ingrained in your mind. Far better to have never placed them there at all.

Have you always given in to anger? Don't expect to automatically ignore the annoyances of life with a shrug of the shoulders. Instead of learning self-control in the first place, you indulged in throwing a fit over every little thing far too long for it to simply disappear without any effort at all.

Have you been part of the gossip chain for years and years? Don't expect your ears to stop tingling when a juicy tidbit floats within earshot just because you claim to now believe in Jesus. You will find some way to make excuses for it if you don't actively make yourself stop.

This is not to discourage you, but to encourage you to work at it and never give up. Things may get easier, but those sins you indulged in regularly will always be a problem. We view sin far too trivially, which is why you hear nonsense like, "Let him sow his wild oats." Sin will have its effect, even after it has been forgiven, simply from the bad habit of it, if nothing else. Usually, though, there is a something else—like pleasure or a sense of belonging, two things that are difficult to give up.

This is also to encourage those who were brought up to know better to treat that as a blessing instead of a curse. Praise God for your good parents. Don't throw those blessings away because you think you need to experience things in order to understand them. Don't start a habit that is hard to break. Sin can be forgiven but the damage cannot be easily undone.

> *Take care, brothers, lest there be in any of you an evil, unbelieving heart, leading you to fall away from the living God. But exhort one another every day, as long as it is called "today," that none of you may be hardened by the deceitfulness of sin. For we share in Christ, if indeed we hold our original confidence firm to the end.*
>
> Hebrews 3.12–14

September 29

Cinders

I married a firebug and raised two more. All the camping we have done, I am sure, was just an excuse to build and sit around campfires, and since we moved to the country we have had a fire pit from the beginning. Once the weather began to turn, we kept the hot dog and marshmallow industries in business almost single-handedly, sometimes with all the trimmings—chili, beans, slaw—other times with just a bag of chips on the side. After the boys went away to college, any weekend they came home, they expected a hot dog roast at least once. From October to April my grocery list always included those all-American sausages, "Nathan's" hot dogs, of course.

Now that the boys are gone, Keith still likes to build a fire on cool nights. Our partially wooded property always produces enough deadfall to keep the fires going, and even here in Florida, the weather is cool enough to make a fire pleasant, rotating yourself like a rotisserie, warming each side in turn.

Keith will often throw a carefully collected and dried pile of Spanish moss on the flame. At first the fire appears smothered, but the heat gradually burns through, producing thick billows of gray smoke that seem almost tactile, finally burning clear and shooting sparks and cinders up toward the sky. We lean our heads on the lawn chair backs to see which will travel highest and glow longest before burning out in the cold blackness above the treetops.

Do you realize that is all an atheist believes life is? We are cinders in a bonfire. Some of us simply dissolve in the fire. Others rise on the updraft, some burning higher, larger, and longer than others, but burning out nonetheless, just like everyone else. How can they survive believing this is all there is to it? Some use that as an excuse to do whatever they want, regardless of who it hurts and the harm it causes. Even then, as they grow older and realize the brevity of life, the pointlessness of it all takes its toll. "When a wicked man dies, his hope perishes; all he expected from his power comes to nothing" (Prov 11.7).

But children of God know better. We are not just nameless cinders in the updraft of a brief blaze. We have not only an eternal existence to look forward to, but a purpose here as well. Very few of us will rise high enough and burn long enough for many to notice and fewer to remember, but we can all give warmth and light in a cold, dark world. Maybe working so hard that we dissolve in the flame without ever rising above it is the better end. How much warmth and light did you ever get out of a single spark anyway?

What are your plans for today? Are you so busy you get tired just thinking about it? And at what? Is it something that will warm someone's heart and light their way? Even things that don't seem likely can be made into an opportunity to do good. If they cannot, maybe we should think twice about doing them. We are all sparks in the fire, or else we are just trying to put it out.

> *You are the light of the world. A city set on a hill cannot be hid. Neither do men light a lamp and put it under a bushel, but on the stand, and it shines unto all who are in the house. Even so let your light shine before men that they may see your good works, and glorify your Father who is in heaven.*
>
> Matthew 5.14–16

September 30

Reality Check

I remembered recently a walk Chloe and I took one morning when she was still a puppy. It was a particularly nice day. The steam bath of a Florida summer had given way to the milder warmth of early fall. Migrating birds had stopped for the breakfast buffet in the nearby woods. My hawk called good morning from high overhead. A breeze fluffed up the grass and sent cotton ball clouds scudding across the sky. Our world was filled with beauty and peace.

All of a sudden, down at my feet, Chloe belched. This was not the dainty puff of air I sometimes hear from our older heeler, who then looks at me with embarrassed, downcast eyes. This was a full-blown, open-mouthed belch that, proportionate to her size, would have rivaled any beer-bellied redneck. I laughed out loud from the sheer shock of it. I had never heard a puppy belch. I didn't even know it was possible.

Puppies are cute; puppies are playful; puppies are sweet and innocent. Hearing Chloe belch certainly ruined *that* image.

Unfortunately, image is one thing and reality is something else entirely. Sometimes we forget that and set ourselves up for a lot of disappointment that could be avoided. And sometimes that disappointment costs us our faith.

Consider this one thing, among many others: how much more shocked are we when a preacher or elder falls? "What hypocrites!" we instantly accuse. Yet, isn't it a poor preacher who cannot preach better than he can practice? Why should *his* inability to be perfect (which we have no problem telling him about otherwise) keep *us* from trying at all? The reality is we *all* fail once in a while, even though our image of them says *they* shouldn't.

Whenever someone says to me, "I'll never go to that church because some of the people there are hypocrites," I usually answer, "Even the apostles had a Judas among them, but they did not let that make them forsake their Lord."

To those who leave the church "because of all the hypocrites," Keith usually says, "And you are going to leave the Lord's church in *their* hands?" You see, what it all boils down to is yet more excuses for our own behavior.

No matter how well put together people seem on the outside, everyone has problems. Sometimes the worst problem anyone can have is trying to live up to another person's image of him. If anyone knows he is *not* perfect, it is usually the one whom everyone else thinks is. Not preachers, not elders, not elders' wives, not great Bible scholars—no one is without fault.

That person you think is a perfect wife? Once in a while she nags. That person you think is a great husband? Once in a while, he leaves his dirty clothes in the floor. That couple you think have a perfect family? Once in a while their children roll their eyes at their parents and actually rebel a little. That one you think is always so kind and sweet? Once in a while she loses her temper.

Never blame your own faithlessness on the imperfections of others. No one is perfect. Don't let your image of how things ought to be, rob you of your faith when reality checks in.

Even puppies belch.

> *If you, O Jehovah, should mark iniquities, who could stand? But there is forgiveness with you that you may be feared. I wait for Jehovah, my soul does wait, and in his word do I hope. ...O Israel, hope in Jehovah, for with Jehovah there is lovingkindness, and with him is plenteous forgiveness.*

Psalm 130.3–4, 7

October 1

The Best Cup of Coffee

I think maybe I have discovered something that will help me a lot.

The best cup of coffee is not the four-dollar, imported-from-some-exotic-place, freshly roasted, even more freshly ground cup you get at that boutique coffee shop. The best cup of coffee is the one you drink from a cracked ceramic cup in front of a campfire on a chilly morning, the smell of bacon mingling with the smoke from that same wood fire and the vapors of the coffee, maybe even a few drops of bitter oils floating on top of it because the propane camp stove is harder to control and sometimes the coffee comes just a little too close to a simmer. When you are cold, nothing tastes better than something warm.

Even tomato soup from that red and white can tastes pretty good. It doesn't matter if the seasoning is not well-balanced (too much sugar and salt and little else). It doesn't matter if there is no complex depth of flavor, just candied tomatoes and tin can. Those niggling little details make no difference to you at that moment. It's warm and you appreciate that. If you have never been truly cold, so cold that your insides quiver and you can hardly make your hands work and keep your mind functioning, you have never tasted a truly good cup of coffee or a good bowl of soup, no matter how much either cost you, or how many gourmets raved about it.

So why will that help me get through life? Just think about this: How do people who have a terrible disease, or who have experienced one calamity after the other, or who are unfairly oppressed for their beliefs, or who come within inches of death, still smile and laugh, still enjoy life and keep their faith? Because when you have a *real* problem, suddenly you understand what is important. You are able to find pleasure in the little things. You can feel joy in watching a sunset. You can find happiness in seeing children play. You can experience contentment in even just one moment of normalcy. You can enjoy peace in the company of those who love you, even if they are not perfect. Suddenly their imperfections become insignificant.

I cannot think of any instance where griping is anything but a sign of ingratitude. When we whine about the inconsequential things, when we complain about the traffic, the weather, the petty grievances against others and the annoyances of life, then maybe we need a catastrophe to wake us up to what really matters. Sadly, that is often what it takes to get our priorities in order. Some things are just more important than others, but, just as it takes a nearly hypothermic person to enjoy what he might ordinarily consider a mediocre cup of coffee, it often takes a disaster to force us to recognize how blessed we truly are.

We could be even happier if we did not always have to learn that the hard way.

Behold, what I have seen to be good and fitting is to eat and drink and find enjoyment in all the toil with which one toils under the sun the few days of his life that God has given him, for this is his lot. Everyone also to whom God has given wealth and possessions and power to enjoy them, and to accept his lot and rejoice in his toil—this is the gift of God. For he will not much remember [brood about] the days of his life because God keeps him occupied with joy in his heart.

Ecclesiastes 5.18–20

October 2

Jesus' Grandmother

Now, now—I can see those eyebrows. No, I don't know her name, but I sure know a lot about her, and so do you, if you think about it.

We need to start back a few generations. Luke tells us that Mary and Elizabeth were close relatives (1.36). If one is from the tribe of Judah, a descendant of David, and the other a "daughter of Aaron" from the tribe of Levi, how could they be "close?"

Under the Jewish system, unless there were no sons to inherit property, daughters were allowed to marry outside their tribe and were absorbed into their husbands' tribes. Luke's genealogy shows that Mary was a direct descendant of David. Yet he also says she was a "near kinswoman" of Elizabeth, a "daughter of Aaron." For Elizabeth to be past child-bearing age, she must have been at least two generations older than Mary, the same generation as Mary's grandmother. Thus it is likely that a sister from the previous generation married into the tribe of Levi, the family of Aaron. The mother of those two earlier sisters must have been a righteous woman to raise two daughters who then raised yet more generations of righteous Jews, one of whom bore John the forerunner of the Messiah, and another the grandmother of the Messiah himself.

This brings us to the woman in question—Jesus' grandmother. We know she had at least two daughters, Mary being the more famous. Now get a sheet of paper, if your mind needs to see this in black and white like mine usually does. Read Matthew 27.56, Mark 15.40, and John 19.25. List the women who stood at the cross and start matching them up. Matthew says they were Mary Magdalene, Mary the mother of James and Joses, and the mother of the sons of Zebedee. Mark says they were Mary Magdalene, Mary the mother of James the Less and Joses, and Salome. John says that besides Jesus' mother Mary, they were Mary Magdalene, Mary the wife of Cleopas (or Clopas or Cleophas), and Jesus' mother's sister.

Look how much you learn from such a simple exercise. Besides finding yet another Mary, we find out that James the Less had a brother named Joses. We find out that his father Alphaeus (Matt 10.3) was also called Cleopas. He was probably the Cleopas on the road to Emmaus in Luke 24.18.

More to the point, we find out that James and John, the sons of Zebedee, were also the sons of Salome, and that she was Mary's sister. If John were the "baby cousin," no wonder he was especially dear to Jesus. This might also mollify any bad feelings some have toward Salome. She really wasn't all that presumptuous. She was His aunt after all, and her sons were Jesus' only blood relatives among the apostles. Why not think they should be His first and second lieutenants?

So following those righteous women down the line we have one branch of the distant family bringing about the Forerunner of the Messiah, the Elijah of the New Testament, a martyr for the Lord's cause. In the other branch we have two twigs, one bringing forth the Messiah, the writers of two epistles (James and Jude, two of Jesus' brothers) and an elder in the Jerusalem church (the same James); and the other bearing two of the apostles, one of whom would be the first apostle martyred (James in Acts 12) and the other who would write one gospel, three epistles, and the final Revelation—the apostle John.

I have often thought of Mary and her dilemma when she discovered that she was told she would be a pregnant virgin. At that point she was a young teenager, poor and unmarried. Imagine having to tell her parents. Would you believe your daughter? Of course, in this age things like that no longer happen, but when was the last miracle these people had seen? How long had they been living with the promise of a Messiah who had yet to come? They knew how they had raised their daughter. They knew she was telling the truth. Or maybe God "helped" them know as He helped Joseph, and their faith kept them strong through what must have been a difficult and awkward time with the rest of the community.

I wonder if God could find such a family today, especially one whose righteousness He could count on to continue through several generations. What about the family I raised? What about yours? What will happen two or three generations from now? Did we give our children enough ammunition to fight Satan that long?

One of the reasons God said he could trust Abraham, one of the reasons he was chosen was "I have known him to the end that he may command his children and his household after him, that they may keep the way of Jehovah to do righteousness and justice *to the end that Jehovah may bring upon Abraham that which he has spoken to him*" (Gen 18.19).

Jesus grandparents and great-grandparents, poor, uneducated by our standards, and living in a vassal nation, still accomplished what even the wealthiest and most powerful could not. They probably never knew the end result during their lifetimes. We may never know what our efforts have accomplished either, but it may be something wonderful. Don't ever think that teaching your children won't matter to the rest of the world. Your influence, for good or bad, could go on for generations.

> *Therefore we said, Let us now build an altar, not for burnt offering, nor for sacrifice, but to be a witness between us and you and between our generations after us, that we do perform the service of the Lord in his presence with our burnt offerings and sacrifices and peace offerings, so your children will not say to our children in time to come, "You have no portion in the Lord."*
>
> Joshua 22.26–27

October 3

Aliens Among Us

I went into the grocery store a few months ago with my check ledger in hand. I had written a check for groceries that, after two months, had not shown up at the bank. Usually that store processes my checks faster than anyone, so it seemed obvious that they had somehow lost the check, and my groceries had not been paid for.

I asked for the manager, and the young lady behind the desk went to find him after I assured her that I really did need him and she could not handle the problem. "Uh oh," her eyes said, obviously expecting a serious complaint. When the manager came, I opened my ledger, explained the problem, and offered to rewrite the check, less the stop payment charge on the first one. They were the ones who lost it after all.

For a moment he just stood there. He was so shocked that the words would not come, not even to okay this solution to the problem. Finally he said, "I appreciate your honesty. Give me a few days and we will see if the check is around here somewhere." I said that was fine, but as I walked away I felt his eyes on my back. I was some sort of alien creature, he probably decided. Anyone else would have jumped at the chance for a week's worth of free groceries.

Honesty is a rare commodity these days. For a country that claims to be "Christian" this is a travesty. Honesty is perhaps the most important factor in whether or not we will be saved. Jesus himself said that the Word could only grow in hearts that were "*honest* and good" (Luke 8.15), and how will I ever know I need the Lord if I am never honest with myself?

I think that nothing makes me angrier than to have someone accuse me of lying. Yet, I know that others lie every day. Keith's work is totally infested with it. Lies are a criminal's stock in trade. What is so funny is that when they get started, he usually interrupts them and finishes their stories. They look at him in amazement. "Don't think you are so smart," he tells them. "I've heard them all before."

And they usually trip themselves up anyway. How about the guy who "accidentally" killed his girlfriend? "You fumbled the gun in an armload of stuff and accidentally shot her? What bad luck. Where did you hit her?" Keith prompted.

"In the leg. The second time I got her in the face," he answered. The second time. Accidentally. *Suuure.* "Lying lips are an abomination to Jehovah, but they who deal truly are his delight" (Prov 12.22).

Too many people who, technically, are not criminals think they can get away with dishonesty as well. They cheat every little chance they get, bending the truth in their favor, or keeping part of it secret, the part that will benefit them. "False balances are an abomination to Jehovah, but a just weight is his delight" (Prov 11.1).

Dishonesty may seem small when compared to other sins, but God places it among what we would consider the worst, including murder (Rom 1.28ff; 1 Tim

1.9–10). Over and over the New Testament enjoins Christians to live an honest life in every area (2 Cor 4.1–2; Eph 4.25; Phil 4.8; Col 3.9; 1 Thes 4.11–12) and it ends with this promise: "But the fearful and unbelieving and abominable, and murderers and fornicators and sorcerers and idolaters *and all liars,* their part shall be in the lake that burns with fire and brimstone, which is the second death" (Rev 21.8).

Go out there today and make someone look at you funny. Make someone wonder what planet you came from. Tell the truth. Pay your debts. Don't take advantage of someone else's poor math. He may snicker behind your back because you were so naïve as to be honest, actually paying what you owe rather than getting away with something, but his opinion is not the one that matters.

> *He who walks righteously and speaks uprightly, he who despises the gain of oppression, that shakes his hands from taking a bribe, who stops his ears from hearing of blood and shuts his eyes from looking upon evil, he shall dwell on high, his place of defense shall be the munitions of rocks, his bread shall be given him, his water shall be sure.*
>
> Isaiah 33.15–16

October 4

Clearing Out the Trees

Two of our near neighbors just broke our hearts. They had a timber company come in and cut down all of their pine trees. I do understand that pine trees are not as good as oaks. They fall over much more easily, they don't really give that much shade, and they can carry those pesky pine bark beetles. But instantly, our screening vanished

In just a few years the oaks that are left will grow up and out and fill in the holes, but it will be a long few years. We lost a lot of the sound barrier when the machines that come in to clip the trees at ground level cleared out the brush in their passage. The neighbor noise and traffic noise has increased exponentially. In fact, one of their dogs can see movement through the openings now and barks at us constantly.

But there is something to be said for cleaning things out. When I clean out a closet I find things I thought I had lost. I also find room I didn't know I had. Sometimes we need to clean out our lives the same way. It isn't so much all the "wrong" things we are doing, as it is the sheer number of things we are doing. Our lives are so cluttered we no longer have time for the good things that need doing, for helping one another, and for helping ourselves to grow. We are too busy working. We are too busy having fun. We are too busy living an earthly life to spend much time on the spiritual. No wonder many of us are often as carnal as the Corinthians.

I think of Paul's request to those Corinthians, especially as I read it recently in the CEV: "Friends in Corinth, we are telling the truth when we say that there is room in our hearts for you. We are not holding back on our love for you, but you are holding back on your love for us. I speak to you as I would speak to my own children. Please make room in your hearts for us" (2 Cor 6.11–13). I can imagine God thinking exactly the same thing about us. "Make room for Me, people!"

And then there is the room we need to make in our minds. In the past I have had days when my mind was racing with things I needed to do, trying my best to create a logical order so I could get it all done. Other times, I am ashamed to say, my mind has been so filled with things I would like to say to someone who has hurt me that there was simply no room for anything else. Prayer? I couldn't even get past the first sentence before I started telling God exactly what I wanted to say to that person.

We need to make room in our lives for the things that truly matter. We need to make room in our minds for the Word of God. We need to make room in our hearts for others. Clear out the brush that obscures your vision; clear out the useless trees that can cause more harm than good. Make room for the good things, for the things that last forever.

> *I cling unto your testimonies: O Jehovah, put me not to shame. I will run the way of your commandments, When you enlarge [make room in] my heart. Teach me, O Jehovah, the way of your statutes; And I shall keep it unto the end.*
>
> Psalm 119.31–33

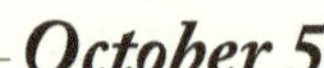

October 5

Acting Like A Child

"Stop acting like a child!" has become a staple line of many arguments. Yet one time, Jesus said the very opposite.

"Verily I say unto you, Except you turn, and become as little children, you shall in no wise enter into the kingdom of heaven" (Matt 18.3). Unfortunately, whenever this event in Jesus' life comes up in Bible classes, we totally ignore the context and instead start listing all the wonderful qualities of children. By the time we have finished, it's a wonder we can't find dozens of passages telling us to act like children instead of dozens telling us to grow up! "Till we all attain unto the unity of the faith, and of the knowledge of the Son of God, unto a *full-grown* man, unto the measure of the stature of the fullness of Christ" (Eph 4.13). Worse than that, we miss the point Jesus is making.

Look what was happening immediately before. The Twelve were arguing about which of them was the greatest in the kingdom. Surely that had something to do with Jesus' admonition.

The verse after the one we all quote so often specifies, "Whosoever shall humble himself as *this* little child..." (v 4). What was it about this particular child? He had no status or rank, no wealth, and nothing to offer in worldly terms at all. All he did was come the minute he was called and trust the one who called implicitly. Don't you think that made those men squirm in embarrassment at their previous behavior?

Then Jesus went on to add, "But whoso shall cause one of these little ones that believe on me to stumble, it is profitable for him that a great millstone should be hanged about his neck, and that he should be sunk in the depth of the sea" (v 6). Here He included those metaphorical children who would come to Him with the same humility and trust. How we treat them determines our fate as much as how we live our lives, or even how we worship or where.

Do you think the early disciples did not need this lesson? Besides their constant bickering about who was the greatest, those early churches had arguments about who had the greatest spiritual gift and who should get the most "floor time" with his gift (1 Cor 12–14). They bragged about which preacher baptized them (1 Cor 1). They showed off their wealth in bringing so much Lord's Supper that it constituted a braggadocio feast instead of a memorial supper (1 Cor 11). Their women had to be reminded not to dress up to show off their wealth (1 Tim 2). They were told that how they received guests into their assembly could condemn them as easily as committing adultery or murder (Jas 2). Clearly, personal humility and acceptance of others regardless of rank was a lesson they needed from the beginning.

Why was that important? Because, as Jesus tells the sheep in that great parable of the judgment in Matthew 25, when they wonder how they had served the Lord by feeding, clothing, and visiting Him, he answers them this way, "Inasmuch as you did it unto one of these my brethren, *even these least,* you did it unto me" (Matt 25.40). Any time we reject a brother because we think we are better than he, whether because of wealth, education, race, or anything other consideration, we are rejecting the Lord *for the same reason.*

So the next time this passage comes up in Bible class, let's see if, instead of listing all the sweet things our children do, we can actually get the lesson Jesus intended from it. It's a whole lot more important than we seem to think.

And he took a little child, and set him in the midst of them: and taking him in his arms, he said unto them, Whosoever shall receive one of such little children in my name, receives me: and whosoever receives me, receives not me, but him that sent me.

Mark 9.36–37

October 6

Order in the Court

A lot of folks think that there is no place for "order" in their religious lives, nor for orders, either. Order, though, is an important concept in the scriptures beginning as early as Genesis.

One would ordinarily think that when he reads, "Noah was 500 years old when he begat Shem, Ham and Japheth," that the order in which the sons are listed is birth order: Shem was the eldest, the first of Noah's "begetting." In fact, whenever Shem is found in any crossword puzzle I do, the clue is invariably, "Noah's eldest." Not so fast—I can prove he was not.

Genesis 5.32: "And Noah was five hundred years old, and Noah begat Shem, Ham, and Japheth." Noah had his first son at the age of 500.

Genesis 7.6: "And Noah was six hundred years old when the flood of waters was upon the earth." That means his eldest son would have been 100 at the time of the flood.

Genesis 11.10: "Shem was one hundred years old and begat Arpachshad *two years after the flood.*" That means that Shem was only 98 at the time of the flood and could not have been the eldest.

Then we have the case of Terah's three sons, "Abram, Nahor, and Haran." Was Abram the eldest?

Genesis 11.26: "Terah lived seventy years and begat Abram, Nahor, and Haran."

Acts 7.4: "Then [Abram] came out of the land of the Chaldeans and dwelt in Haran, and from there, *when his father was dead, God removed him to this land,* wherein you now dwell."

Genesis 11.32: "And the days of Terah were 205, and Terah died in Haran." That means his oldest son would have been (205 minus 70 equals) 135 years old when he died.

Genesis 12.4: "So Abram went as Jehovah had spoken unto him. …And Abram was 75 years old *when he departed out of Haran.*" So since he left Haran after his father's death, he was only 75 when the eldest son would have been 135. Abram was certainly not the eldest son. In fact, he could well have been the youngest.

In the New Testament order is important as well. We have "Barnabas and Saul" in Acts 12.25 and 13.2, 7, until suddenly in 13.13 we have "Paul and his company," and "Paul and Barnabas" from 13.43 on. I think all those are enough to show us that in the Bible, people are listed according to their importance, and their amount of involvement in the activity in question. Shem and Abraham, the ancestors of the Christ were certainly more important than their brothers, and Paul gradually took over as the leader of the missionary journeys.

So why might that be important? For one thing look at Acts 18.26, where we have a man named Apollos who was taught better by "Priscilla and Aquila." If the principle about order means anything, it means Priscilla did much more than just sit there and nod in agreement, and that of necessity means that it is possible for a woman to teach a man, at least in private, without violating the principle not to teach "over" a man (1 Tim 2.12).

"Order" meant a lot of things in the New Testament church. They were commanded to do things "decently and in order" (1 Cor 14.40). Yet in the same context we find that they were shouting out hearty amens (14.16). That tells me we should be careful about imposing our own culture's sense of order upon an order which God plainly approved. If one reads the chapter carefully, we are once again talking about doing things in sequence—don't let two talk at once, take turns; don't let someone speak in tongues unless there is someone who can interpret afterward.

Paul left Titus in Crete to "put things in order." Among other things that meant to appoint elders (Tit 1.5). Think about this: He had told Timothy that a new Christian was not suitable material for an elder, and he did not appoint anyone immediately upon that man's baptism. Yet, here is another sense in which "order" is important: these men obviously set their lives in good order because in a relatively short amount of time, they had matured enough to take the leadership position. Maybe the reason there are churches without qualified men today is that those men do not have their lives in a godly sort of order. Everything—career, recreation, physical fitness, education—*everything* seems more important than time spent on spiritual growth, and that is the wrong order.

Funny how many tidbits you can pick up by simply studying one word or concept in the scriptures, isn't it? Perhaps the most important tidbit today is this: God expects us to put our lives in His order, to run our families in His order, to put the church, the body of His son, in His order; always His order, not ours. Anyone who is "out of order" will be found in contempt of that righteous Judge.

> *For though I am absent in body, yet I am with you in spirit, rejoicing to see your good* ***order*** *and the firmness of your faith in Christ. Therefore* ***as you received*** *Christ Jesus the Lord,* ***so walk*** *in him, rooted and built up in him and established in the faith,* ***just as you were taught****, abounding in thanksgiving.*
>
> Colossians 2.5–7

October 7

Medical Charts

I saw a new tech at the eye clinic the last time I was there. Most of the others know me by sight and name, but this one couldn't pronounce my name, so I knew she had not been there long, and certainly I had never been prepped by her before.

She nearly dropped my chart and said, "Wow! This is a huge one. Have you been coming here all your life?" No, just eight years now. If I had been going there my whole life, the chart would have been in volumes instead of just three inches thick.

You see, everything to do with my eyes is in that chart—every test, every procedure, every surgery, every referral, every appointment of which there have been as many as three dozen in one year. The doctor regularly writes two or three pages of notes at every visit.

That always makes me think of that other book being written that *does* cover my lifetime. I know there are pages in it I would love to remove. If I want them removed, imagine how a holy and righteous God feels about them. Doesn't that make it even more amazing when we realize that He has taken out so many? "I have blotted out, as a thick cloud, your transgressions, and, as a cloud, your sins: return unto me; for I have redeemed you" (Isa 44.22). I hope when He finished blotting out the bad, it wasn't totally empty, that there was at least a page or two of good left.

We sometimes seem to have that mistaken belief, that God has all the good stuff written on one side and all the bad written on the other, and that as long as there is more good than bad, we're safe. Wrong. If He has any bad pages left, that means we haven't repented of those evil things. Sin is so bad that it only takes one unforgiven sin to cost us our souls. "When I say to the righteous, that he shall surely live; if he trust to his righteousness, and commit iniquity, none of his righteous deeds shall be remembered; but in his iniquity that he has committed, therein shall he die" (Ezek 33.13). We simply don't understand the enormity of sin when we treat any of them as small and inconsequential.

The next time you visit the doctor, take a look at that chart. How large is it? Imagine one a hundred times bigger, and then remember that probably a million or so pages have been removed due to the grace of God, and rejoice.

And I saw a great white throne, and him that sat upon it, from whose face the earth and the heaven fled away; and there was found no place for them. And I saw the dead, the great and the small, standing before the throne; and books were opened: and another book was opened, which is the book of life: and the dead were judged out of the things which were written in the books, according to their works. …And if any was not found written in the book of life, he was cast into the lake of fire.

Revelation 20.11–12, 15

October 8

Nursery Tales

I was a lucky young mother. When my babies were small, I worshipped with church families that had no nurseries. I did not realize at the time what a blessing it was.

When Lucas was a baby, we met with a small congregation that rented a union hall. The union must not have been very popular. At the end of a narrow hall was the only room big enough for meeting together, and 30 of us filled it up. Five of us were nursing mothers, and since that was over half the families in the congregation, the men agreed that we should be able to simply step out of the room to get ourselves situated, then come back in to sit and listen to the sermons or Bible classes while we nursed our babies. New babies have a tendency to nurse for long periods of time. We might have missed a full hour if these men had not been so mature-minded, and we ladies gratefully learned early how to stay modest while nursing. I doubt anyone walking in would have even known what we were doing.

When Nathan was a toddler we had moved to a place with an actual meetinghouse. It was an old building way out in the country with absolutely no modern conveniences except electric lights, and certainly no nursery. You walked in the door and there you stood in the open auditorium. That meant when you had to deal with unruly children, you dealt with them and then came right back into the assembly.

So why do I think I was lucky? Because I did not have the source of temptation that so many young mothers must deal with today. When you have no choice, there is no temptation. Young mothers today must be much stronger than I ever had to be.

I gleaned advice from several older women during those years. My mother, for instance, was happy to tell me about how she foiled my attempts to ruin her worship services. I always acted up and she would take me to the nursery—she lived in the city. Finally, when I was 18 months old, she realized that she had not trained me, *I* had trained *her*—all I had to do was wiggle and squeal a little and I got to go play! The next Sunday, she took me, not to the nursery, but outside, and applied her hand to my bottom in a less than comforting way. Then she marched me right back into the auditorium. She said I looked at her with outrage, as if to say, "This is *not* how it works! You broke the rules!" But I was not a stupid child; I learned the new rule quickly: being taken out of the assembly is *not* a pleasant experience.

I went to visit her once at this same meetinghouse. Suddenly, my baby needed a diaper change and needed it then. To have stayed sitting there any longer would have broken the commandment to "Love thy neighbor."

So I got up and took my 20-month-old to the nursery. I was stunned when I walked in. Several young mothers, and a few who looked like grandmothers, were sitting in there chatting away. A playpen had been placed in the middle of the room, full of toys. The side of the playpen was lowered and each baby was sitting around it, reaching in and playing with both the toys and each other. Could the women see the preacher? Yes, there was a large picture window in front of them. Could they hear the preacher? Well, there *was* a speaker on the wall, but their talking and laughing drowned it out.

After the diaper change, I got out of there as quickly as I could. I recognized the siren call immediately. I had dealt with two babies at once, while their father preached. We never lived close to family so I never had a grandparent to help out either. It was often tiring, frustrating and embarrassing to try to train my children to behave in the assembly. To have a place to go where I would no longer have to wrestle with them, where they could play and squeal to their heart's content, would have been wonderful. But it would not have taught them how important the group worship of God is, how precious the rituals we follow are, how much it meant to me and therefore how much it should mean to them.

Being a parent is not for the weak of heart, mind or body. You are on duty 24/7 and you must do what you must do no matter what else is going on in your life. Children will not wait. You cannot easily "unteach" what you later wish you had not taught. I would give anything to undo a lot of the mistakes I made, but it just won't happen. In the end you hope you did more right than wrong, and that those right things were more lasting and impressive.

Think about what you do, when you do it, and how. Think about what those little eyes see and those little ears hear. Think the most about what those little minds infer from what they see and hear you doing. Your children aren't stupid either. Whatever it is you do, when *you* do it, it stays with them the longest.

> *And [Hannah] said, "Oh, my lord! As you live, my lord, I am the woman who was standing here in your presence, praying to the Lord. For this child I prayed, and the Lord has granted me my petition that I made to him. Therefore I have given him to the Lord. As long as he lives, he is given to the Lord." And he worshiped the Lord there.*
>
> 1 Samuel 1.26–28

October 9

Fat Free Living

I accidentally made some healthy cookies a few weeks ago. I had not taken the time to pick up my glasses and the magnifying glass. I had just concentrated hard and was sure the recipe said, "1½ sticks of butter." After the cookies came out of the oven, I was disappointed in their dry, cakey texture, when I had expected something chewy and rich. So I picked up my glasses and looked again—"1½ *cups* of butter." That is three whole sticks. What I had done was cut the butter in half. Low fat cookies were not what I had in mind, but it did help to say to myself, "For low fat, they're not that bad."

As Christians we often focus so often on what we cannot do—all those "thou shalt nots"—that it is amazing we can endure. Our faith becomes negative instead of positive. It is all about what we do not do, not what we do. That may explain why so many of us are bitter and why we never manage to spread the good news—to us it isn't such good news.

It also explains why we lose so many of our children. Your home should be a place of safety, a place of contentment, a place of love and laughter. It should be a haven for your children and their friends. Do you want to know where they are, what they are doing, and with whom? Make your home a pleasant place to be, not a prison they hope to break out of someday, and you will know where they are, because *home* is where they are, and where they want to be.

Christians should be known for what they do, not for what they don't do, for who they are, not who they aren't. If your friends were asked to describe Christians based on their knowledge of you, what would they say? "Christians are people who don't drink, who don't gamble, who don't go to clubs, who don't curse, who don't engage in non-marital sex, who don't smoke or take drugs, who don't watch certain movies and TV shows," and on and on. Or would they say, "Christians are happy, generous people who help others whenever a need arises, who are always having people in their homes—you can hear the laughter going on all evening. They are honest and forgiving. You know you can trust them because you never hear them gossip. They are pleasant to be around and seem to be able to handle anything life throws at them, and handle it well. They are the best people on earth. I wish I was more like them."

God has always promised his people "fat" lives. He told the Israelites they would have "a land flowing with milk and honey" (Exod 3.8). When Nehemiah brought them back from captivity, he reminded them that they had taken "fortified cities, and a fat land, and possessed houses full of all good things, cisterns hewn out, vineyards, and oliveyards, and fruit-trees in abundance: so they did eat, and were filled, and became fat, and delighted themselves in [God's] great goodness" (9.25). But they focused only on the restraints of righteous living instead of the blessings, finally fell away to the heathens whose lives they envied, and God sent them away to punishment.

Yet still, He had Ezekiel tell them of another good land, a Messianic kingdom that would bring joy and peace. "And I will bring them out from the peoples, and gather them from the countries, and will bring them into their own land; and I will feed them upon the mountains of Israel, by the watercourses, and in all the inhabited places of the country. I will feed them with good pasture; and upon the mountains of the height of Israel shall their fold be: there shall they lie down in a good fold; and on fat pasture shall they feed upon the mountains of Israel" (34.13–14). That is exactly where we find ourselves today, in that "fat" Messianic kingdom, so why do we so often insist that the life of a Christian is a miserable one?

God has never required "fat-free living"; in fact, He has promised just the opposite. Concentrate today on the peace that living as a child of God brings to your life. Focus on the joy of salvation and the fellowship of a spiritual family. Contemplate the good in your life. The rest of the world deals with addictions, legal problems, disrupted families, purposeless lives, and finally, illness and death without hope and comfort. Talk about a negative life.

Go out and enjoy the fat in your life today.

The thief comes not, but that he may steal, and kill, and destroy: I came that they may have life, and may have it abundantly.

John 10.10

October 10

The Cookie Cup

When we camp we eat more convenience food than any other time of the year. When you are trying to pack a week's worth into one cooler and two 2 x 1 x 1½ foot plastic containers, and when there is no place to put leftovers, a packaged pasta or rice mix and a small can of vegetables is the perfect-sized accompaniment for whatever meat Keith is grilling that night. Let's face it, an inch thick rib chop, seasoned with herbs and spices and cooked over a wood fire is the star of the show anyway.

As for dessert, store-bought cookies are a staple. However, my family is spoiled by homemade cookies so just any old Chips Ahoy won't do, not even Oreos. So we splurge a bit on the cookies.

A box of Walker's Pure Butter Shortbread Bars, imported from Scotland, are a favorite. Melt-in-your-mouth-rich with the flavor and mouth-feel of real butter, and barely sweetened, they are the perfect accompaniment to a cup of instant hot chocolate—another camping necessity.

Another standby is any Pepperidge Farm cookie, depending upon what's available when I hit the stores the week before a campout. Walker's Shortbread makes them look like a bargain, so I buy two kinds rather than just one. If you have ever had any, you know they come in fluted paper cups, like big, white, muffin pan liners, either nestled in a variety box or stacked in a tall foil-lined paper bag.

To minimize the amount of trash we need to stow away from the raccoons, possums, and bears, we usually toss anything that will burn into the campfire as we finish its contents. On our last trip we tossed the cup from the first layer of Chewy Fruit and Nut Granola Cookies into the fire. Somehow in the draft of the fire it landed right side up in the middle of a scrap board Keith had just thrown in as well. Both sat right in front of an oak log that had coaled up on the bottom, but not yet begun to burn.

Temperatures were in the forties that night, so we had a good hot fire going with backlogs to reflect the heat our way and glowing embers several inches deep. Ordinarily a thin piece of paper in a fire like that won't last five seconds, including burn time. Because of how it landed, that little cup sat there five full minutes. Once, a gust of wind tried to blow it into the fire, but the fire's updraft on either side of it pushed it right back to the middle of the board. Only a small dark singe mark on its pleated edge showed how close a call it had been.

Finally, though, the board itself began to burn from either end and the flames crept inexorably toward the paper cup. Suddenly, in one rapid whoosh, the cup caught fire and was gone in less than a second, its final glowing ash floating into the air before finally winking out in the cold black above.

Too many times we are like that little fluted paper liner. We get ourselves into a place we have no business being, into circumstances that should have ended badly. Yet because God is good, we are saved from the world of hurt we deserved. Then, instead of appreciating the second chance and removing ourselves from that dangerous place, we stay there and gloat. "See? Nothing happened. I'm just fine. I told you I could handle it."

We sit there smug and confident, certain that everyone who cautioned us was wrong, while disaster sneaks up closer and closer. In fact, we reach a point where the danger around us seems normal. We no longer even notice. We may have a close call or two, but for so many it just adds to the feeling of superiority instead of waking us up.

And so suddenly, one day, we are gone in a flash—without warning it seems. But no, we had just become blind to the warnings all around us, fooling ourselves into believing we were safe, while everyone else saw the fire creeping in from all sides.

Pay attention to where you are today. Take a mental step back and see the whole picture, not just the safe little ledge you think you have built. Listen to those around you who can often see much more clearly than you can in the midst of all that smoke and glare. They wouldn't say anything and endure your scorn if they didn't care.

But you, beloved, building up yourselves on your most holy faith, praying in the Holy Spirit, keep yourselves in the love of God, looking for the mercy of our Lord Jesus Christ unto eternal life. And on some have mercy, who are in doubt; and some save, snatching them out of the fire; and on some have mercy with fear; hating even the garment spotted by the flesh.

Jude 20–23

October 11

Ask and It Shall Be Given You

I recently did a personal study about prayer, particularly using passages in the epistles. One thing that struck me immediately was how much the early Christians prayed. It was not merely a respite between songs or a punctuation mark at the end of the sermon; it wasn't just a ritual at home performed before meals or at bedtime. It was an important part of their lives and of their assemblies.

Another thing I noticed was what these people prayed for. Think a minute. The last time you specifically asked someone to pray for you, it was about your physical health wasn't it, or the health of a family member or friend? Here is a challenge for you: pick up a concordance and look up every use of the words *pray, prayer, prayed, praying,* or any other form of the word. Confine yourself to the books of Acts through Revelation, since the point here is how early *Christians* prayed. As you read through those passages, make a note of everything they prayed for or about. Out of 52 passages, I found once or twice where physical health was mentioned or even alluded to—well, three or four if you count all three times Paul says in the same verse that he prayed for his thorn in the flesh to be removed.

So what does that say about them and us? Here were people, the majority of whom had come out of paganism, who had to make drastic lifestyle changes, who, despite their immaturity in the faith—as we who were "raised in the church" or at least grew up in a "Christian nation" would define immaturity—these people, could see that the spiritual mattered much more than the physical. As Paul might have worded it, they were spiritual and we are carnal. Ouch!

Does that mean it is wrong to pray for "the sick and afflicted"? Of course not, since we do have a few examples. I have asked for a lot of prayers lately. But what is our motive in praying for health or safety? What was theirs? As Paul says in Philippians, do I want to stay here for the sake of others, for the sake of the gospel? Do I want to stay healthy so I can serve the Lord and his people? Or have I just not been everywhere and done everything I wanted to? Am I just so sold on this life that the next holds no appeal for me?

Once you have completed the little challenge I gave you earlier, try this one: pray one prayer that does not mention anyone's physical health at all. You know what will happen? If you are like me, a very short prayer. You sit there and wonder, what do I say? That was a sure indication to me that my prayers were not as spiritual as they ought to be.

Here are some passages that may help you start changing the emphasis of your prayers: Ephesians 1.15–19; Philippians 1.9–11; Colossians 1.9–18; 4.2–4; 2 Thessalonians 1.11–12. You can also refer to the list you made earlier. The point is not to remove all prayers for the physically ill, but to add more for our spiritual needs, the things which should be most important to a Christian.

You know that passage that says "Ask and it shall be given you"? You will find that when praying these more spiritual prayers, when God answers them, your life will change for the better, no matter what your state of health.

But if any of you lack wisdom, let him ask of God, who gives to all liberally and does not upbraid, and it shall be given him. But let him ask in faith, nothing doubting;

for he who doubts is like the surge of the sea, driven by the wind and tossed. For let not that man think he shall receive anything of the Lord, a doubleminded man, unstable in all his ways.

James 1.5–8

October 12

Fuel for the Fire

Magdi is getting old. Her red coat is turning white. She cannot hear as well as she used to and often sleeps through things that have Chloe up and running. Her gait is crooked and her joints stiff. Sometimes she loses strength in her hind legs and they simply fall out from under her. But pick up a tennis ball, bounce it once or twice, hold it out for her to see, and instantly the years melt away. Her ears prick, her posture straightens, and she crouches ready to run as soon as you throw it. Her eyes practically *will* you to throw it. When you do, she runs as if she doesn't hurt at all, and will even jump into the air like old times to snatch it on the bounce. This dog loves nothing more than to chase a tennis ball, and would do it until she collapsed if we let her.

If you have never visited with an older Christian, you should. I am no longer surprised by their life stories. Most of these good people have lived far more exciting lives than I, and have been through suffering I hope to never experience. The wisdom in their words will stand you in good stead if you pay attention.

Their knowledge of the scriptures is like that tennis ball to Magdi. They may sit and talk quietly, or hardly talk at all, but then you mention the Bible and it isn't just a light that shines in their eyes, it's a fire that starts burning and gets brighter as they continue. They seem to tap into a hidden energy source, sit up straighter and lean forward with an intent look that will burn itself into your heart, along with the accumulated knowledge and experience they want so badly to impart. It is their legacy, and too often we don't claim it because old people are "boring"—visiting with them is simply a duty we fulfill as seldom as possible. Besides, who can count on their minds to be clear anyway—nothing useful can come from them. So our society trains us, and so we continue to make the foolish mistakes of the naïve when the help is there for the taking.

We have another problem in our society—the desire for instant gratification. Wisdom comes from accumulated experiences and from taking in the word of God—the source of all wisdom—on a regular basis year after year after year. The reason those older folks have a fire burning in their hearts is because they feed it daily. We are too immature to stick it out. We want it now—read a few chapters and become a sage overnight, or at least within a month or two, we seem to think.

If we are not careful, when it comes our turn to be the old wise heads, we will have no fuel to burn, no warmth and glow to pass on to the next generation.

So today's thought is two fold. Go visit some older folks. Sit and listen and take in what they have to offer. Then go home and get yourself ready to be that older generation. It takes more smarts, more strength, and more diligence than you think.

> *God, you have taught me from my youth; and I still declare your wondrous works. Yea, even when I am old and grayheaded, O God, forsake me not, until I have declared your strength unto the next generation, your might to every one that is to come.*
>
> Psalm 71.17–18

A Divine Ought

For when by reason of time you ***ought*** *to be teachers, you have need again that one teach you the rudiments. …Be not many of you teachers, my brethren.* (Heb 5.12; Jas 3.1)

We often shake our heads at people who do their best to make the Bible contradict itself. If they would only check the context, if they would only approach it with the same fair attitude they want others to have toward them, they could see the truth. Yet we are no better when it comes to passages we don't want to deal with.

I am certain that every time a lesson is taught on speaking to our friends and neighbors about our faith someone has said, "But the Bible says, 'Be not many of you teachers.' Teaching is not my talent."

I think it is fair to say that God does not expect everyone to stand in front of a group and teach: "He gave *some* to be… teachers" (Eph 4.11). But that does not mean there is not some aspect of teaching He expects of us all; that is the only way to reconcile those passages above, and reconcile them we must. Otherwise, why bother to believe any of it?

First, God expects us to help teach ourselves. Whether or not we learn from the teaching that is available is entirely up to us. We should be studying outside of the formal setting laid before us by the elders and preachers, spending time on our own meditating on what we have heard, looking things up, making notes in class and out, and sifting through them. You can't do that when you miss those Bible studies to begin with. Whether or not the teacher is a good one makes no difference. There is more to being a student than sitting there waiting to have the facts pumped in. A student with the right attitude can learn something regardless the teacher. Parents, you would do well to remember that the next time your high school age child complains about his Bible class teacher too.

God also expects us to reach the point that we can give good advice. The older training the younger (Tit 2.3–5) is a principle that transcends any time period or culture. The only excuse we have is dying young! How many of you are up for that?

He says we should be able to restore the wayward (Gal 6.1). Who should do that? "You who are spiritual." Do you want to claim to be otherwise before your Maker?

Finally, Peter says we should be "ready always to give answer" (1 Pet 3.15). He doesn't say we should know the answer to every question anyone might ask, but to give "a reason concerning the hope that is in you." Certainly we should know why we believe what we believe. If you don't know why, then how can you be sure your faith is your own and not something simply handed down by tradition?

And that leads us right back around to where we started. Are you attending Bible studies? Are you studying on your own? Are you asking for help from those who might give good advice and have better knowledge concerning the scriptures? Are you taking advantage of the training offered in how to study, which tools to use, and which methods are most helpful? God said, you ought to be teachers. Are you still in need that someone should teach you the basics?

This is a serious matter—a Divine "ought"—more simply put, an order straight from God. Don't let the fact that you have been a Christian for 20 years or more keep you from asking for help. If you wait any longer, it will only be worse. You will be even older and still "need again that someone teach you."

The fear of the Lord is the beginning of knowledge, but fools despise wisdom and instruction.

Proverbs 1.7

October 14

A Life of Luxury

A couple of months ago we had one of those weeks to end all weeks. Besides the tropical storm that dumped 13 inches of rain over us and left us without power for several hours, the pump on the well went out, the phones, and thus the modem, went out, the satellite dish went out, the air conditioning in the car went out, and we each had a respiratory virus.

As I was sitting in the mechanic's air conditioned waiting room, leaning back on his padded couch with a television droning on should I care to watch and a cup of free coffee between my hands, bemoaning all my misfortunes, I suddenly realized what a luxury it was to do so. A tropical storm had moved almost directly over us, yet we only lost power for a few hours. Thirteen inches of rain had fallen, yet we could still get up and down our road to a dry home; we just couldn't use the telephones and modem for four days. The air conditioning in the car, something I never even had as a child, was out, but I could still drive it to the dealership, sit in comfort while they fixed it, and my warranty covered it completely. The pump was out so I had to do without running water for five hours. A hundred years ago I wouldn't have even known what I was missing. What a luxury to be able to complain about such things.

I saw a promo on television the other night. Some rich, show biz personality was "going ballistic" because the $100 lipstick she bought did not match her evening gown, and she had broken a nail right after a $300 manicure. I remember feeling outraged and downright disgusted with her, but am I any better?

Compared to most people in the world, we live lives of luxury and don't even realize it. I am sure many of those impoverished people would have felt the same outrage at me had they heard me complaining.

In the Old Testament, Israel became so wealthy that all they cared about was living lives of ease. They stopped being concerned about the things a true people of God should be concerned with, like sin and evil in the world. While many did not actually partake of those things, they simply let them keep on existing. The important things to them were building large, comfortable homes, entertaining in style, and having others wait on them. That is one of the reasons they were destroyed, as Amos plainly put it. The elite, the "first" in the nation, were the first to be carried away captive.

The next time we start our "poor little me" lists, we need to take a good look at them. Let's at least realize what a luxury it is to have such things to complain about and be grateful, and let's save our real complaints for things that truly matter.

Woe to those who are at ease in Zion, and to those who feel secure on the mountain of Samaria. ... Woe to those who lie on beds of ivory and stretch themselves out on their couches, and eat lambs from the flock and calves from the middle of the stall, who sing idle songs to the sound of the harps and like David, invent themselves instruments of music, who drink in bowls and anoint themselves with the finest oils, but are not grieved over the ruin of Joseph. Therefore they shall now be the first of those who go into exile, and the revelry of those who stretch themselves out shall pass away. The Lord God has sworn by himself, declares the Lord, the God of hosts, I abhor the pride of Jacob and hate his strongholds, and I will deliver up his city and all that is in it.

Amos 6.1, 4–8

October 15

Suppertime

When my boys were still at home, family meal time was important. We all made an effort to be together as many nights a week as possible, even as their schedules became busier in the high school years. The majority of the time, we managed to do so.

I recently read a couple of articles discussing the importance of families eating together. A family that eats together has better nutrition and the girls have fewer eating disorders. The children do better at school. They develop better language skills. They are less likely to take drugs, smoke, or drink. Eating together, especially the evening meal, helps maintain accountability. It is a "check-in time" which fosters a sense of togetherness (www.sixwise.com).

"Dinnertime should be treated like a reunion, a respite from the outside world, a moment of strengthening relationships, and a pleasant experience that should always be cherished," Ron Afable, "Eating Together as a Family" (www.adam.org).

When I read that last quote I was stunned. Was he talking about family dinnertime or the Lord's Supper? God tells us we are to have this meal when we are "gathered together," not each in his own home. The reasons are precisely those reasons. When I walk into the church's gathering place I should have a feeling of relief, a "Whew! I made it!" moment. This is my haven; these people are my support group; this is where I gather the strength to face another week of trials and temptations. Is it any wonder God chose something that was part of a family meal to celebrate our one-ness with Him, with our Savior, and with each other?

The denominational world says that having this meal as often as the first Christians did—every Sunday—makes it less special, yet what does the world say about families having meals together on a regular basis? Surely that applies here as well. We are better nourished spiritually, we grow in the knowledge of the Word, we sin less because of the accountability regular meetings require, and we develop stronger relationships with one another. Funny how God knew what He was doing, isn't it?

We often say that we should forget the outside world during this special time, but more than that, we should remember our "inside world"—our bond with one another. Disagreements should melt away. Aggravations with others should be covered by our love. Personality problems should take the place they deserve—the bottom of the barrel. To do otherwise is to make a mockery of the feast, and "drink damnation to ourselves."

Our Father calls us to this special suppertime to reunite, to rest and recover, and to remember who we are and how we got here. This special dinnertime should always be cherished. Don't make a habit of missing it.

The cup of blessing which we bless, is it not a communion of the blood of Christ; the bread which we break, is it not a communion with the blood of Christ? Seeing that we who are many are one bread, one body, for we all partake of the one bread.

1 Corinthians 10.16–17

October 16

Wage Earners

I was watching a ball game a few weeks ago when the school promos aired. Evidently one of them now has the slogan "I can only count on what I earn." I must have heard it ten times in that 30-second spot.

Every Christian ought to jump back in horror when they hear such a thing. What I earn? My life is a hopeless downhill plunge to destruction if I am counting on what I earn. "For all have sinned and fall short of the glory of God" (Rom 3.23).

Okay, you say, but they are talking about getting along in life, not the afterlife. Really? I can count on my money, my career, my social status? All these things can be taken away in a flash by an illness, an accident, a bad investment, a downturn in the economy, even someone else's crime. How can I count on those for anything? You see, that is the problem when you don't believe in God, as a good many professors no longer do. What a miserable life to live.

What's that? You are not miserable because you can do what you want to do instead of answering to a higher power? I suppose, but then you live a life without hope, without purpose. One of these days that will hit you right between the eyes and you *will* be miserable. All the intellectualism in the world has yet to find a cure for that.

I can only count on God, on His help, on His promises, on His love and grace and mercy. A God by the way, who changes not, who has proven Himself to His people for thousands of years. A God who is always there regardless of the balance in my bank account, the progress of my career, or my status in society.

What are you depending on today, a life of uncertainty, or a God who inhabits eternity and controls it all?

> *But now being made free from sin and become servants to God you have your fruit unto sanctification, and the end eternal life. For the wages of sin is death, but the free gift of God is eternal life through Christ Jesus our Lord.*
>
> Romans 6.22–23

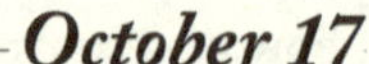

October 17

Practice Makes Perfect

The gospel is nothing if not practical. God was more interested in helping us live our lives every day than equipping us to sit in dusty rooms arguing theology. So today let's be eminently practical.

I am sure you have heard "practice makes perfect" your entire life. *It is wrong.* The only thing practice makes is permanent.

One of the things I had to train many of my piano students to do was to practice correctly. They would come in with the same mistakes week after week. First they played the wrong note (the same wrong note in the same piece at every lesson), and then they would correct it. What they had taught themselves to do was to play the wrong note first, then stop and play the right one. Correcting it did not make the competition judge happy. He wanted a perfect performance the first time.

When their poor practice habits became obvious, we had to start all over. First I had them tell me the name of the correct note, saying the name aloud several times which I then repeated to them. "Right, it's an F#, an F#, an F#." Then I had them find that note and play it with the correct finger, while saying its name over and over. Then I had them play the note before it and after it until they played that three note sequence correctly no less than three times in a row. If they made a mistake, we started counting all over.

Then we backed up one measure and played past it one measure, once again until they could do it correctly three times in a row. Then we backed up one phrase and played past it one phrase until they could play the three phrases correctly three times in a row. You get the picture. We practiced it correctly over and over, using as many senses as possible, hearing ourselves say the correct name of the note, feeling the correct note under the finger, seeing the correct note both on the page and as we played it, and then playing through without the bad habit of doing it wrong first. Usually that took care of the problem.

What do we do as Christians? Do we teach ourselves to do it wrong first, then pray for forgiveness over and over, constantly making the same mistakes? Practice makes permanent. Maybe it is time to do a little analysis.

Why do I keep doing the same thing again and again? "That's just the way I am," is not an acceptable reason; it is a lame excuse. God expects us to change the way we are. If it took such detailed, tedious work to undo a bad habit in a piano piece, why do we think we don't have to really work at it to undo a bad habit in our thoughts or behaviors, where Satan is actively pulling against us? Some of my students may have been little devils, but that is not why they played wrong notes! So why should sin be easier to fix?

Often just the fact that I am owning up to my sin and thinking about the problem will do a world of good, but if you really want to make progress—and I assume we all do—it takes more effort than that.

Make a plan and follow it. Find three times in the day to pray about that particular problem. Find three passages about that sin and read them over and over. The next day pray again and find three more passages. Do that every day, praying, listing and reading. Keep a journal of all the times that problem rears its ugly head. Write down every detail of the situation, how it happened, what caused it, and how you handled, or mishandled, it—*without blaming anyone else*. When you finally have a victory, celebrate with a prayer of thanksgiving and your favorite hymn. Call a friend with whom you have shared your problem (Jas 5.16) and tell them about it so they can rejoice with you.

You do not have to do all of these things in all of these particular ways and numbers, but do *something* to help yourself kick the habit. Think about how you set about to lose weight, keeping track of what you eat (including the no-noes) and how much you exercise each day. Remember how those nicotine patch commercials show people stepping down one level at a time till they reach their goal? But you should be stepping *up* one level at the time to reach yours.

Practice makes permanent. Make sure you are practicing correctly.

> *No one born of God makes a practice of sinning, for God's seed abides in him, and he cannot keep on sinning because he has been born of God.*
>
> 1 John 3.9

October 18

Making Allowances

Four letters, "weight allowance." I have seen it in crossword puzzles so many times that I automatically write in "tret," even though I have no idea what it is talking about. Finally I looked it up. Tret is (or was?) the weight allowance given to buyers of certain commodities, usually four pounds per hundred, to make up for deterioration during transit and impurities like sand and dust. So if they order 100 pounds, they actually receive 104, the idea being that they will have at least 100 pounds of product in that 104 pounds.

That made me think about grace. God supplies what we lack in perfection because of our sin. Only the ratio is backwards—I am sure He allows at least 100 pounds of grace for every four pounds of our faith and obedience, probably far more.

We also make such allowances for each other. When we know someone has been through a rough time, it is easier to take their snappy comment with equanimity. When we love as we ought, our "love covers a multitude of sins" (1 Pet 4.8).

However, the need to make allowances for things like that should eventually disappear as we all grow to maturity in Christ. Shouldn't a man who has been a Christian 40 years no longer be watching and waiting for the Bible class teacher or preacher to make a comment he can raise a fuss about? Yet how many times have I heard young preachers told, "It's just old brother So-and-So. That's just the way he is." Why is he still that way? Hasn't anyone told him how much he hurts people with that behavior? I wonder how many young preachers were expected to make so many allowances for so many things that they just gave up preaching. Why doesn't anyone make allowances for them?

Is old sister So-and-So still managing to take offense at everything anyone says and jumping on them with both feet? Hasn't anyone told her that she is wrong to treat people that way? Oh yes, I know what they will hear back, but we are not doing her any favors to let her keep on this way. The Lord certainly won't make allowances for it.

But the larger question for me is this: are people continually making allowances, "tret," for *me?* Am I the one causing consternation, making people walk on eggshells around me, and stealing everyone's pleasure with my bad attitude? God's grace works for people who are trying their best to do right and still fail, not for those who make a career out of bitterness, criticism, and cynicism and expect everyone, including God, to just accept it. My "tret" should become smaller and smaller as I mature as a Christian, leaving infancy behind and becoming full-grown.

Where do I stand today? A 50-year-old baby is no longer cute, and to take the grace of God for granted in such a way must surely be an abomination to Him.

> *For if we go on sinning deliberately after receiving the knowledge of the truth, there no longer remains a sacrifice for sins, but a fearful expectation of judgment, and a fury of fire that will consume the adversaries. Anyone who has set aside the law of Moses dies without mercy on the evidence of two or three witnesses. How much worse punishment, do you think, will be deserved by the one who has spurned the Son of God, and has profaned the blood of the covenant by which he was sanctified, and has outraged the Spirit of grace?*
>
> Hebrews 10.26–29

October 19

Motivators

Several years ago I was teaching the fourth grade Bible class when the subject of Heaven came up. One of our nine-year-olds was refreshingly candid. "From what I hear about Heaven," she began, "it's going to be just like going to church forever what with all that singing and praising God, and I am not sure I want to do that."

I laughed that day, but I have thought about it a lot. All those descriptions of Heaven are supposed to be motivators, and this little girl was not motivated: "If you're good you get to sit still forever and listen to boring sermons." What have we done? We *know* those descriptions are figurative. We *know* there will be no streets paved with gold. Gold is notoriously soft. Can you imagine what it would look like by the time we all walked on it? Yet, even though we *know* these things, we seem to have missed the point.

Those first century Christians lived a day to day existence. They prayed for their "daily bread" because they had no idea if they would have enough that day, let alone tomorrow. The farmers among them existed at the mercy of the weather and natural disasters. The shopkeepers and artisans lived at the mercy of the economy. No one was going to "bail them out."

To those people, a place so wealthy that gold and precious jewels were used as *construction material,* meant security. It meant rest from working long hours day after day to simply exist.

Those people lived under the rule of a foreign king. Doubtless they had all seen wars and battles. They knew, in fact, that the Barbarian Hordes could still come over the mountains and wipe them out. Did 9/11 cause you some concern? Has it made you worry more about the possibility of terrorists under every bush? Those first century Christians lived with that sort of uncertainty every day of their lives. In fact, they probably had more safety as a conquered people than ever before. But the picture of a huge city with huge walls meant safety and peace *forever.* Security—that is what those pictures of Heaven were all about, not materialism. I have no doubt that if John were writing to us, he would use other motivators.

And that is my point today—give your children motivation that means something to them. Say something like, "Heaven is a place where you never have to go to bed. It's a place where you can play all day and never be scolded." And as they get older perhaps, "Heaven is a place with no homework, a place where you can play video games as long as you want without your thumbs aching, a place you can hang out with your buddies forever." You tell them that whatever Heaven is like, it is as wonderful to the soul as these physical things are to their physical lives. As they get older, you will have directed their training and teaching so that the motivators become more spiritual and less material.

But you know what? There are still days I think Heaven should be a big kitchen I can cook in all day without my back hurting, with the dishes magically cleaning themselves, and with all the finished products looking exactly like the pictures in the cookbooks and tasting just as wonderful! Sometimes you need that sort of motivation and so do your children.

But at this stage of our lives, Keith and I have a different motivation—he knows he will *hear* those beautiful songs, and I know I will *see* the glory of God. Is that still just a little physically-minded and materialistic? Maybe, but it works.

> *And I saw a new heaven and a new earth: for the first heaven and the first earth are passed away; and the sea is no more. And I saw the holy city, new Jerusalem, coming down out of heaven of God, made ready as a bride adorned for her husband. ...Having a wall great and high; having twelve gates, and at the gates twelve angels; and names written thereon, are of the twelve tribes of the children of Israel. ...And the building of the wall thereof was jasper: and the city was pure gold, like unto pure*

glass. The foundations of the wall of the city were adorned with all manner of precious stones. The first foundation was jasper; the second, sapphire; the third, chalcedony; the fourth, emerald; the fifth, sardonyx; the sixth, sardius; the seventh, chrysolite; the eighth, beryl; the ninth, topaz; the tenth, chrysoprase; the eleventh, jacinth; the twelfth, amethyst. And the twelve gates were twelve pearls; each one of the several gates was of one pearl: and the street of the city was pure gold, as it were transparent glass. …And there shall in no wise enter into it anything unclean, or he that makes an abomination and a lie: but only they that are written in the Lamb's book of life.

Revelation 21.1–2, 12, 19–21, 27

October 20

Double Vision

I don't see like you do. I don't even see like those of you who have less-than-perfect vision. Normal vision has never been a part of my life. I suppose that's natural when you have a congenital eye disorder.

When I was a child, no one ever told my parents exactly what was wrong with me, just, "She has really bad vision." As a teenager I began to figure out that it was worse than I thought when my doctor allowed all the student doctors to examine me and give their opinions, then sat back and told them all why they were wrong. Then after I married and we moved out of state, I actually had a doctor tell me he wished I had never walked into his office. I never did again.

So how do I see? That groundbreaking surgery on June 13, 2005, which has saved my vision for six extra years now, has left some interesting effects. Depending upon the day, the light, the internal pressure at any particular moment, I have double vision, tunnel vision, blurry vision, foggy vision, white reflections that block most of the view, ghost images, black specks, pale yellow splotches, starbursts, gold concentric circles, a fish-eye lens effect, spinning black and silver pinwheels on the periphery that move toward the front—and shaky equilibrium!

But I think that makes me understand Jesus' statement in Matthew 6.22 better than most: "The lamp of the body is the eye; if therefore, your eye is single, your whole body shall be full of light."

Jesus is talking about focus. What do I focus on, this physical life or the spiritual? The immediate context is the contrast between spiritual treasures and earthly treasure (vv 19–20), God and mammon (v 24), the concern for physical needs versus righteousness and the kingdom (vv 31–33).

I often become distracted by things that get in the way of my vision. I am down to one eye I am still legal to drive with now, and concentration on the road is important. I have to consciously make an effort to ignore the specks, the splotches, the circles, the starbursts, the reflections, and on days when the blur is too much, I simply cannot drive if I want to avoid a mishap.

In the same way it is easy for our spiritual "eye" to become distracted by all the things in front of us, by a concern for wealth, acceptance, and security, but also by necessities like food, clothing, and shelter—things which certainly are not wrong in themselves. But when that is the thing we focus on, our eye is no longer single but, as Jesus plainly says in verse 23, "evil." Sooner or later we will have a spiritual "wreck."

That is probably where Satan gets the majority of us—we have to provide for our families. Worrying about that can actually make us do more than we need to, perhaps even push us over into a covetous attitude of always wanting more, not relying on God, and putting Him and his kingdom so far down on the list that we never even get to it any more. And that means that our "eye" is no longer light but darkness, making us see things in ways that deceive us—we *can* serve God while we serve this world and its treasures, can't we?

Jesus appeals to our common sense. Two different things cannot be the "most" important. We have to make a choice—which one comes first? Which one do we focus on? Whom do we serve, God or mammon?

Take it from someone who knows—double vision doesn't work.

> *Lay not up for yourselves treasure upon the earth, where moth and rust consume and where thieves break through and steal; but lay up for yourselves treasures in heaven, where neither moth nor rust consume, and where thieves do not break through and steal, for where your treasure is, there will your heart be also. The lamp of the body is the eye;* ***if your eye is single****, your whole body shall be full of light. But if your eye is evil, your whole body shall be full of darkness. If therefore, the light that is in you becomes darkness, how great is the darkness! No man can serve two masters; for either he will hate the one and love the other, or else he will hold to one and despise the other. You cannot serve God and mammon.*
>
> Matthew 6.19–24

October 21

Lessons from Lappidoth

"Now Deborah, a prophetess, the wife of Lappidoth, she judged Israel at that time" (Jdg 4.4).

Do you know anything about Lappidoth? I know he was Deborah's husband and that is all. He is mentioned nowhere else in the entire Bible. Yet because of his amazing wife his name was written down for everyone to read for thousands of years.

No, it was not because God ordained that a wife have no identity without her husband, as some feminists might try to argue. Have you ever googled your own name or simply looked it up in your city's telephone directory? Somewhere in the world there is someone else with the same name as you, first and last. Imagine how many there are with just your first name. I can find six Marys in the New Testament alone.

It was necessary to identify people in the scriptures by their parents or spouses or children in order to make it plain who was being talked about. There was at least one other Deborah in the Bible, the nurse of Rebekah (Gen 35.8). I imagine there were many other little girls named Deborah throughout Israel, especially after the time of Judges 4. Miriam, after all, is the Hebrew for the Aramaic Mary, of whom we have so many in the first century AD. Surely the great woman judge was a worthy namesake too.

So what is the big deal about Lappidoth? Just this: he was mentioned because of his wife, and he is respected because of his wife. Whom you marry can make or break you in your career, in your reputation in the community, and most important, as a servant of God.

How many times have you heard it said, or even said yourself, "He would make a good (elder, preacher, Bible class teacher, deacon) if not for his wife"? God made woman so man would not be alone and so he would have a suitable helper in life. David says, "[Jehovah] is our help" in Psalm 33.20, using exactly the same Hebrew word describing God as the one God used of woman in Genesis 2.18. Part of the help God gives men is the women who stand beside them. There is nothing demeaning about being a tool in the hand of the Lord.

Maybe the problem is men who do not recognize their duty to spiritually lead the family, "nourishing and cherishing" their brides, as Christ did the church. Keith is the one who taught me how to study. "And created a monster," he always adds.

Inevitably though, the onus falls on women who will not be led, who will not grow, who use their freewill instead to rebel against God.

Jesus told a parable in Luke 14 about people who would not follow Him. The point of the parable was the lame excuses people will make, but I can read at least one of those excuses in a different way. When the Lord presents him an opportunity, I would hate for my husband to have to say, "I have married a wife and therefore I cannot come."

A worthy woman who can find? For her price is far above rubies. The heart of her husband trusts in her and he shall have no lack of gain. She does him good and not evil all the days of his life. ...Her husband is known in the gates where he sits with the elders of the land. ...Grace is deceitful and beauty is vain, but a woman who fears Jehovah, she shall be praised.

Proverbs 31.10–12, 23, 30

October 22

Stuck in a Rut

I hear an awful lot these days about people being "stuck in a rut," especially when it comes to their religious practices. For some reason that is supposed to excuse every departure from the scriptures. Some groups, for instance, have decided that the first century practice of taking the Lord's Supper every Sunday must be changed to monthly, quarterly, or only on certain holidays. When one does it too often, they say, it becomes merely habit and loses its meaning.

Others, who claim to understand the importance of following the pattern God set for group worship, still want to change things around on a regular schedule, the incidental things that scripture does not regulate. That's fine. I am the last person to bind where God has not bound, but consider a few things with me.

The way we are doing things now in my church family, while still scriptural, is *not* the way we did them when I was a child. It is *not* the way my grandparents did them. It is not even the way we did them 15 years ago. Society and culture have changed and so have the various expedients we use to fulfill God's requirements. So what is this about ruts?

When Jesus appeared on the scene in the first century, the Jews had been practicing the same law, including a Sabbath *every* Saturday, for 1,500 years by a much more exacting standard than we have under the new covenant. "Aha!" some will say, "and look what happened. Along came the Pharisees to whom the Law was nothing but a set of rules to keep. It had totally lost its meaning to them as a religion of the heart."

Had it? What about Nicodemus and Joseph of Arimathea? What about Saul of Tarsus who "lived before God in all good conscience" (Acts 23.1)? Surely they were not the only Pharisees to whom the Law still meant something. And what about the rest of the people? Did Anna, Simeon, Zacharias and Elisabeth, Mary and Joseph, Salome and Zebedee, Mary, Martha, and Lazarus practice a religion out of habit that had totally lost meaning to them because they had been stuck in a rut for a millennium and a half? How in the world did Jesus manage to find 12 apostles if everyone practicing Judaism was "stuck in a rut"?

It seems to me that when someone complains that his religion no longer has meaning for him because he is "stuck in a rut," it says more about him than it does about the religion he practices. While babes in Christ may need special care, mature Christians should be past the need for coddling. It is my responsibility to keep my heart and my attitude right in my service to God and to keep myself out of the rut of rote ritual, even if God tells me to do exactly the same thing in exactly the same way for 10,000 years. Exactly who is it that is being worshipped anyway? It certainly isn't me and my likes and dislikes—at least it shouldn't be.

If we need to change the things we can change, by all means, let's change them. But when the reason becomes "how I feel" instead of what is best for the body of Christ and the mission God gave us, we need to stop and take a better look at ourselves.

Today I will strive to put my heart into my service to others and to God, even if that service is the same as yesterday's, or last week's, or last year's. That is, and will always be, *my* responsibility and no one else's.

> *And now Israel, what does the Lord your God require of you but to fear the Lord your God and to walk in all his ways, to love him, to serve the Lord your God with all your heart and all your soul, and to keep the commandments and statutes of the Lord, which I am commanding you this day for your good.*
>
> Deuteronomy 10.12–13

October 23

Now Where Did I Put That Hatchet?

If there is one thing I have never understood about grudge-holders, it is how they can think they have a monopoly on being hurt or injured. These are the folks that, though they profess forgiveness, and years later are acting kindly toward their victims—at least in public—can at a moment's notice give a laundry list of every bad deed that person has done to them. And they will, any time you want to hear it. In fact, they will happily do so before you even ask.

But somehow they think they are perfect. They have never done anything hurtful to anyone, and would be horrified if you started making your own laundry list against them! They *must* think that, or surely they would be more merciful, wouldn't they?

You see, grudge-holding is the worst kind of self-centeredness. It says, "My hurts count more than yours." It infers, "I have never done anything as bad as this to you." And then it rationalizes, "What you did to me is so bad, it does not have to be forgiven."

If you said that to a grudge-holder, he would be horrified, especially if he claimed to be a Christian. Unfortunately, that is another aspect of this sin—it keeps you from seeing yourself as you really are. We become so blinded by our "injured innocence" that we cannot see the truth—*no one* is innocent; we *all* mess up once in awhile. It is bad when this sort of selfishness causes animosity between neighbors, sad when it causes rifts in families, and tragic when it causes a lack of unity in the family of God.

Jesus said I cannot be forgiven if I don't forgive. Forgiveness means I don't spread it around, I don't let it fester in my mind, I don't bring it up again at any opportunity, *ever*. Forgiveness means I understand that I have done my fair share of hurts to others, whether intentional or not, and since I hope they will not hold them against me, I certainly won't hold things against them. That is exactly what Peter meant when he said, "Love covers a multitude of sins" (1 Pet 4.8). I think Peter uses that word "sin" in an ironic way. We cannot cover real sins against God, and are not supposed to, but in our self-centeredness, we place what amounts to minimal slights in the same category as real sin. And Peter also makes it plain that no matter what I say about the matter, if I do not forgive and I show that lack of mercy by my constant grudge-holding, I do not love.

Forgiveness means having enough humility to recognize that no one has done to me anything remotely similar to what I have done to the Lord. Holding grudges means the opposite—I have made my feelings just as important as Christ's, therefore I am just as important as He is—just as important as God.

Didn't they used to stone people for that?

> *Therefore is the kingdom of heaven like a certain king who made a reckoning of his servants. ...One was brought to him that owed him* [about 60,000,000 days' pay, Lenski]. ...*The servant therefore fell down and said, Lord have patience with me and I will pay all. And the lord of that servant, being moved with compassion, released him and forgave him the debt. But the servant went out and found one of his fellow servants who owed him* [about 100 days' pay, *Ibid.*]... *and said, Pay what you owe. ...Then the Lord called unto him and said, You wicked servant, I forgave you all your debt...Should you not have had mercy on your fellow servant as I had mercy on you? And the lord was wroth and delivered him to the tormentors. ...So shall also my heavenly Father do unto you if you forgive not your brother* ***from the heart.***
>
> Matthew 18.21–35

What A Horrible Idea

I happened to think the other day, what if someone followed me around with a tape recorder all day, on any given day, and then made me listen to it in the evening? It popped into my mind after I had said something I should not have said to someone, and they wisely stood there and said nothing back. You know what happens when someone does that? *All of a sudden you actually hear yourself.* And boy, are you embarrassed.

So just imagine for a moment that you answer a knock on the door late one evening, just after you brush your teeth and put on your pajamas, and there on the welcome mat lies a tape of everything you have said all day long. Just how welcome would it be? What would you find yourself listening to? Complaining? Gossip? Slander? Nagging? Petty arguments? Insults? Snide comments? Bitter resentment? Boasting? Cruel comments? Foul language? Deceit? Insincere flattery? Excuses for all the above? Just who are we trying to fool? "For out of the abundance of the heart, the mouth speaks" (Luke 6.45).

How loud would it be? How cold would it sound? What would come after each thing I said? Someone laughing, or someone crying?

I have a feeling that no one is really aware of exactly how he sounds. We do not realize that the things we say are as *often* and as *whiny* as they are, that most of our complaints are petty and selfish, that the majority of our comments about others are negative instead of positive, that the impression we give others about our marriages, our families, our church brothers and sisters would make those around us want to avoid those relationships altogether.

Maybe this idea is not so horrible after all. Maybe we all need to pretend today that the tape recorder is running, and do our best to make it "good listening." Someone *is* listening after all.

For there is not a word in my tongue, but lo, O Jehovah, you know it altogether.

Psalm 139.4

October 25

For Mature Audiences Only

Keith and I have wondered out loud lately, how a word that should be a compliment, "adult," has come to mean something bad—adult bookstores, adult movies, adult shops. If a person knew no better, and walked into one of those places what would he see that could be described as "mature" the way the scriptures use the word? It reminds me of Isaiah's warning: "Woe unto those who call evil good and good evil; who put darkness for light and light for darkness, who put sweet for bitter, and bitter for sweet" (5.20).

I think there should be a new movie rating: AM. It stands for "adolescent mentality." Any movie that uses such a meager vocabulary that most of the words have only four letters, that has no dramatic, tension-building dialogue lasting longer than 90 seconds before throwing in an explosion or gunfight to get the audience's attention again, and of course, one that attempts to satisfy the prurient interests of the hormonally-explosive adolescent would get my new rating. Then those of us who want to behave like real adults, who have larger vocabularies, who don't need voyeurism to get our kicks, and who have an attention span longer than a minute or two can actually enjoy real adult entertainment.

The problem with having an adolescent mentality when it comes to entertainment is that it is not confined to that arena. Can I sit still long enough to pray? Make yourself pray at least ten minutes today, by the clock. Can you? You see, once you get past the standard phrases, two minutes at most, you can really open up to your God, and talk to him. If you cannot sit still that long, you may have never really prayed.

Can I follow a rational argument long enough to study the first 11 chapters of Romans, arguably Paul's greatest thesis? Can I study without being led by the hand, or do I simply rely on someone else to do it for me? Do I have the maturity to honestly examine myself and actually try to do better? Being a Christian may mean fighting some important battles, but the biggest are usually fought inside yourself and against yourself, with quiet implosions, not loud explosions.

When we start out, we are all babes in Christ, but He expects us to grow up eventually. That means some tedious work listening to sermons, attending classes, doing our own Bible study. Adults understand that not everything can be fun. It means some long, quiet moments with God. It means some painful moments of self-discovery. Are we adult enough to handle it? Our society's brand of entertainment speaks otherwise, and unfortunately, society usually winds up worming its way into the body of Christ.

When Paul told the Corinthians to "act like men" (1 Cor 16.13), he was bringing the epistle to its logical end. While "act like men" refers to courage under fire, maybe it can mean something else as well. In chapter three he calls them "babies," but now perhaps he is also saying, "Act like adults." Would he say the same thing to us?

> *But I, brothers, could not speak to you as spiritual men, but as carnal, as babies in Christ. I fed you with milk, not with meat, for you were not able, and even now you are not able, for you are yet carnal. ...For everyone who partakes of milk is without experience in the word of righteousness, for he is a baby. But solid food is for full-grown men who by reason of use have their senses exercised to discern good and evil. ...Be watchful, stand firm in the faith. Act like men, be strong.*
>
> 1 Corinthians 3.1–3; Hebrews 5.13–14; 1 Corinthians 16.13

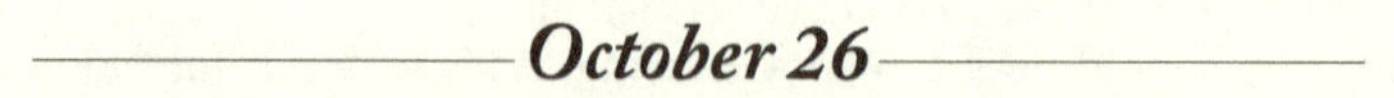

October 26

Notes from a Wilderness Trail: Trekking Poles

We have just returned from the first "normal" camping trip we have been able to take in four years. "Normal" means we camped in the mountains for five days and we hiked. Those quotation marks mean we carried a pile of medications and a doctor's letter explaining my problems, along with three cards detailing all the hardware in my eyes. They also mean I was careful not to overdo it.

Because of all this, Keith bought me a pair of trekking poles from an outfitter. At first I thought he had spent an exorbitant amount of money for two sticks. Then I used them. With two repaired Achilles tendons and reduced vision, my usual klutziness on mountain trails has increased exponentially. My ankles easily turn and twist on rocks and roots, and I trip over anything that sticks up even half an inch off the ground simply because I cannot see it.

But these poles made all the difference in the world. The cork handles conform to your fingers with a knob that keeps them from sliding, and a flat top on which your thumb rests and from which you can help yourself with a little boost. Two straps wrap around your wrists—if you somehow lose hold of a pole, you do not even need to bend over to pick it up. With just a twist you can shorten or lengthen them, not just to suit your particular height, but whether you are going uphill or downhill as well.

I did not stumble once. I did not twist either ankle. Keith did not need to drag me up a single hill or catch me as I rolled down one. And we made what was labeled a four hour hike in just three and a half.

I am not too proud to say I used trekking poles. Should you make a habit of hiking even once or twice a year, you should get some too, especially if, like me, Grace is *not* your middle name. It's no shame to need a little help once in awhile. In fact, I am told avid mountaineers who could hike rings around me backwards and blindfolded use these things.

So why are we so ashamed to ask for help spiritually? Why is it such a big deal to admit we might be wrong about something or have a fault? Why is advice from those who are more experienced seldom sought and even less often taken? Why are we always letting our pride get in the way of our soul's salvation? Even the strong need a hand once in a while.

Find yourself a pair of friendly poles to make the trek with you. You will be glad you did, and much more likely to make the end of the trail.

Then came Amalek and fought with Israel in Rephidim. And Moses said to Joshua, Choose us out men and go out, fight with Amalek; tomorrow I will stand on the top of the hill with the rod of God in my hand. So Joshua did as Moses had said to him and fought Amalek; and Moses, Aaron, and Hur went up to the top of the hill. And it came to pass when Moses held up his hands that Israel prevailed, and when he let down his hands, Amalek prevailed. But Moses' hands grew weary; and they took a stone and put it under him, and he sat thereon, and Aaron and Hur held up his hands, the one on the one side and the other on the other side, and Moses' hands were steady unto the going down of the sun. And Joshua overwhelmed Amalek and his people.

Exodus 17.8–13

Notes from a Wilderness Trail: A Moderate Hike

The first day of our camping trip we warmed up with a one mile nature trail labeled "easy, a half hour walk." And it was. The trail was wide and smooth, the grades so minimal you "stepped" up rather than climbing. Many educational signs along the way gave you a natural respite as you stopped to read. We were shocked when it ended so soon, and we—meaning me, mainly—had energy to spare.

So the next morning we set out on the trail labeled "moderate, four hours travel time." Either "moderate" has changed meaning or the past two years have taken more out of me than I thought. Most of this trail ran either straight up or straight down, with stone "steps" matching the natural rise or drop of a six foot or more man, not a five-four or less woman. Rocks and tree roots paved the way, except for a few places lined with slick wet leaves just begging for a big piece of cardboard so you could sled down them. But for women my age, anything even resembling a fall is to be avoided at all costs no matter how much fun it might look like.

Three-and-a-half hours later we emerged from the woods, puffing and panting. Every muscle below waist level ached. I hit the camp chair with an Aleve and a cold soda. If this was their idea of moderate, I did not think I was quite up to the one labeled "strenuous, more than a full day's hike."

So why do I put myself through this? I could give you a lot of answers. After a hike like that, pure water tastes like nectar. Food is delicious, even the simple fare cooked over a campfire. Crawling into a warm sleeping bag is heaven and you sleep like the proverbial log. When you stay busy and wear yourself out with it, you enjoy even the simplest pleasures far more, and complaining about your lot in life is no longer even in your vocabulary, at least for a day. I am sure you can make that application for yourself.

But also, I made up my mind several years ago that as long as I could, I would, because the longer you do, the longer you can. I am trying now to apply that to everything, not just hiking. It is one thing to grow old gracefully. It is another to lie down and die at a time of my choosing instead of God's, when there is plenty more for me to do, even if I must be a little creative and extra-observant to see it. Growing old gracefully may mean that when you come steaming along behind me, I give you room to pass, but don't expect me to completely step off the trail out of your way!

I find it unfortunate that the translators chose the word "talent" as in "The Parables of…" in Matthew 25. It creates a mindset that has *us* deciding whether or not we are capable of doing things. Those pieces of money do not represent "talents" as in abilities. Jesus himself said the talents (money) were distributed "according as each had ability," so they cannot be the same thing. Those pieces of money represent opportunities. God gives us opportunities according to our abilities. He will not give us opportunities we do not have the ability to handle.

We have no right to say, "I don't have the talent (ability) to take this opportunity." God knows we do or He would not have sent it.

The same is true as we age or become disabled, and grow physically weaker. God may give us fewer opportunities, opportunities that are not as showy or public—like picking up the phone to call a shut-in, giving a word of encouragement, or simply being a consistent example of faith and endurance. But whatever the opportunity, He expects us to take advantage of it. God expects us all to live by this motto: As long as I can, I do.

> *And having gifts differing according to the grace that was given to us, whether prophecy, let us prophesy according to the proportion of our faith; or serving, let us give ourselves to our service; or he who teaches to his teaching; or he who encourages to his encouraging, or he who gives let him do it with liberality; he who rules with diligence, he who shows mercy with cheerfulness.*
>
> Romans 12.6–8

October 28

Notes from a Wilderness Trail: Bridging the Brooks

Our hike took us to the top of a mountain and back, and several times over a creek or brook, none more than a foot or two deep, but plenty deep enough to get cold and wet if there had been no bridge.

The first bridge was a wooden plank affair with handrails, nothing fancy, but solidly constructed. We walked across it without thinking about it one way or the other—it was a bridge, it filled the need.

The next "bridge" was a bit more challenging. Large stones led across the brook and kept your feet dry as long as *you* kept your balance. But the stones were solidly set and not slippery, so aside from having to think where to put your foot on each one, it was not too difficult. Still, it did take *some* thought.

The next also had stepping stones, but these were wetter, which meant slicker, and one teetered when you put your weight on it. If not for my trusty trekking poles, I would have had wet feet, if not something a bit larger wet as well.

Then came the fourth "bridge." Even Keith made a noise when he saw it up ahead. The Georgia Department of Natural Resources had laid four logs across the brook. Not flat planks, mind you, but rounded logs; not large logs, but more like fence posts—small fence posts, not tied together, but each about four inches apart, just far enough for a foot to slip through. With my weak ankles and poor vision, they might just as well have asked me to walk a tightrope.

Keith said, "Had you rather get wet?"

I did not dignify that with an answer. I just started across—slowly sliding my feet an inch or two at a time. Don't tell me that the faster you go, the easier it is. You are talking to a klutz, remember, a half-blind one at that! Those seven or eight feet seemed more like 70 or 80, but I only slipped once, and by then I was close enough to the other side that Keith could reach out and steady me.

As we continued on I reflected on the fact that the "bridges" were getting less and less like real bridges, and was pondering what might come next. One log that rolled as you walked? I found myself praying, stepping stones please, even ones that teeter, but no more logs!

Funny how a hurdle you manage later in life makes the earlier ones seem so much smaller. But which of us would begin weight training with a 200 pound weight or run a marathon the first time we ever jogged?

Don't you know that our Father is watching out for us? A life without any trials would leave us weaklings. But He is careful: the first bridge we cross will make us strong enough for the second, and the second for the third, and so on throughout our lives.

As it turns out those four logs were the last bridge on our trail. God knows which bridge is the most difficult we can manage at any given time. Especially the last one.

> *There has no temptation taken you but such as man can bear; but God is faithful, who will not suffer you to be tempted above that you are able, but will with the temptation make also the way of escape that you may be able to endure it.*
>
> 1 Corinthians 10.13

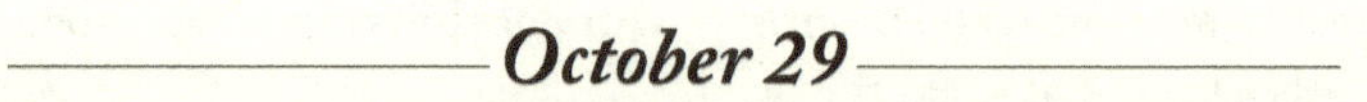

October 29

Notes from a Wilderness Trail: Testimony of the Wilderness

THE LAND BEYOND THIS POINT IS WILDERNESS—TRAVEL WITH CAUTION

This sign greeted us as we headed out that morning. On the board next to it were other warnings about bears, snakes, poisonous plants and insects, and one that said, "Between October 11 and May 1 hikers should wear bright colors. Whistling is also recommended." Various hunting seasons began and ended during that period, bow hunting, black powder, rifle and shotgun, used during the various game seasons.

Still we hiked on. We had seen all these warnings before in the many years we have camped and hiked. The only dangerous game we'd ever seen was the back end of a black bear as he plodded steadily away from us—the best view of a bear there is in my opinion. Still we were careful.

The wilderness can be a scary place if you are careless or arrogant. Besides the bears, snakes, and panthers, paths follow the edges of steep precipices with no guardrails should you lose your footing. Limbs litter them, having died, rotted, and fallen at a slight breeze. Once one fell not ten seconds after I had walked that particular spot. Runs drivel down the slopes, ready to rush into a flash flood should a rain come up, as it often does. It does not take much to remind you how helpless you are.

Keith says that one of the Louis L'Amour westerns tells of travelers leaving piles of rocks to the Native American gods of the trail. No one with an open mind can spend any time in the outdoors without recognizing that it took Divine Intelligence to create it. Twice we passed piles of stones laid on boulders or stumps, a hundred or more, some carefully positioned on end, so they did not just happen to roll there. Our society, I have heard, has gotten more spiritual as of late, but why has that spirituality turned toward paganism like the gods of the trail, instead of Jehovah God? Is it more interesting, more fun? Or is it that paganism carries no moral responsibility to its gods other than a token nod to their supposed existence?

Jehovah God expects certain behavior from us. He requires our service. He demands our lives. And He deserves so much more.

Some day soon take a walk in the wilderness, or even just your backyard, and let it teach you all about Him.

> *For the wrath of God is revealed from heaven against all ungodliness and unrighteousness of men, who hinder the truth in unrighteousness; because that which is known of God is manifest in them.* ***For the invisible things of him since the creation of the world are clearly seen, being perceived through the things that are made, even his everlasting power and divinity, that they may be without excuse;*** *because that, knowing God, they glorified him not as God, neither gave thanks, but became vain in their reasoning, and their senseless heart was darkened. Professing themselves to be wise, they became fools, and exchanged the glory of the incorruptible God for the likeness of an image of corruptible man, and of birds, and four-footed beasts, and creeping things. Wherefore God gave them up. . . .*
>
> Romans 1.18–24

October 30

Notes from a Wilderness Trail: Uphill vs. Downhill

We have a saying: "It's all downhill from here," meaning the hard part is over, and the rest is easy. So this will surprise you: walking a mountain trail is much more difficult going downhill than it is going uphill. I know it does not make any sense, but every time we hike, we learn the lesson yet again.

Going uphill will strain your hamstrings and Achilles tendons with every step. Your pulse and respiration will rise. But as long as you have the breath to, you can keep going at a steady clip.

Going downhill, however, will do a number on your quads—not just with each step, but constantly because even on a smooth slope they will be in continuous braking mode so that your speed does not get ahead of your feet. Where nature has made steps in the form of boulders or tree roots, they never match your foot or leg length, and are as steep as the rungs of a ladder. You wind up grabbing a tree to go one step at a time, sometimes backwards like a real ladder, or sitting on the rocks sliding down one at a time—unless you are as young and agile as a mountain goat. Even then, one slip in a downhill run could see you topple head over heels for 20 or 30 feet which, by the way, would be the only way to make any real time going downhill. If you slow to two miles per hour going uphill, you will be lucky to make one going down.

Satan will always get you when you least expect it. When life is good, when trials are over—for today at least—and we let our guards down, we will get to going too fast, speaking faster than we can think, reacting faster than self-control can kick in. And there we go, tumbling down the hill like Jill tumbling after Jack, who broke his "crown," by the way. And what will happen to ours?

So when life is easy, when suddenly the ascent levels out or even begins a downward slope, be careful. You can still take a nasty fall that lasts longer than you would have ever imagined.

> *Now these things happened unto them by way of example, and they were written for our admonition, upon whom the ends of the ages are come. Wherefore let him who thinks he stands take heed lest he fall.*
>
> 1 Corinthians 10.11–12

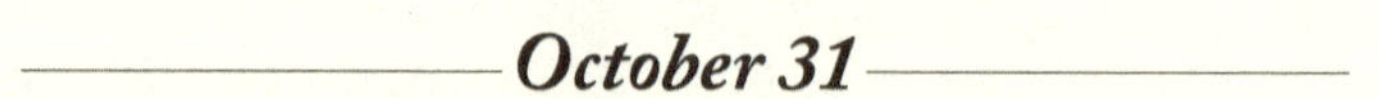

Notes from a Wilderness Trail: A Life in the Wilderness

When Keith and I are hiking we don't talk much. He cannot hear me and I am too busy watching the trail, trying to figure out where to put my foot next. Occasionally I stop and take a moment to look up, but for the most part all I see is the trail. Keith is the one who sees the scenery.

Is that fair? Of course it is. I'll tell you why. While I am looking down, I am *hearing* the scenery: the screaming of hawks, the whining call of the yellow-bellied sapsucker, the raucous laugh of the woodpecker and its beak pounding the trunk of a tree, the gentle susurration of leaves in the breeze and their nearly imperceptible fall to their fellows on the thickly padded forest floor, the buzz of deerflies, the chirring of chipmunks and lower pitched chattering of squirrels, brooks gurgling in the hollows, small waterfalls splashing on rocks at the bottoms of slopes, the fog dripping off of the trees. Keith cannot hear any of that. If he doesn't see it, he misses it.

But then I also see a lot on the trail that he doesn't see because he is looking up: a forest floor covered with bright yellow poplar leaves, orange-red persimmon leaves, deep red sumac leaves, and once, a leaf bigger than a platter; rocks of all shapes and sizes, quartz, granite, slate, mica, limestone; holes and burrows at the edge of the trail and just off to the side in hollow tree trunks; and once, a wasp digging a hole, laying its eggs, then burying another insect it had paralyzed with its venom on top of the eggs, so its young would have food to eat when they hatched. Have you ever seen that?

Many years ago Keith and I used to joke that one day I would *hear* when someone knocked on the door and he would go *see* who it was. That someday is getting closer and closer. But over the years we have adapted. We have adapted to things you probably never even thought about. Do you talk at night after the lights are out? We can't. Keith cannot hear anything without his hearing aids, and needs light to read my lips. Do you banter back and forth while you work together? No, Keith has to be closely watching my mouth to know what I am saying. Do you call to one another from separate rooms in the house? Well, you get the idea. We have lived this way for so many years we don't even give it a second thought any more.

On this past trip we had more things to adapt to. I usually read the maps and navigate while he drives. I cannot read a map any more without two or three magnifiers, and time to focus and concentrate. This time we took out the map the night before we left. Keith read the road numbers and cities, and I wrote them on a sheet of paper in large letters. We made our trip just fine, and we always will. You know what? Other people have it just as rough, or even worse.

Do you remember that old hymn that goes, "Every day I'm camping toward Canaan's happy land?" Just like the Israelites, we live in a dangerous wilderness. We never know what lies before us. Anything can happen, and often does. So life is about change. It is about adapting to your circumstances. If we ever think it is about us deciding how things will turn out, we will be sorely disappointed. And if this life is so important that we let ourselves become miserable because it isn't what we expected, have we really learned the lesson about priorities? Do we really believe that it is not even a drop in the bucket compared to Eternity? Is our faith so weak we must have everything perfect now (according to our definitions of perfection) in order to believe in a perfect Heaven?

Things are not easy for the two of us. We do have days when we wonder why all this has happened. But we strive to remember that our lives are "a vapor that appears for a little while and then vanishes away" (Jas 4.14). These momentary problems will vanish as well. I think James meant that to be a warning, but let it be a comfort to you as well. Some day we will leave the wilderness and arrive in a Promised Land. Everything *will* be better in the end.

> *Now I rejoice in the Lord greatly...for I have learned in whatever state I am to be content. I know how to be abased and I know also how to abound; in everything and in all things have I learned the secret both to be filled and to be hungry, both to abound and to be in want: I can do all things through him who strengthens me.*
>
> Philippians 4.10–13

November 1

Excess Baggage

I hate packing for a trip. I hate unpacking when I get home worse. That is one thing so exciting about the trip to Heaven. I won't have to do either one!

And you know what? When we decide to make that move into the kingdom, we don't have to pack for that either. In fact, Jesus wants us to leave *all* our baggage behind. Not just our lives of sin, but all those biases that keep us from seeing clearly.

Sometimes I let the difficult times I have been through color my view of everything else. It can affect how I view my brethren, always expecting the worst and even looking for it. It can affect my faith so that I cannot totally surrender my life to God; I feel a need to "help Him out" just a little. It can affect my view of the kingdom itself, so that I want to protect it by building walls closer inside to help keep it pure, and even make me less than welcoming to others who need a haven. It can make me too sober, too serious, too unwilling to crack a smile and rejoice!

I may have fought some serious battles for the Lord, but that does not make me the only good judge of what is and is not good for the health of the kingdom.

I may have come from a religious group that does many things contrary to the law of Christ, but that does not mean that "what those people did" is the authority for deciding what God's people cannot do. Ninety-five percent of rat poison is good rat food; otherwise the rats would never eat it! So what we do may in some cases match what they do—the scriptural parts anyway.

I may have learned that a doctrine is unscriptural but that does not mean that a full 180 degree turn in the other direction is necessary. We often overreact just to make sure we do not do something wrong, and wind up being wrong in the opposite direction. The Pharisees were good at that.

I need to remember that I should come to Christ with empty hands, bringing nothing from the old life. "Wherefore if any man is in Christ, he is a new creature; the old things have passed away; behold they have become new" (2 Cor 5.17). All the old things have changed to new things. No old baggage to deal with any longer.

If I truly have faith in my Lord, I don't need anything from that old life. It's a little scary, but that is the nature of trust, isn't it?

> *Peter began to say to him, Lo we have left all and have followed thee. Jesus said, Truly I say to you, there is no man who has left house or brothers or sisters, or mother, or father, or children, or lands, for my sake, and for the gospel's sake, but he shall receive a hundredfold now in this time, houses, and brothers, and sisters, and mothers, and children and lands, with persecutions, and in the world to come eternal life.*
>
> Mark 10.28–30

November 2

Steel Wool

I was born and raised a city girl. We never had a mouse in our house. Cartoons like "Tom and Jerry" and "Pixie and Dixie" seemed like fairy tales to me. Then we moved to a farming community in Illinois. Our house sat on the last street on the edge of the small town, right next to a cornfield. One morning in September I got up to find that our dog had had a playmate all night long—one who was much the worse for wear, and who, unfortunately, had brought several friends in with him.

One of the farm wives in the church told us to stuff steel wool beside every pipe coming up through the floor—the kitchen sink, bathroom lavatory, hot water heater, washer, *etc.* Pipes are the main highway for mice entering a home, and steel wool is the only flexible thing they cannot chew through. I bought the small town out of steel wool and frantically stuffed it all down those offending holes. Our mouse problem suddenly improved. Once in awhile in the years that followed we had an interloper, but he was usually a lone pioneer in what we tried to make a hostile frontier.

How much sense would it have made, though, for me to say, "Steel wool won't take care of them all, so why bother?" About as much sense as it would to say, "A criminal can always find a way into your home if he wants to, so why bother locking the door?" There are some occasions where the word "stupid" legitimately applies.

So why do I hear my brethren constantly harping on the inevitability of sin? "We will all sin sooner or later no matter how hard we try." When I ask why, I hear, "Let him who stands take he lest he fall" (1 Cor 10.12). Translation: the minute you start thinking you can overcome, you have become proud and before you know it, you will be down the tubes! Surely there is a difference in recognizing, "With the help of my Savior, I can overcome," and spouting, "I'm such a strong Christian I'd never do anything like that!" Whatever happened to "I can do all things through him who strengthens me"? Sometimes it sounds like we think that Divine help is at best, anemic, and at worst, impotent. Or is it just that we don't believe what we say?

Why can't I use the fact that I overcame one temptation as an encouragement to overcome some more? Are we denying that God expects us to grow and get stronger every day? None of us would allow our children to play for a team whose coach told them they could never win, that even if they managed a win, they would lose sooner or later. Yet we are so afraid of sounding like we believe in that notion of "once saved always saved," that we openly discourage one another and wear it as a mark of soundness.

Paul was ever mindful of his status as a sinner, "the chiefest" in fact. But he was not afraid to tell the Corinthians about his successes. "I set an example for you by foregoing my rights for the sake of my brother's soul. Now do what I did," (the context of 1 Corinthians 8–10, concluding with 11.1). He did not mean it as a boast, but someone surely could have taken it that way. And when his life was over he said, "I have fought the good fight, I have finished the course, I have kept the faith. Henceforth there is a crown of righteousness waiting for me" (2 Tim 4.7–8). Was he bragging? Of course not. It was a declaration of hope for a job well done. Let's not stand on the sidelines just waiting to jump on a brother and accuse him of a lack of humility when he sees his own progress and is encouraged by it, daring to say, "With the Lord's help, I can win."

Instead, let's stand with the apostles and their view of things.

> *For the death that he died he died unto sin once, but the life that he lives, he lives unto God. Even so, reckon also yourselves to be dead unto sin, but alive unto God in Christ Jesus.* ***Let not sin reign in your mortal bodies*** *that you should obey the lusts thereof, neither present your members as instruments of unrighteousness, but present yourselves unto God as alive from the dead and your members as instruments of righteousness unto God.* (Rom 6.11–13)

> *There has no temptation taken you but such as man can bear, but God is faithful, who will not let you be tempted* ***above what you are able****, but will with the temptation make also the way of escape* ***that you may be able to endure it.*** (1 Cor 10.13)

> *Stand therefore, having girded your loins with truth, and having put on the breastplate of righteousness, and having shod your feet with the preparation of the gospel of peace, and taking up the shield of faith* ***with which you shall be able to quench all the fiery darts of the evil one.*** (Eph 6.14–16)

> *The Lord knows* ***how to deliver the godly out of temptation.*** (2 Pet 2.9)

> *My little children, these things I write unto you* ***that you may not sin****, and if we sin, we have an Advocate with the Father, Jesus Christ the righteous.* (1 John 2.1)

Get out the steel wool. Plug the holes where you can. Don't let the fact that a sin here and there may find its way into your life cause you to roll out the red carpet for every temptation that comes along. Take advantage of the *encouragement* God meant you to have and don't give up the battle before you even start fighting.

November 3

Cooped Up

Keith says I have a personality disorder—I think my name is Francis and I was born in Assisi. Can I help it if the hawk insisted on having a conversation with me this morning?

I haven't been out for awhile due to one thing and another, but he must remember me from all the times I went out while he was a baby and spoke to him up in his nest. So whenever I am outside and he is anywhere nearby, he gives me a shout, and I say hello.

I had my trekking poles so I could give Chloe a little bit of exercise. She is a bit like her mistress, prone to gaining weight at the slightest sniff of food, forget about actually eating it, and she needed a walk. After our first greeting across the fence from one another, the hawk flew behind me and caught up, still staying in the trees on the other side of the boundary, but a little closer this time.

I told him he should come on over. If he wanted to stay safe, we had plenty of trees, plenty of food—he should have known that anyway. His parents had sat on the tomato fence in our garden, diving for mice, squirrels, rabbits, and other goodies that they took to him for supper every night. I kept walking and again he flew to catch up, but once again landed on the other side of the fence.

When we reached the point where the path cut inward to the center of our property, I told him it was time for him to make his decision. "Come on," I told him. "You've been here before. You grew up here. You know it's a good place and a safe place. If you stay over there, who is going to look after you?"

I waited a minute then turned and headed down the path toward the drive. His wings flapped behind me like a big rug flapping on a clothesline in the wind. I turned, only to see he was headed away, deeper into the woods.

I suspect I will still hear from him once in awhile and even see him again. At least until that time when something nabs him and he stops showing up. It's a pity. He would last longer if he stayed close by, but now some neighbor may shoot him just for fun, or he may stray into some other hawk's territory and lose the fight for it. That's what happens when you turn your back because all you can see are restrictions instead of safety, and when all you *want* to see of the other side of the fence is freedom instead of danger. Sooner or later, one way or the other, it will be too late to come back.

> *In the fear of Jehovah is strong confidence; and his children shall have a place of refuge. The fear of Jehovah is a fountain of life, that one may depart from the snares of death.*
>
> Proverbs 14.26–27

November 4

What's in a Name?

I have an unusual first name. Sometimes that is a good thing, sometimes not. When I was a child and someone told the teacher I had done something, I could not say, "It was the other Dene, not me." There was never any question which "Dene" it was because there was never any other "Dene."

On the other hand, I remember the year that Miss America was Debra Dene Barnes. Now that was exciting. When someone asked how to spell my name, I just said, "You know, like Miss America does."

In a new doctor's office I can always tell when it's my turn before the nurse even calls me, poking her head out the door with file in hand—she always hesitates. I have been called "Den-ay," "Dee-nah," even "Danny" once. You can always tell who learned to read with phonics—long "e" plus silent "e" always equals the correct pronunciation.

Sometimes I wish I had chosen to go by my middle name, Teresa. At least all these doctor appointments would have been easier on everyone. When I was young, I even looked like I thought a "Teresa" ought to look—long curly black hair. Now I just look like Mother Teresa.

Some time ago, I started pronouncing it by the pet name my parents always called me, and which Keith has taken up, "Denie." For some reason, when people look at "Dene" that makes more sense to them. And so "Denie" I have become, though still spelled "Dene." It is still fairly unusual and I cannot hide behind the anonymity of a common name.

Names have always been important to God. He has even changed people's names to suit Himself when He thought it was important. But far more important is for us to be called by God's name.

Under the Old Covenant people understood that being called by God's name offered them protection (Deut 28.10). They understood that being called by God's name meant bearing the responsibility to act in certain ways (Isa 63.19), and that wearing His name was not permission to wander from His commandments without consequence (Jer 14.9ff).

But it also meant that He would have compassion on them, that He would love them even while they sinned, and that He wanted their repentance as much as any Father could want his wandering child to return home.

Today we still wear the name of God, Christian. Wearing that name still means all those things it meant so long ago. Are we living up to the responsibility that demands, or is God out there calling us back home? After all, "In none other is there salvation: for neither is there any other name under heaven that is given among men, wherein we must be saved" (Acts 4.12).

> *Fear not; for I am with you: I will bring your seed from the east, and gather you from the west; I will say to the north, Give up; and to the south, Keep not back; bring my sons from far, and my daughters from the end of the earth; every one that is called by my name, and whom I have created for my glory, whom I have formed, and whom I have made.*
>
> Isaiah 43.5–7

November 5

Gleanings

Keith and I teach a class called Preparation for Marriage and Parenting. Below are a few comments we throw in during these classes that are not in the lesson book we compiled, but which probably ought to be. For what they are worth…

- Headship is not about getting to do whatever you want to do. It is about carefully considering the needs of the entire family and doing what is best for them, whether it is what you want to do or not.
- Any woman who has difficulties with subjection has difficulties with being a Christian. Submission is what being a disciple of Christ is all about.
- A man who makes subjection difficult for his wife might as well get himself sized for a millstone. The same is true for a woman who ignores her husband's sexual needs.
- There are many different ways to handle problems in a marriage. The first and most important thing you should do is make up your minds that you *will* make it through this. Never keep a divorce lawyer on your speed dial.
- It doesn't matter whether you understand women or not. It doesn't matter whether you understand men or not. What matters is understanding that your spouse does not think like you do.
- If you ladies are going to use your hormones as an excuse for bad behavior, then you should allow your husband to use male hormones as an excuse for his.

- Marriage is a high maintenance relationship. As soon as you start neglecting it, it will go downhill.
- Spouses who do not communicate well and on a regular basis will soon be total strangers.
- Letting her talk is useless if you don't listen.
- Your children are not your own. They are merely souls God has given into your care, and He expects them to be returned in good shape.
- You are teaching your children whether you intend to or not. What textbook are you using? Look in the mirror.
- Make no mistake about it—you are waging a war with your toddlers, which you should win before they reach school age. Any time you "give in," you have lost a battle and retaking that territory will take twice as long at twice the cost to your relationship with your child.
- Too many parents don't train their children, their children train them.
- A father who won't change dirty diapers probably won't be much use to his children when the real messes of life afflict them either.
- If you tell your child, "If you do that again, I am going to __________ you," and then don't __________ them when they do it again, you have lied to your child.
- Don't tell me that a child is too young to comprehend punishment before the age of two. My child is smarter than any puppy dog I ever saw. So is yours.
- Raising kids is hard work. Our society and its children are suffering from parents who were either too lazy or too selfish to do the job right.

Gleaning in the field sometimes gives you choice produce that was simply overlooked. Other times there is a reason it was left there. So this morning choose from the list and take what is most helpful.

> *Except Jehovah build the house they labor in vain that build it. …Lo, children are a heritage of Jehovah, and the fruit of the womb is his reward. As arrows in the hand of a mighty man, so are the children of youth. Happy is the man who has his quiver full of them; they shall not be put to shame when they speak with their enemies in the gate.*
>
> Psalm 127.1, 3–5

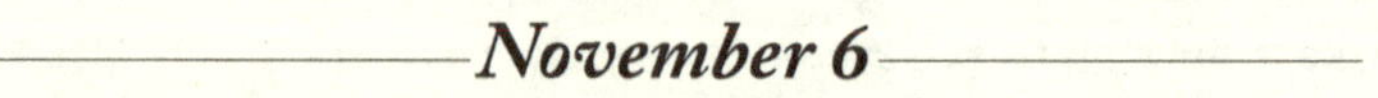

November 6

Homesick

In Thomas Wolfe's novel *You Can't Go Home Again*, George Webber concludes, "You can't go back home to your family, back home to your childhood, …back home to a young man's dreams of glory and of fame... back home to places in the country, back home to the old forms and systems of things which once seemed everlasting but which are changing all the time... ."

Whenever Keith talks about Arkansas, he says, "Back home." It used to bother me a little. Home should be where I am, shouldn't it? Then I realized that I could never have the feelings of a place that he did. I never lived in just one place as a child, and the place I lived longest is not the place I go to when I visit my parents. They left that place a year after I married and have lived in nearly half a dozen places since.

It is ironic that one of my sons lives there now, the place I would have called home, but when I go visit him, it has been so long since it was home, and it has changed so much, that I never even think of it that way any more. The longest I have ever lived in any one place is the place I live now, and as Keith and I head into our senior years, I can foresee a time, though I hope not too soon, when we will have to leave it. Even as small a plot as five acres takes a lot of labor, and it is a long way from the folks we count on to care for us when we become too old and disabled to take care of it and ourselves.

Christians should be careful about those feelings of "home." Home should never be about a place, but about people, and about Truth. I have seen churches divide over doctrines, divisions that were necessary. Yet people who should have known better stayed—they were converted to a place, a building, not to the Lord.

And Christians in our society have another problem—one that the poverty stricken brethren in places like Nicaragua and Zimbabwe never have to deal with—we have become entirely too comfortable. We are so "at home" in our rich lives that we don't want to give them up. Persecution, even simply the ridicule and criticism of others, is too much to bear. There is always a good reason not to speak up when sin becomes accepted, and not to behave differently. Even if there is no persecution, we have a problem singing, "This world is not my home, I'm just a passing through." This is home and we want to stay as long as possible.

We must make ourselves see beyond the here and now. We must force ourselves to realize that where and how we are living today is not our goal. Eternity is difficult enough to comprehend without focusing on what is right in front of us as if it were the only thing that counted. Here is the truth of the matter: compared to Eternity our lives are not even a drop of water in the entire ocean.

Christians have the promise that one day we will never again be homesick. Heaven is the home we have all been looking for, the place we will live forever. We will never have to leave. We will never sit pining and wishing for the good old days. The "dreams of glory" Thomas Wolfe spoke of will be there and then. But perhaps in Eternity "then" will no longer have a meaning. It will be Now—a capital letter Now that never ends.

Being therefore always of good courage, and knowing that, while we are at home in the body, we are absent from the Lord. ...We are of good courage, I say, and are willing rather to be absent from the body, and to be at home with the Lord.

2 Corinthians 5.6, 8

Let's Pretend

Let's play a game. Consider the elders in your church—if you have none, then the men who do the majority of the work. Pretend the government has carted them off to prison, and just this morning you find out one has been executed. Not only is the populace *not* upset about it, they are clamoring for the execution of the other man too. It quickly becomes clear that none of you is safe. You keep your doors locked and the curtains drawn. Even a knock causes your stomach to lurch and your heart to pound as you carefully peek through the drawn blinds.

Your home is large, in the middle of town, just a short walk from the jail. It is not exactly difficult to find. Would you allow the brethren to meet there to pray? Would you have the courage to draw attention to yourself with the long line of cars parked on the street, and the constant coming and going during a time when finding an excuse to arrest and murder people of your persuasion is the latest fad?

Or how about this scenario—you are an outsider where you live, an out-of-towner who owns her own business and depends upon the good will of the citizens there to keep you afloat financially. Since it is a small, family-run business it would not take much to ruin you. Yet you have come across a faith that makes wonderful sense and you believe it whole-heartedly. Still, the men who have taught you, a couple of well-known preachers of this belief, have been arrested. The whole city thinks of them as troublemakers. Only yours and one other family has actually "signed on."

Are you willing to take them into your home? To *insist* that they take advantage of your hospitality, and even make a place for them when they escape from prison? What about your family if you are thrown into prison for "aiding and abetting?" What about your business when people find out you are backing these scalawags?

Mary of Jerusalem, the mother of John Mark (Acts 12), and Lydia, a native of Thyatira living in Philippi (Acts 16), did these things—*women*, mind you, who were not afraid to act and support regardless of what it might have cost them. They did not sit back waiting for men to do the scary stuff—they put their necks on the line, along with the necks of their families, and the good of their livelihoods and homes. They could have lost everything. Yet this is all reported so matter-of-factly that you wonder if they took more than a second to make the decisions they did.

What about us? The time may come when who we are and who we associate with could cost us reputations, jobs, homes, even our lives. Take a minute to "pretend" with real people's names, with real thought about what it might cost. Could we do as well as they did? *Will* we do as well as they did?

I worry that too many of us find excuses that have to do with "propriety." "How will we ever reach anyone if people think we approve of actions like that?" we rationalize. At what point will it ever look appropriate to support someone the world labels a troublemaker simply because he teaches the truth?

We use the word "stewardship" as our alibi. "Why, if we go out of business, we will have less contact with the community and be unable to influence them," we say to justify ourselves. At what point will it ever be good stewardship of our wealth to put our financial future on the line in support of the truth and those who preach it?

So take a moment today and play the game, "Let's pretend. . . ." Remember the example these faithful women have set, and others like them through the centuries. Make sure that when the time comes, we don't look for excuses. Instead, we make our pretensions real, regardless the cost.

> *Only let your manner of life be worthy of the gospel of Christ, so that whether I come and see you or am absent, I may hear of you that you are standing firm in one spirit, with one mind striving side by side for the faith of the gospel, and* ***not frightened in anything by your opponents****. This is a clear sign to them of their destruction, but of your salvation, and that from God.*
>
> Philippians 1.27–28

November 8

Sweeping the Middles

Now that we have this wood floor, it seems I am sweeping all the time. I simply can't stand the sound or feel of sand under my feet when I walk in the house, and living in the country where there is no outside concrete for it to fall on beforehand, we track it in several times a day, despite door mats and runners. Those treads on sneakers must surely have glue in them that wears off the moment you step indoors.

At least once a week I do "the clean sweep." I pull everything out, pick everything up, and sweep every square inch I can possibly get to, followed by the dry sweeping cloths that pick up things the broom missed, as well as all the dust bunnies under the beds and sofa. The rest of the week I make do by "sweeping the middles"—every place I can reach without moving anything. It isn't perfect, as evidenced by what I sweep up on the day of "the clean sweep," but it will do. I really have more important things to do than clean the floors.

I looked up "sweep" and "broom" in the concordance and found that God does not believe in "sweeping the middles." Three evil kings were told that God would "utterly sweep away their houses" (1 Kgs 14.10; 16.3; 21.21). Notice that word "utterly." In addition God said of Babylon, "And I will make it a possession of the hedgehog, and pools of water, and I will sweep it with the broom of destruction" (Isa 14.23). Do you want a good picture of how God sweeps? Read the first chapter of Zephaniah. God moves the furniture and gets under the beds when He decides to destroy sinners.

So how do we avoid that? By not just sweeping the middles when it comes to our lives. We need to clean up every nook and cranny, every hidden corner of our minds, every space beneath the larger items in our lives that we think can hide the sin from God. And grace means that after we do our best to clean the place up, God will come in to clean up what we could not, in the places we cannot reach.

When it comes to life, don't ever be satisfied with just "sweeping the middles." Do "the clean sweep" every day of your life so you don't get caught up in "the broom of destruction."

> *I indeed baptize you in water unto repentance: but he that comes after me is mightier than I, whose shoes I am not worthy to bear: he shall baptize you in the Holy Spirit and fire: whose fan is in his hand, and he will thoroughly cleanse his threshing-floor; and he will gather his wheat into the garner, but the chaff he will burn up with unquenchable fire.*
>
> Matthew 3.11–12

November 9

The Two Sides of God

I don't know how many times in my life I have heard unbelievers make fun of the scriptures, but they obviously do not realize what they show themselves to be when they do. Most of them would call themselves intellectuals, but the statements that come out of their mouths prove they are simply ignorant—at least of the thing they have chosen to ridicule.

Have you ever heard them talk about "the God of the Old Testament" and "the God of the New Testament?" They do this to "prove" that our beliefs are based upon our society, subject to change just as society does, which means that it is all an invention of man. Everyone knows, they affirm, that the God of the Old Testament was a cruel, angry God who punished indiscriminately for even the most minor infraction, while the God of the New Testament is a mild, friendly, grandfatherly sort who forgives anything whether we repent of it or not. Study the two paragraphs below for a few minutes this morning.

> And Jehovah passed before him and proclaimed, Jehovah, Jehovah, a God merciful and gracious, slow to anger, and abundant in lovingkindness and truth. / Jehovah is slow to anger and abundant in lovingkindness, forgiving iniquity and transgression.

> / Know therefore that Jehovah your God, he is God, the faithful God, who keeps covenant and lovingkindness to those who love him and keep his commandments to a thousand generations. / The earth is full of the lovingkindness of Jehovah, / Your lovingkindness, O Jehovah, is in the heavens, your faithfulness reaches to the skies. / Great are your tender mercies, O Jehovah. / Jehovah is good to all, and his tender mercies are over all his works.

> And these shall go away into eternal punishment. / where their worm dies not and the fire is not quenched. / with angels in flaming fire rendering vengeance on those who know not God and obey not the gospel. / It is a fearful thing to fall into the hands of the living God. / Our God is a consuming fire. / But the fearful and unbelieving, and abominable, and murderers, and fornicators, and sorcerers, and idolaters, and all liars, their part shall be in the lake that burns with fire and brimstone, which is the second death.

If you know your scriptures, you probably recognize that the first paragraph is taken entirely from the Old Testament and the second from the New. In fact, I found that the Old Testament uses descriptions of God like "merciful, gracious, and lovingkindness" 312 times, while the New Testament only uses them 200 times! Considering that a good portion of the Old Testament is history rather than teaching about God, that seems significant. So much for the intellectuals and all their theories about God.

Do you want to see a God full of compassion and mercy? Read the book of Hosea (an *Old* Testament prophet) and hear the ache in God's voice as He describes His people, first as a wife He loved who betrayed Him (2.19) and then as a son He cared for and taught, who turned against His father (11.1–4).

Remember Jonah, that *Old* Testament prophet who tried to run from his mission to preach to the wicked city of Nineveh? What did he say about why he ran? "I hasted to flee to Tarshish because I knew you are a gracious God and merciful, slow to anger, and abundant in lovingkindness, and would repent of the threatened judgment" (Jon 4.2). Jonah knew God would forgive, and he didn't want those people saved!

God has not "changed with the times" because He was not invented. Look at the Greek gods through their mythology and see what types of gods men create. The true God could never have come from the mind of any man, no matter how intellectual he thinks he is. A God who gave His creatures the freewill to reject Him? A God who gave up His Son for creatures who did not deserve it? A God who lowered Himself to become human, and allowed those same creatures to torture Him?

Don't let the ignorant fools of the world steal your faith. They have no answers at all for what they believe. Our God loves us—look at what He did for us. But our God will only save those who trust Him, obey Him, and live faithfully. His prophets have been speaking this message for thousands of years—the same message, an unchanging message, a message so far above the intellect of man that no man anywhere could have made it up.

> *Where is the wise? Where is the scribe? Where is the disputer of this world? Has not God made foolish the wisdom of this world? For seeing that in the wisdom of God the world through its wisdom knew not God, it was God's good pleasure through the thing preached to save those who believe. Seeing that Jews ask for signs and Greeks seek after wisdom, but we preach Christ crucified, unto Jews a stumblingblock, and unto Gentiles foolishness; but unto those who are called, both Jews and Greeks, the wisdom of God. Because the foolishness of God is wiser than men, and the weakness of God is stronger than men.*
>
> 1 Corinthians 1.20–25

November 10

City Slickers

It never ceases to amaze me. Folks from the city move out here and, even though they believe they are so much more sophisticated and knowledgeable than we country people, they will soon learn at least one lesson the hard way, possibly more, and we country people will just shake our heads. It's okay not to know; but it certainly is arrogant to act like you know when you have absolutely no experience to back it up.

A few years back a couple moved out with their dog, letting it remain outside with no pen or fence installed, "so he can run free like animals are supposed to." When farmers near them started losing livestock it couldn't be that "my sweet Scruffy" had anything to do with it. They did not understand that dogs are pack animals and when they are left alone at night, "free to run," they will join up with the strays and wreak havoc. They didn't understand until a farmer called the sheriff and there lay three or four dogs shot dead, next to an equally dead calf, nearly torn to bits. Among the dead dogs was Scruffy, the calf's blood smeared all over his mouth, throat, and chest. The farmer, of course, was not at fault—he was protecting his livestock from a pack of wild dogs. At least he only lost one calf that time.

On a less somber note, we have one now who would not listen when Keith told him he needed to ditch the edges of his dirt driveway. It may be the dry season now, but when the summer rains start, he will soon be looking for a friendly farmer with a tractor to pull him out of the muddy drive that has nowhere to drain.

We once had a neighbor who moved to the country "because there are so many more stars out here." He wondered why he couldn't see them after he moved in. Probably because of the street light he had installed outside his door. The reason the country seems so much starrier is the lack of light pollution. The more city people move out here, the fewer stars we can see because they are so scared of the dark. Far better to install a motion detector floodlight than a constant mercury lamp, one high enough to avoid the rambling raccoons and possums.

And then there is the garden. Thirty-five years ago I was a city slicker too. I thought having a garden from which you could pick what you wanted for supper every night was a wonderful idea. Unfortunately, that is not the way it works. You don't tell the garden what you want when you want it. It tells you what there is and when it is ready, and if you do not want it to go to waste, you take care of it then regardless of your schedule. If you wait, the produce will ruin. If you do not plan to tend it when it needs tending, pick when it needs picking, and put up when the crop comes in, don't plant one. Do not spend a hundred dollars on supplies, then let a thousand dollars worth of groceries spoil.

I could go on and on, but this is not a treatise on country vs. city. Let's take this lesson today. I recently heard someone say that Christians were people who had one foot in this world and one foot in the next, like that made them weird. Isn't that the way we are supposed to act? In fact, maybe we should have a little more of the second foot in the next world too.

No, we do not act like ordinary people—at least we shouldn't. As new Christians we have to learn a new way of living. Our citizenship is in Heaven. Our minds are set on spiritual things. The cares of this world do not upset us the same way they upset others, because they do not mean as much to us. We have far better things to think about.

City slickers may think country people are a little strange, but guess who knows how to get along out here the best? If the world thinks you are strange, don't worry. You will manage far better than they. One day, they will call frantically and ask for your help. Hope and pray it is not because the trumpet just sounded, but because they have finally figured out that you knew more than they thought, and there is still time to do something about it.

You are of God, little children, and have overcome them: because greater is he that is in you than he that is in the world. They are of the world: therefore speak they as of the world, and the world hears them. We are of God: he that knows God hears us; he who is not of God hears us not. By this we know the spirit of truth, and the spirit of error.

1 John 4.4–6

November 11

Changing of the Guard

My high school class was just a year or two too young to lose many to the Vietnam War, but we knew upperclassmen who went, and Keith was in the Marine Corps from '67 to '71. My life could easily be different now.

The way those men were greeted when they came home from that horror is a shame to our country. They did not start that war; they were just pawns on a larger political chessboard. The ones who spat on them and called them names were, by and large, a younger group who had never fought in a war, never experienced any sort of economic deprivation, but rather, had their lives handed to them on a silver platter.

In 1994 another group of veterans was finally given the honor they deserved in the many 50th anniversary observances of D-Day. They were called "the Greatest Generation," for making it through the Great Depression and then going on to fight for their country. Many gave the ultimate sacrifice, as we call it. Others still suffer from the injuries they incurred. Many more still bear the pain of emotional scars from that awful conflict. Truly they deserve our respect and our gratitude.

So what has happened? 1994 is gone. I live in Florida, where a great many retirees, many of whom are veterans, finish their lives. They are regularly the brunt of jokes and disrespect from a generation that may never know the trials that group went through, solely because those people went through those trials. Funny how time can wreak such havoc with attitudes isn't it?

Unfortunately, I have seen the same thing happen in the Lord's body. A younger generation sneers at an older one because it *is* older, because it doesn't understand that society is a bit different, and what was once expedient no longer is. Yet, that older generation is the one who saw the problems in the work force during the '40s, a war machine grinding out supplies at a pace unheard of before. *They* were the ones who saw the need for a Sunday evening service so that those Christians who were working shifts would not be left out of the group activities, so they too could experience the encouragement that comes from praising and thanking God *together*.

You know what? When they came up with that idea, *it was new, it was different—it broke all the traditions.* Don't sit there on your high horse and accuse them of not being able to change with the times.

That is why those things are so hard for them to give up. Yes, for some there may be an attitude problem, perhaps a willfulness or stubbornness that should be dealt with, but I would suggest that is not the case for most. Just because someone has a difficult time seeing the need for an expedient change, does not mean he is a Pharisee, which seems to be the accusation *du jour*. Too many times we act towards them with a disrespectful scorn and impatience, while at the same time being happy to stand on those same tired, hunched shoulders, shoulders that bore the burden of fighting the battles that have kept the church sound and faithful to the Lord. Where would we be now without them?

My generation and the one just younger need to be careful. Trying to withhold respect and honor and cloaking it as righteousness is simply another facet to the same Phariseeism we claim to abhor (Mark 7.8–13). Our Lord would not like it now any more than he did two thousand years ago.

So please, be a little more careful how you speak to *and about* the old warriors. Be understanding of the feelings they must have, seeing their world change perhaps more than any other generation before. Be grateful to them for what they have been through and the battles they have fought. One of these days, another generation will come along and look at you and the things you don't want to change. What kind of example will you have left them?

> *You shall stand before the gray head and honor the face of the old man,* ***and you shall fear your God. I AM Jehovah.***
>
> Leviticus 19.32

November 12

Good Enough

We just spent $90 on dirt. We live in the country. At that rate the top six inches of our five acres is worth about a $125,000.

My herb garden had a few problems last year. When your perennial rosemary cannot seem to top six inches and all of your super-easy-to-grow basil and parsley die despite watering and fertilizing, you begin to suspect it has more to do with the ground than the color of your thumb.

So Keith spent a weekend recently digging out the whole bed. Then he bought landscaping timbers, Miracle-Gro garden soil and Black Kow composted manure to fill it with. This bed will grow in spite of itself, yet I could not help but think, "Ninety dollars for dirt!"

"No," he told me, "ninety dollars for all those better meals we will eat due to the flavoring and nuance of home-grown fresh herbs—plenty for a change, instead of a rationed amount."

My old herb garden was good enough. We ate a lot of good meals out of it, but it was beginning to falter. It needed a little help to improve.

Too many times we are satisfied with "good enough" in our lives as Christians. The number of times we meet with our brethren, the amount of time we spend studying and praying, the amount we give in both time and money to spread the Gospel and to help those in need may very well be "good enough." I am not one of those to take the passage "To him who knows to do good and does not do it, to him that is sin," and use it as a hammer to pound feelings of fear and inadequacy into people who are doing their best.

So you stopped your Bible study last night after just an hour so you could play with your children awhile. You know what? That is okay.

So you missed Sunday evening services this week because your widowed mother is gravely ill and it's your only chance to take a turn sitting with her. That is fine. Our choices are not always between good and bad, but between good and better, and it is an individual decision you must make for yourself. No one has the right to judge.

In fact, you may indeed be doing as much as you possibly can. The problem is the attitude that looks for nothing more than "good enough." *When one has that attitude, he isn't.*

As Christians we are *slaves* to God, we are *living sacrifices*. Neither of those words gives us the right to decide that "enough is enough." We are always looking for ways to improve ourselves, for ways to grow, for ways to become more and more like God. That might mean that we must do a lot of extra work here and there (like a slave), and spend more in time and resources (like a sacrifice) in order to improve. But slaves want to please their masters more than themselves, and sacrifices are not sacrifices if they are cheap and easy. We don't want to be "good enough"; we want to be the best!

> *Even so you also, when you shall have done all the things that are commanded you, say, We are unprofitable servants; we have done that which it was our duty to do.*
>
> Luke 17.10

November 13

Mission Accomplished

> *And He said to them, let us go elsewhere into the next towns, that I may preach there also, for to this end came I forth.* (Mark 1.38)

Jesus was a worker. He got up early (Mark 1.35), and sometimes even missed a meal because He was so busy working (John 4.31–34). He was always ready to move on to the next place, the next group of people. His philosophy seemed to be, "There's not much time so let's keep working." Why? Because He understood His mission: this is why I came.

That is not today's philosophy. Instead I hear, "There's plenty of time to work, so let's go play," or "Life is short, so have fun." Maybe we don't work like we ought to because we don't know our mission like He did.

In our culture everything is about me—whether I am happy, whether I get to do the things I want to do, whether I feel fulfilled—and the things that we find fulfilling are usually money, fame, and pleasure.

We are simply too rich. Ask a Christian in a third world country what his mission in life is and you are far more likely to get the right answer. He scarcely has a roof over his head, much less one over a couple of thousand square feet of luxury home—and his leaks! His existence is day to day, hand to mouth, and he works longer hours—for a miniscule fraction of your pay (if indeed he has a job)—than you think is humane. Yet all his spare time is used studying his Bible, attending Bible classes, and speaking to his neighbors. We can hardly find the time to simply sit in the pews, even though we probably work more than a dozen hours less a week than that man.

We seem to be teaching our children the same mindless egocentrism. They "deserve" to have fun. They are so busy with earthly pursuits every minute of the day that they don't even spend 30 minutes a week filling out a Bible lesson—and their parents are too busy to check to see if they did, or sigh with regret and say, "But they needed a little down time." Can't their down time involve something spiritual? Can't we teach them how satisfying it is to take meals to the poor, to visit the elderly and the sick, to do their yard work and run errands for them? If they are not learning it now, when will they? If they are not learning it from you, then who will teach them?

Four times the Hebrew writer says Jesus "sat down" (1.3; 8.1; 10.12; 12.2). Jesus did not sit down because He was tired and needed to rest, or because He needed some time to Himself. He sat down because He had accomplished His task. He told His disciples, "We must work the works of Him that sent me, while it is day; the night comes when no man can work" (John 9.4).

My mission is not about me. My mission is about Jesus and His family—serving Him by serving them; serving Him by serving my friends and neighbors. When you know what your mission is, you are more likely to keep working at it, and less likely to worry about whether you are having enough fun. Those things become your "fun"; they become your fulfilling moments; they become your treasure stored in Heaven.

Accomplishing those things will finally give you the opportunity to sit down and rest.

> *He who overcomes, I will give to Him to sit down with me in my throne, as I also overcame and sat down with my Father in His throne.*
>
> Revelation 3.21

November 14

A Cow Is a Cow Is a Cow—Or Maybe Not

Due to the huge number of college football games seen in my home lately, that commercial in which cows turn on lights, parachute onto a football field, and stand on top of a car pestering the little boy in the back seat has evidently made an impression on me. A survey company called the other day. A long time ago I made a few dollars doing phone surveys and appreciated anyone who did not slam the phone down, so I answered their questions. "Which fast food chain comes to mind first?" I answered immediately, not with any of the hamburger, pizza, sandwich, or taco joints; but the chicken place with the name I never knew how to pronounce until I was grown.

Those commercials stand out to me for a reason—those are dairy cows! They don't need to worry about becoming someone's hamburger.

Does it make a difference? Only to purists, I suppose. The commercials certainly do what they are designed to do as evidenced by my quick answer to the survey question.

But for some things it does make a difference. Jesus warned that blind leaders will cause others to fall into the ditch too; God wasn't going to save them because someone led them the wrong way. John tells us in his first epistle that God expects us to "prove the spirits" because many false ones have gone out into the world. Paul marveled that the Galatians had been fooled so soon after their conversion. None of them told us not to worry, that God would save us if we were tricked into believing something that wasn't so.

A long time ago, a prophet was sent to warn King Jeroboam about his sinful ways. God told that prophet not to stop anywhere on his way home. An older prophet sent word for him to come by for dinner. When the younger prophet told him he could not, the older prophet lied, saying, "God said it was all right for you to eat with me." Instead of checking with God first, the younger prophet stopped by the older prophet's home. Before they had finished their meal God came to him and told him he would be punished for his disobedience, and, sure enough, on the way home he was killed by a lion (1 Kgs 13).

Not knowing the difference between what God said and what this man had said, even a prophet of God, cut his life short. God expected that young man to check with Him when he heard a command other than the original. God expects the same of you and me. And even though this young prophet probably thought he could rely on one of his own, one older and supposedly wiser as well, that didn't mean the message was correct.

One cow is not the same as the other, no matter what it looks like, or what we think about it. Believe me, you could tell the difference between steaks cut from dairy cattle and those cut from beef cattle. And the first time you tried to milk a steer would definitely be the last. Believing a false message, no matter who tells you and no matter what you want to believe, will not make that message true, and the results will be much more serious than a tough steak or even a kick in the head.

> *But evil men and impostors shall wax worse and worse, deceiving and being deceived. But you abide in the things which you have learned and have been assured of, knowing of whom you have learned them.*
>
> 2 Timothy 3.13–14

Hannah and Prayer

Most of us know the story of Hannah who asked God for a son and promised to give him back. She certainly made an amazing vow and an astounding sacrifice I can scarcely understand. But do we consider her many examples in prayer?

Hannah was the second wife of a man of Ephraim, a Levite (1 Chron 6.33–38) named Elkanah. The story reminds me a bit of Leah and Rachel, except that Hannah and Peninnah were not sisters, and Hannah, the favored wife, was far more righteous and God-fearing than Rachel, who stole her father's household gods (Gen 31.19) and nagged Jacob to death about her inability to conceive as if it were his fault (Gen 30.1–2). Going to God was Rachel's last resort, after first badgering Jacob, then offering her handmaid (Gen 30.3) and finally using mandrakes (Gen 30.14), the aphrodisiac of the day. You should take a few minutes sometime and read the meanings of her children's names (by her handmaid) if you want a flavor of her mindset, and compare them with the names of Leah's children. Then of course, there was Joseph. When God answered her prayer for her own child, she named him, "Give me another one." Look at the marvelous contrast of Hannah, who after asking for a child and receiving him, *gave him up to God, with no promise that she would ever have another.*

Hannah shows us what prayer is supposed to be—not some halfhearted muttering of ritual phrases, but a "pouring out of the soul" (1 Sam 1.15). She prayed so fervently that Eli, watching her, thought she was drunk. As she told Eli, "Out of the abundance of my complaint and my provocation have I spoken" (v 16). Her prayer life was such that her relationship with Jehovah gave her the confidence to tell him exactly how she felt, in the plainest of speech, evidently. You do not speak to someone that way unless you have spent plenty of time with him and know him intimately. Are we that close to God?

She also teaches us what prayer should do for us. Look at the contrast between verse 10 and verse 18. Before her prayer, "She was in bitterness of soul… and wept sore." Afterward, she "went her way and did eat, and her countenance was no more sad."

Of course, Hannah had the reassurances of a priest and judge that God would give her what she had prayed for, but don't we have the assurance of the Holy Spirit through the word He gave that God listens and answers our prayers? Shouldn't we exhibit some measure of ease after our prayers? In whom do we have our faith? If the doctors say it is hopeless, do we pray anyway? Do we carry our umbrellas, even though the weatherman says, "No rain in sight"? Do we pray on and on and on, even when it seems that what we ask will never come to pass? God does not run by a timetable like we do. Hannah had the faith that says, "It's in God's hands now," and she was able to get on with her life. Life does go on, no matter which answer we get, and God expects us to continue to serve Him with a "thy will be done" attitude.

"The effectual fervent prayer of a righteous man avails much," James tells us

(5.16). Hannah shows us it works for righteous women as well. Can people tell by our lives that we believe it?

> *Hear my cry, O God; attend unto my prayer. From the end of the earth will I call unto you, when my heart is overwhelmed; lead me to the rock that is higher than I. For you have been a refuge to me, a strong tower from the enemy. I will dwell in your tabernacle forever. I will take refuge in the covert of your wings.*
>
> Psalm 61.1–4

November 16

Mind Over Matter

I have often read Hebrews 10.34 with amazement: "You took joyfully the plundering of your own property since you knew that you have a better possession, and an abiding one." Those people had truly progressed to the point that they had "the mind of the spirit," as Paul calls it in Romans 8, rather than "the mind of the flesh." The mind of the flesh cares about losing earthly possessions. The mind of the spirit knows that something better awaits, even if it cannot be seen yet.

What is your mind set on this morning? Are you concerned about a bill that needs paying, a doctor's appointment that might reveal a serious problem, a job interview that could raise your standard of living, or simply how to fit that to-do list all in one 24 hour period?

Being responsible does mean taking things seriously, meeting one's obligations regardless the cost, and fulfilling promises made to others. The question is, have those things consumed us to the point that they control our mindset? Are we anxious, irritable, and miserable, and do we allow that to effect our relationships with others?

Paul contrasts true spirituality with carnality in 1 Corinthians 3. He says that one is maturity and the other is "walking after the manner of men"—allowing the physical things of this life to direct our steps rather than the spirituality that should be our goal. Certainly if those first century brethren did not despair when their belongings were confiscated, shouldn't we be able to live a life of joy in the relative ease we have today, even when by the world's standards the things we must deal with at the moment are not that easy?

What is your mind on this morning?

> *For those who set their minds on the flesh mind the things of the flesh, but those who set their minds on the spirit, mind the things of the spirit. To set the mind on the flesh is death, but to set the mind on the spirit is life and peace.*
>
> Romans 8.5–6

November 17

Writing Class: Orange-Colored Water

I had a great writing teacher and I still remember the things she taught me. One of the best things she ever said was, "Don't fall in love with your own words."

I had a habit of going off on tangents, especially in expository writing. I kept making asides, ideas that had nothing to do with my main point. "You are confusing people," she said. "Your main point is coming across as one of several in a list instead of something vital. If those other things are that important, make a whole new essay about each of them. If they aren't important enough for that, they certainly aren't important enough to ruin what *is* important."

I have tried to follow that advice for nearly 40 years now. It is a lesson speakers need as well. While tutoring home-schoolers, preachers "in training," and a few "full-fledged" preachers with their writing, I have finally come up with the perfect analogy. Grab a can of orange juice concentrate and read the directions. Pour the concentrate into the pitcher and add three cans of water. Guess what happens if you add more than three cans? You dilute the juice, and the more you add the weaker it gets. Before long you just have orange-colored water.

When you have a point to make and use too many words to say it or drown it in a sea of words that do not apply, you weaken your point. A short pithy statement will stay in people's minds long after they finish reading (or listening).

The same thing is true in life. When we need to rebuke someone don't we add all sorts of extra words to soften the blow? Often that is a good idea. Just the right amount (three cans) can help someone listen to what they need to hear. But sometimes we add so many that they go away agreeing with us, never realizing it was them we were talking about. What was that statement Nathan made to David? "Thou art the man." Four little words pierced David's heart to the core. We often forget to say that part, not because we are wise and loving, but because we are cowards, not loving enough to say what needs to be said.

Then there is this sad fact of life: the more you talk, the more likely you are to put your foot in your mouth. That is why I try not to judge preachers, elders, and Bible class teachers. Their job is to talk. Inevitably something will come out wrong. Be kind in your assessments.

Be careful out there. The more you talk, the more likely you are to hurt someone, the more likely you are to embarrass yourself (and your spouse), and the more likely you are to sin with your tongue. But when the time comes to speak, be careful not to add too much water to the juice out of fear, but just the right amount to help someone find his way back to the Lord. God wants pure orange juice Christians. If He will spew out lukewarm Christians, surely He will spew out the orange-colored water Christians as well.

Be not rash with your mouth, and let not your heart be hasty to utter anything before God; for God is in heaven and you upon earth: therefore let your words be few. For a dream comes with a multitude of business, and a fool's voice with a multitude of words.

Ecclesiastes 5.2–3

Writing Class: The Abstraction Ladder

One of my writing teacher's favorite metaphors was something she called "the abstraction ladder." She told us we wrote in forgettable generalities. "You have to bring it down the ladder," she said. Then she began to show us what she meant.

On the board she wrote, "Meat cooking in a pan." What kind of meat? What kind of cooking? What kind of pan? "Bring it down the ladder," she said. "Make it appeal to as many senses as possible."

Under the offending phrase she drew a large ladder. Then, as we answered each question, she rewrote the original phrase, placing each clarification down another rung on the ladder. Gradually that blah little phrase became more and more concrete. At the bottom of the ladder we wound up with, "Bacon sizzling in a cast iron skillet." Suddenly you could see it, you could hear it, you could even smell it.

Learning all the Bible stories is essential to a Christian. All those narratives make the abstract commands more concrete. "Flee fornication," Paul says in 1 Corinthians 6.18. The concrete illustration is Joseph in Genesis 39. Look at all the things Joseph did to help himself—first he said no to the woman, then he did his best to avoid being alone with her, and when finally she caught him, literally, he simply ran.

But even recognizing that does not bring it down the ladder far enough. I must apply it to my own life. What temptations do I struggle with? Do I even get past the point of saying no? Do I avoid the temptation or try to see how close I can get? Do I think I need to prove something and so stand there and try to overcome the temptation when the wiser thing would be to run away?

That is just a small example of how the Scriptures should affect my life. Men stand and pray at the end of practically every sermon that we will "make application" to our lives. Too often we don't even try. Too often even the sermons themselves are void of specific concrete examples to help us find a way to apply them. In actually making pointed applications, even made-up situations, the preacher is likely to hit a nail right on the head accidentally. Maybe that is why we don't hear too many specific applications. That means we need to try even harder to do it for ourselves.

God meant for the scriptures to lead us to Heaven. We have the mistaken notion that we need to stay at the top of the ladder to get there. But in this case, the closer we get to the bottom, the more likely we will make it.

> *This book of the law shall not depart out of your mouth, but you shall meditate thereon day and night, that you may observe to do according to all that is written therein: for then you shalt make your way prosperous, and then you shall have good success.*
>
> Joshua 1.8

November 19

Writing Class: The Last Word

My writing teacher taught me that the final sentence can make or break a story, essay, or speech. What she actually said was, "Too many people don't know when to shut up." She told us to make the last line, or at least the last phrase, short and punchy so it would stick in people's memories for at least a while after they put our writing down or walked away from our speeches. If you keep on going, you weaken the impact of what *should* have been the last sentence, and no one will remember it.

There have been times the last sentence took me *days* to come up with. I ended the essay just to get it finished, then walked away and turned the thing over in my head until *finally,* as long as a week later, I came up with that punchy last line. There have also been times when I never found it—I just hoped I hadn't ruined the whole thing with my failure.

The last word of our lives is just as important. Sometimes we want to rest on our laurels, laurels that become bigger to us as the years go by, so big we often get lost in their branches. I once heard an old retired preacher who could not sit in the Bible class without reminding everyone of all he had done in the past. The subject at hand made this particularly ironic. It must have finally struck him that everyone else was talking about their past mistakes and the things they had learned in life which had helped them develop humility. He finally spoke up with, "Oh, as I became older I realized I had been wrong about a few things when I was young—but not very many!" Since we were visiting and he was quite elderly, I went away hoping that did not turn out to be his last word before the Lord.

We cannot count on things we did long ago to save us; we cannot choose what will be our last word and expect God to forget what came after. God told Ezekiel, "When I say to the righteous, that he shall surely live; if he trust to his righteousness, and commit iniquity, none of his righteous deeds shall be remembered; but in his iniquity that he has committed, therein shall he die" (33.13). God expects us to continue doing right as long as we live. He expects us to continue serving others in whatever way we can. Those right things may change as our circumstances do; our "serving" may reach the point of simple example as our bodies deteriorate. We may actually become the tool to allow others to serve—saying "yes" when others offer to help is just as important, and humble, as offering the help. For many of us, "Thank you," to a loving brother or sister may be the last words we utter.

God, the Righteous Judge, will be the one with the last word in our final judgment. Nothing I say or do can change the fact that I have sinned and deserve eternal punishment, but the grace of God gives me hope. The last word I want to hear before I leave the realm of Time and enter Eternity is, "Forgiven."

> *This is **the end of the matter**; all has been heard: fear God, and keep his commandments; for this is the whole of man.*
>
> Ecclesiastes 12.13

November 20

Performance Anxiety

I started taking piano lessons when I was about seven years old. It was not "formal" training in a studio, but just a few lessons from a friend of my mother's to see if I was interested. I still remember the first lesson, the first book I had, and the first tune in it. "C-D-E made a boat; round and round the pond he'd float."

A few months later this friend told my parents I needed a "real" teacher. Frankly, I think she was just fine as a teacher. I learned the keys, the notes, and how to count in a few short weeks, but she insisted so off we went.

My next teacher had recitals. I still remember that first recital too, and I can still play my first recital piece: "Arab Horsemen" by Hazel Cobb. Those horsemen were a long way from the guy named "CDE" and his boat. Instead of one hand playing three notes, I had both hands running over six octaves on the piano, and a whole page played with my arms crossed!

As I sat in the student row waiting my turn to play I saw other students wringing their hands or wiping sweat off their palms onto their skirts or pants. What was the problem, I wondered? It never dawned on me that they were nervous about playing in front of people. I wasn't nervous. I knew my piece and could play it flawlessly. What was the big deal?

A few years later we had moved and the new teacher entered me in a talent competition in the County Fair. Once again I was mystified by the nervous entrants around me. I had a great piece and knew it inside and out. I had spent three hours one particular day analyzing every note, every nuance of phrase, and every dynamic marking. I got up and played it, and won a blue ribbon.

The next year I entered another competition. This time the piece was more difficult. It was written only a year or two before by Aaron Copland, a contemporary American composer. It did not make much sense to my classically oriented ear. Going from this note to that seemed totally at random to me and I had a difficult time memorizing it. But the rules for that category said I had to play it.

For the first time in my life I was not comfortable waiting my turn. Then when I got up to play, it happened—I went totally blank. I could not even start the piece. The judges were kind. They let me look at the first line. Then I walked back to the piano and my daily practice automatically kicked in. I played it perfectly, and aced the Beethoven rondo that followed. In fact, Beethoven felt like an old friend at that point.

Ever since that day I have experienced what everyone else does—performance anxiety. I played a solo professional recital once and was sick to my stomach about five minutes before I walked on. That one time when I forgot what to play has never left me. From then on I knew I was as mortal as anyone and I always wondered when it would happen again. Actually it did happen once in the middle of my senior recital, a requirement for a degree in music education. I was playing a sonata and made up about four bars on the second page of the first movement before Haydn's music found its way back into my hands. Good thing you get points for covering up a slip when you perform. I still got my A.

Can you imagine how those apostles felt when Jesus, the one they had always counted on to have the right answer at the right time suddenly left them? He knew what would happen and gave them this promise: "And when they bring you to trial and deliver you up, be not anxious beforehand what you are to say but say whatever is given you to say, for it is not you who speak, but the Holy Spirit" (Mark 13.11). Can you imagine a more comforting promise? I suppose that is why I have always had difficulties with those who claim that Paul misspoke in Acts 23.3, and that he had to apologize. Don't they believe that God kept His promise to these brave men? Try reading what Paul said with the same tone Elijah must surely have had when he spoke to the prophets of Baal in 1 Kings 18. It wouldn't be the first time that God used sarcasm through the voice of a man. Either that or He broke His promise to Paul, you can't have it both ways.

Wouldn't it be great to have that promise today? But wait a minute—in a way we do. Those men did not have the written word. Paul himself promised that one day the gifts that allowed one to prophesy a part and another to prophesy another part would be done away because the entire revelation would be "perfect," complete in all details (1 Cor 13.8–12). That is what we have—the whole shebang.

So why do we experience performance anxiety when someone asks a question, or when it comes time to speak up in the face of false teaching? Is it because we are just a little anxious about choosing exactly the right way to say it, or is it because we didn't prepare ourselves with daily practice, analyzing and memorizing? One is understandable, the other is inexcusable. We may not have all the answers on the tips of our tongues as they did, but we have the source of those answers if we will just take the time to look. "I don't know, but I can find out," may be a better testimony than acting like we do know it all. It tells our friends, if an ordinary guy like him can find it, so can I.

Those 13 men never knew when they would be called upon to speak up for God. We don't either. Start practicing what to say; start considering all the possibilities. God has given you what you need, but it's up to you make use of it.

> *I will hope continually and praise you yet more and more. My mouth will tell of your righteous acts, of your deeds of salvation all the day for their number is past my knowledge. With the mighty deeds of the Lord GOD I will come; I will remind them of your righteousness, yours alone.*
>
> Psalm 71.14–16

November 21

Picky Eaters

The other day I was talking with a friend who loves to cook as much as I do. We both spoke of how much more fun it is to cook for people who were not picky eaters. When all that effort sits in the bowls and platters on the table with scarcely a dent made in them because this one prefers this and that one prefers that, it is hard not to be offended. The very fact that I know so many more picky eaters these days than I did as a child emphasizes how wealthy this society has become. Truly hungry people are not picky eaters.

Real hunger is not a concept we understand. We eat by the clock instead of by our stomachs, which may be the biggest reason so many of us are overweight. If we only ate when we were truly hungry, would we eat too much on a regular basis? A celebratory feast, which used to happen only once or twice or year, has become a weekly, if not daily, occurrence for many.

And because we do not understand true physical hunger, we cannot understand Jesus' blessing upon those who hunger and thirst after righteousness. We think being willing to sit through one sermon a week makes us worthy, when that is probably the shallowest application of that beatitude. We don't want a spiritual feast. We want something light, with fewer calories, requiring little effort to eat. In fact, sometimes we want to be fed too. Spiritual eating has become too much trouble.

How many of us skip Bible classes? How many daydream during the sermons, plan the afternoon ahead, even text message each other? If more than one adult class is offered on Sunday mornings, how many choose the one that requires more study or deeper thinking? When extra classes are offered during the week, what percentage of the church actually chooses to attend? How many of us are actively pursuing our own studies at home, studies beyond that needed for the Sunday morning class? If we won't even eat the meals especially prepared for us by others, how in the world will be seek righteousness on our own and how will we ever progress past simple Bible study in satisfying our spiritual hunger?

Picky eaters suddenly become omnivores when they really need to eat. For some reason we think we can fast from spiritual food and still survive. Amazing how we can deceive ourselves so easily.

So, what's on your menu today, or have you even planned one?

Oh how love I your law! It is my meditation all the day. Your commandments make me wiser than my enemies; for they are ever with me. I have more understanding than all my teachers; for your testimonies are my meditation. I understand more than the aged, because I have kept your precepts. I have refrained my feet from every evil way, that I might observe your word. I have not turned aside from your ordinances; for You have taught me. How sweet are your words to my taste! sweeter than honey to my mouth! Through your precepts I get understanding: therefore I hate every false way.

Psalm 119.97–104

November 22

Understanding God?

I heard something the other day that made me stop and think. Some fellow of some offbeat religion had decided that Jesus was going to come on some given date. One of my brethren immediately said, "Well I guess we know one day Jesus *won't* come."

Now wait just a minute. I understand that concept comes from the passage that says no one knows the day of the Lord's return except God, but God can choose any day He wants to choose, even one I choose, if I were of a mind to. Before long, someone is going to come up with the ridiculous notion that if everyone takes turns choosing a day, then we can keep the world from ever ending. No wonder the world makes fun of us when our thinking is as shallow as that.

Sometimes in an effort to explain the unexplainable we overstate our case. We talk about what God would and wouldn't do, how He would and wouldn't feel, what He just could not do if He were really a loving God, and I want to cringe just waiting for the lightning to strike. "Behold God is great and we know him not" (Job 36.26). God is so far beyond our comprehension we truly cannot understand Him. We need to be careful not to be so presumptuous as to declare what He will and will not do, how He does and does not feel. Yes, I can gauge His reactions to my life based upon how He reacted to others, but making unqualified statements about God's will is pretty arrogant for the created to say about the Creator.

Sometimes we say things like, "I know we'll understand some day." Frankly, I don't know any such thing. God never promised that I will understand everything, or even that I would be able to. "Have you not known, have you not heard? The everlasting God, Jehovah, the creator of the ends of the earth, faints not, neither is weary; there is no searching [no measure] of his understanding" (Isa 40.28). It may be that once I live on a plain of spiritual existence, inhabiting eternity along with Him, that many things will become clear on their own, but God does not owe me an explanation for anything. We seem to have forgotten who holds the IOU.

This is what I know. God loves me. He sent his Son to save me. He has given me every spiritual blessing. I can talk to Him any time I choose, not just when I need help. But when I do need help, He will be there. Those things alone should amaze me and give me plenty of motivation to be faithful to Him.

He is the all-powerful Creator. He owes me nothing; I owe Him everything, including my obedience and loyalty in a life that is sometimes sad, sometimes grueling, sometimes problematic—and He is not required to explain why I must put up with those things—but a life that is also joyous because of the peace I have now and the promises He has given me for the future, even though I don't deserve them. That is all I need to know.

> *For thus says the High and Lofty One who inhabits eternity, whose name is Holy: I dwell in the high and holy place with him also who is of a contrite and humble spirit, to revive the spirit of the humble, and to revive the heart of the contrite.*
>
> Isaiah 57.15

November 23

An Old Dog

Magdi is now ten years old. She was the first dog we ever had that would not only chase a ball and bring it back, but catch it in the air like a fly ball, or chase a ball on the bounce, leaping four feet into the air to catch it. If you said, "Bring me a ball," she ran to the nearest one, picked it up, and brought it to you. If you said, "Give it to me," she would drop it on the ground next to your feet or place it in your hands if you bent over. It was almost as if she really understood English.

She also loved to play "soccer," chasing a soccer ball around the field, then guarding it when one of us ran up as if to take it away, and take off again after she caught her breath, even balancing it on her shoulders or head *or nose* as she ran. She had a large exercise ball, nearly a foot higher than her shoulders, that she would treat the same way. Once in awhile, it rolled so fast that as she tried to jump up to grab it, it threw her over the top. She would simply get up and go again.

Her bones and joints have steadily betrayed her this last year. She drags one hind foot occasionally because it hurts too much to pick it up. Her knees are swollen and stiff and some days she doesn't even try to get up when we go outside; she simply looks up and gives one floppy tail wag—thump, glad to see you, boss. She has stopped racing to the gate to greet us when we come home, but if we have been away awhile, she will slowly walk until she gets there. I always feel so bad when we get the gate closed and start down the drive before she makes it. She has to turn and retrace those several hundred steps, but if we stand and wait at the door, she will eventually make it for a pat on the head and the words she wants most to hear, "Good dog."

Pick up a ball, though, and her ears stand up even if she does not. If you bounce it, she will rise to her feet, though a bit unsteadily, and stand poised ready to run. We have learned to merely toss it now, rather than throwing it as hard and far as we can, and she hobbles after it, all thought of pain and age and weariness abandoned.

The other day Keith blew off the roof, leaving piles of leaves around the house, and wads of moss clinging in the topmost branches of the azaleas. I spent the next morning trying to "rake" it down to the ground. Magdi thought I had something—something that might be interesting, like a snake or a lizard—and she was up instantly, running from bush to bush, even standing precariously on her aching hind legs, trying to help me get whatever it was I didn't want in those bushes. She has "taken care of" many snakes and lizards over the years, as well as moles, tortoises, armadillos, and possums. It's her job, and since all these surgeries started, she has taken her duty as my protector much more seriously. Despite her creaking joints she was ready to work and if necessary, rescue me from whatever monster lurked in the azaleas.

I have been reading through the Old Testament laws concerning the elderly lately for some classes I have been teaching. What has become most apparent is how carefully God made arrangements for those and other equally helpless people like orphans and strangers, to be taken care of. Did you know that the penalty for oppressing a widow or orphan was death (Exod 22.22–24)? Did you know that sin is listed in the same category as adultery and witchcraft (Mal 3.5)? Truly we need to take this more to heart than we usually do.

But I also noticed God's expectations for those same people themselves. The older men and women are to train the younger (Tit 2). In times of struggle they should be fonts of wisdom, not buckets of bitter resentments and regrets. In the midst of fiery disputes they should be sources of temperance and cooling thoughts not fanners of the flame.

As to the widows indeed, widows with no family who had met certain qualifications and were still able-bodied, they were to pledge themselves to work for the church in return for monetary support. All those women were over 60 mind you, yet God said if they could still work for Him, they should (1 Tim 5.9–12).

What about Anna? She stayed at the temple, prophesying every day. She might possibly have been one of those women who worked there (Exod 38.8), even though she was over 80.

Simeon, who was also elderly, was still actively searching for the Messiah when Mary and Joseph brought Jesus to the Temple that first time. The Spirit sent him that special day not only to see the answer to his many prayers, but to testify to the identity of the young babe.

People of God work for God and serve Him as long as they possibly can. Working for God takes one's mind off himself, off her own problems and pains. As long as I can, I should do what I can, perhaps adapting to new circumstances, but never sitting back and saying, "Well that's it, I'm done." I have known mortally ill Christians who were still talking with people who needed help, still holding the hands of those who came to visit and cheering *them* up instead, while only days from death.

I know an old dog who still loves to play, who still wants more than anything to please her masters. I think she will probably die with a ball in her mouth, trying to bring it back for one last throw. I hope I never drop the ball for the Lord.

The righteous shall flourish like the palm tree; he shall grow like a cedar in Lebanon. They are planted in the house of Jehovah; they shall flourish in the courts of our God. They shall still bring forth fruit in old age; they shall be full of sap and green to show that Jehovah is upright; He is my rock and there is no unrighteousness in Him.

Psalm 92.12–15

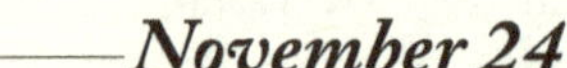

November 24

Making Choices

We live in Florida. So does Mickey Mouse. When my boys were in school, it seemed like every other year the school decided a "field trip" to that Orlando park was in order. (Whatever happened to "field trips" to the firehouse or the water plant or the art museum?) You sent $40 to the school—this was 25 years ago, remember—and your children got on a bus at 6:00 AM, which drove up to the park and unloaded about 9:00 AM. At 3:00 PM, the kids climbed back aboard and came home. Meanwhile, you had also sent at least $15 more so they would not go hungry.

We were on a tight budget and, as adults, we could easily see that the scant amount of time there was not worth the money. So we spelled it out carefully and gave them the choice—no more of these so-called field trips. Instead, if they wanted to, we would save money for a year and "do it right." Four nights in the Disney campground (the hotels were out of the question), complete with all the transportation around the park and free Disney movies every night at an outdoor theater with park benches to sit on. Four four-day park passes and supper one night in the castle, plus all the special shows they never had time to see before, like the Main Street electrical parade and the laser show at Epcot, and a souvenir of their choice at any park shop.

What made the choice difficult? For the next year, when their classmates piled into the buses, they stayed behind. Usually I showed up at the school to take them out for "early dismissal," but the next day they endured questioning about why they did not go to Disney with the rest of the group, and listened to the stories about all the fun they had. None of their classmates ever did understand, even when the boys told them the whole story. Why not do both? they wanted to know. It is always hard to tell your friends that you are not as well off as they are, especially when you are young and don't really understand it yourself. Yet the boys thought about it, and made the choice. "Doing it right" was by far better, they decided.

So we saved for a year, all of us. The boys picked up aluminum cans and coke bottles, and even set aside birthday money, which we had encouraged grandparents to send instead of gifts—they knew the plan. Seven hundred dollars later, we had the vacation of a lifetime, and the boys felt even better because they had helped pay for it. Don't tell me that having Cinderella lean over you during dinner is unimportant to a 12-year-old boy. You have never seen such bashful blushing in your life.

Growing up is all about learning to make choices. If you miss that valuable lesson, you may face a life of misery that could have been avoided. Learning to weigh options, both their pros and cons, is the key.

Just think about sin for a moment. Sin is pleasurable or it would not be a temptation. But weigh the choices.

A life of purity will give you a renewed mind (Eph 4.22–24). A fresh, optimistic outlook on life can get you through a world of trouble.

The decision to remain pure will lead to better relationships with those you deal with and the self-respect that comes with self-control (1 Thes 4.1–8). Self-control is not a prison—it is freedom from things that rule your life; it is you making the choices not your appetites. That is empowering.

Pure living will give you not only the hope of a life to come, but hope for the life now too (1 Tim 4.7–8). It promises you that God will never forsake you (Heb 13.4–6), and will cause others to glorify God (1 Pet 2.11–12). And talk about comforting—living a pure life leaves you unafraid to stand before God and give an account of it (1 Pet 4.1–5).

And the other option? Let's see, a life of impurity could give you STDs along with ensuing pain and infertility and possible death, cirrhosis of the liver, ulcers and other stress-induced conditions, a suspended driver's license, a criminal record, a broken home and family who won't talk to you any longer, fair-weather friends who leave when you need them the most, a ruined reputation, financial ruin caused by alimony and child support payments, and gambling debts you can never repay, not to mention those eternal consequences which include facing the wrath of God (Col 3.5–11), and the second death (Rev 21.8).

Hmm. Doesn't really sound like such a difficult choice to me.

> *By faith Moses, when he was grown up, refused to be called the son of Pharaoh's daughter; choosing rather to share ill treatment with the people of God, than to enjoy the pleasures of sin for a season; accounting the reproach of Christ greater riches than the treasures of Egypt: for he looked unto the recompense of reward.*
>
> Hebrews 11.24–26

November 25

Taking the Time to Notice

Lucas is manager in a supermarket deli. He had to run to another store, one he had worked in a year and a half before, to pick up something his store had run out of. Several customers recognized him, asked how he was, told him how much they missed him since his promotion, and asked where he was working. It made him feel good; what would have done even more for him, was for those same folks to take the time to tell the store manager the same thing or, better yet, go to the company website and send an email to corporate, or a snail mail to the district office. "Lucas Ward is a great guy. We really miss him at the Spring Hill store. He deserves a promotion." (If you live in the area, please take careful notes!)

Lucas tells us that for every compliment, the store receives at least five or six complaints. It isn't because the store is so bad, or the employees. It is because we are all far quicker to complain than to compliment. When you remember that your words can make or break a career, shouldn't Christians be far more careful about this? I have made it a point in the past few years to compliment workers who go out of their way for me. I also try to speak to a manager or send a letter. I listen for people's names and repeat them back at some point. If you are not receiving good service, you might be surprised at how much better your service instantly becomes when the server knows you can call him by name. They know you have noticed them as people. Isn't that what Jesus always did, notice the folks that no one else ever paid any attention to?

In our travels to other cities for my medical treatments, we stayed in one hotel twice within a six month period. On the second visit, the waitress in the restaurant remembered us. "You are the only ones who ever talked to me like I was a real person," she said. "The others treat me like furniture." That same morning I left my purse in the restaurant. Most of our travel money was in that purse, which was why I did not leave it in the room. That waitress did not know our names, but she described us to the front desk—"A couple from Florida. The wife is here for eye surgery"—and was standing outside our hotel room door with the purse before I even noticed it was missing. The hotel received a letter about her after we returned home. I hope it helped her as much as she helped us.

Christians should never be the ones making a scene at the supermarket because we opened up the flour and found weevils in it. Christians simply take it back and quietly ask for a refund or a replacement. Christians should never be the ones ordering waitresses around as if they were slaves, or barking at every little thing that isn't just right. Surely we can ask for something in a civil tone and say thank you when the item is brought to us. Surely we can say, "I'm sorry to cause you trouble but this steak is a little underdone. Could you possibly give it another minute or two?" How much does it hurt to be kind instead of mean? How much does it hurt to be like Jesus?

And think about this: What if that waitress walks into services Sunday morning because she has seen a sign or a tract, or a neighbor has invited her, and there sits the biggest grouch she ever waited on? What is it the Lord said about millstones and stumblingblocks?

If instead, she sees some of the nicest people she has ever served, I bet she will be more likely to listen and then to come back. I had much rather be in that situation than the other.

> *Give no occasions of stumbling, either to Jews, or to Greeks, or to the church of God: even as I also please all men in all things, not seeking my own profit, but the profit of the many, that they may be saved.*
>
> 1 Corinthians 10.32–33

November 26

Running Water

I wonder if it means as much to us. I wonder if it would have even gotten our attention. We take so much for granted, so many things people have not always had access to, things they would marvel at were they alive today.

Noon on a hot, dusty day saw a thirsty man sitting by a well after a long walk.

A woman trudged up, not during the normal hours of drawing water; a woman, we would later discover, who was on the fringes of her society, a society that was on the fringes itself, especially to people like this man, who sat where she had hoped to find no one. To her utter amazement, he asked her for a drink. It was not just that she was from a hated caste, but she was a woman, and men seldom talked to women in public, especially not one with her background. And not only that, but he offered her something wonderful—she would never have to come draw water from this well again. She was so excited she ran to tell the others in the town, even the ones who before would not speak to her because of her questionable morals.

He stayed for two days, teaching about this miraculous water, water they eventually realized was not wet or even real, as the world counts reality, but far more real in the dawning light of a spiritual kingdom that would accept them all, not just those other people who hated them. Soon, everyone would have this living water available, and no one in that kingdom would be considered "second class."

I wonder if Jesus would have gotten my attention with this talk? I don't have to draw water from a well in the heat of the day—enough water to clean, bathe, cook, and stay alive. But one day, nearly 30 years ago, that little story meant a whole lot more to me than it ever had before.

We came home from a trip to discover that our well had collapsed. We did not have the several hundred dollars it would have cost at the time to fix it. Keith had to dig a new well himself. For a month, every night after he finished the studying and home classes he conducted as a preacher, he worked on that well, even in the cold January rain, even running a fever.

A farmer neighbor filled and carted a 500 gallon tank outside our door. That tank had held things not good for human consumption, so we used that water to carry in five gallon buckets for flushes, and pressure canners full for bathing. Every morning I went to another neighbor's house to fill up gallon jugs for the water we used to brush teeth, make tea and coffee, and wash dishes. The boys were five and three, way too little to help cart water. I learned the value of carrying a bucket in each hand—balance was everything if you wanted to slosh as little as possible all over your carpets.

We learned to conserve water without even thinking about it—no more water running in the lavatory while brushing teeth, shaving, or putting in contact lenses! Suddenly, carrying water was a time-consuming, back-breaking job. Modern homes are simply not geared to anything but *running* water. It would have been much simpler to have had an outhouse in the backyard, and a pump handle in the kitchen. The amount of water that needed hauling would have been cut in half.

And after a month of that, I understood what this woman must have thought, what a luxury the concept must have seemed to her hot, weary body. Do we feel that way about "living water"? Is salvation such a luxury that we marvel at it and run to tell others? Or do we take it for granted like running water in our kitchens and bathrooms? I would not wish the month we endured on anyone else, but you know what? I think it was good for all of us.

Therefore with joy shall we draw water out of the wells of salvation. And in that day shall you say, Give thanks unto Jehovah, call upon his name, declare his doings among the peoples, make mention that his name is exalted.

Isaiah 12.3–4

When the Going Gets Tough

In our women's study we recently spent some time on the first century church's attitude toward persecution. We found several passages that told us the results of persecution. What would you guess they were? The group diminished in size and visibility, becoming timid and fearful, hiding when they worshipped, and keeping their faith a secret from their neighbors, right? Although we all knew better than that, we were still surprised by what we discovered.

In Acts 5 persecution left the early Christians with even more determination to preach so that in Acts 8 when persecution scattered them, the church spread over all the known world. And why should we emulate these people? In Romans 8 we found that we will be glorified if we suffer and in 2 Corinthians 4 we manifest the life of Christ when we are persecuted. Philippians 1 tells us we have a token of our salvation when we suffer, and 2 Thessalonians says that our faith grows, our love abounds and we are counted worthy of the kingdom. Peter tells us in various chapters of his first epistle that persecution proves our faith, gives us a blessing, and that the Spirit will rest on us when we endure it. Then in Revelation, the brethren are promised that if they endure their coming trials they will wear white robes, they are washed and cleansed, they will live with Christ in His kingdom and have rest (chs 6, 7, 20).

So how should we feel about persecution? The class decided it might just be necessary, even desirable. Those first century brothers and sisters rejoiced in it (Acts 5.40–42), took pleasure in it (2 Cor 12.10), and considered it a privilege (Phil 1.27–30). Maybe we should be rethinking our attitudes about persecution.

I asked what they thought would happen if we were really persecuted today. At first the women said, "The church would shrink a whole lot." Then, remembering what we had discovered about the early church, we decided it wouldn't. We would just see who was *really* part of the Lord's body, not who showed up and sat in the pews. And if history is any indicator, when the world saw how we stood for the Lord, even in the face of pain or death, they might understand that this is something worthwhile, something they might need in their lives as well, something worth any sacrifice called for. Isn't that what happened in the first century?

So should we be thanking God that we can worship "without fear of molestation?" As big a coward as I am, I might still do so, but frankly, I am not so certain I should any more.

> *Blessed are they that have been persecuted for righteousness's sake, for theirs is the kingdom of heaven. Blessed are you when men shall reproach you and persecute you, and say all manner of evil against you falsely for my sake. Rejoice and be exceeding glad, for great is your reward in heaven, for so persecuted they the prophets that were before you.*
>
> Matthew 5.10–12

November 28

Returning the Favor

In the past few years people have done things for me that I could not even have imagined. They have cleaned my house, they have put up my garden produce, they have brought meals, they have taken me to the doctor over and over and over, putting about 120 miles on their cars each time. They have shopped for me and then conveniently forgotten how much I owe them. They have walked up to me and in the midst of a hug slipped a hundred dollar bill in my pocket to help pay for surgeries, medicines and medically necessary trips that were not covered at any percentage by insurance because they were too "experimental." Many, many more have told me that they get down on their knees and pray for me every day, and many of those knees are frail and aching.

What do you say to people like that? What can you do for people like that? "Thank you," seems so lame.

And what can we do for God and Christ? Most of us understand that nothing will repay the debt we owe Them. That is what grace means—you receive mercy you don't deserve and cannot repay. Then why do we still act like our "service" is indeed plentiful payment for our salvation? Why do we question our trials as if God is letting us down "after all we've done"?

Just think for a moment about the absurdity of this: God had the power to create the complexities of this vast universe; Christ "is the image of the invisible God, the firstborn of all creation; for in Him were all things created, in the heavens and upon the earth, things visible and things invisible, whether thrones or dominions or principalities or powers; all things have been created through Him, and unto Him; and He is before all things, and in Him all things consist" (Col 1.15–17); and so, dear Father and Jesus, because of all that, I will try real hard not to sin today. That is my idea of service?

God deserves all of me, not just a few little commandments I try to keep. He deserves my service everyday, not just on Sundays. He deserves my heart, not just my outward posture. When I give myself to God there should be nothing leftover for me or anyone else.

And He deserves this even when things in my life are not particularly good. God is the Creator, He is the Almighty, He is the Ruler of the Universe. That is why He deserves my service, not because He has been good to me. We truly do not stand in awe of God if we think otherwise. Today, think about the power of God and what it should mean in your service to Him.

> *Ascribe to the Lord, O heavenly beings, ascribe to the Lord glory and strength. Ascribe to the Lord* ***the glory due his name****; worship the Lord in the splendor of holiness. The voice of the Lord is over the waters; the God of glory thunders... over many waters. The voice of the Lord is powerful; the voice of the Lord is full of majesty. The voice of the Lord breaks the cedars; the Lord breaks the cedars of Lebanon. ...The voice of the Lord flashes forth flames of fire. The voice of the Lord shakes the wilderness. ...The voice of the Lord makes the deer give birth and strips the forests bare, and in his temple all cry, "Glory!" The Lord sits enthroned over the flood; the Lord sits enthroned as king forever.*
>
> Psalm 29.1–5, 7–10

November 29

Satan Isn't Stupid

Last month I celebrated yet another birthday. Once that first number hits five, though, they suddenly become less than exciting. But all these years have given me one thing that I find invaluable, at least now that I am past them—a boatload of experiences. In fact, you may be getting tired of hearing about them.

Here is one that struck me just the other day: I now need more than two hands to count the number of times a Christian has told me about having his horoscope read, having a tarot card reading, or going to a palm reader—"just to see what it's like"—and have him tell me how astounded he was. "I know it isn't real, but it was so close, it was uncanny."

And do you think Satan is going to allow them to be so far off that you won't even be tempted to believe in them? Really now, Satan is not that stupid. But sometimes I wonder about us! Excuse me, I guess the word should be "gullible," or perhaps the more politically correct "naïve." Solomon was not nearly so concerned about being politically correct. The word he used when a child of God put himself into a position to be deceived was "fool."

Because deception is what surely follows if we are not careful. This "uncanny" ability to be so accurate (we think) draws us closer and closer, until finally we are relying on those things *more* than God, and eventually *instead* of God. Yes, it can happen to you. I have heard Christians I thought were strong tell me they could not make a decision until they had read their horoscopes for the day.

And you know what is even scarier? When it becomes obvious that we *want* to rely on these things instead of God, He will allow it. "And for this cause God sends them a working of error, that they should believe a lie, that they might all be judged who believed not the truth, but had pleasure in unrighteousness" (2 Thes 2.11–12). He considers all such things "idolatry" because they are more important to the person than He is, and "adultery" because that person has been unfaithful to Him. This is a serious matter. That is another way Satan can get to you. He will tell you it is just a fun little pastime. Read Ezekiel 16 sometime today and see exactly how God depicts this "harmless" recreation: "I will judge you as women who commit adultery and murder are judged, and I will bring upon you the blood of wrath and jealousy" (Ezek 16.38).

So think about it today. What are we doing that seems harmless but that could have dire consequences if we let it go to its natural end? Satan has dozens of beautifully crafted lures to draw us in, set the hook, and catch us before we even realize we are in danger. He is not so stupid that he will make the traps obvious. Be careful out there today. Rely on God and Him alone. Be faithful to Him and He will never be unfaithful to you.

> *For such men are false apostles, deceitful workers, fashioning themselves into apostles of Christ. And no marvel, for even Satan fashions himself into an angel of light. It is no great thing therefore if his ministers also fashion themselves as ministers of righteousness, whose end shall be according to their works.*
>
> 2 Corinthians 11.13–15

November 30

Fashion Plate

Have you noticed the new tops that fashionable young women are now wearing? I have seen them before, and worn them—30 years ago when I was pregnant. They look like nothing more than maternity smocks. I had only three maternity tops and three maternity dresses, so they wore out their welcome in a hurry. Besides, like most women, I thought they made me look like a whale. It's safe to say I won't be buying any tops till this style changes. I will say this about the new ones, though. They are better than the last fad—tops so short, yet cut so low they practically met in the middle, and tight enough to double as corsets.

Then there are the men's pants that seem to stay up by magic. I saw a teenager bussing tables at a restaurant a few months ago whose belt was literally around his thighs, the crotch of his khaki pants suspended between his knees, and the bulk of the legs bunched up above his ankles like a squeezed accordion. He walked with the mincing steps of a woman in a long tight skirt. If my schedule had allowed that day, I would have dallied over my coffee until his shift ended, just so I could see how he managed to get down the steps outside the door.

But have you noticed this about style? It doesn't change; it just rotates around the circle. Young people have been wearing the same hip-hugging wide-legged pants my generation wore as teenagers, and they think it's new. The capris women have worn the past few years are the pedal pushers we wore in the '50s and '60s. I guess it's true that you should never throw anything away because it will eventually come back into style.

God's word, however, never goes out of style. Oh, believing it and living by it goes out of style. That's not the point. Some clothing styles are called "classic" because they always work—they look nice, they're comfortable, practical and always appropriate. Doesn't that describe God's word? If everyone lived by it, think how much better this world would be.

Just a small "for instance": 20 percent of American adults now have genital herpes. That's one in five, folks. Talk about an epidemic. And why? Because people do not want to live God's way—one man for one woman for one lifetime.

One million cases of pelvic inflammatory disease occur annually. There are more cases of syphilis now than at any time since the discovery of penicillin. One-point-three million new cases of gonorrhea surface every year, as well as four million cases of Chlamydia. And these statistics are ten years out of date. Imagine what it's like now. A medical investigation done at UC Berkley discovered that 47 percent of the female students there carried the human papilloma virus.

And why has all this happened? Because it is now out of style to teach your children self-control, to wait for marriage—in other words, God's way of doing things. Instead, society teaches them the lie called "safe sex." If promiscuity were so safe, how could I find figures like these?

This is something we need to remember every day. If anyone should know how to make our lives here happy, shouldn't the One who made us? Do you realize that the laws God set down in the Old Testament put the ancient Jews thousands of years ahead of their time in public health and sanitation? Don't you get it? In any situation you can imagine, handling things God's way is safer, healthier, and happier in the long run. All this, and Heaven too. Indeed, Father knows best.

Let your steadfast love come to me, O Lord, your salvation according to your promise; then shall I have an answer to him who taunts me for I trust in your Word. And take not the word of truth utterly out of my mouth, for my hope is in your rules. I will keep your law continually forever and ever, and I shall walk in a wide place for I have sought your precepts. I shall speak of your testimonies before kings and shall not be put to shame, for I find my delight in your commandments which I love. I shall lift up my hands to your commandments, which I love, and I will meditate on your statutes.

Psalm 119.41–48

Bored to Death

I suppose it is the time of year. The mailbox has been spewing out six inch high piles of catalogues lately. Usually they wind up in the trash, but I opened up one of the less familiar ones the other day. The prices made it obvious this was for people of means, not folks like us, and so did the items themselves.

A Marshmallow Blaster (a pneumatic gun to shoot marshmallows up to 40 feet, $39.95)

A Touchscreen Portable Video Poker Game ($99.95)

A Rotating Dual Disco Ball ($59.95)

A Fish-Finding Watch ($139.95)

A Laser-Guided Pool Cue ($79.95)

A Balance Board Trainer (helps you improve your balance without having to go to a gym, $479.95)

An Authentic Scottish Practice Chanter (the first step for those who wish to learn to play the bagpipes, $49.95)

Obviously, the people who would want these things are either so wealthy that they truly need nothing, or else bored to death—possibly both.

That's what happens when you count on this world to make you happy. Solomon did exactly that and came to the conclusion that "all things are full of weariness; man cannot utter it: the eye is not satisfied with seeing, nor the ear filled with hearing. That which hath been is that which shall be; and that which hath been done is that which shall be done: and there is no new thing under the sun" (Ecc 1.8–9)—despite what Hammacher Schlemmer comes up with.

Boredom can get to us in every way when things are too easy. We recently sent care packages to Zimbabwe that included powdered Concord grape juice. Evidently grapes are not a native crop over there, and with the drought, rampant inflation, and food shortages, they were having difficulty even fulfilling the obligation to observe the Lord's Supper on Sunday mornings. At one point, they were reduced to boiling raisins and using the decanted water.

And here some of my brethren sit arguing about whether or not to call it an "act of worship," how big a piece of bread to break off, whether the bread should contain oil or shortening, whether it can be sweet, and other assorted nitpicky items. Our destitute brethren could teach us a thing or two about how precious this observance should be, precious enough to even think of buying the grape juice *instead of food*, and certainly not a source of contention.

When things become so easy that our worship to God becomes tedium so that we argue about it to fill the time, remember how it got to be that way—because we are so blessed in the first place. Maybe there is a reason that the last beatitude is "Blessed are those who are persecuted for righteousness's sake." Maybe our blessings would mean a whole lot more to us if they were harder to come by.

> *For from the rising of the sun even unto the going down of the same my name shall be great among the Gentiles; and in every place incense shall be offered unto my name, and a pure offering: for my name shall be great among the Gentiles, says Jehovah of hosts. But you profane it, in that ye say, The table of Jehovah is polluted, and the fruit thereof, even its food, is contemptible. You say also, Behold, what a weariness is it! and you have snuffed at it, says Jehovah of hosts; and ye have brought that which was taken by violence, and the lame, and the sick; thus you bring the offering: should I accept this at your hand? says Jehovah.*
>
> Malachi 1.11–13

December 2

A Bad Taste in the Mouth

Not too many weeks ago when I had a check-up with the cornea specialist, she discovered that my vision had decreased markedly and my eye pressure had more than doubled. My other doctor, the one who deals with the rare things, was away, so she made an appointment for his next available opening, less than a week from then. They gave me the time and day and said, "Will that work?"

This has been a long journey with a lot of pain and anxiety, but I was relatively calm. If I became hysterical every time I received a bad report, I would have completely worn myself out by now. But maybe that is why they felt the need to ask—to make sure I was taking things seriously. "I will make it work," I told them. If it had meant canceling a dozen other plans or walking the whole 30 miles I would have made it work.

Too many times we don't take our sin seriously. We act like it is no big deal, except big enough to get mad at anyone who might actually point out our faults. We know enough to say, "I am not perfect," but certainly let us not admit a specific fault under any circumstance. Do we think it will simply go away?

If I had ignored my appointment, the pressure would not have gone down. It would have risen to the point that I lost my vision almost immediately, instead of over the long haul. So why do we think ignoring our sins will make them go away?

Israel did the same thing in the Old Testament. Though there were priests and prophets who could heal their spiritual ailments, they not only ignored them, they persecuted them and even killed them. Along came the later generations of the New Testament, and they killed their Physician too.

How ridiculous is it when people will not take their medicine just because it tastes bad, and so they become sicker, or even die? And how ridiculous is it when we will not take care of our spiritual illnesses just because we are too proud to admit we might be wrong about something?

Yet they both happen. I would say, though, that most of us take our physical lives far more seriously than the spiritual. One day we will understand how misplaced those priorities are. I hope that bit of wisdom comes soon enough.

> *For the wound of the daughter of my people is my heart wounded; I mourn, and dismay has taken hold on me. Is there no balm in Gilead? Is there no physician there? Why then has the health of the daughter of my people not been restored?*
>
> Jeremiah 8.21–22

December 3

Servants at Every Position

I learned a long time ago that any position of authority comes with more responsibility than the right to wear the title is worth. As head of the string section of our district competition, having to deal with teachers who would stalk the judges if their students did not get the ratings they thought they deserved (anything less than a superior regardless how they performed), I had to learn how to confront those same teachers while cajoling judges to return even after the word had spread about the unprofessional behavior in our district. I had to deal with parents who wanted their child to be the exception to every rule. I had to decide when an exception was truly warranted and when it wasn't, then live with the flak my decision caused.

When I was appointed head of the vocal department for the *state* competition, things just got worse. Everyone knew how to do my job better than I did, even if they had never had a voice lesson in their lives. They might think that diphthongs were women's underwear, but they could judge a voice better than a man with a doctorate in vocal performance and 20 years experience on the stage.

The more authority you have, the more responsibility you have, and the more troubles are laid at your door. Anyone who goes around looking for it had better love the cause since he or she will get far more grief than he or she ever bargained for. And that is only right because headship is not about privilege; it is about doing what is best for those in your charge, even when it isn't what you really want to do.

Miriam forgot that. Miriam found herself leader of those Israelite women who fled Egypt along with their men. After the victory at the Red Sea, she led them in song, praising God for their victory. God also made her one of His prophetesses. Micah makes it plain that God considered her a leader: "For I brought you up out of the land of Egypt, and redeemed you out of the house of bondage; and I sent before you Moses, and Aaron, and Miriam" (6.4).

But Miriam was not happy with her calling. In Numbers 12.2 she and Aaron came before God and dared to say, "Has Jehovah indeed spoken only with Moses? Has he not also spoken with us?" Notice in verse 1 that Miriam's name is listed first, which usually means something in the scriptures. In addition I found at least one commentary that says the literal Hebrew in that verse is, "And *she* spake, Miriam and Aaron, against Moses," making it clear that Miriam was the ringleader of this little rebellion.

Miriam was not satisfied with the place of honor God gave her—it wasn't enough. She could tell that God held Moses in higher esteem, even than her brother Aaron, and she was not happy about it. Yet she had proved that she was not capable of handling the responsibilities of the job.

In Exodus 32, when Moses left the people in her and Aaron's charge, she allowed them to make the golden calf. How did she allow it? By saying nothing. As a leader she should have spoken out against their sin. God expects that of any leader, and she failed miserably. No, Aaron did not do any better, but then was he the one who complained in Numbers 12? No, he just went right along with it like he did in Exodus 32. Nothing about Aaron changed from one time to the next. Miriam's complete failure to stem the tide of idolatry at the foot of Mt. Sinai showed her unfit to be a leader of God's people. For her to then come along and demand that position in Numbers 12 showed that she wasn't even perceptive enough to see her own failures, much less lead a group that failed over and over in the years that followed.

So what does God expect of us?

How does a man react to his selection as an elder? Does he follow the path of least resistance when it is time to make a decision? Does he avoid making a decision at all, hoping to avoid unpleasant consequences? Or does he make the tough decisions that are best for the good of those he shepherds, even knowing it will cause him problems with those same people?

How does a man handle the headship of his family? Is it all about getting to do things his way, and only his way? Is it all about telling everyone else what they should be doing, while sitting around being waited on? Or does he do what is best for each member of his family, even if it makes more work and worry for him?

How about an older woman in the church, in a family, in a community? Does she stand for the truth in whatever capacity she finds herself? Is she strong enough to do right even when it isn't popular, or when it causes her personal pain? Can she remove herself and her feelings far enough from a situation to see the problems and help solve them, even if it means others will disagree? Can she stand for the truth even when it breaks her heart?

Too many people desire the perks and not the works. Jesus came looking for servants at every level, not just the bottom rung of the ladder, and those servants are judged by the deeds they do, not the glory they receive from men. Be careful what you wish for.

> *Likewise you younger, be subject to the elder. Yea all of you gird yourselves with humility that you may serve one another. For God resists the proud, but gives grace to the humble*
>
> 1 Peter 5.5

December 4

Story Time

If you are familiar with the prophets, you know they often told stories and then made spiritual application. We can read from Jewish histories that the rabbis did the same thing. It was a standard teaching method. In fact, some of the stories had the same elements, just as many jokes begin, "A rabbi, a priest, and a lawyer...." I have read in at least one source that the rich man and the poor beggar were staple characters in teaching stories all across the mid-east, even as far west as Egypt, one reason we should be careful about calling Luke 16 a "true story." Jesus was known as a rabbi because he used some of the same methods.

I have known people who insisted that preachers and teachers should not "tell stories." The Bible has plenty, they say, so use them. While in the past I agreed more than I disagreed, I have come to a change of mind. Yes, Jesus used some of the events from the Old Testament in his teaching, but far more often he used the events of every day life in stories we call parables. So I tell stories too.

Some people ask me how in the world I come up with the applications to all my stories. The answer to that is another reason I tell them. Some of them come easily but often I have to think for awhile to find a spiritual application. Guess what I am *not* doing while my mind is busy with spiritual things? Guess what does *not* happen while I search the scriptures trying to find pertinent passages? Far better to spend your time searching for applications to the events in your life than to brood over them, becoming depressed and bitter. Far better to see a way to improve yourself than to blame others as if the whole world were out to get you and you are the only one these things happen to.

Life is the training ground for an eternal existence. If I cannot become spiritual enough to handle things here, how will I ever become suitable for a spiritual existence with a Spirit Deity? That is our goal, but the way some of us lead our lives, never learning from them, I wonder if we know it, or even care.

Try today to make some spiritual applications from the things that happen to you. Think about your past and the many times you could have learned a lesson if your eyes and ears had been open to them. It is really not that difficult. If I can do it, anyone can.

> *And the disciples came, and said unto him, Why do you speak to them in parables? And he answered and said unto them, Unto you it is given to know the mysteries of the kingdom of heaven, but to them it is not given. For whosoever has, to him shall be given, and he shall have abundance: but whosoever has not, from him shall be taken away even that which he has. Therefore I speak to them in parables; because seeing they see not, and hearing they hear not, neither do they understand. And unto them is fulfilled the prophecy of Isaiah, which says, By hearing you shall hear, and shall in no wise understand; And seeing you shall see, and shall in no wise perceive: For this people's heart is waxed gross, And their ears are dull of hearing, And their eyes they have closed; Lest haply they should perceive with their eyes, And hear with their ears, And understand with their heart, And should turn again, And I should heal them. But blessed are your eyes, for they see; and your ears, for they hear. For verily I say unto you, that many prophets and righteous men desired to see the things which you see, and saw them not; and to hear the things which you hear, and heard them not.*
>
> Matthew 13.10–17

December 5

Leftovers

Have you finished the leftover turkey marathon yet? Turkey pot pie, turkey divan, turkey enchiladas, turkey soup, turkey salad, and anything else that will use up a good-sized portion of that leftover bird. It seems they all have something in common—some sort of sauce, gravy, or broth to make the endlessly heated up, dried out meat palatable. If you like turkey leftovers, it is not the turkey you like—it is what the turkey becomes, a new dish with flavorful moist ingredients that fill you up and satisfy your hunger. You can only reheat unadorned meat so many times before it turns into sawdust.

While my family enjoys leftover turkey dishes, God most emphatically does not like leftovers.

If you are a gardener, you understand the concept of first-fruits. The first pickings, like the first serving of turkey, are always the best. By the end of the summer the beans are tough, the corn is starchy, the squash is wormy, and the tomatoes are small and hard or half-rotten. That is why you doll them up in casseroles and sauces. I always make the tomato sauce in July. The June tomatoes are ripe, sweet and juicy, far too good to turn into sauce.

God has always expected the first-fruits from His people. "The first of the first-fruits of your ground you shall bring into the house of Jehovah your God" (Exod 23.19). He expected the first-fruits of everything to be given to His servants, the priests, who waited on Him night and day: "And this shall be the priests' due from the people, from them that offer a sacrifice, whether it be ox or sheep, that they shall give unto the priest the shoulder, and the two cheeks, and the maw. The first-fruits of your grain, of your new wine, and of your oil, and the first of the fleece of your sheep, shall you give him" (Deut 18.3–4).

The Israelites in Malachi's day discovered exactly how God felt about offerings that were less than the best: "You offer polluted bread upon my altar. And you say, Wherein have we polluted you? In that you say, The table of Jehovah is contemptible. And when you offer the blind for sacrifice, it is no evil! And when you offer the lame and sick, it is no evil! Present it now to your governor; will he be pleased with you? Or will he accept you? says Jehovah of hosts" (Mal 1.7–8).

We usually cite these verses when it comes time to put money in the plate. Certainly we should be planning ahead, "purposing in our hearts" what we will give to God, rather than reaching for the leftover change in our pockets. But what about the rest of our "offerings"?

Too many of us give God our leftover time. Rather than planning to pray and study, scheduling time in the week to care for our brothers and sisters in need, and putting our assemblies at the top of our agendas, we wait till we have finished what *we* consider necessary, then look to see if we can give any time and energy to God. Usually it is too late, or we are too tired, or something else that really cannot be rescheduled takes the last few minutes of our day. If there is time, we are tired, our energy flagging and our concentration poor. No wonder some of the children I have taught in Bible classes treat the concept of a family Bible study as something unheard of. No wonder the adults in Bible classes sit close-mouthed with little to offer to edify their brothers and sisters, or spout out something that even a quick study of scripture would prove to be wrong.

It only makes sense for us to give God our best. God has given us His best too, an only begotten Son, "the firstfruits of them that are asleep" (1 Cor 15.20), as a hope of the resurrection.

God not only expects us to give our first-fruits, he expects us to be one. "Of his own will he brought us forth by the word of truth, that we should be a kind of firstfruits of his creatures" (Jas 1.18). Maybe that is the problem—our lives do not match the concept. Instead, we are the blemished fruit, the tough, small, wormy, and half-rotten. How can we give God anything else when that is all we have to offer? This business of leftover offerings covers far more than the collection plate, far more than we would like to believe.

Turkey leftovers are one thing. They have a place, especially in the lives of those trying to be good stewards of their blessings. But leftovers in my service to God might as well be fed to the dog.

Honor Jehovah with your substance, and with the first-fruits of all your increase: So shall your barns be filled with plenty, and your vats shall overflow with new wine.

Proverbs 3.9–10

December 6

Second Chances

"Do you love me, Peter?"
"Lord, you know I love you."
"Feed my sheep."

Most of us are familiar with the scene on the seashore recorded in John 21. I think we make a lot of fuss over the word "love" in its various permutations because we have read a Greek dictionary and think we have suddenly become scholars with great insight. In reality there is considerable disagreement about what Jesus and Peter may or may not have intended.

However, most people agree that Jesus repeats the question three times because of Peter's three denials. Peter had already repented in bitter tears and was surely forgiven, but this gave him the opportunity to make amends in another, more direct way.

Peter takes a lot of grief for his failings. I have heard many say, and have more than likely said myself, "Peter gives me hope. If the Lord will take him, surely he will take me." Why do we think we are any better than Peter?

Is it any less a denial of the Lord as the master of my life when I fail to act as He would? Is it any less a denial when I fail to speak His word in an age of political correctness? Is it any less a denial when I fail to follow His example in forgiving my neighbor, my brother, my spouse, or simply the other driver or shopper or the waitress or store clerk? Is it any less a denial when my life matches the world instead of my Savior's? I may stand up and confess His name on Sunday morning, but it's how I live my life the rest of the week that truly tells the story, and neither the circumstances nor the provocation matter. *All of my reactions to the circumstances of life and to other people are either a confession or a denial of Jesus as the Lord of my life.*

How many times should the Lord ask me, "Do you love me?" How many second chances do I need? How many will I need *just today?*

> *But he was wounded for our transgressions, he was bruised for our iniquities; the chastisement of our peace was upon him; and with his stripes we are healed. All we like sheep have gone astray; we have turned every one to his own way; and Jehovah hath laid on him the iniquity of us all.*
>
> Isaiah 53.5–6

December 7

Tracks

On our recent camping trip we had a lot of wildlife for company. Yet it was neither frightening nor bothersome. The only animal we saw besides the usual birds and squirrels that lived in the campground itself was a young raccoon who moseyed up to the woodpile, so interested in the spot where Keith had slung some cold coffee that he didn't see us until about the same time we saw him. All of us were startled and he fled for cover. Yet I am positive we had much more company out in the woods.

If I did not see them, how do I know? Because as we hiked the park's 15 miles of trails over the next four days, we saw their tracks: the cloven hoof prints of many deer, the tiny handprints of other raccoons, the small padded paws of bobcats, and the deep, heavy prints of wild boars, along with places they had torn up the ground rooting and wallowing. There were not just a few of these tracks either. We saw far more animal tracks than people tracks on our daily hikes.

I bet you believe me, don't you? Yet God's fingerprints are all over this world of ours and it seems that every year fewer people believe in Him. They might as well believe that animals don't exist in the forest; it would make about as much sense.

But people have been behaving this way for thousands of years. I am reminded of Moses performing his signs before Pharaoh. The Egyptian ruler did not want to believe in Jehovah as the one true God. He had his many magicians replicate Moses' signs with their tricks. Finally though, they reached a point where they could not do so.

"This," they said to Pharaoh, "is the finger of God."

Would that men would be so honest today.

> *For the invisible things of Him since the creation of the world are clearly seen, being perceived through the things that are made, even His everlasting power and divinity; that they may without excuse, because that knowing God, they glorified Him not as God, neither gave thanks, but became vain in their reasonings and their senseless heart was darkened. Professing themselves to be wise, they became fools, and changed the glory of the incorruptible God for the likeness of an image of corruptible man, and of birds, and four-footed beasts, and creeping things. Wherefore God gave them up....*
>
> Romans 1.20–24

December 8

Teaching and Admonishing Yourselves

Quite a few of you are probably scratching your heads and saying, "There is something not quite right about that quote." Look at good old Colossians 3.16 and many versions have "teaching and admonishing *one another* in psalms, hymns, and spiritual songs."

I was doing a study of all the "one another" passages recently, and discovered, to my great surprise, that this passage is *not* a "one another" passage. All those other passages, like "greet one another" (1 Cor 16.20); "confess your faults to one another" (Jas 5.16); and "love one another" (1 John 3.23), use a completely different Greek word from this one in Colossians.

The word here is simply a pronoun, in this instance much better translated "yourselves." The other word also involves reciprocal action—both parties *greeting, confessing, loving* or whatever else in all the passages where it is used. The pronoun in Colossians does not. In fact, in many cases it is a singular pronoun, herself, himself, itself, yourself. "If any would follow me let him deny *himself*" (Mark 8.34); "let a man examine *himself*" (1 Cor 11.28); "he humbled *himself* and became obedient" (Phil 2.8). If you check those out, you will see that reciprocal action is not a necessary element of that pronoun. In fact, as a scholarly brother recently pointed out in one of our Bible classes, the assembly of the church is nowhere in sight in the context of Colossians 3.16 so there can be no thought of reciprocation. All of this applies to Ephesians 5.19 as well. Same word, same type of context.

So that's interesting, and something you might not have ever realized before. What of it? Just this—we have so often pigeonholed certain acts into the assembly that we may have missed out on one of God's greatest teaching devices. I am supposed to be teaching and admonishing *myself,* day in and day out, by singing. Think for a minute: how did you learn your alphabet? Is there anyone out there who did not sing those letters to the tune of "Twinkle, Twinkle Little Star?" How did you learn the books of the Bible, the twelve apostles, the twelve sons of Jacob? (Shhh! Don't tell, but if I want to get those twelve sons in birth order and make sure I do not leave someone out, I *still* have to sing that song!)

God knew a long time before modern educational theory and Saturday morning *Schoolhouse Rock* figured it out that you can learn by singing. Not only can it help you memorize a list or a scripture, but a song can get you safely through a temptation. It can cheer up a depressed moment. It can make you realize exactly how blessed you are. Some of those words we sing can even shame us into better behavior.

It isn't just that we *are allowed* to sing in places other than the assembly. It is that we are *told* to. Paul, the writer of Colossians, followed his own instructions. What did he and Silas do while languishing in stocks in a Philippian prison, not sure what the next day might hold? They prayed and sang hymns to God.

So turn off that radio, get that iPod out of your ears, unless of course, you have chosen spiritual songs to listen to and sing with all day. Teach and admonish *yourself* in psalms, hymns, and spiritual songs. Don't lose out on the hours of teaching that God intended us all to have.

Let my lips utter praise, for you teach me your statutes. Let my tongue sing of your word, for all your commandments are righteousness.

Psalm 119.171–172

December 9

Meow

I came across an interesting proverb the other day: "As a madman who casts firebrands, arrows and death, so is the man who deceives his neighbor and says, 'Am I not in sport?'" (Prov 26.18–19).

My understanding of that proverb is that a man who vents his malice toward his neighbor with all sorts of slanderous accusations is like a man who is so enraged he just shoots at everything, and then claims he was only joking and didn't mean to hurt anyone.

I know you've seen it happen—someone makes a snide comment, then when it becomes obvious that his words will get him into trouble, he smiles and says, "I was only teasing." But anyone close to the situation, who knows it well, knows that it was anything but teasing. We women have a special word for remarks like that:

"catty." They are instantly recognizable and, in our embarrassed silence, those of us within earshot become complicit because no one wants to make a scene. It would just embarrass the victim further, we rationalize. But doesn't that just reward the miscreant so that he continues on to hurt others? I wonder sometimes if a woman shouldn't say to the smug little tabby cat, "That was an ugly thing to say"; if an honorable man shouldn't stand up to the smirking tom in question and say, "That isn't funny—you have crossed a line." Would it really cause more embarrassment than has been forced on everyone already?

God wants a joyful people. He wants people who enjoy their lives here as much as possible, and who enjoy each other as well, even joking and teasing one another. Jesus, with his hilarious metaphors—running around with a log sticking out of your eye, or straining at a gnat while swallowing a camel—showed us that a sense of humor is not sinful, that we do not have to live with a sober, serious look on our faces all the time. Sometimes a sense of humor is the only thing that gets us through a difficult situation—perhaps that is one reason God gave us one, as a defense against Satan and the trials of life. To use it maliciously seems, well, irreverent somehow.

Today I will be especially careful to watch my tongue and how I use that wonderful sense God gave me. All you have to do is look at a hippopotamus to know that He has it too.

> *Behold this is the joy of his way; and out of the earth shall others spring. ...He will fill your mouth with laughter and your lips with shouting. They that hate you shall be clothed with shame, and the tent of the wicked shall be no more.*
>
> Job 8.19, 21–22

December 10

'Tis the Season

'Tis always the season for what I am talking about this morning: "Preach the word, be urgent in season and out of season, reprove, rebuke, and exhort with all longsuffering and teaching" (2 Tim 4.2). While we all understand a certain concept of "a wrong time," that concept does not stretch to mean that when I do not want to hear it, I don't have to. When exactly do any of us *want* to be reproved or rebuked? Exhorted maybe, but not reproved and certainly not rebuked. I have yet to find a person who will tell me a time when hearing about his faults is "in season," including me. Yet that is exactly what Timothy the evangelist was commanded to do, tell them when they want to hear it and when they don't.

As Paul goes on to tell the preacher, people will want you to scratch their "itching ears," what today we might call stroking someone's ego. And this has always been, for Old Testament Israel was bad about listening to the prophets they wanted to listen to instead of the ones who told them the truth. Ahab told Jehoshaphat, who had asked if a *real* prophet was anywhere around, "There is yet one man by whom we may inquire of Jehovah, Micaiah the son of Imlah, but I hate him, for he does not prophesy good concerning me, but evil" (1 Kgs 22.8). Funny how it never dawned on Ahab that he could fix that problem himself without touching a hair of Micaiah's head.

I have been known to say that our society is worse about this than in the past—a bunch of namby-pambies who cannot take criticism—and maybe it is worse today than a hundred years ago, but the scriptures make it plain that God's teachers have always had to deal with arrogant people who think they need no correction about anything at all. I suppose it will always be so. But we should do our best to make sure we are not among them because neither God nor Jesus ever had anything good to say about people like that. In fact, some of Jesus' strongest condemnations were to people who claimed to be the most righteous. He said that their attitude of self-righteousness made them just the opposite, a brood of vipers, among other harsh accusations.

Examining ourselves and learning to do better are always in season simply because they are always necessary. I shouldn't blame the preacher, or any other caring brother or sister, because he does as God commands when I am the one at fault.

'Tis the season, whether we think so or not. Fa, la, la, la, la—la, la, la, la!

A wonderful and a horrible thing is come to pass in the land; the prophets prophesy falsely and the priests bear rule by their means, and my people love to have it so, and what will the end thereof be? ...They have healed also the hurt of my people slightly saying, "Peace, peace," when there is no peace.

Jeremiah 5.30–31; 6.14

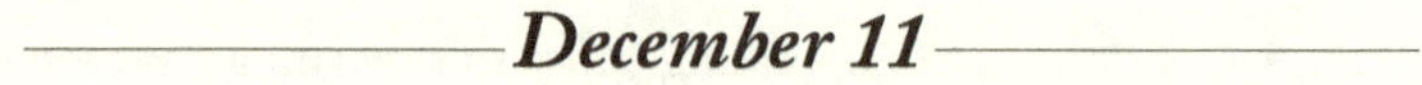

December 11

Shooting from the Lip

I am not a gun nut. I don't know a whole lot about shooting. But I do know some things that should be obvious, yet apparently are not. For example, when you shoot a gun, the bullet has to come down somewhere.

We live in the country. That means we do not have to worry about the laws against discharging a weapon in the city limits. Since we have a lot more poisonous snakes, rabid coons, and bobcats ravaging the chicken coops than they do in town, that is a good thing. Still, we must be careful.

One reason many people use shotguns out in the country is that the load will scatter and not do much harm after a few feet. If you shoot a rifle, you must constantly be careful of what is behind your target and the pitch of your gun barrel. It *must* be pointing down so that if you miss your target, the spent bullet will hit the ground harmlessly not too far beyond. If you miss what you are aiming at, the bullet keeps going until it either runs out of energy or hits something else. And yes, even those supposedly harmless shots they fire in the air in all the old Westerns do eventually come down, and can still kill someone. Evidently people who are *not* gun nuts, and certainly not physicists, write all those scripts because they regularly show their ignorance in these matters.

Words are like that. Too many times we become angry, carelessly "shooting from the lip" or firing a few verbal bullets into the air, unaware of how those words may hurt those who may be within earshot. Even words meant only for ourselves can cause damage to others when spoken aloud—there is always the chance that someone else will hear. If a target needs a well-chosen word, chances are something spoken in haste was not well chosen anyway. I need to keep it to myself until I am certain my aim is correct, the background is clear, and no one else is in danger.

Just like a bullet, a word can come to rest in the heart of an innocent bystander. Be sure you don't make a tragic mistake.

I tell you on the day of judgment people will give account for every careless word they speak, for by your words you shall be justified, and by your words you shall be condemned.

Matthew 12.36–37

December 12

The New Neighbor

We were standing on the carport one evening when I saw movement out of the corner of my eye. I turned just in time to push Keith out of the path of a garter snake determinedly chugging his way up the slope to the concrete slab. We called the dogs off and allowed him to meander under the mower and off the edge of the pad to the cool darkness under the porch. A few days later he made another appearance and we discovered his home when he wriggled away—the hollow pipes supporting the metal roofing of the carport.

I have come a long way in 35 years—from a city girl who screamed and ran from a foot long, pencil-thick, bright green garden snake to a country woman who understands the value of a snake on the property—God's original mousetrap. I will never be a snake lover. I went out one afternoon and found him stretched out at the foot of my lounge chair. I got the broom and shooed him back into his pipe. My dogs can sit at my feet and have their heads scratched, but with Mr. Snake it is only a matter of "live and let live."

Too many times we take that attitude with Satan. Yes, he is out there every day. Sometimes we even bump elbows in passing, but we don't have to stop and politely say, "Excuse me." Don't give him a cool spot on the carport and an idle belly rub with your bare toes.

If this garter snake were one of the four poisonous varieties we have in this area—all of which we have seen on our land—he would not be tolerated. Although my guys may tell funny stories about me and snakes, they cannot deny that I know how to make like Annie Oakley when a bad one comes along. I have killed them with a shotgun, a .22 rifle, and a .22 pistol. I have killed them with rat shot and buckshot. When necessary I have used a shovel. I have lost count of how many poisonous snakes I have killed. They get fewer every year.

How are we doing with Satan? Does he think his presence is tolerated, even welcome? Or does he know that it's dangerous to be around us? He is fighting a losing battle and he knows it, but that won't keep his poison from killing us if we allow him to get too close.

Do not give opportunity to the Devil.

Ephesians 4.27

December 13

Roll and Wrestle

When I had boys I was scared to death. Growing up there was just my sister and I, and most of the boys I knew at church were wild. In fact, quite a few left the church as soon as they could. I just knew I would never be able to raise good boys.

I had never reckoned with Keith. He was determined to raise those boys "in the nurture and admonition of the Lord." He never expected me to do it alone, and he started when they were young. Even if he could not nurse them, he got up when they cried in the night and brought them to me. He often sat there talking to them while they nursed, when he could have been sleeping, so they would early on associate both our voices with that comforting process.

Every evening he gave them their baths so I would have enough uninterrupted time to do the things I needed to do—wash the evening dishes, finish folding the laundry, and other necessary things. A few times he sent me out right after the afternoon nursing to "do whatever you want," while he sat with them, usually playing or reading to them. Other times I would hear their voices wafting through the kitchen window, singing about the "wee little man." while he held them up on the lowest limb of "the Zaccheus tree," a sapling in the backyard

Play usually involved acting out Bible stories. It was so handy that Daddy was bigger than they, so he could be Goliath, or "the big fish," swallowing them up by covering them with his body until they had prayed for "three days and nights." As they grew older, the play became more spirited. "Let's play 'roll and wrestle,' Daddy," was followed by thumps and giggles, and muffled shrieks of laughter as they took turns tackling Daddy in the middle of the living room floor and then rolling around as far as they could without knocking something over. They never knew that Daddy was watching out for the furniture and carefully moderating his strength so he would not hurt them. They just knew that Daddy would get down in the floor and play with them whenever they asked him to.

My favorite snapshot from those days is the one I took standing in the front door looking down on three mud-covered bodies. It was summer and a soft, warm rain made it perfect for a mud fight. They went out and had the time of their lives, then knocked on the front door. I opened it to see Nathan on Keith's shoulders and Lucas standing just in front of his legs, head about waist high, all three shirtless in grungy, mud-spattered cut-offs. I think. I did see three sets of eyes and grinning white teeth somewhere in all that brown mud. Clean-up was just as much fun since it involved using a hose before they could even step inside the house.

He didn't just involve himself in their fun. He taught them how to work, how to be gentlemen, and how to study the Bible, among other manly pursuits.

Keith started being a dad before those boys were even born, and has kept it up. He was not above changing diapers. In fact, one of his own original sayings is that if a Dad cannot change the messy diapers, he won't be much use in later years when the messes of life afflict his children either.

Keith will tell you that 90 percent of the convicted felons who sit across the desk from him did not have fathers in their homes. He does not bother to check out what kind of father, or whether the marriage was a good one. That makes that little fact even more important. Even the mere presence of a father can make a huge difference. Imagine the difference it would make if he were really trying to be a good one.

Dads, you know what you need to do today. The buck stops at you.

***Fathers,** provoke not your children to wrath: but bring them up in the nurture and admonition of the Lord.*

Ephesians 6.4

December 14

Have a Nice Day

I saw a bumper sticker in a parking lot: DON'T TELL ME WHAT KIND OF DAY TO HAVE. I must be slow because it took me several minutes to figure it out. Here was someone so mad at the world that he couldn't even handle a common courtesy. He obviously did not want to have a nice day, thank you very much, and I suspect that he didn't, not that day nor any other.

I have heard similar things about other polite phrases. "You don't care how I am, why ask?" Everyone with any sense knows that "How are you?" is not a question; it's a greeting. Do these people need a course in semantics or what?

No, what they need is an attitude adjustment, the kind you get from becoming a disciple of Christ. Christians are not afraid to take risks, to put themselves out there for people like that to step all over, because Christians understand that treating others well, regardless of how they are treated, is the signature of a follower of Christ. More than anything else, it shows who we are. We choose to believe the best about people; we choose to offer help whether it is accepted or not, whether we are taken advantage of or not; we choose to show a spirit of forgiveness whether the other person deserves it or not.

Those others, the grumpy, the bitter, the cynical, the ones who view the world with a jaundiced eye, the ones who deride us for our stupidity, as they categorize it, who think themselves so much smarter and better than us with their snide sarcastic sayings—"Don't tell me what kind of day to have"—are in actuality cowards. They are afraid of being hurt, afraid of being used, afraid of losing the only thing they have—confidence in themselves and how they choose to live. They will not take risks, while we thrive on it. We know that anything we lose here was not worth that much anyway—it will all perish in the end. The things they count on could be gone in a flash, but they are not smart enough to figure that out.

So there you have it—they are cowards and not very smart ones at that. Don't worry when they laugh at you for your willingness to take risks. When you think about it, we aren't taking any risks at all—*they* are the ones with everything to lose.

And by the way, have a nice day!

You have heard that it was said, An eye for an eye, and a tooth for a tooth: but I say unto you, resist not him that is evil: but whosoever smites you on the right cheek, turn to him the other also. And if any man would go to law with you, and take away your coat, let him have your cloak also. And whosoever shall compel you to go one mile, go with him two. Give to him that asks you, and from him that would borrow of you turn not away. You have heard that it was said, You shall love your neighbor, and hate your enemy: but I say unto you, love your enemies, and pray for them that persecute you; that you may be sons of your Father who is in heaven: for he makes his sun to rise on the evil and the good, and sends rain on the just and the unjust. For if you love them that love you, what reward have you? Do not even the publicans the same? And if you salute your brethren only, what do you more than others? Do not even the Gentiles the same? You therefore shall be perfect, as your heavenly Father is perfect.

Matthew 5.38–48

December 15

Aroma Therapy

Yesterday I stepped onto the curb outside my supermarket and the scent instantly sent me back to my childhood, when artificial Christmas trees were unheard of, and the whole house smelled of fir, spruce, pine, or whatever evergreen we found at the local lot that happened to fit that special spot in the living room for those few weeks every year. Funny how a smell can bring back so many memories.

It happens with the change of every season. Right now the cold air carries the smell of wood fires from all the hearths in the neighbors' houses. And isn't it odd that on winter mornings the aroma of bacon can travel for hundreds of yards when it won't any other time of year? Soon the smells will change to jasmine, gardenia, and other heavily scented tropical flowers, and the air, while still cool, will gain a little weight in the morning from fog. Then summer will carry the smell of new-mown grass, afternoon rain blowing in on humid breezes from the west, and all too often the chicken farm a mile down the highway. Finally, the air will begin to crisp and the fires will come from leaf piles and field burns, a less pleasant odor than the wood fires, which will once again permeate the air soon after.

Aromas mean a lot to God as well. He told his people several times that when they offered acceptable sacrifices the "sweet savor" of their offerings pleased Him (*e.g.*, Exod 29.18; Lev 1.9; Ezra 6.10). Ezekiel told them that God would "accept them as a sweet savor" when they returned from exile, a penitent and purified nation (Ezek 20.39–44). On the other hand, He used a reeking garbage dump in the valley of Hinnom, where even the bodies of the dead were often thrown, to symbolize the punishment He had in store for the faithless (Isa 66.24; Jer 7.31–34).

They say that certain smells can energize you, calm you, lift your spirits, ease your tensions, and just about anything else you can imagine. God has used our sense of smell and the power it has to conjure up thoughts to symbolize the pleasure He has in our gifts to Him, the fear we should have in displeasing Him, and the grace He offers to such weak, sinful creatures as us, who deserve nothing but His disapproval. Take a good whiff and see what you can smell this morning.

Be ye therefore imitators of God, as beloved children; and walk in love, even as Christ also loved you, and gave himself up for us, an offering and a sacrifice to God for an odor of a sweet smell.

Ephesians 5.1–2

December 16

An Unfair Fight

She took him into her home. She fed him. She offered him a place to rest, a place he felt safe. Then, when he was sound asleep, she knelt next to him and pounded a tent pin through his temple.

Many times I have heard Jael, the wife of Heber, described as a sneaky, devious, blood-thirsty woman. We in our civilized, politically correct, white collar world decry any ancient blood-letting as barbaric, even though people of our own era commit atrocities, from the mega-massacres of Stalin and Hitler to the mob mentality that runs rampant in both the inner cities and suburbia at the lowest flashpoint, be it outrage or fear. So, in our blindness to our own hidden savagery, we read the account in Judges 4 with a jaundiced and arrogant eye. If we had spent any time at all on the song of Deborah in Judges 5, we would have avoided contradicting divinely inspired opinion about Jael's actions. "Blessed above women shall Jael be" (v 24).

Certainly that should settle the matter. Just for the added emphasis of common sense, though, let's ponder this question: What was this nomadic shepherd woman, alone at home, supposed to do? Should we require that she meet a trained warrior, the captain of a mighty army, in a fair fight? Indeed, I read that the customs of the day said for a man to force his way into another man's tent, or to merely enter that same tent when the man was not at home, was an action worthy of death.

But how do we reconcile this type of behavior with Jesus' teaching? "I say unto you, love your enemies, do good to them who hate you; bless those who curse you; pray for those who despitefully use you. To him who smites you on the one cheek, offer the other also; and from him who takes away your cloak, withhold not your coat also. Give to everyone who asks and from him who takes away your goods, ask them not again. And as you would that men should do to you, do also unto them likewise" (Luke 6.27–31). Some would say, "Jael was under the old law. Things are different now." While that is so, it only skims the surface of the matter.

Old Testament Israel was a physical kingdom with a physical king sitting on a physical throne. They fought physical wars using physical weapons. Isaiah prophesies a coming kingdom where "they shall beat their swords into plowshares and their spears into pruning hooks, nation shall not lift up sword against nation, neither shall they learn war any more" (2.4); a kingdom that would have no physical boundaries, but would encompass the whole world, one into which "all nations shall flow" (2.2). Jesus established that kingdom, the church, his throne not on this earth but in Heaven.

Yet we still fight battles. Paul spent a good amount of time detailing our armor (Eph 6), our weapons and battle tactics (2 Cor 10), and the characteristics of a faithful soldier (2 Tim 2).

Every time we overcome temptation, we win a battle; every time we speak of our faith to others, we take an enemy captive; every time a Christian leaves this world, having been faithful to the end, we pound a tent pin into the temple of Satan. If we are too politically correct to fight a battle, if we are too finicky for hand-to-hand combat, if we are too "civilized" to pick up a sword and slash our way through the enemy forces, we don't have what it takes to be a follower of Christ.

Make no mistake about it. You are going to war today. Be prepared to fight in it.

Suffer hardship as a good soldier of Christ, for no soldier on service entangles himself in the affairs of this life, that he may please him who enrolled him as a soldier.

2 Timothy 2.3–4

December 17

Walking the Walk

Keith and I met at college. It took most of the first year for us to actually become an "item" because of a lot of things—mainly our differences: country boy vs. city girl, 24-year-old ex-Marine vs. naïve 17-year-old girl. We lost count of how many people told us it would never work. Even today, people who have met us separately and then finally see us as a couple say, "I never would have put you two together."

The campus was small so you parked and walked everywhere. Few knew the extent of my vision problems back then. I had learned to watch people move, and usually recognized them across campus by their walks.

I did not realize exactly how distinctive a walk could be until I met Keith. I still can't quite figure it out. He keeps the top portion of his body completely still and swings his legs from the hips—at least that is the best way I can describe it. Whatever it is, I recognized him from a farther distance than I ever had anyone before. He says it has something to do with growing up on the side of a mountain. I have seen that mountain and the remains of that old house, and it brings to mind the old joke about cows in the mountains having legs of different lengths.

I wonder how people in the world recognize us. Could it be that our walk gives us away?

John tells us that as followers of Christ, we ought to walk "even as He walked" (1 John 2.6), and that would certainly make people notice. If they don't, then are we really behaving as we ought? If we use the same language, engage in the same activities, dress the same way, and react in the same way as the rest of the world, who exactly are we walking like? Sounds like the rest of the world to me.

People in the neighborhood, in the office, in the school, in the grocery store or doctor's office should all be able to see a difference in how we behave and how the rest of the world behaves. Yet it is not just a matter of being "different." They should know what that difference means. *They should be able to recognize the walk!*

It is not enough to just follow His footsteps—a lot of people do that with little or no thought. It keeps them out of trouble, it keeps them in good standing with the elders, it satisfies them that they have fulfilled the commandments. But a child can stand in one of his father's footprints and then jump to the next without making a new impression in the sand. Is he really walking like his father walks?

What really needs to happen is the full body awareness, swinging your arms the same way, holding your head the same way, lifting your feet and setting them down the same way—everything exactly the same because now Christ lives in you. You have reached a point where you no longer need to struggle to leap from footprint to footprint in order to stay on track. Your walk actually fits into His.

How are you walking this morning? Is it a recognizable walk? And exactly how would a stranger describe it? If you are walking as He did, there should be no question about it.

> *If we say that we have fellowship with him and walk in the darkness, we lie, and do not the truth: but if we walk in the light, as he is in the light, we have fellowship one with another, and the blood of Jesus his Son cleanses us from all sin.*
>
> 1 John 1.6–7

December 18

Rocking Horses

My boys survived on hand-me-downs, including hand-me-down toys. An acquaintance gave us one of those molded plastic "rocking horses" that hang suspended by four large springs on a tubular steel frame. The boys were so young we had to hold them on it at first, but before long they could mount it and ride on their own, the steady, groaning sproing, sproing, sproing reaching my ears as I worked in the kitchen. As they grew older and gained experience with western heroes, particularly a certain Texas Ranger who wore a mask, I often heard shouts of, "Giddy-up," "Whoa," and finally, "Hi-yo Silver, awaaaaaay!"

In their active little minds they traveled everywhere on that horse, despite the fact that they never left the room. Sometimes we have the same problem.

I have seen good, sincere, faithful Christians hamstring themselves by riding a certain hobby nearly to death. No matter what subject comes up, they can finagle it around to their favorite topic. After awhile you learn to avoid certain words that function like detonators on a land mine. We often accuse preachers of this problem, but it can happen to us just as easily, not only about topics, but about people too.

When you can only focus on the aggravating things about a person, you fail to see the good in them. When all you can see are the annoyances in the church, you fail to gain the encouragement you need from the assembling together of a spiritual family. When one pet peeve is all you see in any passage of scripture, you fail to see the things you yourself need in order to grow and improve. Obsession can rob you of any influence you might otherwise have because everyone will just say, "There he (or she) goes again," automatically dismissing anything you say.

It is even worse when the thing the "equestrian" goes on about is actually a good and right thing. He simply makes more of it than it deserves because to him it has become a holy grail. He can make it seem that anyone who does not share his opinion has some sort of deep-seeded problem with a) love; b) authority; c) faithfulness; d) all of the above, choose whatever fits the occasion. So division often occurs, if not in fact, then in spirit, because in his arrogance he believes that this "thing" is the root of every other problem we might possibly have and important enough to cause a fuss about.

The rider may think he sees better than others, but all he is seeing is one tiny corner of the Word, while the rest remains hidden behind his self-imposed blinders. He may think he is enjoying an amazing ride on a marvelous steed, but he is sitting on a swayback nag in the middle of a field, going nowhere. At least the children eventually get off the horse.

It is a whole lot easier to get on the horse than to get off it. Sometimes we don't even realize that is what we have done. Do you need to get off yours and take a new look around? It might surprise you how far you have *not* come—but it's the first necessary step to going farther.

> *Of these things put them in remembrance, charging them in the sight of the Lord, that they strive not about words, to no profit, to the subverting of those who hear. Give diligence to present yourself approved unto God, a workman who does not need to be ashamed, handling aright the word of truth.*
>
> 2 Timothy 2.14–15

December 19

Man and Machine

I am a technophobe. I hate all these new contraptions with all their buttons and all their directions. Whenever something goes wrong and I have to fiddle with them, I get so worried about it that I get sick to my stomach. I have absolutely no aptitude for them.

I recently had a run-in with my TV. Somehow the thing decided to take the picture and squish it in from the sides, elongating all the faces in the process. To make up for that, it chopped off the tops of heads and the bottoms of chins. I tried to fix it myself. A good friend told me there was nothing I could do that could not be undone. She had not reckoned with anyone like me. I hit a button I did not mean to hit and the whole picture disappeared. So I hit it again to undo it, right? Wrong! All I got was a baby blue box telling me there was no signal.

"No signal?" I said aloud to my television. "If you are so smart, tell me something I cannot figure out myself!" I hate it when a machine riles me to the point that I actually talk out loud to it.

After several frantic hours, my good friend arranged a conference call between the tech support people and the two of us. (I don't like to talk with them. There is no way I can hide the fact that I am an idiot.) We got my picture back, but it took sliding a lever that I was warned never to touch, and never had—I promise! Like I said, I can really mess things up.

During all of this I learned that I have an amazing TV. It can let me watch several channels at once. It can take messages for me. It can lull me to sleep and then turn itself off. I never knew all that. But you know what I want? I want a TV with an on/off switch, a channel changing knob, and a volume knob. Period. Well, maybe I wouldn't mind if it brought me a cup of coffee every morning. But do they make a TV like that? Of course not.

I have issues with my computer too. I want it to type and print, and I have gotten attached to the e-mail function, as well. But that is all I want. It infuriates me when it tells me that I cannot do what I want to do. Then when it tells me I am doing something illegal, I really get mad. I guess there is a reason Keith keeps his hammer in the shed.

But now that I think about it, we do the same thing to God. How many times do we hear, or even make the statement ourselves, "I don't think God would mind this." "I think God will understand." Or the even more arrogant and judgmental, "I can't believe God would let this happen," as if we had a right to approve or disapprove God's actions.

What would you do if you changed the channel one day, and the TV flipped it to another? After several tries, the baby blue box pops on the screen saying, "You cannot watch that other show. I like this one better."

What would you do if you tried to delete a file on your computer, and the "save" box kept coming up instead? After several tries that gray box pops up and says, "I don't want to delete this. I like it. Hit the save button."

Aren't we glad God doesn't have a hammer handy? Not that he couldn't just create one out of thin air, which emphasizes the point. He is patient, when many times we do not deserve it. I need to take note of my aggravation with the aggravating machines in my life, and make sure I am no longer an aggravating creation to him.

He says it, I do it. Period.

The Lord is not slack concerning his promise, as some count slackness, but is longsuffering toward you, not wishing that any should perish, but that all should come to repentance.

2 Peter 3.9

Shopping Lists

I make a shopping list every week. When you live 30 miles from town and the price of gas has risen so high, you learn to plan. Running up to the store for a forgotten item is not in the works.

I know what I am going to cook each night that week, what I need for each dish, what is missing from the staples in the pantry, and what is on sale where before I leave the house. Keith and I also spend a few minutes the evening before trying to think of every other piece of business I can take care of in the same trip. Used to be I had to make as many stops as the grocery store, the pharmacy, the dry cleaners, the bank, the discount store, the music store, and the office supply store, then fit the women's Bible study in there somewhere, making certain I accomplished everything in time to be home, unloaded, dinner either in the oven or the crockpot or everything set out for a quick fix meal, and then the studio set up and ready for music students by 2:30 for four hours of instruction.

I learned to use one of the reply envelopes supplied by all the credit card companies who want us to go into debt up to our ears. I kept a stack in my kitchen drawer and each week listed all my stops, numbered for time and gas efficiency, and what I needed to do or pick up at each stop on the outside of the envelope. Inside I put coupons and claim tickets. When I came home those had been replaced with receipts and new claim tickets, depending upon what was happening that week. I seldom forgot anything thanks to my "system."

The other day as I was talking to God, I realized that I had strayed into my shopping list format. Very matter-of-factly I was telling Him what I needed when and how I would like it served. I reminded myself of Captain Picard standing in front of the replicator in his ready room barking out, "Tea—Earl Gray—hot!" Suddenly I remembered to Whom I was talking and shivered a little. What in the world was I thinking?

God is not a grocery store. He is not a waiter at the restaurant waiting for me to make my order, giving Him extra directions so it will be exactly what I want—pastrami on rye, pressed, extra mustard, hold the mayo, slaw on the side. Yet isn't that exactly how we treat Him sometimes? Yes, I can tell Him all my desires; in fact, He expects me to do that, and He wants to satisfy me, His child. But when I start expecting Him to parcel it out in only the way I want it, as if I can send it back with a reprimand if it doesn't suit me, I have overstepped the bounds.

We have all seen children make their lists for birthdays and for Christmas, but don't we all think better of the children who have learned that wanting something doesn't mean they ought to have it, that wanting for others is even better than wanting for themselves, and that they should be grateful for whatever they receive, not complain about it.

My parents taught me to never greet a guest, especially a grandparent or favorite aunt or uncle with, "What did you bring me?"

"They might think that is the only reason you want to see them, and that would hurt their feelings," it was explained to me. I think I need to relearn that lesson about God.

> *And at the evening oblation I arose up from my humiliation, even with my garment and my robe rent; and I fell upon my knees and spread out my hands unto Jehovah my God, and I said, Oh my God, I am ashamed and blush to lift up my face to you my God; for our iniquities are increased over our head, and our guiltiness is grown up unto the heavens.*
>
> Ezra 9.5–6

December 21

A Long Hard Winter

Today is the winter solstice, the first day of winter. In Florida that means very little, but a year or so ago we had a different sort of winter—long cold spells with lows below freezing and highs only in the 40s, and frosts as late as April. Snow fell in the panhandle and in the north central peninsula. Usually we are sorry to see the heat return, but that year we were longing for it.

The spring was different too. The azaleas bloomed two months later, and all at the same time, so profusely you couldn't even see the branches. The blueberries had more fruit on them than any time in the five years past. The hostas not only came up again but multiplied, sending up four plants where each one plant sat the year before. The spring wildflowers were beautiful, turning fields first into blankets of blue and lavender, then red and maroon, and finally pink and white. The oak pollen fell so thickly the lawn looked like wall to wall brown carpeting. And the garden produced better than it had in years.

I wondered, could one thing have to do with the other? Could a long, hard winter be the cause of good crops and beautiful flowers in the spring?

"And they arrested [Peter and John] and put them in custody until the next day because it was already evening. But many of those who heard the word believed and the number of men came to about five thousand" (Acts 4.3–4). That is not the only case in the New Testament where rapid growth of the kingdom followed hard on the heels of persecution. A long hard winter of trial always seemed to make for a springtime of growth among God's people.

Then there is the personal aspect. I have seen so many times how a personal trial has led to spiritual growth in a Christian. I have experienced it myself. Something about trial inures us to the pains that might otherwise cost us our souls. We grow stronger little by little, gradually learning the lessons of faith, endurance and strength in the service of God.

That may be why I cringe when I see a young mother turn every little scrape on the knee or cut on the finger into a life-threatening crisis worthy of the loudest wails, instead of helping her child learn to laugh it off. I have seen too many of those children grow into men and women who complain about everything that does not go their way. If it's okay to whine and cry like the world is ending when you fall and skin your knees, why isn't it okay to scream at other drivers who get in your way? If it's okay to pout and mope when you don't get to play your favorite video game, why isn't it okay to complain long and loud when the boss asks you to work overtime? If it's okay to pitch a fit when some mean adult tells you to straighten up, why isn't it okay to stand in the parking lot complaining about the church, the preachers, the elders, and anyone else who doesn't see things your way?

God needs people who are strong, who can take pain and suffering for His sake, who understand that their way doesn't really matter if it is not His way, and that the good of the kingdom and its mission may have nothing to do with them having an easy, perfect life here in this world, but everything to do with a perfect life in the next.

Just as with everything else, our culture is affecting us. The strong silent type who can take the worst the world has to offer and keep going is no longer the hero. Instead we reward jerks and boors and idolize intemperance. Prodigality and lavish lifestyles are our measure of success; striking back is our measure of character, and throwing tantrums is our measure of strength.

I see a day coming when the church will once again be in the middle of a long, hard winter of persecution. The way we are going we may not survive it at all, let alone have a bountiful spring because trials and persecution only work to build strength when you learn from them. They only produce character when you have the toughness to take the bad with the good without whining about it.

What kind of spring will you have next year?

And not only so but we rejoice in our tribulations, knowing that tribulation works steadfastness; and steadfastness approvedness; and approvedness hope; and hope puts not to shame, because the love of God has been shed abroad in our hearts through the Holy Spirit which was given unto us.

Romans 5.3–5

December 22

Greetings

Salute one another with a holy kiss. (Rom 16.16)

Over the years I have heard a lot of people make a big deal out of this, asking, if we are going to be so picky about things, why we don't go around kissing one another all the time. They usually stand there smiling, completely satisfied with themselves for having "caught" us. It is perfectly easy to answer. We can find many different greetings in the scriptures, all of which appear to be acceptable to God—kissing, embracing, bowing, or simply speaking to one another with standard greetings of the day. Greetings vary from culture to culture and by not specifying one, God has given us tacit authority to practice them all.

As usual, these folks have focused on the wrong part of the phrase. It isn't the "kiss" that we should emphasize; it is the type of kiss—a holy one. In fact, the choice of greeting in this illustration seems the perfect one to use since it was a dissembling kiss that betrayed our Lord. Today we Americans would simply say, "Greet one another with a holy handshake."

So what makes a greeting "holy"? Sincerity obviously, and especially so if we are contrasting it with a kiss of betrayal. Do we shake hands with good feelings in our hearts, or is there a metaphorical knife hidden in the other hand, ready to stab the person we seem to be accepting as soon as they turn around? Will we say pleasant things to their faces, then slander them when they leave? Or perhaps less obvious but more prevalent, will we call one another "brethren" when we really don't want to be around one another any longer than we must?

A lot of people hang on to *agape* with glee, spouting that handy definition, "seeking the other's good whether you like him or not." It's almost like they are shouting, "Oh goody! I don't have to like that brother after all!"

Pardon me?

"It's not *phileo*," they say, "so it doesn't mean we really have to like one another." What then do they do with all the passages that talk about brotherly love and kindheartedness? Do they just cut them out of their Bibles?

For one thing, we have made too big a distinction in those two words. In the early first century, *agape* was not looked on with the approval we do now. How exactly would you feel if someone said to you, "I care what happens to you, but I don't much like you"? I think I might be insulted, and that may be one reason Peter had such a hard time in John 21 accepting Jesus' question, "Do you *agape* me?" To him, it was far more important to *phileo* the Lord. It took the rest of the century and into the next for that word to become the deeper love we often talk about.

Do a little research and you will find that the two words are often used interchangeably in the New Testament, much of which was written closer to the middle of the first century, when the meaning of *agape* was still evolving. In 1 Corinthians 8.3 and 16.22 we are told to love God. One uses *agape*, the other *phileo*. In Ephesians 5.25 and Titus 2.4 we are told to love our spouses. One uses *agape*, the other *phileo*. In John 13.23 and 20.2 we hear about "the disciple whom Jesus loved." Guess what? That's right, one uses *agape* and the other *phileo*. That little tidbit only took me about five minutes to look up.

You can tell a lot about people by what they emphasize in the scriptures—their pet peeves, their personal interests, even who they have a hard time loving. Make sure that your greetings, whether a handshake, a kiss, a hug, or a simple wave of the hand, are holy.

> *Seeing you have purified your souls in your obedience to the truth unto unfeigned love of the brethren [phileo + adelphoi], love [agapao] one another from the heart fervently.*
>
> 1 Peter 1.22

December 23

Fudge

This time of year I usually try to make a batch of chocolate fudge. I say "try" because I usually fail. Peanut butter fudge I have down. Nineteen out of 20 times it will turn out right, but not the chocolate variety. I am talking about real fudge, not the newer recipes that add things like marshmallow crème, and wind up changing the texture just so it won't flop on you. If it shines, it isn't fudge; if it's soft, it isn't fudge; if it's grainy, it isn't fudge; if it must be kept refrigerated, it isn't fudge. Real fudge is matte to the eye, firm to the touch, creamy in your mouth, and sits just fine on the countertop without changing consistency.

So a couple of years ago I found a recipe for foolproof fudge in a cooking magazine that I ordinarily trust implicitly. I made their recipe, and indeed it did just fine, but it was shiny, it was soft, it had to be stored in the fridge. It wasn't fudge, and I was disappointed beyond measure. However, in the article accompanying the recipe, the author stated that fudge is a tricky thing. If the temperature and humidity are not just right, if your ingredients have sucked up too much moisture from the kitchen atmosphere any time recently, if your candy thermometer is just a degree or two off, your fudge will not "fudge." He went on to say that even seasoned professionals feel frustrated when trying to make this unreasonably difficult recipe. While I am sorry those folks feel that way, it certainly made me feel a lot better. It helped explain my one in ten record of success over the years.

Aren't we glad salvation is not so difficult? Just follow a few simple directions and suddenly you have a relationship that will help you in the trials of this life, and lead you to the joys of the next, the sweetest of treats anyone could possibly enjoy. Why is it that some people feel so obligated to make it more difficult?

My brother-in-law was nearly run out of a church on a rail once because, using the Philippian jailor of Acts 16 as an example, he dared to say that there really is not all that much we have to know before we submit to baptism. Oh no, he was told, we must know all about the plan of God through the ages, about the true nature of the first century church, about the false teachings on salvation and how to combat them, about the "correct" definitions of faith, baptism, and grace, among other things.

Just what was it Philip asked that Ethiopian proselyte when he wanted to be baptized? "If you believe with all your heart, you may, and he said, I believe that Jesus Christ is the Son of God" (Acts 8.37). Funny that Philip never gave him a list of things to memorize and recite before he was allowed in the water. Isn't it wonderful—and amazing!—that our Lord will accept our obedient faith the moment we realize our need for Him?

Yes, there are many things we must all learn. All these years after my baptism there are still many more. That's what the rest of your life is for; that's why Peter said to "grow in the grace and knowledge of the Lord and Savior Jesus Christ" (2 Pet 3.18). We never finish that part. Maybe the problem is, we make this arbitrary list and think once we know it, we *are* finished. Just who made the list in the first place, if God didn't?

One of Satan's most powerful tools is frustration and hopelessness. Let's not help him do his work by making salvation so difficult that people give up before they even get the chance to start.

> *And [the jailor] called for lights and sprang in, and trembling for fear, fell down before Paul and Silas and brought them out and said, Sirs, what must I do to be saved? And they said, Believe on the Lord Jesus and you shall be saved, you and your house; and they spoke the word of the Lord unto him with all that were in his house, and he took them* ***the same hour of the night*** *and washed their stripes and was baptized, he and all his immediately.*
>
> Acts 16.29–33

December 24

Presents

My dogs brought me a present the other afternoon. I walked out onto the carport and there by my chair, where I like to sit in the evening, lay a dead possum. Not just any dead possum—this one they had buried for awhile so it would age properly, then dug up to lay before my "throne." I imagine that when the wind blew the right way, my neighbors knew about my present too.

I have had cats bring me equally lovely gifts before, but this was a first for dogs. As you can imagine, I did not jump for joy. In fact, I hardly expressed any appreciation at all. I had not felt very good that day—these medications do a number on my stomach, and this gift, no matter how sincerely it may have been meant, did not help.

These two small creatures rely on me for everything. I feed them, make sure they have their vaccinations and medications, care for them when they feel bad, and play with them when I have the chance. And for that little bit they want nothing more in this world than to please me. Red heelers are often called "Velcro Dogs" because they stick next to their masters' sides. Magdi and Chloe will even turn their noses up at a treat just so I can pet them. Loving is much more important to them than food.

And if for any reason I am displeased with them, their ears go down, their heads bow, their tails are tucked and they practically crawl on their knees to me. Magdi will rub her head against my leg over and over. I know she is saying, "I'm sorry, I'm sorry, I'm so, so sorry." If she isn't, she certainly has me fooled.

So how do I treat my Master? Do I want nothing more in the world than to please Him? Do I repent on my knees in abject sorrow when I know I don't? Or am I too proud for that? Do I truly understand that any gift I give is really no more to Him than that dead possum was to me? Do I appreciate that I can never repay what He has done for me, and therefore try my best to show gratitude and reverence with the gift of obedience and faith, a gift that still falls far short of repayment?

Sometimes I wonder if dogs show more respect for their masters than we do for ours, and their masters are anything but perfect, holy, and awesome. Maybe we should take a lesson.

> *For we are all become as one who is unclean, and all our righteousnesses are as filthy rags; and we all do fade as a leaf, and our iniquities, like the wind, take us away. . . .*
>
> *Even so you also, when you have done all the things that are commanded you say, "We are unprofitable servants. We have done that which it was our duty to do."*
>
> Isaiah 64.6; Luke 17.10

December 25

Ornaments

If you are like me, it took a long day, or maybe even more than one, to get out those boxes of decorations and turn your homes into fantasy lands of colored lights, sparkly globes and shiny tinsel. Awhile back I finally gave into my sons' groans and stopped hanging the handmade elementary school ornaments. Still, I have a fondness for macaroni glued to a paper plate, spray-painted gold and flecked with green glitter, and toilet paper rolls attired in shiny red paper, white lace, and sequins. They bring back a lot of precious memories my sons will not understand until they have their own masterpieces hanging on an evergreen limb.

And have you ever noticed that people adorn themselves as well? Not their clothing, though this time of year I see magazine and newspaper ads full of expensive, gaudy clothes I would never have a place to wear. I am talking about their behavior. Even the biggest heathen in the world does not want to be called a grinch and struggles to adorn himself with "the holiday spirit." I am glad that at least one month a year we must put up with less grouchiness, less complaining, and less selfish behavior from the public at large. But I wonder what God thinks about it.

The true Christian has the "mind of the spirit" no matter what month the calendar shows. He is liberal in his giving, not just to get in a tax deduction before the end of his fiscal year, but because he truly wants to help others. He is considerate of others, not because someone has reminded him with a poke in the ribs that "it's Christmas," but because he is in the habit of serving others. He smiles and laughs, not because he has indulged in a little too much "holiday cheer," but because he lives a life of joy as a child of God. He shows courtesy in traffic, in parking lots, and in long check-out lines, not because of the lights and wreaths hanging all over town to remind him this is the month for "peace on earth, good will to men," but because he lives that way all year long.

Next week the calendar will change. "January" will signal the start of a new year. Will my behavior change as well? Or do I live the same way regardless of the calendar, as a Christian who follows in the steps of the one I claim to be my Lord—kind, courteous, considerate, joyful, and full of goodwill to all?

> *Put on therefore as God's elect, holy and beloved, a heart of compassion, kindness, lowliness, meekness, longsuffering, forbearing one another and forgiving each other, if any man have a complaint against any, even as the Lord forgave you, so also do you. And above all these things, put on love which is the bond of perfectness.*
>
> Colossians 3.12–14

December 26

Clearance Sale!

The biggest clearance sales of the year start today. I clip coupons all the time, but clearance sales are good, too, and a clearance sale that I can use a coupon on makes my day.

Where we live, I often resort to catalogues. The shipping works out about the same as the gas it would cost to go to the store, and when you add in the time, there is no contest. As you might guess, I am not one of those "Born to shop" women. I only shop when I need something. But when a clearance catalogue hits my mailbox, I usually try to think ahead to what I might need in the near future.

Of course you know the problem with clearance catalogues. They only have some of the colors left, in only some of the sizes—usually the weird colors and odd sizes, say, chartreuse size zero or fluorescent orange plaid size XXXL. If you want the good stuff you have to call in early, preferably the same day you get the catalogue, and have several options on your list. That way you might get one or two things you need in the correct size and a reasonably non-hideous color.

If something is totally free, I am not quite as picky. I had a coupon once for a free 12 pack of one of those odd new Dr Pepper flavors, if I also bought a regular 12 pack. Keith is the Dr Pepper drinker in this house, but he doesn't like his favorite things fooled around with—not his coffee, not his iced tea, not his Coke, and certainly not his Dr Pepper. I almost did not use the coupon. Then I thought, hey, it's free! If he doesn't like it, I can give it to someone else. We were nearly out of drinks and the regular Dr Pepper was on sale, so it was no loss to us if that is what happened.

Isn't it amazing how people line up for good sales, and go nuts for things that are free, but no one is lining up for the most important free thing there is—eternal life! You can't even tell anyone about this great deal without them looking at you askance and walking away in the middle of a sentence—or making a pronouncement like, "I don't discuss religion and politics."

Unfortunately the majority of the world hasn't a spiritual bone in its body. People are all too consumed with the here and now, with immediate results, with instant gratification of any and every desire. It's interesting that Paul calls such people "babies" in his letter to the Corinthians. It takes spiritual maturity, an ability to see beyond the present and to weigh the true importance of things, to understand that this world is not what counts.

A baby will cover his face with a blanket and think no one can see him. He has not yet learned that there is any other perspective than his own. He thinks if he cannot see you, then you cannot see him. That seems to be how many adults live their lives as well. The only things that matter to them are what *they* are going through, and how it affects *them*. The self-centeredness of an infant has grown into the selfishness of an adult.

So it is difficult for people to realize that they are sinners in need of salvation. That is the first hurdle to cross. You cannot convert a person who thinks he is spiritually safe. That is why Jesus had more luck with harlots and publicans than with the religious leaders of his day. And the sad thing is that if they could ever realize their need, the solution is free! No coupons needed. Yet they miss the greatest clearance sale ever. Salvation has been on sale for thousands of years. One hundred percent off, totally free.

Don't let pride and immaturity make you miss the bargain of your life.

So then as through one trespass the judgment came unto all men to condemnation, even so through one act of righteousness the free gift came unto all men to justification of life.

Romans 5.18

December 27

Fowl Weather Friends

The catbird is back. Finally the weather is turning and he is back for an easy meal. Funny how he only comes to the feeder when finding his own food becomes too difficult. The rest of the year I do not have the pleasure of his handsome company. He is flying out there enjoying himself with scarcely a thought in my direction.

How many times do we usually pray in a day? How many conversations do we have with a Father who loves us more than anything else? If you are like me, I call many more times when things are difficult than when they are going well. That may be normal, but does that make it right? Any parent worth the name wants his child to call when he needs help, would, in fact, be angry if he did not receive such a call, but it certainly goes down better when those calls come at other times too, doesn't it?

Solomon set forth the principle in Proverbs when he personified wisdom as a woman offering her gift to any who needed it. Too few take her up on the offer and she says, "Because I have called and you refused to listen, I have stretched out my hand and no one has heeded, because you have ignored all my counsel and would have none of my reproof, I also will laugh at your calamity; I will mock when terror strikes you, when terror strikes you like a storm and your calamity comes like a whirlwind, when distress and anguish come upon you. Then they will call upon me, but I will not answer; they will seek me diligently but will not find me" (Prov 1.24–28).

Oh, but that would never happen with God, some will say. Jesus loves everyone, even the vilest sinner. Neither will ever refuse to help someone who asks. Listen to the words God spoke through Isaiah to his chosen people, who continually fell away, repented when times got hard, only to fall away yet again. "I will destine you to the sword, and all of you shall bow down to the slaughter, because when I called, you did not answer; when I spoke, you did not listen, but you did what was evil in my eyes and chose what I did not delight in" (Isa 65.12).

We want this relationship to be one with a revolving door—we can come in and out of it as we please. We want to live like we choose to live and then come running to God for help when our foolish choices bring us pain and misery. We expect Him to snatch us from the jaws of disaster and make everything right again. That's what He's supposed to do! But God will not tolerate being used; He has a right to expect certain behavior from us. Even if He were not so good to us, He is still our Creator and that gives Him the ultimate authority in everything we do. Perhaps one of the biggest dangers of living in a democracy is thinking we have rights when it comes to our dealings with an Almighty God.

Are you like the catbird who only comes calling when times are tough, or are you there every day, building a relationship with your Father through constant communication, obedience, and dependence? Maybe you should make an appointment with Him sometime in the next few minutes.

> *They have turned back to the iniquities of their forefathers, who refused to hear my words. They have gone after other gods to serve them. . . . Therefore do not pray for this people, or lift up a cry or prayer on their behalf, for I will not listen when they call to me in the time of their trouble.*
>
> Jeremiah 11.10, 14

December 28

The Ad Man

Have you noticed the number of commercials and advertisements for weight-loss products, nicotine patches, fitness equipment, and gym memberships? The ad man is not dumb. This is the week we decide on our resolutions. It happens every year.

Just think about the grocery flyer you see each week. Next month we will see specials for diet foods. February it will be chocolate, strawberries, and roses, and in March it will be corned beef and cabbage. Candy, eggs, ham, and legs of lamb will top the list in April. May through August will feature ribs, ground beef, steaks of all sorts, hot dogs, potato salad and baked beans—typical summer cook-out fare. Then September will devote a whole page to notebooks, paper, and pencils. And you know what the fall brings—chili beans, apples, turkeys, cranberries, sweet potatoes, and standing rib roasts. And we all buy most of that "in season" don't we? Then we load our carts with salads, yogurt, and Lean Cuisines on January 1, and begin the whole sequence all over.

They have us pegged. They pay attention to our habits. They even know when a trend is *about* to start so they can cash in from the beginning. Low fat gave way to low carb, and now the buzzword is "organic." It seems to me that labeling food "organic" is a bit redundant, but that's another topic for another day.

If men can figure us out that easily, why don't we understand that our adversary can too? He knows *what* will tempt us the most and *when* it will, and he is persistent. We can get rid of him for a time, "resist the Devil and he will flee from you" (Jas 4.7), but he will always come back and try again. Just like those ad men, he uses the things he knows will work, and is never afraid to branch out and try a new tack.

When you pick up that flyer in the Thursday paper, use it as a reminder to be careful. Our lives are an open book, in more ways than one.

For this is the love of God that we keep his commandments, and his commandments are not grievous. For whosoever is begotten of God overcomes the world, and this is the victory that overcomes the world—our faith. And who is he who overcomes the world but he who believes that Jesus is the Son of God.

1 John 5.3–5

Inflated Expectations

I have learned a lot of things over the years, among them these: No matter how well you keep your house, the morning that you get busy with something early on and decide to finish before you dress and do the usual morning chores, will always be the morning the neighbor stops by and finds you still in your bathrobe at 11, the breakfast dishes scattered over the countertop, and the bed unmade—and the more you try to explain that this is unusual for you, the more unbelievable you will sound. When someone tells you a joke you don't "get," you will suddenly comprehend the punch line and laugh raucously the next morning while standing at the checkout behind a woman who has just told the cashier that her mother has a terminal illness. And your baby will always choose the moment after the preacher reads Habakkuk 2.20—"Jehovah is in His holy temple, let all the earth keep silence before Him"—to fill his diaper as noisily as possible.

Part of learning how to live is learning how to cope with annoyances and embarrassments on an every day basis, realizing that you are not the only one this happens to.

So why do we let disappointments ruin our faith so easily? Yes, the church is God's perfect institution, but as long as it is filled with people like you and me, it will not always behave itself perfectly. Even the chosen 12 had a Judas among them. Even the first Christians had a couple like Ananias and Sapphira, who gave for the praise they would receive rather than from a heart of love. Even the first church had instances of social bias that caused uproar over the care of widows. Yet they got over it, continuing to work and grow by leaps and bounds. Why can't we?

It is good to have ideals, but be realistic as well. God will never disappoint you, but His people will. Until you can present to them a perfect example of righteousness, don't expect them to do so for you. Rather, understand that we are all growing together.

Someone someday will lie about you, perhaps even a Christian. Realize this—most of the time they don't even know they are lying. For some reason or other their attitude of depression or bitterness at that moment has put a winding road in their ear canals that twists everything they hear into something hurtful. By the time they tell someone else what they "heard," they really think that is exactly what you said. You know what? It won't kill you. People who know you (or the other person) will either dismiss the comment entirely or ask you about it, giving you a chance to set the record straight. Anyone who believes it has their own problems to deal with. In ten years, no one will care, because no one will remember. I know. These days it only costs me one night of sleep instead of a year's worth of worry. Progress!

Stop expecting perfection where there is none. Stop blaming God for the sins of His children. Remember to whom you were converted—to the Lord, and not to a group of forgiven sinners who sometimes backslide. Learn not to expect more than you can deliver yourself. It's a whole lot easier on your faith.

> *And he said unto his disciples, It is impossible but that occasions of stumbling should come; but woe unto him, through whom they come. ...For there must be also factions among you, that they that are approved may be made manifest among you.*
>
> Luke 17.1; 1 Corinthians 11.19

December 30

The Quota System

I have heard it all my life and never noticed the problem until recently. "Do one good deed every day." How many New Year's resolutions have you heard that include that phrase? How many times have you heard people talk about trying to better themselves by doing "one good deed every day"? How many speak as if they are proud of that very accomplishment?

Then it struck me. One good deed a day? *That* is supposed to make me a good person? One? Hey! If I get it done by 8:00 or 9:00 in the morning, I don't have to worry about another one, right? If I do five today, I can take the rest of the week off. I'm not expected to work on the weekends surely. Something is terribly wrong if we think doing one good deed a day is a wonderful accomplishment for a Christian.

> Depart from evil, *and do good;* Seek peace, *and pursue it.* (Psa 34.14)
>
> Trust in Jehovah, *and do good.* ...Depart from evil, *and do good.* (Psa 37.3, 27)
>
> I know that there is nothing better for them, than to rejoice, *and to do good so long as they live.* (Ecc 3.12)
>
> But I say unto you that hear, Love your enemies, *do good to them that hate you.* (Luke 6.27)
>
> *But to do good and to communicate forget not:* for with such sacrifices God is well pleased. (Heb 13.16)

> *And let us not be weary in well-doing:* for in due season we shall reap, if we faint not. So then, *as we have opportunity, let us work that which is good* toward all men, and especially toward them that are of the household of the faith. (Gal 6.9–10)
>
> Let love be without hypocrisy. Abhor that which is evil; *cleave to that which is good.* In love of the brethren be tenderly affectioned one to another; in honor preferring one another; communicating to the necessities of the saints; given to hospitality. Bless them that persecute you; bless, and curse not. Rejoice with them that rejoice; weep with them that weep. Be of the same mind one toward another. Render to no man evil for evil. Take thought for things honorable in the sight of all men. If it be possible, as much as in you lies, be at peace with all men. Avenge not yourselves, beloved, but give place unto the wrath of God: for it is written, Vengeance belongs unto me; I will recompense, says the Lord. But if your enemy hunger, feed him; if he thirst, give him to drink: for in so doing thou shalt heap coals of fire upon his head. Be not overcome of evil, but *overcome evil with good.* (Rom 12.9–10, 13–21)

Do I really think I can overcome evil with one good deed a day?

Christians don't work by the quota system. They know they should be looking for good things to do, as well as reacting in good ways to things done to them, all day long, every day. Yet even that is not enough to repay the debt we owe for our forgiveness.

I think we need to stop counting.

December 31

The Trash Bin

My father was a young boy in the Depression and grew up on a small farm where they made use of everything. He cannot stand to see something going to waste, even if he can't at that moment find a use for it. Before his retirement he often pulled stacks of paper out of the company trash bins, that old, wide, green and white striped computer paper with the holes in the sides. He pulled out card stock that had been run through a printer of some sort leaving thin black lines on one side only. Then he brought them all to me.

We were usually with a small church all those years ago, with a limited budget, and our own was even more limited. What did I do with all that paper and cardstock? The computer paper graced the walls of many a Bible class. You want to know how tall Goliath was? Unroll a ten foot long length of it, tear it off along the perforations and then measure out Goliath's six cubits and a span on it and tack it to the wall. In a high ceiling-ed room it was easy, but in others Goliath had to bend over, with the paper running up the wall then along the ceiling. Suddenly you really understood what a "giant" was. It wasn't just the height. It was how massive his body must have been to support that height.

You want to know how tall Saul was? The scriptures say he was "from his shoulders upward" taller than any of the men of Israel. So we asked the tallest man in the church to come in and stand by our computer paper. We marked his height, then went up as much more as his head and shoulders. Saul was no Lilliputian himself. Those lengths of paper also made great time lines. Other times they were "missionary journeys," an attendance chart for each student, each one measured out according to scale and then "journeyed" with a felt pen to the next stop each time a student came to class. If he didn't make it back to Antioch or Jerusalem by the time we finished the lesson book it was a sure sign he had missed too many classes!

And the card stock? I must have cut out thousands of flash cards for memory verses, apostles, judges, and prophets, anything that could be represented with a line drawing and a stick man, as well as the question cards for board games I made and Bible Jeopardy boards I constructed. The trash that no one else wanted found a spiritual use that helped hundreds of children learn about God and His word.

God has a habit of taking things that no one else wants and making use of them too. "For behold your calling brethren, that not many wise after the flesh, not many mighty, not many noble are called" (1 Cor 1.26). Jesus did not go to the "in crowd"; He did not go to the rich and powerful. In fact, most of the time those people became his followers it was because they came seeking Him, not the other way around. No, Jesus went to the poor, the disenfranchised, and those whose lives were filled with problems that filled others with disgust. Fishermen may not have been the dregs of society, but they were the working class poor. Matthew the publican was despised. Simon the Zealot was a fanatic from whom others might have shied away. Zacchaeus, though wealthy, was another despised tax collector. Mary Magdalene had had seven demons. He healed ten lepers and the only one of that shunned group that even came back to thank Him was a Samaritan, the lowest of the low.

Why did these people flock to Him so? Because He gave them hope. He gave them purpose. He made something of them when everyone else had given up on them. And He will do the same for you and for me. It matters not how far you have fallen, nor how little anyone else values you. God valued you enough to give His son for you. He can pull you out of the world's trash can and make you a "vessel of honor, sanctified, meet for the Master's use" (2 Tim 2.21). If you think otherwise then you don't really believe in the Almighty God.

Thus says the LORD, Let not the wise man boast in his wisdom, let not the mighty man boast in his might, let not the rich man boast in his riches, but let him who boasts boast in this, that he understands and knows me, that I am the LORD who practices steadfast love, justice and righteousness in the earth. For in these things I delight, declares the LORD.

Jeremiah 9.23–24

Afterword

Now I invite you to turn back to the first page tomorrow morning and journey through the year with me again. If you are like me, memory grows worse as the years pass by, and perhaps you won't be bored.

Many of the New Testament writers talked about putting ourselves in "remembrance" of things we already know. I find that the more I study, the more likely I am to have a passage at the ready when I need its encouragement. I hope these little articles have helped you in the same way, and perhaps the ones that meant less will come at a time when they are more needful in your life the next time through. God's amazing providence has a way of working its way into our lives when we trust Him implicitly and depend upon Him for our every need.

Thanks for reading.

> *Wherefore brethren, give the more diligence to make your calling and election sure; for if you do these things you shall never stumble; for thus shall be richly supplied unto you the entrance into the eternal kingdom of our Lord and Savior Jesus Christ. Wherefore I shall be ready always to put you in remembrance of these things, though you know them and are established in the truth which is with you. And I think it right as long as I am in this tabernacle to stir you up by putting you in remembrance.*
>
> 2 Peter 1.10–13

ALSO FROM DEWARD PUBLISHING:

Beneath the Cross: Essays and Relfections on the Lord's Supper
Jady S. Copeland and Nathan Ward (editors)

The Bible has much to say about the Lord's Supper. Almost every component of this memorial is rich with meaning—meaning supplied by Old Testament foreshadowing and New Testament teaching. The Lord's death itself is meaningful and significant in ways we rarely point out. In sixty-nine essays by forty different authors, Beneath the Cross explores the depths of symbolism and meaning to be found in the last hours of the Lord's life and offers a helpful look at the memorial feast that commemorates it. 329 pages. $14.99 (PB); $23.99 (HB).

Invitation to a Spiritual Revolution
Paul Earnhart

Few preachers have studied the Sermon on the Mount as intensively or spoken on its contents so frequently and effectively as the author of this work. His excellent and very readable written analysis appeared first as a series of articles in Christianity Magazine. By popular demand it is here offered in one volume so that it can be more easily preserved, circulated, read, reread and made available to those who would not otherwise have access to it. Foreword by Sewell Hall. 173 pages. $9.99 (PB).

Boot Camp: Equipping Men with Integrity for Spiritual Warfare
Jason Hardin

According to best-selling author Stephen Arterburn, "This is a great book to help us men live opposite of this world's model of a man." Boot Camp: Equipping Men with Integrity for Spiritual Warfare is the first volume in the new IMAGE series of books for men by Jason Hardin. It serves as a Basic Training manual in the spiritual war for honor, integrity and a God-glorifying life. 237 pages. $13.99 (PB); $24.99 (HB).

Prepared to Answer: A Guide to Christian Evidences
Rob van de Weghe

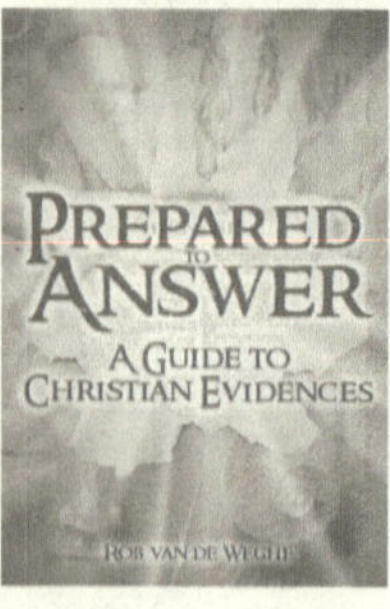

Follow the personal odyssey of a man of science as he journeys from skepticism to faith. Logic, science, and history become bridges instead of barriers, as doubt is transformed into confidence. Scrutinize the evidence that compels the verdict that Christian faith rests upon truth and fact, not legend and myth. 450 pages. $18.99 (PB).

The Growth of the Seed: Notes on the Book of Genesis
Nathan Ward

A study of the book of Genesis that emphasizes two primary themes: the development of the Messianic line and the growing enmity between the righteous and the wicked. In addition, it provides detailed comments on the text and short essays on several subjects that are suggested in, yet peripheral to, Genesis. 537 pages. $19.99 (PB).

Things Most Surely Believed
Forrest D. Moyer

In these 16 brief sermons, Forrest Darrell Moyer has stated with beautiful clarity and simplicity, yet with compelling force, the Christian's "reason for hope" that is in him. He deals with the greatest themes the race has ever known—God, Christ, the cross, sin and redemption, the church, heaven and hell—yet he does it in language that the man in the pew, unskilled in the intricacies of theological vocabularies, can easily grasp. These sermons partake of that same quality which characterized the initial preaching of the gospel by Christ himself, of whom it was said, "and the common people heard him gladly." Foreword by Doy Moyer. New Introduction by Jefferson David Tant. 142 pages. $9.99 (PB)

The Big Picture of the Bible
Kenneth W. Craig

In this short book, the author summarizes the central theme of the Bible in a simple, yet comprehensive approach. Evangelists across the world have used this presentation to convert countless souls to the discipleship of Jesus Christ. Bulk discounts will be available, as will special pricing for congregational orders. Foreword by Daniel DeGarmo. 45 pages, full color. $6.99 (PB)

For a full listing of DeWard Publishing Company books, visit our website:

www.deward.com

www.ingramcontent.com/pod-product-compliance
Lightning Source LLC
LaVergne TN
LVHW050913080826
845145LV00001B/68

* 9 7 8 1 9 3 6 3 4 1 1 1 5 *